D1591336

Astronomers, Scribes, and Priests

Astronomers, Scribes, and Priests

Intellectual Interchange between the Northern Maya Lowlands
and Highland Mexico in the Late Postclassic Period

Edited by Gabrielle Vail and Christine Hernández

For E. Wyllys Andrews V on the occasion of his
retirement from teaching—esteemed colleague, dedicated
mentor, valued friend.

Library of Congress Cataloging-in-Publication Data
Astronomers, scribes, and priests : intellectual interchange between the
    northern Maya lowlands and highland Mexico in the late postclassic
    period / edited by Gabrielle Vail and Christine Hernández.
        p. cm.
Includes index.
    A collection of papers based on a symposium sponsored by Dumbarton
        Oaks at the Library of Congress, October 6–7, 2006.
    ISBN 978-0-88402-346-3 (hardcover : alk. paper)
1. Mayas—Intellectual life—Congresses.
2. Maya astronomy—Congresses.
3. Indians of Mexico—Intellectual life Congresses.
4. Indians of Central America—Intellectual life—Congresses.
5. Indians of Mexico--Antiquities—Congresses.
6. Indians of Central America—Antiquities—Congresses.
7. Mexico—Antiquities—Congresses.
8. Central America—Antiquities—Congresses.
I. Vail, Gabrielle.   II. Hernández, Christine L.   III. Dumbarton Oaks.
F1435.3.I57A86   2009
306.4′2097265097240902   dc22

www.doaks.org/publications

Contents

Preface

Dumbarton Oaks has held numerous meetings concerning one or another of the great Pre-Hispanic cultures of Mesoamerica, and a smaller number of meetings concerning interactions among the great cultures—polities that have often been considered distinct and quite separate interaction spheres. The 2006 Pre-Columbian symposium, "Astronomers, Scribes, and Priests: Intellectual Interchange between the Northern Maya Lowlands and Highland Mexico in the Late Postclassic Period," was the first to examine specifically the exchange of ideas between specialists in central Mexico—home to Aztecs, among others—and in Maya polities on the Yucatán Peninsula on the eve of the arrival of Europeans into Mexico.

The symposium was the fruit of several years of planning. In 2004 Gabrielle Vail and Christine Hernández spoke with Jeffrey Quilter, then director of Pre-Columbian Studies at Dumbarton Oaks, about the possibility of organizing a symposium on the topic of connections between the Maya region and central Mexico. Professors Vail and Hernández had previously noted intriguing correspondences between manuscripts from these regions and felt the time was right to explore the nature and means of such apparent interactions. The scope of the gathering was broadened to include an examination of the topic through approaches drawn from archaeology, astronomy, linguistics, art history, and related disciplines.

The Music Room of Dumbarton Oaks is the traditional setting for our annual symposia, but in late 2004 the Main House was closed for renovations. Taking this opportunity to work collaboratively with our sister institutions in the Washington, D.C. area, we held the fall 2006 symposium at the Library of Congress. I am very grateful to our colleagues there, in particular Georgette Dorn and Barbara Tenenbaum of the Hispanic Division and Mark Dimunation of the Rare Book and Special Collections Division. I also extend my gratitude to Arthur Dunkelman, formerly of the Rare Book and Special Collections Division. Thanks are also due to Jai Alterman and Emily Gulick of Dumbarton

Oaks for their logistical help at the symposium, and in the case of Emily, in the preparation of the publication.

It is particularly appropriate that this symposium was at the Library of Congress, as one central focus of the symposium was the exchange of information via books, specifically the exquisite screenfold manuscripts that were produced in both regions in Pre-Hispanic times. In turn I am delighted that the ideas shared at the symposium have now been preserved in a more permanent form in the present volume, a book that will ultimately have a home in the Library of Congress and Dumbarton Oaks. I thank Gabrielle Vail, Christine Hernández, and the contributors for their great efforts over these past few years in the realization of this book—a volume that will surely be a spark for further intellectual interchange among scholars internationally.

Joanne Pillsbury
Director of Studies, Pre-Columbian Program

Abbreviations

B	Borgia Codex
D	Dresden Codex
FM	Codex Fejérváry-Mayer
INAH	Instituto Nacional de Antropología e Historia
M	Madrid Codex
P	Paris Codex
pUA	proto-Uto-Aztecan
UA	Uto-Aztecan
UNAM	Universidad Nacional Autónoma de México

Chapter One

Astronomers, Scribes, and Priests

An Introduction

Gabrielle Vail and Christine Hernández

THE QUESTION of a possible relationship between the Maya of the northern lowlands and Nahuatl speakers and related groups from highland central Mexico during what we now call the Late Postclassic period has excited generations of researchers. Early studies, beginning with the work of scholars such as Eduard Seler (1904) and Cyrus Thomas (1884), focused on a comparative analysis of Pre-Hispanic manuscripts from the two regions, known today as the Maya and Borgia Group codices. The iconographic, calendrical, and structural similarities they documented can be interpreted in various ways— as resulting from an underlying common religious/cultural tradition shared across much of Mesoamerica, diffusion from one area to another through either direct or indirect means, or an active interchange among members of both areas. The goal of this volume is to explore the lines of evidence for connections between the two regions (fig. 1), assess past and current interpretations of the data, and further the development of models for understanding Late Postclassic interaction.

Our focus with respect to the data sets examined within the following chapters is specifically on interaction among those who made up the "intellectual" class of elites—astronomers, priests, scribes, and artisans. Who were these people? We use the term *priest* to refer to the class of ritual specialists described in Tozzer's translation of Landa's *Relación de las cosas de Yucatán* as follows: "The office of the priest was to discuss and teach their sciences, to make known their

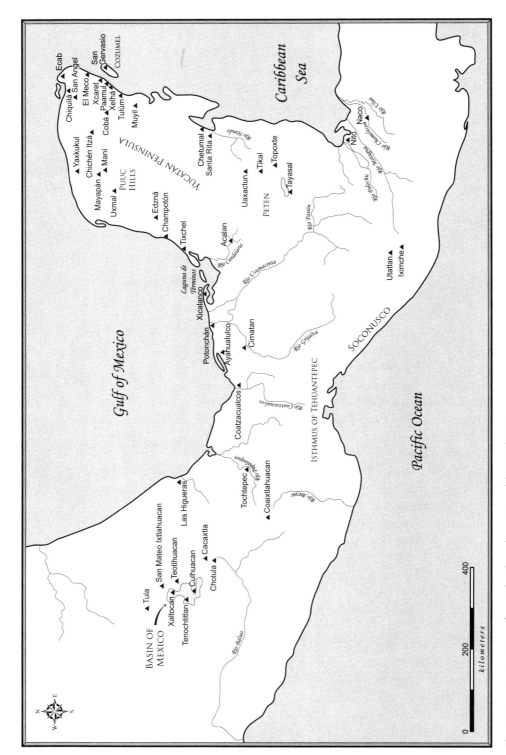

Fig. 1. Mesoamerican sites referenced in this volume. Artwork by David R. Hixson.

2

needs and the remedies for them, to preach and to publish the festival days, to offer sacrifices and to administer their sacraments" (Tozzer 1941: 111–112). To function in this capacity, priests required a broad educational background in all of the arts and sciences, yet we know that there were also specializations within the priesthood for particular social functions. Ethnohistoric sources describe several categories of ritual specialist (including soothsayer, sorcerer, and sage) in Aztec society who would have provided the services just listed (Boone 2007: 20–28). One of those specialties was likely to include astronomy. We are not necessarily advocating that "astronomers" as titled practitioners formed a separately recognized profession in ancient Maya and central Mexican societies, but we do contend that there existed a practice of an indigenous astronomy in Mesoamerica and that members of the elite class were schooled in certain of its fundamentals. An astronomer, according to *Webster's New Encyclopedic Dictionary*, is "one who makes observations of celestial phenomena." Some of the elite students trained to become priests and scribes learned to track and record the movements of celestial bodies across the sky, understood the cyclical nature of those movements, and mastered the indigenous mathematics involved in calculating the periodicities implied by patterning found in observational data—in other words, they practiced astronomy.[1]

The papers in this volume—presented originally at the October 2006 Dumbarton Oaks Pre-Columbian Symposium in Washington, D.C.—represent the latest research addressing issues of interchange among Mesoamerican intellectuals. The work is informed by over a century of previous research built on rich data sets, summarized here as an introduction to the themes discussed in the succeeding chapters.

Evidence previously cited as suggesting connections between the Maya area and the central Mexican highlands (including the Basin of Mexico and the Mixteca-Puebla region encompassing southern Puebla and northern Oaxaca) includes the following:

- Codical data, including iconographic, calendrical, and structural connections among almanacs (see the Glossary) in the Maya and Borgia Group codices. The best-known examples are the related almanacs on Fejérváry–Mayer 1 and Madrid 75–76 (plates 1–2) and the Dresden Venus table and cognate Venus almanacs from the Borgia Group (cf. Bricker, ch. 10: figs. 1 and 4, this volume).

- Stylistic similarities and a common symbol set appearing in murals and portable art from throughout various parts of Mesoamerica, including the Maya area and the Mixteca-Puebla region (see fig. 2 in Introduction to Part II). This International style of murals is best known in the Maya area from sites like Tulúm, Santa Rita, and Mayapán.

- Archaeological and ethnohistoric evidence for trade networks. Distinct spheres appear to have been operating in the Maya peninsular area and in highland Mexico. Research by a number of scholars (see, e.g., Berdan et al. 2003; Gasco and Berdan 2003) suggests that the two were connected by trade through the Gulf Coast region.
- Linguistic evidence, including the presence of words having a Uto-Aztecan (Nahua) origin in hieroglyphic texts from both the Classic and Postclassic periods.
- Ethnohistoric evidence suggesting the presence of Mexican/Nahuatl speakers in various parts of the Maya area and Central America.
- Sculpture and architecture at the northern Maya site of Mayapán that resemble art from central Mexico, and Mexican deities depicted in Maya codices and in *incensarios* from Mayapán.

Early explanations of these connections had the disadvantage of focusing almost exclusively on the Maya as passive receptors of Mexican culture; they also lacked an understanding of the truly "international" nature of the stylistic and iconographic connections among various regions. Recent studies have shown the importance of Maya-Mexican connections during the Late Postclassic period, as documented by the ongoing archaeological work at Mayapán and other late Pre-Hispanic sites across Mesoamerica (e.g., Andrews and Andrews 2001; Kepecs 2003; Masson 2000; Masson and Sabloff 2003; Milbrath and Peraza Lope 2003; Smith 2000; Smith and Berdan 2003); ethnohistoric research (Gasco and Berdan 2003; Robles 2007); and studies of Late Post-classic murals, codices, architecture, and pottery (Aveni 1999; Aveni et al. 2004; Boone 2003; Bricker 2001; Drapkin n.d. [2002]; Hernández and Bricker 2004; Just 2004; Masson 2003; Milbrath and Peraza Lope 2003; Pohl 2003, 2004; Vail and Aveni 2004: ch. 1).[2] Linguistic studies document both episodic and extended periods of contact evident in borrowings across Mesoamerican languages throughout much of the Pre-Hispanic period (see, e.g., Dakin and Wichmann 2000; Justeson et al. 1985; Macri and Looper 2003), presumably as a result of what Macri (ch. 6, this volume) terms "mutual economic and intellectual sharing."

Previous theories for explaining "Mexican" traits in the Maya area include migrations of substantial groups of people from central Mexico to the northern Maya lowlands, travel by religious specialists carrying codices or textiles, the promotion of "Aztec" traits in preparation for imperial conquest, and indirect influence such as the diffusion of "waves of influence." Ringle and his colleagues suggest a model in which elite interaction in Mesoamerica during the period immediately before the Late Postclassic was based on the cult of Quetzalcoatl/Kukulcan (Ringle 2004; Ringle et al. 1998); indoctrination into the cult occurred primarily through pilgrimages and investiture ceremonies.

Other recent models for understanding the types of interaction character-izing the Late Postclassic period are outlined in *The Postclassic Mesoamerican World* (Smith and Berdan 2003). Smith and the other authors in that volume note that, although many of the traits under discussion were first identified in central Mexico, it is now clear that they developed in many different parts of Mesoamerica and were truly international in scope. They suggest that the spread of common art styles and iconography in Postclassic Mesoamerica was the result of stylistic interaction and information exchange, rather than the imposition of elements from a dominant central Mexican culture on their weaker neighbors.

Smith and his colleagues promote a world systems approach that incorporates processes of information exchange as well as economic exchange. Although the latter may have opened the door to other types of interchange, Smith (2003; Boone and Smith 2003), following Ringle et al. (1998), argues that Mesoamerican elites deliberately chose to use specific stylistic elements and symbols to foster social and political interactions both within and outside their communities. The presence of particular institutions or complexes of traits that can be linked to central Mexico in the Maya area—a relatively rare occurrence—does not justify claims that the Maya or other Mesoamerican cultures became Mexicanized through the adoption of these particular features. It is far more likely that local elites chose to adopt specific foreign ideas and/or traits for their own purposes (Smith 2003: 185). World systems theory, then, focuses attention on the interplay of cultures, each acting to promote its own interests; it veers away from models that portray the Maya, Mixtec, and other groups as passive agents in a Late Postclassic Mesoamerican world dominated by central Mexican cultures. The chapters that follow clearly show that the Maya of the northern lowlands were active agents in the cultural interchange that characterized Mesoamerica in the centuries just before the Spanish conquest.

Impetus for the Symposium and Volume

Several collaborative sessions at Tulane University, involving many of the contributors to the present volume, highlighted for us significant parallels in the structure and content of the Maya and Borgia Group codices, adding to data published earlier in seminal studies by Eduard Seler (1904) and Cyrus Thomas (1884). The present volume builds on a century of scholarship on this subject, highlighted most recently in Elizabeth Boone's chapter "A Web of Understanding" in Smith and Berdan (2003) and in part III of *The Madrid Codex: New Approaches to Understanding an Ancient Maya Manuscript* (Vail and Aveni 2004).

The idea for the Dumbarton Oaks symposium arose as a result of these studies and their findings of explicit structural and calendrical parallels between highland Mexican and Maya codices (Boone 2003; Drapkin n.d. [2002];

Hernández and Bricker 2004; Just 2000, 2004), which led to models suggesting that Maya scribes may have had actual physical access to Borgia-style codices and contact with the scribes who produced these manuscripts (Boone 2003; Hernández and Bricker 2004). Our interest was in documenting when and where such interaction could have occurred within the context of Late Postclassic Mesoamerica. To address this issue, we invited scholars working in the fields of Mesoamerican archaeology, epigraphy, art history, archaeoastronomy, linguistics, and ethnohistory to meet and discuss data sets pertaining to intellectual interchange among elite members of Maya culture inhabiting the northern lowlands of Yucatán and highland central Mexican cultures, including Nahuatl speakers from the Basin of Mexico as well as the authors of the Borgia Group manuscripts.[3] The diverse chapters in this volume are a result of this scholarly interchange.

Contributions of Current Studies

We have grouped the discussions of particular data sets into three parts, based on the types of information that are examined. The chapters in Part I are concerned with archaeological and ethnohistoric data; Part II is focused on texts, language, and imagery; and Part III on the hieroglyphic and pictorial codices and the laying out of space.

Part I contains chapters by Fernando Robles, Marilyn Masson and Carlos Peraza, and Anthony Aveni. Robles presents a comprehensive overview of the archaeological and ethnohistoric data pertaining to the interaction between central and eastern Mesoamerica before and during the Culhua Mexica ("Aztec") expansion. His chapter provides an important framework for the discussions in the remainder of the volume, and his interpretation of recent chronological data is especially significant to our understanding of the Postclassic period within the context of earlier Mesoamerican history.

Masson and Peraza focus more specifically on one site—that of Mayapán in Yucatán, which has long been of interest to scholars because of statements made during the early colonial period suggesting a "Mexican" presence at the site (Tozzer 1941: 32). However, Masson and Peraza find that, despite strong indications of stylistic influences from the Mexican highlands, material evidence suggesting that enclaves of Mexican people were living at the site is ambiguous at best.

The chapters by Robles and by Masson and Peraza raise several issues worthy of further discussion. First, they make an important point concerning the chronology of Mayapán and how it relates to that for the Basin of Mexico and the surrounding highlands. Although it is frequently linked to Aztec Tenochtitlan in the literature, Mayapán was abandoned before the Mexica began their expansion beyond the territorial limits of the Basin of Mexico. "Mexican" influences at the site, therefore, are likely to be linked to groups other than the ethnic Mexica. In addition, both chapters highlight the importance of the Gulf Coast region in mediating trade and other relationships between the northern Maya lowlands and the Mexican highlands. As Scholes and Roys (1968: 23) suggested almost forty years ago, "Mexican" influences in Yucatán are probably not the result of migrations of central Mexican populations but rather came about indirectly from inhabitants of southern Mexico and the Gulf Coast region. It is within this region, we believe, that the types of Maya-Mexican interactions associated with long-distance trade and the movement of people, objects, luxury items, and food stuffs discussed later in the volume are most likely to have occurred.

In the final chapter in Part I, Aveni considers the evidence for Postclassic Mexican-Maya interchange with respect to the use of shared cosmographic schemes for founding settlements and aligning important structures within urban centers. Alignment data compiled for this study suggest to Aveni that not only are the plans for aligning public structures in Postclassic northern Yucatán more diverse than in previous eras in terms of the astronomical and seasonal events that they target, but that they also reflect similar schemes found at coeval sites in the central highlands. Aveni proposes that late changes in site plans at urban Yucatec Maya centers may be part of a larger and more comprehensive shift in calendrical and ritual programs focused on agricultural concerns that are also recorded by scribes in the Pre-Hispanic codices. What remains in question is whether these changes were brought about by information exchanged directly between Maya and Mexican scribes and architects or if instead they were the result of parallel cultural development as both regions responded to similar environmental changes. Although the alignment data cannot answer questions of this nature, other lines of evidence (discussed below) suggest the possibility of direct exchange.

The papers in Part II provide a broad frame of reference for interpreting evidence of a stylistic, linguistic, and textual nature from the Late Postclassic period suggestive of interaction between the northern Maya area and highland Mexico. The first three chapters, by Karl Taube, Martha Macri, and Karen Dakin, illustrate that interchange between lowland Maya and highland Mexican cultures was of a long-standing nature and can be documented at least as early as the Late Preclassic period. Taube examines this interaction in the artistic record, noting that the Maya area played as significant a role in innovation as did highland Mexico. Macri, who considers the visual record from a glyphic perspective, also finds evidence of interaction flowing in both directions. Their chapters, as well as that of Dakin, provide evidence for multiple avenues of communication, involving not only the areas previously discussed but also highland Guatemala. Although we chose to focus more narrowly on the northern Maya lowlands, the question of how the Guatemalan highlands were integrated into Late Postclassic networks of interaction is a topic that clearly requires further consideration and discussion.

The final chapter in Part II by Timothy Knowlton extends the frame of reference for evidence of interchange to the colonial period. In his examination of a text entitled the "Song of the Fall of Chichén Itzá," Knowlton points to the presence of Nahua vocables (syllables used exclusively for their sound value), which he suggests were employed to reinforce the "Mexican" affiliation of the Itzá groups who controlled Chichén Itzá during the Terminal Classic period. The use of specific syllables from the Nahua tradition is clear evidence, as Knowlton suggests, of a highland Mexican influence on Maya music and texts at some point in the Pre-Hispanic past.

Part III consists of chapters by Merideth Paxton, Victoria Bricker, and Christine Hernández and Gabrielle Vail. These contributors focus on investigating correspondences between almanacs (calendrical instruments) in the Maya and Borgia Group codices, and, in the case of Paxton's chapter, colonial era diagrams and maps associated with rituals of foundation. All three chapters consider the almanacs on pages 75 and 76 of the Madrid Codex and page 1 of the Codex Fejérváry-Mayer (plates 1–2), although they propose different interpretations of how they were used. When evaluating the various models, it is important to keep in mind that they may each provide significant information about the function and use of these instruments by the Late Postclassic cultures of Mesoamerica. One thing that has become increasingly clear to codical scholars in recent years is that almanacs were ingenious devices for modeling multiple calendrical, seasonal, and astronomical cycles and their interrelationships, meaning that they frequently had more than a single use or function.

Paxton's chapter, like Knowlton's in the previous section, provides a bridge between the Late Postclassic and colonial periods. She looks specifically at the influence of an abstract image of the apparent annual motion of the sun across the sky that appears in two Pre-Hispanic almanacs—pages 75 and 76 of the Maya Madrid Codex and page 1 of the Codex Fejérváry-Mayer—on colonial period renderings of geographic space for the town of Yaxkukul in northern Yucatán and Tenochtitlan and San Mateo Ixtlahuacan in the Basin of Mexico. While she notes that both the Maya and Mexican Pre-Hispanic schemes of solar cartography transcend the Postclassic period to influence early colonial descriptions and illustrations of settlement geography, she does not find persuasive evidence of late cross-cultural sharing of such schemes but rather a more general pattern of similarity, suggesting long-held pan-Mesoamerican concepts.

The chapters by Bricker and by Hernández and Vail address the question of interchange between codical scribes from Yucatán and central Mexico by considering cognate almanacs from the extant Maya and Borgia Group codices. The results of both studies suggest that the similarities one sees on the surface, specifically in terms of iconography and almanac layout, hint at an even deeper set of connections in almanac structure, function, and calendrical reckoning. Such an exchange and mutual understanding of esoteric information would seem to argue for more intimate modes of interaction beyond the mere swapping, copying, and possession of objects.

The volume concludes with two chapters that serve as a further discussion of the data sets and themes considered by the contributors to Parts I–III. Anthony Andrews comments on the archaeological evidence presented in Part I, and Alfonso Lacadena discusses Parts II and III. In addition to their insightful commentaries, Andrews and Lacadena provide further data relevant to the consideration of interchange among highland Mexican and Yucatec Maya astronomers, scribes, and priests in Late Postclassic Mesoamerica.

One thing that remains puzzling, as Andrews points out, is the apparent contradiction between historic sources that describe a vigorous commercial interaction between the two areas, and the material record, which to date reveals very little evidence of this thriving trade. Andrews notes that various factors may have contributed to the sparse material evidence for interaction, the most significant being that only a very small percentage of the archaeological record pertinent to the Postclassic period has been sampled and investigated. As Lacadena observes, the record for contact between the two areas is much more robust when one examines modes of communication, including written and spoken language, symbols, and pictures, in conjunction with the items that are used to communicate—books, mural paintings, textiles, and carved objects, to name a few. He reminds us that the sharing and exchange of symbolically laden information implies personal, perhaps even collegial, forms of interaction that result in the transmission of the original meanings of words, symbols, and pictures before innovation and transformation can take place. This implies that the evidence for intellectual exchange in the Postclassic period documented in this volume must be the result of a long and continuous history of cultural contact between the central highlands and the Maya area that has ebbed and flowed over many centuries, but one that can only be understood as involving intellectual peers.

Note on Orthography

We have left the choice of orthography when spelling words in one of the indigenous Mesoamerican languages to the discretion of each author. As a result, the same word may occur a number of different ways across the volume; for example, the twentieth day of the 260-day Maya calendar can be rendered as Ahau, Ahaw, or Ajaw. Similarly, the name of this ritual calendar is spelled *tzolkin* in some chapters and *tzolk'in* in others.

For language and site names and for geographic regions, we follow a standard orthography throughout the volume. It is fairly complex but is meant to take into account the preferences of our Latin American colleagues as well as of indigenous groups in Mexico and Guatemala.

Language names. We defer to the spellings of the Academia de las Lenguas mayas de Guatemala for all languages within Guatemala. The traditional spellings of language names are used for Mexico (e.g., Yucatec rather than Yukatek and Huastec instead of Wastek). These are listed on the map showing the distribution of Mayan and Uto-Aztecan languages at the time of contact (Dakin, this volume, fig. 1).

Maya site and geographic names. Again, we follow a different system for sites and areas within Guatemala and those in Mexico. The preference in Guatemala today is not to use accents for Maya words, so that what was formerly spelled as Petén is now Peten and Yaxhá is now Yaxha. Accents are still retained in Spanish words (e.g., Río). Accents are also still used with the names of sites and geographic regions within Mexico (e.g., Mayapán, Yucatán).

Nahuatl/Uto-Aztecan site names. Like the current Guatemalan system, accents are no longer used for indigenous site names when they were introduced as part of the Spanish orthography (e.g., Tenochtitlán is now Tenochtitlan). We follow recent publications of the Instituto Nacional de Antropología e Historia to determine the current preferences, in particular Fernando Robles's *Culhua México: Una revisión arqueo-etnohistórica del imperio de los mexica tenochca* (2007).

Occasionally, the authors of different chapters use variant spellings of the same site name (e.g., Xicalango/Xicalanco or Champoton/Chanpoton). We have left the choice of which form to use, which is based on variant spellings in the literature, to their discretion.

Acknowledgments

The chapters in this volume are the result of a multiyear process of collaboration among the contributors, accomplished via the Internet, a working group session at the Society for American Archaeology meetings in San Juan (April 2006), and the October 2006 Pre-Columbian Studies symposium sponsored by Dumbarton Oaks and hosted by the Library of Congress. We would like to extend our gratitude especially to Joanne Pillsbury, Jeffrey Quilter, Jai Alterman, Bridget Gazzo, Emily Gulick, Kathy Sparkes, and Sara Taylor of—or formerly of, in the case of Jai Alterman and Jeffrey Quilter—Dumbarton Oaks; Georgette Dorn and Barbara Tenenbaum of the Hispanic Division of the Library of Congress; Arthur Dunkelman formerly of Rare Books and Special Collections, and the Kislak Collection of the Library of Congress; and the contributors, discussants, and participants who attended the Pre-Columbian Studies symposium and engaged in a lively and productive exchange on the question of interchange among Late Postclassic cultures in the northern Maya lowlands and highland Mexico.

We are also indebted to the National Endowment for the Humanities for supporting our research on interrelationships among the Maya and Borgia Group codices and would especially like to thank our program officers, Elizabeth Arndt and Lisa Kahn, for their support. Discussions with a number of colleagues, including Tony Andrews, Tony Aveni, Victoria Bricker, Karen Dakin, Dan Healan, Martha Macri, Merideth Paxton, and Fernando Robles, have been extremely helpful during the process of writing and editing this book. Finally, we greatly appreciate the editorial expertise of James Coffey and Cynthia Vail, the assistance of Alejandro Figueroa, Mary Grove, José Moreno, and Jessica Wheeler, and the support of the New College glyph group.

Notes

1. See Aveni's discussion concerning the ethnohistoric and ethnographic evidence for ancient Mesoamerican astronomers in chapter 2 of *Skywatchers* (2001).
2. Space considerations preclude an exhaustive bibliography of current research on these issues. The reader is referred to the sources referenced for a more extensive list of resources that are relevant to the present discussion.
3. The codices of the Borgia Group are generally referred to with the name following "Codex" (e.g., Codex Fejérváry-Mayer), whereas the Maya codices are designated by the city where they were found, followed by "Codex" (e.g., Madrid Codex). In the chapters that follow, we deviate from this convention on occasion by referring to the Borgia as the Borgia Codex rather than Codex Borgia. We follow the standard format in referring to the other codices, however.

References Cited

Andrews, E. Wyllys, V, and Anthony P. Andrews
    2001   Northern Maya Lowlands. In *The Oxford Encyclopedia of Mesoamerican Cultures: The Civilizations of Mexico and Central America*, vol. 2 (Davíd Carrasco, ed.): 378–385. Oxford University Press, New York.

Aveni, Anthony F.
    1999   Astronomy in the Mexican Codex Borgia. *Archaeoastronomy* (Supplement to *Journal for the History of Astronomy*) 24: S1–S20.
    2001   *Skywatchers*. Rev. ed. University of Texas Press, Austin.

Aveni, Anthony F., Susan Milbrath, and Carlos Peraza Lope
    2004   Chichén Itzá's Legacy in the Astronomical Oriented Architecture of Mayapán. *RES* 45: 123–143.

Berdan, Frances F., Marilyn A. Masson, Janine Gasco, and Michael E. Smith
    2003   An International Economy. In *The Postclassic Mesoamerican World* (Michael E. Smith and Frances F. Berdan, eds.): 96–108. University of Utah Press, Salt Lake City.

Boone, Elizabeth H.

    2003   A Web of Understanding: Pictorial Codices and the Shared Intellectual Culture of Late Postclassic Mesoamerica. In *The Postclassic Mesoamerican World* (Michael E. Smith and Frances F. Berdan, eds.): 207–221. University of Utah Press, Salt Lake City.

    2007   *Cycles of Time and Meaning in the Mexican Books of Fate.* University of Texas Press, Austin.

Boone, Elizabeth H., and Michael E. Smith

    2003   Postclassic International Styles and Symbol Sets. In *The Postclassic Mesoamerican World* (Michael E. Smith and Frances F. Berdan, eds.): 186–193. University of Utah Press, Salt Lake City.

Bricker, Victoria R.

    2001   A Method for Dating Venus Almanacs in the Borgia Codex. *Archaeoastronomy* (Supplement to *Journal for the History of Astronomy*) 26: S21–S44.

Dakin, Karen, and Søren Wichmann

    2000   Cacao and Chocolate: A Uto-Aztecan Perspective. *Ancient Mesoamerica* 11: 55–75.

Drapkin, Julia

    n.d.   Interpreting the Dialect of Time: A Structural Analysis and Discussion of Almanacs in the Madrid Codex. Honors thesis, Department of Anthropology, Tulane University, New Orleans, 2002.

Gasco, Janine, and Frances F. Berdan

    2003   International Trade Centers. In *The Postclassic Mesoamerican World* (Michael E. Smith and Frances F. Berdan, eds.): 109–116. University of Utah Press, Salt Lake City.

Hernández, Christine, and Victoria R. Bricker

    2004   The Inauguration of Planting in the Borgia and Madrid Codices. In *The Madrid Codex: New Approaches to Understanding an Ancient Maya Manuscript* (Gabrielle Vail and Anthony Aveni, eds.): 277–320. University Press of Colorado, Boulder.

Just, Bryan R.

    2000   Concordances of Time: *In Extenso* Almanacs in the Madrid and Borgia Group Codices. *Human Mosaic* 33 (1): 7–16.

    2004   *In Extenso* Almanacs in the Madrid Codex. In *The Madrid Codex: New Approaches to Understanding an Ancient Maya Manuscript* (Gabrielle Vail and Anthony Aveni, eds.): 255–276. University Press of Colorado, Boulder.

Justeson, John S., William M. Norman, Lyle Campbell, and Terrence Kaufman

    1985   *The Foreign Impact on Lowland Mayan Language and Script.* Middle American Research Institute Publication 53. Tulane University, New Orleans.

Kepecs, Susan M.

    2003   Chikinchel. In *The Postclassic Mesoamerican World* (Michael E. Smith and Frances F. Berdan, eds.): 259–268. University of Utah Press, Salt Lake City.

Macri, Martha J., and Matthew G. Looper

    2003   Nahua in Ancient Mesoamerica: Evidence from Maya Inscriptions. *Ancient Mesoamerica* 14: 285–297.

Masson, Marilyn A.

2000 *In the Realm of Nachan Kan: Postclassic Maya Archaeology at Laguna de On, Belize.* University Press of Colorado, Boulder.

2003 The Late Postclassic Symbol Set in the Maya Area. In *The Postclassic Mesoamerican World* (Michael E. Smith and Frances F. Berdan, eds.): 194–200. University of Utah Press, Salt Lake City.

Masson, Marilyn A., and Jeremy A. Sabloff

2003 Developments in Northern Yucatán Archaeology. In *Escondido en la selva: Arqueología en el norte de Yucatán; Segundo Simposio Teoberto Maler, Bonn, 2000* (Hanns J. Prem, ed.): 417–424. Universidad de Bonn, Bonn and Instituto Nacional de Antropología e Historia, México, D.F.

Milbrath, Susan, and Carlos Peraza Lope

2003 Revisiting Mayapan: Mexico's Last Maya Capital. *Ancient Mesoamerica* 14: 1–46.

Pohl, John M. D.

2003 Ritual and Iconographic Variability in Mixteca-Puebla Polychrome Pottery. In *The Postclassic Mesoamerican World* (Michael E. Smith and Frances F. Berdan, eds.): 201–206. University of Utah Press, Salt Lake City.

2004 Screenfold Manuscripts of Highland Mexico and Their Possible Influence on Codex Madrid: A Summary. In *The Madrid Codex: New Approaches to Understanding an Ancient Maya Manuscript* (Gabrielle Vail and Anthony Aveni, eds.): 367–413. University Press of Colorado, Boulder.

Ringle, William M.

2004 On the Political Organization of Chichen Itza. *Ancient Mesoamerica* 15 (2): 167–218.

Ringle, William M., Tomás Gallareta Negrón, and George J. Bey III

1998 The Return of Quetzalcoatl: Evidence for the Spread of a World Religion during the Epiclassic Period. *Ancient Mesoamerica* 9: 183–232.

Robles Castellanos, Fernando

2007 *Culhua México: Una revisión arqueo-etnohistórica del imperio de los mexica tenochca.* Instituto Nacional de Antropología e Historia, México, D.F.

Scholes, France V., and Ralph L. Roys

1968 *The Maya Chontal Indians of Acalan-Tixchel: A Contribution to the History and Ethnography of the Yucatan Peninsula.* University of Oklahoma Press, Norman.

Seler, Eduard

1904 Venus Period in the Picture Writings of the Borgian Codex Group. *Bureau of American Ethnology, Bulletin* 28: 355–391. Smithsonian Institution, Washington, D.C.

Smith, Michael E.

2000 Long-Distance Trade under the Aztec Empire: The Archaeological Evidence. *Ancient Mesoamerica* 1: 153–169.

2003 Information Networks in Postclassic Mesoamerica. In *The Postclassic Mesoamerican World* (Michael E. Smith and Frances F. Berdan, eds.): 181–185. University of Utah Press, Salt Lake City.

Smith, Michael E., and Frances F. Berdan (eds.)

    2003   *The Postclassic Mesoamerican World*. University of Utah Press, Salt Lake City.

Thomas, Cyrus

    1884   Notes on Certain Maya and Mexican Manuscripts. In *Third Annual Report of the Bureau of American Ethnology, 1881–82*: 7–65. Smithsonian Institution, Washington, D.C.

Tozzer, Alfred M.

    1941   *Landa's* Relación de las cosas de Yucatan: *A Translation*. Papers of the Peabody Museum of American Archaeology and Ethnology 18. Harvard University, Cambridge, Mass.

Vail, Gabrielle, and Anthony Aveni (eds.)

    2004   *The Madrid Codex: New Approaches to Understanding an Ancient Maya Manuscript*. University Press of Colorado, Boulder.

Part I

Archaeological Evidence

Introduction

Christine Hernández, Anthony P. Andrews,
and Gabrielle Vail

THE CHAPTERS IN PART I go directly to the heart of the question of interaction between central Mexican and Yucatecan populations during the Postclassic period in their emphasis on the use and exchange of foreign objects and commodities. Clearly, the archaeological record is bound to contain the most tangible and obvious types of material evidence for face-to-face contact between the Maya of the northern lowlands and Nahuatl-speaking people and related groups from highland central Mexico during the Postclassic period (ca. 1100–1542 CE). Therefore, the chapters in Part I examine narratives from ethnohistoric documents, items of foreign material culture (ceramics, lithics, and figurines, to name a few), and cultural patterns (burial configurations and architectural orientations, for example) preserved within the archaeological record. Recent studies of pan-Mesoamerican interaction and imperial expansion during the Postclassic period (Berdan and Smith 1996; Smith and Berdan 2003) suggest that archaeological evidence for contact between the Mexican highlands and the Maya lowlands in the post-Toltec, post–Chichén Itzá era is nominal and restricted to representations of elite information exchange recovered primarily from Maya sites (Smith 2003). These findings imply that much of the positive material evidence for long-distance interaction is to be found in Yucatán and very little is to be expected from the central highlands. The apparent absence of material traces of contact with the Postclassic lowland Maya in this region may be due in part to the infrequent excavation of Late Postclassic contexts in areas of particular interest to the current study, such as the Puebla-Tlaxcala region and the southern Gulf Coast. Or it may be that the evidence has been destroyed, built over, or is simply not there.

These initial impressions are not too surprising, given that this period came immediately after the cessation of the intense commercial, political, and proposed cult activities (Ringle et al. 1998) that had previously tied these regions closely together for more than a century after the end of the Classic period. However, evidence from early colonial sources from both regions alludes to sustained commercial and possibly intermittent political interaction between areas of central Mexico, the Gulf Coast, and northern Yucatán during the later Postclassic and Protohistoric periods (discussed later; see also Robles, ch. 2, and Taube, ch. 5, this volume). This evidence, in combination with recent discoveries in the extant Maya codices and mural art as well as at major archaeological sites in northern Yucatán, reveals new and important information on the subject. In Part I, we consider what the archaeological record can tell us about the renewal and reconfiguration of pan-Mesoamerican communication that may have taken place in the aftermath of the central Mexican Epiclassic and Maya Terminal Classic periods. The chapters by Fernando Robles and by Marilyn Masson and Carlos Peraza employ the latest chronological revisions and new material data to complement the ethnohistory in order to better understand when, where, and under what conditions interchange among Mexican and Maya intellectuals could have taken place. Anthony Aveni's contribution highlights changes in architectural alignments from the Classic to Postclassic periods that may be a result of interchange among calendrical specialists based in highland Mexico and the northern Maya lowlands.

Postclassic Period Chronology

The final centuries of the Pre-Hispanic era are commonly (but mistakenly, as we will show) viewed as a period characterized by the cultural decline of ancient Mesoamerican civilization. As its label implies, the Postclassic period comprises the interval of time after the events defining the end of the Classic period up to the point at which the Spanish arrived in Mesoamerica (table 1). In the Basin of Mexico, archaeologists break the Postclassic period into two (Early and Late) or three (Early, Middle, and Late) subdivisions (e.g., Parsons et al. 1996: fig. 1; Sanders et al. 1979: table 5.1, 93), and it is generally seen as the time interval following the decline of major regional urban centers, including Cholula, Xochicalco, Tenango del Valle, Cantona, Cacaxtla, and El Tajín. The Early Postclassic coincides with the settlement, flourishing, and subsequent abandonment of the site of Tula in southern Hidalgo, a major regional capital from ca. 950 to 1100/1150.[1] The latter episode, or "Late" Postclassic, is further broken down into two shorter subperiods. The first subdivision, sometimes referred to as the "Middle Postclassic," encompasses the two centuries following the decline of the urban center at Tula when new, Nahuatl-speaking populations from northern central Mexico are believed to have begun to migrate southward into the Basin of Mexico and surrounding areas, and when the balkanization of the central highlands into a number of small political entities

Table 1 Select chronologies from the central highlands of Mexico and northern Yucatán[1]

Date (CE)	Cultural periods central Mexico[2]	Basin of Mexico sites[2]	Tula[3]	Cholula[4]	Cultural periods northern Yucatán[5]	Chichén Itzá[5]	Mayapán[6]
1550		Tlatelolco (Aztec IV)					
1500	Late Postclassic		Palacio	Late Chollan			
1450		Tenochtitlan (Aztec III)					
1400							
1350		Tenayuca (Aztec II)			Postclassic	Tases	Tases
1300	Middle Postclassic		Fuego	Early Chollan			
1250		Culhuacan (Aztec I)					
1200							
1150				Late Tlachihualtépetl			
1100							Tases / Hocabá
1050	Early Postclassic	Mazapan	Tollan			Sotuta-Hocabá	
1000							Cehpech
950				Early Tlachihualtépetl	Terminal Classic	Sotuta	
900	Epiclassic						

1. Compiled by Christine Hernández, Fernando Robles, and Anthony P. Andrews.
2. Parsons et al. (1996)
3. Cobean and Mastache (1989)
4. McCafferty (1996)
5. Andrews et al. (2003)
6. Peraza Lope et al. (2006)

occurred (1150–1350 CE). The second subdivision is generally associated with the emergence and imperial expansion of the Aztec state directed by the ruling Mexica elite of Tenochtitlan (ca. 1367–1521 CE).

In Yucatán, a similar two-part breakdown of the Postclassic period has been applied to the archaeological record. The Early Postclassic has traditionally been defined as the time following the collapse of the Classic Maya polities throughout the lowlands and the continued florescence of the Terminal Classic northern regional capitals of Uxmal, Kabah, Izamal, and Ek Balam, among others, in concert with the fortunes of the site of Chichén Itzá. However, it has recently been suggested that the Yucatecan Early Postclassic be redefined as part of the previous Terminal Classic period because there is strong chronological evidence that Chichén Itzá's florescence as an urban center is contemporary with the apogee of the Puuc cities to the south, and that Chichén survived as a regional urban capital for only a few decades, or perhaps even a century, after their demise. It is now widely believed that the Itzá capital ceased to be a major seat of power sometime between 1050 and 1100 CE (Andrews et al. 2003).

The subsequent Late Postclassic period can therefore be best defined as the Postclassic period proper. As in central Mexico, this period can be divided into two subphases. Unlike the situation in the central highlands, the first subphase was a time of regional political centralization and stability that saw the ascendancy and decline of the Mayapán polity and the growth of communities along the east coast of the peninsula (in present-day Quintana Roo). The fall of Mayapán in ca. 1450 and the fragmentation of its former territory into a cluster of politically unstable "provinces," or *cuchcabaloob*, marks the beginning of the second subphase. During this final century before the conquest, the towns and cities of Quintana Roo continued to flourish, Tulúm most prominently. This walled city rose to regional preeminence, most likely owing to its role as a commercial trading center and possibly also to its strong ties to the expanding imperial networks emanating from the Basin of Mexico.

The present volume takes up the question of interregional interchange during what was previously called the Late Postclassic period. It is consequently of paramount importance to our enterprise that we have at our disposal the best possible chronological models available for tracing the culture history and trajectories of social development in both the Maya lowlands and the central Mexican highlands. They are essential, as we will see, to understanding the timing and context of whatever forms of cultural contact can be documented by the archaeological evidence.

History of Archaeological Research

A number of early colonial sources discuss historic contacts between Mexicans and the Yucatec Maya in the centuries immediately preceding the arrival of the Spanish in 1519. Bishop Diego de Landa, in his 1566 manuscript *Relación de las cosas de Yucatán*, was one of the first to do so, recounting the historico-mythical story of the migration of the central Mexican ruler and deity Quetzal-coatl to northern Yucatán, where the local chronicles record his arrival under the name Kukulcan, and his founding of Chichén Itzá and/or Mayapán (Tozzer 1941: 20–24). Other chroniclers also discuss this migration event, as originally detailed in the native chronicles of central Mexico and the Maya area. Although the particulars vary from account to account, the most widely told narrative holds that Quetzalcoatl was one of the last rulers of Tollan (generally held to be the archaeological site of Tula, Hidalgo) and that he came to Yucatán with his followers and founded Chichén Itzá several centuries before the arrival of the Spaniards.[2]

Bishop Landa also gives specific details regarding the history of the city of Mayapán, which had been abandoned shortly before the conquest:

> The Governor Cocom began to covet riches and for this reason he arranged with the troops of the garrison, which the kings of Mexico kept at Tabasco and Xicalango, to hand over the city to them. And thus he brought the Mexican people into Mayapán, and oppressed the poor and made many slaves, and the lords would have put him to death but for the fear they had of the Mexicans. And the Yucatecans, finding themselves in this situation, learned from the Mexicans the use of arms, and they soon became masters of the bow and arrow, the lance and the axe, their shields and jackets made strong with the salt and cotton, as well as other instruments of war, so that finally they neither admired the Mexicans nor feared them; on the contrary they took little account of them (Tozzer 1941: 32–35).[3]

Trading activities were the main crucible for the movement, not only of goods, but also of travelers, political communication, and cultural influences. Much of the trade between central Mexico and Yucatán apparently went through the intermediate trading ports of the Tabasco/Campeche coast, and particularly Xicalango, a strategic trading node referred to in many early chronicles. Goods traded from Yucatán included cotton, cotton cloth, dyes, honey, wax, and various other items, whereas central Mexico supplied the Maya lowlands with obsidian, turquoise, weapons, decorated cloth, and artifacts made from crystal, gold, and copper.[4]

Most of the early colonial accounts were shelved and forgotten during the later colonial period, and the subject of Mexican-Maya interactions did not reemerge until the nineteenth century, when the older accounts were rediscovered and published, at the same time that explorers began investigating the abandoned ruins of the Pre-Hispanic Maya.

Perhaps the earliest archaeological explorer to revive the subject was John L. Stephens, who, with the English artist Frederick Catherwood, traveled throughout the Maya area between 1839 and 1842. In the course of their travels, Stephens, who was acquainted with most of the historical and archaeological literature on ancient Mesoamerica then available, made reference to the Toltec/Quetzalcoatl/Kukulcan migration myth, and he observed several features in the architecture, sculpture, and paintings of Chichén Itzá that suggested to him that they had a central Mexican or Toltec origin. He was also the first to note the similarity of the ballcourts of Uxmal and Chichén Itzá to the "tennis courts" of central Mexico, and he remarked on the likely Mexican origin of several Maya obsidian artifacts he encountered at Kantunilkin (Stephens 1843).

Another scholarly explorer who delved into the subject was the French photographer Désiré Charnay, who, in the course of his extensive travels in Mesoamerica, conducted detailed explorations and excavations at both Tula and Chichén Itzá between 1880 and 1882. Charnay noted similarities in the architecture and sculpture of the two sites, notably the ballcourts and colonnaded halls, and associated relief panels and sculptures.[5] The recently discovered *chacmool* statue, in particular, attracted his attention, and he compared the statues from Chichén Itzá and Tlaxcala (Charnay 1887: 95–96, 332–368, 375–376).[6] All of these similarities were noted in support of the Toltec migration myth, which was by then acquiring historical status.[7] In Charnay's view, Chichén Itzá, Mayapán, and the Xius and Cocoms were all descendants of the Toltecs, and they constituted the Toltec-Maya civilization (Charnay 1887: 357–358).[8]

Subsequent travelers and scholars in the late nineteenth and early twentieth centuries continued to make observations on and conduct studies of similarities and evidence of contact between the northern Maya and the Mexican cultures. Many of the observations centered on the architecture and artwork at Chichén Itzá, although "Mexican" features and artifacts were reported from a number of other sites as well. Some of the more prominent investigators who added valuable contributions to the subject of Mexican-Yucatec interactions were Edward Thompson and William Holmes, who conducted fieldwork at several sites in Yucatán (and in the case of Holmes, at sites in central and southern Mexico as well, which provided him with an excellent comparative perspective).[9] Another scholar who contributed to the subject was the great Americanist Eduard Seler, who made three visits to Yucatán between 1902 and 1911. In his lifetime Seler traveled throughout the continent and visited many archaeological sites in Mesoamerica. His collected works on Mesoamerican linguistics and archaeology are a monumental legacy, combining a prodigious amount of synthesis with his own observations in the field. Among his many publications are several that recap and discuss the observations of previous scholars, including his own on many aspects of Mexican-Maya interaction, such as the Quetzalcoatl/Kukulcan myth and shared features in the architecture, sculpture, relief panels, murals, and codices.[10]

In the course of the twentieth century, fieldwork conducted by the Carnegie Institution of Washington at Chichén Itzá, Mayapán, and sites along the east coast of Yucatán, and by other institutions at Teotihuacan, Tula, Xochicalco, and Cacaxtla in central Mexico; at Kaminaljuyu, Utatlan, Mixco Viejo, and Iximche in highland Guatemala; and at Tikal and other sites in the Maya lowlands has yielded considerable archaeological information on Mexican-Maya commercial, artistic, religious, and political interaction. Much of this work focuses on the Late Preclassic and Early Classic periods (Teotihuacan and related sites in the Maya area) and the Terminal Classic/Early Postclassic period (Tula, Chichén Itzá, and sites in highland Guatemala).[11] The primary focus of the studies in this volume concerns the question of cultural contact and long-distance interaction in the final two centuries of the Postclassic period (ca. 1350–1542 CE); thus the remainder of this brief survey examines the history of research dedicated to the last centuries of the Pre-Hispanic era.

Much of the archaeological information on this subject for this period in Yucatán comes from the work at Mayapán, conducted by the Carnegie Institution of Washington from 1949 to 1955 and, more recently, by the Instituto Nacional de Antropología e Historia (INAH) under the direction of Carlos Peraza.[12] Mayapán, the capital of the last large regional state in the Maya lowlands, emerged as the paramount economic and political urban center in Yucatán sometime in the late eleventh or early twelfth century, went into decline around 1400, came to an abrupt and calamitous end around 1441(?), and was abandoned and in ruins when the Spanish arrived in the sixteenth century. Because it inherited a large part of the extensive trade networks of the earlier capital of Chichén Itzá, Mayapán became a wealthy and metropolitan center in its own right. Archaeologists have known for some time that its architecture and artwork, while clearly Maya, had a strong Mexican flavor. Beyond the obvious external influence, it is difficult to define the exact nature of the Mexican "presence" in the city. The chapters in Part I present new information and a revised chronology that unveils a more complex scenario of the possible archaeological footprints of foreigners in the urban area and who those foreigners could have been.

Extensive fieldwork has also been carried out at a number of Postclassic sites throughout Quintana Roo,[13] where evidence of cultural connections to central Mexico are apparent in architecture, sculpture, and mural painting. Ever since Samuel Lothrop published his landmark survey of the sites along the Quintana Roo coast in 1924, the notion of a Postclassic "East Coast style" of architecture became embedded in the archaeological literature. Many of the salient architectural and related sculptural features of this style have long been recognized as having central Mexican affinities, which are generally attributed either to their presence in the earlier regional state capital of Chichén Itzá or to direct influence from Mexico during the Postclassic period. These features include serpent columns, serpent balustrades, columns with carved or stuccoed figures, balustrades with vertical upper zones, *chacmool* statues, colonnaded structures, inset panels above doorways, sloping or battered bases of temple walls, round structures, and Mixtec and Toltec motifs in mural paintings (Andrews and Andrews 1975). Robles suggests that if there is evidence of Aztec *pochtecas* to be found in northern Yucatán, it would be at these sites along the eastern Quintana Roo coast.

The first comprehensive study of Maya art, published by Herbert Spinden in 1913, highlighted the round structures found in many Terminal Classic and Postclassic sites in central Mexico and Yucatán. These are generally believed to be astronomical observatories and/or temples dedicated to Quetzalcoatl/ Ehecatl, the god of wind, who was a prominent deity among Postclassic period societies in central Mexico and the Mixteca region of Oaxaca.[14]

Perhaps the most compelling evidence of central Mexican influence in northern Yucatán occurs in the mural paintings found at several sites in Quintana Roo and Mayapán. These paintings have been the subject of substantial research in the last three decades. A seminal work is that of Donald Robertson (1970), who proposed the notion of an International style linking codices and murals from the Mixteca-Puebla region to those of the northern Maya area, notably at Tulúm and at Santa Rita in Belize. Further studies along these lines have been conducted by Jacinto Quirarte (1982), Arthur Miller (1982), Martine Fettweis-Vienot (n.d.a [1973], 1980, n.d.b [1981], 1983, 1987), Sonia Lombardo de Ruiz (1987, 2001), Tomás Gallareta and Karl Taube (2006), and Gabrielle Vail and Christine Hernández (Vail 2008; Vail and Hernández n.d.).

Mayapán and the Ethnohistory of Yucatán and Tabasco

According to ethnohistoric accounts, Mayapán was settled by Cocom émigrés from the site of Chichén Itzá and Xiu groups who came from the Puuc region to the south of the site (Farris 1984: 245; Roys 1967: 194; Tozzer 1941: 40). Archaeologically, feathered-serpent imagery at Mayapán seems to be linked to the Cocom, who, according to colonial sources, represented the ruling lineage at Chichén, where they were referred to as Itzá. Bill Ringle et al. (1998) propose that the Itzá may not have been an ethnic group but rather a religious affiliation linked to the spread of the Quetzalcoatl/Kukulcan cult in Mesoamerica. They suggest that the cult had its origins in the Tlaxcala area and spread from there during the Epiclassic/Terminal Classic period along trade routes formerly dominated by Teotihuacan. They further believe that the Itzá cult was part of a military incursion, forced on local populations previously engaged with them in trade relationships.

The Cocom were the most powerful of the various elite lineage groups residing at Mayapán and are said to have used another group, the Canul, as mercenaries to increase their power base. According to Landa (Tozzer 1941: 31–37), the ruling families of other towns from throughout the peninsula lived at Mayapán until the Xiu mounted a revolt, at which time they each returned to their separate territories.

The Xiu were also part of the confederacy government. Although they claimed to be of local descent, ethnohistoric data suggest that they came originally from Tabasco (Tozzer 1941: 30–31). The word *Xiu* itself is Nahuatl (Milbrath and Peraza 2003: 33),[15] which supports a western origin, as does Edmonson's (1982: 9, n. 119) statement that the Mayapán Xius included seven lords with Nahuatl names who took part in the revolt that destroyed the city. After this, the lineage moved to Maní, where they founded a Xiu settlement (Tozzer 1941: 40, n. 194).

According to the Book of Chilam Balam of Maní, the Tutul Xius came from the west, from the land of Tulapan, via the Peten (Craine and Reindorp 1979: 138–139). They arrived at Uxmal in *k'atun* 2 Ahaw (possibly 751 CE; Schele and Mathews 1998: 259) and are associated with Puuc architecture both at Classic period sites and at Mayapán. Another style of architecture at Mayapán includes colonnaded halls associated with Hocabá pottery and Peto Cream wares from the east coast of the peninsula, suggesting that Mayapán was truly a cosmopolitan center (Milbrath and Peraza 2003: 35; Proskouriakoff 1962: 132; see also Masson and Peraza, ch. 3, this volume).

The most foreign of the groups residing at Mayapán were the Canuls, who can be identified as Nahua speakers originally from Xicalango, on the Laguna de Términos in Campeche (Milbrath and Peraza 2003: 35; Tozzer 1941: 39). Xicalango is known to have housed Mexican traders and perhaps warriors as well. Ethnohistoric documents confirm the presence of *pochteca* merchants in the Gulf Coast region by the late fifteenth century (Sahagún 1950–1982, bk. 9: 3, n. 1, 17, n. 2).

The *Relación de la villa de Santa Maria de la Victoria* suggests that the Aztec ruler Montezuma (Moctezuma II) had a fortress at Xicalango and that he was about to launch an invasion of Yucatán at the time of the Spanish conquest. Scholes and Roys (1968: 34–36) believe that this claim is exaggerated, but they note that a close relative of Moctezuma appears to have been in charge of a colony of Mexican merchants at Xicalango and may have been planning to extend his commercial activities into Yucatán around the time that Cortés seized Tenochtitlan. Fernando Robles discusses these events in Chapter 2 of this volume.

At the time of the Spanish conquest, the peninsula of Yucatán and adjoining lands along the Gulf of Mexico and the Caribbean formed an economic unit that was held together by commercial relations. Yucatán had a monopoly on salt production and also exported cotton cloth and slaves. In exchange, they received cacao, obsidian, copper, gold, feathers, and other luxury items from Tabasco and the Caribbean (Andrews 1990, 1993; Andrews and Andrews 2001; Gasco and Berdan 2003; Scholes and Roys 1968). Tabasco's prosperity can be attributed to its cacao production. It is located on what were the main trade routes connecting the Veracruz slope, the Valley of Mexico, and the highlands of Chiapas with Yucatán and the rich coast of northern Honduras. At the time of the Spanish conquest, there were at least eight and possibly more Mexican-speaking towns in Tabasco (Scholes and Roys 1968: 27–28).

The province of Acalan, inhabited by people who spoke the Chontal language of Tabasco, occupied a strategic position within this economic unit. At the time of the Spanish conquest, Acalan dominated the drainage of the Río Candelaria, which flows into the Laguna de Términos, and played an important part in the trade carried on between the Gulf and Caribbean coasts.[16] Ethnohistoric documents indicate that the Acalan ruling family came from northeast Yucatán, although they were originally from Tabasco. Subsequently, this group occupied the Usumacinta Valley near Temosique, the region around Laguna de Términos, and the Candelaria area, where Cortés found them in 1525 CE. The term *Chontal* was originally applied to the inhabitants of Tabasco by the Mexicans; *chontalli* is an Aztec term meaning "foreigner." Acalan is a Nahuatl word derived from *acalli*, "canoe"; the name has been translated as "place of the canoes" (Scholes and Roys 1968: 48–52).

Nahua-speaking peoples were living among the Chontal of Tabasco at the time of the conquest. They may have come from the Gulf slope of southern Veracruz or the adjacent part of Tabasco west of the Maya area. According to Scholes and Roys (1968: 23), the spread of Nahua languages to these regions appears to have been the result of actual migrations that included women as well as men. Indigenous sources and reports by Spanish chroniclers indicate that Mexican enclaves and towns were established in other parts of the Maya area during this period as well, including Ulua in Honduras and several areas of highland Guatemala. Nahua-speaking colonies were also reported by early Spanish explorers in parts of El Salvador and Nicaragua (Scholes and Roys 1968: 21).

Three important commercial centers existed in Tabasco proper—Cimatan, Xicalango, and Potonchán. The first two were either wholly or partly Nahuatl speaking, whereas Potonchán was Chontal speaking. Xicalango was probably ruled by a merchant class who spoke Nahuatl, although the bulk of the population would have been Chontal. A third language, Zoque, was spoken in six prosperous towns on the southern border of Tabasco and was involved in the same economic sphere (Scholes and Roys 1968: 31–38).

At least four Zoque towns are known to have been subject to Cimatan. This site clearly controlled the most important trade routes from the highlands of Chiapas as well as those from the Valley of Mexico. Xicalango enjoyed a very similar advantage in regard to Yucatán, Acalan, and the Usumacinta Valley. Xicalango shared this commerce with Potonchán (Scholes and Roys 1968: 32–34).

Pilgrims (probably merchants) from both sites, and from Champotón and Campeche in southwest Yucatán, visited the shrine of the goddess Ix Chel on Cozumel Island. Moreover, the brother of Acalan's ruler governed the section of Nito in Honduras occupied by merchants from that province. Merchants from both Yucatán and Xicalango had warehouses and factories on the Río Ulua in Honduras. At the time of his father's death, the son of the murdered Cocom ruler of Mayapán was away from home, conducting business in Ulua (Scholes and Roys 1968: 57–58).

Statements made by several chroniclers indicate that various Ch'olan dialects were understood in Yucatán. Alonso de Avila, for example, noted in 1533 that he was able to use the same interpreter in Yucatán and in northern Honduras (reported in Scholes and Roys 1968: 3). This suggests a substantial degree of contact between the two Maya groups. It is of interest in this regard that the word for rulership represented in the codices is *ahawle* (the Chontal form) rather than *ahawlil* (the Yucatec form).

Mayapán is the subject of Chapter 3, by Marilyn Masson and Carlos Peraza. In light of the claims summarized earlier for significant trade and other relationships between populations residing in the Yucatán Peninsula and farther to the west, one of the topics discussed in detail in their chapter is the archaeological evidence for economic and political relationships between Mayapán and port-of-trade settlements in Tabasco and along the southwestern coast of Yucatán that formed important nodes in pan-Mesoamerican trade networks. In addition, they consider whether there is substantiation for foreign merchant enclaves or mercenaries in the archaeological record.

Recent excavations at Mayapán indicate a diversity of artistic styles, including possible connections with central Mexico, as reflected in murals and sculpture from the later levels at the site (Milbrath and Peraza 2003). These data suggest connections with the Late Postclassic International style more commonly seen along the Caribbean coast of the peninsula and also with the Maya Dresden and Madrid codices. These connections indicate that Mayapán was, in Milbrath and Peraza's words, "at a crossroads of cultural contact between central Mexican and Maya areas of Late Postclassic Mesoamerica" (2003: 40).

Studies of architecture and architectural alignments from Mayapán and other Late Postclassic sites, the subject of Chapter 4 by Anthony Aveni, also make a significant contribution to the discussion of long-distance intellectual exchange, specifically pertaining to the realm of shared calendrical and ritual programs and cosmological site planning. Aveni considers two structures from Mayapán in particular: the Castillo pyramid (Q162) and the Caracol or Round Temple (Q152). Although these structures appear to be poorly executed imitations of a pair of similar structures from earlier Chichén Itzá, Aveni suggests that, rather than being mere copies used in a program of revivalism, changes made to elements and structure positioning may in fact have more to do with a Late Postclassic revision of the calendar and cosmological programs for agricultural and solar rituals than with reviving the Classic period past.

The exchange of such esoteric and highly restricted information must have occurred via the elite scribal priests who were responsible for keeping and creating the calendrical tools necessary for reckoning, divining, and programming rituals in accordance with the fates prescribed for any number of sacred and secular events taking place throughout the solar year. These tools—called almanacs—were recorded in codices, and some of our best evidence for the sharing and exchange of the kinds of calendrical and cosmological knowledge encoded into the architecture at Mayapán can be discerned from comparative analyses of codical almanacs like the studies highlighted in Chapter 10 by Victoria R. Bricker, and in Chapter 11 by Christine Hernández and Gabrielle Vail, this volume.

Milbrath and Peraza (2003: 24–31) note that trade goods at Mayapán are evidence of connections with highland Guatemala (obsidian), the Caribbean Coast (pottery), the Gulf Coast (Fine Orange pottery), and Oaxaca and highland Mexico (metalwork). Materials recovered from central Mexico (i.e., Maya Blue pigments believed to come from the area around Mayapán in contexts dating from 1375–1427 CE) hint at a Mexican interest in the northern Maya lowlands, where the largest salt beds in Mesoamerica were also located.[17] Milbrath and Peraza (2003: 29) also comment on similarities between the latest murals at Mayapán and early examples of Aztec art from Tenochtitlan, which are evident in the subject matter as well as in the costuming, pose, and proportions of the figures. In addition, they note that the standard-bearers pictured in the murals associated with Structure Q161 at Mayapán (see Milbrath and Peraza 2003: fig. 29) are quite similar to those from Phase II of the Templo Mayor (ca. 1375–1427 CE). These commonalities lead Milbrath and Peraza to suggest a period of heightened contact with central Mexico. Indeed, they propose that these Mexican traits may have been introduced by the Canul inhabitants of Mayapán, who are described by Landa (Tozzer 1941: 32, 36) as Mexicans from Tabasco and Xicalango who were invited to live in the city by the Cocom rulers because of their connections with the lucrative Gulf Coast trading networks linking the Mexican highlands with the Yucatecan peninsular trade. It is even possible, they suggest, that central Mexican artists invited by the Canul were commissioned to create the Mexican-style murals that depict standard-bearers as well as sculptures that portray Mexican deities.

Since the publication of their article in *Ancient Mesoamerica* (Milbrath and Peraza 2003), several additional field seasons have been undertaken at Mayapán, providing additional data to address the question of a possible Mexican presence at the site (Masson and Peraza, ch. 3, this volume). These data can be appreciated more fully in light of the broader archaeological, chronological, and ethnohistoric data for this time period, as summarized by Robles in Chapter 2, this volume. The studies in both chapters suggest that the question of cultural interaction between residents of Mayapán and inhabitants of central Mexico will require archaeological investigation of sites along the southern Gulf Coast and their ties to commercial centers in the southern highlands of Mexico.

Notes

1. The date of the fall of Tula is still disputed, and a variety of historic and contemporary sources place it anywhere between 1000 and 1200 CE, although recent research favors a date between 1050 and 1150. For discussions of the chronology of Tula, and in particular, of the date of its demise as a political capital, see chapter 2 in this volume, a critical reanalysis of the Tula chronology by George Cowgill (1996), and the essays in the recent volume on Tula and Chichén Itzá edited by Jeff Karl Kowalski and Cynthia Kristan-Graham (2007). The chapters by Kristin-Graham and Kowalski, Patricia Fournier and Victor Bolaños, and Michael E. Smith in the latter volume are particularly relevant to the subject.

2. For a discussion of the major central Mexican sources on the Quetzalcoatl myth, see H. B. Nicholson (2001) and chapter 2, this volume. The primary native sources on Kukulcan in Yucatán are the Books of Chilam Balam of Chumayel (Edmonson 1986; Roys 1967) and of Tizimín (Edmonson 1982). For additional sources on native history and culture before the conquest, see Alfred Tozzer's (1941) annotations to his edition of Landa and the relevant historical works of Ralph Roys (1943, 1967). A recent essay by Susan Gillespie (2007) presents an excellent in-depth discussion of both the Maya and the Mexican sources and the history of their interpretation.

3. This passage has given rise to considerable confusion, as some writers have interpreted it as evidence of an Aztec presence in Yucatán. However, as numerous scholars have noted, if there is any basis for it, it must refer to pre-Aztec Mexicans because Mayapán was abandoned well before the Aztecs established outposts at Xicalango and other localities on the periphery of the Maya area (see Robles, ch. 2, this volume).

4. The sources on Mexican-Yucatecan trade are numerous. Much of the information has been summarized in the works of Crescencio Carrillo y Ancona (1897), Frans Blom (1932), Alfred Tozzer (1941), Ralph Roys (1943), and Román Piña Chan (1978).

5. Some of the Mexican sculptures he mentioned are in fact probably Aztec, a group he believed to be descended from the Toltec. He also noted similarities between Yucatec ceramics and those of Teotihuacan (Charnay 1887: 375–376). A more detailed discussion of Charnay's views on Mexican-Mayan cultural connections, and a critique of those views by Daniel Brinton, is available in the recent overview of the subject by Jeff Karl Kowalski and Cynthia Kristan-Graham (2007).

6. The misnamed "chacmool" statue was unearthed from beneath the Platform of the Eagles and Jaguars by Augustus LePlongeon in 1875. This was the first such statue to be reported; subsequent statues have been found from Michoacán to El Salvador, dating from the Terminal Classic through Postclassic periods. The majority have been recovered at Tula and Chichén Itzá, as well as several Aztec sites. Placed at the tops of temples, they are believed to be a representation of a rain god or a fallen warrior, who holds a receptacle in which the hearts of sacrificial victims were placed.

7. A subsequent in-depth study of the original native sources led the historian Wigberto Jiménez to put forth a detailed reconstruction of Toltec history in 1941, which enhanced the historical veracity of the migration story and many of the details that became enshrined in textbooks and popular books for several decades.

8. During his travels Charnay also visited the site of El Bellote on the Tabasco coast, noting that one of the main pyramids "was identical in all respects with those at Tula and Teotihuacan" (Charnay 1887: 188). Subsequent investigations of this site have revealed a history of occupation extending from the Late/Terminal

Classic period, when it was the main port for Comalcalco and a conduit for east-west trade along the Gulf Coast (Berlin 1956; Ensor 2003). Thus, it was likely a key trading node between central Mexico and the Maya lowlands in Classic and possibly Postclassic times.

9. For an overview of Thompson's work, see the biography by Robert Brunhouse (1973), which also contains a list of his publications. Holmes's studies were published by the Field Museum of Chicago (Holmes 1895–1897).

10. Most of Seler's publications are available in his collected works in German and English (Seler 1902–1923, 1990–2000). The frontmatter of the English edition (Comparato 1990) contains a complete list of his travels and publications and a list of biographies.

11. Summaries and overviews of this research are available in volumes edited by Arthur Miller (1983), Michael Smith and Frances Berdan (2003), and Geoffrey Braswell (2003). Other key studies include those of Zelia Nuttall (1930), Harry Pollock (1936), J. Eric S. Thompson (1953), Alfred Tozzer (1957), George Kubler (1961), Alberto Ruz (1964, 1971), Evelyn Rattray (1987; see also papers in Rattray 1998), and Carlos Navarrete (1996).

12. The main report of this research was published by Pollock et al. (1962). Numerous additional reports, published by Carnegie and through other sources, are cited in the Pollock volume. The INAH work is still ongoing; preliminary reports and interpretations of the results obtained to date are available in the recent publications of Carlos Peraza, Marilyn Masson, and Susan Milbrath, which are cited, along with further discussions, in this volume.

13. See Andrews and Andrews (1975) and Con Uribe (2005) for histories of this research.

14. For a more detailed treatment of Mesoamerican round structures, see the studies by Zelia Nuttall (1930) and Harry Pollock (1936). For a discussion of their astronomical functions, see Anthony Aveni (ch. 4, this volume), which also includes citations to many sources on this subject.

15. We follow Milbrath and Peraza here, and Scholes and Roys (1968) in a later discussion, in labeling these speakers as Nahuatl. It may be more appropriate, however, to use the undifferentiated term *Nahua* (see discussion in the introduction to Part II).

16. For recent research on the prehispanic and early Colonial political geography and archaeology of the Tabasco-Xicalango-Acalan region, see the studies of Ana Luisa Izquierdo (1997) and Ernesto Vargas (2001).

17. The significance of the use of Maya Blue at Tenochtitlan must be reevaluated in light of recent findings of other sources of the clay that contain the diagnostic ingredient in other parts of Mesoamerica, several of which are closer to Tenochtitlan (Susan Milbrath, personal communication, February 2007). For a discussion of sourcing methods, see Arnold et al. (2007).

References Cited

Andrews, Anthony P.
    1990   The Role of Ports in Maya Civilization. In *Vision and Revision in Maya Studies* (Flora S. Clancy and Peter D. Harrison, eds.): 159–167. University of New Mexico Press, Albuquerque.

1993   Late Postclassic Lowland Maya Archaeology. *Journal of World Prehistory* 7
        (1): 36–69.

Andrews, Anthony P., E. Wyllys Andrews V, and Fernando Robles Castellanos
2003   The Northern Maya Collapse and Its Aftermath. *Ancient Mesoamerica*
        14: 151–156.

Andrews, E. Wyllys, IV, and Anthony P. Andrews
1975   *A Preliminary Study of the Ruins of Xcaret, Quintana Roo, Mexico.*
        Middle American Research Institute Publication 40. Tulane University,
        New Orleans.

Andrews, E. Wyllys, V, and Anthony P. Andrews
2001   Northern Maya Lowlands. In *The Oxford Encyclopedia of Mesoamerican
        Cultures: The Civilizations of Mexico and Central America*, vol. 2 (David
        Carrasco, ed.): 378–385. Oxford University Press, New York.

Arnold, Dean E., Hector Neff, Michael D. Glascock, and Robert J. Speakman
2007   Sourcing the Palygorskite Used in Maya Blue: A Pilot Study Comparing the
        Results of INAA and LA-ICP-MS. *Latin American Antiquity* 18 (1): 44–58.

Berdan, Frances F., and Michael E. Smith (eds.)
1996   *Aztec Imperial Strategies.* Dumbarton Oaks Research Library and
        Collection, Washington, D.C.

Berlin, Heinrich
1956   Late Pottery Horizons of Tabasco, Mexico. *Contributions to American
        Anthropology and History* 12 (59): 95–153. Carnegie Institution of
        Washington Publication 66. Washington, D.C.

Blom, Frans
1932   *Commerce, Trade and Monetary Units of the Maya.* Middle American
        Research Institute Research Series 4: 531–556. Tulane University,
        New Orleans.

Braswell, Geoffrey
2003   *The Maya and Teotihuacan: Reinterpreting Early Classic Interaction.*
        University of Texas Press, Austin.

Brunhouse, Robert
1973   *In Search of the Maya: The First Archaeologists.* University of New Mexico
        Press, Albuquerque.

Carrillo y Ancona, Crescencio
1897   El comercio en Yucatán antes del descubrimiento. In *Actas del XI Congreso
        Internacional de Americanistas*: 203–208. Mexico. [Republished in 1987
        by Salvador Rodríguez Losa, along with a biography of Carrillo y Ancona
        written by Gustavo Martínez Alomia in 1906, in *Cuadernos de Yucatán* 3,
        Consejo Editorial de Yucatán, Mérida.]

Charnay, Désiré
1887   *Ancient Cities of the New World: Being Voyages and Explorations in Mexico
        and Central America from 1857–1882* (J. Gonino and Helen S. Conant,
        trans.). Harper & Brothers, New York.

Cobean, Robert, and Guadalupe Mastache

1989   The Late Classic and Early Postclassic Chronology of the Tula Region. In *Tula of the Toltecs* (Dan M. Healan, ed.): 34–46. University of Iowa Press, Iowa City.

Comparato, Frank E.

1990   Introduction to the English Edition. In *Collected Works in Mesoamerican Linguistics and Archaeology: English Translations of German Papers from Gesammelte Abhandlungen zur amerikanischen Sprach- und Alterthumskunde*, vol. 1 (Frank E. Comparato, gen. ed.): ix–xii. Labyrinthos, Culver City, Calif.

Con Uribe, María José

2005   The East Coast of Quintana Roo: A Brief Account of Archaeological Work. In *Quintana Roo Archaeology* (Justine M. Shaw and Jennifer P. Matthews, eds.): 1–29. University of Arizona Press, Tucson.

Cowgill, George L.

1996   Discussion. *Ancient Mesoamerica* 7 (2): 325–332. [Special Section: Recent Chronological Research in Central Mexico.]

Craine, Eugene R., and Reginald C. Reindorp

1979   *Codex Pérez and the Book of Chilam Balam of Maní.* University of Oklahoma Press, Norman.

Edmonson, Munro S.

1982   *The Ancient Future of the Itza: The Book of Chilam Balam of Tizimin.* University of Texas Press, Austin.

1986   *Heaven Born Merida and Its Destiny: The Book of Chilam Balam of Chumayel.* University of Texas Press, Austin.

Ensor, Bradley E.

2003   Islas de los Cerros: A Coastal Site Complex near Comalcalco, Tabasco, Mexico. *Mexicon* 25 (4): 106–111.

Farris, Nancy M.

1984   *Maya Society under Colonial Rule: The Collective Enterprise of Survival.* Princeton University Press, Princeton, N.J.

Fettweis-Vienot, Martine

1980   Las pinturas murales de Cobá: Periódo posclásico. *Boletín de la Escuela de Ciencias Antropológicas de la Universidad de Yucatán*: 2–50.

1983   Cataloguing Mayan Mural Painting. *Mexicon* 5 (3): 53–54.

1987   Iconografía de la pintura mural. In *La pintura mural en Quintana Roo* (Sonia Lombardo de Ruiz, ed.): 49–78. Instituto Nacional de Antropología e Historia, México, D. F.

n.d.a   Prospections archéologiques sur la Côte Est du Quintana Roo. Contribution a l'étude de l'architecture et de la peinture murale. M.A. thesis, Universidad de Lovaina, Belgium, 1973.

n.d.b   Les peintures murales Postclasiques du Quintana Roo. Du cataloque au dechiffrement, recherché d'une méthode et applications a deux cas: Cobá et Xelhá. Ph.D. dissertation, École des Hautes Études en Sciences Sociales, Paris, 1981.

Gallareta, Tomás, and Karl Taube

2006   Late Postclassic Occupation in the Ruinas de San Ángel Region. In
        Quintana Roo Archaeology (Justine M. Shaw and Jennifer P. Mathews, eds.):
        87–111. University of Arizona Press, Tucson.

Gasco, Janine, and Frances F. Berdan

2003   International Trade Centers. In *The Postclassic Mesoamerican World*
        (Michael E. Smith and Frances F. Berdan, eds.): 109–116. University of Utah
        Press, Salt Lake City.

Gillespie, Susan D.

2007   Toltecs, Tula, and Chichén Itzá: The Development of an Archaeological
        Myth. In *Twin Tollans: Chichén Itzá, Tula, and the Epiclassic to Early
        Postclassic Mesoamerican World* (Jeff K. Kowalski and Cynthia Kristan-
        Graham, eds.): 85–128. Dumbarton Oaks Research Library and Collection,
        Washington, D.C.

Holmes, William Henry

1895–1897   *Archaeological Studies among the Ancient Cities of Mexico.*
        Anthropological Series 1 (1). Field Museum of Natural History, Chicago.

Izquierdo, Ana Luisa

1997   *Acalán y la Chontalpa en el siglo XVI. Su geografía política.* Centro de
        Estudios Mayas, Universidad Nacional Autónoma de México, México, D.F.

Kowalski, Jeff Karl, and Cynthia Kristan-Graham (eds.)

2007   *Twin Tollans: Chichén Itzá, Tula, and the Epiclassic to Early Postclassic
        Mesoamerican World.* Dumbarton Oaks Research Library and Collection,
        Washington, D.C.

Kubler, George

1961   Chichen-Itza y Tula. *Estudios de cultura maya* 1: 47–80.

Lombardo de Ruiz, Sonia (ed.)

1987   *La pintura mural en Quintana Roo.* Instituto Nacional de Antropología e
        Historia, México, D.F.

2001   Los estilos en la pintura mural maya. In *La pintura mural prehispánica en
        México: Área maya, tomo III: Estudios* (Leticia Staines Cicero, ed.): 85–154.
        Universidad Nacional Autónoma de México, México, D.F.

McCafferty, Geoffrey G.

1996   The Ceramics and Chronology of Cholula, Mexico. *Ancient Mesoamerica* 7
        (2): 299–325.

Milbrath, Susan, and Carlos Peraza Lope

2003   Revisiting Mayapan: Mexico's Last Maya Capital. *Ancient Mesoamerica*
        14: 1–46.

Miller, Arthur G.

1982   *On the Edge of the Sea: Mural Painting at Tancah-Tulum, Quintana Roo,
        Mexico.* Dumbarton Oaks, Washington, D.C.

Miller, Arthur G. (ed.)

1983   *Highland-Lowland Interaction in Mesoamerica: Interdisciplinary
        Approaches.* Dumbarton Oaks, Washington, D.C.

Navarrete, Carlos
    1996   Elementos arqueológicos de mexicanización en las tierras altas mayas. In *Temas mesoamericanos* (Sonia Lombardo and Enrique Nalda, eds.): 305–342. Instituto Nacional de Antropología e Historia, México, D.F.

Nicholson, H. B.
    2001   *Topiltzin Quetzalcoatl: The Once and Future Lord of the Toltecs.* University Press of Colorado, Boulder.

Nuttall, Zelia
    1930   The Round Temples of Mexico and Yucatan. *Art and Archaeology* 30 (6): 229–233.

Parsons, Jeffrey R., Elizabeth Brumfiel, and Mary Hodge
    1996   Developmental Implications of Earlier Dates for Early Aztec in the Basin of Mexico. *Ancient Mesoamerica* 7 (2): 217–230.

Peraza Lope, Carlos, Marilyn A. Masson, Timothy S. Hare, and Pedro Candelario Delgado Kú
    2006   The Chronology of Mayapan: New Radiocarbon Evidence. *Ancient Mesoamerica* 17 (2): 153–175.

Piña Chan, Román
    1978   Commerce in the Yucatan Peninsula: The Conquest and Colonial Period. In *Mesoamerican Communication Routes and Cultural Contacts* (Thomas A. Lee and Carlos Navarrete, eds.): 37–48. Papers of the New World Archaeological Foundation 40. Brigham Young University, Provo, Utah.

Pollock, Harry E.
    1936   *Round Structure of Aboriginal Middle America.* Carnegie Institution of Washington Publication 471. Washington, D.C.

Pollock, Harry E., Ralph Roys, Tatiana Proskouriakoff, and Alfred Ledyard Smith
    1962   *Mayapan, Yucatan, Mexico.* Carnegie Institution of Washington Publication 619. Washington, D.C.

Proskouriakoff, Tatiana
    1962   Civic and Religious Structures of Mayapan. In *Mayapan, Yucatan, Mexico* (Harry E. D. Pollock, Ralph L. Roys, Tatiana Proskouriakoff, and A. Ledyard Smith, eds.): 87–164. Carnegie Institution of Washington Publication 619. Washington, D.C.

Quirarte, Jacinto
    1982   Santa Rita Murals: A Review. In *Occasional Papers of the Middle American Research Institute* 4: 43–59. Tulane University, New Orleans.

Rattray, Evelyn C.
    1987   Los barrios foráneos de Teotihuacan. In *Teotihuacán: Nuevos datos, nuevas síntesis, nuevos problemas* (Emily McClung de Tapia and Evelyn C. Rattray, eds.): 243–274. Instituto de Investigaciones Antropológicas, Universidad Nacional Autónoma de México, México, D.F.

Rattray, Evelyn C. (ed.)
    1998   *Rutas de intercambio en Mesoamerica. III Coloquio Pedro Bosch Gimpera.* Instituto de Investigaciones Antropologicas, Universidad Nacional Autónoma de México, México, D.F.

Ringle, William M., Tomás Gallareta Negrón, and George J. Bey III
  1998   The Return of Quetzalcóatl: Evidence for the Spread of a World Religion
          during the Epiclassic Period. *Ancient Mesoamerica* 9: 183–232.

Robertson, Donald
  1970   The Tulum Murals: The International Style of the Late Post-Classic. In
          *Verhandlungen des XXXVIII Internationalen Amerikanistenkongresses,
          Stuttgart-München, 1968*, vol. 2: 77–88. Kommissionsverlag Klaus Renner,
          Munich.

Roys, Ralph L.
  1943   *The Indian Background of Colonial Yucatan*. Carnegie Institution of
          Washington Publication 548. Washington, D.C.
  1967   *The Book of Chilam Balam of Chumayel*. University of Oklahoma Press,
          Norman. [Originally published 1933, Carnegie Institution of Washington.]

Ruz L., Alberto
  1964   Influencias mexicanas sobre los mayas. In *Desarollo cultural de los mayas*
          (Evon Z. Vogt and Alberto Ruz L., eds.): 195–227. Centro de Estudios Mayas,
          Universidad Nacional Autónoma de México, México, D.F.
  1971   Influencias mexicanas sobre los mayas. In *Desarollo cultural de los mayas*
          (Evon Z. Vogt and Alberto Ruz L., eds.): 203–235. 2nd ed. Centro de
          Estudios Mayas, Universidad Nacional Autónoma de México, México, D.F.

Sahagún, Fray Bernardino de
  1950–1982   *Florentine Codex: General History of the Things of New Spain*. 12 vols.
          (Arthur J. O. Anderson and Charles E. Dibble, trans. and eds.). University
          of Utah, Salt Lake City and School of American Research, Santa Fe, N.Mex.

Sanders, William T., Jeffrey Parsons, and Robert Santley
  1979   *The Basin of Mexico: The Ecological Processes in the Evolution of a
          Civilization*. Academic Press, New York.

Schele, Linda, and Peter Matthews
  1998   *The Code of Kings: The Language of Seven Sacred Maya Temples and Tombs*.
          Scribner, New York.

Scholes, Frances V., and Ralph L. Roys
  1968   *The Maya Chontal Indians of Acalan-Tixchel: A Contribution to the History
          and Ethnography of the Yucatan Peninsula*. University of Oklahoma Press,
          Norman. [Originally published 1948, Carnegie Institution of Washington.]

Seler, Eduard
  1902–1923   *Gesammelte Abhandlungen zur Amerikanischen Sprach- und
          Alterthumskunde*. 5 vols. A. Asher & Company, Berlin.
  1990–2000   *Collected Works in Mesoamerican Linguistics and Archaeology:
          English Translations of German Papers from Gesammelte Abhandlungen
          zur amerikanischen Sprach- und Alterthumskunde*. 7 vols. (Frank
          E. Comparato, gen. ed.). Labyrinthos, Culver City, Calif.

Smith, Michael E.
  2003   Information Networks in Postclassic Mesoamerica. In *The Postclassic
          Mesoamerican World* (Michael E. Smith and Frances F. Berdan, eds.): 181–
          185. University of Utah Press, Salt Lake City.

Smith, Michael E., and Frances F. Berdan (eds.)
  2003   *The Postclassic Mesoamerican World*. University of Utah Press, Salt
         Lake City.

Stephens, John L.
  1843   *Incidents of Travel in Yucatan*. John Murray, London.

Thompson, J. Eric S.
  1953   *The Civilization of the Mayas*. Chicago Natural History Museum, Chicago.

Tozzer, Alfred M.
  1941   *Landa's* Relación de las cosas de Yucatan: *A Translation*. Papers of the
         Peabody Museum of American Archaeology and Ethnology 18. Harvard
         University, Cambridge, Mass.
  1957   *Chichen Itza and its Cenote of Sacrifice: A Comparative Study of
         Contemporaneous Maya and Toltec*. Peabody Museum, Cambridge, Mass.

Vail, Gabrielle
  2008   El tema del sacrificio en el arte y los textos mayas del Posclásico Tardío.
         Temas Antropológicos 30 (3): 5–31.

Vail, Gabrielle, and Christine Hernández
  n.d.   Cords and Crocodilians: Creation Mythology in Late Postclassic Maya
         Iconography and Texts. In *The Maya and their Sacred Narratives: Text and
         Context of Maya Mythologies; Proceedings of the Twelfth Annual European
         Maya Conference* (Geneviève LeFort, Raphaël Gardiol, and Sebastian
         Matteo, eds.). Verlag Anton Saurwein, Markt Schwaben, Germany. In press.

Vargas Pacheco, Ernesto
  2001   *Itzamkanac y Acalan: Tiempos de crisis anticipando el futuro*. Instituto
         de Investigaciones Antropológicas, Universidad Nacional Autónoma de
         México, México, D.F.

Chapter Two

Interaction between Central and Eastern Mesoamerica before and during the Culhua Mexica Expansion

Fernando Robles Castellanos

Translated by Christine Hernández

T HE LATE POSTCLASSIC CONSTITUTES the last period of indigenous
cultural-historical development in Mesoamerica, during which time a new
multiethnic stage and geopolitical order emerged. Also at this time, the material culture of the ruling elites in central and eastern Mesoamerica underwent
a process of relative cultural homogenization that followed the canons of the
so-called Mixteca-Puebla or International style. This concept, outlined initially by George Vaillant (1940), is a descriptive term that refers to the artistic style
that presumably derived from the area comprising southern Puebla and northern Oaxaca and became widely distributed throughout Mesoamerica during
the Late Postclassic period (see Boone and Smith 2003; see also the introduction to Part II and Taube, ch. 5, this volume, for a broader discussion). The idea
of a unipolar diffusion of the Mixteca-Puebla style across Mesoamerica still
prevails, despite the well-known fact that the style derives from the dichotomy of a single body of art called "Toltec." This style was developed jointly by
two distant metropolises, Chichén Itzá and Tollan, during the Terminal Classic
(or Early Postclassic) period from preexisting Mesoamerican cultural traits in
northern Yucatán and central Mexico, respectively (fig. 1).

It is clear that a certain amount of cultural similarity existed among ruling

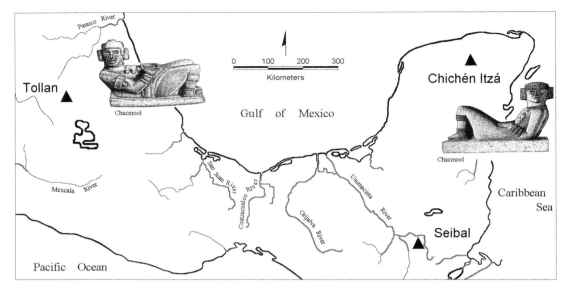

Fig. 1. The regional capitals of Tollan and Chichén Itzá exhibit the widespread cultural similarities marking the climax of the Epiclassic period and establishing the paradigm of cultural-historical development in the Postclassic period. Artwork by Fernando Robles.

elites of diverse ethnic origin and from distant polities during the Postclassic period. Nevertheless, it still remains to be clarified at which place or places the International Mixteca-Puebla style appeared in a syncretic form, the manner of its dispersal across Mesoamerica, and the mechanisms subsequently used to maintain the legitimacy of this tradition throughout the little more than 400 years that made up the Late Postclassic period (discussed later).

A consensus has emerged among scholars that the centralized regimes at Chichén Itzá and Tula ended at more or less the same time and that, after their decline, a new and dynamic sense of change was set in motion throughout Mesoamerica. The recent revisions of the archaeological and chronological evidence suggest that this historical event probably occurred a little before 1100 CE (Andrews et al. 2003; Cobos 1997, 1998; Ringle et al. 1998; Schmidt 1998). Be that as it may, what remains in little doubt is that the political and cultural legacy of both regional capitals was transcendental in shaping the historical events that were to follow in the Late Postclassic period.

It is well known that Chichén Itzá and Tula are characterized by close similarities in their monumental architecture and in their sculpture and iconography that can be traced to the immediate antecedents of the Mixteca-Puebla style. The so-called Toltec art at Chichén Itzá and Tula is the immediate precursor of the Mixteca-Puebla style in central and eastern Mesoamerica, and may well be considered the last expression of the artistic and esoteric manifestations of the regional capitals of the Epiclassic/Terminal Classic, of which Chichén Itzá and Tula were the culmination. As Peter Schmidt (1998) has suggested, Cacaxtla, Xochicalco, and El Tajín, as well as Tula and Chichén Itzá, were all regional post-Teotihuacan capitals or "Tulas" that together contributed, to a greater or lesser degree, to the formation of the symbolism and iconographic patterns that would later be defined as the Mixteca-Puebla style in its strictest sense by George Vaillant (Nicholson 1982). In fact, "it is striking how we can read in the language of the Postclassic codices much of the imagery in the reliefs from Chichén Itzá" (Schmidt 2003: 59).

Thus it is after the fall of Chichén Itzá and Tula that the Late Postclassic epoch, interpreted as one single Postclassic period without divisions, began in Mesoamerica. Its cultural-historical development extended for more than 400 years, until the arrival of Hernán Cortés in 1519 CE, which marked the moment when its lengthy decline began.

The First Phase of the Late Postclassic (1050/1100–1441/1461 CE)

The Ascendancy of Coaixtlahuacan and Mayapán in Central and Eastern Mesoamerica

In various regions of Mesoamerica, the Late Postclassic represents the most recent period of the Pre-Hispanic past, a time when written sources come to the aid of the archaeological record in reconstructing local events that took place at a given moment. Archaeological and ethnohistoric research suggest that, after the decline of Chichén Itzá and Tula in their former spheres of influence, two similar but separate processes of cultural change began to take place; these changes set the standard for the political and cultural development in central and eastern Mesoamerica up to the middle of the fifteenth century, at which time the Mexica imperial expansion began. In spite of this dichotomy and the large distance that separated these two regions during this first phase of the Late Postclassic period, the ruling elites in both areas shared the same "official" art that followed the canons of the aforementioned Mixteca-Puebla tradition (obviously with their own regional distinctions), and a common ideology centered on the tutelary cult of Quetzalcoatl/Kukulcan, who was the plumed serpent god of Tula and Chichén Itzá (Rincón 1995: 62; Ringle et al. 1998).

CENTRAL MESOAMERICA   According to the most reliable primary sources of indigenous historiography, internal dissent led to political fissioning and the abandonment of Tula by Toltec factions in the year 1 Flint, or 1064 CE (*Códice Chimalpopoca* 1975: 14–15; *Historia Tolteca-Chichimeca* 1976: 141–142).[1] From that moment on, the ethnohistoric and archaeological records indicate that central Mesoamerica entered a period of political balkanization that resulted in the formation of diverse sociopolitical spheres (Marcus and Flannery 1983; Sanders et al. 1979). At that time, a number of diverse groups of elites burst onto the historical stage. They were loosely organized, politically and ethnically distinct from previous rulers, and began progressively to take control of large parts of the land in central and southeastern Mesoamerica. For example, the Matlatzinca (Otopame) took over the Toluca Valley (Carrasco 1950; Quezada 1972); the Tlalhuica (Nahua), the Valley of Morelos (Smith n.d. [1983]); the Couixca (Nahua), northern Guerrero (Barlow 1948); the Cuetlaxteca (Popoloca), central Veracruz (Medellín 1952; Melgarejo 1989); and the Cuexteca (Huaxteca), the northern regions of Puebla and Veracruz (Ochoa 1979; Palacios 1941). Later in the Postclassic, Quiché elites (Mayas) occupied the central Guatemalan highlands (Carmack 1968, 1981). In a still more distant setting, Nahua-Pipil groups of elites, like the Cuscateca, Nicarao, and Cholulteca, spread south into Central America, where they settled in what are today the nations of El Salvador, Nicaragua, and Honduras (Estrada Belli 1999; Fowler 1989; Lothrop 1926; Stone 1949, 1982) (fig. 2).

As they arrived, the leaders of these elite groups proceeded to mark out the limits of their newly acquired domains; though owing to the intrinsic political instability of the ruling elites who governed these territories, we know that the boundaries continuously changed over time. In fact, several of the first domains to have emerged quickly fragmented into small autonomous polities or disappeared altogether, as their territories were absorbed into different politico-territorial formations that emerged later in the Postclassic period.

In the majority of cases, the new regions were named after the occupying faction's ruling lineage, for example, Cuextlan, "region of the [ruling] Cuexteca [Huaxteca]" and Matlatzinco "place of the [ruling] Matlatzinca." Nevertheless, these new dominions did not constitute unified entities, nor did they have a central government. Rather, each of them consisted of an unstable conglomerate of autonomous domains or *señoríos*, each governed by dynastic rulers generally from the same lineage who had established their political seats in the most important towns (Caso 1966; Robles 2007: 45–47).

With respect to ideology, we know that several rulers, like those who governed the Cuexteca, Cuauhtinchantlaca-Chichimeca, Olmeca-Uixotzin, and the Quiché, perpetuated the idea that their respective lineages were descended from the Tolteca or that their ancestors originally formed part of the "Great Tollan" (Carmack 1968; Kirchhoff 1985; León-Portilla 1965; Melgarejo 1989; Reyes 1988; Scholes and Warren 1965). Whether fact or myth, the purpose of this was to appropriate a symbolic means of demonstrating their authority that was also capable of lending prestige, sanctioning their acquired dominance, and ideologically countering any rivals with similar pretensions, as they set out to govern their newly acquired lands.

Above all, the same ethnohistoric sources emphasize the history of three

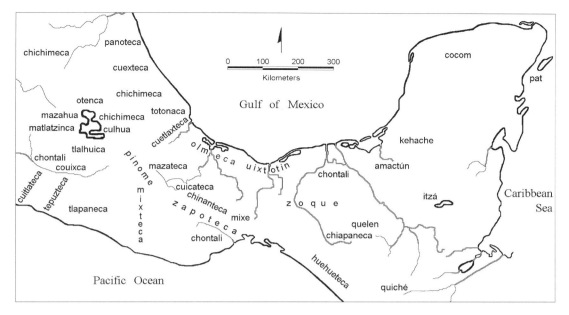

Gulf of Mexico

Caribbean Sea

Pacific Ocean

Fig. 2. Mesoamerica showing the location of the important ruling ethnic groups after the decline of Tula and Chichén Itzá. Artwork by Fernando Robles.

specific Toltec factions that left Tollan: the Tolteca-Chichimeca, the Culhua, and another group who were led by a Toltec leader called Atónal, who was a native of Totitlan (Cuauhtitlan). They settled at Chollolan (Cholula, Puebla), Culhuacan (today, Culuacán, D.F.), and Coaixtlahuacan (Coaixtlahuaca, in the northern Mixteca Alta of Oaxaca), respectively. The leaders of these factions were the supposed direct descendants of the ancient rulers of Tollan, through whose ranks they assumed the *tlapializtli*, or "duty to guard or preserve" the legitimacy of the Toltec legacy of cultured society, or *toltecáyotl*, in the new order that emerged in central Mesoamerica (Davies 1980; León-Portilla 1980: 15–35).

CHOLLOLAN   It is known that, after the arrival of the Tolteca-Chichimeca at Chollolan around the beginning of the twelfth century CE, the ancient city was transformed, not only into the principal religious center of the cult of Quetzalcoatl in central Mexico but also into the prestigious Toltec regional seat of government, where nobles from the polities of Quauhtinchan and Totomihuacan (corresponding to central and southern Puebla today) were anointed as the rulers of their respective domains (Reyes 1988: 76–88; *Historia Tolteca-Chichimeca* 1976: 180–208). Consequently, the city acquired the "official" name Tollan Chollolan Tlachiuhaltépetl. A council of priests, led by those with the titles of *aquiach* and *tlalquiach*, governed the city throughout the Postclassic

Fig. 3. Tollan Chollolan in the *Mapa de las migraciones chichimeca* of the *Historia Tolteca-Chichimeca.* An immense platform built in ancient times (Tlachiuhaltépetl) is at the center of the site, on top of which was placed the Temple of Quetzalcoatl during the Late Postclassic period. After *Historia Tolteca-Chichimeca* (1976: 181).

period. At the same time, Chollolan became (or better yet, reclaimed its former status as) an important commercial center, and an immense platform built in ancient times (Tlachiuhaltépetl) was reused to support a temple dedicated to Quetzalcoatl, which became a sacred site for the entire elite class throughout the central highlands of Mexico (fig. 3). So holy was the Great Temple of Quetzalcoatl in Chollolan, that even the Mexica, in the midst of their imperial expansion, respected the autonomy of the "city-state," and their rulers made pilgrimages to the city to honor Quetzalcoatl (Davies 1968: 102–103; Díaz del Castillo 1904, 1: cap. 83; *Relación (descripción) de Cholula* 1927–1928: 159–164).

CULHUACAN The *Anales de Cuauhtitlan* (*Códice Chimalpopoca* 1975: 15) and Chimalpahin (1982: 68) record that soon after the Toltec factions split in year 1 Flint (1064 CE), Huehue Nauhyotzin, leader of the Culhua (Nahua) faction, led his people out from Tula and later founded the Toltec kingdom of Culhuacan in the southern Basin of Mexico. It was his lineage that later produced "those nine [great rulers] who succeeded to the throne and government of Mexico Tenochtitlan" (Chimalpahin 1982: 61–62, 68; see also Chimalpahin 1950; Hodge 1984: 100; *Relación de Coatépec (Chalco)* 1905: 66, *Relación de la genealogía* 1891: 268–271).

With the arrival of Huehue Nauhyotzin, Culhuacan began to rule over the fertile region between the Ixtapalapa peninsula and the Ajusco mountain range in the freshwater-fed area in the southern Basin of Mexico (Hodge 1984: 100) (fig. 4). In addition, the Chichimec (Otopame) leaders who had recently arrived began to establish themselves as a new elite class. To legitimize their right to rule over the rural communities in the central and northern reaches of the Basin of Mexico, they began merging with the ancient "Toltec" ruling class, through marriage alliances with Culhuacan princesses who were speakers of "the Nahua language, the Toltec language" (Chimalpahin 1982: 74; *Códice Chimalpopoca* 1975: 27–31; Davies 1973: 21–22; Hodge 1984: 58, 70; *Relación de Tequisquiac* 1957: 289).

However, between 1268 and 1304 CE the southwest corner of the Basin of

Fig. 4. The approximate limits of the Toltec (Nahua) territory of Culhuacan south of the Basin of Mexico and the neighboring Chichimec (Otopame) areas to the north, ca. 1270 CE. Artwork by Fernando Robles.

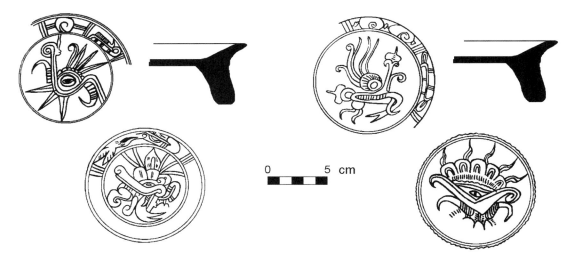

Fig. 5. Examples of Aztec I Black-on-Orange pottery from Culhuacan with serpent mandible motifs, which are representations of Quetzalcoatl, the tutelary deity of the Toltec Culhua lords of Culhuacan. After Peterson (1957).

Mexico was gradually occupied by multiethnic groups later known as Chalca; at about the same time, the Xochimilcas (Nahua) and then the Mixquic-Cuitlahuacas (Nahua) arrived and seized territory in the Ajusco Mountains south of Lake Xochimilco and Lake Chalco. From approximately the beginning of the fourteenth century, the Culhuacan territory was reduced to the western half of the Ixtapalapa Peninsula, including a portion of the southwestern edge of Lake Texcoco between Tizapan (El Pedregal) to the south and Cerro Chapultepec to the north (Chimalpahin 1982: 60, 72–73, 164–169; Hodge 1984: 37–40, 82; *Relación de la genealogía* 1891: 273).

Culturally, the ascendancy of Culhuacan in the southern Basin of Mexico is correlated with the presence of Aztec I ceramics, which are a regional variant of the Mixteca-Puebla pottery tradition (fig. 5). Moreover, the ceramics and the written sources suggest cultural and commercial interaction between the Culhuas and the inhabitants of Chollolan. This suggests that both groups of elites likely lived by a similar principle: that of being authentic keepers of the Toltec legacy of cultured society (Davies 1973: 25–26; Hodge 1984: 82). It is likely that this concept was zealously exploited to defend ideologically the patrimony of Culhuacan and Chollolan against the Chichimec groups (Tepaneca [Otopame], Acolhua [Otopame], and Uexotzinca [Nahua]) to the north who had adopted Toltec cultural patterns after having become sedentary farmers (Carrasco 1950).

Historically, the ascendancy of Culhuacan over the Basin of Mexico came to an end in the year 11 Reed, or 1347 CE, when internal dissent led to political fractioning of the ruling class, and members of the elite left to live elsewhere in the Basin of Mexico (*Anales de Tlatelolco* 1948: 46; *Códice Chimalpopoca* 1975: 29; *Relación de la genealogía* 1891: 271). The political and cultural legacy of the Culhua Toltec lords nevertheless survived as they doggedly revived their society within the Basin of Mexico. Their descendents later acceded to the throne of Mexico Tenochtitlan, the capital city of the Culhua Mexica Empire, which became the largest and most stable state of the Toltec tradition to emerge in the final era of Postclassic Mesoamerica (Davies 1987).

COAIXTLAHUACAN The *Anales de Cuauhtitlan* relate that, after leaving Tollan in the year 1 Flint (1064 CE), a group of Toltecas stayed behind in Cuauhtitlan (today, Cuautitlán Ixcalli, north of Mexico City) to await the arrival of a Toltec dignitary who was either the ruler or a native son of Tamaçolac of Totitlan

> named Atónal who along with others then brought his subjects. The Toltecs immediately left . . . to go to and enter towns, some were established at Chollolan, Teohuacan, Cozcatlan, Nonohualco, Teotlillan, Coyixtlahuacan, Tamaçólac, Copilco, Topillan, Ayotlan, Maçatlan, until the rest of them settled in all parts of the land of Anahuac, where they now live (*Códice Chimalpopoca* 1975: 14–15; see also *Historia Tolteca-Chichimeca* 1976: 131–141).

The place names where followers of this Toltec group finally settled (some of them the Nonoualca-Chichimeca) are found in an area that extends from central Puebla to northern Oaxaca, where contact period inhabitants spoke Chocho-Popoloca, Nahua, Ixcatec, and Mazatec languages, neighboring the Mixtec speakers to the north. In other words, they occupied the geographic region of Mexico where presumably the syncretic and archetypical Mixteca-Puebla style first appeared (fig. 6).

"The land of Anahuac," on the other hand, the place where other groups with Toltec affiliation later settled, alludes to the far regions of the Tabasco-Campeche coast along the Gulf of Mexico and to Soconusco along the coast of Chiapas and Guatemala, the ports of entry to the Maya world.[2] In effect, *Anahuac* means "on the edge of the water [or sea]," and, as Eduard Seler (1894: 211) makes clear:

> This original and general meaning of the word anahuac is most closely connected with the special technical meaning, which the word has preserved in Mexican usage, and in the history of P. Sahagún, in the *Anales de Quauhtitlan, Anales de Chimalpahin*, etc. Thus the Mexicans denoted by this word the hot maritime regions of the north and south sea, which were rich in all kinds of tropical products, the lands on the gulf coast and on the Pacific coast, and indeed especially the regions to which the great commercial expeditions were undertaken from the

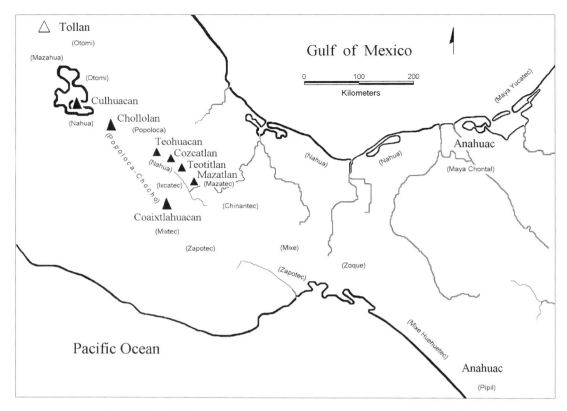

Fig. 6. Tolteca-Chichimeca settlements in central Puebla and northern Oaxaca. The languages spoken by the inhabitants are indicated in parentheses. Artwork by Fernando Robles.

cities of the plateau, which were allied with Mexico, and which are described in full in the ninth book of Sahagún's history (trans. J. Eric Thompson and Francis B. Richardson; see also Chimalpahin 1982: 228; *Códice Chimalpopoca* 1975: 52; Sahagún 1938, 2: ch. 4).

Ethnohistoric sources relate that Atónal and his party finally settled in Coaixtlahuacan (Place of the Serpent's [Quetzalcoatl's?] Plain), where Atónal founded a new royal Toltec dynasty guided by the god Quetzalcoatl/Ehecatl and where successive dynasties of Chocho-Popoloca stock appear to have taken the name of their founder as their royal title. In addition, Atónal (the ruler 7 Reed of the Chochon tradition?), along with another local leader of Mixtec ethnicity, began to co-rule a kingdom located on the northern edge of the Mixteca Alta called *Tocnijñuhuó* (fig. 7) (Caso 1977, 1: 231–239; Dahlgren 1954: 127–128; Parmenter 1982; Reyes 1988: 60–62; Rincón 1995: 62, 2000, 2005: 61–63, fig. 73).

More importantly, indigenous sources from central Mexico relate that

Fig. 7. The toponym of Coaixtlahuacan, Place of the Serpent's (Quetzalcoatl's?) Plain, in the post-conquest Seler II Codex. After his departure from Tollan, Atónal founded at Coaixtlahuacan a new royal Toltec dynasty guided by the god Ehecatl-Quetzalcoatl (9 Wind) and, along with another leader of Mixtec ethnicity, began to co-rule a kingdom called Tocuijñuhuó. Artwork by Fernando Robles, after Ringle et al. (1998).

Atónal, or to be more accurate, the series of rulers who took his name as title, began to build Coaixtlahuacan into the famed *tianquiztli*, or interregional market, where the exchange of exotic products like gold, quetzal feathers, rubber [*hule*], cacao, and "other riches" from the tropical regions of Anahuac took place. Before the Mexican *pochteca* took control, the merchants of the Coaixtlahuacan *tianquiztli* controlled the exchange of exotic merchandise along ancestral long-distance commercial routes between central Mesoamerica and Anahuac (*Códice Chimalpopoca* 1975: 52; Dahlgren 1954: 226–227; *Noticias relativas* 1944: 178–179; Seler 1894):

> Cohuayxtlahuacan [was] where the great king [*hueytlatoani*] Atónal then ruled, who was heavily dedicated to the management of trade and tribute revenues from all parts of Anáhuac. It is said that this Atónal was the son of toltecs and a native of Tamaçolac of Toltitlan, from where he left, when the toltecs ruined themselves and left [Tollan] (*Códice Chimalpopoca* 1975: 52).

Because Coaixtlahuacan is situated on the northern edge of the Sierra Mixteca, which descends eastward to the adjacent Cuicatlán Cañada in Oaxaca, one can suppose that this strategic geographic location contributed to the development of Coaixtlahuacan into a center of interregional exchange. There, the Santo Domingo River cuts a deep, narrow canyon through the Sierra Madre Oriental to connect the Mixteca Alta with the south-central coast of Veracruz. The Tonto River near Tuxtepéc, Oaxaca, and the Santo Domingo River come together at the edge of the coast to form the Papaloapan River, which flows into Lake Alvarado in central-southern Veracruz. From there, one can easily access the shores of Anahuac by navigating through the intricate river system that connects southern Veracruz with Tabasco or by cutting through to the northern coast of the Isthmus of Tehuantepec.

To the north, the basin (plains) of Coaixtlahuacan connects with the Tehuacán Valley via a natural route of passage to central Puebla and the Basin of Mexico. To the south, Coaixtlahuacan connects with the Etla arm of the central Oaxaca Valley; a few kilometers east of the Tlacolula arm, the Tehuantepec River's flow cuts a mountain pass through the ranges of the Sierra Madre del Sur and the Sierra Mixe to pass west of the Pacific Plains and into the southern Isthmus of Tehuantepec. Since time immemorial, this geographic corridor has served as the principal route for Chocho, Mixtec, and Zapotec merchants who went to "*teguantepeque* and the *provincias* of Soconusco and Guatemala" to traffic in exotic goods (Ball and Brockington 1978; *Relación de Iztepexi* 1905: 16–17; *Relación de Nexapa* 1984: 349–353; *Relación de Tehuantepec* 1927–1928: 166). These merchants, in the service of the interregional market at Coaixtlahuacan and independent of their own ethnic backgrounds, contributed to the maintenance and diffusion of the legitimacy of the Toltec Mixteca-Puebla traditional canons among the rulers and clients of the heterogeneous Postclassic period communities in central and southern Mesoamerica, who were encountered along the route followed by these long commercial expeditions.

The modern town of Coaixtlahuaca is constructed over the remains of the indigenous settlement. In fact, the splendid sixteenth-century church was constructed over the ruins of a pyramidal platform. Ignacio Bernal (1949) explored the site in the late 1940s and focused his excavations in the best-preserved architectural group, called Inguiteria, which is situated atop a hill immediately west of the town's center. This site spreads over an area 1 kilometer long by 400 meters wide. At the center of the site, public structures delimit rectangular patio areas. The slopes of the hill support a series of residences. In his excavations, Bernal found abundant Late Postclassic ceramics, including locally made Mixtec polychrome types, Yanhuitlán Red-on-Cream, and Gris Delgado Monte Albán V (G3M), along with a considerable amount of Aztec III pottery. A cremation burial associated with Aztec III vessels was also found in the site center.

Because the Mexica razed Coaixtlahuacan and repopulated the site with

Chocho and Mixtec people and a Mexica military attachment, which controlled the region during imperial times (Chimalpahin 1982: 103; *Relación de Atlatlauca* 1905: 165–166), it is likely that the structures Bernal excavated in the Inguiteria group date to the period of Mexica occupation rather than to the time of ancient Coaixtlahuacan. Currently, the only thing we can say is that ancient Coaixtlahuacan, the ruins of which are buried under the modern town, must have been a settlement a little larger than the neighboring Mixtec, Cuicatec, and Popoloca capitals with which Coaixtlahuacan maintained close cultural and economic ties (and continuous conflicts over regional authority) (Rincón 2000: table 2). In addition, historical narratives tell of merchants from contemporary communities in the Basin of Mexico who frequented the *tianquiztli* of Coaixtlahuacan (*Noticias relativas* 1944: 178).

Be that as it may, the commercial ascendancy of Coaixtlahuacan in central Mesoamerica began to be eclipsed in 1461 CE, when Moctezuma Ilhuicamina (r. 1441–1469), who was greedily consolidating resources for the emergent Culhua-Mexica state, finally decided to take control of the mercantile operations of the famed *tianquiztli* by force:

> After the city of Cohuayxtlhuaca was seized, from there, for the first time, gold, quetzal feathers, rubber, cacao, and other riches began to enter here [to Tenochtitlan]; and with the income of the resulting tribute the Mexica monarchy began its consolidation, etc. (*Códice Chimalpopoca* 1975: 52, trans. Fernando Robles and Anthony P. Andrews; see also *Anales Tepaneca* 1900: 66).

Shortly afterward, in 1469, the successor of Moctezuma Ilhuicamina, Axayácatl (r. 1469–1481), ordered the suppression of the local dynasties and, in reprisal for having sided with his rivals, had Coaixtlahuacan razed (Chimalpahin 1982: 103). From that point on, the *hueytlatoque* ("supreme lords") of Mexico intensified their expansionist campaigns which led, within a few decades, not only to the subjugation of vast swaths of central and southern Mesoamerica but also to control of the mercantile trade along the ancient long-distance commercial routes between central Mexico and Anahuac (Sahagún 1938, 2: 355–356).

The Road to Anahuac: The Coatzacualco Province and the Nonohualco Region as a Node of Communication between Central Mexico and the Maya Lowlands

Indigenous sources tell us that the commercial routes leaving central Mexico (from Coaixtlahuacan at that time) for Anahuac pass through part of the Gulf of Mexico to end at the northwestern limits of the Maya lowlands in a region known to central Mexicans as Nonohualco (the Tabasco-Campeche alluvial plain); this is the port of entry to far eastern Tlapallan, which most probably alludes to the world of the Maya in Yucatán (Chimalpahin 1982: 29, 166; see also Carmack 1968: 65–70; Roys 1943: 98; Scholes and Roys 1968: 2; Torquemada 1975, 1: 381, 2: 256).[3] However, before arriving at Nonohualco, one had to

50

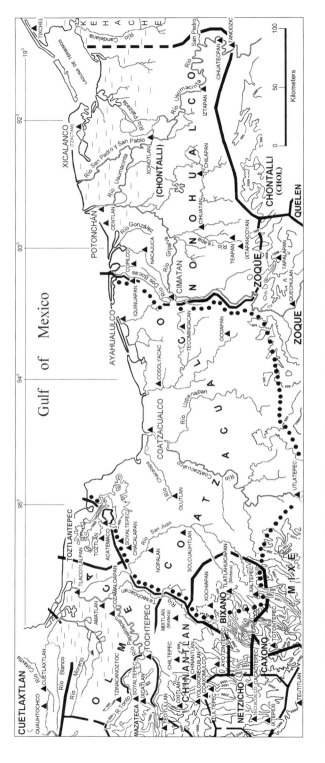

Fig. 8. Approximate limits of the indigenous territories of the Veracruz-Tabasco coastal plain toward the end of the fourteenth century CE. After Robles (2007: 268, fig. 39).

cross the wide basin of the Coatzacualco (Cuitlaxcolapa) River, located in Veracruz on the northern Isthmus of Tehuantepec (fig. 8). It appears that several Nahua-speaking groups (the historic Uixtotin?) arrived in this area just before the fall of Chichén Itzá and Tula, where they founded a series of autonomous domains and imposed their linguistic and cultural influences on the older Popoloca-Zoque populations. Later, other Nahua groups crossed the Tonalá River and occupied the west coast of Tabasco as far as the Dos Bocas (Seco) River, which marks the western limits of Nonohualco and where several towns were founded that colonial sources call the "Agualulcos" from the name Ayahualulco, which at the time of European contact was the most important capital (García de León 1976: 9–17; *Relación de la provincia de Coatzacualco* 1984: 115–126; Scholes and Roys 1968: 91–92, n. 24; Scholes and Warren 1965: 780).

Unfortunately, the written sources do not tell us anything about the communities around the source of the Coatzacualco River before the fifteenth century, nor do we know much about their material culture (Coe 1981: 136–139). To judge by later events, after their arrival on the Gulf Coast, the Nahua leadership began to intervene in the mercantile trade so that, by the middle of the fifteenth century, they had an interregional *tianquiztli* established at Coatzacualco ("Place of the Caged Serpent"). At that time, Coatzacualco was the region's dominant town and was located to the east of the mouth of the Coatzacualco River, which gave it control over communications with all of the northern Isthmus of Tehuantepec and allowed it to profit as an intermediary in exchanges between central Mexico and Anahuac (Durán 1965, 1: 229–230; Sahagún 1938, 1: 355). Undoubtedly, the strong influence that the Nahua had on the Mayan Chontal language (and by extension the neighboring Maya Yucatec language as well) derived from the vigorous interaction that the Nahuas of the "provinces" of Coatzacualco and Ayahualulco sustained throughout the Postclassic period with the Chontal Maya of the Nonohualco region on their eastern border (Izquierdo and Figueroa 1978; Justeson et al. 1985: 24–26).

By the middle of the fourteenth century, the settlements east of the Dos Bocas (Seco) River, Cimatan and Xicalanco, constituted the highest seats of gov-ernment, or *tecpanes*, in the adjacent Maya Chontal region of Nonohualco (Roys 1943; Sahagún 1938, 2: 355; Scholes and Roys 1968). The capital of Cimatan (Tecpan Cimatan or Cimatécatl) was a town situated on the shores of the Grijalva River, near Cárdenas, Tabasco, and fortified by palisades. Likewise, Xicalanco (Tzactam, in Chontal) was a coastal port town located on the north shore of Lake Pom (a western extension of the Laguna de Términos) in Campeche. It may be one and the same as the archaeological site of Los Cerrillos, which consists of modest public structures and platforms filled with the remains of mollusks that supported perishable wood constructions with straw roofs (Jakeman 1952; Ochoa and Vargas 1979: 75).

Fine Orange "U" pottery, or Cunduacán, predominates in Cimatan's sphere

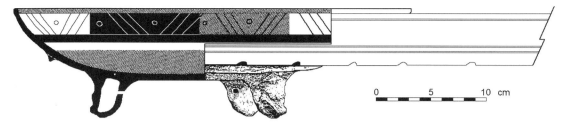

Fig. 9. Vessel form representative of Mantillas (V) Fine Orange pottery from the Late Postclassic occupation at El Meco, Quintana Roo. Artwork by Fernando Robles.

of influence east of the Grijalva River. Likewise, in satellite towns of Xicalanco located east of the Grijalva River and below the Usumacinta River, the predominant ceramic is Fine Orange "V," or Matillas pottery, whose most representative forms are tripod bowls with zoomorphic or effigy supports and polychrome decoration that are incised or gouged (fig. 9) (Ball 1985: 236–238; Ochoa and Casasola 1978: 38).[4] Matillas Fine Orange is a luxury ceramic that was also used exclusively by Yucatec Maya elites of the Pat lineage, who ruled the distant island of Cozumel and adjacent sites along the east coast of Quintana Roo, and also by the Cocom, who governed Mayapán, the capital city of Yucatán (Ochoa n.d. [2004]; Peraza n.d. [1993]; Robles 1986; Smith 1971, 1: 234–238), and who undoubtedly acquired the pottery thanks to the productive exchange network they had established with the Xicalanco province (Landa 1973: 15–17, 39).

Several native sources relate that, in the "time of their heathenism," the Maya of Yucatán went by land as far as Tixchel in the extreme north of the Sabancuy estuary of the Laguna de Términos, bringing with them local products such as marine salt, copal incense, vegetable dyes, cotton (or cotton textiles), feathers, and precious purple and yellow sea shells. From there the goods would be shipped to their ultimate destination at Xicalanco, where merchants from all over the Maya world came to trade. In addition, through other coastal ports adjoining the adjacent Tabasco coast, such as Potonchán and Centlan, Xicalanco established active dealings with Coatzacualco and commercial routes leading to central Mexico (Gil y Sáenz 1872: 77; *Relación de la villa de Santa María* 1898: 346–347; Roys 1943; Sahagún 1938, 3: 355; Scholes and Warren 1965: 784).

At the end of the fourteenth century, a bellicose group called Amactún, who departed from the island of Cozumel, established themselves at Tixchel with the objective of gaining part of the lucrative mercantile trade dominated by Xicalanco. To safeguard their threatened mercantile interests, Xicalanco joined forces with Pontonchán and Champotón and expelled the Amactún from Tixchel. The Amactún later regrouped at Itzamkanac, on the Candelaria River, then part of the southern Campeche domain of the Yucatec Maya

Kehache lords. There they seized control over the surrounding area and organized a new kingdom of their own called Tamactún (also called Acalan, 'the
place of canoes,' by the central Mexicans). From there, they discreetly secured
a waterway passage through which "they all go out to the bay or the port called
Términos, through which by canoe they have great trade with Xicalanco and
Tabasco [Potonchán]" (Cortés 1981: 237). From then on, Itzamkanac began to
compete with Xicalanco, and their rivalry lasted until Cortés arrived in the region in 1524 CE (Scholes and Roys 1968).

THE NORTHERN YUCATÁN PENINSULA   After the fall of Chichén Itzá, Yucatec
Maya communities in northern Yucatán underwent a series of changes aimed
at restructuring the political and cultural organizational foundation of the ancient Itzá order. These efforts took divergent courses in the western and eastern
parts of the peninsula, and they led to the formation of two principal political-
cultural entities led by Mayapán and Cuzamil, respectively (fig. 10) (Robles and
Andrews 1986: 90–97). In spite of this dichotomy, both Yucatec Maya entities
shared the same "official" art and subscribed to the canons of the poorly named
Mixteca-Puebla style, but in this case, they created new models derived from the

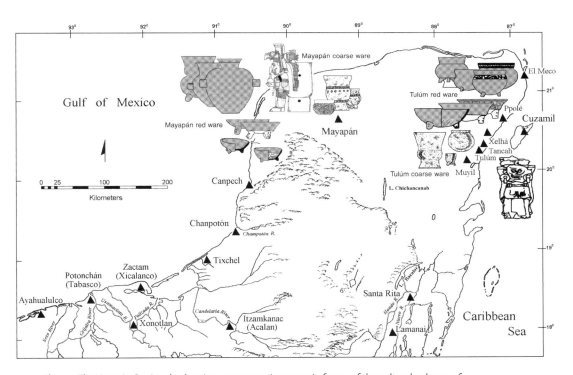

Fig. 10. The Yucatán Peninsula showing representative ceramic forms of the cultural spheres of
Mayapán and Cuzamil. Artwork by Fernando Robles.

ancient cultural tradition of the Itzá. Their leadership set a standard for cultural and economic development in the rest of the Maya lowlands during the first phase of the Late Postclassic period.

CUZAMIL AND ALLIED SITES ALONG THE EASTERN YUCATÁN COAST   At the end of the eleventh century, when Chichén Itzá no longer ruled over northern Quintana Roo, the ancient seat of the Itzá at Tantúm in Cuzamil (today San Gervasio on the island of Cozumel) was transformed into the largest and most powerful settlement in the region before Tulúm's emergence (Sierra 1994: 100–112). The foundations of residential structures dispersed around San Gervasio eventually covered an area of 800 by 1,400 square meters, and important public structures erected at the site include the temples and colonnades of the central group as well as the basal pyramidal structure for the temple dedicated to Ixchel. Subsequently, after the Itzá abandonment of Cozumel, the public structures at San Gervasio were built according to the canons of the East Coast architectural style (Vargas n.d. [1992]).

San Gervasio (Cuzamil) is, in fact, not the only Pre-Hispanic site to have reached its highest level of sociocultural complexity during the Late Postclassic period; this is also true for most of the adjacent sites along the eastern coast of Yucatán, which together constitute an independent cultural unity. Proof of this are the numerous temples, altars, outlying palaces, and other public works that were built along the northern Quintana Roo coast during the Late Postclassic, which all show characteristics of the East Coast architectural style (inset panels above the doorways, flat roofs, three-member moldings, and so forth) (fig. 11) (Andrews and Robles 1986; Toscano n.d. [1994]; Vargas n.d. [1992]; see also Andrews and Andrews 1975). According to Lourdes Toscano (n.d. [1994]), this architectural style derives from the structures built during the Itzá epoch at San Gervasio that exhibit architecture imitative of Chichén Itzá. Leticia Vargas (n.d. [1992]: 247–248), who conducted excavations of the public architecture at San Gervasio, labeled this style "Provincial Chichén." It includes distinctive features such as *talud-tablero* walls, balustrades with upper vertical zones, sloping ramps, and colonnaded hallways. In addition, mural paintings in several of the structures built in the East Coast style show pictographic representations in a manner similar to the Mixteca-Puebla style of the Maya codices (fig. 12), and have direct antecedents in the mural painting and imagery of the reliefs at Chichén Itzá (see, for example, Fettweis 1976; Lombardo 1982; Miller 1982: 64–71, fig. 98, plate 6; Roys 1967: plate 1-c; Schmidt 2003: 59, figs. 2–3). Moreover, sites exhibiting the East Coast style also belong to a distinct regional ceramic sphere characterized by the predominance of Tulúm Red vessels (Payil Group) and smoothed jars of the Nabulá type as well as anthropomorphic Chen Mul modeled censers (although they are not as elaborate as their counterparts

Fig. 11. Structure 32a at San Gervasio. Note the architectural elements of East Coast Postclassic style: inset panels above the doorways, flat roofs, and three-member moldings. Photograph by Fernando Robles.

Fig. 12. Fragment of a Maya-style Mixteca-Puebla mural preserved in the interior of the House of the Jaguar at Xelhá, Quintana Roo. Artwork by Fernando Robles, from a drawing by Martine Fettweis, Archive of the Cobá INAH Archaeological Project, 1974–1976.

found at Mayapán) (see fig. 10) (Canché n.d. [1992]; Mayer 1984; Ochoa n.d. [2004]; Peraza n.d. [1993]; Robles 1986; Robles and Andrews 1986: 94).

It is likely that, through bonds of marriage with the ruling elite at sites along the east coast of Yucatán, the *halach uinic*, or "supreme ruler," of Cuzamil (San Gervasio) and head of the Pat lineage implemented a strategy designed to strengthen alliances and forge ties of reciprocity to restructure and stabilize a regional political organization (Oviedo y Valdés 1851–1855, 1: 226–227; Scholes and Roys 1968: 77–78). He also established the ideological foundations for the development of regional cultural uniformity. The success of these political innovations was such that this regime was abolished only as a result of the Spanish conquest around the middle of the sixteenth century.

We know from written sources that during the Postclassic period numerous pilgrims converged on Cuzamil, bringing with them products and riches from the far corners of the Maya world to be offered at the sanctuary of the goddess Ixchel; while they were there, they also took advantage of the opportunity to engage in trade (Landa 1973: 48; Roys 1957; Roys et al. 1940; Scholes and Roys 1968: 77). We also know that people came on pilgrimages from Tabasco (Potonchán), Xicalanco, Champotón, and Campeche (*Relaciones histórico-geográficas* 1985, 2: 187). There is little doubt that, during the Late Postclassic period, Cuzamil constituted a significant focal point for the diffusion of the Mixteca-Puebla style, ideology, and iconography in the eastern part of the Maya area and adjacent regions of Central America.

To the south, the cultural supremacy of Cuzumil extended at least as far as the "province" of Chetumal in northern Belize (Chase and Chase 1988; Masson 2000). Sailing along the southern coast of Belize provided access to the "land of the Ulua" in the Gulf of Honduras, which was a trade node for Central America and Tabasco (Landa 1973: 18, 39). In the famed commercial port of Nito, Chontal leaders from Xicalanco, and later the Amactún (Acalanes) from Itzamkanac, established trading posts to administer their trade with Cozumel and Central America (Scholes and Roys 1968: 34).

It is likely that the great site of Tulúm (Zama) constituted a late commercial enclave established by powerful foreign groups. The political moment and urban and architectural influences common to central Mexico and seen at Tulúm clearly relate this site to the economic and cultural processes generated by the imperial and commercial expansion of the Culhua-Mexica in the Toltec tradition of the later phase of the Postclassic period (fig. 13) (León-Portilla 1980; Robles and Andrews 1986: 96; discussed later). In addition, the obvious absence of an established population and historical local tradition suggests that Tulúm must have been founded in a sudden manner, probably toward the second half of the fifteenth century, and later abandoned in a similar manner with the arrival of the Spaniards.

Fig. 13. El Castillo at Tulúm is a late example of the East Coast architectural style. Photograph by Fernando Robles.

MAYAPÁN, CAPITAL OF THE LAST STATE-LEVEL SOCIETY IN YUCATÁN   Oral tradition holds that after the fall of Chichén Itzá the city of Mayapán began to rule the territory that today includes most of the modern state of Yucatán. Sanctioned by its resemblance to the ancient cultural-political tradition of the Itzá, the new capital began to govern under the rule of the noble Cocom dynasty, the most powerful of the various noble groups who lived in the city and who were descendants of a ruling Yucatec Maya faction originally from Chichén Itzá (Landa 1973: 12–17; Milbrath and Peraza 2003: 31–35; Proskouriakoff 1955; Ringle 1990; Roys 1966).

A series of 38 new radiocarbon dates, most of which come from current excavations at Mayapán and its environs, convincingly suggests that the city was founded around 1100 CE and that it originally constituted a settlement of modest size. Later, during the thirteenth and first half of the fourteenth century, the site was transformed into the metropolis visible today, as indicated by the fact that the majority of the monumental architecture is associated with radiocarbon samples that date to this time period. It is probably the case that the lofty position held by Mayapán as regional capital of Yucatán during the Postclassic period was obtained after a long process of political centralization and was not inherited from Chichén Itzá as alluded to by historic sources (Peraza et al. 2006). Thus it was probably around the beginning of the thirteenth century that a new era began when the Cocom nobles finally succeeded in consolidating a

Fig. 14. The temple-pyramid of the Castillo at Chichén Itzá. Photograph courtesy of Ed Kurjack, Archive of the Atlas Arqueológico del Estado de Yucatán, Centro INAH Yucatán.

centralized regime among the Yucatec Maya communities of north-central and northwestern Yucatán. With this accomplished, they inaugurated a period of more than 200 years of relative political stability, and the inhabitants of Mayapán transformed themselves into the most complex sociocultural entity of their time, not only in the Maya area but in all of Mesoamerica (only to be emulated and eclipsed later by that of the Mexica at Tenochtitlan).

There is no doubt that Mayapán continued the "cultured" tradition of Chichén Itzá and that the Cocom found in its cultural-political canons an effective means of legitimizing their supreme rule over the other subordinate elite factions (Canul, Chel, and later the Xiu, and so on) who were brought into the *multepal*, or "joint government," that is alluded to in the written sources (Roys 1967: 49, 137).

Following the Itzá legacy, the principal temple at Mayapán was also dedicated to Kukulcan (Quetzalcoatl), the tutelary god of the ruling dynasty of the Cocom (Landa 1973: 14). Emulating the architecture of the main pyramid at Chichén Itzá, the temple to Kukulcan at Mayapán also has traces of serpent heads situated at the base of the balustrades of the north stairway, although the heads are modeled in stucco and not carved in stone like those at Chichén Itzá.

Fig. 15. The temple-pyramid of Kukulcan at Mayapán. Note that it faithfully replicates the same architectural details as that of the Castillo at Chichén Itzá. Photograph courtesy of Susan Milbrath.

Both basal pyramids consist of nine stepped levels, have stairways with balustrades on each of the four sides, and are crowned by temples whose entrances face north and display twin columns in the form of feathered serpents. Nevertheless, the basal pyramid at Mayapán is only 15 meters high (fig. 15), whereas the one at Chichén Itzá is 24 meters high (a total of 32 meters with its crowning temple) (fig. 14). Likewise, Mayapán also has a "Round Temple," which is a smaller imitation of the Caracol at Chichén Itzá; incorporated into its architectural design, among other similarities, are Puuc-style Chaak masks (Milbrath and Peraza 2003: 8–21; for a further comparison of the Chichén Itzá and Mayapán buildings, see Aveni, ch. 4, this volume).

According to Roys (1957, 1962), the jurisdiction of the Mayapán *multepal* comprised the provinces of Ah Canul, Chakán, Cehpech, Hocabá, Maní, Ah Kin Chel, Sotuta, and Cochuah. Canpech and Chanpotón to the south apparently were outside Mayapán's direct control, although their rulers must have come to some form of political understanding with the Cocom because the central coast of Campeche was the main route to Xicalanco, which at the time was the key node of exchange with the southwest Maya lowlands and central Mexico.

Fig. 16. A small temple from the mural on the Temple of the Niches (Q80) at Mayapán. After Proskouriakoff (1962).

There is evidence to suggest that the leadership of Mayapán maintained commercial ties with central Mesoamerica and, in particular, with the region of Coaixtlahuacan. This is suggested by pictorial representations in the public architecture of Mayapán, which have an affinity to the archetypical iconography of the Mixteca-Puebla art style from the distant Chocho-Mixtec region of northern Oaxaca, where the Coaixtlahuacan emporium operated. On the other hand, painted murals at Mayapán share greater similarities with pictorial representations at Postclassic Maya sites on the nearby east coast of Yucatán (figs. 16 and 17) (Milbrath and Peraza 2003: 26–28; Proskouriakoff 1962).

A recent analysis revealed that Mayapán obtained obsidian mainly from the mines at Ixtepeque (85.13 percent), El Chayal (12.13 percent), and San Martín Jilotepeque (1.36 percent) in the Guatemala highlands, whereas much smaller quantities came from various mines located across the central highlands

Fig. 17. A fragment of the mural in the Temple of the Fisherman (Q95) at Mayapán. Photograph courtesy of Carlos Peraza.

and Gulf Coast of Mexico (Escamilla n.d. [2004]). These data suggest that, in contrast to Chichén Itzá, commercial activities at Mayapán focused preferentially on exchange with neighboring communities in the Maya lowlands and the Guatemalan highlands and, to a lesser extent, with communities in central Mesoamerica.

Although exchange between Mayapán and central Mexico was relatively restricted, being guided by Xicalanco as an intermediary to the east, we know from written sources that the Cocom of Mayapán channeled trade with the highlands of Guatemala and northern Honduras through the port of Nito. Nito was situated in the Bay of Amatique (Honduras) where "there was a lot of trading from all quarters . . . Being a trading center, a lot of news was had from all over" (Cortés 1981: 246–248; Henderson 1979; Roys 1962; Strong 1935). In fact, it was on account of being away on a trade mission that "the son of the ruling

Cocom escaped death because he was away in Ulua, which is beyond the small town of Salamanca [Bacalar], conducting business; it was there that he learned about his father's death and the destruction of the city" (Landa 1973: 18).

According to most reliable documentary sources, this event occurred in Katun 8 Ahaw (1441–1461 CE), when a rebellion led by the seditious Xiu faction succeeded in destroying the city of Mayapán (Landa 1973: 12–19; Roys 1962). Afterward, the ancient Cocom domain split into a group of unstable political jurisdictions (or provinces) called *cuchcabal* (pl. *cuchcabaloob*), whose respective leaders, in constant internal and external conflict, lacked sufficient military force or political clout to reestablish a stable order. As a result, most of the northern half of the peninsula sank into a morass of continuous conflicts over lands and rights of succession—with the only exception being the east coast, which continued as a stronghold of Maya civilization until the arrival of Adelantado Francisco de Montejo, slightly over 100 years later.

The Second or Late Phase of the Late Postclassic (1458/ 1469–1521 CE): The Imperial and Commercial Invasion of the Culhua Mexica in Central and Eastern Mesoamerica

The story of the Aztecs has its beginnings in the fourteenth century. The primary indigenous historiographic sources relate that a few years after the founding of the Tepanec polity at Mexico Tlatelolco, a rebel Mexica faction led by Tenoch left Tlatelolco and founded the *tecpan* of Mexico Tenochtitlan. After 1367 CE, the Mexica Tenochas chose Acamapichtli to be their ruler, "because he is of Culhua lineage and was born at Culhuacan itself" (Chimalpahin 1982: 79, 82, 182; *Códice Chimalpopoca* 1975: 31; *Relación de la genealogía* 1891: 274–276). The *hueytlatoque*, or supreme lords, who ruled in Mexico Tenochtitlan had to be descended from the Culhua Toltec lineage of Acamapichtli; beginning with Itzcóatl (r. 1426–1441), they employed warfare to unify the Chichimec (Otopame-speaking) ruling elites in distant parts of the Basin of Mexico into a centralized government, and they imposed "the Nahua language, the Toltec language" as their official language (Carrasco 1950: 31–34).[5] In addition, marriage alliances united the lineages of the leaders of the more pugnacious Chichimec ("Aztec") factions and those of the "house" of Culhua in Mexico (Motolinía 1971: 205–206; Robles 2007: 81–91). Leading the new alliance of Culhua elites, the successors of Itzcóatl to the throne of Mexico over the following 80 years succeeded in conquering vast territories in central and southern Mesoamerica. In addition, the Culhua Mexica leadership officially named the extensive dominion they recently acquired with the patronym of their illustrious ancestral lineage: "[The] lord of México tenuxtitlan and the other culúa lords (so that when the name of culúa [Culhua] is invoked, it is understood by all the lands and provinces of these parts [of New Spain] to be subjects

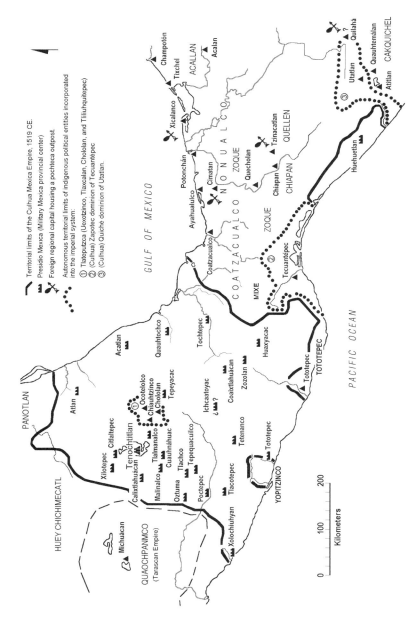

Fig. 18. The territorial extension and areas of imperial Culhua Mexica (Aztec) influence in central and eastern Mesoamerica at the time of Hernán Cortés's arrival, 1519 CE. After Robles (2007: Mapa del Imperio).

of tenuxtitlan)" (fig. 18) (Cortés 1981: 110; see also Díaz del Castillo 1904, 1: ch. 44). Moreover, after the middle of the fifteenth century, the language "of [the] culúa, that is Mexican" acquired the character of a lingua franca among the diverse ethnic groups of central and eastern Mesoamerica, and it outstripped the Nahua language of the Gulf Coast as the dominant language of commercial trade between central Mexico and the regions of Anahuac (Díaz del Castillo 1904, 1: ch. 36).

It is interesting to note that the Coaixtlahuacan emporium in central Mesoamerica was eclipsed at approximately the same time as the collapse of Mayapán. As we have seen, by order of Axayácatl, *hueytlatoani* of Mexico, Coaixtlahuacan was razed, and the interregional trade network with Anahuac that it controlled was restructured to favor the Mexica. Soon after, around 1489 CE, Ahuízotl, who reigned from 1481 to 1502, conquered Tochtepec (today Tuxtepéc, Oaxaca), a small Popoloca-Zoque village situated at the source of the headwaters of the great Papaloapan River. At Tochtepec, the Mexica ruler established a garrison whose lead captain assumed responsibility for securing Mexica dominion of the lush tropical region of south-central Veracruz (*Relación de Chinantla* 1905: 61–62; Robles 2007: 266–281).

According to the Tlatelolcan informants of Sahagún, Ahuízotl was the first ruler to sponsor the *pochteca,* allowing them to extend their trading business from Tochtepec toward the distant region of Anahuac Xicalanco (Sahagún 1938, 2: 341–356). At the beginning of his reign, Moctezuma Xocoyótzin (r. 1502–1520) established militarized Mexica trading posts at Cimatan and Xicalanco to monitor long-distance trade and provide security to the *pochteca.* As noted previously, these towns had been established long before as trading centers in the Chontal district (Chontalpa) of Nonohualco (*Relación del pueblo de Dzonot* 1983: 91; *Relación de la villa de Santa María* 1898: 346–347; Scholes and Roys 1968: 31–36).

Slightly more than 40 years after the ancient metropolis of Mayapán lay in ruins, the *pochteca* in the service of Mexico finally succeeded in establishing their interests in Xicalanco. From there, they acquired products directly from northern Yucatán, such as marine salt, cotton, valuable red and yellow shells, dyes, precious feathers, and fine textiles, many destined for the Tlatelolco market in Mexico.

Some contemporary writers have suggested that the "Mexicans," who lent military support to the Cocom of Mayapán in their struggle to gain control over rival elite factions led by Xiu conspirators, were Aztec mercenaries from Xicalanco (Okoshi 2001) and that the art of Mayapán displays "Aztec" influence (Milbrath and Peraza 2003; Proskouriakoff 1955). This is not possible. When Mayapán faded from the historic scene, the Mexica ("Aztecs") had just barely finished consolidating their rule over the Basin of Mexico and neighboring areas and had not yet taken control of the Coaixtlahuacan market, whose great ruler still directed the merchants' contacts and cultural relations with the distant "lands of Anahuac." By the time the Mexica established their trading outposts on the coast of Tabasco and Campeche, Mayapán was no more.

Considering themselves the legitimate heirs of the cultured Toltec or Toltecáyotl legacy, the supreme Culhua Mexica not only claimed as their own the canons of the Mixteca-Puebla tradition but also gave a final impetus to its diffusion (León Portilla 1980).[6] Proof of this lies in the late "Mexican" influences of the Mixteca-Puebla style in the architecture and mural painting of distant sites like Kumarcaaj (Utatlan) and Iximché (Quauhtemallan), the contemporary capitals of the Maya Quiché and Cakchiquel kingdoms in the Guatemalan highlands (founded ca. 1400 and 1470 CE, respectively), and Tulúm (Zama) on the eastern coast of Yucatán. The cultural development of these sites is correlated historically with the main period of imperial expansion of the Culhua Mexica, and they too ended up succumbing to the onslaught of the Spanish conquistadors in the following century (Brown 1985: 276–281; Carmack 1981: 143, 264–303; Guillemin 1977).

Closing Remarks

In closing, it is now evident that the central Mexican and northern Maya Postclassic had parallel early and late phases, which, in both cases, grew out of cultural traditions of the earlier Epiclassic/Terminal Classic period, that is, Toltec in the highlands and Itzá in the northern lowlands. While these developments followed both similar and different trajectories, and ultimately played out in unique ways, they also shared a common heritage and similar artistic and ideological canons, such as the Mixteca-Puebla art style and the cult of Quetzalcoatl. That they were parallel processes is now clear; the emergence of autonomous political entities in central Mexico after the fall of Tula and the rise of Mayapán after the collapse of the Itzá state were complementary cultural manifestations. They were also different in that Mayapán quickly developed a centralized state level of organization, while in central Mexico competing elites created a loose and unstable political situation. In spite of these differences, trade flourished and both regions enjoyed an era of relative prosperity.

In the end, the trajectories of the two regions bifurcated during the short "later" phase of the Postclassic. Mayapán collapsed, to be replaced by centrifugal, competing, and loosely organized political entities, while the opposite took place in central Mexico, with the emergence of the Culhua Mexica as the paramount ruling lineage and the eventual crystallization of the Aztec Empire.

Although both phases of the Postclassic in these two distant regions shared a common legacy and the artistic canons of the Mixteca-Puebla style, there was a fundamental shift in ideology in the later part of the period. During the first phase, the elites of both regions were linked through extensive commercial ties and a common ideology in which the cult of Quetzacoatl played a crucial role. In the latter phase, Quetzalcoatl lost ground: in central Mexico to the militaristic imperial cult of Huitzilopochtli (the god of war and tutelary deity of the Culhua Mexica) and in the Maya area to a host of lesser deities.

Even if a shared ideology was the driving force in both regions during the early phase, it is not clear why the trajectories diverged during the second phase, ultimately leading to such radically different outcomes. These developments were the result of complex processes that still remain poorly understood, and their explanations stand as a major challenge to future research.

Notes

1. The *Anales de Cuauhtitlan*, as well as the *Leyenda de los Soles* and the *Historia Tolteca-Chichimeca*, give the year 1 *técpatl* (1 Flint), or 1064 CE of the Mexica calendar, as the date for the political fractioning among the Toltecs of Tollan (*Códice Chimalpopoca* 1975: 14–15, 127; *Historia Tolteca-Chichimeca* 1976: 141–142). For his part, Chimalpahin (1982: 61) records that "the city of Tollan . . . in the year 1-Reed, 1031, was destroyed." The seventeenth-century glosses written about Toltec history by the chroniclers Fernando Ixtlilxóchitl and Fray Juan de Torquemada are not used because we know that the former misrepresented the original dates and accounts given in the *Anales de Cuauhtitlan*, and the latter based his arguments on a reinterpretation of Chimalpahin's work.

2. Subsequently the Mexica designated both tropical regions by the names Anahuac Xicalanco (for the Tabasco-Campeche coast) and Anahuac Ayotlan (for the Chiapas-Guatemalan coast) (Sahagún 1938, 2: ch. 4).

3. Several indigenous sources refer to the account of how the Toltec ruler Ce Acatl Topilzin Quetzalcoatl left Tollan at the insistence of Tezcatlipoca and traveled to the east, to Tlapallan "the land of red color or East." The *Historia de los Mexicanos por sus pinturas* corroborates Chimalpahin's (1982: 166) location of Tlapallan: "Tezcatlipoca came to him and told him that toward Honduras, at a place that is today also called Tlapalla, you had your house [temple] ready, and there you had to go and to be and to die, and to have to leave Tula, and in that place they had you as their god Ce Acatl." As we understand it, Tlapallan alludes to the enigmatic world of the Maya in Yucatán (from the perspective of the communities in central Mexico, obviously). This interpretation is based on the fact that the Yucatán Peninsula closes off the Gulf of Mexico to the east; therefore, the most important temples dedicated to Quetzalcoatl/Kukulcan in all of the Maya area are those that were first built at Chichén Itzá and later at Mayapán.

4. Recent reevaluation of stratigraphic evidence and spatial distribution of Fine Orange "V" (Matillas) and Fine Orange "U" (Cunduacán) ceramics of the Cintla phase has allowed Joseph Ball (1985: 236–238) to discern that the two vessel types do not correspond to two sequential periods of ceramic production, as Heinrich Berlin (1956; see also Smith 1971, 1: 20) initially thought; they actually represent distinct cultural-geographic zones of the Tabasco-Campeche coast that emerged in the Postclassic period.

5. The notion of the "Triple Alliance," which refers to the supposedly tripartite political regime that ruled the "Aztec" Empire, was a historic fabrication of the early colonial period, the rudiments of which can be traced back to post-conquest

Texcocan historiographic glosses. The purpose of this sophism was to erase historically the supremacy that the Culhua rulers of Mexico held over the traditional hierarchy of the Chichimec (Aztec) lords after they eliminated the Tepanec hegemony over the Basin of Mexico in 1430 CE. This subtlety favored the dynastic pretensions of those *caciques principales* of the Culhua regime of lesser rank, such as Ixtlilxóchitl the Second, whom Cortés placed on the throne of Texcoco Acolhuacan. Ixtlilxóchitl was committed to the cause of the Spanish conquest, having much to gain by lessening the supremacy of the Mexica lords. His supposed descendants, Juan Pomar Bautista and Fernando de Alva Ixtlilxóchitl, who later wrote the Texcocan chronicles, were also promoting their own interests, which provided a basis for the privileges to which they claimed they were entitled. Undermining the historical legitimacy of the native ruling elites also furthered the cause of the conquistadors (Robles 2007: 347–360).

6. The Culhua Mexica inherited this tradition from their Culhua Toltec ancestors from Culhuacan, who were ultimately historically linked to ancient Tollan.

References Cited

Anales de Tlatelolco
    1948 [1528]   *Unos anales históricos de la nación mexicana y códice de Tlatelolco.* Fuentes Para la Historia de México 2. Antigua Librería Robredo, México, D.F.

Anales Tepaneca (México-Atzcapotzalco) 1426–1585
    1900 [ca. 1589]   (Sr. F. Galícia Chimalpopoca, trans.). *Anales del Museo Nacional de México*, época I, 7: 49–74.

Andrews, Anthony P., E. Wyllys Andrews V, and Fernando Robles Castellanos
    2003   The Northern Maya Collapse and Its Aftermath. *Ancient Mesoamerica* 14: 151–156.

Andrews, Anthony P., and Fernando Robles Castellanos (eds.)
    1986   *Excavaciones arqueológicas en El Meco, Quintana Roo, 1977.* Colección Científica 158. Instituto Nacional de Antropología e Historia, México, D.F.

Andrews, E. Wyllys, IV, and Anthony P. Andrews
    1975   *A Preliminary Study of the Ruins of Xcaret.* Middle American Research Institute Publication 40. Tulane University, New Orleans.

Ball, Hugh G., and Donald L. Brockington
    1978   Trade and Travel in Prehispanic Oaxaca. In *Mesoamerican Communication Routes and Cultural Contacts* (T. A. Lee Jr. and C. Navarrete, eds.): 107–144. Papers of the New World Archaeological Foundation 40. Brigham Young University, Provo, Utah.

Ball, Joseph W.
    1985   The Postclassic Archaeology of the Western Gulf Coast: Some Initial Observations. In *The Lowland Maya Postclassic* (Arlen F. Chase and Prudence M. Rice, eds.): 235–244. University of Texas Press, Austin.

Barlow, Robert H.
    1948   Apuntes para la historia antigua de Guerrero. In *El occidente de México*: 181–190. Sociedad Mexicana de Antropología, México, D.F.

Berlin, Heinrich
  1956   Late Pottery Horizons of Tabasco, Mexico. In *Contributions to American Anthropology and History* 12 (59): 95–153. Carnegie Institution of Washington Publication 66. Washington, D.C.

Bernal, Ignacio
  1949   Exploraciones en Coaixtlahuaca, Oaxaca. *Revista mexicana de estudios antropológicos* 10: 5–76.

Boone, Elizabeth H., and Michael E. Smith
  2003   Postclassic International Styles and Symbol Sets. In *The Postclassic Mesoamerican World* (Michael E. Smith and Frances F. Berdan, eds.): 186–193. University of Utah Press, Salt Lake City.

Brown, Kenneth L.
  1985   Postclassic Relationships between the Highland and Lowland Maya. In *The Lowland Maya Postclassic* (Arlen F. Chase and Prudence M. Rice, eds.): 270–281. University of Texas Press, Austin.

Canché Manzanero, Elena de la Cruz
  n.d.   La secuencia cerámica de Xelhá, Quintana Roo. Tesis profesional, Facultad de Ciencias Antropológicas de la Universidad Autónoma de Yucatán, Mérida, 1992.

Carmack, Robert M.
  1968   *Toltec Influence on the Postclassic Culture History of Highland Guatemala.* Middle American Research Institute Publication 26, pt. 4: 49–92. Tulane University, New Orleans.
  1981   *The Quiché Mayas of Utatlán: The Evolution of a Highland Guatemalan Kingdom.* University of Oklahoma Press, Norman.

Carrasco, Pedro
  1950   *Los otomíes: Cultura e historia de los pueblos mesoamericanos de habla otomiana.* Instituto de Historia, Universidad Nacional Autónoma de México (Primera serie 15), México, D.F.

Caso, Alfonso
  1966   La época de los señoríos independientes. *Revista mexicana de estudios antropológicos* 20: 147–154.
  1977   *Reyes y reinos de la mixteca*, 2 vols. Fondo de Cultura Económica, México, D.F.

Chase, Diane Z., and Arlen F. Chase
  1988   *A Postclassic Perspective: Excavations at the Maya Site of Santa Rita Corozal, Belize.* Pre-Columbian Art Research Institute Monograph 4. Pre-Columbian Art Research Institute, San Francisco.

Chimalpahin Cuauhtlehuanitzin, Francisco de San Antón Muñón
  1950   Das memorial breve acerca de la fundación de la ciudad de Culhuacan und weitere ausgewählte Teile aus den "Diferentes historias originales de los reynos de Culhuacan y México, y de otras provincias" (Walter Lehmann and Gerdt Kutscher, trans.). Quellenwerke zur alten Geschichte Amerikas aufgezeichnet in den Sprachen der Eingeborenen 7. Stuttgart.
  1982 [ca. 1620]   *Relaciones originales de Chalco Amecamecan* (Silvia Rendón, trans. and ed.). Fondo de Cultura Económica, México, D.F.

Cobos, Rafael

1997   Katún y Ahau: Fechando el fin de Chichén Itzá. In *Identidades sociales en Yucatán* (Ma. C. Lara Cebada, ed.): 17–40. Facultad de Ciencias Antropológicas, Universidad Autónoma de Yucatán, Mérida.

1998   Chichén Itzá y el clásico terminal en las tierras bajas mayas. In *XI Simposio de investigaciones arqueológicas en Guatemala* (J. P. Laporte and H. Escobedo, eds.): 791–799. Museo Nacional de Guatemala, Guatemala.

Códice Chimalpopoca

1975   *Anales de Cuauhtitlan* [1570] y *Leyenda de los Soles* [1558]. Instituto de Investigaciones Históricas, Primera Serie Prehispánica 1 (trans. from the Náhuatl by Primo Feliciano Velázquez). Universidad Nacional Autónoma de México, México, D.F.

Coe, Michael D.

1981   San Lorenzo Tenochtitlan. In *Handbook of Middle American Indians*. Suppl. 1: *Archaeology* (Jeremy A. Sabloff, ed.): 117–146. University of Texas Press, Austin.

Cortés, Hernán

1981 [1519–1526]   *Cartas de relación de la conquista de México*. 12th ed. Serie Sepan cuantos 7. Editorial Porrúa, México, D.F.

Dahlgren de Jordán, Barbro

1954   *La mixteca: Su cultura e historia prehispánica*. Cultura Mexicana 11. Imprenta Universitaria, México, D.F.

Davies, Nigel

1968   *Los señoríos independientes del imperio azteca*. Serie Historia 19. Instituto Nacional de Antropología e Historia, México, D.F.

1973   *Los mexicas: Primeros pasos hacia el imperio*. Instituto de Investigaciones Históricas, Universidad Nacional Autónoma de México, México, D.F.

1980   *The Toltec Heritage: From the Fall of Tula to the Rise of Tenochtitlan*. University of Oklahoma Press, Norman.

1987   *The Aztec Empire: The Toltec Resurgence*. University of Oklahoma Press, Norman.

Díaz del Castillo, Bernal

1904 [1568]   *Historia verdadera de la conquista de la Nueva España*, 2 vols. Tipografía de la Secretaría de Fomento, México, D.F.

Durán, Fray Diego

1965 [ca. 1581]   *Historia de las indias de Nueva España y islas de tierra firme*, 2 vols. (Notes by José Fernando Ramírez.) Editorial Nacional, México, D.F.

Escamilla Ojeda, Bárbara

n.d.   Los artefactos de obsidiana de Mayapán, Yucatán. Tesis profesional, Facultad de Ciencias Antropológicas de la Universidad Autónoma de Yucatán, Mérida, 2004.

Estrada Belli, Francisco

1999   *The Archaeology of Complex Societies in Southeastern Pacific Coastal Guatemala: A Regional GIS Approach*. BAR International Series 820. Oxford, England.

Fettweis, Martine
    1976   Algunos sitios con pintura mural de la costa oriental de Quintana Roo. In *Investigaciones arqueológicas en el sureste. Cuaderno de los centros* 27: 125–150. Centro Regional del Sureste, Instituto Nacional de Antropología e Historia, México, D.F.

Fowler, William R., Jr.
    1989   *The Cultural Evolution of Ancient Nahua Civilization: The Pipil-Nicarao of Central America.* University of Oklahoma Press, Norman and London.

García de León, Antonio
    1976   *Pajapan: Un dialecto mexicano del Golfo.* Colección Científica 43. Instituto Nacional de Antropología e Historia, México, D.F.

Gil y Sáenz, Manuel
    1872   *Compendio histórico, geográfico y estadístico del estado de Tabasco.* Tabasco, Mexico.

Guillemin, George F.
    1977   Urbanism and Hierarchy at Iximche. In *Social Process in Maya Prehistory: Essays in Honour of Sir J. Eric S. Thompson* (Norman Hammond, ed.): 227–264. Academic Press, New York.

Henderson, John S.
    1979   The Valley of Naco: Ethnohistory and Archaeology of Northwestern Honduras. *Ethnohistory* 24 (4): 363–377.

Historia Tolteca-Chichimeca o anales de Quauhtínchan
    1976   *Manuscrito de mediados del siglo XVI.* Instituto Nacional de Antropología e Historia-SEP, México, D.F.

Hodge, Mary G.
    1984   *Aztec City-States.* Memoirs of the Museum of Anthropology of Michigan 18. Studies in Latin American Ethnohistory and Archaeology 3. Ann Arbor, Mich.

Izquierdo, Ana Luisa, and Tolita Figueroa
    1978   Las influencias nahuas entre los chontales. In *Estudios preliminares sobre los mayas de las tierras bajas noroccidentales* (L. Ochoa, ed.): 71–89. Universidad Nacional Autónoma de México, México, D.F.

Jakeman, Wells M.
    1952   An Archaeological Reconnaissance of the Xicalango Area of Western Campeche, Mexico. *Bulletin of the University Archaeological Society* 3: 16–47. Provo, Utah.

Justeson, John S., William M. Norman, Lyle Campbell, and Terrence Kaufman
    1985   *The Foreign Impact on Lowland Maya Language and Script.* Middle American Research Institute Publication 53. Tulane University, New Orleans.

Kirchhoff, Paul
    1985   El imperio tolteca. In *Mesoamérica y el centro de México* (J. Monjaráz-Ruiz, R. Brambila, and E. Pérez-Rocha, eds.): 249–272. Colección Biblioteca del Instituto Nacional de Antropología e Historia, México, D.F.

Landa, Fray Diego de

1973   *Relación de las cosas de Yucatán.* Biblioteca Porrúa 13. Editorial Porrúa, México, D.F.

León Portilla, Miguel

1965   *Los huaxtecos, según los informantes de Sahagún.* Estudios de Cultura Náhuatl. Instituto de Investigaciones Históricas, Universidad Autónoma de México, México, D.F.

1980   *Toltecáyotl, aspectos de la cultura náhuatl.* Fondo de Cultura Económica, Mexico, D.F.

Lombardo de Ruíz, Sonia (ed.)

1982   *La pintura mural maya en Quintana Roo.* Colección Fuentes, Instituto Nacional de Antropología e Historia–Gobierno del Estado de Quintana Roo, Mexico.

Lothrop, Samuel K.

1926   *Pottery of Costa Rica and Nicaragua,* 2 vols. Heye Foundation, Museum of the American Indian, New York.

Marcus, Joyce, and Kent V. Flannery

1983   The Postclassic Balkanization of Oaxaca. In *The Cloud People* (Kent V. Flannery and Joyce Marcus, eds.): 217–226. Academic Press, New York.

Masson, Marilyn A.

2000   *In the Realm of Nachan Kan: Postclassic Maya Archaeology at Laguna de On, Belize.* University Press of Colorado, Boulder.

Mayer Guala, Pablo

1984   Interpretaciones preliminares de la cerámica de Can-Cún. In *Investigaciones recientes en el área maya. XVII Mesa Redonda,* vol. 2: 167–175. San Cristóbal de las Casas, Chiapas.

Medellín Zenil, Alfonso

1952   *Exploraciones en Quauhtochco.* Departamento de Antropología Gobierno del Estado de Veracruz, Jalapa, Mexico.

Melgarejo Vivanco, José Luís

1989   *Historia de Cotaxtla.* Universidad Veracruzana, Xalapa, Mexico.

Milbrath, Susan, and Carlos Peraza Lope

2003   Revisiting Mayapan, Mexico's Last Maya Capital. *Ancient Mesoamerica* 14: 1–46.

Miller, Arthur G.

1982   *On the Edge of the Sea: Mural Painting at Tancah-Tulum, Quintana Roo, Mexico.* Dumbarton Oaks, Washington, D.C.

Motolinía, Fray Toribio de Benavente

1971 [ca. 1543]   *Memoriales;* o, *Libro de las cosas de la Nueva España y de los naturales de ella* (Edmundo O'Gorman, ed.). Instituto de Investigaciones Históricas, Universidad Nacional Autónoma de México, México, D.F.

Nicholson, Henry B.

1982   The Mixteca-Puebla Concept Revised. In *The Art and Iconography of Late Post-Classic Central Mexico* (Elizabeth H. Boone, ed.): 227–254. Dumbarton Oaks, Washington, D.C.

Noticias relativas al reinado de Moctezuma Ilhuicamina
  1944 [ca. 1583–1587]   In *Códice Ramírez* (resumen fragmentario al parecer de los
          testimonios indígenas allegados por el jesuita Juan de Tovar; examen de la
          obra, con un anexo de la cronología Mexicana por el Lic. Manuel Orozco y
          Berra): 173–184. Editorial Leyenda, México, D.F.

Ochoa Rodríguez, José Manuel
  n.d.   La secuencia cerámica de Xcaret, Quintana Roo, México. Tesis profesional,
          Facultad de Ciencias Antropológicas de la Universidad Autónoma de
          Yucatán, Mérida, 2004.

Ochoa S., Lorenzo
  1979   *Historia prehispánica de la Huaxteca.* Serie Antropología 26. Instituto de
          Investigaciones Históricas, Universidad Nacional Autónoma de México,
          México, D.F.

Ochoa S., Lorenzo, and Luis Casasola
  1978   Los cambios del patrón de asentamiento en el área del Usumacinta. In
          Estudios preliminares sobre los mayas de las tierras bajas noroccidentales (L.
          Ochoa, ed.): 19–43. Universidad Nacional Autónoma de México, México,
          D.F.

Ochoa S., Lorenzo, and Ernesto Vargas P.
  1979   El colapso maya, los chontales y Xicalango. *Estudios de cultura maya* 12:
          61–91.

Okoshi Harada, Tsubasa
  2001   Gaspar Antonio Chi Xiu: el que "perpetuó" la imagen de los Xiu. In
          Maya Survivalism (U. Hostettler and M. Restall, eds.): 60–72. Acta
          Mesoamericana 12. Verlag Anton Saurwein, Markt Schwaben, Germany.

Oviedo y Valdés, Gonzalo Fernández de
  1851–1855 [1555]   *Historia general y natural de las Indias, islas y tierra-firme del
          Mar Océano,* 4 vols. Madrid.

Palacios, Enrique Juan
  1941   Perspectivas emanadas del vocablo "huasteca." In *Los mayas antiguos*
          (César Lizardi Ramos, ed.): 87–97. El Colegio de México-Fondo de Cultura
          Económica, México, D.F.

Parmenter, Ross
  1982   *Four Lienzos of the Coaixtlahuaca Valley.* Studies in Pre-Colombian Art
          and Archaeology 26. Dumbarton Oaks, Washington, D.C.

Peraza Lope, Carlos A.
  n.d.   Estudio y secuencia del material cerámico de San Gervasio, Cozumel.
          Tesis profesional, Facultad de Ciencias Antropológicas de la Universidad
          Autónoma de Yucatán, Mérida, 1993.

Peraza Lope, Carlos, Marilyn A. Masson, Timothy S. Hare, and Pedro Delgado Kú
  2006   The Chronology of Mayapan: New Radiocarbon Evidence. *Ancient
          Mesoamerica* 17: 153–175.

Peterson, Fredrick A.
  1957   El "motivo serpiente" en la cerámica de Culhuacán. In *Motivos decorativos
          de la cerámica azteca* (by José Luís Franco C. and Fredrick A. Peterson): 37–
          48. Serie Científica 5. Museo Nacional de Antropología, México, D.F.

Proskouriakoff, Tatiana

1955 Mayapan: The Last Stronghold of a Civilization. *Archaeology* 7 (2): 96–103.

1962 Civic and Religious Structures of Mayapan. In *Mayapan, Yucatan, Mexico* (H. E. D. Pollock, R. L. Roys, T. Proskouriakoff, and A. L. Smith, eds.): 87–164. Carnegie Institution of Washington Publication 619. Washington, D.C.

Quezada Ramírez, María Noemí

1972 *Los matlatzincas: Época prehispánica y época colonial hasta 1650.* Instituto Nacional de Antropología e Historia, México, D.F.

Relación de Atlatlauca y Malinaltepec

1905 [1580] Hecha por el corregidor de ambos pueblos, Francisco de La Mezquita. In *Papeles de Nueva España*, vol. 4 (Francisco del Paso y Troncoso, ed.): 163–177. Sucesores de Rivadeneyra, Madrid.

Relación de Chinantla

1905 [1579] Hecha por el corregidor del pueblo, Diego de Esquivel. In *Papeles de Nueva España*, vol. 4 (Francisco del Paso y Troncoso, ed.): 58–68. Sucesores de Rivadeneyra, Madrid.

Relación de Coatépec (Chalco) y su partido

1905 [1579] Hecha por el corregidor de todo el partido, Comendador Cristobal de Salazar. In *Papeles de Nueva España*, vol. 6 (Francisco del Paso y Troncoso, ed.): 39–86. Sucesores de Rivadeneyra, Madrid.

Relación de Iztepexi

1905 [1579] Suscrita por el corregidor de dicho pueblo, Juan Ximénez Ortíz. In *Papeles de Nueva España*, vol. 6 (Francisco del Paso y Troncoso, ed.): 9–23. Sucesores de Rivadeneyra, Madrid.

Relación de la genealogía y linaje de los señores que han señoreado esta tierra de Nueva España

1891 [ca. 1530] In *Nueva colección de documentos para la historia de México (siglo XVI)*, vol. 3 (Joaquín García Icazbalceta, ed.): 263–281. Imprenta de Francisco Díaz de León, México, D.F.

Relación de la provincia de Coatzacualco, villa del Espíritu Santo

1984 [1580] Hecha por el alcalde mayor, Suero de Cangas y Quiñones. In *Relaciones geográficas del siglo XVI: Antequera*, Book 1 [vol. 2 of the series] (René Acuña, ed.): 111–126. Universidad Nacional Autónoma de México, México, D.F.

Relación de la villa de Santa María de la Victoria de la provincia de Tabasco

1898 [1579] In *Colección de documentos inéditos*, vol. XI: *Relaciones de Yucatán*, vol. 1: 341–374. Sucesores de Rivadeneyra, Madrid.

Relación de Nexapa

1984 [1580] Hecha por Fray Bernardino de Santa Maria. In *Relaciones Geográficas del siglo XVI: Antequera*, vol. 2 (René Acuña, ed.): 341–360. Universidad Nacional Autónoma de México, México, D.F.

Relación de Tehuantepec y su provincia

1927–28 [1580] Hecha por el alcalde mayor de la villa, Juan de Torres De Lagunas. In *Revista mexicana de estudios históricos* II, append.: 164–175. México, D.F.

Relación de Tequisquiac, Citlaltepec y Xilocingo
   1957 [1579]   Hecha por el corregidor del partido de Citlaltepec, Antonio de Galdo. In *Tlalocan* 3 (Ignacio Bernal, ed.): 289–308.

Relación del pueblo de Dzonot
   1983 [1579]   Hecha por el encomendero del pueblo, Giraldo Díaz de Alpuche. In *Relaciones histórico geográficas de la gobernación de Yucatán*, vol. 2 (Mercedes de la Garza, Ana Luisa Izquierdo, Ma del Carmen León Cásares, and Tolita Figueroa, eds.): 83–92. Universidad Nacional Autónoma de México, México, D.F.

Relación (descripción) de Cholula
   1927–28 [1581]   Hecha por el corregidor de la ciudad, Gabriel de Rojas. In *Revista mexicana de estudios históricos* I, append.: 158–170. México, D.F.

Relaciones histórico-geográficas de la gobernación de Yucatán
   1985   Fuentes para el estudio de la cultura maya 1. Universidad Nacional Autónoma de México, México, D.F.

Reyes García, Luís
   1988   *Cuauhtinchan del siglo XII al XVI (formación y desarrollo de un señorío prehispánico)*. Fondo de Cultura Económica, México, D.F.

Rincón Mautner, Carlos A.
   1995   The Ñuiñe Codex from the Colossal Natural Bridge on the Ndaxagua: An Early Pictographic Text from the Coixtlahuaca Basin. *Institute of Maya Studies Journal* 1 (2): 29–66.
   2000   La reconstrucción cronológica del linaje principal de Coixtlahuaca. In *Códices y documentos sobre México: Tercer simposio* (Constanza Vega, ed.): 25–43. Serie Historia, Colección Científica 409. Instituto Nacional de Antropología e Historia, México, D.F.
   2005   The Pictographic Assemblage from the Colossal Natural Bridge on the Ndaxagua, Coixtlahuaca Basin, Northwestern Mixteca Alta of Oaxaca, Mexico. *Ketzalcalli* 2: 2–69.

Ringle, William M.
   1990   Who Was Who in Ninth-Century Chichen Itza. *Ancient Mesoamerica* 1: 233–243.

Ringle, William M., Tomás Gallareta Negrón, and George J. Bey III
   1998   The Return of Quetzalcoatl: Evidence for the Spread of a World Religion during the Epiclassic Period. *Ancient Mesoamerica* 9: 183–232.

Robles Castellanos, Fernando
   1986   Cronología cerámica de El Meco. In *Excavaciones arqueológicas en El Meco, Quintana Roo, 1977* (Anthony P. Andrews and Fernando Robles Castellanos, eds.): 77–130. Colección Científica 158. Instituto Nacional de Antropología e Historia, México, D.F.
   2007   *Culhua México: Una revisión arqueo-etnohistórica del imperio de los mexica tenochca*. Colección Obra Diversa. Instituto Nacional de Antropología e Historia, México, D.F.

Robles Castellanos, Fernando, and Anthony P. Andrews

1986   A Review and Synthesis of Recent Postclassic Archaeology in Northern
       Yucatan. In *Late Lowland Maya Civilization: Classic to Postclassic* (Jeremy
       Sabloff and E. Wyllys Andrews V, eds.): 53–98. University of New Mexico
       Press, Albuquerque.

Roys, Ralph L.

1943   *The Indian Background of Colonial Yucatan.* Carnegie Institution of
       Washington Publication 548. Washington, D.C.

1957   *The Political Geography of the Yucatan Maya.* Carnegie Institution of
       Washington Publication 613. Washington, D.C.

1962   Literary Sources for the History of Mayapan. In *Mayapan, Yucatan, Mexico*
       (H. E. D. Pollock, R. L. Roys, T. Proskouriakoff, and A. L. Smith, eds.): 24–
       86. Carnegie Institution of Washington Publication 619. Washington, D.C.

1966   Native Empires in Yucatan: The Maya-Toltec Empire. *Revista mexicana de
       estudios antropológicos* 20: 153–177.

1967   *The Book of Chilam Balam of Chumayel.* University of Oklahoma Press,
       Norman.

Roys, Ralph L., France V. Scholes, and Eleanor B. Adams

1940   Report and Census of the Indians of Cozumel, 1570. *Contributions to
       American Anthropology and History,* no. 30. Carnegie Institution of
       Washington Publication 523. Washington, D.C.

Sahagún, Fray Bernardino de

1938 [ca. 1576]   *Historia general de las cosas de Nueva España.* 4 vols. Editorial
       Pedro Robredo, México, D.F.

Sanders, William. T., Jeremy R. Parsons, and Robert S. Santley

1979   *The Basin of Mexico: Ecological Process in the Evolution of a Civilization.*
       Academic Press, New York.

Schmidt, Peter J.

1998   Contacts with Central Mexico and the Transition to the Postclassic:
       Chichén Itzá and Central Mexico. In *Maya* (Peter J. Schmidt, Mercedes de
       la Garza, and E. Nalda, eds.): 427–449. Rizzoli, New York.

2003   Siete años entre los itzá: Nuevas excavaciones en Chichén Itzá y sus
       resultados. In *Escondido en la selva* (A. J. Prem, ed.): 53–63. Universidad de
       Bonn, and Instituto Nacional de Antropología e Historia, México, D.F.

Scholes, Frances V., and Ralph L. Roys

1968 [1948]   *The Maya Chontal Indians of Acalan-Tixchel.* University of Oklahoma
       Press, Norman.

Scholes, Frances V., and Dave Warren

1965   The Olmec Region at Spanish Contact. In *Handbook of Middle American
       Indians*, vol. 3, pt. 2 (Gordon R. Willey, ed.): 776–787. University of Texas
       Press, Austin.

Seler, Eduard

1894   On the Words Anáuac and Náhuatl (trans. from the Spanish by J. Eric
       S. Thompson and Francis B. Richardson). *Compte rendu de la Xeme session
       du Congrès International des Américanistes, Stockholm*: 211–244. On file,
       Tozzer Library, Harvard University, Cambridge, Mass.

Sierra Sosa, Thelma Noemí

1994 *Contribución al estudio de los asentamientos de San Gervasio, isla de Cozumel.* Colección Científica 279. Instituto Nacional de Antropología e Historia, México, D.F.

Smith, Michael E.

n.d. Postclassic Culture Change in Western Morelos, Mexico: The Development and Correlation of Archaeological and Ethnohistorical Chronologies. Ph.D. dissertation, University of Illinois at Urbana–Champaign, 1983.

Smith, Robert E.

1971 *The Pottery of Mayapan.* Papers of the Peabody Museum of Archaeology and Ethnology 66, 2 vols. Harvard University, Cambridge, Mass.

Stone, Doris

1949 Los grupos mexicanos en la América Central y su importancia. *Antropología e historia de Guatemala* 1: 43–47.

1982 Cultural Radiations from the Central and Southern Highlands of Mexico into Costa Rica. In *Aspects of Mixteca-Puebla Style and Mixtec and Central Mexican Culture in Southern Mesoamerica* (J. S. H. Brown and E. W. Andrews V, eds.): 60–70. Middle American Research Institute, Occasional Paper 4. Tulane University, New Orleans.

Strong, William D.

1935 Archaeological Investigations in the Bay Islands, Spanish Honduras. *Smithsonian Miscellaneous Collections* 94 (14): 7–19. Washington, D.C.

Torquemada, Fray Juan de

1975 [1615] *Monarquía indiana.* 3 vols. Introducción por Miguel León Portilla. Editorial Porrúa, México, D.F.

Toscano Hernández, María de Lourdes

n.d. Secuencia arqueológica de la arquitectura pública de Xélhá, Quintana Roo. Tesis profesional, Facultad de Antropología de la Universidad Veracruzana, Jalapa, 1994.

Vaillant, George C.

1940 Patterns in Middle American Archaeology. In *The Maya and Their Neighbors: Essays on Middle American Anthropology and Archaeology* (Clarence L. Hay, Ralph L. Linton, Samuel K. Lothrop, Harry L. Shapiro, and George C. Vaillant, eds.): 295–305. D. Appelton-Century, New York.

Vargas de la Peña, Leticia

n.d. Estudio de la arquitectura pública de San Gervasio, Cozumel. Tesis profesional, Facultad de Ciencias Antropológicas de la Universidad Autónoma de Yucatán, Mérida, 1992.

Chapter Three

Evidence for Maya-Mexican Interaction in the Archaeological Record of Mayapán

Marilyn A. Masson and Carlos Peraza Lope

Tʜᴇ ᴘᴏsᴛᴄʟᴀssɪᴄ ᴍᴀʏᴀ ᴄɪᴛʏ of Mayapán is rumored to have been a cosmopolitan place. Established by a confederation of noble headmen who represented a mosaic of northern Maya towns, this city was also settled by commoners whose labor sustained the metropolis and "foreigners" who were often the object of disdainful regard by colonial period chroniclers. Who were those foreigners, and what was their social position within the city? We draw here on the material record of Mayapán to investigate the ever-slippery question of ethnicity. *Ethnicity* refers to "self-conscious identification" with a distinct social group that is linked to some extent to concepts of an origin or place, although Shennan (1989: 14) points out that this definition poses a problem for archaeologists, because we cannot directly access the consciousness of past peoples. The archaeological study of ethnic groups in recent decades customarily recognizes that each group is a "dynamic and situational phenomenon," and style should not be used as the sole criteria for identifying ethnicity in the archaeological record (Jones 1997: 110). Jones observes that ethnic groups are fluid and change through time and space as agents accommodate identity to their strategic goals; economic and political stress in particular can augment the differentiation of identity (Jones 1997: 110). Scholars have effectively critiqued the use of stylistic variation to identify cultural groups due to the fact that style can be adopted through a variety of mechanisms. Nevertheless, in some cases spatio-stylistic distributions do in fact seem to reflect meaningful, diverse social entities. Some of the best examples in Mesoamerica are known from Teotihuacan (Millon 1981: 222), its hinterland site Matacapan (Santley et al. 1987), and the Peten Lakes (Cecil n.d. [2001]; Pugh 2003).

Foreigners at Mayapán: Documentary Accounts

Foreigners at Mayapán were described as mercenaries who purportedly assisted with Kukulcan/Hunac Ceel's founding of the site and resolved a later Cocom-Xiu conflict (Barrera and Morley 1949: table 6; Roys 1962: 59; Tozzer 1941: 36). Allies who ultimately betrayed the elusory Hunac Ceel character of Mayapán—whom Tozzer (1941: 34, n. 172) argued was the same person or office as Nacxit Kukulcan—clearly had Mexican names, including Cinteotl Chan, Tzontecome, Tlaxcallan Pantemitl, Xichihuehuetl, Itzcóatl, and Cacalacatl (Tozzer 1941: 34, n. 172; Edmonson 1982: 9), although the chronology of their activities is difficult to pinpoint from the Chilam Balam books. In a famous documentary passage, Landa notes "Governor Cocom began to covet riches and for this reason he arranged with the troops of the garrison, which the kings of Mexico kept at Tabasco and Xicalango, to hand over the city to them. And thus he brought the Mexican people to Mayapán" (Tozzer 1941: 32). In the Chilam Balam of Chumayel, four rulers of the land are named, including Zacaal Puc, who is said to have come from Mexico (Tozzer 1941: 34, n. 172). At a later point in Mayapán's history, more Mexican forces were again brought to the site to resolve internal Cocom-Xiu conflicts, according to Tozzer (1941: 34, n. 172). Other Nahuatl names in Yucatán listed by Roys (1940) include Cetzal, Chimal, Iuit, Nauat, Pan/Pantli, Tepal, Ueuet, and Xiu (Victoria Bricker, personal communication, September 2006).

Foreign merchants likely maintained homes and facilities at Mayapán. Historical accounts reveal that Xicalango merchants had warehouses, family members, and other agents on the Ulua River in Honduras, and Acalan agents had employees and slaves quartered at Nito (Piña Chan 1978: 43, 47; Scholes and Roys 1968: 34). There are many examples of similar facilities at key trading sites (Scholes and Roys 1968: 317). It is said that the Aztec emperor Moctezuma had a fortress at Xicalango at the time of Spanish contact and harbored intentions of expanding to Yucatán when the Spanish conquest intervened (Scholes and Roys 1968: 35). This account implies that central Mexican agents were not in a dominant military or political position at Mayapán before Spanish contact, although they might have held offices beneath local Yucatecan paramounts. Tozzer (1941: n. 171) disputes the presence of Mexica garrisons on the Gulf Coast. Mexicanized groups from the Maya Gulf Coast (Campeche, Tabasco) were clearly moving about the peninsula and were involved in forging and maintaining emergent Postclassic polities (Scholes and Roys 1968: 76).

What did *foreign* mean at Mayapán? This category could have encompassed all groups who were not local to northwest Yucatán (the stronghold of the Mayapán confederacy), including the east coast or southern polities to which the settlements of Cozumel, Tulúm, Santa Rita, Caye Coco, Laguna de On, Lamanai, or the Peten Lakes belonged, as well as to linguistically diverse entities from the Gulf Coast, Honduras, and highland Chiapas/Guatemala. In accordance with the theme of this volume, we concentrate specifically on potential "Mexican" groups at the city, although we are fairly certain that this referent included borderland societies like those of the Gulf Coast. It is likely that Mayapán had more prolonged direct contact with Gulf Coast intermediaries than with central Mexican groups.

Scholarly opinions are divided on the matter of Mexican contact in the Postclassic Maya area. Some investigators see evidence for direct central Mexican contact, conquest, or other forms of strong political presence in the art and architectural programs of Mayapán (Barrera and Peraza 2001; Milbrath and Peraza 2003), Tulúm (Miller 1982: 75), and highland Utatlán (Fox 1987). However, in some cases, artistic imitation could be the result of local adoption of international styles emulated by elites throughout the Postclassic Mesoamerican world (Masson 2003; Masson and Peraza 2007; Smith 2003a: 182–184; Smith and Heath-Smith 1980). Style is a notoriously ambiguous factor on which to form an opinion on the matter of foreign contact. This debate echoes longstanding arguments for the site of Chichén Itzá, where traditional elements of Maya cosmological and creation myth symbolism are represented using international conventions (e.g., Kowalski and Kristan-Graham 2007; Schele and Matthews 1998), although intensive participation in a pan-Mesoamerican elite interaction sphere is also evident for that site (Ringle 2004; Ringle et al. 1998; Taube 1994). As Ringle and colleagues (1998) point out, major Mesoamerican cities were in close contact and shared conventions of feathered serpent religious cultic practice, principles of council government, and institutions of investiture during the Epiclassic and Terminal Classic periods. We feel that Mayapán was also an international city as a result of similar processes. The style of the city's public art shows considerable foreign and international inspiration (Barrera and Peraza 2001; Milbrath and Peraza 2003). Other papers in this volume argue for important shared elite traditions across regions in the Late Postclassic period. To what degree did this stylistic and symbolic exchange reflect the ethnic diversity and relative regional autonomy of Mayapán?

Chronology and Mexican Interaction with the Maya Area

Most of Mayapán's contact with central Mexico (table 1), either direct or via Gulf Coast intermediaries, would have been with the city-state kingdoms of the highland Early Aztec period (1150–1350 CE) and the first century of occupation at Tenochtitlan (1325–1428 CE), as defined by Michael Smith (2003b:

Table 1. A general comparison of Tenochtitlan and Mayapán chronologies

Time range (CE)	Tenochtitlan chronology	Time range (CE)	Mayapán chronology
1428–1521	Triple Alliance	1400–1441	Terminal Mayapán
1325–1428	First 100 years of Tenochtitlan (1372) First Mexica king	1350–1400	Conflicts
		1200–1350	Height of Mayapán
1150–1350	Early Aztec	1100–1200	Rise of Mayapán

37–43). Mayapán was at the height of its power from around 1250–1400 CE, during the century before the appointment of the first Mexica king at Tenochtitlan in 1372 CE (Smith 2003b: 44) and for three subsequent decades. The historic date for Mayapán's fall is around 1441 CE, only 13 years after the formation of the Imperial Aztec Triple Alliance in 1428 (Smith 2003b: 47), but mass graves, burned houses, and public buildings at the site indicate that it was in decline by 1400 CE and perhaps during the century leading up to this date, probably due to conflicts internal to Yucatán (Peraza et al. 2006). Although an external attack on Mayapán cannot be ruled out based on current evidence, there are no material indications of a subsequent "foreign" occupation. Radiocarbon ranges for late violent events at Mayapán extend from 1250 to 1400 CE, and thus could have occurred before the rise of Tenochtitlan's first king in 1372. While we have no reason to suspect that Mayapán was subject to the authority of central Mexican kingdoms during the early years, it is curious that Mayapán's prolonged decline coincides with the rise of Tenochtitlan, perhaps due to greater economic competition, rife factionalism, and the stressful effects of the Little Ice Age in Yucatán (Hodell et al. 2005).

Mexicans at Mayapán: Material Record

In this section, we review the spatial distributions of architecture, rare pottery, figurines, and censers, weaponry, and cremations to evaluate the nature of foreign involvement at the city. Our efforts concentrate on archaeological data not previously considered by Milbrath and Peraza (2003), who have documented important similarities in Mayapán and Mexican art.

Architecture

The ritual and public architecture of Mayapán follows precedents established at Chichén Itzá, including colonnaded halls, radial or partly radial temples, Venus platforms, shrines, occasional *sacbes*, and burial shaft temples (Masson et al. 2006; Proskouriakoff 1962). Some of Chichén Itzá's innovations were not repeated at Mayapán, including ballcourts and gallery-patio groups, and the use of cenotes for depositing mortuary remains and large scale offerings (Masson et al. 2006). The lack of ballcourts and sweatbaths at Mayapán distinguishes it from central Mexican sites; sweatbaths were common features even in Aztec villages (Evans 1988: 34, 2000). One group, T-70 to T-72 (fig. 1), next to Cenote X-Coton by the far eastern portion of the city wall, has a double temple, a feature sometimes seen at Aztec sites although also common in the Maya area (Smith 2003a: 184). The pottery from Carnegie investigations within the X-Coton cenote itself and at the double temple group reveals nothing unusual about this area's Postclassic assemblage.

The elite residences at Mayapán share general features with those from smaller central Mexican city-states, such as their organization around a quadrangular patio; the presence of multiple small rooms; and the use of a frontal

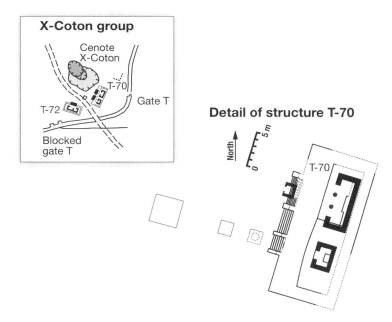

Fig. 1. Cenote X-Coton group, by a far eastern gate of the city wall, includes a double temple/shrine (T-70) and an additional ritual structure (T-72). A cremation was found in T-72, an oratory. Modified from Shook (1953: fig. 1) and Jones (1962).

gallery and adjoining courtyard for meeting, entertaining, and ceremony (Evans 1988; Smith 1992: fig. 7.1; Vaillant and Sanders 2000: fig. 206, 207). However, this general organization of elite residences is common cross-culturally and is observed in earlier Maya traditions (Inomata 2001: 33; Pillsbury and Evans 2004). We have argued that noble residences overlapped in function with colonnaded halls at Mayapán, based on parallel forms of ritual paraphernalia found in both types of features (Masson and Peraza n.d.b [2004]); this observation has been made for other Maya Postclassic sites (Freidel and Sabloff 1984: 41; Wallace 1977). Nobles held political meetings and hosted ceremonies and feasts in their homes in central Mexico (Evans 1988) and at Postclassic Maya sites (Chase 1985).

Domestic architecture at Mayapán is dominated by typical two- or three-bench rectangular house forms; this plan was a widely adopted trademark of the city, represented at 71 percent of mapped houses (Masson et al. n.d. [2006]; Smith 1962). Examples of Mayapán's typical house plan are not observed in published drawings of Aztec houses, but general construction techniques, such as single- or double-wall foundations, cobble patio surfaces, and clearing of bedrock surfaces, are reported (Smith 1992: 293, 297, 299). Other parallels include the presence of unroofed platforms in domestic groups and platform houses (Smith 1992: 317, 319). Three uncommon house forms that we have documented at Mayapán are large, square houses; rectangular multiroom alignments without benches; and massive platforms with room blocks (Hare et al. n.d. [2006]). Such house styles are common in the lowlands from the Gulf to Caribbean coasts outside of Mayapán (Alexander 2005: fig. 10.4; Carmean et al. 2004: fig. 19.4; Freidel and Sabloff 1984: 9, 145; Williams-Beck 1999: fig. 7), and massive platforms common in Veracruz may also represent warehouses (Sanders 1955: 185–188). Aztec houses can also be square or rectangular, with or without internal room divisions that lack benches (Evans 2000; Smith 1992: figs. 3.6, 3.11, 4.1, 4.3, 4.10), not unlike a minority of Mayapán houses. A degree of diversity in house form is thus observed at both Mayapán and rural Aztec sites. Massive platform P-114 is the only aberrant form associated with rare pottery (Palmul Incised), also seen at nearby houses. Minimally, this settlement cluster may represent an enclave of households engaged in trading, whether foreign or not. House types may indicate distinct social groups at Mayapán, but we cannot tie house form to specific areas of origin. The diversity of aberrant house types may simply represent a range of variation acceptable for northern Yucatán.

Rare Pottery

Not a single Aztec polychrome sherd has been found at Mayapán. It is noteworthy that Aztec pottery is found, in low quantities, in the Soconusco, a distant tributary province of the empire (Voorhies and Gasco 2004: fig. 6.10), which indicates that polities with direct ties to central Mexico did receive Aztec vessels. Their absence at Mayapán implies few direct ties. In contrast, Matillas

Fine Orange Gulf Coast pottery (Bishop 2003; Forsyth 2004), while not abundant at Mayapán, is regularly found at the site. If Fine Orange vessels were being transported to Mayapán, then it seems likely that other vessels (such as painted Aztec pottery) could also have been imported, in the same way that Tohil Plumbate made its way around the Mesoamerican world before the Late Postclassic. Two other rare types of pottery may indicate foreign ties: the Buff Polbox group (including Tecoh Red on Buff and Pele Polychrome types), and Palmul Incised. The latter is a common Caribbean coast type, and external inspiration for the former types has not yet been determined. Fine Orange is more common than either Buff Polbox or Palmul Incised at Mayapán. In 152 PEMY (Proyecto Económico de Mayapán) house-lot contexts, 60 percent had at least one sherd of Fine Orange, whereas only 45 percent had Buff Polbox and only 7 percent had Palmul.

Kenneth Hirth (1993: 125) argues that imported pottery was obtained in the marketplace at large central cities such as Xochicalco, and this was also likely true for Mayapán. Certainly, the large number of contexts (60 percent) in which low quantities of Fine Orange were recovered at Mayapán suggests that some of this pottery was obtained by ordinary households from the site's marketplace. High percentages of rare types do occur at multiple contexts in the same *milpa* areas (table 2), but large quantities of different kinds of rare pots almost never co-occur in the same domestic context (Hare et al. n.d. [2006]). This pattern supports the idea that "suppliers" might have retained more of the specific types of pots they brought to the site. If marketplace exchange were the only mechanism for obtaining rare pottery, consumers of higher quantities of rare pots would be more likely to obtain a variety of rare vessels, rather than one specific type. Of ten contexts with Palmul Incised pottery, seven are concentrated in a residential zone just outside of the western margin of the site center, and five of these seven contexts are clustered in the western/southern parameters of this sample area at or near the P-114 massive platform. Because close ties are documented between Cozumel and Acalan (Scholes and Roys 1968: 10, 77), Gulf Coast traders of Mayapán, navigating the waters of the peninsula, may have obtained some of this east coast incised pottery (Hare et al. n.d. [2006]); thus this concentration of Palmul Incised could reflect Gulf or Caribbean coast connections. Matillas Fine Orange pottery is found in high proportions at four clustered house-lot groups and also at isolated localities, the latter suggesting that distribution does not always occur in enclave-like patterns. Residential groups with different trading ties may have sometimes lived in close proximity (Hare et al. n.d. [2006]).

At the far eastern edge of the city, the outlying prominent Itzmal Ch'en temple/hall group showed no large clusters of rare pottery in either our samples or those reported by Carnegie investigators, and houses near Itzmal Ch'en had high proportions of different types of rare pottery. This locality was likely a nexus of interaction and exchange. We cannot yet postulate a potential ethnic

Table 2. PEMY and Carnegie domestic zone contexts with high percentages of rare pottery[1]

Context	Palmul and High Buff Polbox	High Fine Orange
Carnegie Milpa 11, Str. R-204		4.1%
Carnegie Milpa 11, Str. R-103		2.4%
PEMY Milpa 15, Str. S-10c		2.2%
PEMY Milpa 16, Str. I-55		5.1%
PEMY Milpa 16, Str. H-24		3.6%
PEMY Milpa 1b, Open area		3.1%
PEMY Milpa 24, Str. M-61		2.1%
Carnegie Milpa 1, Str. P-23e		1.9%
Carnegie Milpa 1, Str. P-28b		1.7%
Carnegie Milpa 10, Str. R-126°		2.4%
Carnegie near Milpa 32, Str Y-2ad		1.7%
Carnegie Milpa 10, Str. R-142c/e	Polbox 8.2%	1.4%
PEMY Milpa 14, open	Polbox 7.7%	7.7%
PEMY Milpa 24, Str. M-12	Polbox 3%	
PEMY Milpa 6, Str. Y-45a	Polbox 11.4%	
PEMY Milpa 7, Str. X-45c	Polbox 2.9%	
PEMY Milpa 17, Str. F-12a	Polbox 2.7%	
PEMY Milpa 12, Str. P-151	Polbox 3.6%	
PEMY Milpa 6, Str. Y-111	Polbox 3%	
PEMY Milpa 1a, Str. P-114	Palmul	
PEMY Milpa 1a, Str. P-115	Palmul	
PEMY Milpa 1, Str. Q-303	Palmul	
PEMY Milpa 1, Str. Q-42	Palmul	
PEMY Milpa 1, Str. Q-188	Palmul	
PEMY Milpa 1, Str. Q-193	Palmul	
PEMY Milpa 1, Str. Q-176	Palmul	
PEMY Milpa 11a, Str. R-155	Palmul	
PEMY Milpa 2, Str. Z-47	Palmul	
PEMY Str H-20, Itzmal Ch'en	Palmul	

1. High Fine Orange and Buff Polbox defined as values ≥1 standard deviation above the mean. Palmul Incised is tracked by its presence in any proportion.

affiliation for Itzmal Ch'en. This group has long been thought to be linked to the Kowoj (who later migrated to the Peten) based on a documentary reference naming this lineage as the "guardians of the east gate" (Pugh 2003; Roys 1962: 79). Minimally, families living around Itzmal Ch'en were actively engaged in trade. The west gate guardian lineage was Zulim Chan, and the southern gate of the site was guarded by a Mexican-named lineage—Nahuat (Roys 1962: 79); yet we see no concentrations of Fine Orange in the southern *milpas*.

Figurines

In a recent paper on Mayapán figurines, we determined that there is little evidence for Mexican deity figurines at Mayapán (Masson and Peraza n.d.a [2006]). However, the presence of a well-developed figurine tradition at Mayapán does represent a strong parallel with contemporary, earlier, and later central Mexican sites. The use of figurines at Mayapán is far more prevalent than recorded for the northern Belize sites of Laguna de On and Caye Coco, where only two figurine fragments were recovered. Figurines from caches at Santa Rita Corozal (Chase and Chase 1988: figs. 25, 32, 33) are primarily animals and often represent different taxa from Mayapán's figurines, such as sharks and crocodiles, although a few of the deer and serpent figurines may be analogous. Female figurines, which are so abundant at Mayapán, have not been reported from Santa Rita. The widespread use of animal and female figurines is a common shared practice between Mayapán and central Mexico.

The subject and stylistic attributes of the figurines imply local inspiration (figs. 2–6). Key identifying features of two goddesses prevalent in central Mexican assemblages analyzed by Kaplan (2007), Coatlicue and Xochiquetzal, are practically absent at Mayapán, including the former entity's serpent- or diamond-patterned skirt and the latter's beaded and banded turban or three-rosette headdress (Otis Charlton 1994: fig. 8.4b). Only two examples from Mayapán (figs. 7–8) exhibit the double side loop headdress and rimmed mouth that Kaplan associates with Coatlicue (Kaplan 2007: 15, 20, figs. 6, 8, 18; see also Brumfiel 2005: fig. 4.20a; Masson and Peraza n.d.a [2006]; Otis Charlton 1994: fig. 8.3a), but no bodies with diagnostic skirt elements of this entity were found. These examples come from Q-163, a hall next to the Castillo pyramid, and Q-208, an elite residence near the site center. One other aberrant figurine from Q-62 in the site center may not be local to Mayapán; the eyes of this figure are painted with a black band (fig. 2h).

Another aspect of central Mexican figurines is that they are regularly shown holding children, emphasizing the importance of Aztec women in the role of reproduction and child rearing (Brumfiel 1996: 146; Otis Charlton 1994: 206, fig. 8.3b). Mayapán figurines do not display this trait. Females with their arms at their sides or with one arm on their abdomen are common at Mayapán (fig. 6); the former are also known from Morelos (Otis Charlton 1994: fig. 8.4c).

Fig. 2. Typical female figurines, such as this example from Mayapán, show little formal similarity to those of other regions. See also figures 3–5. Artwork by Wilberth Cruz Alvarado for PEMY.

Fig. 3. A Mayapán female figurine. See also figures 2, 4, and 5. Artwork by Wilberth Cruz Alvarado for PEMY.

Fig. 4. A Mayapán female figurine. See also figures 2, 3, and 5. Artwork by Wilberth Cruz Alvarado for PEMY.

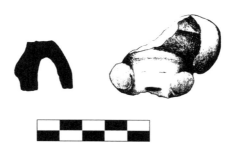

Fig. 5. A Mayapán female figurine. See also figures 2–4. Artwork by Wilberth Cruz Alvarado for PEMY.

Fig. 6. Female figurines from Mayapán are generally in standing positions with their arms at their sides.

Fig. 7. One of two female figurines from Mayapán that exhibits the headdress and rimmed mouth of the central Mexican deity Coatlicue (Kaplan 2007). See also figure 8. Artwork by Wilberth Cruz Alvarado for PEMY.

Fig. 8. Central Mexican example of Coatlicue, according to Flora Kaplan. Artwork by Kendra Farstad; redrawn after Kaplan (2007: fig. 3).

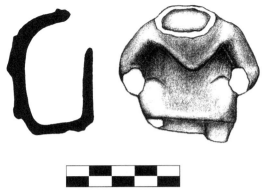

Fig. 9. Female figurines from Mayapán with swollen, possibly pregnant, bellies.

Fig. 10. Squatting female figurine, possibly in a childbirth posture. Artwork by Wilberth Cruz Alvarado for PEMY.

Only a few female figurines at Mayapán reflect the theme of reproduction: five have protruding bellies, and one squatting figurine is perhaps shown in a childbirth posture (figs. 9–10). Mayapán also has all three figurine technologies known for the Postclassic Basin of Mexico—hollow, solid, and jointed or puppet figurines (Otis Charlton 1994: 204)—but it lacks Ehecatl figurines or the corn goddesses with offering cups like those made at Otumba (Otis Charlton 1994: 206). Jointed or puppet figurines originated at Teotihuacan (Leonard 1971: fig. 11); they continued in the Postclassic Basin of Mexico (Otis Charlton 1994) and are found in low numbers at Mayapán.

Only a small number of Mexican deities are visible in the effigy censer assemblage. Two examples of Tlazolteotl and nine examples of Xipe censers were reported from the Carnegie investigations (Thompson 1957),[1] and our analysis of 265 effigy censers and cups from the Carnegie, Instituto Nacional de Antropología e Historia (INAH), and PEMY projects have recovered no other Mexican entities. The proportion of Mexican entities in this assemblage stands at 3.8 percent (Peraza et al. n.d. [2005]). In all contexts in which Xipe or Tlazolteotl were recovered, the assemblages were numerically dominated by effigies of local Maya gods (Peraza et al. n.d. [2005]). The frequencies of Xipe censers (and potentially related "closed eyed" male figures) are shown in figure 11A, and the frequencies of local Maya gods are shown in figure 11B, for the same structures. Wherever Xipe occurs, local gods were also used in rituals. This pattern suggests that foreign symbols were incorporated and assimilated into Maya deity repertoires.

Figure 12 shows the distribution of artifacts and features that potentially signal greater contact with Mexico at Mayapán (table 3). These items are

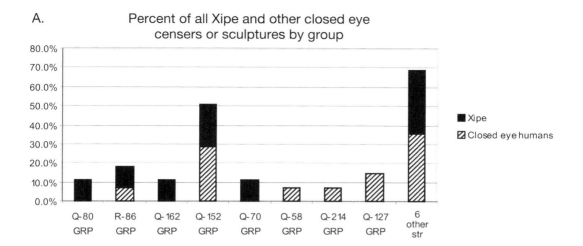

A. Percent of all Xipe and other closed eye censers or sculptures by group

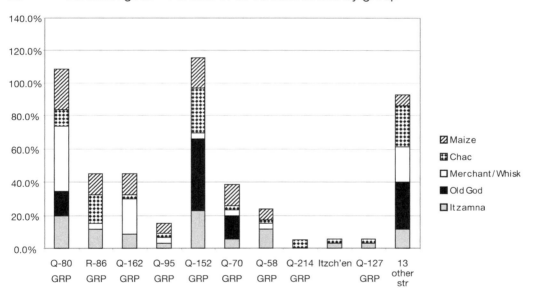

B. Common gods—Percent of all censers at site by group

Fig. 11. A. Contexts where Xipe Totec or related closed eye male figurines were recovered.
B. Contexts where local Maya gods were recovered.

Table 3. Selected list of potential foreign diagnostics
from Carnegie/INAH contexts[1]

Structure	Censers, figurines, and sculptures with Mexican features[2]	Cremation	Palmul and Buff Polbox[3]	High Fine Orange[4]
Q-95	Death cups			
Q-90				1.2%
Q-92				1.1%
Q-93			Polbox, 0.3%	
Q-208	Rimmed mouth figurine			
	Xipe (2)			
	Tlazolteotl (1)			
Q-64				1.9%
Q-62	Atypical figurine			
Q-61	Puppet (2)			
T-72		Yes		
Q-172		Yes		
Q-165		Yes		
Q-169		Yes		
S-133b	Puppet (1)	Partial		
Q-59a	Ladle (8)	Partial		
Q-59b	Xipe mask			
R-86-90	Xipe (1)			
	Tlazolteotl			
Q-163	Rimmed mouth figurine			
Q-163a			Polbox, 0.5%	
Q-162	Tlaloc		Palmul, 0.3%	
Q-161	Ehecatl (3)		Polbox, 0.3%	
Q-80	Xipe			
Q-81	Tlazolteotl		Palmul, 0.1%	
Q-79	Venus (1)		Polbox, 0.4%	
Q-82	Venus (3)		Palmul, 0.2%	
Q-72b/	Xipe (1)			
Q-72				
Q-70				
Q-88a/b	Xipe (2)			
Q-87a			Polbox, 0.3%	1.7%
Q-83	Tlatecuhtli			
152/151	Atypical figurine, painted			
Q-152			Polbox, 0.1%	
Q-152c				
Q-151				

(table continues)

Table 3. Selected list of potential foreign diagnostics from Carnegie/INAH contexts *(continued)*

Structure	Censers, figurines, and sculptures with Mexican features[2]	Cremation	Palmul and Buff Polbox[3]	High Fine Orange[4]
Q-159	Tlatecuhtli			
Q-119	Xipe mask (1)			
Q-244	Xipe mask (2)			
H-18a	Tlatecuhtli			
Q-218	Gouged eyeball snake			
Q-56				
Q-66			Polbox, 0.2%	
Z-8b	Mexican flint glyph on monkey panel			
Z-4b	Puppet (1)			
AA-37	Puppet (1)			

1. Full pottery frequencies not available for all structures.
2. Numbers in parentheses in column two indicate the number of examples from the context.
3. Tracked by presence in any proportion.
4. Defined as values ≥ 1 standard deviation above the mean.

strongly concentrated in the site center where most of the investigations have focused. The centralized pattern may thus be related to sample size. High quantities of Fine Orange, or cremations (discussed later), are often found without figurines, effigy censers, or sculptures that depict Mexican gods. The site center shows a wide distribution of low frequencies of Mexican figurines and sculptures across many different groups. These data indicate that particular public buildings or residences cannot be distinguished from others based on their Mexican artifacts (fig. 13). Instead, this pattern suggests that the noble class in general at Mayapán coveted and obtained foreign objects, likely through their involvement in distant trading. Figure 14 illustrates the kinds of Mexican-like features and artifacts found at specific groups. Many groups tend to have a few such objects. Figure 15 lists additional groups that show the same patterns in the site center—of widespread use, in low frequencies, of potential Mexican-style artifacts. To further demonstrate this point, examples of censers portraying local and nonlocal deities from a couple of intensively excavated groups are shown in figures 16–21. The R-86-90 palace had representations of Xipe (figs. 16–17) and Tlazolteotl, along with Ek Chuah, the merchant god (fig. 18), and Itzamna (fig. 19). Similarly, the Q-208 nobles' residence had Xipe (fig. 20), Tlazolteotl, and a rimmed-mouth figurine along with Chac, Itzamna (fig. 21), diving gods, and other local representations.

(text continues on page 96)

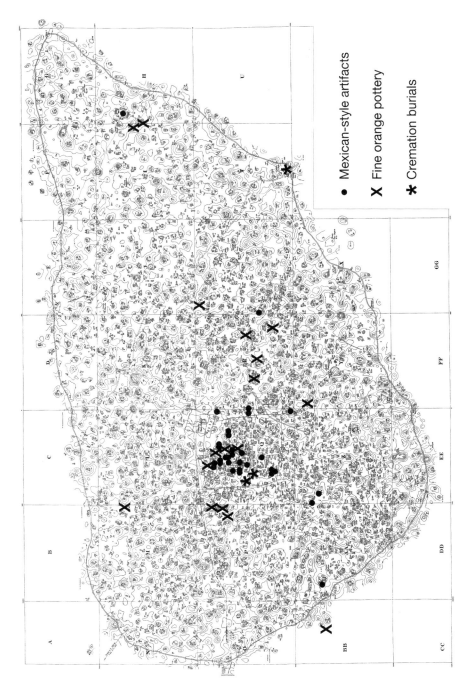

● Mexican-style artifacts

X Fine orange pottery

✳ Cremation burials

Fig. 12. Distribution of Mexican-style artifacts, high quantities of Matillas Fine Orange pottery, and cremation burials at Mayapán. Modified from Jones (1962).

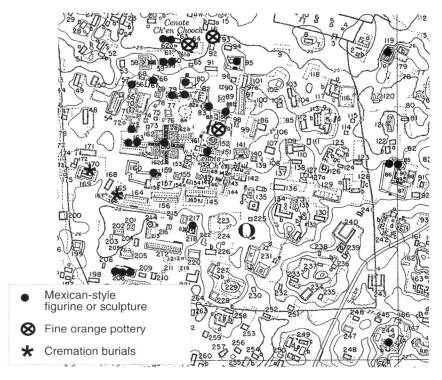

Fig. 13. Distribution of Mexican-style artifacts, high quantities of Matillas Fine Orange pottery, and cremation burials at Mayapán's monumental center. Modified from Jones (1962).

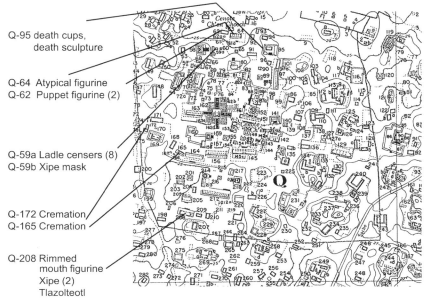

Q-95 death cups, death sculpture

Q-64 Atypical figurine
Q-62 Puppet figurine (2)

Q-59a Ladle censers (8)
Q-59b Xipe mask

Q-172 Cremation
Q-165 Cremation

Q-208 Rimmed mouth figurine Xipe (2) Tlazolteotl

Fig. 14. Mexican-style artifacts found at selected contexts in Mayapán's monumental center. Many contexts have a few artifacts. Modified from Jones (1962).

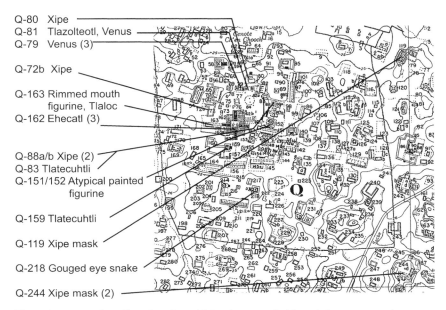

Q-80   Xipe
Q-81   Tlazolteotl, Venus
Q-79   Venus (3)

Q-72b Xipe

Q-163 Rimmed mouth
          figurine, Tlaloc
Q-162 Ehecatl (3)

Q-88a/b Xipe (2)
Q-83 Tlatecuhtli
Q-151/152 Atypical painted
          figurine

Q-159 Tlatecuhtli

Q-119 Xipe mask

Q-218 Gouged eye snake

Q-244 Xipe mask (2)

Fig. 15. Mexican-style artifacts found at additional contexts in Mayapán's monumental center. Modified from Jones (1962).

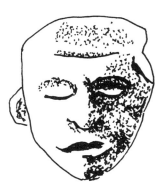

Fig. 16. Xipe effigy ceramic face from palace group R-86–90. Artwork by Anne Deane from Proskouriakoff and Temple (1955: fig. 22).

Fig. 17. Xipe effigy ceramic face from palace group R-86–90. Artwork by Anne Deane from Proskouriakoff and Temple (1955: fig. 22).

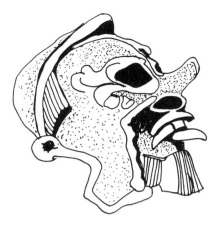

Fig. 18. Ek Chuah (merchant god) effigy ceramic face from palace group R-86–90. Original artwork by Anne Deane from Proskouriakoff and Temple (1955: fig. 22).

Fig. 19. Itzamna effigy ceramic face from palace group R-86–90. Artwork by Anne Deane from Proskouriakoff and Temple (1955: fig. 22).

Fig. 20. Xipe effigy ceramic face from elite residence Q-208. Artwork by Anne Deane from Thompson (1954: fig. 2).

Fig. 21. Itzamna effigy ceramic figurine from elite residence Q-208. Artwork by Anne Deane from Thompson (1954: fig. 2).

Fig. 22. This carved monkey panel from Mayapán has a Mexican-style personified flint glyph that resembles the pointed knives common in the tool assemblage from the site. After Proskouriakoff (1962: fig. 11b).

Weaponry

On a more utilitarian note, projectile points and knives at Mayapán are highly similar to those of central Mexico, as noted by Pollock (1962: 14). In addition to trade and elite symbolic or diplomatic exchanges, warfare was a common venue for interregional interaction, and this seems to have culminated in similar weaponry across Mesoamerica during the Late Postclassic period. Side-notched projectile points that are not always fully bifacially flaked and are often made of obsidian or local chalcedonies/cherts are common throughout Maya lowland regions, including Mayapán, northern Belize, and Tipú, as well as the Soconusco (Masson 2000: fig. 5.2; Shafer and Hester 1988: 112–113, fig. 57; Simmons 1995; Voorhies and Gasco 2004), although curiously not at Colhá (Michaels n.d. [1987]: fig. 26; Shafer and Hester 1988: 112). Similar forms are reported from Aztec sites such as Texcoco and Chiconautla (González 1979: fig. 2; Tolstoy 1971: fig. 30). Shorter, more triangular side-notched points common throughout Postclassic Mesoamerica are distinct from the elongated side-notched form (Shafer and Hester 1988: 112) based on the former's tiny size and shorter triangular shape; both forms occur at Mayapán and at Laguna de On and Caye Coco, leading us to infer that they are contemporary.

The pointed bifacial knives of Mayapán are more similar to central Mexican forms than are the knives of the east coast/Belize region. Proskouriakoff (1952: 257) identified a Mexican flint glyph (Tecpatl) on an inscribed monkey panel from Structure Z-8b at Mayapán (fig. 22); it is personified with teeth, as is common in Mexican art. The actual tools closely resemble the form of the knife glyph. Postclassic Belize lenticular and lozenge-shaped bifaces are analogous (Michaels n.d. [1987]: 146, 150, fig. 27), but their proximal lateral edges are straighter than those at Mayapán. Although smaller in size than published "Mexica" knives from such renowned deposits as the Templo Mayor and elsewhere (e.g., González 1979: 7, fig. 1), the Mayapán pointed bifaces are quite similar in shape, and no doubt function, to Aztec knives. One such knife was found embedded in the rib cage of a skeleton from a human mass grave located at the northwest entrance to the Main Plaza (Adams 1953: fig. 1). If this form was inspired by contact with Mexico, it was quickly adopted, made of local materials, and was used in many house-lots for a range of tasks. Mayapán's lords also used agricultural tools such as axes for warfare. Wedge-shaped triangular axes were used for violent ends in codex scenes that depict them in the context of captive sacrifice (Masson et al. n.d. [2006]); these are common at Mayapán and are regularly found at Maya sites in Belize (Michaels n.d. [1987]: fig. 30), although they have not been reported from Mexican sites.

Cremation Burials

Cremation was a common form of burial in Aztec villages (Evans 1988: 35; Smith 2003b: 207–208, 210). Some Aztec nobles were buried in chambered tombs in residential patios or in mass graves of cremated or noncremated individuals (Smith 1992: 367, 369). Mayapán cremations are from elite residential or public contexts. Multiple interments at high-status houses are common at Mayapán, and this pattern, along with the use of chambered tombs, is shared with central Mexico. Family tombs are so common at Mayapán, however, that it is unlikely that they indicate Mexican identity.

If cremation is an Aztec signature at Mayapán, it is rare. Only three true cremations were reported by Carnegie investigators (Oratory T-72, and elite houses Q-172 and Q-165). Structure T-72 had a small burial shaft into which at least four cremated adults were placed (fig. 1) (Shook 1953: 209).[2] This structure is one of four burial shaft temples at the site, but none of the others have cremated burials. It is also part of the only twin temple group at the site, near Cenote X-Coton and east Gate T (fig. 1).

The other two cremations are located in adjacent groups, which may signal an ethnic cluster. Structure Q-172 is an oratory situated within an elite residential group on the south margin of the site center. The cremation in Q-172 was placed in a jar, and four adult skeletons were also found in the altar, partly articulated (Thompson and Thompson 1955: 236). A vaulted tomb at residence Q-169 represents a third variant in burial type for the group, which had mixed mortuary practices overall. Q-165 is an oratory that is part of an elite residential compound that is adjacent to Group Q-172/Q-169, which also had a cremation. Beneath Q-165 was a natural cave with at least three regular burials and one cremation jar with the ashes of human and animal bone (Chowning and Thompson 1956: 435). Thus, of the three true cremations at Mayapán, two are interred in groups or features that also had noncremated individuals. None of the full or partial cremation groups showed high proportions of Fine Orange pottery.

Elite Symbolic Interaction

Although the evidence we have summarized for the settlement zone is sketchy with respect to the presence of foreign artifacts and features, this is not the case for characteristics pertaining to Mayapán's administrative and ritual features (Barrera and Peraza 2001; Masson and Peraza 2007; Milbrath and Peraza 2003). In this regard, Mayapán differs little from earlier sites in the region such as Uxmal and Chichén Itzá that have international elements incorporated into monumental art and architectural programs (e.g., Schele and Matthews 1998). As an exercise in comparison, we compiled two lists of selected, shared aspects of Mayapán-Mexican ritual art and architecture. Similar features at the Templo Mayor and various Mayapán buildings include pairs of temples with opposing or dual deity themes, skull platforms, splayed earth monster imagery in association with Kukulcan/Quetzalcoatl, mass graves of sacrificial victims, and death god effigies (table 4). Comparing Mayapán to a variety of Mexican highland locations beyond the Templo Mayor yields a much longer list of parallels in the symbolic realm, such as International-style murals, creation myths involving Kukulcan and a death god, Ehecatl (Masson and Peraza 2007), round temples, and a similar range of mortuary patterns (table 5). This list also extends to highly specific attributes, such as types of ritual and domestic artifacts—including weapons, musical instruments, the use of figurines, censer styles, and even hairstyles—shared deities, and the existence of sacred and secular offices of authority. The overlap in elite symbols utilized by Mayapán, its central Mexican contemporaries, and their descendants clearly indicates the city's strong international ties and the open exchange of ideas, information, and goods across borders during the Postclassic period, as recently documented extensively in Smith and Berdan's book *The Postclassic Mesoamerican World* (2003).

These ties are likely best explained by interregional institutions that originated in earlier periods and became amplified late in Mesoamerican history. The practices of investiture and pilgrimage became widespread during the Epiclassic period throughout Mesoamerica. Ringle (2004) and Pohl (2003b: 62–63) present compelling descriptions of institutions that integrated elite culture across political boundaries. Traveling to key world cities to receive the vestments of office became a central component for the sanction of authority

Table 4. Shared features of the Templo Mayor and various Mayapán public buildings

Templo Mayor	Mayapán
Dually opposing deities	Dual opposing temples (Q-95, Q-58) with potential dedication to dual deities (Monkey Scribe, Kukulcan)[1]
West-facing skull platform, Structure B	West-facing skull platform, Q-89
Tlaloc/Tlatecuhtli splayed monster sculptures	Tlatecuhtli splayed monster sculpture at H-18 (Itzmal Ch'en)
Mass grave (children)	Mass graves, burial shaft temples or shrines Q-95, Q-58, T-72, H-18
Death god sculpture near mass grave	Death god sculpture/effigies at burial shaft (mass grave) temple Q-95

1. Masson and Peraza Lope (2007)

(Boone 2003: 212; Byland and Pohl 1994: 138–151; Pohl 1994: 83–93). Foreign, sacred legitimization was linked to important trade ties and the establishment of political and religious rulership. The cultivation of external foundations of authority often carried the potential of military partnerships (Pohl 2003b). The readiness of Mexican agents for periodic intervention in Mayapán's affairs at the behest of local Maya usurpers implies the regular maintenance of firm diplomatic ties, perhaps cultivated through institutions of alliance networks, intermarriage, pilgrimage, and investiture. Pilgrimage, market events, and periodic calendrical rituals were highly integrated occurrences and have been well documented for many areas of Postclassic Mesoamerica (Berdan et al. 2003: 103; Freidel 1981; Freidel and Sabloff 1984: 186–187; Gasco and Berdan 2003: 110–111; Pohl 2003c: 172–173). For example, ritual feasts on a massive scale were sponsored by merchant-lords from Cholula in conjunction with festivities honoring Quetzalcoatl (Pohl 2003c: 173), who was both the patron god for an interregional market system and an expert luxury craftsman (Pohl 2003c: 174, 176). Economic exchange, currency, and production were thus deeply embedded in deity constructs and events hosted on their behalf. Mesoamerican nobles engaged in prestigious long-distance mercantile ventures, and a complex hierarchy of merchants and traders provided a variety of luxury and utilitarian goods to consumers in Maya towns (Feldman 1978).

The use of foreign sanctions for local legitimacy is a common cross-cultural phenomenon in that geographically distant places are often associated with sacred, cosmopolitan localities (Braswell 2003b: 301; Masson 2003: 194, 200;

Table 5. Shared attributes—central Mexico and Mayapán

Central Mexico	Mayapán
International style (codices, murals)	Pescador Temple Q-95, Sun Disk Hall Q-161
Quetzalcoatl/Kukulcan and Tlatecuhtli Underworld creation myth	Burial shaft temples/art:[1] Pescador Temple Q-95, Kukulcan/death god Itzmal Ch'en H-18/H-18a Tlatecuhtli) Riders on serpent columns Q-159, other sculpture Q-83
Skeletal stucco reliefs (Zaachila, Oaxaca)	Early Kukulcan Temple (Q-162a)
Ehecatl aspect of Quetzalcoatl	Sculptures at Kukulcan Temple group
Round temples	Q-152, Q-214, Q-126, H-18
Mass sacrifices	Q-79/79a mass grave Itzmal Ch'en (H-15) mass grave Burial shaft temples Q-95, Q-58, T-72, H-18
Skull caches (e.g., Teopanzolco, Tlatelolco)[2]	Q-152 Round Temple skull concentration in alley between Q-152 and Q-152c
Diversity in mortuary patterns Ossuaries, stone cist tombs Cremations	Commonly found (ossuaries, stone cist tombs) Q-172, Q-165, T-72 (only three true cremated)
Artifacts: Side-notched partly bifacial points Pointed knives Rasps made of human long bones[3] Female figurines (with rimmed mouths, double-side loop headdresses) Animal figurines	All common at Mayapán, except rimmed-mouth figurines (N = 2)
Foodways: Grater bowls common	Grater bowls common
Animal warrior guilds[4]	Bird and reptile headdresses on possible warrior effigy censers (and sculptures) at Mayapán
Cropped hairstyle of males portrayed in effigy ceramics[5]	Numerous examples at Mayapán
Death bonnet effigies[6] Death effigy vessels[7] Xipe Totec Tlazoltéotl Tlatecuhtli Fire god	Numerous examples at Mayapán Death effigy vessels (concentrated at Q-95) Occasional examples at Mayapán
Miniature temple effigies[8]	Example at Mayapán, Q-66
Dual governing institutions, ranked secular political offices and priestly offices[9]	Well developed for Mayapán and Chichén Itzá[10]

1. Masson and Peraza Lope (2007) discuss Kukulcan/Quetzalcoatl and Tlatecuhtli myths at Mayapán.
2. Smith (2003b: 228).
3. Long bone rasps from Aztec sites reported by Evans and Abrams (1988: 76), Evans (2000: pl. 155b), and Smith (2003b: 210).
4. Animal headdress worn by Aztec warrior shown by Solis (2004: pl. 63); Roys (1962: 44) also discusses a "snakes and jaguars" reference for conflicting factions within Mayapán's government.
5. Solís (2004: pl. 63), for example.
6. Evans (2000: pl. 154b), for example.
7. Pohl (2003a: fig. 26.2b), "Eastern Nahua."
8. Marquina (1960: figs. 3–6), for example.
9. Ringle (2004), for example.
10. Masson et al. (2006) and Ringle (2004).

Restall 2001: 370–375; Smith 2003a: 185). Both foreign and local funds of power are needed for effective justification of authority. One of many ethnographic examples is that described by Sahlins (1981: 10–12) for Hawaii. Usurper chiefs of the island's volatile political history claimed to come from Kahiki, a distant, mythical place on the horizon, but intermarriage into local lines was also a critical dimension of their ultimate consolidation of power. Restall (2001: 372) points out that foreign claims in Yucatán may have been for the primary purpose of legitimization, and he observes the contradictory nature of the use of foreign place names and directional associations. The Cocom of Mayapán made both local and foreign identity claims (Restall 2001: 372–373), and the incorporation of the Kukulcan myth at Mayapán may have fulfilled the need for distant legitimacy (Masson 2000: 260). Shared heroic histories and creation stories helped unite elite culture and their polities across large portions of Mesoamerica and fostered alliance building and the establishment of confederacies (Pohl 2003b). Alliances were consolidated with elite intermarriages across boundaries; such marriages provided economic advantages because royal women were skilled at crafts such as weaving (Pohl 2003c: 177)

Discussion

Santley et al. (1987) advocate the use of multiple lines of evidence to identify potential foreign ethnic enclaves at archaeological sites, and their example of Matacapán stands as a formidable model against which other sites can be measured. Contexts with numerically robust multiple indicators of ethnicity are currently elusive at Mayapán. Unusual house types at Mayapán used primarily local pottery, and contexts with high proportions of imported pottery are commonly found at typical house forms for the site. Only one atypical structure, the P-114 platform, has a concentration of East Coast Palmul Incised sherds, as do more typical Mayapán structures in the platform's immediate vicinity. Unlike Matacapán, we have no distinctive "Mexican" architectural types at Mayapán that do not also have analogs at Chichén Itzá or other sites of the Yucatán Peninsula.

Lynn Meskell (1999: 148) argues that distinct social identity can most often be tracked by the distribution of rare, unusual, and idiosyncratic items such as those we list in Table 5. Following her reasoning, we anticipated finding signatures of potential Mexican groups at Mayapán through concentrations of Fine Orange pottery or by tracking the location of low frequency, rare artifacts. However, both of these criteria have proven unsatisfying. A total of 60 percent of our contexts have Fine Orange pottery; it was clearly available in the site's markets. Where Fine Orange concentrates in high amounts, it does not correlate spatially with artifacts or architecture of nonlocal style. The distribution of Mexican-style artifacts is in fact widespread at Mayapán, and it seems that most noble families possessed an exotic object or two. Given the documented involvement of Mayapán's nobles in distant trading, it makes sense that these family groups represented nodes for importation and incorporation of Mexican objects and ideas. Thompson (1957: 621) proposed that the use of Mexican effigy censers advertised the "Mexican connections" of certain noble families, and he noted the association of foreign symbolism with the upper class at the site, who also drew on a range of local gods.

We do not doubt that Gulf Coast Mexican agents and allies settled at Mayapán. However, if they did so, they have thus far been camouflaged archaeologically and resemble the majority of Mayapán's nobles. It may have been advantageous to marry into local lineages quickly, a process of rapid assimilation that would have contributed to rendering them less visible in the material record. Oudijk (2002) observes that marriage between communities for alliance building among Postclassic Zapotec city-states had the effect of raising polity above ethnicity as a primary marker of social identity; Pohl (2003b) makes a similar argument for interacting polities of central and southern Mexico. We suspect that this principle was also operating at Mayapán.

Our review of the archaeological data does not clearly reveal whether clusters of nonlocal artifacts represent groups occupied by foreigners or, alternatively, noble or affluent commoner class merchant families. The same interpretive problem was faced at Teotihuacan in regard to the "Merchants' Barrio," which had high quantities of Gulf Coast and Maya ceramics. Millon (1981: 226) chose to name it the Merchants' Barrio because he did not think it was occupied by foreigners. The edifice with the greatest concentration of these materials at Teotihuacan was a multiroom structure that may have been used as a warehouse (Millon 1981: 226), perhaps like the P-114 platform at Mayapán.

Two different categories of merchant institutions at Mayapán may have involved foreign residents. Foreign merchants may have established their own households, either independently or in barrio clusters, and these families might have been lesser ranked (affluent commoners) in the Mayapán social hierarchy. The P-114 platform may represent a facility operated and/or occupied by one such group, as massive platforms have been identified as provisional warehouse facilities at other sites involved in Postclassic trade (Freidel and Sabloff 1984: 136–137, 190–191; Gasco and Berdan 2003: 111). A second category of merchants and/or foreigners might have been allied nobility who married into Mayapán's elite families. Such personae may have been linked to upper-status houses or public buildings at the site where foreign objects were used. These two kinds of merchants may have been involved in the exchange of different material classes; the lower-ranking category could have traded pottery and other distant, valuable utilitarian goods, and noble traders could have handled a greater proportion of luxury and ritual goods. Berdan et al. (2003: 102–103) describe these two categories of merchants—regional merchants and high-status merchants—who were classified according to their respective commoner and elite social status. Regional merchants brokered bulk luxury (cotton, cacao, salt) items across regions, and high-status merchants operated over greater distances and also transported low-bulk luxury goods (Gasco and Berdan 2003: 116); the latter include the central Mexican *pochteca* of commoner birth, as well as noble traders of the Maya area. A third type of merchant was the petty vendor who operated on a more local scale (Berdan et al. 2003: 102–103).

It is possible that the nature of our investigations in the residential zone has hampered our ability to identify foreigners at Mayapán. Surface data and small test pit samples have limited capacities for addressing this research problem compared to large horizontal excavations (Hendon 1991: 896, 1992), and full excavation may be necessary to recover unusual features or artifacts attesting to foreign occupancy. We fully excavated one outlying elite house, Y-45a, where residents had smashed a large quantity of their fancy serving wares on the floors of two rooms before abandonment (Masson and Peraza 2005). This assemblage revealed anomalously high proportions of Pele Polychrome pottery (Buff Polbox group) as well as a lower tier of rooms that is unlike any other house form yet documented at Mayapán. Full excavation of other such houses might reveal greater diversity at Mayapán than we have been able to document to date, and complete investigation of contexts where cremations were found may refine our understanding of foreign residents at Mayapán.

In terms of Mayapán's economy, the greatest number of imports seem to have been from within the Maya lowlands and highlands, including salt from coastal regions, as surmised from historic accounts and coastal factories that are documented archaeologically (Kepecs 2003). Obsidian was largely from the Ixtepeque source in highland Guatemala (Masson et al. n.d. [2006]). In this respect, Mayapán was less dependent on external sources than Chichén Itzá, as the latter center obtained a considerable amount of obsidian from central Mexico (Andrews et al. 1989: 361; Braswell 2003a: 140–141). If Mayapán relied on any resource from central Mexico for daily life, such items would have been perishable and were not preserved for us to track archaeologically. We do feel that documentary allusions to extensive trade between northern Yucatán and Xicalango (and beyond to central Mexico) are likely correct (Kepecs 2003). As the political capital of northern Yucatán, Mayapán would have been heavily invested in regional tribute and distant exchange systems. However, Mayapán merchants may have accepted payment primarily in the form of shell beads, copper bells, cacao beans, or cotton mantles, items used for currencies in the city's marketplace (Tozzer 1941: 37, n. 179; 94, n. 417), as has been suggested for late sites in the Chikinchel polity (Kepecs 2003: 267). Receiving money for distant trade would have allowed merchant nobles from the city to reinvest their profits into projects at the city or in additional inventory for export to distant lands. Unfortunately, perishable currencies like cacao beans and cloth cannot be tracked archaeologically.

Nobles and lower-ranked merchant families also engaged in distant trading and drew on their international connections to provide themselves and other residents of the city with exotica from afar. Some of these goods were available in local markets at the site, enabling commoners to sometimes possess a small number of imported goods. Smith (2003a, 2007) has called for better models with which to interpret stylistic, symbolic, and economic interaction among late Mesoamerican city-states, such as the use of a world systems perspective. Our search for Mexicans at Mayapán suggests that Smith (2003a: 183–184) offers a viable alternative for moving "beyond Mexicanization" and sidestepping the empirical dead end of attributing goods of diverse origin as evidence of foreign migration, occupation, or conquest. He argues that a more productive approach is to draw on the comparative anthropological literature in analyzing interregional interaction among elites and commercial trading partners (Smith 2007). This approach has been compellingly applied in recent works (Boone 2003: 220; Oudijk 2002; Pohl 2003b; Ringle 2004; Ringle et al. 1998; Smith and Berdan 2003). As summarized by Smith (2003a: 184), "stylistic interaction and the exchange of information were two-way processes that easily crossed political borders in Postclassic Mesoamerica, and . . . old models of Mexicanization are not up to the task of accounting for the explosion of internationalization in the Postclassic world system." Another key observation is that, during the Postclassic period, the wide distribution of "Aztec" styles in painting, sculpture, and architecture in other regions actually predates the rise of the Aztec Empire, which indicates the spread of such styles through exchange and communication networks, rather than through processes of imperialism (Boone and Smith 2003: 191–192).

Our renewed examination of the distribution of materials at Mayapán concurs with the statement by Harry Pollock (1962: 14):

> Broadly speaking, there is a distinct overlay of foreign culture, not always specific but broadly "Mexican" in character, at Mayapán. This does not of necessity imply direct communications with the valley of Mexico. . . . The inhabitants of the city must have been aware of a world much larger than the ancient homeland of the northern Maya.

Notes

1. Taube (1992: 125, fig. 66) argues that a Mexican fire god (Huehueteotl) is also present among the censer assemblage.
2. Because this grave was looted, there may have been more individuals.

References Cited

Adams, Robert M., Jr.
  1953   Some Small Ceremonial Structures at Mayapan. *Current Reports* 9: 144–179. Department of Archaeology, Carnegie Institution of Washington, Washington, D.C.

Alexander, Rani T.
  2005   Isla Civlituk and the Difficulties of Spanish Colonization in Southwestern Campeche. In *The Postclassic to Spanish-Era Transition in Mesoamerica: Archaeological Perspectives* (Susan Kepecs and Rani T. Alexander, eds.): 161–182. University of New Mexico Press, Albuquerque.

Andrews, Anthony P., Frank Asaro, Helen V. Michel, Fred H. Stross, and Pura Cervera Rivero
  1989   The Obsidian Trade at Isla Cerritos, Yucatan, Mexico. *Journal of Field Archaeology* 16: 355–376.

Barrera Rubio, Alfredo, and Carlos Peraza Lope
  2001   La pintura mural de Mayapán. In *La pintura mural prehispánica en México: Área maya, tomo IV: Estudios* (Leticia Staines Cicero, ed.): 419–446. Universidad Nacional Autónoma de México, México, D.F.

Barrera Vásquez, Alfredo, and Sylvanus G. Morley
  1949   *The Maya Chronicles*. Carnegie Institution of Washington Publication 585, Contribution 48, Washington, D.C.

Berdan, Frances F., Marilyn A. Masson, Janine Gasco, and Michael E. Smith
  2003   An International Economy. In *The Postclassic Mesoamerican World* (Michael E. Smith and Frances F. Berdan, eds.): 96–108. University of Utah Press, Salt Lake City.

Bishop, Ronald L.
  2003   Five Decades of Maya Fine Orange Investigation by INAA. In *Patterns and Process: A Festschrift in Honor of Dr. Edward V. Sayre* (Lambertus van Zelst, ed.): 81–91. Smithsonian Center for Materials Research and Education, Suitland, Md.

Boone, Elizabeth H.
  2003   A Web of Understanding: Pictorial Codices and the Shared Intellectual Culture of Late Postclassic Mesoamerica. In *The Postclassic Mesoamerican World* (Michael E. Smith and Frances F. Berdan, eds.): 207–224. University of Utah Press, Salt Lake City.

Boone, Elizabeth H., and Michael E. Smith
  2003   Postclassic International Styles and Symbol Sets. In *The Postclassic Mesoamerican World* (Michael E. Smith and Frances F. Berdan, eds.): 186–193. University of Utah Press, Salt Lake City.

Braswell, Geoffrey E.
  2003a   Obsidian Exchange Spheres. In *The Postclassic Mesoamerican World* (Michael E. Smith and Frances F. Berdan, eds.): 131–158. University of Utah Press, Salt Lake City.
  2003b   K'iche'an Origins, Symbolic Emulation, and Ethnogenesis in the Maya Highlands, A.D. 1450–1524. In *The Postclassic Mesoamerican World* (Michael E. Smith and Frances F. Berdan, eds.): 297–306. University of Utah Press, Salt Lake City.

Brumfiel, Elizabeth M.

1996　Figurines and the Aztec State: Testing the Effectiveness of Ideological Domination. In *Gender and Archaeology: Essays in Research and Practice* (Rita P. Wright, ed.): 143–166. University of Pennsylvania Press, Philadelphia.

2005　Ceramic Chronology at Xaltocan. In *Production and Power at Postclassic Xaltocan* (Elizabeth M. Brumfiel, ed.): 117–152. Instituto Nacional de Antropología e Historia, México, D.F., and University of Pittsburgh, Pa.

Byland, Bruce E., and John M. D. Pohl

1994　*In the Realm of 8 Deer: The Archaeology of the Mixtec Codices.* University of Oklahoma Press, Norman.

Carmean, Kelli, Nicholas Dunning, and Jeff Karl Kowalski

2004　High Times in the Hill Country: A Perspective from the Terminal Classic Puuc Region. In *The Terminal Classic in the Maya Lowlands: Collapse, Transition, and Transformation* (Arthur A. Demarest, Prudence M. Rice, and Don S. Rice, eds.): 424–449. University Press of Colorado, Boulder.

Cecil, Leslie G.

n.d.　Technological Styles of Late Postclassic Slipped Pottery from the Central Petén Lakes Region, El Petén, Guatemala. Ph.D. dissertation, Department of Anthropology, Southern Illinois University at Carbondale, 2001.

Chase, Diane Z.

1985　Ganned but Not Forgotten: Late Postclassic Archaeology and Ritual at Santa Rita Corozal, Belize. In *The Lowland Maya Postclassic* (Arlen F. Chase and Prudence M. Rice, eds.): 104–125. University of Texas Press, Austin.

Chase, Diane Z., and Arlen F. Chase

1988　*A Postclassic Perspective: Excavations at the Maya Site of Santa Rita Corozal, Belize.* Precolumbian Art Research Institute Monograph 4. San Francisco.

Chowning, Ann, and Donald E. Thompson

1956　A Dwelling and Shrine at Mayapan. *Current Reports* 33: 425–442. Carnegie Institution of Washington, Department of Archaeology, Washington, D.C.

Edmonson, Munro S.

1982　*The Ancient Future of the Itza: The Book of Chilam Balam of Tizimin.* University of Texas Press, Austin.

Evans, Susan Toby

1988　Cihuatecpan: The Village in Its Ecological and Historical Context. In *Excavations at Cihuatecpan: An Aztec Village in the Teotihuacan Valley* (Susan T. Evans, ed.): 1–49. Vanderbilt University Publications in Anthropology 36. Nashville, Tenn.

2000　Research at Cihuatecpan (T.A. 81) in 1984: A Summary. In *The Teotihuacan Valley Project Final Report.* Vol. 5: *The Aztec Period Occupation of the Valley, Part 2, Excavations at T.A. 40 and Related Projects* (William T. Sanders and Susan Toby Evans, eds.): 789–834. Occasional Papers in Anthropology 26. The Pennsylvania State University, University Park.

Evans, Susan T., and Elliot M. Abrams

    1988   Archaeology at the Aztec Period Village of Cihuatecpan. In *Excavations at Cihuatecpan: An Aztec Village in the Teotihuacan Valley* (Susan T. Evans, ed.): 50–238. Vanderbilt University Publications in Anthropology 36. Nashville, Tenn.

Feldman, Lawrence H.

    1978   Moving Merchandise in Protohistoric Central Quauhtemallan. In *Mesoamerican Communication Routes and Cultural Contacts* (Thomas A. Olee Jr. and Carlos Navarrete, eds.): 7–17. Papers of the New World Archaeological Foundation 40. Brigham Young University, Provo, Utah.

Forsyth, Donald W.

    2004   Reflexiones sobre la ocupación postclasica en Champotón a traves de la cerámica. *Los investigadores de la cultura maya* 12 (1): 33–37.

Fox, John W.

    1987   *Late Postclassic State Formation.* Cambridge University Press, Cambridge.

Freidel, David A.

    1981   The Political Economics of Residential Dispersion among the Lowland Maya. In *Lowland Maya Settlement Patterns* (Wendy Ashmore, ed.): 371–382. University of New Mexico Press, Albuquerque.

Freidel, David A., and Jeremy A. Sabloff

    1984   *Cozumel: Late Maya Settlement Patterns.* Academic Press, New York.

Gasco, Janine, and Frances F. Berdan

    2003   International Trade Centers. In *The Postclassic Mesoamerican World* (Michael E. Smith and Frances F. Berdan, eds.): 109–116. University of Utah Press, Salt Lake City.

González Rul, Franciso

    1979   *La lítica en Tlatelolco.* Colección Científica 74. Instituto Nacional de Antropología e Historia, México, D.F.

Hare, Timothy S., Marilyn A. Masson, and Carlos Peraza Lope

    n.d.   The Spatial and Social Organization of Mayapán. Paper presented at the Society for American Archaeology meetings, San Juan, Puerto Rico, April 2006.

Hendon, Julia A.

    1991   Status and Power in Classic Maya Society: An Archaeological Study. *American Anthropologist* 93: 894–918.

    1992   The Interpretation of Survey Data: Two Case Studies from the Maya Area. *Latin American Antiquity* 3: 22–42.

Hirth, Kenneth G.

    1993   Identifying Rank and Socioeconomic Status in Domestic Contexts: An Example from Central Mexico. In *Prehispanic Domestic Units in Western Mesoamerica: Studies of the Household, Compound, and Residence* (Robert S. Santley and Kenneth G. Hirth, eds.): 121–146. CRC Press, Boca Raton, Fla.

Hodell, D. A., M. Brenner, J. H. Curtis, R. M. Gonzalez Medina, M. F. Rosenmeier, and T. P. Guilderson

    2005   Little Ice Age on the Yucatan Peninsula. *Quaternary Research* 63: 109–121.

Inomata, Takeshi

    2001   King's People: Classic Maya Courtiers in a Comparative Perspective. In *Royal Courts of the Maya*. Vol. 1: *Theory, Comparison, Synthesis* (Takeshi Inomata and Stephen Houston, eds.): 27–53. Westview Press, Boulder, Colo.

Jones, Morris R.

    1962   Topographic Map of the Ruins of Mayapan. In *Mayapan, Yucatan, Mexico* (Harry E. D. Pollock, Ralph Roys, Tatiana Proskouriakoff, and A. Ledyard Smith, eds.): map inset. Carnegie Institution of Washington Publication 619. Washington, D.C.

Jones, Siân

    1997   *The Archaeology of Ethnicity: Constructing Identities in the Past and Present.* Routledge, London and New York.

Kaplan, Flora Siegel

    2007   *The Postclassic Figurines of Central Mexico.* Institute for Mesoamerican Studies Occasional Publication 11. State University of New York, Albany.

Kepecs, Susan

    2003   Chikinchel. In *The Postclassic Mesoamerican World* (Michael E. Smith and Frances F. Berdan, eds.): 259–268. University of Utah Press, Salt Lake City.

Kowalski, Jeff, and Cynthia Kristan-Graham (eds.)

    2007   *Twin Tollans: Chichén Itzá, Tula, and the Epiclassic to Early Postclassic Mesoamerican World.* Dumbarton Oaks Research Library and Collection, Washington, D.C.

Leonard, Carmen Cook de

    1971   Ceramics of the Classic Period in Central Mexico. In *Handbook of Middle American Indians*, vol. 10, pt. I (Gordon Ekholm and Ignacio Bernal, eds.): 179–205. University of Texas Press, Austin.

Marquina, Ignacio

    1960   *El Templo Mayor de México.* Instituto Nacional de Antropología e Historia, México, D.F.

Masson, Marilyn A.

    2000   *In the Realm of Nachan Kan: Postclassic Maya Archaeology at Laguna de On, Belize.* University Press of Colorado, Boulder.

    2003   The Late Postclassic Symbol Set in the Maya Area. In *The Postclassic Mesoamerican World* (Michael E. Smith and Frances F. Berdan, eds.): 194–200. University of Utah Press, Salt Lake City.

Masson, Marilyn A., Timothy S. Hare, and Carlos Peraza Lope

    2006   Postclassic Maya Society Regenerated at Mayapan. In *After Collapse: The Regeneration of Complex Societies* (Glenn M. Schwartz and John J. Nichols, eds.): 188–207. University of Arizona Press, Tucson.

Masson, Marilyn A., and Carlos Peraza Lope

    2005   Nuevas investigaciones en tres unidades residenciales fuera del área monumental de Mayapán. In *Investigadores de la cultura maya* 13 (2): 411–424.

2007   Kukulkan/Quetzalcoatl, Death God, and Creation Mythology of Burial
        Shaft Temples at Mayapán. *Mexicon* 29 (3): 77–85.
n.d.a   Figurines and Social Diversity at Mayapán. Paper presented at the
        International Congress of Americanists, Seville, July 2006.
n.d.b   A New Look at Household and Administrative Facilities at the Postclassic
        Maya City of Mayapán. Paper presented at the Society for American
        Archaeology meetings, Montreal, April 2004.

Masson, Marilyn A., Carlos Peraza Lope, and Timothy S. Hare
n.d.   The Political Economy of Mayapán. Paper presented at the Society for
        American Archaeology meetings, San Juan, Puerto Rico, April 2006.

Meskell, Lynn
1999   *The Archaeologies of Social Life: Age, Sex, Class, Et cetera in Ancient Egypt.*
        Blackwell Press, Oxford.

Michaels, George H.
n.d.   A Description of Early Postclassic Lithic Technology at Colha, Belize. M.A.
        thesis, Department of Anthropology, Texas A & M University, College
        Station, 1987.

Milbrath, Susan, and Carlos Peraza Lope
2003   Revisiting Mayapan: Mexico's Last Maya Capital. *Ancient Mesoamerica*
        14: 1–47.

Miller, Arthur G.
1982   *On the Edge of the Sea: Mural Painting at Tancah-Tulum, Quintana Roo,
        Mexico.* Dumbarton Oaks, Washington, D.C.

Millon, René
1981   Teotihuacan: City, State, and Civilization. In *Supplement to the Handbook
        of Middle American Indians.* Vol. 1, *Archaeology* (Jeremy A. Sabloff, ed.):
        198–243. University of Texas Press, Austin.

Otis Charlton, Cynthia
1994   Plebeians and Patricians: Contrasting Patterns of Production and
        Distribution in the Aztec Figurine and Lapidary Industries. In *Economies
        and Polities in the Aztec Realm* (Mary G. Hodge and Michael E. Smith, eds.):
        195–219. Institute for Mesoamerican Studies, Albany, N.Y.

Oudijk, Michael
2002   The Zapotec City-State. In *A Comparative Study of Six City-State Cultures*
        (Mogens Herman Hansen, ed.): 73–90. Historisk-filosofiske Skrifter 27. The
        Royal Danish Academy of Sciences and Letters, Copenhagen.

Peraza Lope, Carlos, Marilyn A. Masson, Timothy S. Hare, and Pedro Candelario
Delgado Kú
2006   The Chronology of Mayapan: New Radiocarbon Evidence. *Ancient
        Mesoamerica* 17 (2): 153–175.

Peraza Lope, Carlos, Marilyn A. Masson, and Bradley W. Russell
n.d.   Spatial Patterns of Effigy Censer and Sculpture Use at Mayapán. Paper
        presented at the Segundo Congreso Internacional de Mayistas, Mérida,
        Yucatán, México, March 2005.

Pillsbury, Joanne, and Susan T. Evans

2004   Palaces of the Ancient New World: An Introduction. In *Palaces of the Ancient New World* (Susan T. Evans and Joanne Pillsbury, eds.): 1–6. Dumbarton Oaks Research Library and Collection, Washington, D.C.

Piña Chan, Román

1978   Commerce in the Yucatec Peninsula: The Conquest and Colonial Period. In *Mesoamerican Communication Routes and Culture Contacts* (T. A. Lee and C. Navarrete, eds.): 37–48. Papers of the New World Archaeological Foundation 40. Brigham Young University, Provo, Utah.

Pohl, John M. D.

1994   *The Politics of Symbolism in the Mixtec Codices.* Vanderbilt University Publications in Anthropology 46. Vanderbilt University, Nashville, Tenn.

2003a   Ritual and Iconographic Variability in Mixteca-Puebla Polychrome Pottery. In *The Postclassic Mesoamerican World* (Michael E. Smith and Frances F. Berdan, eds.): 201–206. University of Utah Press, Salt Lake City.

2003b   Creation Stories, Hero Cults, and Alliance Building: Confederacies of Central and Southern Mexico. In *The Postclassic Mesoamerican World* (Michael E. Smith and Frances F. Berdan, eds.): 61–66. University of Utah Press, Salt Lake City.

2003c   Ritual Ideology and Commerce in the Southern Mexican Highlands. In *The Postclassic Mesoamerican World* (Michael E. Smith and Frances F. Berdan, eds.): 172–177. University of Utah Press, Salt Lake City.

Pollock, Harry E. D.

1962   Introduction. In *Mayapan, Yucatan, Mexico* (Harry E. D. Pollock, Ralph Roys, Tatiana Proskouriakoff, and A. Ledyard Smith, eds.): 1–23. Carnegie Institution of Washington Publication 619. Washington, D.C.

Proskouriakoff, Tatiana

1952   Sculpture and Artifacts from Mayapan. *Carnegie Institution of Washington Year Book* 51: 256–259.

1962   Civic and Religious Structures of Mayapan. In *Mayapan, Yucatan, Mexico* (Harry E. D. Pollock, Ralph Roys, Tatiana Proskouriakoff, and A. Ledyard Smith, eds.): 87–164. Carnegie Institution of Washington Publication 619. Washington, D.C.

Proskouriakoff, Tatiana, and Charles R. Temple

1955   A Residential Quadrangle—Structures R-85 to R-90. *Current Reports* 29: 289–362. Carnegie Institution of Washington, Department of Archaeology, Washington, D.C.

Pugh, Timothy W.

2003   The Exemplary Center of the Late Postclassic Kowoj Maya. *Latin American Antiquity* 14: 408–430.

Restall, Matthew

2001   The People of the Patio: Ethnohistorical Evidence of Yucatec Maya Royal Courts. In *Royal Courts of the Maya.* Vol. 2: *Data and Case Studies* (Takeshi Inomata and Stephen D. Houston, eds.): 335–390. Westview Press, Boulder, Colo.

Ringle, William M.

2004   On the Political Organization of Chichen Itza. *Ancient Mesoamerica* 15: 167–218.

Ringle, William M., Tomás Gallareta Negron, and George J. Bey III
   1998   The Return of Quetzalcoatl: Evidence for the Spread of a World Religion during the Epiclassic Period. *Ancient Mesoamerica* 9: 183–232.

Roys, Ralph L.
   1940   Personal Names of the Maya of Yucatan. *Contributions to American Anthropology and History* 31. Carnegie Institution of Washington Publication 523. Washington, D.C.
   1962   Literary Sources for the History of Mayapan. In *Mayapan, Yucatan, Mexico* (Harry E. D. Pollock, Ralph Roys, Tatiana Proskouriakoff, and A. Ledyard Smith, eds.): 25–86. Carnegie Institution of Washington Publication 619. Washington, D.C.

Sahlins, Marshall D.
   1981   *Historical Metaphors and Mythical Realities: Structure in the Early History of the Sandwich Islands Kingdom.* Association for Social Anthropology in Oceania Special Publication 1. University of Michigan Press, Ann Arbor.

Sanders, William T.
   1955   An Archaeological Reconnaissance of Northern Quintana Roo. *Current Reports* 24: 154–264. Department of Archaeology, Carnegie Institution of Washington, Washington, D.C.

Santley, Robert, Clare Yarborough, and Barbara Hall
   1987   Enclaves, Ethnicity, and the Archaeological Record at Matacapán. In *Ethnicity and Culture: Proceedings of the Eighteenth Annual Conference of the Archaeological Association of the University of Calgary* (Réginald Auger, Margaret F. Glass, and Scott MacEachern, eds.): 85–100. University of Calgary Archaeological Association, Calgary, Canada.

Schele, Linda, and Peter Matthews
   1998   *The Code of Kings: The Language of Seven Sacred Maya Temples and Tombs.* Scribner, New York.

Scholes, France V., and Ralph L. Roys
   1968   *The Maya Chontal Indians of Acalan-Tixchel.* University of Oklahoma Press, Norman.

Shafer, Harry J., and Thomas R. Hester
   1988   Appendix III: Preliminary Analysis of Postclassic Lithics from Santa Rita Corozal, Belize. In *A Postclassic Perspective: Excavations at the Maya Site of Santa Rita Corozal, Belize* (by Diane Z. Chase and Arlen F. Chase): 111–117. Pre-Columbian Art Research Institute Monograph 4. San Francisco.

Shennan, Stephen
   1989   Introduction. *Archaeological Approaches to Cultural Identity* (Stephen Shennan, ed.): 1–32. Unwin Hyman, London.

Shook, Edwin M.
   1953   The X-Coton Temples at Mayapan. *Current Reports* 11: 207–221. Department of Archaeology, Carnegie Institution of Washington, Washington, D.C.

Simmons, Scott
   1995   Maya Resistance, Maya Resolve: The Tools of Autonomy from Tipu, Belize. *Ancient Mesoamerica* 6: 135–146.

Smith, A. Ledyard

1962   Residential and Associated Structures at Mayapan. In *Mayapan, Yucatan, Mexico* (Harry E. D. Pollock, Ralph Roys, Tatiana Proskouriakoff, and A. Ledyard Smith, eds.): 165–320. Carnegie Institution of Washington Publication 619. Washington, D.C.

Smith, Michael E.

1957   Deities Portrayed on Censers at Mayapan. *Current Reports* 40: 599–632. Department of Archaeology, Carnegie Institution of Washington, Washington, D.C.

1992   *Archaeological Research at Aztec-Period Rural Sites in Morelos, Mexico.* Vol. 1: *Excavations and Architecture.* Memoirs in Latin American Archaeology 4. University of Pittsburgh, Department of Anthropology, Pittsburgh, Pa.

2003a   Information Networks in Postclassic Mesoamerica. In *The Postclassic Mesoamerican World* (Michael E. Smith and Frances F. Berdan, eds.): 181–185. University of Utah Press, Salt Lake City.

2003b   *The Aztecs.* Blackwell, Malden, Mass.

2007   Tula and Chichén Itzá: Are We Asking the Right Questions? In *Twin Tollans: Chichén Itzá, Tula, and the Epiclassic to Early Postclassic Mesoamerican World* (Jeffrey Kowalski and Cynthia Kristan-Graham, eds.): 579–618. Dumbarton Oaks Research Library and Collection, Washington, D.C.

Smith, Michael E., and Frances F. Berdan (eds.)

2003   *The Postclassic Mesoamerican World.* University of Utah Press, Salt Lake City.

Smith, Michael E., and Cynthia Heath-Smith

1980   Waves of Influence in Postclassic Mesoamerica? A Critique of the Mixteca-Puebla Concept. *Anthropology* 4: 15–20.

Smith, Robert Eliot

1971   *The Pottery of Mayapan.* Papers of the Peabody Museum of Archaeology and Ethnology 66. Harvard University, Cambridge, Mass.

Solís, Felipe

2004   *The Aztec Empire.* Guggenheim Museum Publications, New York.

Taube, Karl A.

1992   *The Major Gods of Ancient Yucatan.* Studies in Pre-Columbian Art and Archaeology 32. Dumbarton Oaks Research Library and Collection, Washington, D.C.

1994   The Iconography of Toltec Period Chichén Itzá. In *Hidden among the Hills: Maya Archaeology of the Northwest Yucatan Peninsula* (Hanns Prem, ed.): 212–246. Acta Mesoamericana 7. Verlag von Flemming, Möckmühl.

Thompson, Donald E., and J. Eric S. Thompson

1955   A Noble's Residence and Its Dependencies at Mayapan. *Current Reports* 25: 225–252. Department of Archaeology, Carnegie Institution of Washington, Washington, D.C.

Thompson, J. Eric S.

1954   A Presumed Residence of the Nobility at Mayapan. *Current Reports* 19: 71–88. Department of Archaeology, Carnegie Institution of Washington, Washington, D.C.

Tolstoy, Paul

1971   Utilitarian Artifacts of Central Mexico. In *Handbook of Middle American Indians*, vol. 10, pt. 1 (Gordon F. Ekholm and Ignacio Bernal, eds.): 270–296. University of Texas Press, Austin.

Tozzer, Alfred M.

1941   *Landa's* Relación de las cosas de Yucatan: *A Translation*. Papers of the Peabody Museum of American Archaeology and Ethnology 18. Harvard University, Cambridge, Mass.

Vaillant, George C., and William T. Sanders

2000   Excavations at Chiconauhtla. In *The Teotihuacan Valley Project Final Report*. Vol. 5: *The Aztec Period Occupation of the Valley, Part 2, Excavations at T.A. 40 and Related Projects* (William T. Sanders and Susan T. Evans, eds.): 757–788. Occasional Papers in Anthropology 26. Pennsylvania State University, University Park.

Voorhies, Barbara, and Janine Gasco

2004   *Postclassic Soconusco Society: The Late Prehistory of the Coast of Chiapas, Mexico*. Institute for Mesoamerican Studies, State University of New York, Albany. Distributed by the David Brown Book Co.

Wallace, Dwight T.

1977   An Intra-Site Locational Analysis of Utatlan: The Structure of an Urban Site. In *Archaeology and Ethnohistory of the Central Quiche* (Dwight T. Wallace and Robert M. Carmack, eds.): 20–54. Institute for Mesoamerican Studies, State University of New York, Albany.

Williams-Beck, Lorraine

1999   *Tiempo en trozos: Cerámica de la región de los Chenes, Campeche, México*. Gobierno del Estado de Campeche, Instituto de Cultura de Campeche, Universidad Autónoma de Campeche, Consejo Nactional para la Cultura y las Artes, Campeche, Mexico.

Chapter Four

Cosmology and Cultural Landscape

The Late Postclassic Maya of North Yucatán

Anthony F. Aveni

WERE LATE POSTCLASSIC SITES in north Yucatán astronomically aligned? And if so, whence the tradition? Can the central Mexican worldview be involved? These are the questions I will consider in this chapter.

Urban architectural traditions in many ancient cultures are thought to have been influenced by cosmological principles. Most notable are the Greeks (Dinsmoor 1939), the Etruscans (Aveni and Romano 1994), the Chinese (Wheatley 1971), and the Cambodians (Manikka 1996).

The laying of squares upon the earth dates back at least to the earliest Egyptian dynasties. It began with the reestablishment of boundaries following the receding of the waters after the annual flooding of the Nile, and it symbolized the return to order from primeval watery chaos. Because the reordering of the earth followed changes in the human order, each year the temple astronomer, aware of certain alterations in celestial configurations that portended changing social dimensions, might require slight shifts and particular placements in the built environment to accord with them. This activity of earth measuring was passed on to the ancient Greeks, who called it *geometrein*—geometry to us.

In a recently published forum in the *Cambridge Archaeological Journal* (Carl et al. 2000), regional specialists (mostly British) were asked to respond to the question: Were cities built as images? It is surprising that, with the exception of brief mention of Teotihuacan, nothing was addressed in regard to Mesoamerica. Very little was mentioned about celestially aligned buildings anywhere. Respondents repeatedly separated praxis or "day-to-day needs of the urban community" (Carl et al. 2000: 327) from symbolic imagery, and most based their arguments entirely on Western concepts; thus the question (raised in the context of the pre-polis city of Egypt): How is it that evidently complex and coordinated topographies might arise in the absence of a developed geometry? Carl (2000) presupposed that there is only one kind of geometry.

Before embarking on a discussion of the role of cosmology in Late Postclassic Maya sites (or any ancient sites for that matter), we would do well to remind ourselves that the habit of dichotomizing human behavior acquired from Enlightenment thinking has a tendency to lead us to regard indigenous concepts of space as (unlike Greek geometry) illogical. (For some examples of the non-orthodox nature of Maya geometry, see Aveni and Hartung 1982.)

Maya City Planning

Why should we entertain the question of whether Mesoamerican sites were astronomically aligned? That the depiction of the cardinal directions of space might have had something to do with events taking place in the sky in Mesoamerica is suggested by cosmologically related diagrams. Page 1 of the Codex Fejérváry-Mayer (plate 2), for example, pictures a centrally located fire god (Xiuhtecuhtli) upon whom streams of blood converge and who appears surrounded by the qualities associated with each of the cardinal directions as well as with the flow of time (Seler 1963, 2: 85). Thus the trees, birds, gods, colors, and the names of the days that symbolize those directionally based qualities are framed within one of the four appropriate arms of a Maltese or Formée cross. Time envelops space, as the count of the 260-day sacred calendar proceeds counterclockwise, dot by dot, in segments of 13 days around the border of the diagram (see Introduction to Part III, this volume). In the middle of the top flap of the cross, which represents the direction east, the place where the sun is born, one finds the disk of the rising sun perched on an altar at the base of the eastern tree. On the opposite side (west), the place where the sun dies, an open-mouthed figure appears. Note that the east and west segments of the cross, unlike the opposing pair, which may represent north–south or possibly up–down, are attached to the central frame of the diagram as if to assign greater importance to this axial direction. Madrid 75–76 (plate 1), a Maya version of this diagram, bears a striking resemblance to its counterpart from central Mexico, even down to the depiction of 260 days around the horizon, walked by footprints seen in the figure.

We know that the Poptí' Maya have long conceived of the measurement of time as a pacing off of duration "in feet" (cf. Milbrath 1999: 60, 71). The basic subdivision of their year is 40 days, which they call "one foot of the year" and which they term *yoc habil*, the word *yoc*, or *oc*, meaning 'foot, footprint, or track' in the Poptí' Mayan language. In the Book of Chilam Balam of Chumayel (Roys 1967: 116–117), we learn of the creation of the *uinal* by the first priest:

> "What shall we say when we see man on the road?" These were their words as they marched along, when there was no man <as yet>. Then they arrived there in the east and began to speak. "Who has passed here? Here are footprints. Measure it off with your foot." So spoke the mistress of the world. Then he measured the footstep of our Lord, God, the Father. This was the reason it was called counting off the whole earth, *lahca* (12) Oc. This was the count, after it had been created by <the day> 13 Oc, after his feet were joined evenly, after they had departed there in the east.

Statements from sacred Maya books such as the *Popol Vuh* imply a craftsperson (dare one say cosmic "intelligent designer"?) at work squaring off the finished product of creation, which is conceived as a performative act (Tedlock 1985: 72):

> The fourfold siding, fourfold cornering,
>   measuring, fourfold staking,
> halving the cord, stretching the cord
> in the sky, on the earth,
> the four sides, the four corners.

In some parts of Mesoamerica there seems little doubt that objects and events gleaned from the sky played a major role in planning urban structure. For example, in Tenochtitlan a chronicler tells us explicitly that Moctezuma II needed to tear down the Templo Mayor and rebuild it because it was not square with sunrise at the equinox, a statement corroborated by the archaeological record (Aveni and Gibbs 1976). It is also well established that the skewed pristine grid of the great city of Teotihuacan was laid out at least in part in accord with celestial phenomena that took place at the western (Aveni 2000) and possibly eastern horizon (Šprajc 2000).

All of the foregoing textual inferences notwithstanding, whether one can "read" cosmology in ancient Maya city plans remains a subject of heated debate (cf. Ashmore and Sabloff 2003; Smith 2003, 2005; Šprajc 2005). Before moving on to our area of concern in this volume, allow me to elaborate on a few aspects of the debate surrounding this subject. Most scholars agree that the Twin Pyramid complexes at Tikal (fig. 1) and similar structures at Yaxha are recognizable architectural manifestations of the so-called cosmograms in the codices. Each complex (dated ca. 600 CE) is close to cardinally oriented and composed of two large pyramids positioned on the dominant east–west axis of a plaza, with smaller structures located on the opposing north–south axis. A stela and altar pair on the north (symbolically "up") building provides information about the ruler who commissioned the complex, likely to celebrate the *katun* ending (approximately 20-year period) in which he had ruled. This building is open to the

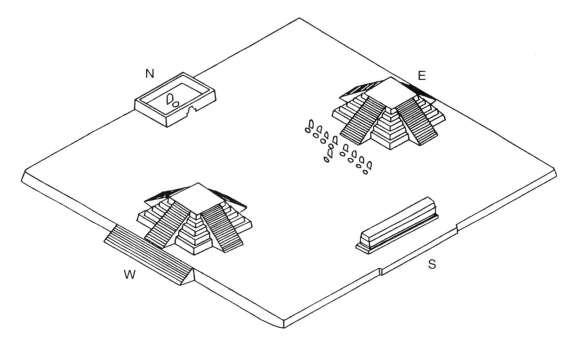

Fig. 1. Tikal's Twin Pyramid complexes. Note hints of structural principles evident in the Fejérváry-Mayer and Madrid cosmograms. After Aveni (2001: fig. 87).

zenith, whence he derives his power. The southern ("down") structure is a low-range building that consists of nine doorways, the same as the number of levels of the underworld.

Drawing on Maya quadripartite designs in specialized complexes such as these, Ashmore (1989, 1991) has singled out five cosmologically related components of a model or template of the architectural setting of the entire Classic Maya city that illustrate its role in politico-religious statements. The principal components of the pattern are (1) a strongly marked north–south axis; (2) a mutually complementary functional dualism for construction and spaces at the north and south ends of that axis, in which north stands for the celestial supernatural sphere and south, for the underworld or worldly sphere; (3) the appendage of subsidiary eastern and western units to form a triangle with the north; (4) the common but not invariant presence of a ballcourt as mediator between north and south; and (5) the frequent use of causeways to underscore the linkage between various elements and thereby stress the symbolic coherence of the whole. With Sabloff (Ashmore and Sabloff 2000), Ashmore argues that such a scheme occurs at Copán as well as at a number of other Classic period sites.

On the contrary, Smith (2003: 221) finds such arguments "vague, weak, and unconvincing," claiming that they offer no rigorous method of "investigation" and little hard evidence to corroborate the hypothesis (cf. Ashmore and Sabloff 2003 for a rebuttal). Responding to more specific claims by other scholars, Flannery and Marcus (1993: 267) concur when they state that "when we see cosmology derived solely from the alleged orientation of a building to a particular star . . . we have a right to be skeptical." In my view, the rigor Smith calls for must derive from quantitative archaeological data systematically acquired from a significant number of sites of similar temporal provenience. This can help strengthen or lessen doubts regarding the intentions of the builders.

Alignment Evidence from North Yucatán

Systematic alignment trends that can be explained by the incorporation of astronomical/calendrical correlations in city plans seem to be present in certain Maya cultural phases. An example rich in data emanates from the Terminal Classic (800–1000 CE) Puuc of northwest Yucatán. As Pollock and other archaeologists had noted, the civic plans of many of the larger sites in this area are similar in at least three regards: (1) the buildings often are grouped about a general north–south axis, (2) the buildings in a given complex often face inward toward the center of that complex, and (3) there is a tendency "for single structures and larger architectural complexes to face toward the ceremonial or civic center of the site" (Pollock 1980: 652). When Pollock noted the clockwise-skewed (from north) axiality of Puuc cities, he offered no explanation for it; nor did he discuss how such a consistent absolute directional alignment might have been executed in practice.

In a detailed study based on measurements taken at a large number of sites (Aveni and Hartung 1986), we noted a sharp concentration of Puuc city orientation axes averaging 14° east of cardinal north (or 14° S of E), a marked contrast to Late Formative and Early Classic orientations, which tended to peak at the solstices. We found it difficult to conceive how Maya architects might have laid out their cities on so narrowly focused a direction over such a wide area without the use of astronomical bodies at the horizon as reference objects. Moreover, we noted that in the latitude of north Yucatán the 14° skew pointed to sunsets/sunrises counted 20 days from the points where the sun rose/set on the day it passed the zenith. One can think of such an arrangement as a spatial transformation of a temporal idea—a clever and highly visible, unwritten way of expressing the manner in which the counting of time and the laying out of space in the city go together. We argued that this calendar was a modified form of a solar zenith-based calendar that emanated (along with many other architectural and iconographic traits) from the Peten (cf. Gendrop 1983). This turns out to be consistent with the results of our more recent investigation of the E-type groups (Aveni et al. 2003; see Glossary).

Late Postclassic Site Axes and a Possible Mexican Connection

Until relatively recently, Late Postclassic north Yucatán was regarded as a declining cultural backwater devoid of the sort of esoteric wisdom and concomitant energy that might have led to the incorporation of precise astronomical knowledge in urban design plans. After all, the Long Count had been abandoned, and, except for the codices, inscriptions were scant and even then only crudely rendered. Their architects were generally regarded as inattentive and unskilled, "their workmanship hardly worth a passing glance" (Proskouriakoff 1954: 96). Thus there was little motivation to undertake studies related to city planning and cosmology in Late Postclassic north Yucatán.

Now there is abundant evidence in the ethnohistoric and epigraphic literature that places Maya calendrical and astronomical knowledge during the Late Postclassic period in a divinatory astrological context, close to the center of a rather all-pervasive religious ideology. The content of the almanacs in the Dresden and Madrid codices demonstrates that the Maya went to great lengths to hone their calendar toward divinatory ends, specifically to formalize rituals relating to agriculture. Some aspects of this written calendar—for example, the Venus and eclipse tables in the Dresden Codex—indicate a deep interest in precise knowledge of celestial events. Recently, scholars studying the Madrid Codex have postulated testable methodologies leading to the conclusion that, despite the absence of Long Count dates, celestial events—among them the stations of Mars, solar and lunar eclipses, and seasonal phenomena such as summer solstice and vernal equinox, all couched in a real-time framework—are recorded in that document (cf., e.g., Bricker and Bricker 1988; Bricker et al. 1997; Bricker 1997; Graff 1997).

The written record provides further evidence concerning possible ways of marking the sowing and harvest dates and of establishing the times for rainfall, harvest, rites of debt payment to the agricultural gods, etc.; thus we might say that the written calendar is as much "agrilogical" as it is astrological. As Landa put it,

> The sciences which they [the keepers of the codices] were taught were the computation of the years, months, and days, the festivals and ceremonies, the administration of the sacraments, the fateful days and seasons, their methods of divination and their prophecies (cited in Tozzer 1941: 27).

We can imagine enclaves of priests from the urban centers visiting the surrounding towns with their codices tucked under their arms, ready to prescribe a particular ritual for a given event in the agricultural cycle by consulting their sacred books.

Scholars also have revealed profound evidence, especially during the second half of the fifteenth century, of cross-cultural contact with central Mexico

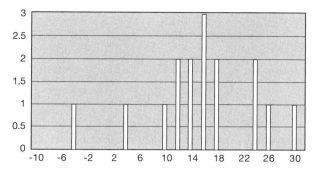

Fig. 2. Distributions of alignments of Late Postclassic sites in north Yucatán. Zero signifies north; east of north is to the right; west of north is to the left.

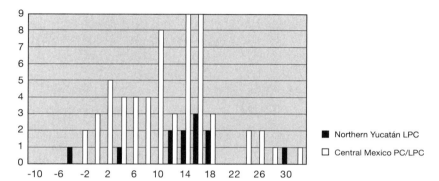

Northern Yucatán LPC

Central Mexico PC/LPC

Fig. 3. Distributions of alignments of Postclassic (PC) and Late Postclassic (LPC) sites in central Mexico. Zero signifies north; east of north is to the right; west of north is to the left.

that may have impinged on the problem of the reconfiguration of time in the codices. This evidence is manifest in the discovery of specific iconographic and calendrical parallels between the Madrid and the Borgia Group codices (see, e.g., Hernández 2004; Hernández and Bricker 2004; Just 2004).

Such written evidence raises the question: Might the built environment have played a role in the expression of calendrical change resulting from cross-cultural contact? To begin to test this hypothesis, I offer a collection of earlier and more recently acquired alignment data. Figure 2 shows the distribution of the axial alignments about the horizon of Late Postclassic site axes in north Yucatán folded about the astronomical north–south direction (vertical axis). Despite the relatively small number of points, this plot shows a concentration of alignments in the 14°–18° region, skewed to the east from north on the horizontal axis. Compare this plot with that in figure 3, which samples a much larger data set consisting of alignments measured at Postclassic sites in the Mexican highlands (after Šprajc 2001 and personal communication, November 2005; see also Aveni and Hartung 1986: fig. 2b; Aveni and Gibbs 1976). Although additional data are still wanting to decide the case, the general similarity between these histograms supports the hypothesis that central Mexican alignments may have influenced Late Postclassic north Yucatán, or vice versa. (For a more detailed treatment of the data, see the appendix to this chapter.) Thus the template that governs the arrangement of sacred and civic space may be added to the panoply of cross-cultural elements transferred between the highlands and north Yucatán discussed in this text.

Specialized Structures Manifesting Astronomical Alignments in Late Postclassic North Yucatán

Finally, we look at individual structures in light of the same hypothesis about cross-cultural influence. We can think of cosmically influenced city plans in at least three ways. At a symbolic level, they represent the sanctified materialization of the union of space and time, "whose importance in the Mesoamerican worldview is attested in different sources" (Šprajc 2005: 211–212); at the political level, they constitute a manifest attempt of royalty, befitting its political ideology, to legitimize its power (like the Egyptians) by reenacting and perpetuating the cosmic order in the theater of the built terrestrial environment. Finally, at a more practical level, we can interpret Maya architecture as a contrivance that must be so arranged that the celestial bodies arrive in the proper place at the correct time, lest a particular ritual or debt payment might not be effective. It is in this latter sense that we have come to speak of certain preferentially aligned structures as "observatories," a term that often can be misleading if taken to imply the existence of structures possessing unwarranted precision, utilized by scientific astronomers such as we find in the West.

Individual buildings possessing an unusual shape and/or orientation relative to other structures at a given site further prompt investigations into possible astronomical motivation on the part of the builders. In the Maya world, the House of the Governor at Uxmal and the Caracol of Chichén Itzá come to mind. Among the unusual Late Postclassic buildings whose designs may have been inspired by earlier structures of similar design are the "Castillo" (Q162) and "Caracol" or Round Temple (Q152) of Mayapán.

Umberger (1987: 67) proposed that the pan-Mesoamerican concept of cyclic time and history might tend to promote revivalism as a way of setting up a dialectic between past and present. Thus Chichén Itzá's legacy at Mayapán may have taken the form of replication of certain components of the city. Such replication might be expected to reveal calendrical change. We found some curious

Fig. 4. A. Castillo of Chichén Itzá showing the equinox hierophany. Photograph by Anthony Aveni. B. Castillo of Mayapán showing the winter solstice hierophany. Photograph courtesy of Susan Milbrath.

parallels when we examined these buildings in detail (Aveni et al. 2004). For example, whereas Chichén's Castillo has 364 steps (91 on a side), the Castillo of Mayapán has 260 (65 on a side). They differ in orientation by some 15°, the former exhibiting its so-called hierophany (a manifestation of the sacred in the built or natural environment) around the equinoxes, the latter around the summer solstice (fig. 4). The similarity in form of the plans of these radial

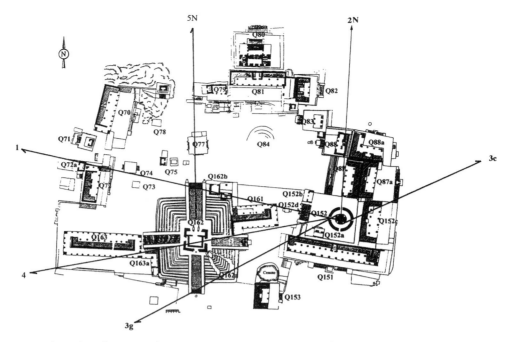

Fig. 5. Plan of Mayapán showing the relevant sunset alignments from Q152 over the Castillo (Q162) at the spring equinox (4) and on April 30 (1). After Aveni et al. (2004: fig. 6).

pyramids and the Formée cross almanacs in the Fejérváry-Mayer and Madrid codices should not pass unnoticed (compare the plan of Structure Q162 shown in figure 5 with plates 1 and 2).

The round temples, also differently oriented (by more than 10°), offer a curious contrast as well. For example, Structure Q152, the so-called Caracol of Mayapán, lacks a hollow interior chamber and access way to the turret. Instead, four outer doorways give access to an interior circular chamber that confronts a solid cylindrical core marked only by four (approximately intercardinal) niches. We have argued (Aveni et al. 1975 and subsequent publications; see Aveni 2001 for a list of references) that the Caracol at Chichén, quite isolated from the Castillo, appears to incorporate alignments to Venus. On the other hand, Q152, the Mayapán counterpart, is positioned close to the west side of the Castillo, its slightly skewed doorway fronting the east side of that building (the skew is nearly identical to that at Chichén) (fig. 6).

The most logical astronomical orientation targets sunsets along the northern facade of Q162 (fig. 5). Thus the sight line over the top of the Castillo, viewed from the doorway of Q152, points to the equinox sunsets (recall that the Aztec Templo Mayor offers a Mesoamerican precedent for sighting the sun over the

Fig. 6. A. The Caracol of Chichén Itzá. B. The Round Temple (Q152) of Mayapán. Note the nearly identical (rightward) skew of the central doorway from the central axis of the stairway. Photographs by Anthony Aveni.

top of a temple at the equinoxes) (fig. 5, alignment 4). The alignment across the base (alignment 1) fixes the sunset on April 30 and August 13 (Gregorian). The solar dates tied to the base alignment are identical to those that fit the skewed Teotihuacan east–west orientation (Šprajc 2001: 405), thus possibly reflecting a continuation of a very early Mesoamerican agricultural calendrical tradition. During the crucial 40-day period between the spring equinox (March 20) and April 30 (approximately between 60 and 20 days before the first solar zenith passage), the setting sun, watched from day to day, gradually descends the steps of the Castillo—that is, it walks "one foot of the year." Now the period March 20 to April 30 marks the beginning of the end of the local dry season, which is documented in the Madrid Codex during the fifteenth century as that period during which rituals pertaining to planting in anticipation of the rainy season were conducted (Hernández and Bricker 2004). This makes sense, because it is during this critical period that one anticipates the coming of the rains, which fuels the motivation for conducting rain-bringing rituals to pay the debt to the gods to ensure a bountiful harvest. The enhancement of a solar cult at Mayapán is supported by evidence in the mural painting on Structure Q161, a building attached to the east side of the Castillo, which depicts multiple images of the sun disk on its north and south facades.

Summary

Were the Maya "laying squares" upon the earth? It would appear from the evidence gathered at a significant number of sites that there are likely preferential building alignments in Late Postclassic north Yucatán. Although the prescription for orientation seems not as rigid as that practiced in the Terminal Classic Puuc cities, distribution plots of the alignment data hint at a different, perhaps more loosely applied, calendrical dictum. It too focused on a solar zenith–based calendar, and it bore a not too distant resemblance to what was going on at that time in central Mexico. Such a development might have been anticipated, given the evidence of a strong similarity in regard to calendrical/ritual practice in the Borgia and Maya codices. To further demonstrate the reality of cultural transfer of cosmically based site planning in the Late Postclassic, I refer to a specialized Late Postclassic architectural structure, the round tower (Q152) of Mayapán. It emerges as something more than a mere nonfunctional imitation of its earlier, more famous counterpart at Chichén Itzá. Rather, it may be regarded as a revisionist reflection of a calendrical ritual program that underwent studied change. In this sense, imitation is not simply a sincere form of flattery. It is a reflection of creativity, independence, and change. Did the ideology of the learned daykeepers embrace an altered view of the cosmos or were the priests simply responding to hitherto unrecognized environmental changes? We will probably never know.

An Astronomer's Personal Afterword

Are architectural alignments metaphoric or literal? Symbolic or practical? Must one choose? I believe the overused word *observatory* often opens the gate to the ethnocentric pathway of belief that any measured quantity that does not yield a precise fit can have had nothing to do with astronomy. But here there is safety in numbers. As I have argued, the analysis of a significant number of sites can unveil real trends. Detailed comparisons of individual buildings and a rigorous examination of the data can also reveal intentionality, especially when an orientation is backed up by iconographic, epigraphic, and ethnohistoric evidence.

When it comes to the question of the role of cosmology in city planning, I prefer to think that ceremonial architecture might have provided not so much a laboratory for the acquisition, documentation, and analysis of precise, quantitative astronomical information (what happens in a modern astronomical observatory), as a sacred place where the conduct of cosmically based ritual could be rendered most efficacious in the eyes of the practitioner. For a differing point of view, see Aimers and Rice (2006: 86). In the practical architectural sense, this would have amounted to laying squares in such a manner that Venus, Mars, the sun, or whatever celestial object or phenomenon might have been configured into the divinatory process would be delivered to the proper place, be it the top of a temple, the doorway of a building, or the open plaza where a debt payment would be transacted with the gods, at the correct time. Such a perspective places ancient Maya astronomy and cosmology as much in the realm of theater as science.

Acknowledgments

I am indebted to Ivan Šprajc, Dominique Rissolo, Tomás Gallareta, and Fernando Robles for providing alignment data and other information, some of it in advance of publication; and to Gabrielle Vail, Susan Milbrath, Chris Hernández, Tony Andrews, and Mike Smith for comments on earlier drafts of this paper.

APPENDIX
Interpreting Alignments: Some Astronomical and Topographic Details

There are 16 data points for north Yucatán (see table 1 for the relevant data), and 56 for central Mexico. Mean (and median) alignments are, respectively, 19°.1 (18°) and 11°.6 (12°). Closer examination of the histograms reveals a strong clustering in the 10°–20° range in each data set. To the right of the peak lie some sites that, despite their late dates of construction, exhibit the (likely) archaic solstice alignment trend due either to an insistence on maintaining tradition

Appendix Table 1. Orientations of Late Postclassic sites in north Yucatán

Site	Azimuth	Notes/references
El Meco	19° 40′	Str. 1: Andrews and Robles (1986)
El Rey	12° 02′	Conjunto El Rey: Vargas (1978)
Playa del Carmen	33°	Average of three groupings (B, C, D): Andrews and Andrews (1975)
San Angel	15° 37′	Colonnaded structure in principal group (contains remnants of mural paintings in the Borgia style): Tomás Gallareta (personal communication, December 2006)
Xelhá	18°	Aveni (1980)
Muyil	18°	Witschey (1988). Measurements taken in January 2007; revised Aveni (1980)
Tancah	22° 44′	Str 12. Measurements taken in January 2007; revised Aveni (1980)
Xcaret	43° 59′	Group D: Aveni (1980)
Akumal	24° 09′	Measurements taken in January 2007
P. Islote, Cozumel	13° 14′	Aveni (1980)
El Cedral, Cozumel	19° 05′	Aveni (1980)
Str. 13, Cozumel	16° 01′	Aveni (1980)
Str. 14, Cozumel	28° 02′	Aveni (1980)
Str. 15, Cozumel	26° 27′	Aveni (1980)
El Real, Cozumel	16° 27′	Aveni (1980)
Mayapán Ch'en Mul Group (Mayapán core)	12°	Aveni et al. (2004); Masson (2000); Pugh (2005)
Mayapán Itzmal Ch'en Group	11° 22′	Masson (2000); Pugh (2005). Measurements taken in January 2007. Despite their wide separation, the two Mayapán groups have the same orientation.

or to erecting structures over earlier foundations, perhaps simply for convenience. Alignments below 10° in the central Mexican data set appear to reflect some other orientation principle, perhaps a crude attempt at achieving cardinality. If these data are removed from the picture, then the means, and standard deviations therefrom, become for north Yucatán 17°.1 ± 0°.9 (10 data points), and for central Mexico 13°.8 ± 0°.5 (34 data points).

The relatively small sample of data points from north Yucatán notwithstanding, this is the basis for suggesting that there may be a hint of central Mexican influence in the general orientation of Late Postclassic sites in north Yucatán.

References Cited

Aimers, James J., and Prudence M. Rice
  2006   Astronomy, Ritual, and the Interpretation of Maya "E-Group"
          Architectural Assemblages. *Ancient Mesoamerica* 17 (1): 79–96.

Andrews, Anthony, and E. Wyllys Andrews IV
  1975   *A Preliminary Study of the Ruins of Xcaret, Quintana Roo, Mexico.*
          Middle American Research Institute Publication 40. Tulane University,
          New Orleans.

Andrews, Anthony, and Fernando Robles Castellanos (eds.)
  1986   *Excavaciones arqueológicas en El Meco, Quintana Roo.* Colección Científica
          158. Instituto Nacional de Antropología e Historia, México, D.F.

Ashmore, Wendy
  1989   Construction and Cosmology: Politics and Ideology in Lowland Maya
          Settlement Patterns. In *Word and Image in Maya Culture: Explorations in
          Language, Writing and Representation* (William F. Hanks and Don S. Rice,
          eds.): 272–286. University of Utah Press, Salt Lake City.
  1991   Site-Planning Principles and Concepts of Directionality among the Ancient
          Maya. *Latin American Antiquity* 2: 199–226.

Ashmore, Wendy, and Jeremy A. Sabloff
  2000   El orden de espacio en los planes civicos mayas. In *Arquitectura e ideología
          de los antiguos mayas: Memoria de la Segunda Mesa Redonda de Palenque*
          (Silvia Trejo, ed.): 14–23. Instituto Nacional de Antropología e Historia,
          México, D.F.
  2003   Interpreting Ancient Maya Civic Plans: Reply to Smith. *Latin American
          Antiquity* 14: 229–236.

Aveni, Anthony F.
  1980   *Skywatchers of Ancient Mexico.* University of Texas Press, Austin.
  2000   Out of Teotihuacan: Origins of the Celestial Canon in Mesoamerica. In
          Mesoamerica's Classic Heritage: From Teotihuacan to the Aztecs (David
          Carrasco, Lindsay Jones, and Scott Sessions, eds.): 253–268. University Press
          of Colorado, Boulder.
  2001   *Skywatchers.* Rev. ed. University of Texas Press, Austin.

Aveni, Anthony F., Anne S. Dowd, and Benjamin Vining
  2003   Maya Calendar Reform? Evidence from Orientations of Specialized
          Architectural Assemblages. *Latin American Antiquity* 14: 159–178.

Aveni, Anthony F., and Sharon Gibbs
  1976   On the Orientation of Pre-Columbian Buildings in Central Mexico.
          American Antiquity 41 (4): 510–517.

Aveni, Anthony F., Sharon L. Gibbs, and Horst Hartung
  1975   The Caracol Tower at Chichen Itza: An Ancient Astronomical Observatory?
          Science 188: 977–985.

Aveni, Anthony F., and Horst Hartung

1982   Precision in the Layout of Maya Architecture. In *Ethnoastronomy and Archaeoastronomy in the American Tropics* (Anthony Aveni and Gary Urton, eds.): 63–80. Annals of the New York Academy of Sciences 385. New York.

1986   Maya City Planning and the Calendar. *Transactions of the American Philosophical Society* 76 (7): 1–87.

Aveni, Anthony, Susan Milbrath, and Carlos Peraza Lope

2004   Chichén Itzá's Legacy in the Astronomically Oriented Architecture of Mayapan. *RES: Anthropology and Aesthetics* 45: 123–144.

Aveni, Anthony, and Guiliano Romano

1994   Orientation and Etruscan Ritual. *Antiquity* 68: 545–563.

Bricker, Harvey M., Victoria R. Bricker, and Bettina Wulfing

1997   Determining the Historicity of Three Astronomical Almanacs in the Madrid Codex. *Archaeoastronomy* (Supplement to the *Journal for the History of Astronomy*) 22: S17–S36.

Bricker, Victoria R.

1997   The "Calendar-Round" Almanac in the Madrid Codex. In *Papers on the Madrid Codex* (Victoria R. Bricker and Gabrielle Vail, eds.): 169–180. Middle American Research Institute Publication 64. Tulane University, New Orleans.

Bricker, Victoria R., and Harvey M. Bricker

1988   The Seasonal Table in the Dresden Codex and Related Almanacs. *Archaeoastronomy* (Supplement to the *Journal for the History of Astronomy*) 12: S1–S62.

Carl, Peter

2000   City-Image vs. Topography of Praxis. *Cambridge Archaeological Journal* 10: 329–334.

Carl, Peter, Barry Kemp, Ray Laurence, Robin Coningham, Charles Higman, and George L. Cowgill

2000   Viewpoint: Were Cities Built as Images? *Cambridge Archaeological Journal* 10: 327–365.

Dinsmoor, W.

1939   Archaeology and Astronomy. *Proceedings of the American Philosophical Society* 80: 95–173.

Flannery, Kent, and Joyce Marcus

1993   Cognitive Archaeology. *Cambridge Archaeological Journal* 3: 260–270.

Gendrop, Paul

1983   *Los estilos Río Bec, Chenes y Puuc en la arquitectura maya.* Universidad Nacional Autónoma de México, México, D.F.

Graff, Donald H.

1997   Dating a Section of the Madrid Codex: Astronomical and Iconographic
        Evidence. In *Papers on the Madrid Codex* (Victoria R. Bricker and Gabrielle
        Vail, eds.): 147–167. Middle American Research Institute Publication 64.
        Tulane University, New Orleans.

Hernández, Christine

2004   Yearbearer Pages and Their Connection to Planting Almanacs in the
        Borgia Codex. In *The Madrid Codex: New Approaches to Understanding an
        Ancient Maya Manuscript* (Gabrielle Vail and Anthony Aveni, eds.): 321–
        366. University Press of Colorado, Boulder.

Hernández, Christine, and Victoria R. Bricker

2004   The Inauguration of Planting in the Borgia and Madrid Codices. In *The
        Madrid Codex: New Approaches to Understanding an Ancient Maya
        Manuscript* (Gabrielle Vail and Anthony Aveni, eds.): 277–320. University
        Press of Colorado, Boulder.

Just, Bryan R.

2004   *In Extenso* Almanacs in the Madrid Codex. In *The Madrid Codex: New
        Approaches to Understanding an Ancient Maya Manuscript* (Gabrielle Vail
        and Anthony Aveni, eds.): 255–276. University Press of Colorado, Boulder.

Manikka, Eleanor

1996   *Angkor Wat: Time, Space, and Kingship.* University of Hawaii Press,
        Honolulu.

Masson, Marilyn

2000   *In the Realm of Nachan Kan: Postclassic Archaeology at Laguna de On,
        Belize.* University Press of Colorado, Boulder.

Milbrath, Susan

1999   *Star Gods of the Maya: Astronomy in Art, Folklore, and Calendars.*
        University of Texas Press, Austin.

Pollock, Harry

1980   *The Puuc: An Architectural Survey of the Hill Country of Yucatán and
        Northern Campeche.* Memoirs of the Peabody Museum of Archaeology and
        Ethnology 19. Harvard University, Cambridge, Mass.

Proskouriakoff, Tatiana

1954   Mayapan: The Last Stronghold of a Civilization. *Archaeology* 7: 96–103.

Pugh, Timothy

2005   Caves and Artificial Caves in Late Postclassic Maya Ceremonial Groups.
        In *Stone Houses and Earth Lords: Maya Religion in the Cave Context*
        (Keith Prufer and James Brady, eds.): 47–70. University Press of Colorado,
        Boulder.

Roys, Ralph

1967   *The Book of Chilam Balam of Chumayel.* University of Oklahoma Press,
        Norman.

Seler, Eduard

   1963   *Comentarios al Códice Borgia.* (Mariana Frenk, trans.). Vols. 1–3. Fondo de
          Cultura Económica, México, D.F.

Smith, Michael E.

   2003   Can We Read Cosmology in Ancient Maya City Plans? Comment on
          Ashmore and Sabloff. *Latin American Antiquity* 14 (2): 221–228.

   2005   Did the Maya Build Architectural Cosmograms? *Latin American Antiquity*
          16 (2): 217–224.

Šprajc, Ivan

   2000   Astronomical Alignments at Teotihuacan. *Latin American Antiquity* 11
          (4): 403–415.

   2001   *Orientaciones astronómicas en la arquitectura prehispánica del centro de
          México.* Instituto Nacional de Antropología e Historia, México, D.F.

   2005   More on Mesoamerican Cosmology and City Plans. *Latin American
          Antiquity* 16: 209–216.

Tedlock, Dennis

   1985   *Popol Vuh: The Mayan Book of the Dawn of Life.* Simon & Shuster,
          New York.

Tozzer, Alfred M.

   1941   *Landa's* Relación de las cosas de Yucatan: *A Translation.* Papers of the
          Peabody Museum of American Archaeology and Ethnology 18. Harvard
          University, Cambridge, Mass.

Umberger, Emily

   1987   Antiques, Revivals, and References to the Past in Aztec Art. *RES:
          Anthropology and Aesthetics* 13: 63–105.

Vargas Pacheco, Ernesto

   1978   Los asentamientos prehispánicos y la arquitectura en la Isla Can Cun,
          Quintana Roo. *Estudios de cultura maya* 11: 93–112. Universidad Nacional
          Autónoma de México, México, D.F.

Wheatley, Paul

   1971   *Pivot of the Four Quarters.* Aldine, Chicago.

Witschey, Walter

   1988   Recent Investigations at the Maya Inland Port City of Muyil (Chunyaxché),
          Quintana Roo, Mexico. *Mexicon* 10 (6): 111–117.

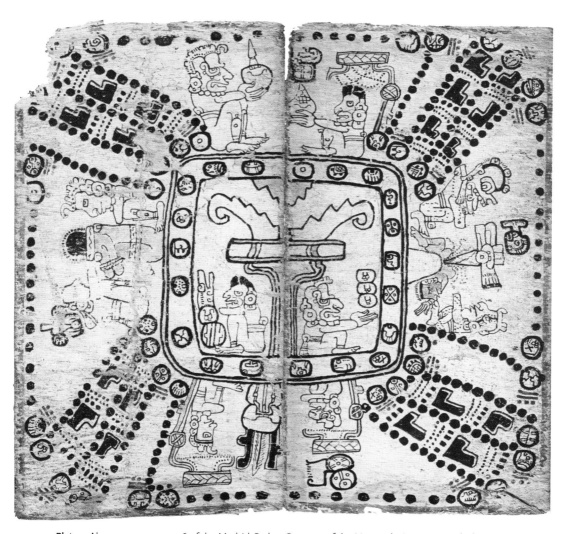

Plate 1. Almanac on pp. 75–76 of the Madrid Codex. Courtesy of the Museo de América, Madrid.

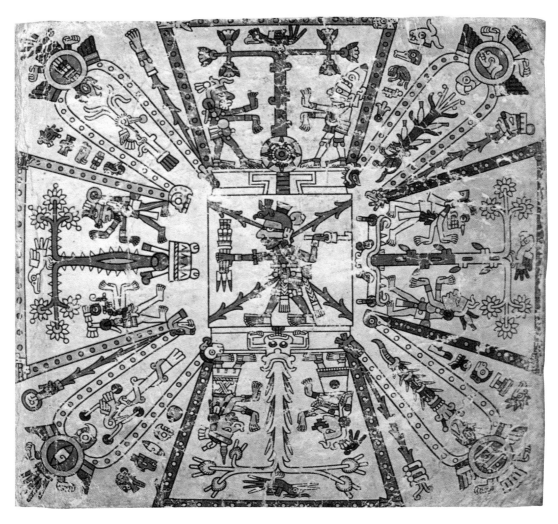

Plate 2. Almanac on p. 1 of the Codex Fejérváry-Mayer. Copyright National Museums Liverpool, World Museum Liverpool.

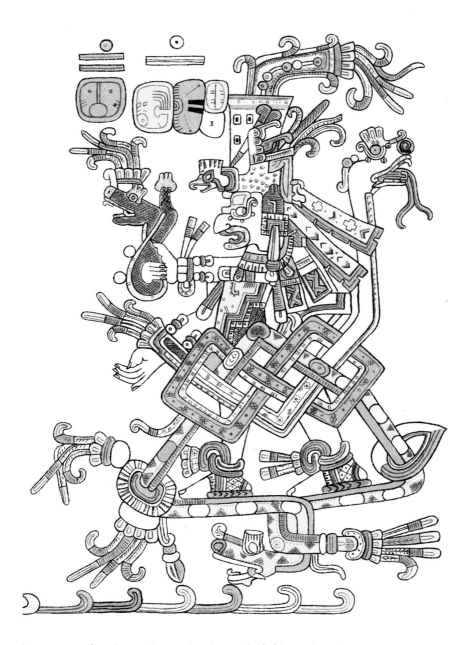

Plate 3. Figure 8 from the mural painted on the west half of the north wall, Mound 1, Santa Rita. After Gann (1900: pl. 30).

Plate 4. Temple of the Fisherman mural, Mayapán. Photograph courtesy of Carlos Peraza.

Part II

Texts, Language, and Imagery

Introduction

Gabrielle Vail and Christine Hernández

P HYSICAL EVIDENCE, in the form of material remains such as those discussed in the preceding part, provide one of several means of examining
questions of interaction among Late Postclassic cultures and people of Mesoamerica. The chapters in this part are concerned with other types of evidence
for interchange—as documented through the study of hieroglyphic and alphabetic texts, linguistic relationships, and art portrayed in various media, including ceramics, murals, codices, and sculpture.

Languages of Postclassic Mesoamerica

The linguistic history of Pre-Hispanic Mesoamerica has been the subject of
considerable research within the past 40 years (see, e.g., Campbell and Kaufman 1976; Campbell 1997; Hill 2001; Justeson et al. 1985; Macri and Looper
2003, and references therein). Our interest lies especially in contacts that can be
documented through textual or historical linguistic evidence between speakers
of Yucatec Maya in the northern Yucatán Peninsula and Chontal, Zoque, and
Totonac speakers along key coastal trade routes (fig. 1), and with inland populations in central Mesoamerica (Zapotec, Mixtec, Totonac, and Nahuatl).

The distribution of ethnic and linguistic groups in Postclassic Mesoamerica is explored in detail by Fernando Robles in Chapter 2. To this discussion,
the chapters in Part II add a diachronic perspective, examining the earlier linguistic history of the two regions under consideration and the nature of the interactions characterizing the relevant linguistic groups. In addition to noting
influences from the Uto-Aztecan language family on Maya texts, Macri presents evidence suggesting that Zapotec and Maya speakers may have been in
contact during the Classic period.

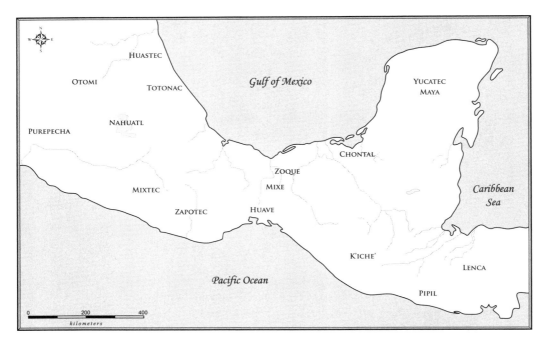

Fig. 1. Selected languages spoken in Postclassic Mesoamerica. For a tentative mapping of the distribution of language families at ca. 1500 CE, see figure 1 in Chapter 7. Artwork by David R. Hixson; modified after Weaver (1981: map 2).

In Chapter 7, Dakin considers the early history of the Uto-Aztecan languages in Mesoamerica and linguistic evidence for relationships between Uto-Aztecan and Mayan speakers. Although traditionally believed to have originated in the American Southwest or northern Mexico, Jane Hill (2001) places the homeland of proto-Uto-Aztecan groups within Mesoamerica and suggests a subsequent northern migration (see discussion in Dakin, ch. 7, this volume). Within Mesoamerica, two main branches of the Uto-Aztecan language Nahua can be differentiated—Eastern and Western Nahua.[1] The former appears to have an earlier history in Mesoamerica than the latter and can be linked to Nahua dialects spoken in southern Mesoamerica (including the Gulf Coast) and El Salvador. In addition, evidence suggests that parts of Tlaxcala and central Guerrero were also settled by Eastern Nahua speakers (Dakin 2001: 364).

The western branch may have had a homeland in northern Mexico. Migrations into Mesoamerica appear to have included groups that moved west and down the coast from Michoacán to Oaxaca, and others who moved into northern Guerrero and the state of Mexico (Dakin 2001: 364). Dakin notes that the latter were the founders of Tenochtitlan and other Nahuatl communities in

Morelos, Puebla, and Tlaxcala. It appears that a third dialect, resulting from contact between speakers of the Eastern and Western Nahua languages, developed in central Mexico and led to what is termed "Classical Nahuatl" (the colonial period dialect), as Dakin discusses in her chapter.

Several southward migrations of Nahua speakers can be reconstructed, including a major one during the Late Classic period. One scenario has Nahua populations moving south to southern Veracruz and later to the Soconusco (Campbell 1985, 1997). Thereafter, they were displaced and continued southward, establishing colonies in Guatemala, El Salvador, and Nicaragua, as well as isolated communities in Costa Rica and Panama. The southward migration from the Soconusco is believed to have begun around 800 CE (Campbell 1985; Maxwell 2001), although there is some evidence to suggest that it may have been earlier (Dakin and Wichmann 2000).

Scholes and Roys (1968) report Nahua-speaking populations residing in the Gulf Coast region of Tabasco and a Nahua enclave at Ulua in Honduras, as determined from ethnohistoric sources. Reports of a Mexican lineage (the Canul) resident at Mayapán are also found in ethnohistoric documents (Tozzer 1941: 39 and note 190). It has been suggested that they were originally based at Xicalango (also spelled Xicalanco).

The question of an earlier presence of Nahua speakers in the Yucatán Peninsula, associated with the site of Chichén Itzá, is one of the topics addressed by Timothy Knowlton in Chapter 8. He explores the various overlays of "Mexican" culture on Yucatec Maya society from the viewpoint of an indigenous colonial text called the "Song of the Fall of Chichén Itzá."[2] Also relevant to this inquiry is Karen Dakin's discussion of the "language of Zuyúa" in the Books of Chilam Balam, which is believed to have Mexican antecedents.

The existence of written texts aids significantly in the reconstruction of linguistic relationships in Pre-Hispanic Mesoamerica (see, e.g., Dakin and Wichmann 2000; Justeson et al. 1985; Macri and Looper 2003), although scholars do not always agree on the particulars. One debate that is still fiercely being contested involves the presence of Nahua speakers in southern Mesoamerica before the Terminal Classic period (see the recent discussion in Kaufman and Justeson 2006 and reply in Macri 2009). Macri and Looper (2003) provide compelling evidence from Maya glyphic texts suggesting that there is a Nahua basis for a number of the graphic signs commonly employed by Classic period Maya scribes. In addition, Macri (2005) reports evidence of Nahua words spelled syllabically on an Early Classic ceramic vessel from Río Azul. An early Nahua presence in Mesoamerica is given further consideration in the chapters by Macri (ch. 6) and Dakin (ch. 7). Their discussions suggest that Uto-Aztecan (Nahua) speakers first interacted with Mayan speakers by the Early Classic period (400 CE or earlier).

At a much later time period, there is evidence of a continuing relationship between Mayan and Nahua speakers, as documented in the eighteenth century Books of Chilam Balam (Bricker 2000). Timothy Knowlton (ch. 8, this volume) considers one aspect of the Chilam Balam texts that has not been previously discussed: the presence of Nahua vocables (syllables chosen for their sound value alone) in the "Song of the Fall of Chichén Itzá."

Relationships with other linguistic/ethnic groups in highland Mexico appear to have played a significant role in lowland Maya culture during the first part of the Late Postclassic period as well as earlier, as Karl Taube (ch. 5, this volume) documents in his discussion of shared motifs, symbols, and styles that characterize the art of highland Mexico and the Maya area.

Mesoamerican Art and the International Style

A common thread throughout many of the chapters in the volume is a consideration of similarities in the art of various sites from both the northern Maya lowlands and the Mexican highlands, as seen in their style, subject matter, and the inclusion of particular symbols and motifs (cf. plates 1–2). Because it is found at sites throughout Mesoamerica and is, for the moment, the best empirical evidence we have suggesting a connection between the two regions, this art style is now commonly referred to as the "International style." However, in the past it was identified with the Mixteca-Puebla area (and hence became known as the Mixteca-Puebla style), primarily because the greatest concentration of objects in this style was found in the highland regions of Puebla, Tlaxcala, and Oaxaca, and it was believed to have originated in this region (Vaillant 1938, 1940, 1941). It is defined by a number of motifs with a widespread distribution and a particular style of painting, which may be seen, for example, in the Mixtec and Borgia Group codices (see plate 2), as well as in murals from various sites, including Tulúm and Santa Rita in the Maya region (see, e.g., Nicholson 1982; Robertson 1970; see also plates 3–4). However, the symbols and pictorial style are separate components and should be considered as such, as Elizabeth Boone and Michael Smith (2003) caution in their recent discussion on this subject.

The style is characterized by stiff lines and renders forms as flat; figures and objects are "almost geometric in their shape" (Boone and Smith 2003: 187). They have black outlines and are brightly colored, although neither modeling nor shading is used, producing a two-dimensional effect. Little attention is given to perspective, and figures frequently appear to be floating in space or portrayed in relation to a painted line defining the bottom of a scene or register (Boone and Smith 2003: 186–187; see also plates 2–4).

Examples of International-style art occur in many different regions of Mesoamerica and have come to be separated into distinct substyles—one centered in the Mixteca-Puebla area and characterized by the Mixtec and Borgia Group codices as well as polychrome ceramics; another in the Aztec area; a third in

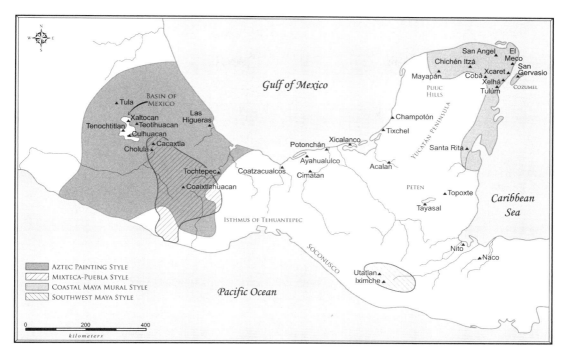

Fig. 2. Postclassic Mesoamerica showing the regional variants of the Late Postclassic International style. Artwork by David R. Hixson; modified after Smith (2003: fig. 23.1).

the eastern Maya coastal area, which is best known from the murals from this region; and a fourth in the highland region of Guatemala (fig. 2). Although each is distinct in its way, the four substyles are characterized by the use of similar symbols and motifs and a common subject matter, with an emphasis on animals, plants, skybands, ritual objects, and deities. Karl Taube discusses various examples of the International style, focusing on the Tulúm and Santa Rita murals, in Chapter 5.

Early discussions of the International style (then called Mixteca-Puebla) focused on an origin in the highlands of central Mexico via codices, polychrome ceramics, and murals (see, e.g., Ekholm 1942; Nicholson 1966, 1982; Vaillant 1940). Murals in this style in the Maya area were therefore seen as evidence of Mexican influence on Maya populations. In some instances (e.g., Miller 1982: 71–75), they were cited as evidence for Mexican incursions within the Maya area, and at times they continue to be interpreted in this way (Milbrath and Pereza 2003: 29–31).

Recent discussions, however, such as that by Marilyn Masson (2003), emphasize the role played by these murals in information-exchange networks in

Mesoamerica. Masson (2003: 200) notes that "the importance of external connections to Postclassic Maya elites is illustrated in the prominence and abundance of international symbols in Maya murals, as well as the use of a variant of the Postclassic international style." Theories like Arthur Miller's for explaining their presence in the Maya area, she suggests, can no longer be supported. Rather, it is now clear that much of the iconography used in the International style did not originate with the Aztecs (Nahuatl populations), and that the style and symbol set actually diffused throughout Mesoamerica before the rise of the Aztec Empire (see table 1, ch. 3, this volume).

Masson suggests that Maya artists at Tulúm and elsewhere were selective in their use of foreign styles and symbols, employing these in mural programs that were largely focused on local themes, perhaps as a way of sanctioning local authority within larger-scale trade networks involving visiting elites from throughout the peninsula. She concludes by noting that "the Postclassic Maya murals provide one of the best examples of the blending of local and international elements in the Postclassic world system" (Masson 2003: 200).

John Pohl's (2003) study of painted polychrome ceramics from the Mixteca-Puebla region of central and southern Mexico is also of interest in terms of his discussion of the adoption of pan-Mesoamerican versus regional and local ideologies. He finds that, while the spread of the International style had the effect of facilitating communication among elites residing in Tlaxcala, Puebla, and Oaxaca, it was also employed (through variations in vessel form and iconography) to communicate the diversity of worldviews among the different regions.

Karl Taube provides a detailed discussion of the International style and symbol set in Chapter 5, focusing on earlier antecedents for the elements and motifs that came to be considered diagnostic during the Late Postclassic period. Rather than indicating a uniform origin in the highland area, he notes that many of the symbols and motifs were adopted into the Mixteca-Puebla region and central Mexico from the Maya area and that the eastern Maya area had a special symbolic significance within pan-Mesoamerican belief systems.[3] It should be stressed, in light of earlier models that focused on highland Mexico as the innovator, that Taube's chapter, like those that discuss the linguistic and textual evidence, clearly reinforces the idea of cross-cultural interchange as a multilateral process.

Acknowledgments

We thank Karen Dakin and Martha Macri for providing references and information pertaining to our discussion of the languages of Postclassic Mesoamerica. We also extend our gratitude to Cynthia Vail for her editorial assistance.

Notes

1. We follow other scholars in using the term *Nahua* to refer to varieties of these languages spoken during the Classic and Terminal Classic/Epiclassic periods.

2. We use the term *Mexican* to refer to cultures based in the central Mexican highlands.

3. Taube's discussion of Tulúm as representative of the eastern realm in Mesoamerica
   is presaged by the work of Arthur Miller (1982: ch. 5); see also Merideth Paxton's (2001: ch. 6) discussion of the sacred geography of the Late Postclassic Yucatán Peninsula.

References Cited

Boone, Elizabeth H., and Michael E. Smith
    2003   Postclassic International Styles and Symbol Sets. In *The Postclassic Mesoamerican World* (Michael E. Smith and Frances F. Berdan, eds.): 186–193. University of Utah Press, Salt Lake City.

Bricker, Victoria R.
    2000   Bilingualism in the Maya Codices and the Books of Chilam Balam. *Written Language and Literacy* 3 (1): 77–115. [Special issue: Language and Dialect in the Maya Hieroglyphic Script (Gabrielle Vail and Martha J. Macri, eds.).]

Campbell, Lyle
    1985   *The Pipil Language of El Salvador.* Mouton, New York.
    1997   *American Indian Languages: The Historical Linguistics of Native America.* Oxford University Press, New York.

Campbell, Lyle, and Terrence Kaufman
    1976   A Linguistic Look at the Olmecs. *American Antiquity* 41 (1): 80–89.

Dakin, Karen
    2001   Nahuatl. In *The Oxford Encyclopedia of Mesoamerican Cultures: The Civilizations of Mexico and Central America*, vol. 2 (Davíd Carrasco, ed.): 363–365. Oxford University Press, New York.

Dakin, Karen, and Søren Wichmann
    2000   Cacao and Chocolate: A Uto-Aztecan Perspective. *Ancient Mesoamerica* 11: 55–75.

Ekholm, Gordon
    1942   Excavations at Guasave, Sinaloa, Mexico. *Anthropological Papers of the American Museum of Natural History* 38 (2): 23–139.

Hill, Jane
    2001   Proto-Uto-Aztecan: A Community of Cultivators in Central Mexico? *American Anthropologist* 103: 913–934.

Justeson, John S., William M. Norman, Lyle Campbell, and Terrence Kaufman
    1985   *The Foreign Impact on Lowland Mayan Language and Script.* Middle American Research Institute Publication 53. Tulane University, New Orleans.

Kaufman, Terrence, and John Justeson

2006   The History of the Word for "Cacao" and Related Terms in Ancient Meso-America. In *Chocolate in Mesoamerica: A Cultural History of Cacao* (Cameron L. McNeil, ed.): 117–139. University of Florida Press, Gainesville.

Macri, Martha J.

2005   Nahua Loan Words from the Early Classic Period: Words for Cacao Preparation on a Río Azul Ceramic Vessel. *Ancient Mesoamerica* 16: 321–326.

2009   Tempest in a Chocolate Pot: The Origin of Word *Cacao*. In *Chocolate: History, Culture, Heritage* (Louis E. Grivetti and Howard-Yana Shapiro, eds.): 17–26. Wiley, Hoboken, N.J.

Macri, Martha J., and Matthew G. Looper

2003   Nahua in Ancient Mesoamerica: Evidence from Maya Inscriptions. *Ancient Mesoamerica* 14: 285–297.

Masson, Marilyn A.

2003   The Late Postclassic Symbol Set in the Maya Area. In *The Postclassic Mesoamerican World* (Michael E. Smith and Frances F. Berdan, eds.): 194–200. University of Utah Press, Salt Lake City.

Maxwell, Judith M.

2001   Languages at the Time of Contact. In *Archaeology of Ancient Mexico and Central America: An Encyclopedia* (Susan T. Evans and David L. Webster, eds.): 395–399. Garland Publishing, New York and London.

Milbrath, Susan, and Carlos Peraza Lope

2003   Revisiting Mayapan: Mexico's Last Maya Capital. *Ancient Mesoamerica* 14: 1–46.

Miller, Arthur G.

1982   *On the Edge of the Sea: Mural Painting at Tancah-Tulum, Quintana Roo, Mexico.* Dumbarton Oaks, Washington, D.C.

Nicholson, Henry B.

1966   The Problem of the Provenience of the Members of the "Codex Borgia Group": A Summary. In *Summa anthropologica en homenaje a Roberto J. Weitlaner* (A. Pompa y Pompa, ed.): 145–158. Instituto Nacional de Antropología e Historia, México, D.F.

1982   The Mixteca-Puebla Concept Revisited. In *The Art and Iconography of Late Post-Classic Central Mexico* (Elizabeth H. Boone, ed.): 227–254. Dumbarton Oaks, Washington, D.C.

Paxton, Merideth

2001   *The Cosmos of the Yucatec Maya: Cycles and Steps from the Madrid Codex.* University of New Mexico Press, Albuquerque.

Pohl, John M. D.

2003   Ritual and Iconographic Variability in Mixteca-Puebla Polychrome Pottery. In *The Postclassic Mesoamerican World* (Michael E. Smith and Frances F. Berdan, eds.): 201–206. University of Utah Press, Salt Lake City.

Robertson, Donald

1970 The Tulum Murals: The International Style of the Late Post-Classic. In *Verhandlungen des XXXVIII Internationalen Amerikanistenkongresses, Stuttgart-München, 1968,* vol. 2: 77–88. Kommissionsverlag Klaus Renner, Munich.

Scholes, France V., and Ralph L. Roys

1968 *The Maya Chontal Indians of Acalan-Tixchel: A Contribution to the History and Ethnography of the Yucatan Peninsula.* University of Oklahoma Press, Norman.

Smith, Michael E.

2003 Information Networks in Postclassic Mesoamerica. In *The Postclassic Mesoamerican World* (Michael E. Smith and Frances F. Berdan, eds.): 181–185. University of Utah Press, Salt Lake City.

Tozzer, Alfred M.

1941 *Landa's* Relación de las cosas de Yucatan: *A Translation.* Papers of the Peabody Museum of American Archaeology and Ethnology 18. Harvard University, Cambridge, Mass.

Vaillant, George C.

1938 A Correlation of Archaeological and Historical Sequences in the Valley of Mexico. *American Anthropologist* 40 (4): 535–573.

1940 Patterns in Middle American Archaeology. In *The Maya and Their Neighbors: Essays on Middle American Anthropology and Archaeology* (Clarence L. Hay, Ralph L. Linton, Samuel K. Lothrop, Harry L. Shapiro, and George C. Vaillant, eds.): 295–305. Appelton-Century, New York.

1941 *Aztecs of Mexico: Origin, Rise and Fall of the Aztec Nation.* Doubleday, Doran, Garden City, N.Y.

Weaver, Muriel P.

1981 *The Aztec, Maya, and Their Predecessors: Archaeology of Mesoamerica.* Academic Press, New York.

Chapter Five

At Dawn's Edge: Tulúm, Santa Rita, and Floral Symbolism in the International Style of Late Postclassic Mesoamerica

Karl Taube

THE MURALS OF TULÚM AND SANTA RITA constitute some of the most elaborate artistic programs known for the Late Postclassic Maya (see fig. 1 in ch. 1 for the location of these and other sites discussed). In contrast to the extant screenfold Maya codices, the mural surfaces are far larger, allowing for complex scenes involving many figures engaged in a variety of acts. Although those from Tulúm and Santa Rita are the best known (plate 3), similar murals occur at other Late Postclassic sites in Quintana Roo and northern Belize, including Tancah, Rancho Ina, Cobá, Xelhá, and San Angel (Gallareta Negrón and Taube 2005; Lombardo de Ruiz 1987; Martos López 2001; Miller 1982). Important murals are also known for Mayapán (plate 4), the major Yucatec capital of the northern Maya lowlands during the Late Postclassic period (Barrera Rubio and Peraza 2001). In addition, murals have been excavated in the Maya highlands at Utatlan and Iximche, the Late Postclassic capitals of the K'iche' and Kaqchikel, respectively (Navarrete 1996).

In this chapter, I examine the antecedents of elements from the Tulúm and Santa Rita murals that are identified with the International style and symbol set (defined later in the chapter), demonstrating that the point of origin of this complex does not lie in the Mixteca-Puebla region, as previously assumed, but rather that the Maya and other Mesoamerican cultures each contributed to the body of material grouped under this label over a period of many centuries.

The term *Mixteca-Puebla* was coined by George Vaillant (1938: 565; 1940: 299–300; 1941); he noted that it constituted one of the late widespread defining traits of ancient Mesoamerica, extending as far north as Sinaloa and as far south as Nicaragua. During the Late Postclassic period, there were many distinct regional developments deriving from local as well as foreign traditions. Because it occurs over such a wide area, Donald Roberston (1970: 88) preferred the term *International style* (rather than Mixteca-Puebla) for describing the Tulúm murals. Indeed, despite the presence of "Mixteca-Puebla" motifs such as skybands, solar rays, and starry eyes, the murals of Tulúm and Santa Rita are still strongly Maya, with Maya deities, offerings, and other symbolic themes.

In the edited volume *The Postclassic Mesoamerican World* (Smith and Berdan 2003), the authors concur that the term *Postclassic International style* be used rather than Mixteca-Puebla, which instead represents "a subset of the more inclusive Postclassic international style" (Smith 2003: 182). The four regional subsets are Aztec, Mixteca-Puebla, coastal Maya mural style (typified by the murals of Tulúm and Santa Rita), and artistic traditions of highland Guatemala (Boone and Smith 2003: 187; Smith 2003: 182). In this study, I use the term International style for this multiethnic art of the Late Postclassic period, with Mixteca-Puebla referring more specifically to its manifestation in northern Oaxaca and neighboring Puebla and Tlaxcala.

I focus on the murals of Tulúm and Santa Rita for several reasons. For one, they are especially well documented (see Gann's [1900] renderings of the Santa Rita murals and the excellent paintings by Felipe Davalos of the Tulúm murals in Miller [1982]). The murals from these two sites are by far the most elaborate and best preserved of those known for the Late Postclassic Maya. Even more important for this discussion, they are filled with floral imagery and symbolism, including flowers as items of costume, exhaled breath, celestial and solar signs, and markers of supernatural loci, such as pathways or roads in the form of plumed serpents. Rather than being limited to the coastal Maya region, this floral symbolism and imagery appears widely in International-style art. In this study, I examine the antecedents of International-style floral symbolism, much of which can be readily traced to the Classic Maya.

Flower World in Ancient Mesoamerica

In International-style art, flowers are not only items of pleasure and beauty but also symbolize the life spirit and the paradise of the sun. In her groundbreaking 1992 study, linguist Jane Hill called attention to a widespread spiritual complex present in both Mesoamerica and the American Southwest. Terming it *Flower World*, Hill (1992) noted that this paradisal solar realm is expressed not only through colorful flowers, but also by bright and shining items such as precious birds and polished stones. Hill (1992: 125) notes that "the image of the flowery road, with its prototype in the path of the sun across the heavens, is one of the most widely diffused Flower World metaphors." The Flower World complex is especially well developed among Uto-Aztecan-speaking peoples, including the Aztec, Huichol, Yaqui, O'odham (Pima and Papago), and Hopi (Hill 1992). The Aztec Flower World was a solar garden of heroic kings and warriors, where the honored dead fluttered as birds and butterflies sucking the nectar of sweet flowers (Sahagún 1950–82, bk. 3: 49; bk. 6: 163). Geronimo Mendieta (1980: 97) recorded a similar belief among the Nahuatl of Tlaxcala, where the souls of nobles became mists, clouds, beautiful birds, and shining jewels. In addition, John Pohl (2003: 201) notes that many motifs appearing in Mixteca-Puebla art (e.g., birds, butterflies, and jewels) concern the souls of the dead. Butterflies, for example, beyond being natural pollinators, symbolize the souls of dead warriors, a concept that can be traced to Early Classic Teotihuacan (Berlo 1983; Taube 2000, 2005a, 2006).

The Flower World complex is of great antiquity and may also be found among the Classic Maya (250–900 CE), where it was also highly developed. As in the case of central Mexico, the Classic Maya floral paradise was a solar region inhabited by quetzals and other precious birds, as well as gods and noble ancestors. Fragrant blossoms closely relate to concepts of the soul, especially the life force contained in the breath (Taube 2001a, 2004a, 2005b; see also Houston and Taube 2000; Looper and Kappelman 2001). Examples may be found in Hopi ritual (see Wright 1973: 94, 103, 105), as well as in ancient Mesoamerican art, where blossoms exhale breath, often as symmetrical, outwardly curling volutes (figs. 7C–E, 8, 9). Rather than being passive, inert objects, flowers are dynamic vehicles for the passage of gods and ancestors, and often appear as cave-like portals or supernatural paths (see discussion below).

One of the basic traits of Flower World in Mesoamerican thought is its relation to the east, the place of the dawning sun. Thus, the celestial solar paradise of Aztec warriors is in the east: "the brave warriors, the eagle-ocelot warriors, those who died in war, went there to the house of the sun. And they lived there in the east, where the sun arose" (Sahagún 1950–82, bk. 6: 162). In ancient Mexico, east was not simply an abstract concept but rather a geographical region— the land of the Maya. In the Borgia Group codices, the directional temples and trees of the east are consistently portrayed with jade and quetzal birds, precious goods derived from the eastern Maya realm (Taube 1994: 224–225), and the directional god of the east is the sun god Tonatiuh (fig. 3B). There is good evidence to suggest that Tonatiuh derives from Early Postclassic portrayals of a Maya solar king at Chichén Itzá (Taube 1994: 224–225 and discussed later).

In a far-ranging study concerning the geographic symbolism of east and west in the Maya region, Arthur Miller (1974: 46) argues that, while Copán may have been the primary eastern center of the Classic Maya, coastal Quintana Roo had a similar symbolic significance during the Late Postclassic, representing "an area suggesting birth and rebirth." Miller's (1974, 1982) studies of the Tulúm murals also focused on the motif of twisted cords as a cosmic umbilicus. At Tulúm and Santa Rita, however, these cords are the bodies of plumed serpents, also creatures of the east. In Mesoamerica, the plumed serpent known as Quetzalcoatl is consistently identified with the east, as is his stellar form Tlahuizcalpantecuhtli, or "Lord of the Dawn." In terms of natural phenomena, the identification of Quetzalcoatl and the plumed serpent with the east is concerned not only with the morning star but also with the wind (Graulich 1992; Taube 2001a). In Mesoamerica, the critically important rain-bringing spring and summer winds come from the east (see Vivó Escoto 1964: fig. 4). It is for this reason that Quetzalcoatl, as depicted from Early Classic Teotihuacan to the sixteenth century, is covered with plumage from the quetzal, a bird deriving squarely from the Maya region.

The eastern themes of solar imagery, plumed serpents, quetzals, and jade are major motifs of the Tulúm and Santa Rita murals and are also basic to the Flower World complex of ancient Mesoamerica. Many of the themes appearing in International-style art pertain to the eastern realm of the Maya, and it is surely no coincidence that a great deal of this symbolism and imagery derives from earlier Classic and even Preclassic Maya traditions.

The International Style and Its Origins

Whereas Vaillant (1941: 22) posited a local origin for the Mixteca-Puebla style of highland Mexico, recent studies consider lowland Veracruz and the Maya region to be of great importance as well. Soon after Vaillant's original discussions of Mixteca-Puebla culture, Wigberto Jiménez Moreno (1942: 128–129) noted the similarity of the earliest Aztec and Cholula ceramics to wares from Veracruz. Largely from this observation, Nicholson (1960: 616) suggested that the Olmeca-Xicalanca from the southern Gulf Coast region may have been the creators par excellence of the International style. With the discovery in 1975 of spectacular murals at Cacaxtla, it has become increasingly clear that the Olmeca-Xicalanca elite, who founded Cacaxtla as their new capital following their expulsion from Cholula (Armillas 1946), had an extensive knowledge of Maya art and iconography, including concepts of sacred landscape and the attributes of particular Maya deities.

More recent discussions of the Mixteca-Puebla style include Michael Lind's (1994) work documenting its regional development through the systematic study of archaeologically excavated ceramics. Following a suggestion by John Paddock, Lind (1994: 98) noted that Cholula polychrome vessels probably derived from Late Classic Maya polychrome traditions. Dating to roughly 950–1150 CE, the prototypes of Late Postclassic Cholula polychrome vessels commonly display floral motifs (fig. 17A). Based on this research, Lind (1994: 98)

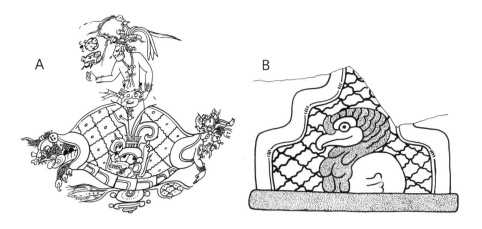

Fig. 1. The netted earth motif. Artwork by Karl Taube. A. Late Classic Maya bowl with earth turtle marked with netted motif. From Taube (1993: 77). B. Hill of the Turkey toponym with netted earth sign, Red Temple, Cacaxtla. Redrawn after Stuart (n.d. [1992]: 131).

concluded that the Olmeca-Xicalanca were indeed involved in the development of the Mixteca-Puebla style, with much of the symbolism deriving from the southern Gulf Coast and Maya lowlands. Pohl also suggested that the Terminal Classic Olmeca-Xicalanca created "variants of Maya polychrome" that gave rise to the Late Postclassic *policromo laca* of Cholula and that the technology for creating Mixteca-Puebla–style pottery also probably derived from the Late Classic Maya (Pohl 2003: 201, 322n2).

With clear evidence of contact with the Classic Maya, Cacaxtla would be a logical place to observe the adoption of Maya motifs into highland Mexican iconography. Indeed, there is a specific motif at Cacaxtla that is found first with the Classic Maya. Occurring initially in Early Classic Maya art, the "earth net" motif appears as wavy, crossed diagonal lines and commonly occurs on water lily pads and turtle shells, the latter being a well-known Maya symbol of the earth (fig. 1A; see Quenon and Le Fort 1997: 897–898). A bench within the Red Temple at Cacaxtla featuring a "Turkey Mountain" toponym (place glyph) has the hill marked with the earth net motif, the earliest known example from highland Mexico (fig. 1B). In Late Postclassic and early colonial highland Mexican manuscripts, this motif marks mountains and the earth (fig. 5D).

As mentioned earlier, the Late Postclassic Tonatiuh probably derived from portrayals of a Maya solar king at Early Postclassic Chichén Itzá. There, he wears a late form of the Jester God diadem and sits on a jaguar throne, both emblems of Classic Maya kings (fig. 3A). In Late Postclassic Mixteca-Puebla–style art of the Borgia Group and Mixtec codices, this jade jewel was reinterpreted as a butterfly head with an upwardly curving proboscis (fig. 3B; for butterfly identification, see Caso 1949: fig. 12; Franco 1961: 198). Although this diadem is most diagnostic of the sun god, it appears also with other beings in the Mixteca-Puebla codices. Similar forms are worn by deities in the Tulúm and Santa Rita murals. Although they may have ultimately derived from the Classic Maya jester god, the late Maya examples are clearly the Mixteca-Puebla–style butterfly jewel (fig. 3C–G). As noted later, a Santa Rita deity wearing this device is probably the youthful sun god (fig. 3D). With its projecting facial beads and down-curving proboscis, the brow piece is notably similar to a butterfly head appearing in a Cholula-style polychrome bowl (see Parsons 1980: no. 159).

Both Aztec and Mixteca-Puebla–style motifs are clearly present in the Late Postclassic Maya lowlands. For example, page 4a of the Dresden Codex portrays Quetzalcoatl in the garb of the Aztec Ehecatl-Quetzalcoatl, which includes a turquoise headdress flanked by a pair of knots (see Taube 1992: 60). This particular headdress is exclusively Aztec and does not appear in Mixteca-Puebla–style art. At Santa Rita, Arlen Chase and Diane Chase discovered a cache containing an effigy vessel of God N emerging from his conch (fig. 2A). According to D. Chase (1985: 112), the figure wears a "horned jaguar head" as his headdress. However, this vessel actually pertains to central Mexican portrayals of legged mollusks, including examples from the Florentine Codex, Late Classic Cacaxtla, and Teotihuacan (fig. 2B–G).

A specific convention appearing in the Borgia, Vaticanus B, and Cospi codices of the Borgia Group is the "swirling grass" commonly seen on green hills and fields as a spiral rimmed by short lines of grass (fig. 4C–D). Although rare in Mixtec art, it also appears in Cholula-style polychrome, including a fragmentary vessel from Ocotelulco, Tlaxcala (fig. 4B). The vessel depicts a schematic dart with the swirling forms, probably a reference to the field of battle. Another example is found on a shield in the Late Postclassic murals from Tehuacán Viejo (fig. 4A). The twisted grass motif also appears in Late Postclassic Maya art of the northern lowlands, and versions can be seen in the thatch of the four temples in the Dresden Codex New Year's pages (fig. 5A). In addition, especially clear examples occur in portrayals of green zoomorphic hills from Structure Q80 at Mayapán (fig. 5B–C). Both the Dresden and Mayapán examples are marked with short, parallel black lines, a trait that also appears with a burning field in the Vaticanus B Codex (fig. 4E). With their serpent maws, the Mayapán hills closely resemble the toponymic sign for Tepetlaoztoc appearing in the early colonial Codex Kingsborough of central Mexico (fig. 5D).

One of the striking traits of the Late Postclassic International style is the elaborate concern with textiles, both as costumes and as sources for designs. In part, this may derive from the great economic importance of textiles as items of tribute and trade during the Late Postclassic period. However, as in the central Andes, light and durable textiles were probably important vehicles

Fig. 2. Portrayals of legged mollusks in ancient Mesoamerica. Artwork by Karl Taube. A. Late Postclassic ceramic figure from Santa Rita, Belize. Redrawn after Chase (1985: fig. 7). B and C. Early colonial portrayals from the Florentine Codex. Redrawn after Sahagún (1950–82, bk. 11: figs. 200, 198). D and E. Terminal Classic depictions from Structure A, Cacaxtla. Redrawn after Matos Moctezuma (1987: 104, 100). F. Early Classic mollusk emerging from bivalve, Teotihuacan. Redrawn after Miller (1973: fig. 128). G. Legged *Spondylus* creature, detail of Teotihuacan-style vessel. Redrawn after Bolz (1975: plate 31).

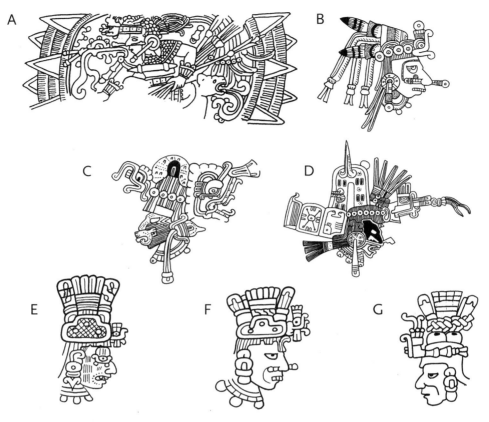

Fig. 3. The jade butterfly brow piece in International-style art. Artwork by Karl Taube. A. Early Postclassic sun god wearing Jester God brow piece of Maya kings, Chichén Itzá. From Taube (1992: fig. 77e). B. Tonatiuh with butterfly brow piece, Borgia 70. C. Figure with butterfly brow piece and plumed serpent at back of head, Santa Rita. Redrawn after Gann (1900: plate 29). D. Probable Tonatiuh figure with butterfly brow piece; compare with example B. Redrawn after Gann (1900: plate 29). E. Chak Chel with butterfly brow piece, Mural 1, Tulúm Structure 5. Redrawn after Miller (1982: plate 28); F and G. Portrayals of Chak Chel with butterfly brow piece, Tulúm Structure 16. From Miller (1982: plate 37).

for transferring artistic styles and religious practices and beliefs. In Peru, it has been suggested that the complex iconography and ritual of Early Horizon Chavín was brought to the southern coast by painted textiles hung on walls of temple shrines (Burger 1992: 198; 1996: 76–77; Sawyer 1972). Likewise, painted textiles were an important vehicle for the dissemination of the International style in Postclassic Mesoamerica.

In his initial study of the International style, Nicholson (1960: 614) notes that, among "the most frequent and diagnostic symbol groups is the row of

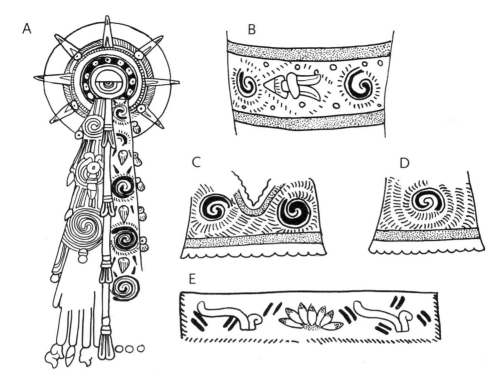

Fig. 4. The swirling grass motif in Mixteca-Puebla–style art. Artwork by Karl Taube. A. From band denoting *tlachinolli,* "fire," Shield 4 of Tehuacán Viejo mural. Redrawn after Sisson and Lilly (1994: fig. 5). B. With schematic dart, detail of Cholula-style vessel from Ocotelulco. Redrawn after Neff et al. (1994: fig. 13). C and D. On hill signs, Borgia 54 and 49. E. Field with flames, flint blades, and thick diagonal bands, Codex Vaticanus B 69.

alternating skulls and crossed bones," often co-occurring with hearts, severed hands, extruded eyeballs, and other emblems of death and gore. In bas-relief carvings and mural paintings from Tenochtitlan, Tenayuca, Tizatlan, and Ocotelulco, these elements are edged with a clear textile motif of cords with crenelated edgings (fig. 6F; see Caso 1967: 135–136; Contreras Martínez 1994: figs. 8–9; Mirambell Silva 1996: 117; Villagra Caleti 1971: fig. 29). Similarly bordered textiles with motifs of death and sacrifice appear in the Borgia Group codices (fig. 6A–B). The early colonial Tudela Codex portrays an old woman with such a cloth held behind her back with her outstretched arms (fig. 6C). The woman is labeled as a *vieja hechicera,* or "old spell-caster," recalling the well-known role of Tezcatlipoca as patron of sorcerers. In addition, Chak Chel, the aged Maya goddess of midwives, divination, and curing, appears as early as the Classic period wearing a black dress or skirt of crossed bones, eyes, and other elements

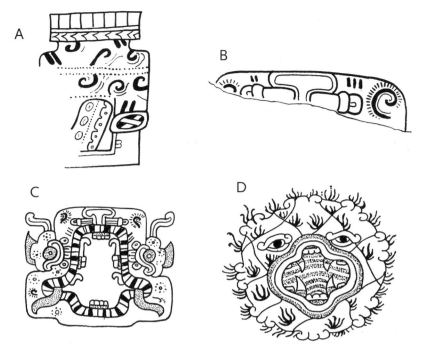

Fig. 5. The swirling grass motif in Late Postclassic Yucatán. Artwork by Karl Taube. A. Temple with thatch marked with grass motif and thick diagonal bands, Dresden 28. B. Detail of Mayapán zoomorphic hill with grass motif and thick bands. Redrawn after Barrera Rubio et al. (2001: fig. 11). C. Zoomorphic hill cave with swirling grass motif, Mayapán Structure Q80. Redrawn after Barrera Rubio and Peraza (2001: fig. 14). D. Zoomorphic hill cave, Codex Kingsborough, fol. 2, fig. B.

(fig. 6D). In fact, this complex of death and sacrifice emblems was fully articulated among the Classic Maya (fig. 6E), and this could well be where this "diagnostic symbol group" of the Aztec and Mixteca-Puebla styles originates.

In addition to the rope and crenelated textile edging, Mixteca-Puebla–style murals feature other clear evocations of textile patterns. The central altar portraying the House of Flints at Ocotelulco depicts textile designs portraying a tie-dye technique documented for the Aztec by Patricia Anawalt (1990). In addition, the lower portions of all four murals of Altar B at Tizatlan portray finely woven textile borders (fig. 6G; see Mirambell Silva 1996: 118–120). The frequent painting of textile motifs on temple benches and altars suggests that such murals constitute more permanent renderings of textiles commonly hung in shrines and temples. Frances Berdan (personal communication, 2006) called my attention to a relevant passage in the Florentine Codex describing an elaborately painted textile placed in front of the image of Huitzilopochtli (Sahagún 1950–82, bk. 2: 72):

Fig. 6. The skull and crossed bones textile motif. Artwork by Karl Taube. A. Textile with severed hand and mirror hanging from arm of Tezcatlipoca, Borgia 17. B. Textile with skull, crossed bones, and severed hand, Codex Vaticanus B 7. C. Woman with crossed bone and skull textile labeled as *vieja hechizera*, Codex Tudela 50r D. Late Classic Maya Chak Chel with textile marked with crossed bones and eyes. From Taube (1992: fig. 51c). E. Fan with eyeballs, crossed bones, and severed hands and feet, detail of Late Classic Maya vase. Redrawn after photo by Justin Kerr [K3924]). F. Mural of crossed bones and skulls with textile border, Tenayuca. Redrawn after Villagra Caleti (1971: fig. 29). G. Mural with lower register of textile elements, Tizatlan Altar B. Redrawn after Villagra Caleti (1971: fig. 28).

> And the cape which they lay covered, which lay spread before him,
> was designed with severed heads, the palms of hands, hip bones,
> ribs, tibias, lower arm bones, footprints. With them it was painted.

Although this account does not mention how this mantle was spread, Durán (1971: 188) describes an altar textile within the warrior House of the Eagles, those destined for the solar paradise:

> Above an altar there hung on the wall a painting done with brush on cloth: the image of the sun: This figure was in the form of a butterfly with wings and around it a golden circle emitting radiant beams and glowing lines.

Both accounts explicitly describe the textiles as painted rather than woven. Not only does this closely resemble the medium of mural painting, but painted rather than woven mantles could more readily convey complex imagery, such as appears in screenfold codices. Two International-style painted textiles from the cave at La Garrafa, Chiapas are probably rare examples of the cloths that would have ornamented temple altars and shrines (see Navarrete 1996: figs. 41–42).

Flower Symbolism and the International Style

Flowers are prominent in the art and architecture of Tulúm, where large blossoms with radiating petals ornament the cornices of buildings and the bodies of serpents (fig. 7). In many examples, a pair of outwardly turning volutes emerge and descend from the center of the blossom (fig. 7C–E). The symmetrical volutes represent aroma and commonly emerge from flowers in ancient Mesoamerican art, including that of the Classic Maya and Teotihuacan, as well as the Late Postclassic Mixtec and Aztec (fig. 8). Symmetrical aroma volutes are especially common in Classic Maya art (fig. 9A–B), a convention that can be traced back to the Late Formative period, ca. 500–100 BCE (fig. 9C–D, 10A–B). A ceramic sherd from El Mirador dating to the third century BCE portrays an early form of the day sign Ajaw, equivalent to the central Mexican day name Xochitl, or "flower," with the same aroma volutes (fig. 9D). David Stuart (n.d. [1992]) notes that the Maya day sign also denotes a blossom, and the recently discovered Late Preclassic murals of San Bartolo provide considerable support for this identification (fig. 9E). In one scene, a snake exhales an Ajaw sign from his mouth, an early version of the breath blossoms commonly found in Classic and Postclassic Maya iconography. The bifurcated breath and fragrance motif is found as early as the Middle Formative Olmec (fig. 9F–G). In ancient Mesoamerican art, earspools are often flowers exhaling breath and moisture (fig. 9G; see Taube 2005b).

Among both the Olmec and later Classic Maya, breath is commonly rendered as a flower or jade hovering before the nose (Houston and Taube 2000; Ketunnen 2005; Taube 2004a: 72; 2005b). This convention continues in Late Postclassic Maya art (fig. 10). At Tulúm, breath blossoms are limited to beings with zoomorphic snouts, such as Chaak, K'awiil, and serpents. However, a roughly contemporaneous mural from Xelhá depicts the Maya sun god exhaling an elaborate floral breath scroll from his nostrils (fig. 10C), and several human figures in the Santa Rita murals display prominent breath blossoms (fig. 10A–B; note that flowers emanate not only from the face of the figure in 10A but from his headdress medallion as well). The broad headband and medallion of this figure (fig. 10A) indicate that he may be the Maya wind god, as is also suggested by his flattened, conical hat, which resembles that worn by the highland Mexican wind god Ehecatl-Quetzalcoatl, or 9 Wind to the Mixtec.

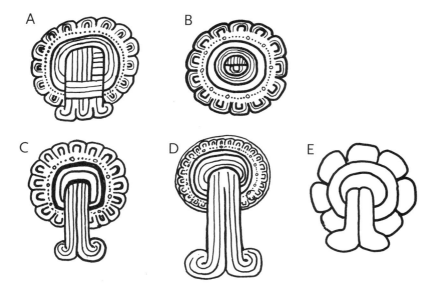

Fig. 7. Portrayals of flowers at Tulúm. Artwork by Karl Taube. A. Blossom with central protruding bud, detail of mural from Structure 16. Redrawn after Miller (1982: plate 37). B. Flower with central eye. Redrawn after Miller (1982: plate 37). C. Flower emanating bifurcated breath scrolls, Structure 5. Redrawn after Miller (1982: plate 28). D. Blossom with breath scrolls, exterior of Structure 5. Redrawn after Miller (1982: plate 25). E. Blossom exhaling breath scrolls, detail of stucco façade, Structure 16. Redrawn after Miller (1982: plate 31).

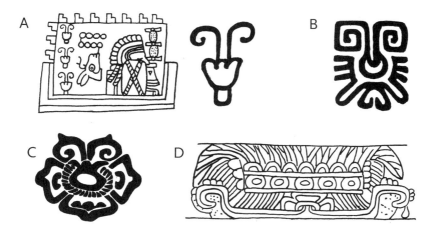

Fig. 8. Highland Mexican depictions of aromatic flowers. Artwork by Karl Taube. A. Late Postclassic Mixtec portrayal of tomb of Lord 8 Deer with flowers on wall, Codex Bodley 14. B. Aztec ceramic seal of flower exhaling bifurcated breath elements. Redrawn after Enciso (1953: 14: 1). C. Aztec seal portraying aroma as sound volutes. Redrawn after Enciso (1953: 43: 1). D. Early Classic Teotihuacan vase depicting floral face with scrolls of aroma or sound. From Taube (2001a: fig. 82e).

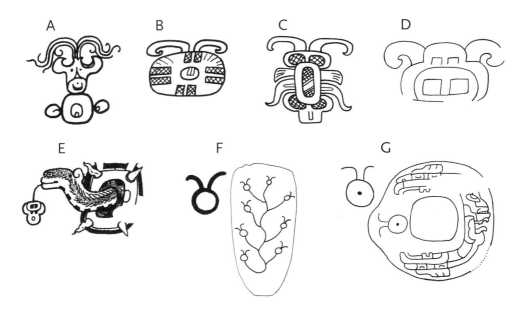

Fig. 9. Aromatic flowers in Maya and Olmec art. Artwork by Karl Taube. A. Late Classic blossom exhaling breath volutes, Lápida de Creación, Palenque. From Houston and Taube (2000: fig. 5g). B. Early Classic flower with bifurcated elements. From Schele and Miller (1986: 309). C. Late Preclassic flower with breath scrolls, detail of incised stone vessel. Redrawn after Kerr (1994: 544 [K4480]). D. Early floral Ajaw sign with bifurcated breath elements; detail of vessel sherd, El Mirador. Redrawn after Fields and Reents-Budet (2005: cat. 24). E. Late Preclassic serpent exhaling Ajaw sign breath blossom; detail of North Wall mural, San Bartolo. From Saturno et al. (2005: fig. 10a). F. Flowering plant with bifurcated breath on Olmec-style celt attributed to Chalcatzingo. From Taube (2001a: fig. 84). G. Olmec jade earspool with floral breath element, La Venta. From Taube (2001a: fig. 81).

Another deity displays a breath element of quetzal plumes emerging from a flower or earspool, a convention also known for the Late Classic Maya (fig. 10B) (see Taube 2005b: fig. 19G). The breath blossoms at Santa Rita clearly derive from Classic Maya traditions and are generally absent from Teotihuacan and Aztec and Mixteca-Puebla–style art.

The earspools worn by the deities at Santa Rita closely correspond to Classic Maya symbolism pertaining to jade and flowers. Classic Maya earspools are commonly depicted as flowers, and many of the Santa Rita examples display prominent petaled rims (fig. 10A–B). In addition, the earpiece of one of the figures is rendered as a flower in profile (fig. 3C) (Quirarte 1982: 52). In this example and others, the central projecting bead is long and flexible, despite the fact that it is probably of jade (figs. 3C, 10A–B). Columns from the Late Classic

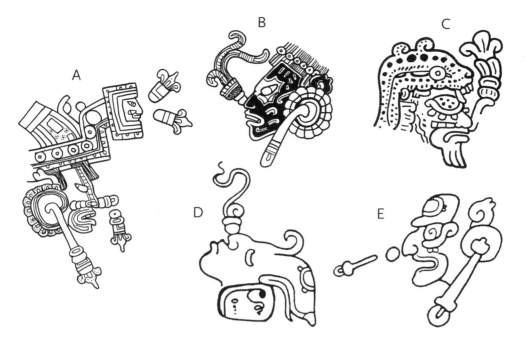

Fig. 10. Floral breath elements in Late Postclassic Maya iconography. Artwork by Karl Taube.
A. Possible Maya wind god with floral breath signs before face and mask plaque in headdress,
Santa Rita. Redrawn after Gann (1900: plate 29). B. Floral breath element with probable quetzal
plumes, Santa Rita. Redrawn after Gann (1900: plate 30). C. Sun god with floral breath scroll,
detail of Xelhá mural. Redrawn after Miller (1982: plate 46). D. Severed head of maize god with
breath element, Dresden 34a. E. Itzamnaaj exhaling breath element, Dresden 9b.

center of Santa Bárbara, Yucatán, portray the central earspool element extending almost the entire length of the torso (see Stanton et al. 2003: figs. 8–10).
Although rare in central Mexico, this convention occurs with the Maya-style
dancing figure from the south jamb of Structure A at Cacaxtla (see Matos
Moctezuma 1987: 123–124). Rather than being realistic portrayals of extremely
long, sinuous beads, such devices underscore the symbolic meaning of the central bead—as the "breath" of the floral earspool (Taube 2005b).

An emerging serpent often embodies the central breath element of Classic
Maya earspools (fig. 11A–C), a convention that continued into the Late Postclassic period (Taube 2005b). In an earspool worn by Chaak in the Dresden Codex, the serpent undulates from the central projecting bead, clearly indicating
that this creature is an idealized portrayal of breath (fig. 11F). At Santa Rita,
a large serpent emerges out of the floral earspool of K'awiil, a motif deriving
from Classic Maya conventions (fig. 11E). A serpent also hangs from the ear of

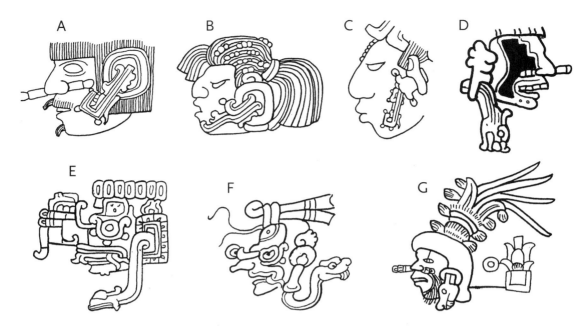

Fig. 11. Serpents emerging from earspools. Artwork by Karl Taube. A–C. Late Classic Maya portrayals of bracket-nosed serpent heads in earspools. From Taube (2005b: fig. 14d–f). D. Deity with serpent passing through ear, detail of mural from Tulúm Structure 16. Redrawn after Miller (1982: plate 37). E. K'awiil with serpent earspool, Santa Rita. Redrawn after Gann (1900: plate 29). F. Chaak with serpent emerging from earspool bead, Dresden 35b. G. Quetzalcoatl with serpent earspool, Codex Telleriano-Remensis, fol. 22r.

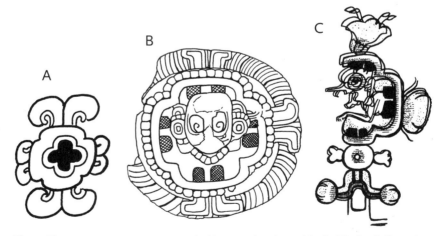

Fig. 12. Flowers as caves or passageways in Mesoamerica. Artwork by Karl Taube. A. Flower in form of quatrefoil cave with bifurcated breath elements, detail of Late Classic Maya vase. From Houston and Taube (2000: fig. 5h). B. Probable skeletal insect emerging from quatrefoil flower, Toniná. Redrawn after Yadeun (2001: 46). C. Skeletal insect in quatrefoil flower, detail of mural from House E, Palenque. Redrawn after Seler (1977: fig. 137).

a deity in Mural 1 of Tulúm Structure 16, although no earspool is present (fig. 11D). Serpent earspools also appear in Aztec and Mixteca-Puebla art, especially with Quetzalcoatl and Tlaloc—gods of rain and fertility (Taube 2005b: 43–44). During the presentation of deity costumes to Hernán Cortés in 1519, one of the items the Aztec included with the regalia of Tlaloc were serpent earspools, called *chalchiuhcoanacoch* (Sahagún 1950–1982, bk. 12: 12). The accompanying Spanish text describes them as "unas orejeras de *chalchíhuitl* anchas que tenía a dentro unas culebritas de chalchiuhuites" (some wide earrings of *chalchihuitl* that had inside some little serpents of jade) (Sahagún 2000: 1168). These Aztec serpent earspools probably derive from more ancient Classic Maya conventions. It is fitting that both Quetzalcoatl and Tlaloc wear such earspools, as the rain-bringing spring and summer winds derive from the eastern Maya realm.

Serpent earspools embody the Mesoamerican concept of flowers as cave-like portals or passageways (Taube 2001a: 109). In Classic Maya art, flowers frequently appear as the cave quatrefoil, at times exhaling volutes of aroma (fig. 12A–C). Creatures often emerge out of the blossoms, including skeletal beings that are probably Maya interpretations of bees, butterflies, and other insects (fig. 12B–C). In Mixteca-Puebla art, birds, mammals, gods, and ancestors may be seen inhabiting or exiting flowers.

The Sun and the Floral Paradise

In ancient Mesoamerica, the sun was often portrayed as a bellicose being ruling the afterlife floral realm of the brave and virtuous. Among the Classic Maya, the sun god was a deity of war and sacrifice (Taube 2001b: 275–276). The stairway of Copán Structure 10L-16 portrays the founder K'inich Yax K'uk' Mo' apotheosized as the sun god engaged in a war dance within a solar shield (Taube 2004b). Ek' Balam Stela 1 similarly depicts the deceased king U Kit Kan Leek in a solar disk wielding a shield and a bicephalic centipede lance (see Grube et al. 2003: fig. 55).

Late Postclassic Maya art also portrays the sun deity as a war god. According to Landa (Tozzer 1941: 144), war dances were performed in honor of the sun god K'inich Ajaw during celebrations of the Muluk New Year. At Xelhá, a Late Postclassic mural depicts the bearded sun god wielding a shield and lance (fig. 13A), and he also holds a lance on page 90 of the Madrid Codex (fig. 13B). In addition, the wooden handle of a flint sacrificial dagger portrays a descending deity with a beard and fangs (fig. 13C). Although it has been attributed to the Aztec or Mixtec (Couch 1988: 51), it is more likely from the northern Maya lowlands. The beard and fangs are common traits of the Late Postclassic Maya sun god. In the west wall mural at Santa Rita, one of the severed heads held by the dancing figure is the bearded sun god with prominent fangs (see Gann 1900: plate 31; Taube 1992: fig. 22F). Page 10 of the Nuttall Codex depicts the Mixtec

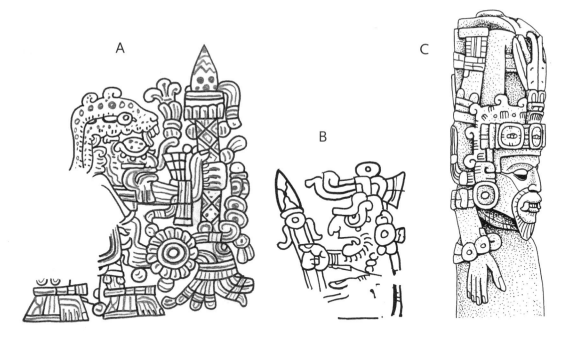

Fig. 13. The Late Postclassic Maya sun god. Artwork by Karl Taube. A. Bearded sun god with shield and lance, detail of Xelhá mural. Redrawn after Miller (1982: plate 46). B. Bearded sun god with lance, Madrid 90d. C. Diving sun god on wooden handle of sacrificial knife. Note beard, fangs, and floral *k'in* signs in headdress. Redrawn after Couch (1988: no. 54).

sun god with fangs, but this is notably rare and may well derive from Maya influence. A turquoise mosaic mask in the collections of Dumbarton Oaks, attributed to Chiapas, also portrays the bearded sun god with inlaid jaguar fangs in the corners of the mouth (fig. 14). The mask originally had a beard and brow fashioned from human hair (now largely missing). Rendered with stepped frets on the cheeks, this mask is a rare portrayal of the bearded Maya sun god depicted in the International style.

Among the ancient Maya, flowers were closely related to the sun. As noted by Eric Thompson (1950: 142), the Maya solar *k'in* sign is based on a four-petaled flower. At times, *k'in* signs can appear within flowers in Classic Maya art (fig. 15A). Thompson also mentioned that the Chilam Balam of Chumayel refers to the sun within a flower: "four-fold [or four-branched] was the plate of the flower, and Ah Kin Xocbiltun [the sun god] was set in the center." The Classic period logograph for flower, or *nik*, has a form resembling but not identical to the conventional Classic *k'in* sign (fig. 15B). The Late Classic Maya increasingly began using the floral *nik* as *k'in* (fig. 15C–D), stemming from a reinterpretation rather

Fig. 14. Turquoise mosaic mask of probable sun god with beard and jaguar fangs. Dumbarton Oaks, Pre-Columbian Collection, Washington, D.C.

than a misidentification of the four-lobed *k'in* glyph. Not only does the Classic solar sign portray a flower, but Late Postclassic floral *nik/k'in* signs in the Dresden Codex are surrounded by explicit flowers (fig. 15D and 17E). The appearance of flowers with the Maya solar sign is entirely consistent with the Flower World complex identified by Hill (1992).

In the International style of the northern Maya lowlands, there is another solar motif that is distinct from the floral *k'in* glyph. The Santa Rita murals portray solar cartouches displaying four solar rays with outflaring bases and four jade signs (fig. 16A–B), which clearly relate to Mixteca-Puebla and Aztec portrayals of the sun. In its most basic form, this motif has four jades and solar rays arranged around a central solar disc (fig. 16C). One of the earliest known examples of this International-style form may be seen in Late Classic polychrome murals from Las Higueras, Veracruz. The floor of the eastern door of the Building of the Paintings features a massive sun sign rimmed with red and green plumes and circular blue disks at the intercardinal points, early versions of the jades placed in the same position in later International-style art (fig. 16D).

Fig. 15. The Maya floral *k'in* sign. Artwork by Karl Taube. A. Four-petaled *k'in* sign within blossom, detail of Late Classic vase. Redrawn after Kerr (1997: 788 [K5436]). B. Floral *nik* glyph appearing in phrase *ah sak nikte'*. Redrawn after Kerr (1990: 276 [K2730]). C. Floral *nik* sign serving as *k'in* glyph on sacrificial vessel, detail of Late Classic Chamá-style vessel. Redrawn after Coe (1978: no. 13). D. Solar sign formed of *nik* version of *k'in* glyph with four blossoms rendered in profile, Dresden 52b.

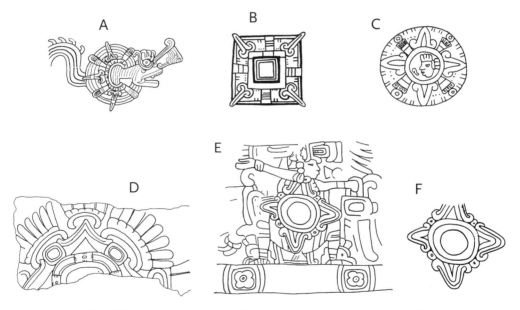

Fig. 16. The solar sign composed of four rays and jades. Artwork by Karl Taube. A. Plumed serpent passing through solar disk, Santa Rita. Redrawn after Gann (1900: plate 29). B. Solar sign with solar rays separated by probable jade elements, Santa Rita. Redrawn after Gann (1900: plate 30). C. Head of sun god in solar disk, Codex Huamantla. D. Late Classic mural of solar disk with rays and probable jade disks, Las Higueras, Veracruz. Note Maya *nik* elements in interior circle. Redrawn after Morante López (2005: 81). E. Figure with solar disk on abdomen, Las Higueras. Note probable versions of Maya *k'in* signs in band below. Redrawn after Morante López (2005: 99). F. Detail of solar disk. Redrawn after Morante López (2005: 99).

In addition, the inner portion of the disk includes the Maya *k'in* glyph, the Late Classic reinterpretation of the *nik* sign. The eastern doorway jambs feature squatting solar figures atop a band containing four-petaled forms of Maya *k'in* signs (fig. 16F). As in the central sun disk on the floor, circular beads separate the rays, probably an early version of the jade and solar rays surrounding International-style forms of the sun disk.

In Late Postclassic highland Mexico, solar-related images frequently appear in the interior of fine polychrome bowls that were probably used in feasting events. One example from central Veracruz has the sun rimmed by an outer border exhibiting jade bead assemblages, probable quetzals, pairs of maguey spine bloodletters, and possible spearthrowers, all associated with the realm of the sun (fig. 17B–C). Beautiful jades and exotic birds relate not only to this paradise but also to war and sacrifice, with the sun being the preeminent "blood drinker." Of special interest is the central disk, containing the visage of a Veracruz sun god surrounded by quadripartite solar rays and flowers (fig. 17D). In addition, the four flowers and the rim band are interspersed with very thin, U-shaped elements, or a pair of parallel lines, which in Mixteca-Puebla and Aztec-style imagery denote solar brilliance (fig. 19B–D). The roughly contemporaneous Dresden Codex also portrays images of the sun with four flowers at the intercardinal points to denote the sun in the realm of Flower World (figs. 15D, 17E). A fragmentary bowl from Cholula probably originally displayed an Early Postclassic version of a central floral element surrounded by four blossoms (fig. 17A). Although the pointed elements near the rim resemble solar rays, their asymmetrical sides suggest that they are more likely maguey spines, as appear in later Mixteca-Puebla–style art (fig. 19C). The other rim element, a flower in profile, closely resembles the Maya Ajaw sign with rudimentary eyes and a mouth (fig. 17A; cf. fig. 9A).

A vessel from a royal Zapotec tomb at Zaachila features a hummingbird drinking from a floral bowl with imagery similar to that appearing on the exterior rims of many Mixteca-Puebla polychrome bowls—a lower segmented portion with, above it, upward-looking heads interspersed with the same thin U-shaped elements commonly found with solar disks (fig. 18). Clearly, the poised bird denotes that the solar bowl is an open flower. For Mixteca-Puebla and Aztec-style polychromes, the rims are usually flowers with open, petaled rims, but more important, such rims vividly display the essential attributes and inhabitants of the floral, solar paradise, which were first described by Hermann Beyer (1969). Beyer called attention to jade and solar rays and the exotic *coxcoxtli* or great curassow (*Crax rubra*), which is native to the Gulf Coast and Maya region, recalling the eastern locale of the quetzal (e.g., fig. 19C, far right) (Howell and Webb 1995: 223–224). He also illustrated other vessel rims having solar rays, jades, forms of the U-shaped "brilliance" element, and explicit flowers

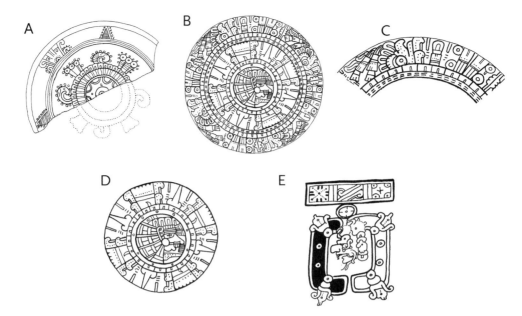

Fig. 17. Floral and solar imagery in Postclassic Mesoamerica. Artwork by Karl Taube.
A. Fragmentary bowl with central blossom, Early Postclassic Cholula. Note probable original design of four surrounding blossoms in profile. Redrawn after Lind (1994: fig. 2c). B. Late Postclassic central Veracruz bowl with celestial solar and floral motifs. Redrawn after Uriarte (1998: cat. 220). C. Detail of celestial rim band with quetzals, jade, maguey bloodletters, and other elements. Redrawn after Uriarte (1998: cat. 220). D. Detail of central solar disk with four blossoms and solar rays. Redrawn after Uriarte (1998: cat. 220). E. Maya solar sign with head of sun god surrounded by four blossoms in profile, Dresden 56a.

Fig. 18. Hummingbird poised on rim of bowl symbolizing an open flower. Artwork by Karl Taube. Redrawn after Paddock (1966: plate 18).

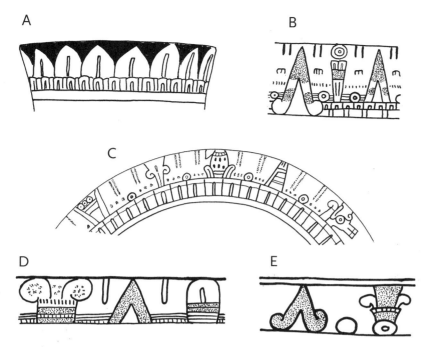

Fig. 19. Floral rims on Mixteca-Puebla–style vessels. Artwork by Karl Taube. A. Rim as open flower. Redrawn after Lind (1994: fig. 15e). B. Rim with petaled band, jade sign, and solar rays. Redrawn after Beyer (1969: fig. 43). C. Petaled rim with flowers, maize, maguey spines, *coxcoxtli* bird, and probable spearthrowers. Redrawn after Parsons (1980: cat. 159). D. Rim with flowers, solar rays, and jade signs. Redrawn after Beyer (1969: fig. 48). E. Rim with solar rays and flowers. Redrawn after Beyer (1969: fig. 45).

(fig. 19C–E), whereas Lind (1994) identified examples of Mixteca-Puebla–style polychrome bowls in the Late Postclassic codices of the Borgia Group. These bowls are portrayed as massive, open blossoms offering views of the solar Flower World. They typically have yellow, petaled rims—yellow being the color used for the day sign Flower and blossoms in general in Mixteca-Puebla–style art (fig. 20A–E). The widespread motif of quetzal birds and butterflies descending to such vessels identify them as cave-like floral passageways for birds, butterflies, and other celestial spirit beings (fig. 20F).

Identical passages in the Borgia and Vaticanus B codices portray Mixteca-Puebla polychrome bowls placed lip to lip as cache offerings. The Borgia example features five jades and a great maize plant surging from the center of the lid (fig. 21B). In the Vaticanus B scene (fig. 21C), a plant sprouts from a lid ornamented with signs of jade and preciousness. On pages 17 and 18 of the Vaticanus B Codex, world directional trees feature cosmic versions of the same

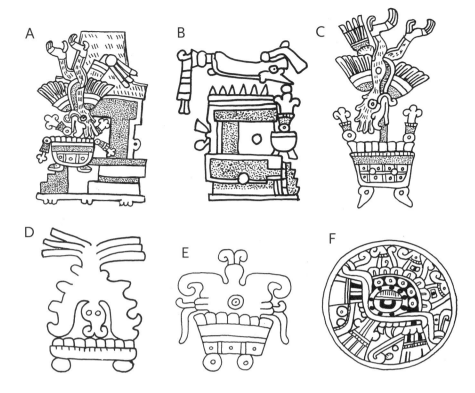

Fig. 20. Portrayals of bowls as open flowers in Mixteca-Puebla–style art. Artwork by Karl Taube. A. Quetzal descending to petaled bowl ornamented with blossom, Borgia 1. B. Hummingbird sipping flower in bowl, Codex Cospi 2. C. Quetzal sipping blood from floral bowl, Borgia 3. D. Butterfly descending to floral bowl, Codex Vaticanus B 4. E. Fiery butterfly emerging from floral bowl, Borgia 6. F. Butterfly head in center of Mixeca-Puebla–style bowl. Redrawn after Solís (2004: cat. 152).

motif, with three of the four trees growing out of the center of inverted Mixteca-Puebla–style bowls (fig. 21D). The upper inverted lid of cache vessels represents the sky (see also Tozzer's [1907: 71] description of the Lacandón Maya practice of placing an inverted ceramic bowl atop a vessel of burning incense to collect black soot symbolic of the rain clouds). In the Maya region, this symbolism is probably of great antiquity. The interior of an Early Classic cache vessel lid from Caracol portrays the Principal Bird Deity flying, with the opposing basal interior featuring a probable portrayal of the severed, lifeless head of the maize god (see Chase and Chase 1987: fig. 41a–c). As Chase and Chase (1987: 46–48) note, the lid and basal scenes refer to the sky and netherworld, respectively.

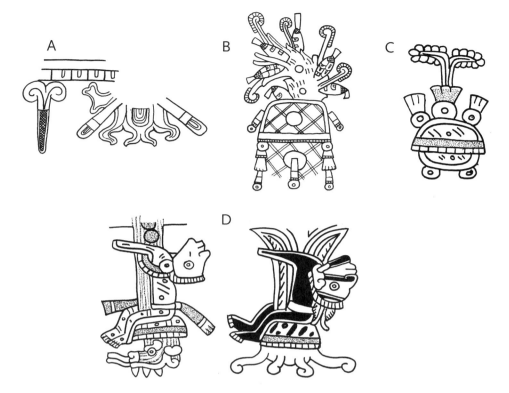

Fig. 21. Inverted bowls and celestial symbolism in International-style art. Artwork by Karl Taube. A. Skyband with petaled edge, Santa Rita. Redrawn after Gann (1900: plate 31). B. Cache vessels with sprouting maize, Borgia 7. C. Cache vessels with sprouting plants, Codex Vaticanus B 7. D. World trees sprouting from inverted bowls, Codex Vaticanus B 17–18.

The quadripartite arrangements seen in many Late Preclassic and Classic Maya cache vessels relate to the basic cosmological meaning of the inverted bowls and world trees such as appear in the Vaticanus B Codex scenes—the division of the four world directions. An especially striking Aztec parallel is the stone box from Tizapán containing a central greenstone image of the maize goddess Chicomecoatl and four directional rain gods hovering above in the interior of the lid (see Solís 2004: no. 86). As on the Caracol lid, the four Tlalocs denote the celestial realm, here as rain falling on the maize goddess below. A pair of large Aztec cache vessels from Chamber 3 of the Templo Mayor feature dual images of Tlaloc and Chicomecoatl on opposite sides (see López Luján 1994: 322–323; López Portillo et al. 1981: 244–245). Both effigy jars contained vast amounts of carved greenstone. One also features a ceramic lid with Tlaloc on the exterior (see López Luján 1998: fig. 15.9); he again inhabits the heavens as he pours rainwater from an inverted ceramic bowl held in both hands.

A

B

C

Fig. 22. Mixtec portrayals of gods and spirits in celestial floral paradise. Details of three carved bones from Tomb 7, Monte Albán. Artwork by Karl Taube. A. Creatures emerging from flowers hanging from skyband. Note flower held by central figure. Redrawn after Caso (1969: fig. 219). B. Heads attached to blossoms in skyband. Redrawn after Caso (1969: fig. 240). C. Figures emerging from flowers. Redrawn after Caso (1969: fig. 177).

The rim of the Aztec lid is segmented with a repetitive, petal-like motif, similar to examples appearing in Late Postclassic skybands and to the aforementioned cache lids in the Borgia and Vaticanus B codices (fig. 21B–D). When fine Mixteca-Puebla polychrome vessels are inverted, many rims exhibit explicit skybands, with solar rays, jade, flowers, and celestial motifs (fig. 19B–E). With its petaled edge and solar rays, the skyband at Santa Rita is very similar to the inverted rims of Mixteca-Puebla–style bowls (fig. 21A). Examples of similar skybands are found on carved bones from Tomb 7 at Monte Albán (fig. 22A–B). Along with petaled edging, one bone also exhibits solar rays (fig. 22B), and the heads of humans, serpents, precious birds, butterflies, eagles, and other beings appear on the skybands in both examples, recalling similarly placed heads on the rims of Mixteca-Puebla–style bowls (figs. 17B–C, 18, and 19C). The heads on the carved bones emerge from or are placed on blossoms as celestial denizens of the solar Flower World.

Quetzalcoatl and the Plumed Serpent

Among the most striking deities in the Santa Rita murals is an old god holding a feather-crested serpent staff (plate 3). Long ago, Gann (1900: 668) identified this being as Quetzalcoatl, due to the accompanying serpents with feather crests. In addition, there are other more subtle but perhaps also more significant indications of his identity. A descending male quetzal, identified by his feather crest and long undulating tail, appears in the lower portion of his headdress (fig. 23A). Classic Maya feather headdresses often feature descending quetzals and other birds, with their tails erect and wings stretched outward to the sides, indicating that the Santa Rita example derived from Classic Maya traditions (fig. 23B–D). However, the Aztec also had the *quetzalpanecáyotl* quetzal plume headdress, such as was presented to Cortés as part of the godly costume of Quetzalcoatl (Sahagún 1950–1982, bk. 12: 11; see Aguilera 2003). An example of such a headdress has been preserved in the Museum für Völkerkunde in Vienna. Although little mentioned, accounts between 1596 and 1730 consistently note that it had a "golden beak" (Feest 1990: 10). The only place for such an item would be the central brow, suggesting that it portrays a descending quetzal with outstretched wings and a vertical tail—essentially the same headdress as the Santa Rita example.

According to the Florentine Codex, a turquoise, serpent-headed spearthrower was another insignia of Quetzalcoatl presented to Cortés (Sahagún 1950–1982, bk. 12: 11). The serpent held in the hand of the Santa Rita figure has a forwardly projecting hook at the tip of the snout, denoting a serpent spearthrower (plate 3). A shallow Cholula polychrome bowl portrays an interwoven rattlesnake with a similar hook on its snout (see Beyer 1969: 451). Because the serpent is atop a prominent dart, it is probably also a symbolic spearthrower.

Fig. 23. Ancient Maya portrayals of headdresses as descending birds. Artwork by Karl Taube. A. Quetzal headdress worn by Quetzalcoatl in the Santa Rita mural. B. Early Classic headdress in form of descending bird, Quiriguá Monument 26. Redrawn after Sharer (1990: fig. 47). C. Woman wearing headdress as a descending quetzal, detail of Late Classic vase. Redrawn after Kerr (1990: 255 [K2695]). D. Headdress as descending quetzal, Naranjo Stela 8. Redrawn after Graham and von Euw (1975: 27).

Much as Gann (1900) originally argued, the Santa Rita figure is Quetzalcoatl and displays some of the same regalia that was presented to Cortés when he arrived on the eastern shores of the Aztec Empire.

In Late Postclassic Maya art, plumed serpents commonly display feathered crests on their brows (fig. 24), in contrast to roughly contemporaneous Aztec and Mixteca-Puebla representations of plumed serpents, which tend to have quetzal plumes along their faces and bodies rather than cranial crests. Nonetheless, both the lowland Maya and highland Mexican creatures are related beings, serpentine embodiments of rain-bringing wind who exhale flowers and quetzal plumes as their precious breath. At Tulúm, they often exhale floral breath elements, a theme that also appears in a Late Postclassic Tikal graffito of a serpent with a feather crest (cf. fig. 24A and H). The convention of plumes emerging from the snouts of plumed serpents identifies their feathered bodies as symbols of breath and wind (fig. 24D–E; Taube 2001a: 121).

Feather-crested serpents are not limited to the Late Postclassic but are also common in Classic Maya iconography and frequently appear with flowers

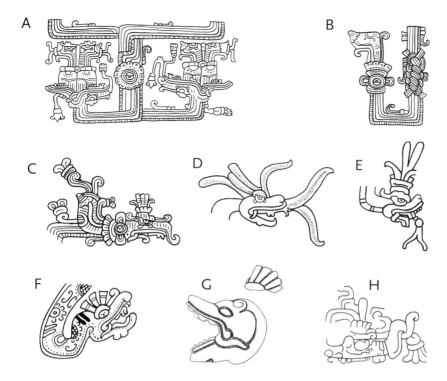

Fig. 24. Plumed serpents in Late Postclassic Maya art. Artwork by Karl Taube. A. Pair of intertwined serpents with flowers on their bodies, Tulúm Structure 16. Redrawn after Miller (1982: plate 37). B. Tail of serpent with blossom, Tulúm Structure 16. Redrawn after Miller (1982: plate 37). C. Serpent with feather crest, Tulúm Structure 5. Redrawn after Miller (1982: plate 28). D. Feather-crested serpent exhaling pair of quetzal plumes, Tulúm Structure 1. Redrawn after Lothrop (1924: plate 4). E. Plumed serpent exhaling bead and pair of plumes, Tulúm Structure 1. Redrawn after Lothrop (1924: plate 4). F. Serpent with feather crest, Madrid 15. G. Balustrade of serpent with feather crest. Redrawn after Gallareta and Taube (2005: fig. 6.6a). H. Tikal graffito of feather-crested serpent with flower at tip of snout. Redrawn after Trik and Kampen (1983: fig. 17a).

(fig. 25). Examples may be seen at Kabah and Sayil (fig. 25A–B), and a crested serpent pair flanks the doorway maw of Hochob Structure 2, much as if they are the breath of the zoomorphic facade (fig. 25C). Breath signs tip their tails (also seen with the Sayil examples). At Hochob, the tail elements are flower and jade signs; feathered serpents with floral tails also appear in the Pyramid of the Plumed Serpents at Xochicalco and in the roughly contemporaneous murals at Cacaxtla. At Cacaxtla, the tail blossoms are the same yellow flowers found in the North Jamb mural of Structure A (see Matos Moctezuma 1987: 109, 113).

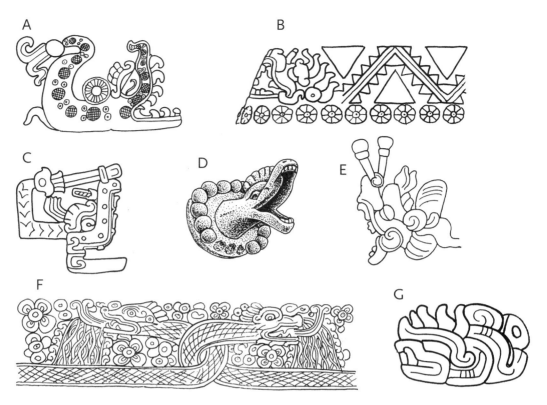

Fig. 25. Classic Maya plumed serpents. Artwork by Karl Taube. A. With flower on back, Structure 2B1, Sayil. Redrawn after Pollock (1980: fig. 202). B. Atop line of flowers, Structure 2C6, Kabah. Redrawn after Pollock (1980: fig. 364). C. With floral tail element, Hochob Structure 2. Redrawn after Gendrop (1983: fig. 73). D. Crested serpent emerging from blossom, detail of Palenque censer. E. Serpent emerging from blossom, Piedras Negras Stela 2. Redrawn after Stuart (2003: 21). F. Pair of intertwined serpents with blossoms, detail of Early Classic Tikal vessel. Redrawn after Culbert (1993: fig. 50b). G. Serpent with feather crest, detail of Early Classic Tikal vessel. Redrawn after Culbert (1993: fig. 20b).

Serpents with feather brows also occur in Early Classic Maya iconography, including vessels from Tikal (fig. 25F–G). In one example, abundant blossoms surround an intertwined pair of crested serpents (fig. 25F). The water spewing from their mouths is clearly a Teotihuacan-derived convention, although crested serpents are generally absent from Early Classic Teotihuacan iconography. At Teotihuacan, feathered serpents also commonly appear with flowers, as seen at the Temple of Quetzalcoatl, which portrays plumed serpents emerging out of massive blossoms (Taube 2004a). In addition, one Teotihuacan mural fragment depicts a plumed serpent with flanking lines of blossoms and a flowering

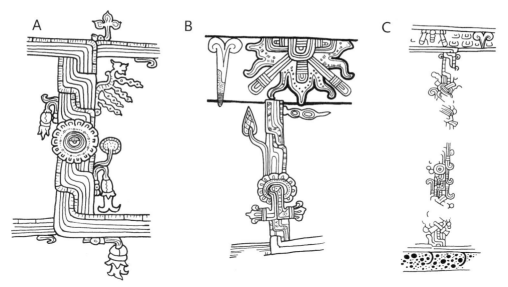

Fig. 26. Intertwined serpent bodies in Late Postclassic Maya murals. Artwork by Karl Taube.
A. Intertwined serpents with flowers, Tulúm Structure 16. Redrawn after Miller (1982: plate 37). B. Intertwined serpents with skyband, Santa Rita. Redrawn after Gann (1900: plate 29). C. Intertwined serpents with skyband, Rancho Ina. Redrawn after Martos López (2001: plate 11).

plant growing from its body (see Berrin 1988: plate 14). However, the relation of the plumed serpent to flowers is of still greater antiquity. The North Wall mural at San Bartolo, dating to the first century BCE, features human figures atop a great plumed serpent exhaling yellow blossoms with another on its back (Saturno et al. 2005). At San Bartolo, as well as in Classic and Postclassic Mesoamerican iconography, this being embodies Flower Road, a path or conduit for forces of life and fertility.

The San Bartolo scene strongly resembles the imagery of the much later murals from Tulúm Structure 16 that portray deities atop plumed serpents with blossoms on their bodies and flowers being exhaled from their snouts (figs. 24A, 26A). The Tulúm serpents, however, are tightly intertwined and resemble a segment of cord or rope. This motif also occurs in the Santa Rita and Rancho Ina murals, in which the belly scutes of the serpents are plainly evident (fig. 26B–C). At both sites, their bodies extend to explicit skybands, denoting them as celestial roads or vehicles. At Santa Rita, the serpent cord connects two deities, the probable Maya wind god and a youthful deity sitting in the maw of a plumed serpent (see Gann 1900: plate 29, figs. 4 and 5). Portrayed with solar rays and the headband of the central Mexican sun god, the seated figure is probably a Maya depiction of Tonatiuh (fig. 3B and D). He is clearly distinct from the bearded

Maya sun god, who stands in the same mural scene wearing a plumed serpent headdress (see Gann 1900: plate 29, fig. 2). The seated deity is accompanied by a glyphic compound that can be read either as *chik'in*, "west," or *k'inich*, the Maya name of the sun god. I favor the latter reading, as he probably is the dawning sun appearing with symbolism of the morning star.

At Santa Rita, the plumed serpent often appears with solar imagery. The Maya sun god wears a plumed serpent headdress not only in the North Wall mural but also in the West Wall scene, in which he emerges from a solar disk (see Gann 1900: plate 31). As an eastern being, the plumed serpent is both the bringer of rain and the vehicle or path for the dawning sun. A Late Postclassic carved bone from Tomb 7 at Monte Albán portrays a pair of rising intertwined feathered serpents carrying a solar disk on their backs (see Caso 1969: fig. 201). The back of the Aztec Stuttgart "Xolotl" statuette also portrays Tonatiuh in a solar disk atop the plumed serpent (see Pasztory 1983: plate 279). Rather than being Xolotl, the statue portrays Tlahuizcalpantecuhtli—that is, Venus as the eastern morning star (Coltman 2007). After his final mythic journey to the east, Quetzalcoatl was reborn as Tlahuizcalpantecuhtli, and plumed serpents are frequently marked with stars to denote the eastern morning star (fig. 27A). Quetzalcoatl as the Morning Star carried the dawning sun into the sky (Miller 1982: 89), a concept still present among the Tzotzil Maya: "At dawn the sun rises in the east preceded by Venus, the Morning Star, a large plumed serpent called *Mukta ch'on*" (Vogt 1969: 89). According to Arthur Miller (1982: 97), the underlying theme of the Tulúm murals concerns the plumed serpent as Venus assisting the emerging sun.

The preeminent weapon of Tlahuizcalpantecuhtli is his spearthrower for shooting his deadly rays of light, the same weapon wielded by Quetzalcoatl. It is therefore highly significant that the Santa Rita plumed serpent supporting Tonatiuh has a vertical dart on its snout, denoting a serpent spearthrower such as appears elsewhere in the mural (plate 3; fig. 27D). Rather than swallowing the solar figure, the Santa Rita serpent carries him into the sky with the darts of dawn, the shooting rays of the morning star.

Carved contact period serpent spearthrowers exist as well, including two virtually identical examples featuring a plumed serpent flanked by star signs rising out of a pool in the maw of the earth monster (fig. 27A–B; Saville 1925: pls. 10–11). In cosmological terms, this refers to the dawn emergence of Quetzalcoatl and Venus out of the eastern sea. A much smaller dart-shooting serpent also emerges out of the water, recalling the upwardly facing plumed serpent supporting Tonatiuh at Santa Rita (fig. 27B–D). The back of the serpent is covered by a "daisy chain" of hummingbirds connected by blossoms near their tails (fig. 27E), probably the souls of warriors rising at dawn out of the eastern sea on the Flower Road of the plumed serpent.

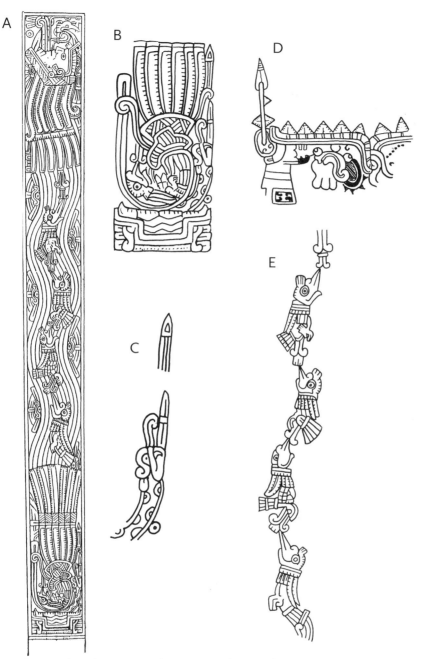

Fig. 27. A plumed serpent spearthrower. A. Wooden spearthrower portraying plumed serpent emerging from pool. From Saville (1925: plate 11). B. Detail of serpent tail and pool. C. Detail of small serpent emitting darts. D. Plumed serpent with dart projecting from snout, detail of Santa Rita mural. Redrawn after Gann (1900: plate 29). E. Detail of hummingbirds and flowers on back of plumed serpent in part A. B–E: Artwork by Karl Taube.

The Mountain of Dawn

For the Classic Maya and ancient Teotihuacan, Flower Mountain was an eastern locale occupied by quetzals and other precious tropical birds (Taube 2004a, 2005a). Although little discussed, mountain imagery is a major theme at two of the most eastern Maya sites, Tulúm and Santa Rita. The frontal side of Tulúm Structure 16 features massive stucco heads of an old man at the cornice corners who wears two plumed serpents in his headdress (fig. 28A). His chapfallen and craggy features closely resemble portrayals of *witz* mountains in the Dresden Codex (fig. 28B), shown as the head of an old man with Kawak markings, denoting stone (for the *witz* identification, see Stuart 1987). The Tulúm heads are strikingly similar to a Codex Laud mountain marked with profile heads at both sides (fig. 28C). The figures' beards indicate that they are old because facial hair commonly designates agedness in the Borgia Group. The location of the heads at the corners of the Tulúm structure recalls the zoomorphic *witz* heads at the corners of Copán Structure 10L-26, as well as many Chenes, Río Bec, and Puuc structures. Moreover, the majority of the so-called Chaak masks of Puuc-style buildings have recently been identified as zoomorphic *witz* heads (Boot 2004; Taube 2004a). Many of these display prominent flowers on their brows, identifying them as Flower Mountain (Taube 2004a).

An extremely elaborate mountain scene appears in the interior of Tulúm Structure 16 (see Miller 1982: plate 37). The mural features a pair of intertwined serpents carrying gods on their backs as they rise out of a pool of water. Rather than depicting a freshwater cenote, the pool, which contains a marine ray, is almost surely the Caribbean, located less than 100 meters to the east. A zoomorphic maw encloses the water, immediately recalling the central Mexican pool in the mouth of Tlaltecuhtli (fig. 27B). However, the Tulúm maw consists of two profile heads with sharply upturned snouts, late versions of the Witz Monster mountain, with its maw being a cave. As is the case of many *witz* appearing on Late Classic Puuc structures, the snout is marked with a series of disks (fig. 29B).

The Santa Rita mural also features a single profile version of the mountain cave maw with very similar teeth and facial markings, including smoke-like vertical scrolls and a petaled band crossing the upturned snout (fig. 29C) (for the entire scene, see Gann 1900: plate 29). Although largely destroyed, the top of the Santa Rita mountain is marked with remnants of a yellow trefoil flower and feather elements, possibly denoting Flower Mountain. The two quetzals in front of it recall the pair of quetzals commonly appearing in scenes of the floral paradise and Flower Mountain of ancient Mesoamerica (Taube 2004a; 2005a: fig. 1). The snouts of the Tulúm examples have blossoming bean and squash plants, probably denoting Flower Mountain as well. Another

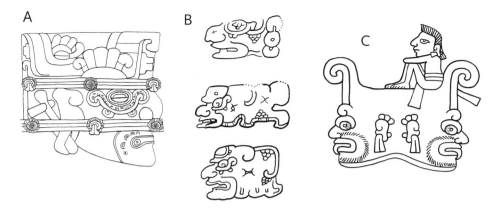

Fig. 28. The old man mountain motif. Artwork by Karl Taube. A. Stucco facade portraying head of old man, Tulúm Structure 16. Redrawn after Miller (1982: plate 31). B. Heads of old men appearing as *witz* mountains, Dresden 66b, 34c, 41a. C. Mountain marked with pair of human heads, Codex Laud 28.

zoomorphic mountain cave appears in the Codex Laud, again with an up-turned snout marked with a petaled band (fig. 29D).

The Tulúm composition with two mountains flanking and containing a cave pool is known for earlier Maya portrayals of Flower Mountain (fig. 30B) (see Taube 2004a: 82). The North Wall mural at San Bartolo depicts Flower Mountain with a great maw and stalactite tusk, clearly an early version of the Tulúm, Santa Rita, and Codex Laud examples appearing in profile as inverted Ls with teeth in their widely open mouths (fig. 30A).

The San Bartolo mountain exhales a massive plumed serpent with yellow flowers on its back and emerging from its snout (fig. 30A). The serpent is a Flower Road for eight figures conveying a basket of tamales and a water gourd out of Flower Mountain, a scene interpreted as the mythic emergence of maize and humans to the surface of the earth (Saturno et al. 2005). A Late Classic vessel with two inwardly facing forms of Flower Mountain shows a human couple at a quatrefoil cave in the basal aquatic area (see Coe 1978: no. 16). Stephen Houston (personal communication, 2003) notes that this vessel probably depicts the emergence of humans out of the watery underworld, greeted by gods presenting the esoteric arts of writing and ritual. The entire composition of Tulúm Temple 16 emphasizes emergence, and much like San Bartolo, the gods carry vessels of tamales and drink atop floral serpents rising out of Flower Mountain. At Tulúm, the mythic event of emergence repeats every day when the sun with the gods and ancestors rises on Flower Road out of the eastern waters of the Caribbean Sea.

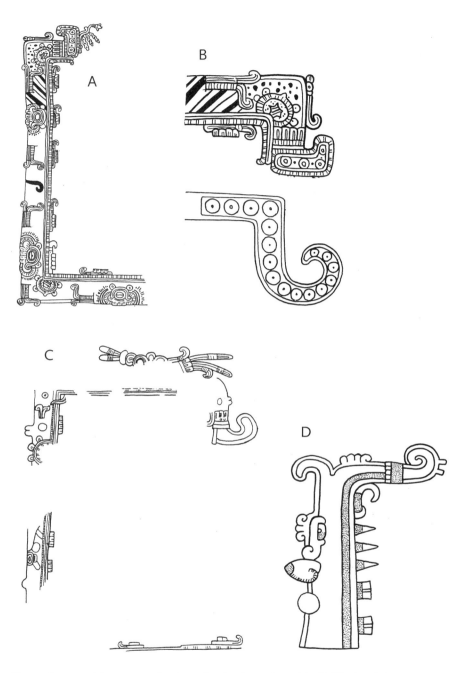

Fig. 29. The mountain cave maw in International-style art. Artwork by Karl Taube. A. Cave maw from mural in Tulúm Structure 16. Redrawn after Miller (1982: plate 37). B. Comparison of snout of Tulúm zoomorphic mountain with *witz* snout from Structure 2C6, Kabah. Redrawn after Miller (1982) and Pollock (1980: fig. 367c). C. Cave maw from Santa Rita mural. Redrawn after Gann (1900: plate 29). D. Cave maw with band across snout, Codex Laud 3.

A

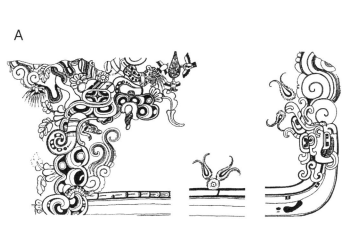

B

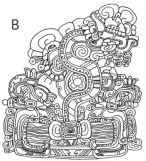

C   D

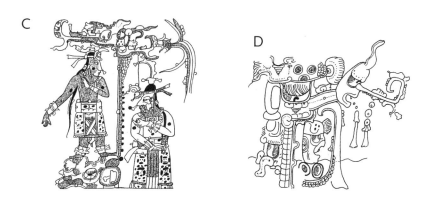

Fig. 30. Ancient Maya portrayals of Flower Mountain. A. Plumed serpent emerging from Flower Mountain. Detail of drawing by Heather Hurst, after Saturno et al. (2005: fig. 12). B. Serpent with sun emerging out of profile portrayals of Flower Mountain, Takalik Abaj Stela 4; partly reconstructed drawing by Karl Taube; from Saturno et al. (2005: fig. 15b). C. Hero Twins at cave maw of Flower Mountain, detail of Late Classic vase. From Taube (2004a: fig. 12d). D. Flower Mountain rising out of pool of water. From Saturno et al. (2005: fig. 12c). B–D: Artwork by Karl Taube.

Conclusions

Among the more dominant themes in International-style art are flowers, butterflies, and precious birds, all related to the eastern solar paradise. A great deal of International-style art concerns this realm, with its imagery of skybands, volutes of music, breath and wind, and spirit souls appearing as disembodied heads, butterflies, and precious birds. In highland Mexico, Flower World appears vividly on ceramic vessels used for feasting with the honored dead as well as the living. Much of this symbolism is of great antiquity in Mesoamerica; even in Late Preclassic Maya art, ancestors appear as celestial, disembodied heads surrounded by swirling clouds (e.g., El Baul Stela 1, Takalik Abaj Stela 2). In addition, the convention of double breath volutes exhaled from blossoms can be traced backward from Late Postclassic Tulúm to the Middle Formative Olmec. It is likely that many conventions appearing in International-style art derived from Late Classic Maya iconography, including the jade brow piece of Tonatiuh, the netted earth motif, and flower symbolism and imagery. However, the relationship of ancestors with butterflies, which occurs in central Mexico, was not widely shared with the ancient Maya, who instead classified butterflies with bug-like insects, skeletal beings of death and darkness, rather than of light and beauty.

One creature widely identified with the celestial flower paradise is the plumed serpent. Often ornamented with flowers on its tail and body, this being embodies Flower Road, the celestial path of the sun, gods, and ancestors. The relationship between the plumed serpent and Venus probably relates to its eastern nature, the east being where both the morning star and sun emerge. Depictions of feathered serpents rising out of water represent their dawn emergence out of the eastern sea. Long before Tulúm Temple 16 was built, the Temple of Quetzalcoatl at Teotihuacan portrayed plumed serpents swimming in a sea of marine shells and emerging from blossoms on Flower Mountain. These beings, the earliest known portrayals of plumed serpents at Teotihuacan, are covered with quetzal plumes from the eastern Maya realm.

The many blossoms ornamenting the facades at Tulúm are not simply adornments but label the structures as floral temples. In the Borgia, Cospi, and Fejérváry-Mayer codices, the eastern temple of Tonatiuh is portrayed as a house of flowers, or *xochicalli*. At Tulúm, however, Structure 16 and the more impressive Castillo (Structure 1) are not simply temples but are symbolic forms of Flower Mountain. The Structure 16 murals feature serpents rising out of the water at Flower Mountain, and the exterior floral cornices display massive heads of old men, late forms of the zoomorphic *witz* masks from Late Classic Maya temples. As a major temple pyramid literally at the shore of the Caribbean, the Castillo probably symbolized the sacred mountain of the east. Although Cozumel is well known as an important pilgrimage center devoted to Ix Chel, the goddess of midwives, the birth metaphor for east clearly derives from the dawning of the sun (see Miller 1982: 85). A great deal of ritual and symbolism at Tulúm surely concerned the daily rebirth of the sun out of the eastern sea. As Miller (1982: 3) notes, the ancient name for this place was Zamal, or "dawn." Among the contemporary Huichol of western Mexico, the peyote pilgrimage replicates the mythic emergence of the gods out of the Pacific to their rebirth with the newly born sun at Cerro Quemado, a hill located in their floral paradise of Wirikuta. From this eastern realm, the pilgrims return westward to their communities with the plumed serpent of rain (Neurath 2002: 169). Similarly, as a place of pilgrimage as well as trade, Tulúm and the eastern Caribbean coast may have been regarded as the paradisal floral realm of the sun and the ancestors in the Late Postclassic world.

References Cited

Aguilera, Carmen
    2003   El penacho de Motecuhzoma. *Arquelogía mexicana* 11 (64): 76–79.

Anawalt, Patricia Rieff
    1990   The Emperor's Cloak: Aztec Pomp, Toltec Circumstances. *American Antiquity* 55 (2): 291–307.

Armillas, Pedro
    1946   Los Olmeca-Xicalanca y los sitios arqueológicos del suroeste de Tlaxcala. *Revista mexicana de estudios antropológicos* 8: 137–145.

Barrera Rubio, Alfredo, and Carlos Peraza Lope
    2001   La pintura mural de Mayapán. In *La pintura mural prehispánica en México: Área maya, Tomo IV: Estudios* (Leticia Staines Cicero, ed.): 419–446. Universidad Nacional Autónoma de México, México, D.F.

Berlo, Janet
    1983   The Warrior and the Butterfly: Central Mexican Ideologies of Sacred Warfare and Teotihuacan Iconography. In *Text and Image in Pre-Columbian Art: Essays on the Interrelationship of the Visual and Verbal Arts* (Janet Berlo, ed.): 79–117. BAR International Series 180. Oxford, England.

Berrin, Kathleen (ed.)
    1988   *Feathered Serpents and Flowering Trees: Reconstructing the Murals of Teotihuacan.* University of Washington Press, Seattle.

Beyer, Hermann
    1969   Explicación de un fragmento de un antiguo plato decorado de Cholula. *El México antiguo* 11: 450–470.

Bolz, Ingeborg
    1975   *Meisterwerke altindianischer Kunst.* Verlag Aurel Bongers Recklinghausen, Germany.

Boone, Elizabeth H., and Michael E. Smith

2003   Postclassic International Styles and Symbol Sets. In *The Postclassic Mesoamerican World* (Michael E. Smith and Frances F. Berdan, eds.): 186–193. University of Utah Press, Salt Lake City.

Boot, Erik

2004   "Ceramic" Support for the Identity of Classic Maya Architectural Long-Lipped (Corner) Masks as the Animated *Witz* "Hill, Mountain." *Mesoweb*. Available at www.mesoweb.com/features/boot/Masks.pdf.

Burger, Richard L.

1992   *Chavín and the Origins of Andean Civilization*. Thames and Hudson, London and New York.

1996   Chavín. In *Andean Art at Dumbarton Oaks* (Elizabeth H. Boone, ed.): 45–86. Dumbarton Oaks Research Library and Collection, Washington, D.C.

Caso, Alfonso

1949   Una urna con diosa mariposa. *El México antiguo* 7: 78–95.

1967   *Los calendarios prehispánicos*. Universidad Nacional Autónoma de México, México, D.F.

1969   *El tesoro de Monte Albán*. Instituto Nacional de Antropología de Historia, México, D.F.

Chase, Arlen F., and Diane Z. Chase

1987   *Investigations at the Classic Maya City of Caracol, Belize: 1985–1987*. Pre-Columbian Art Research Institute Monograph 3. San Francisco.

Chase, Diane

1985   Ganned but Not Forgotten: Late Postclassic Archaeology and Ritual at Santa Rita, Corozal, Belize. In *The Lowland Maya Postclassic* (Arlen F. Chase and Prudence M. Rice, eds.): 104–125. University of Texas Press, Austin.

Coe, Michael D.

1978   *Lords of the Underworld: Masterpieces of Classic Maya Ceramics*. Princeton University Press, Princeton, N.J.

Coltman, Jeremy

2007   The Iconography of the Stuttgart Statuette: An Iconographic Analysis. *Mexicon* 29 (3): 70–77.

Contreras Martínez, José Eduardo

1994   Los murales y cerámica policromos de la zona arqueológica de Ocotelulco, Tlaxcala. In *Mixteca-Puebla: Discoveries and Research in Mesoamerican Art and Archaeology* (H. B. Nicholson and Eloise Quiñones-Keber, eds.): 7–24. Labyrinthos, Culver City, Calif.

Couch, N. C. Christopher

1988   *Pre-Columbian Art from the Ernest Erickson Collection at the American Museum of Natural History*. American Museum of Natural History, New York.

Culbert, T. Patrick

1993   *The Ceramics of Tikal: Vessels from the Burials, Caches, and Problematical Deposits*. Tikal Report 25, part A. The University Museum, University of Pennsylvania, Philadelphia.

Durán, Fray Diego
    1971   *Book of the Gods and Rites and the Ancient Calendar* (Fernando Horcasitas and Doris Heyden, trans. and eds.). University of Oklahoma Press, Norman.

Enciso, Jorge
    1953   *Design Motifs of Ancient Mexico*. Dover Publications, New York.

Feest, Christian F.
    1990   Vienna's Mexican Treasures: Aztec, Mixtec, and Tarascan Works from 16th Century Austrian Collections. *Archiv für Völkerkunde* 44: 1–64.

Fields, Virginia, and Dorie Reents-Budet
    2005   *Lords of Creation: The Origins of Sacred Maya Kingship*. Scala Publishers, London.

Franco, José Luis
    1961   Representaciones de la mariposa de Mesoámerica. *El México antiguo* 9: 195–244.

Gallareta Negrón, Tomás, and Karl Taube
    2005   Late Postclassic Occupation in the Ruinas de San Angel Region. In *Quintana Roo Archaeology* (Justine M. Shaw and Jennifer P. Mathews, eds.): 87–111. University of Arizona Press, Tucson.

Gann, Thomas
    1900   Mounds in Northern Honduras. In *Nineteenth Annual Report of the Bureau of American Ethnology, 1897–98*, pt. 2: 655–692. Washington, D.C.

Gendrop, Paul
    1983   *Los estilos Río Bec, Chenes y Puuc en la arquitectura maya*. Universidad Nacional Autónoma de México, México, D.F.

Graham, Ian, and Eric von Euw
    1975   *Corpus of Maya Hieroglyphic Inscriptions*. Vol 2, pt. 1: *Naranjo*. Peabody Museum of Archaeology and Ethnology, Cambridge, Mass.

Graulich, Michel
    1992   Quetzalcoatl-Ehecatl, the Bringer of Life. In *Ancient America: Contributions to New World Archaeology* (Nicholas Saunders, ed.): 33–38. Oxbow Books, Oxford.

Grube, Nikolai, Alfonso Lacadena, and Simon Martin
    2003   Chichén Itzá and Ek' Balam: Terminal Classic Inscriptions from Yucatán. In *Notebook for the XXVIIth Maya Hieroglyphic Forum at Texas*, pt. 2. Maya Workshop Foundation at University of Texas Press, Austin.

Hill, Jane H.
    1992   The Flower World of Old Uto-Aztecan. *Journal of Anthropological Research* 48: 117–44.

Houston, Stephen D., and Karl Taube
    2000   An Archeology of the Senses: Perception and Cultural Expression in Ancient Mesoamerica. *Cambridge Archaeological Journal* 10 (2): 261–294.

Howell, Steve N. G., and Sophie Webb

    1995   *A Guide to the Birds of Mexico and Northern Central America.* Oxford University Press, Oxford.

Jiménez Moreno, Wigberto

    1942   El enigma de los Olmecas. *Cuadernos americanos* 1 (5): 113–145.

Kerr, Justin

    1990   *The Maya Vase Book*, vol. 2. Kerr Associates, New York.

    1994   *The Maya Vase Book*, vol. 4. Kerr Associates, New York.

    1997   *The Maya Vase Book*, vol. 5. Kerr Associates, New York.

Ketunnen, Harri

    2005   *Nasal Motifs in Maya Iconography.* Annales Academiae Scientiarum Fennicae 342. Academia Scientiarum Fennica, Helsinki.

Lind, Michael D.

    1994   Cholula and Mixteca Polychromes: Two Mixteca-Puebla Regional Sub-Styles. In *Mixteca-Puebla: Discoveries and Research in Mesoamerican Art and Archaeology* (H. B. Nicholson and Eloise Quiñones-Keber, eds.): 79–99. Labyrinthos, Culver City, Calif.

Lombardo de Ruiz, Sonia

    1987   *La pintura mural maya en Quintana Roo.* Instituto Nacional de Antropología e Historia, México, D.F.

Looper, Matthew G., and Julia Guernsey Kappelman

    2001   The Cosmic Umbilicus in Mesoamerica: A Floral Metaphor for the Source of Life. *Journal of Latin American Lore* 21 (1): 3–54.

López Luján, Leonardo

    1994   *The Offerings of the Templo Mayor of Tenochtitlan.* University Press of Colorado, Niwot.

    1998   Recreating the Cosmos: Seventeen Aztec Dedication Caches. In *The Sowing and the Dawning: Termination, Dedication, and Transformation in the Archaeological and Ethnographic Record of Mesoamerica* (Shirley Boteler Mock, ed.): 176–187. University of New Mexico Press, Albuquerque.

López Portillo, José, Miguel Leon Portilla, and Eduardo Matos Moctezuma

    1981   *El Templo Mayor.* Bancomer, México, D.F.

Lothrop, Samuel K.

    1924   *Tulum: An Archaeological Study of the East Coast of Yucatan.* Carnegie Institution of Washington, Washington, D.C.

Martos López, Luis Alberto

    2001   La pintura mural de Rancho Ina, Quintana Roo. In *La pintura mural prehispánica en México: Área maya, Tomo IV: Estudios* (Leticia Staines Cicero, ed.): 461–481. Universidad Nacional Autónoma de México, México, D.F.

Matos Moctezuma, Eduardo

    1987   *Cacaxtla.* Citicorp, México, D.F.

Mendieta, Geronimo

    1980   *Historia eclesiástica indiana.* Editorial Porrúa, México, D.F.

Miller, Arthur G.

1973   *The Mural Painting of Teotihuacan.* Dumbarton Oaks, Washington, D.C.

1974   West and East in Maya Thought: Death and Rebirth at Palenque and Tulum.
        In *Primera Mesa Redonda de Palenque, Part II* (Merle Greene Robertson,
        ed.): 45–49. The Robert Louis Stevenson School, Pebble Beach, Calif.

1982   *On the Edge of the Sea: Mural Painting at Tancah-Tulum, Quintana Roo,
        Mexico.* Dumbarton Oaks, Washington, D.C.

Mirambell Silva, Lorena (ed.)

1996   *Antología de Tizatlán.* Instituto Nacional Autónoma de Antropolgía de
        Historia, México, D.F.

Morante López, Rubén

2005   *La pintura mural de Las Higueras, Veracruz.* Universidad Veracruzana,
        Jalapa.

Navarrete, Carlos

1996   Elementos arquelógicos de mexicanización en las tierras altas mayas. In
        Temas mesoamericanos (Sonio Lombardo and Enrique Nalda, eds.): 305–
        352. Instituto Nacional de Antropología e Historia, México, D.F.

Neff, Hector, Ronald L. Bishop, Edward B. Sisson, Michael D. Glascock, and
Penny R. Sisson

1994   Neutron Activation Analysis of Late Postclassic Polychrome Pottery
        from Central Mexico. In *Mixteca-Puebla: Discoveries and Research in
        Mesoamerican Art and Archaeology* (H. B. Nicholson and Eloise Quiñones-
        Keber, eds.): 117–141. Labyrinthos, Culver City, Calif.

Neurath, Johannes

2002   Venus y el sol en la religion de Coras, Huicholes y Mexicaneros:
        Consideraciones sobre la posibiliidad de establecer comparciones con las
        antiguas concepciones mesoamericanas. *Anales de antropología* 36: 155–177.

Nicholson, H. B.

1960   The Mixteca-Puebla Concept in Mesoamerican Archaeology: A
        Re-examination. In *Men and Cultures: Selected Papers from the Fifth
        International Congress of Anthropological and Enthnological Sciences,
        Philadelphia, September 1–9, 1956* (Anthony F. C. Wallace, ed.): 612–617.
        University of Pennsylvania, Philadelphia.

Paddock, John (ed.)

1966   *Ancient Oaxaca: Discoveries in Mexican Archaeology and History.* Stanford
        University Press, Stanford, Calif.

Parsons, Lee A.

1980   *Pre-Columbian Art: The Morton D. May and the Saint Louis Art Museum
        Collections.* Harper and Rowe, New York.

Pasztory, Esther

1983   *Aztec Art.* Harry N. Abrams, New York.

Pohl, John M. D.

2003   Ritual Iconographic Variability in Mixteca-Puebla Polychrome Pottery.
        In *The Postclassic Mesoamerican World* (Michael E. Smith and Frances
        F. Berdan, eds.): 201–206. University of Utah Press, Salt Lake City.

Pollock, H. E. D.

　1980　*The Puuc: An Architectural Survey of the Hill Country of Yucatan and Northern Campeche, Mexico*. Memoirs of the Peabody Museum of Archaeology and Ethnology 19. Harvard University, Cambridge, Mass.

Quenon, Michel, and Geneviève Le Fort

　1997　Rebirth and Resurrection in Maize God Iconography. In *The Maya Vase Book*, vol. 5 (Justin Kerr, ed.): 884–902. Kerr Associates, New York.

Quirarte, Jacinto

　1982　The Santa Rita Murals: A Review. In *Aspects of the Mixteca-Puebla Style and Mixtec and Central Mexican Culture in Southern Mesoamerica* (Jennifer S. H. Brown and E. Wyllys Andrews V, eds.): 43–57. Middle American Research Institute Occasional Papers 4. Tulane University, New Orleans.

Robertson, Donald

　1970　The Tulum Murals: The International Style of the Late Post-Classic. In *Verhandlungen des XXXVIII Internationalen Amerikanistenkongresses, Stuttgart-München, 1968*, vol. 2: 77–78. Kommissonsverlag Klaus Renner, Munich.

Sahagún, Fray Bernardino

　1950–1982　*Florentine Codex: General History of the Things of New Spain* (Arthur J. O. Anderson and Charles E. Dibble, trans.). School of American Research, Santa Fe, N.Mex.

　2000　*Historia general de las cosas de Nueva España*. Consejo Nacional para la Cultura y las Artes, México, D.F.

Saturno, William, Karl Taube, and David Stuart

　2005　The Murals of San Bartolo, El Petén, Guatemala. Pt. 1: The North Wall. *Ancient America* 7. Center for Ancient American Studies, Barnardsville and Washington, D.C.

Saville, Marshall H.

　1925　*The Wood-Carver's Art in Ancient Mexico*. Museum of the American Indian, Heye Foundation, New York.

Sawyer, Alan R.

　1972　The Feline in Paracas Art. In *The Cult of the Feline* (Elizabeth P. Benson, ed.): 91–115. Dumbarton Oaks Research Library and Collection, Washington, D.C.

Schele, Linda, and Mary Ellen Miller

　1986　*The Blood of Kings: Dynasty and Ritual in Maya Art*. Kimbell Art Museum, Fort Worth, Tex.

Seler, Eduard

　1977　*Observations and Studies in the Ruins of Palenque* (Gisela Morgner, trans.; Thomas Bartman and George Kubler, eds.). Robert Louis Stevenson School, Pebble Beach, Calif.

Sharer, Robert M.

　1990　*Quirigua: A Classic Maya Center and Its Sculptures*. Carolina Academic Press, Durham, N.C.

Sisson, Edward B., and T. Gerald Lilly
　1994　The Mural of the Chimales and the Codex Borgia. In *Mixteca-Puebla: Discoveries and Research in Mesoamerican Art and Archaeology* (H. B. Nicholson and Eloise Quiñones-Keber, eds.): 24–44. Labyrinthos, Culver City, Calif.

Smith, Michael E.
　2003　Information Networks in Postclassic Mesoamerica. In *The Postclassic Mesoamerican World* (Michael E. Smith and Frances F. Berdan, eds.): 186–93. University of Utah Press, Salt Lake City.

Smith, Michael E., and Frances Berdan (eds.)
　2003　*The Postclassic Mesoamerican World.* University of Utah Press, Salt Lake City.

Solís, Felipe (curator)
　2004　*The Aztec Empire: Catalogue of the Exhibition.* Solomon R. Guggenheim Foundation, New York.

Stanton, Travis W., Ramón Carrillo Sánchez, Teresa Ceballos Gallarreta, Markus Eberl, Socorro Jiménez Alvarez, and Julieta Ramos Pacheco
　2003　Puuc Settlement on the Northwest Coastal Plain of Yucatan: Preliminary Research from Santa Barbara. *Mexicon* 25 (1): 24–33.

Stuart, David
　1987　*Ten Phonetic Syllables.* Research Reports on Ancient Maya Writing 14. Center for Maya Research, Washington, D.C.
　2003　*Corpus of Maya Hieroglyphic Inscriptions.* Vol. 9, pt. 2: *Piedras Negras.* Peabody Museum of Archaeology and Ethnology, Harvard University, Cambridge, Mass.
　n.d.　Flower Symbolism in Maya Iconography. Paper presented at the symposium "Origins: Creation and Continuity, Mythology and History in Mesoamerica," Maya Meetings, University of Texas at Austin, March 1992.

Stuart, George E.
　1992　Mural Masterpieces of Ancient Cacaxtla. *National Geographic* 182 (3): 120–136.

Taube, Karl A.
　1992　*The Major Gods of Ancient Yucatan.* Studies in Pre-Columbian Art and Archaeology 32. Dumbarton Oaks Research Library and Collection, Washington, D.C.
　1993　*Aztec and Maya Myths.* British Museum Press, London.
　1994　The Iconography of Toltec Period Chichen Itza. In *Hidden in the Hills: Maya Archaeology of the Northwestern Yucatan Peninsula* (Hanns J. Prem, ed.): 212–246. Acta Mesoamericana 7. Verlag von Flemming, Möckmühl, Germany.
　2000　The Turquoise Hearth: Fire, Self-Sacrifice, and the Central Mexican Cult of War. In *Mesoamerica's Classic Heritage: From Teotihuacan to the Aztecs* (Davíd Carrasco, Lindsay Jones, and Scott Sessions, eds.): 269–340. University Press of Colorado, Niwot.

2001a   The Breath of Life: The Symbolism of Wind in Mesoamerica and the American Southwest. In *The Road to Aztlan: Art from a Mythic Homeland* (Virginia M. Fields and Victor Zamudio-Taylor, eds.): 102–123. Los Angeles County Museum of Art, Los Angeles.

2001b   The Classic Maya Gods. In *Maya: Divine Kings of the Rain Forest* (Nikolai Grube, ed.): 262–277. Könemann, Cologne.

2004a   Flower Mountain: Concepts of Life, Beauty, and Paradise among the Classic Maya. *RES: Anthropology and Aesthetics* 45: 69–98.

2004b   The Stairway Sculptures of Structure 10L-16: Fire and the Evocation and Resurrection of K'inich Yax K'uk' Mo'. In *Understanding Early Classic Copán* (Ellen Bell, Marcello Canuto, and Robert Sharer, eds.): 215–247. University of Pennsylvania Museum of Archaeology and Anthropology, Philadelphia.

2005a   Representaciones del paraíso en el arte cerámico del Clásico Temprano de Escuintla, Guatemala. In *Iconografía y escritura teotihuacana en la costa sur de Guatemala y Chiapas* (Oswaldo Chinchilla and Barbara Arroyo, eds.): 33–54. U Tz'ib, Serie Reportes 1 (5). Asociación Tikal, Guatemala.

2005b   The Symbolism of Jade in Classic Maya Religion. *Ancient Mesoamerica* 16: 23–50.

2006   Climbing Flower Mountain: Concepts of Resurrection and the Afterlife in Ancient Teotihuacan. In *Arqueología e historia del centro de México: Homenaje a Eduardo Matos Moctezuma* (Leonardo López Luján, Davíd Carrasco, and Lordes Cué, eds.): 153–170. Instituto Nacional de Antropología e Historia, México, D.F.

Thompson, J. Eric S.

1950   *Maya Hieroglyphic Writing: An Introduction.* Carnegie Institution of Washington, Washington, D.C.

Tozzer, Alfred M.

1907   *A Comparative Study of the Mayas and the Lacandones.* Macmillan, London.

1941   *Landa's* Relación de las cosas de Yucatan: *A Translation.* Papers of the Peabody Museum of American Archaeology and Ethnology 18. Harvard University, Cambridge, Mass.

Trik, Helen, and Michael E. Kampen

1983   *The Graffiti of Tikal.* Tikal Report 31. The University Museum, University of Pennsylvania, Philadelphia.

Uriarte, María Teresa (gen. ed.)

1998   *Fragmentos del pasado: Murales prehispánicos.* Antiguo Colegio de San Ildefonso, México, D.F.

Vaillant, George C.

1938   A Correlation of Archaeological and Historical Sequences in the Valley of Mexico. *American Anthropologist* 40 (4): 535–573.

1940   Patterns in Middle American Archaeology. In *The Maya and Their Neighbors: Essays on Middle American Anthropology and Archaeology* (Clarence L. Hay, Ralph L. Linton, Samuel K. Lothrop, Harry L. Shapiro, and George C. Vaillant, eds.): 295–305. Appelton-Century, New York.

1941   *Aztecs of Mexico: Origin, Rise and Fall of the Aztec Nation.* Doubleday,
        Doran, Garden City, New York.

Villagra Caleti, Agustín
1971   Mural Painting in Central Mexico. In *Handbook of Middle American
        Indians*, vol. 10 (Gordon F. Ekholm and Ignacio Bernal, eds.): 135–156.
        University of Texas Press, Austin.

Vivó Escoto, Jorgé
1964   Weather and Climate of Mexico and Central America. In *Handbook of
        Middle American Indians*, vol. 1 (Robert C. West, ed.): 187–215. University of
        Texas Press, Austin.

Vogt, Evon
1969   *Zinacantan: A Maya Community in the Highlands of Chiapas.* Bellnap
        Press, Harvard University, Cambridge, Mass.

Von Winning, Hasso
1968   *Pre-Columbian Art of Mexico and Central America.* Harry N. Abrams,
        New York.

Wright, Barton
1973   *Kachinas: A Hopi Artist's Documentary.* Northland Press, Flagstaff, Ariz.

Yadeun, Juan
2001   El museo de Toniná. *Arqueología mexicana* 9 (50): 44–49.

Chapter Six

Scribal Interaction in Postclassic Mesoamerica

Martha J. Macri

CONTINUITY IN TEXTS and images throughout ancient Mesoamerica establishes the presence of active communication among scribes across linguistic, ethnic, political, and geographic regions. The durability of written texts and graphic images allowed this communication across both spatial and temporal barriers. The evidence for scribal interaction is not limited to the Postclassic period, but comes from the earliest known visual imagery in Mesoamerica. Nevertheless, regardless of the date of their earliest appearance, each of the items discussed in this chapter is present in Postclassic scripts and iconography.

The discussion begins with a specific complex graphic symbol, the quadripartite star/Venus glyph, known from the Preclassic period to the sixteenth century.[1] Next, the metaphor of "water-hill" for town, known in languages throughout Mesoamerica, is shown to have been depicted in at least three distinct graphic traditions. Unexplained relationships between certain seemingly unrelated Maya graphemes, such as those for "road" and "snake," make sense when we understand that the Maya scribes who first used these signs were familiar with words and symbols from non-Maya traditions. Certain Maya syllabic signs that look similar but that have different syllabic values may have originated as rebuses using non-Maya words. Finally, Nahua words spelled with syllabic signs can be found in Maya texts from almost every period (discussed later).[2] Several models can be described to explain how foreign traditions, including iconographic images, metaphors, and words in other languages, may have been known to scribes and artists, as well as to their audiences.

Previously I discussed examples of continuity across iconography and script traditions to make the case for a robust exchange of portable objects throughout Mesoamerica, from the Preclassic to the seventeenth century (Macri n.d. [2005]). An active distribution of portable objects, not only paper documents but also carved bones, celts, beads, shells, and wooden objects, as well as painted pots and textiles, played an essential role in the communication of symbols among artists across time and space. Certainly the images from the Late Postclassic and colonial periods are key to understanding the nature of the intellectual interchange between the Maya lowlands and the Mexican highlands.

A Shared Icon: Venus/Star and the Maya Day Lamat

Mesoamerican signs that represent the planet Venus can be grouped into two major categories: a quadripartite sign found in the Isthmian script (Gulf Coast) and Maya texts, and a five-pointed star found in murals at Teotihuacan and Cacaxtla and in the Mexican and Mixtec codices. Both of these forms also occur as what are sometimes called "half stars." Often overlooked is whether these signs depict any heavenly body, all stars, only planets, or specifically the planet Venus. Two lines of evidence suggest that the Maya glyph was used for stars. One is that the sign is prefixed by **chäk**, "great," on one of the doorway panels of Temple 11 at Copán and throughout the Venus table of the Dresden Codex (fig. 1). In this context it would have been read **ek'**, "star."[3] The sign also occurs iconographically in the Bonampak murals, in Room 2 in the upper register, where it represents stars. Three of these signs on the back of a turtle appear to represent the three stars of Orion's belt (Aveni 2001: 204). So, undeniably, in some contexts the sign simply refers to "heavenly body" or to "star." Similar evidence for this is presented in Aldana (2005). Unlike Aldana, however, I conclude, with Closs (1979: 147–148), that when the sign appears in a Maya text, it nearly always signifies the planet Venus.

Fig. 1.
Great/red star, *chäk ek'*, on Dresden
47bG18. After Förstemann (1880).

The origin of the five-pointed star as a Venus symbol, found also in ancient Mesopotamia and Greece, is likely rooted in the 5:8 ratio of the five Venus cycles (5 × 584 days = 2920 days) to eight tropical years (8 × 365 days = 2920 days) (Aveni 2001: 83). A pentagram is formed by the appearance of Venus at five different positions in the zodiac for any specific point in its cycle (first appearance, greatest elongation, etc.). This can be represented by the symmetrical five-pointed star, or, when first heliacal risings as morning star are plotted as observed points on the horizon, as a flattened "half star."[4]

Earliest Depictions of Venus

The Venus/star logograph is depicted on portable objects from the Preclassic, Classic, and Postclassic periods into the sixteenth century. This continuity of an image that is graphically complex and semantically consistent is evidence not of the borrowing of a word or concept but of the transmission of a specific image over an extensive geographic and temporal range. An early example of Venus symbols appears on La Mojarra Stela 1 from the Gulf Coast (Winfield Capitaine 1988), a monument that has two Long Count dates: 8.5.3.3.5 and 8.5.16.9.7, equivalent to the Gregorian dates May 21, 143 CE (Julian day number 1773430) and July 13, 156 CE (Julian day number 1778232). For both days, Venus is about 42° above the horizon (42° 4.6′ above the western horizon in Cancer, and 42° 56′ above the eastern horizon in Orion, respectively). For 143 CE, this is within a week of maximum elongation; for 156 CE it is at maximum elongation. Thus, on the two initial dates on the La Mojarra text, Venus appears as evening star and morning star, in mirror positions, just as the two parts of the La Mojarra text mirror each other. A minor graphic variation may also be relevant to this contrast. The triangles on the star from the right side of the text contrast with circles on the other (fig. 2). If this graphic variation is significant, it may relate to two opposing positions of the planet. Justeson and Kaufman (1993) identify the sign preceding the first "star" in both text segments as "great," analogous to the later Mayan spelling of the name of Venus as "great star."

A second example of the symbol comes from the San Bartolo mural, dated to the Late Preclassic period. The third person/deity on the west wall has a diamond-shaped star sign in his headdress (not unlike images of Quetzalcoatl in the Codex Borbonicus discussed later). Just above and to the left of him is a column of glyph blocks, the last five of which can now be seen (Saturno 2006a: 74) (fig. 3). Saturno (2006b) suggests that the last three glyphs name the person as *Ajaw Ek' Winik,* literally, "Lord Star Man." In Saturno (2006a: 68), he is identified as the Maya maize god. In the San Bartolo text, unlike the La Mojarra inscription, the use of the sign ZQD[5] in a proper name or title does not provide evidence favoring a reading of either "star" or "Venus."

Yet another early example of the Venus symbol can be seen on a carved jade text taken from the cenote at Chichén Itzá, estimated to date from the Late

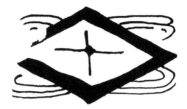

Fig. 2. Venus phrases on La Mojarra Stela 1 at C1-4 and R5-8. Artwork by George Stuart in Winfield Capitaine (1988).

Fig. 3. Venus glyph on painted stone at San Bartolo. After photograph in Saturno (2006a: 74).

Preclassic or Early Classic period (fig. 4; seen in the fifth glyph block). Here again, it is uncertain that Venus is specifically indicated. All three of these early examples resemble each other in that they consist of four circles, diamonds, or curves surrounding a central diamond shape that itself contains a cross or a smaller diamond.

Venus and the Day Sign Lamat

Lamat is the Yucatec Maya name for one of the 20 days in the 260-day Meso-american calendar (*Lamb'at* is the Ch'olan form) (see Dakin, ch. 7, this volume). Signs that represent the day Lamat in hieroglyphic texts can be grouped into several sets and subsets. In its simplest form, the sign is a circle divided into four equal parts, usually with a small circle in each of the parts and another circle, cross, or diamond shape in the center. Many examples resemble the early Venus symbols. Others appear to be quartered circles with a dot in each section. The day Lamat occurs several times in the Postclassic Maya codices. Examples from the Dresden Codex pages 47 and 49 show how, even within a single column, the scribes varied the form of the sign (fig. 5). In some examples, it looks like a square divided into four parts with a dot in each. Other examples have a diamond in the center, making it more closely resemble the Venus sign.

Fig. 5. Examples of the day sign for Lamat on Dresden 47a D6-9 and 49a C7-10. After Förstemann (1880).

Fig. 4. Venus symbol on carved jade text from the cenote at Chichén Itzá. After Proskouriakoff (1974: fig. 12).

Fig. 6. Initial series introductory glyph with the variable element for the month Yax, from Quirigua Stela K. Artwork by Matthew G. Looper.

Initial Series Introductory Glyph

During the Classic period, the Lamat/Venus sign also occurred in initial series introductory glyphs as a variable element (the *haab'* "patron") for dates occurring in the month Yax (fig. 6).[6] These signs show the full range of variation for the day Lamat and Venus, with the addition of it being depicted in the eye of an animal that David Stuart (2005: 70) has referred to as the Starry Deer Alligator.

Codical Examples of Venus

Both the full and half forms of the Lamat/Venus sign are found throughout the Postclassic Maya codices. At least one of the Classic monumental examples, and most of those from the codices, are modified by the adjective *chäk*, signifying "great/red star," the specific Maya name for the planet Venus. These texts demonstrate that, although the sign can be interpreted as "star" in the name "great star," in these contexts Venus is clearly intended even when it occurs without the **chäk** prefix. The range of variation among signs representing Lamat and Venus, though not identical, overlaps in many respects. Whether they are fully equivalent is not clear, but certainly they are graphically, and in some manner semantically, related.

The Five-Pointed Star

The quadripartite examples discussed up to this point contrast with the five-pointed stars from Teotihuacan, dating from approximately the same time as the Maya Late Preclassic and Early Classic periods. Both full five-pointed stars and "half-star" conch shells appear on murals and ceramic vessels from that site. In some cases, many of these stars occur together, suggesting again that the symbol may not be exclusively signifying the planet Venus. Nevertheless, occurrences of the five-pointed star in the murals of Cacaxtla (Carlson 1991) and in Postclassic depictions of Quetzalcoatl suggest an association with Venus (Seler 1904, 1990).

The Mixtec deity born on the day 9 Wind in the Oaxacan tradition is known in Nahuatl as Quetzalcoatl. In the Mixtec Zouche Nuttall Codex, 9 Wind/Quetzalcoatl (or a person dressed as him) appears with the five-pointed conch shell on his belt. In central Mexico, there is a parallel tradition in which Venus is represented by a five-pointed star or a five-pointed half star. As mentioned previously, these five-pointed stars occur throughout Teotihuacan and can be found in the Cacaxtla murals as well as in several Postclassic Mexican codices. In the Mexican tradition, the god Quetzalcoatl is identified with the planet Venus (Aveni 2001: 274; Milbrath 1999: 177). Particularly striking examples of Quetzalcoatl with Venus imagery occur on pages 26, 27, and 36 of the Codex Borbonicus (fig. 7).[7] The five-pointed Venus half star is on his chest and on his shield, and a symbol that resembles the quadripartite Venus glyph is on his headdress. In these images, the Mexican and the Gulf/Maya traditions are combined. The use of these two forms of Venus images spans over 1,400 years, demonstrating a continuity that could not have existed without a strong history of interaction among scribes and artists from a number of ethnicities. The examples from the Codex Borbonicus demonstrate that both of the traditions were known to the painters of Postclassic highland Mexico.

Fig. 7. Quetzalcoatl with Gulf/Maya symbol on headdress and central Mexican conch shell symbol on costume (belt?) and shield. After Anders et al. (1991: 26).

Combining Mesoamerican and Christian Symbols

An interesting case can be made that the Mexican image of Nuestra Señora de Guadalupe combines both Mesoamerican and Christian symbols. The original venerated painted cloth that hangs in the basilica in Mexico City dates from 1531, a mere ten years after the fall of Tenochtitlan. Photographs vary greatly in the colors and the kinds of details that can be seen in them. Over the years, the image has been subject to refurbishing and repainting. Even without knowing how exactly the image of today matches the original, it should be noted that all available images of it bear little resemblance to its namesake, the European Virgin of Guadalupe from Extremadura, Spain.

Celestial imagery abounds: stars decorate the green cape, and the Virgin stands in front of a radiant light (the sun?) on a crescent moon, below which is a winged figure. Mary, the mother of Jesus, was called *Stella Maris*, "star of the sea," as early as the seventh century.[8] *Lux Matutina*, "morning light," and *Stella Marina*, "star of the sea," appear in a twelfth-century Parisian manuscript. The title *Stella Matutina*, "morning star," dates from the fourteenth century, when it was first used in the Padua version of the Litanies of Loretto.[9]

Because Venus is nearer to the sun than is the earth, it is most dramatically visible at the same time as the lunar crescent—that is, near sunset or dawn. The ancient Maya and Nahua peoples, like the Europeans, associated Venus with

Fig. 8.
Our Lady of Guadalupe. Arrows
point to five of the Venus-like stars.
From photograph in public domain.

the dawn. In the Venus table in the Dresden Codex (on pages 46–50), in addition to many examples of the Venus glyph, there are several Venus-related titles that seem to be Nahua words spelled with syllabic signs. The title from page 48, **ta-wi-si-ka-la**, *tawisikal(a),* is a Maya version of the Nahuatl name Tlahuisical, "luz rosacea del amanecer [dawn]" (Macri and Looper 2003b; Whittaker 1986), literally the Homeric phrase "rosy light of dawn."

Venus imagery on the portrait of Our Lady of Guadalupe includes stars and a crescent and may also have been invoked by the quadripartite floral design on her clothing. At least six of these flower-like quadripartite symbols, which resemble the Maya and Gulf (La Mojarra) representations of Venus, appear as decoration on her inner garment. Five of these are marked by arrows on the image in figure 8. The presence of other imagery evoking the Roman Catholic tradition that names Mary as the morning star supports their identification as Venus symbols. Does the Guadalupe image, which includes celestial imagery and otherwise illustrates elements of both European and Mexican visual traditions, also make use of an ancient Mesoamerican sign for Venus? I believe it is possible.

Venus/Star/Lamat Complex

A second item that offers insight into scribal interaction also involves the Venus symbol, but the discussion now moves from simply tracing graphic continuity to examining evidence for the sharing of a metaphor. In moving beyond a simple visual relationship, we encounter a feature that involves not a specific language, but a metaphor that is found throughout Mesoamerica. Several verbs in Maya glyphic texts are associated with war and conquest; for example: *chuk*, "capture"; *pul*, "burn"; *hub'*, "fell"; *ch'äk*, "cut; destroy." One contains a Venus symbol and has been referred to as the "star war" verb (fig. 9). It is composed of a Venus sign, a symbol of war, above a central element that may be the "earth, region" glyph **kab'**, the syllabic sign **yi**, perhaps representing the verbal suffix -*vy*, or the central element of an emblem glyph that names a polity that has been conquered. On both sides of the central element—in the example shown, only on one side—is a representation of water, either as lines of circles or dots or as Maya "water stacks."

Aldana (2005: 313) argues that attempts to associate the dates of "star war" events with significant points in the Venus cycle have been for the most part forced and unsuccessful and suggests, rather, that the Venus sign should be read as the logograph **ek'** used in rebus fashion for the first syllable in the verb *ek'emey*, "to fall." However, in realizing that the "star war" glyph is consistent with other Mesoamerican emblems representing conquest, it is possible to retain the value of the sign as Venus without having to demonstrate that all (or many) such events occur at specific points in the Venus cycle. This emblematic interpretation also explains the presence of the "water" elements surrounding the earth sign and emblem glyphs that occur beneath the star symbol.

Fig. 9. Grapheme for "was conquered," ZQE. Artwork by Matthew G. Looper.

Semantic couplets, also called semantic calques or loan translations (*difrasismos* in Spanish), are one of several traits diagnostic of Mesoamerica as a linguistic area—that is, a region in which languages of various families share a number of linguistic features as a result of significant historical contact (Campbell et al. 1986: 554–555; Smith-Stark 1994). One of these semantic couplets is "water + hill," meaning "town." Its full Nahuatl form is *in atl in tepetl*—literally, "the water, the hill"—to mean "a population, a city" (Garibay 1999: 116). Combined into the compound word *altepetl*, it is a political entity that can be glossed as "community," "town," or "kingdom" (e.g., Boone 2000: 11). This metaphor is not, however, limited to Nahuatl. Campbell et al. (1986: 554) note that this couplet (they call it "water-mountain") occurs in languages representing several distinct families throughout Mesoamerica: Nahuatl, Pochutec, Oluta Popoluca, Sayula Popoluca, Sierra Totonac, and Mazatec. Montes de Oca Vega (2004: 245) gives examples of "water-hill" for "town" from six languages, four of those just listed, plus Otomí and Mixtec.

Representations of towns or regions are typically shown in Mixtec and central Mexican codices by a water-hill—that is, an image of a hill with water curls on it, which constitute a frame or base for icons that provide the specific name. A spear driven into this water-hill shows that the polity so named has "fallen" (fig. 10).

As far as I am aware, the water-hill couplet is not found in contemporary Mayan languages. Nevertheless, it seems this widespread metaphor was known to the ancient Maya scribes and was represented in the complex logograph that is directly analogous to the Mexican water-hill and that substituted in glyphic inscriptions for the intransitive verb "to fall, to be defeated." Figure 11 shows a Maya representation of conquest. In the glyph shown here, the water curls are represented by "water stacks," but they are more typically shown as lines of circles representing droplets of water. The hill seen in central Mexican examples is replaced by the Maya symbol for earth or, in some instances, by the emblem glyph representing the polity that has been conquered. Here the central element is the emblem glyph for the site of Naranjo. In the Maya form, the act of conquest itself is represented by a "half-Venus" war symbol instead of a spear.

That Venus was associated with war and sacrifice has been known from the earliest writings about the Mexica (Sahagún 1959–1982, bk. 7: 62). It is also evident from images showing Venus, or personages representing Venus, using a spearthrower to spear various animals, deities, warriors, and objects. Representations of this can be seen in the Venus pages in codices of the Borgia Group from central Mexico: on pages 53–54 of the Borgia (Anders et al. 1993), pages 9–11 of the Cospi (Anders et al. 1994), and pages 80–84 of the Vaticanus B (Anders 1972), as well as in the figures accompanying the Venus almanac in the Maya Dresden Codex (pages 46–50). On page 46 of the Codex Nuttall, it is Quetzalcoatl (or a priest dressed in his symbols, including the half-star conch

Fig. 10. A conquered polity, Codex Nuttall, p. 46. After Anders et al. (1992).

Fig. 11. Maya glyph for a conquered polity, from Naranjo Hieroglyphic Stairway 1, Step 6 N1. After Graham (1978: 109).

shell at his waist) that introduces a series of speared water-hills conquered by 8 Deer (Anders et al. 1992).

This emblematic interpretation of the star war glyph has two advantages over previous explanations: it is no longer imperative to associate all occurrences of it with events in the cycle of the planet Venus, and it explains the presence of the water stacks/water drops along the sides of the "earth" sign or emblem glyph for the conquered polity. The presence of this metaphor does not imply the borrowing of a foreign word but, perhaps more remarkably, the sharing of a specific metaphor. It provides yet another indication of the interrelatedness of Mesoamerican intellectual traditions.

Snakes and Roads

Evidence that at least some scribes may have been familiar with neighboring languages and foreign graphic traditions comes from two sets of signs that are graphically and semantically related but that have seemingly unrelated syllabic values. The Maya glyph for the syllable **b'i/b'e** is a set of five circles arranged in a quincunx inside a cartouche (XGE) (fig. 12A). Its logographic value is **b'ih/b'éeh**—in Ch'olan languages "road" is *b'ih*; in Yucatecan, it is *b'éeh*. Another glyph for **b'i/b'e** is HTF (fig. 12B), a footprint on a road, also found in Mexican and Mixtecan pictorial manuscripts representing roads, paths, and journeys. The relationship between the sound **b'i** and the footprint for "road" is evident from the Early Classic period in a text from Río Azul on Vessel 15, the "chocolate pot," in which a foot or footprint (HTF) is painted on the face of a snake (AC6) in a spelling of **yu-k'i-b'i**, *yuk'ib'*, "his drinking vessel" (fig. 12C). The glyph for the snake typically shows a head with a snub nose, a cross-hatched area above the eye, fangs, and sometimes lines along the bottom representing reptilian belly plates (fig. 12D). The quincunx on the head of a snake replaces the cross-hatching over 30 times in Classic period texts; the majority of these come from the western region, with 20 examples from Palenque alone (fig. 12E). In the primary standard sequence found on ceramic texts, a footprint covers the eye of the snake, as in the Río Azul example. In several examples, the footprint in a cartouche (HTF) completely replaces the head of the snake (fig. 12B).

Why would the logograph for "snake," **káan/chan** (AC6), be read as syllabic **b'i** when a quincunx (XGE) occurs on its face, or when a foot (HTF) is drawn in its eye? Zapotecan languages offer a possible explanation. By adding a syllabic sign for **b'i/b'e** to a snake head (either XGE or HTF), the scribe may have intended to call to mind the Zapotecan word "snake." Composed of the animal-classifying prefix *b'V-* and the root *el̲*, we find several forms of the word: *bel̲*, Zapotec de Yatzachi (Butler 1997: 13) and Zapotec de Zoogocho (Long C. and Cruz M. 1999: 9); *bäl̲*, Zapotec de Mitla (Stubblefield and Stubblefield 1991: 6); *bèllà*, Zapotec de Juarez (Nellis and Nellis 1983: 14); and *beenda'*, Zapotec del Istmo (Pickett et al. 1979: 68). Although the Zapotec glyph for the fifth day of the 20-day calendar is a picture of a snake (Urcid Serrano 2001: 252, fig. 4.151), there is no confirmation that it was actually read *b'el̲*. Thus, if the Maya examples do have a connection with the Zapotec language, it was restricted to the spoken word "snake" and cannot be confirmed or even supported by images of snakes from Zapotec inscriptions because we do not know if they were read **b'el**. The locations where Zapotecan languages are spoken today, the Isthmus and southern and western Oaxaca, do not directly border the Maya lowlands, but the sites along the Usumacinta River and Palenque, the sources of the majority of the **b'i** snakes, are the Classic Maya sites nearest to Zapotecan regions. Such a web of interrelatedness could be explained by the fact that Maya scribes were familiar with languages and scribal traditions other than their own. Although such musings about the motivations for this example of graphic variation lie beyond our ability to prove, a consideration of words in non-Mayan languages offers some intriguing avenues for further investigation.

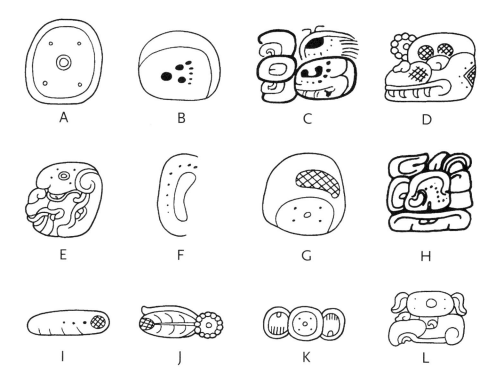

Fig. 12. Maya graphemes related to "road" and the syllables **b'i** and **o**. Artwork by Matthew G. Looper, unless otherwise noted. A. XGE. B. HTF. After Stuart (1988: fig. 2B). C. **yu-k'i-b'i**, *yuk'ib'*, "his drinking vessel." D. AC6. E. AC6. F. HTF. G. YG6. H. Glyph G8, Palenque, Tablet of the Cross at A10. Copyright David Schele, courtesy of FAMSI. I. BT1. J. BT1 variant. K. 32E. L. 32E variant.

Several other Maya graphemes (HTE, YG6, and 1SJ) appear to be graphically, semantically, and phonetically related to the quincunx (XGE) (fig. 12F–H). Each has an elongated, usually cross-hatched or darkened shape, which we now recognize as a stylized foot. The Maya logograph **b'ix**, *b'ix*, "go away" (YG6), includes the quincunx within its cartouche, with an elongated curved cross-hatched shape above it. Its logographic value is confirmed by its substitution for the syllabic sequence **b'i xi** in a representation of *b'ix* in *ho'b'ix*, "five days ago," and *wukb'ix*, "seven days ago," in distance numbers including Glyph D of the supplementary series. The interpretation of the glyph as a foot on a road is certainly compatible with the sense of the Ch'olan verb *b'ix*, "go away." This can be compared to **hul**, *hul*, "to arrive" (HTE), known from early Classic texts, which is composed of a stylized footprint in an elongated cartouche.

Fig. 13. Otontecutli, a lord of the Otomí. After Sahagún (1993: 262r).

The grapheme 1SJ (in the center of fig. 12H) appears earlier and much more frequently than the others. The curved shape of the glyph has inspired such interpretations as the arched body of a snake (Thompson 1962: 55), a bent feather, a shell, or even a decapitated bird (Justeson 1984: 327). It occurs in two calendrical signs: as Glyph G8 in the cycle of G1–G9 of the supplementary series, and as the prefix on the month Kumk'u. An elongated cross-hatched shape is usually on one half of the glyph, and dots or small circles are along the other side of it or in a line coming from the cross-hatched shape. The example in figure 12H is from the Tablet of the Cross at Palenque (A10). The elongated shape is shown here as a foot with toes visible. The line of dots to the right of it suggests a path, similar to how journeying is depicted in some Mixtec and central Mexican books.

Lounsbury (1983) demonstrated that 1SJ substitutes for BT1, known to have the syllabic value of **o** (fig. 12I–J).[10] Another sign that substitutes for the BT1 variants, and consequently is believed to have the value **o**, is 32E (fig. 12K–L). The central element in this grapheme is a quincunx, a "road" sign. But why would signs associated with "road" ever have the value **o**? One explanation is that "road" is *b'éeh* and *b'ih* in Yucatecan and Ch'olan, respectively, and *o'-tli* is "road" in Nahuatl. The dual syllabic values of **b'i/b'e** and **o** for signs with footprints and quincunxes on them may reflect the Maya scribes' knowledge that the Nahua word for "road," *o'tli*, is equivalent to *b'éeh* and *b'ih* in their languages.

An example from a central Mexican document may be related. In Sahagún's *Primeros memoriales,* a lord of the Otomí, *Otontecutli,* is shown carrying a shield with five cotton balls on it (fig. 13). He is one of only two of the series of 36 lords to carry such a shield (the other is Atlaua whose shield is half white and half red). It may be that the quincunx here has the same semantic value ("road") that it has in Maya texts, but with the value **o** derived from the Nahuatl root *o'-,* "road," it cues the first syllable of the name *Otontecutli.*

To add a note of caution to this discussion, among the oldest Mesoamerican examples of the quincunx are those from carved stone monuments from Oaxaca. There the elongated signs containing a quincunx have been associated with either death or subjugation (Marcus 1992: 395, fig. 11.35; Urcid Serrano 2001: 71, fig. 2.31). Some scholars have identified these as images of spearthrowers. Might they somehow be related to the Maya graphemes containing the quincunx?

Models of Intellectual Exchange

Graphic images can be spread in several ways. Either people travel from place to place (in pilgrimage, for trade, for conquest) viewing murals, architectural panels, and stone monuments and reproducing them in other locations, or people travel from place to place carrying books, beads, celts, shells, pottery, or textiles that bear such images that then become known to people in new regions. It may well be that the spread of graphic images occurred as a result of both of these activities. At various times and places, scribes were familiar with more than one language and/or more than one script and/or more than one iconographic system.

Evidence for such knowledge among scribes—and their readers—can be seen in several painted texts. The presence of Venus symbols from the Gulf/ Maya tradition and the central Mexican tradition on the figure of Quetzalcoatl was discussed earlier. Another notable example comes from the Mexican highlands. Figure 14 from the Codex Mendoza shows a scribe painting a Mexican "day" sign (Berdan and Anawalt 1992: 70r). This can be compared with the depiction in the Telleriano-Remensis (fig. 15) of a Mexican scribe painting the Maya and the Mexican "day" signs side by side (Quiñones Keber 1995: 30r).[11] Even though scribes may have been familiar with a variety of iconographic traditions, most of the time scribes and painters kept with their own conventions—especially within written texts. Archaic or foreign elements, when they do appear, are often limited to iconographic images. Examples of this can be seen in the presence of Mexican symbols in Maya skybands. In the skyband in figure 16, from page 56 of the Dresden Codex, we see both the Maya and the Mexican signs for "day," paired in the same manner as in the

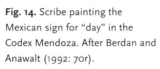

Fig. 14. Scribe painting the Mexican sign for "day" in the Codex Mendoza. After Berdan and Anawalt (1992: 70r).

Fig. 15. Scribe painting the Maya and Mexican signs for "day" in the Codex Telleriano-Remensis. After Quiñones Keber (1995: 30r).

Telleriano-Remensis. Ancient Mesoamerica was rich in recording words and images. The challenge remains for us to discover what these words and pictures can tell us about the relationships between the scribal and artistic traditions of those who created them.

Nahua Loans

It is within this context of a cosmopolitan multiethnic setting that we approach the question of the presence of Nahua words in the Maya texts. Although several linguists have argued that the Nahua language could not have been present in southern Mesoamerica until the tenth or eleventh century (most recently, for example, Kaufman and Justeson 2006: 126), examples of loanwords from Nahuatl or from a closely related Uto-Aztecan language in Maya hieroglyphic texts continues to mount.

Given the unreliability of assigning absolute calendar dates to stages of language diversification, a few centuries more or less would hardly seem significant, yet it is critical to our understanding of sociopolitical relationships between southern Mesoamerica and the central Mexican region. Nahua words spelled with syllabic signs in Classic period inscriptions offer clear and datable evidence of Nahua influence on the peoples of the Maya lowlands well before the Postclassic and suggest that the significant intellectual interchanges among the Maya lowlands, the Gulf region, and the Mexican highlands have a complex and sustained history.

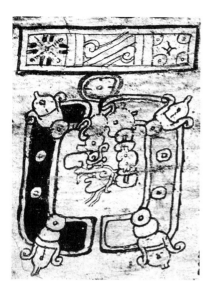

Fig. 16. Maya skyband with Maya and Mexican signs for "day" on Dresden 56a. After Förstemann (1880).

The relationships expressed during the Postclassic, as evidenced by Nahua words in the Maya codices (Macri, in press), were built on even earlier periods of contact. Syllabic spellings on the lidded chocolate pot from Río Azul suggest contact by the Early Classic period (Macri 2005). Another wave of influence appears in the western Maya lowlands during the seventh century (Macri and Looper 2003b). It is unlikely that these are the only periods of contact or that these episodes of contact were identical in either intensity or duration, some probably being best described as episodic, during which contact was brief and perhaps superficial, while others might be better described as extended intervals of mutual cultural and intellectual sharing.

Evidence of Nahua words appears in the hieroglyphic texts in several different forms. In some cases, a logograph is written with a phonetic complement that signals a Nahua loanword. A patterned logograph representing *pik*, "skirt," occurs twice in the Dresden Codex with the phonetic complement **ki** (Dresden 2d). The associated images show Ixik Kab' ("Lady Earth") and the death god holding skirt-like garments. The word *pik*, "skirt," occurs in both Yucatecan and Ch'olan languages, presumably a borrowing related to the Nahuatl verb "to wrap"—for example, *pi:ccatl*, "envoltura" (Karttunen 1983: 193); *pi:qu(i)*, "envolver tamales en hojas cuando los hacen, o cosa semejante; lo envuelve" (Karttunen 1983: 197); and *pi:ki*, "to arrange, to put together, to tie together with string to make something with netting, to assemble, to build" (Campbell 1985: 391). In other instances, a word may be spelled entirely with syllabic signs. This is the case of the Venus deity title **ta-wi-si-ka-la** for the Nahuatl name Tlahuisical, which occurs in the Venus table (Dresden 48eA2).

Words can be shared across languages as a result of direct contact or contact through an intermediary language or languages. Familiarity with the "foreign" language can range from widespread bilingualism to limited bilingualism with knowledge of a subset of vocabulary or even of a single word. The contact may be the result of economic or military expansion, or of migration. It can be sudden or long lasting. And the words can be forever identified as "foreign" or can be fully incorporated into the borrowing language after even a generation, with speakers totally unaware of their origin (see Dakin, ch. 7, this volume, for a more detailed treatment of this phenomenon).

With the invention of alphabetic writing, the representation of information became abstracted from visual imagery. The Mesoamerican scribes, however, did not see a dichotomy between language and art. Not only did they associate their texts with accompanying pictures, but the logographs themselves, the word signs, frequently remained identifiable with the objects they represented. And even when the original referent can no longer be identified, the logographs remain distinct from one another, enabling us to trace their histories through the centuries. Within this tradition, the Maya were among those scribes who also developed an inventory of abstract syllabic signs to record the sounds of their words. Thus they combined both language and visual art to document their rich intellectual environment. The complex interplay between the diverse peoples of the region is chronicled in the sounds and images they passed on to us.

Notes

1. Approximate date ranges for archaeological periods mentioned in this paper follow roughly those developed for the Maya region: Preclassic, 1500 BCE to 200 CE; Classic, 200–900 CE; Postclassic, 900 CE to the sixteenth century.

2. In this paper the term *Nahuatl* refers to the Uto-Aztecan language spoken in Mexico from within a few centuries of the Spanish conquest. I use the term *Nahua* when referring to Classic period loanwords to mean languages in the group that includes Nahuatl and any closely related language varieties that preceded it.

3. Words in Mesoamerican languages are shown here in italics. Words and syllables in boldface type represent word and syllable values of Maya glyphic signs. English glosses (rough translations) of words are shown within quotation marks.

4. A plotting of the positions of the first appearance of Venus at the moment of sunrise for consecutive intervals of 584 days can be seen at freemasonry.bcy.ca/antimasonry/venus.html, accessed January 14, 2007.

5. Graphemes in the Maya script are referred to by the three-digit codes assigned in Macri and Looper (2003a).

6. Initial series dates include the Long Count, which gives the total number of days since the beginning of the current creation, the Calendar Round day and month, and a lunar count. These dates are introduced by a complex glyph that includes the *haab'* patron—that is, a variable element that corresponds to one of the 19 named periods of the solar year.

7. The five-pointed Venus half star, found in the murals at Cacaxtla and in central Mexican codices, can be traced as far back as Teotihuacan (Aveni 2001: 225).

8. See www.newadvent.org/cathen/02149a.htm, accessed on January 11, 2009.

9. See campus.udayton.edu/mary//questions/yq/yq71.html, accessed on September 8, 2006.

10. This grapheme includes signs T99, T279, and T280 in Thompson (1962).

11. This example was brought to my attention by Gabrielle Vail and Christine Hernández.

References Cited

Aldana, Gerardo
    2005   Agency and the "Star War" Glyph: A Historical Reassessment of Classic Maya Astrology and Warfare. *Ancient Mesoameric*a 16: 305–320.

Anders, Ferdinand
    1972   *Codex Vaticanus 3773 (Codex Vaticanus B).* Biblioteca Apostolica Vaticana. Akademische Druck- und Verlagsanstalt, Graz, Austria.

Anders, Ferdinand, Maarten Jansen, and Gabina Aurora Pérez Jiménez
    1992   *Crónica mixteca: El rey 8 Venado, Garra de Jaguar, y la dinastía de Teozacualco-Zaachila.* Akademische Druck- und Verlagsanstalt, Graz, Austria; Sociedad Estatal Quinto Centenario, Madrid; Fondo de Cultura Económica S.A., México, D.F.

Anders, Ferdinand, Maarten Jansen, and Luis Reyes García
    1991   *El libro del Ciuacoatl: Homenaje para el año del Fuego Nuevo. Libro explicativo del llamado Códice Borbónico.* Akademische Druck- und Verlagsanstalt, Graz, Austria; Sociedad Estatal Quinto Centenario, Madrid; Fondo de Cultura Económica S.A., México, D.F.
    1993   *Los templos del cielo y de la oscuridad. Libro explicativo del llamado Códice Borgianus.* Akademische Druck- und Verlagsanstalt, Graz, Austria; Sociedad Estatal Quinto Centenario, Madrid; Fondo de Cultura Económica S.A., México, D.F.

Anders, Ferdinand, Maarten Jansen, and Peter van der Loo
    1994   *Códice Cospi. Calendario de pronósticos y ofrendas.* Facsimile with commentary. Akademische Druck- und Verlagsanstalt, Graz, Austria; Fondo de Cultura Económica S.A., México, D.F.

Aveni, Anthony F.
    2001   *Skywatchers.* Rev. ed. University of Texas Press, Austin.

Berdan, Frances F., and Patricia Rieff Anawalt
    1992   *The Codex Mendoza.* Vol. 3: *A Facsimile Reproduction of the Codex Mendoza.* University of California Press, Berkeley.

Boone, Elizabeth Hill
    2000   *Stories in Red and Black: Pictorial Histories of the Aztecs and Mixtecs.* University of Texas Press, Austin.

Butler, Inez M.

1997   *Diccionario zapoteco de Yatzachi.* Instituto Lingüístico de Verano, Tucson, Ariz.

Campbell, Lyle

1985   *The Pipil Language of El Salvador.* Mouton, Berlin.

Campbell, Lyle, Terrence E. Kaufman, and Thomas C. Smith-Stark

1986   Mesoamerica as a Linguistic Area. *Language* 62: 530–570.

Carlson, John B.

1991   *Venus-Regulated Warfare and Ritual Sacrifice in Mesoamerica: Teotihuacan and the Cacaxtla Star Wars Connection.* Center for Archaeoastronomy, University of Maryland, College Park.

Closs, Michael P.

1979   Venus in the Maya World: Glyphs, Gods and Associated Astronomical Phenomena. In *Tercera Mesa Redonda de Palenque,* vol. 4 (Merle Greene Robertson and Donnan Call Jeffers, eds.): 147–163. Pre-Columbian Art Research Institute, Monterey, Calif.

Förstemann, Ernst

1880   *Die Maya Handschrift der Königlichen öffentlichen Bibliothek zu Dresden.* Mit 74 Tafeln in Chromo-Lightdruck. Verlag der A. Naumannschen Lichtdruckeret, Leipzig.

Garibay K., Angel Maria

1999   *Llave del náhuatl: Colecciónes de trozos clásicos, con gramática y vocabulario nahuat-castellano, para utilidad de los principiantes.* 7th ed. Editorial Porrúa, México, D.F.

Graham, Ian

1978   *Corpus of Maya Hieroglyphic Inscriptions.* Vol. 2, pt. 2: *Naranjo, Chunhuitz, Xunantunich.* Peabody Museum of Archaeology and Ethnology, Harvard University, Cambridge, Mass.

Henry, H.

1907   Ave Maris Stella. In *The Catholic Encyclopedia.* Robert Appleton Company, New York. Electronic document, http://www.newadvent.org/cathen/02149a.htm, accessed January 11, 2009.

Justeson, John S.

1984   Appendix B: Interpretations of Mayan Hieroglyphs. In *Phoneticism in Mayan Hieroglyphic Writing* (John S. Justeson and Lyle Campbell, eds.): 315–362. Institute for Mesoamerican Studies, State University of New York, Albany.

Justeson, John S., and Terrence Kaufman

1993   A Decipherment of Epi-Olmec Hieroglyphic Writing. *Science* 259: 1703–1711.

Karttunen, Frances

1983   *An Analytical Dictionary of Nahuatl.* University of Oklahoma Press, Norman.

Kaufman, Terrence, and John Justeson

2006   The History of the Word for "Cacao" and Related Terms in Ancient Meso-
America. In *Chocolate in Mesoamerica: A Cultural History of Cacao*
(Cameron L. McNeil, ed.): 117–139. University of Florida Press, Gainesville.

Long C., Rebecca, and Sofronio Cruz M.

1999   *Diccionario zapoteco de San Bartolomé Zoogocho, Oaxaca.* Instituto
Lingüístico de Verano, Coyoacán, D.F.

Lounsbury, Floyd G.

1983   Glyph Values: T99, 155, 279, 280. In *Contributions to Maya Hieroglyphic
Decipherment*, vol. 1 (Stephen D. Houston, ed.): 44–49. Human Relations
Area Files, New Haven, Conn.

Macri, Martha J.

2005   Nahua Loan Words from the Early Classic Period: Words for Cacao
Preparation on a Río Azul Ceramic Vessel. *Ancient Mesoamerica*
16: 311–326.

n.d.   Mesoamerican Scripts and Iconography: Evidence for Portable Texts from
the Preclassic to the 16th Century. Paper presented at the symposium
"Recent Progress in Understanding the History of the Area Between the
Basin of Mexico and the Gulf Coast, from Toltec Times to the Present" at
the annual meeting of the American Society for Ethnohistory, Santa Fe,
N.Mex., November 2005.

Macri, Martha J., and Matthew Looper

2003a   *The New Catalog of Maya Hieroglyphs.* Vol. 1: *The Classic Period
Inscriptions.* University of Oklahoma Press, Norman.

2003b   Nahua in Ancient Mesoamerica: Evidence from Maya Inscriptions. *Ancient
Mesoamerica* 14: 285–297.

Marcus, Joyce

1992   *Mesoamerican Writing Systems: Propaganda, Myth, and History in Four
Ancient Civilizations.* Princeton University Press, Princeton, N.J.

Milbrath, Susan

1999   *Star Gods of the Maya: Astronomy in Art, Folklore, and Calendars.*
University of Texas Press, Austin.

Montes de Oca Vega, Mercedes

2004   Los difrasismos: ¿Núcleos conceptuales mesoamericanos? In *La metáfora
en Mesoamérica* (Mercedes Montes de Oca Vega, ed.): 225–251. Estudios
Sobre Lenguas Americanas 3. Universidad Nacional Autónoma de México,
Instituto de Investigaciones Filológicas, Seminario de Lenguas Indígenas,
México, D.F.

Nellis, Neil, and Jane Goodner de Nellis

1983   *Diccionario zapoteco de Juárez: Ca Titsa' Qui' Ri'u.* Instituto Lingüístico
de Verano, México, D.F.

Pickett, Velma, with collaborators

1979   *Vocabulario zapoteco del Istmo.* Instituto Lingüístico de Verano,
México, D.F.

Proskouriakoff, Tatiana

1974   *Jades from the Cenote of Sacrifice, Chichen Itza, Yucatan.* Memoirs of
the Peabody Museum of Archaeology and Ethnology 10 (1). Harvard
University, Cambridge, Mass.

Quiñones Keber, Eloise

1995   *Codex Telleriano-Remensis: Ritual, Divination, and History in a Pictorial
Aztec Manuscript.* Illustrations by Michel Besson. University of Texas
Press, Austin.

Sahagún, Bernardino de

1959–1982   *Florentine Codex: General History of the Things of New Spain,* 12 books
in 13 vols. (Charles E. Dibble and Arthur J. O. Anderson, eds. and trans.).
School of American Research, Santa Fe, and University of Utah Press, Salt
Lake City.

1993   *Primeros memoriales.* University of Oklahoma Press, Norman.

Saturno, William

2006a   The Dawn of Maya Gods and Kings. *National Geographic Magazine*
209: 68–77.

2006b   The Dawn of Maya Gods and Kings. Available at http://ngm
.nationalgeographic.com/2006/01/dawn-of-the-maya/saturno-text,
accessed April 2, 2009.

Seler, Eduard

1904   Venus Period in the Picture Writings of the Borgian Codex Group. *Bureau
of American Ethnology Bulletin* 28: 355–391.

1990 [1898]   Quetzalcoatl-Kukulcan in Yucatan. In *Collected Works in
Mesoamerican Linguistics and Archaeology,* vol. 1 (Frank E. Comparato,
general ed.): 198–218. Labyrinthos, Culver City, Calif.

Smith-Stark, Thomas C.

1994   Mesoamerican Calques. In *Investigaciones lingüísticas en Mesoamérica*
(Carolyn J. MacKay and Verónica Vázquez, eds.): 15–50. Estudios Sobre
Lenguas Americanas 1. Universidad Nacional Autónoma de México,
Instituto de Investigaciones Filológicas, Seminario de Lenguas Indígenas,
México, D.F.

Stuart, David

1988   The Río Azul Cacao Pot: Epigraphic Observations on the Function of a
Maya Ceramic Vessel. *Antiquity* 62: 153–157.

2005   *The Inscriptions from Temple XIX at Palenque.* Pre-Columbian Art
Research Institute, San Francisco.

Stubblefield, Morris, and Carol Miller de Stubblefield

1991   *Diccionario zapoteco de Mitla, Oaxaca.* Instituto Lingüístico de Verano,
México, D.F.

Thompson, J. Eric S.

1962   *A Catalog of Maya Hieroglyphs.* University of Oklahoma Press, Norman.

Urcid Serrano, Javier

2001   *Zapotec Hieroglyphic Writing.* Dumbarton Oaks Research Library and
Collection, Washington, D.C.

Winfield Capitaine, Fernando

1988   *La Estela 1 de La Mojarra, Veracruz, México.* Research Reports on Ancient Maya Writing 16. Center for Maya Research, Washington, D.C.

Whittaker, Gordon

1986   The Mexican Names of Three Venus Gods in the Dresden Codex. *Mexicon* 8: 56–60.

Chapter Seven

Linguistic Evidence for Historical Contacts between Nahuas and Northern Lowland Mayan Speakers

Karen Dakin

INTERACTION BETWEEN highland Mexico and the northern Maya low-lands in the Late Postclassic, in particular the different kinds of ideological interaction that involves scribes, astronomers, and priests, is the focus of the papers in this volume. In this chapter, I discuss various kinds of linguistic data that can be used as evidence in understanding that interaction. I should note as well that the evidence indicates contact between Nahuatl and Mayan speakers in southern Mesoamerica, rather than the presence of Mayan speakers in highland Mexico. The reasons for this probably have to do with a long-time presence of Nahuatl[1] speakers in the southern area. The initial dates of that presence are controversial and the subject of recent research pointing to conflicting analyses of the origins and interrelationships of words such as those corresponding to *cacao* and *chocolate*, and to *Xolotl* and the cork tree, or *jonote*, in various southern Mesoamerican languages (cf. Dakin 2005; Dakin and Wichmann 2000; Justeson et al. 1985; Macri and Looper 2003). However, the influence of Nahuatl in the Maya area in the Late Postclassic is more easily documented and supported by evidence of various kinds. Historical references to languages spoken in the area and linguistic inferences of various kinds for Campeche, Tabasco, and northern Yucatán make it clear that, in the Late Postclassic, Chontal, Yucatec, and Itzaj were in contact with Nahuatl as a lingua franca, and it is very likely that some of these regions had multilingual populations (fig. 1).

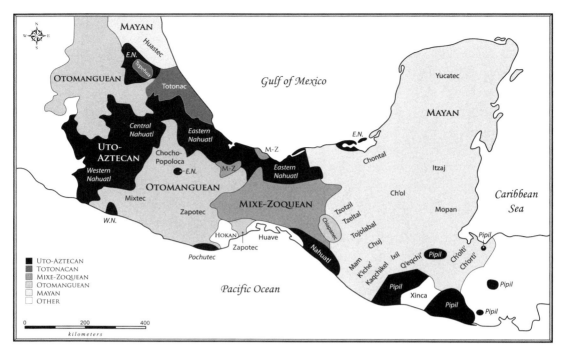

Fig. 1. The approximate distribution of selected language families and languages spoken at the time of contact, with specific emphasis on the regions where Nahuatl can be documented. Nonitalicized text labels are for constituent languages (again not a comprehensive listing). Labels in italics are language dialects discussed in the chapter. The reader should keep in mind that the boundaries are approximate and that they represent the dominant language family that can be reconstructed for a particular area. The linguistic complexity of the Basin of Mexico and surrounding regions is not accurately represented, nor is that of highland Guatemala, due to a lack of space. Map compiled from Terrence Kaufman (1994: Map 13, 34–41) and Robert Longacre (1967: fig. 15). Artwork by David R. Hixson.

Although the Postclassic period was one of intense interaction between Nahuatl-speaking populations from the central area of Puebla-Cholula and speakers of Mayan languages in northern Yucatán, such contact probably was easily established because it was part of a tradition of continuous interaction between groups who spoke various Nahuatl dialects and other ethnic groups in the region. The contacts described suggest that some level of bilingualism, perhaps limited to a scribal or merchant group or to those in power, had existed between Mayan language speakers and Nahuatl speakers for a long period. That interaction was probably not limited to Mayan and Nahuatl speakers because there were also other languages bordering on the area, such as Gulf

Zoque, but the focus of this chapter concerns the contact that can be identified specifically between Nahuatl and Mayan speakers.[2]

In considering the relationship between Nahuatl speakers and Mayan speakers from the northern lowlands and elsewhere, López Austin and López Luján (1999: 141) have proposed the existence of a society with a multiethnic and multilingual population, typically under a confederation with three capitals and based on the plumed serpent. They use the term *Zuyúa* to distinguish this society from Toltec, a name generally associated with a specific place— Tula, Hidalgo. The carriers of the society they term Zuyúa "were of a diverse nature; sometimes the system was brought into a region by aggressive foreigners" following commercial routes, but in other cases it was imposed by local groups on their neighbors (López Austin and López Luján 1999: 142). The linguistic data support such a situation.

Kinds of Linguistic Evidence

Lingua Franca

Let us consider first what we can regard as the linguistic evidence for Nahuatl-Mayan contact in the Late Postclassic period. There are mentions of the use of Nahuatl in the Maya area early after the arrival of the Spanish. For example, Fray Tomás de la Torre, in his description of the journey he made in 1544–1545 with his group of priests from Salamanca to Campeche, and from there to Xicalango and then finally to Ciudad Real, San Cristóbal de las Casas, relates how on their way north from Campeche they would ask, "gueca xicolango," the Nahuatl words / wehka šikalanko/, to inquire, "Is it far to Xicalango?" (Torre 1944–1945: 150).

The Nahuatl area of Tabasco and Campeche bordered on the Maya area. Scholes and Roys (1996: 25) cite a 1533 document to this effect: *Y del río Cupilco-Zacualco adelante es la lengua de la Nueva España* [Náhuatl] *y lo mismo del dicho río de Ulúa adelante es otra lengua* ("And from the Cupilco-Zacualco River on it is the language of New Spain [Nahuatl] and the same from the river of Ulua on it is a different language"). As a result, it would seem likely that many Yucatec Mayan speakers also were able to communicate with Nahuatl speakers.

It is possible to argue as well for the Pre-Hispanic Postclassic use of Nahuatl as a lingua franca in Mayan-speaking areas during the sixteenth century on the basis of the form of the language found in documents. For the early colonial period, we have a body of sixteenth- and seventeenth-century Nahuatl documents from the area where Mayan languages other than Yucatec were spoken. It is interesting, however, that there do not seem to be any specifically from Yucatán. Restall (1997) has done extensive archival work relating to the Yucatán Peninsula, but in his major study of the colonial indigenous documentation, he mentions only manuscripts in Yucatec. This is probably due to the fact that it was a variant of Yucatec Maya rather than Nahuatl that functioned as a lingua franca in that area because of its higher prestige.

We do have published and unpublished documents in Nahuatl from the rest of the southern area: parts of Chiapas and Guatemala, including Chenalhó (Tzotzil) and Amatenango (Tzeltal) in Chiapas; and Antigua (Kaqchikel), Santa Eulalia (Q'anjob'al) (the last in two variants of Nahuatl); and Quetzaltenango (Mam) in Guatemala. In addition, there are colonial documents in Nahuatl from the Nahuatl-speaking Xoconochco (Soconusco), the Lenca area in Honduras, and from the Mixe and Zoque areas of Oaxaca and Chiapas (cf. Dakin 1996b, 2009). Although the use of Nahuatl for documents written in the Roman alphabet is a result of Spanish administrative policy, an analysis of the language employed in them leads us to argue that such usage is also a reflection of the Pre-Hispanic use of an archaic lingua franca variant in the area in the Late Postclassic, one that also differed from the variants spoken by the Nahuas who accompanied Alvarado and his men into Guatemala and further south.

To understand the importance of the existence of these Nahuatl documents in the southern area and the fact that at least two different major dialects of Nahuatl were in contact there, one must consider the historical development and geographical diversification of Nahuatl. The scenario that follows is based principally on Canger's (1988) classification of modern and colonial dialects, but it takes into account the chronology from my own reconstruction (Dakin 1982, 2002). In Canger and Dakin (1985), we described an isogloss involving the two reflexes *i* or *e* of proto-Uto-Aztecan (pUA) *u that represents an early split dividing eastern from western and central dialects, dating from the very formation of the language. Apparently there were Nahuatl speakers from the eastern branch who migrated from a point not yet clearly identifiable into the Valley of Mexico and surrounding areas and who also moved into central Guerrero and the eastern areas of the Huasteca, the Sierra de Puebla, and along the Gulf Coast into the Isthmus and Central America. We still have little reliable linguistic evidence for dating this early expansion south. It would be necessary to find datable written sources, for example, of Nahuatl words showing specific variation written phonetically with the forms corresponding to Eastern Nahuatl in dated Maya inscriptions.

The second branch of this early split, central and western, can be associated with at least one older dialect, the extinct Pochutec from Oaxaca.[3] The Mexica and other later migrating groups that moved down the western area of Mexico, then across into what is now the State of Mexico and into its center, should probably be associated with this second branch. In the central area of the Valley of Mexico, where speakers of the eastern branch had settled first, it appears from linguistic data that the older population mixed with the later immigrants, creating a new dialect with features of the eastern and central branches that, with the growth of the Aztec Empire, gradually spread its influence into

Table 1. Historical classification of Nahuatl dialects[1]

Eastern Nahuatl
    Huasteca
    Central Guerrero
    Sierra de Puebla
    Tehuacan-Zongolica
    Isthmus
    Pipil
Western Nahuatl
    Central Nahuatl
        "Classical" Nahuatl
        Central Nahuatl (D.F., Morelos, Tlaxcala, State of Mexico [Texcoco, etc.])
        North Puebla Nahuatl
        [Lingua franca]
    Western Periphery
        Colima-Durango
        Northern part of the State of Mexico (Almomoloya, Sultepec)
        Jalisco-Nayarit
        Michoacán
        North Guerrero
        Pochutec

1. Based on Canger (1988) and Lastra de Suárez (1986), with modifications by the author.

surrounding areas in Morelos, Tlaxcala, and north Puebla. The classification from this early historical split is detailed in Table 1.

It is important to recognize the dialect split because the colonial Nahuatl documents from the southern part of Mesoamerica are written in the same orthography as that taught to Nahuatl speakers by Spanish priests in the central region of Mexico. The language variant used in the documents is basically uniform, and it is similar to the Central Nahuatl dialect described by the Spanish grammarian priests who arrived in the Valley of Mexico with Cortés and later, but not to the eastern Isthmus and Central American Pipil dialect. However, as mentioned, what is important in terms of Postclassic contact between the central and southern areas of Mesoamerica is how this lingua franca, the language of the documents, differs from that of central Mexico (generally called Classical Nahuatl): some of the key features reflect a more archaic form than that described in early colonial sources for Mexico-Tenochtitlan. The evidence is strong that the lingua franca used in southern Mexico and Guatemala is an earlier Postclassic form of the central dialect, one spread before the arrival of the Spanish.[4]

But, as noted earlier, Yucatec Maya was used in northern Yucatán instead of Nahuatl. Is there any other kind of linguistic and language-related evidence for Late Postclassic contact between this specific area and Puebla-Cholula and the Valley of Mexico? Some attention has been given to a "Zuyúa secret language,"[5] mentioned, unfortunately only briefly, in the Chilam Balam of Chumayel (Barrera Vásquez and Rendón 1982), in which a number of riddles said to originate in that language are cited with interpretations. For instance, one riddle reads "Bring me the sun, my children, to have it on my plate" (Barrera Vásquez and Rendón 1982: 131). The reference is to a fried egg. If there were a bilingual Nahuatl-Mayan language population, it seems possible that there would be clear traces of that bilingualism in the kinds of genres and descriptions used. For example, if they derive from a Nahuatl tradition, one would expect to find the same riddle, or at least similar descriptions, in surviving Nahuatl texts. However, a comparison with the riddles in Sahagún's Florentine Codex based on Mercenario Ortega (2009), as well as with the large collection of modern riddles made by Amith (1997) for central Guerrero Nahuatl, yielded no such examples, although, of course, they could nevertheless exist.

Other possible indications of contact between Yucatec Mayan and Nahuatl speakers would be the sharing of specific details of ritual language. For example, the expression "the sky's brains" is used as a metaphor for copal. In a comparison of the Zuyúa examples with the language of the *Conjuros* collected by Ruíz de Alarcón (1975 [1629]) in Guerrero in the seventeenth century—a body of texts that would be comparable in terms of the use of ritualized language—no specific descriptions or metaphors were found to be shared, although both had similar kinds of metaphorical and rhetorical devices, including the use of paired couplets and of colors in descriptions. Although that does seem to indicate a shared oral tradition, without specific examples it is difficult to consider such similarities as solid evidence for more intense contact between Mayan and Nahuatl speakers. This is especially true because recent research on Native American discourse (cf. Montes de Oca Vega 2005 and Jane Hill n.d. [2001], among others) has shown that many rhetorical practices in ritual language in Mesoamerica, such as paired couplets (*difrasismos*) and obscure metaphors first believed to be traits limited to Mesoamerica, are also found outside the area. For example, *difrasismos* are regularly used in Luiseño, a Uto-Aztecan language spoken in California (see Elliot n.d. [1999]). Although such distribution is not relevant to showing specific Nahuatl-Yucatec contact, it is interesting because it reflects multilingual interaction in a wider area that includes Uto-Aztecan languages to the north as well as in Mesoamerica.

What other kinds of linguistic evidence exist for both Postclassic and earlier contact? Historical and comparative linguistic studies, based particularly on the regularity and logic of sound change, have helped in the reconstruction of pre-history for many parts of the world, a reconstruction that can often be corroborated by knowledge from other fields as well, such as history and archaeology. The kinds of evidence for dating the presence of a language group is summarized in the following sections.

Lexical Statistics

Lexical statistics, which includes the method of glottochronology developed by Morris Swadesh (1950) and applied by him to Uto-Aztecan (1954), is a tool for reconstructing linguistic prehistory that should be mentioned. Although linguists and statisticians continue to generate results using various kinds of lexical statistics, sociolinguistic studies concerning contact between groups and linguistic reconstructions have made us question many of the results of glottochronology that claim to go beyond establishing simple relationships. More knowledge, particularly of the lexicon, of all the languages involved is necessary to establish what the linguistic correspondences among the languages are before we can accurately identify all cognates. Variation in the number of recognized cognates can drastically change results about relative time depth. Finally, the notion of a basic vocabulary in itself has also been shown to be undependable because of the differing structures of semantic systems. However, more sophisticated statistical methods that trace individual rates of retention and loss within such basic vocabulary are being developed, and it may be that they will provide new data that can be used in forming hypotheses based on lexical statistics.

Linguistic Paleontology

The reconstruction of ecological and cultural systems that can be identified with specific areas has often been used for proposing homelands and the early presence of language groups.[6] In Uto-Aztecan studies, Fowler's (1983) important reconstruction of plant and animal names showed that the dispersal point for Uto-Aztecan could not have been much north of the southernmost point of Nevada. Hill (2001) has argued that terms for both water usage and the cultivation of corn can be reconstructed, and she proposes a point of origin in Mesoamerica for Uto-Aztecan languages. Campbell and Kaufman (1976) and Justeson et al. (1985) have used arguments from linguistic paleontology in their more conservative proposals involving loanwords; their work is discussed in more detail later.

As one of the tools of linguistic paleontology, lexical diffusion has long been recognized as evidence of contact in cultural history. Examples discussed here are calques (loan translations), shared metaphors, and loanwords.

CALQUES AND SHARED METAPHORS   The existence of bilingual populations leads to the creation of calques, or loan translations. For example, some bilingual California Spanish speakers use the word *soplahojas* to refer to workers who operate leaf blowers, although the appliance they use is technically known by other names; another example is the Chicano expression *venir para atrás*, instead of *regresar*, when asking someone to "come back." Smith-Stark (1994) did an extensive study of calques created from metaphors lexicalized in Mesoamerican languages. They include expressions such as "mouth of the house" for "door." Although some of his examples have since been found to exist outside of the region as well and their distribution across Mesoamerican languages is not consistent, the latter does reveal interesting patterns that must reflect interaction within the region. Of special interest for this chapter, Smith-Stark (1994: 38) points out that "the Gulf Coast has served as the primary corridor for the spread of areal features." In contrast he notes that the "great core of Otomanguean languages centered on Oaxaca seems to have been only sporadically affected by diffusion" (1994: 38).

LOANWORDS   There are inherent problems that need to be addressed in reconstructing linguistic history using loanwords, including the fact that languages may have continued in contact for a period of time, resulting in the presence of different chronological layers that often, but not always, can be sorted out by careful consideration of the necessary sequence of sound changes. As evident in the earlier summary, one of the problems in considering Nahuatl contact with Mayan speakers is distinguishing these layers. In addition, loans pass through chains of contact—for example, in Mexico, it appears that a number of Spanish words were borrowed into some indigenous languages through contact with Nahuatl speakers rather than through direct contact with Spanish speakers. Conversely, some Nahuatl loans have entered other Mesoamerican languages through Spanish—for example, Itzaj has *jolotej* as the name of what is described by Santamaría (1983: 643) as a river fish without scales, a word borrowed from /šo:lo:-tl/ into colonial Spanish, after which the /š/ went through the Spanish sound change of the palatal [š] to the velar fricative [x] to give the modern form [*xolote*] which then was borrowed into Itzaj. As has often been noted, the use of Nahuatl in the colonial period resulted in the loan of a number of Nahuatl religious and administrative terms adapted to Spanish institutions, such as *totahtzin*, "our father"; *teopantli*, "temple, church"; and *pale:wia*, "to help." These, in turn, were borrowed into other indigenous languages.

In cases of contact having complications such as these, we may find a way to determine the history of contact through the logic of natural sound changes. With time, loans can be adapted phonologically to the borrowing language. An obvious example involves the Nahuatl final *-tli*, which often becomes *-cle* in Spanish, as in *escuincle.* In a K'iche'an loan containing the postvelar consonant *q,* this sound becomes a *k* in languages without that consonant. The fact that the borrowing language has fewer phonological contrasts than the lending one helps distinguish the one from the other.

One of the surest ways to identify the source language is understanding that the word in question should have a valid etymology in that language. In the case of polysynthetic languages such as the Uto-Aztecan ones, which have a relatively small phonemic inventory, the case can be even stronger because what initially may appear to be simple roots can often be shown to derive from more complex structures involving proto-Uto-Aztecan short roots composed of CV (consonant-vowel) and CVCV (consonant-vowel-consonant-vowel) sequences that have fused in different ways in the daughter languages. We can isolate them because they fit into "constellations," a term I use to describe the interlacing of a set of roots with different derivational paradigms that permit us to identify the constants in the meanings for the roots in those word formations. In contrast to Uto-Aztecan languages, Mayan languages have a much larger consonant inventory that permits a greater number of shorter roots, mostly with a CVC (consonant-vowel-consonant) structure, and less dependence on compounding and complex derivational processes. Proto-Uto-Aztecan has a consonant inventory of 12 or 13, whereas proto-Mayan has perhaps 25 or 26.

An important tool, of course, is written evidence, which is also the most precise for dating loanwords. For the Maya area, we have some phonetic spellings indicating a Nahuatl presence, such as the text from Río Azul with a phonetic spelling of *kakaw (ka-ka-wa)*. Macri and Looper (2003: 288–292), in addition to discussing Whittaker's (1986) identification of Postclassic Nahuatl borrowings in the Dresden Codex, have proposed reading specific glyphs from the Classic period as Nahuatl terms. They present evidence, for example, for the syllabic combinations *yo-óol-la* as Nahuatl *yo:l-*, "heart, live" and Yucatec *[y]óol*, with reinterpretation in Yucatec of the initial *y-* as a possessive prefix; and *ko-o- ha-wa* and *ko-ha-wa*, which they interpret as *ko'haw*, "helmet" (noting the sixteenth-century Tzotzil word *kovov*, "helmet"), and suggest that it comes from Nahuatl /k^{w}ay-/ "forehead." For the latter word, another possible interpretation would be that Nahuatl /k^{w}a:w-/, "eagle," is the source of the word, given the use of helmets in the shape of eagles' heads, at least in the later Mexican period.

A chronology for linguistic change is another means of identifying the source language. When it is possible to reconstruct a chronology for certain changes, we can sometimes identify loans as representative of earlier stages of the lending language. For example, *chief* was borrowed into English before the affricate č became š in French. If it had been borrowed later, after the change in French, it would be pronounced *ši:f.*

Lexical Loans into Other Languages in the Area

Although Tozzer (1941: 132, n. 117), in his notes to Landa's *Relación de las cosas de Yucatan,* suggests that Yucatec *metnal* came from Nahuatl *mictlan* /miktlan/,[7] it was Whorf in 1948 and Thompson (1948) in his comments on Whorf's work who first, to my knowledge, made proposals to use loanwords systematically between Mesoamerican languages as evidence of the region's cultural history. Whorf's description of the problems involved is a classic one.[8] A number of linguists working on different languages began to look for indigenous loans between specific languages and families, in particular Kaufman, who in 1971 identified loanwords into Mayan, suggesting various languages as sources for them. Campbell (1977), in his work on K'iche', noted a number of loans from Nahuatl and other languages and proposed criteria for their chronology. Campbell and Kaufman (1976), in their well-known proposal, argue that the Olmecs were Mixe-Zoquean speakers based on their attribution of Mixe-Zoquean origins to loanwords in various cultural fields. Justeson et al. (1985) made more detailed proposals about lowland Mayan contacts with neighboring languages and argued for the identification of Mixe-Zoquean speakers with the Olmecs. A number of papers, including Suárez (1985), Dakin and Wichmann (2000), Dakin (2001, 2003), and Macri and Looper (2003), have since questioned the direction of specific loans, proposing other sources for a number of the terms, and identifying additional diffused words as possible loans from Nahuatl.

Justeson et al. (1985: 24–26, 57–70), in their extensive study of the "foreign" impact on lowland Mayan languages, mention loans from Nahuatl and other languages to Yucatec and Ch'olan, but they identify them as late, in contrast with their set of Mixe-Zoquean loans. They propose that the Nahuatl loans must have come from the Gulf area variants and describe the phonetic changes in Gulf Coast Nahuatl as also being late, no earlier than the Late Classic period on the basis of the pre-Yucatec *t > š change that does not affect the "borrowing of Yucatec *kó:t* and Cholti <coht> "eagle" from Gulf Coast Nahuatl **koh-(ti).*" Justeson and coworkers state that they find such loans only in individual Yucatecan or Ch'olan languages and not widely distributed within these subgroups, so they conclude that they must be late borrowings. However, Wichmann (1999, and personal communication, April 1, 2007) has questioned whether *kó:t,* the key word for their dating, is a loanword from a Gulf Coast variant form derived from Nahuatl *kʷa:w-tli,* because it is found distributed in K'iche'an and Mamean languages as well as in Yucatecan and Ch'olan. I would add in support of his doubts that a final *-t* on the various forms for "eagle" is problematic since, to my knowledge, the word does not end in *t* in any dialect because the Nahuatl absolute suffix has the form *-ti* in Gulf Coast dialects and *-tli* in the central area. The *-t* / *-tl* suffix has an epenthetic vowel when following a final consonant. In addition, the common word for "eagle" in modern Gulf Coast and many other Eastern Nahua dialects appears not to be *kʷawti* or *kohti* but *kʷišin,* a word that refers to hawks in other dialects in which it is found. However, it may also be the case that the word for "eagle" has been lost. The other arguments Justeson et al. (1985: 25) suggest for late dates relate to semantic fields in that they are "apparently associated with Toltec and epi-Toltec influence in the Maya area."

There are some indications of earlier, or at least peripheral, Nahuatl loans, supported by the chronology of sound changes. Yucatec Mayan *tepal,* "ruler," appears to be a borrowing from what may be reconstructed as early or peripheral Nahuatl *te-pal-li,* "throne" (literally "broad stone"). Thompson (1948) and Justeson et al. (1985: 70) suggest that *tepal* is a Nahuatl loan, but derive it from *te-pe:wa,* "to conquer," *tepe:walli,* "conquered." However, the loss of the intervocalic *w* is not consistent in other loans, and the change from "conquered" to "conqueror" seems unlikely. Although the etymology may appear fanciful, there is a regular change in Nahuatl by which *tep- > ikp-, and –pal- is a formant in many words, where it denotes a roundish or oval flat surface, as in *noh-pal-li,* "nopal leaf," from proto-Uto-Aztecan *napu- ("nopal") and *pal-, and *mah-pal-li* ("palm of hand") from proto-Uto-Aztecan *mah- ("hand") and *pal- (cf. Dakin 1991, 1996a). Whorf (1948: 3) had proposed the alternative that *tepal* derived from *tekpan,* but both the loss of the *-k-* and the change of final *-n* to *-l* would involve more changes and ones that are less natural phonologically.

Many of the rest of the Nahuatl loans that Justeson et al. (1985) propose had been previously identified by Whorf (1948). I have eliminated some questionable forms from their list, but others are

Nahuatl *či:mal-li* ("shield") > Ch'olan *čimal* ("shield")

Nahuatl *čina:mi-TL* ("fence, lineage") > Ch'olan *činam* ("pueblo")

Nahuatl *wi:pi:l-li* ("huipil") > Yucatec *i:pil* ("huipil")

Nahuatl *ko:mi-TL* ("pot, jug, pitcher") > proto-Yucatec *kum ("pot")

Nahuatl *pa:n-TLi, pa:mi-TL* ("flag, banner") > Ch'olan *pan* ("flag")

Nahuatl *šikol-li* ("jacket of painted cloth in which the ministers of the idols officiated") > Yucatec *šikul* ("jacket")

Nahuatl *šiwi-TL* ("plant, leaf, vegetation") > Yucatec *ši:w* ("plant"), Mopan numeral classifier *ši:t* ("leaf")

Nahuatl *ȼapa-tl* ("dwarf") > Yucatec *ȼapa* ("dwarf")

Nahuatl *ma:se:wal-li* ("Indian, commoner") > Chontal *masewal* ("Indian, peasant")

Nahuatl *to:nal-li* ("day, alter ego") > Yucatec *ah tunal* ("sorcerer")

Nahuatl *tamal-li* ("tamale") > Yucatec *tamali'* ("tamale")

Nahuatl *to:pi:l-li* ("staff of office, officer") > Yucatec *tupil* ("alguacil, esbirro")

Barrera Vásquez et al. (1995) list a number of patronyms of Nahuatl origin as well that include *iwit* < *ihwi-tl* ("feather"), *kiaw* < *kiyawi-tl* ("rain"), and *šiw* <*šiwi-tl* ("grass, herbs"), mentioned above. From these examples, it is evident that at least by the Late Postclassic, Nahuatl loanwords had become a part of the lowland and Yucatec Mayan lexicons. As Justeson et al. (1985: 26) describe it: "The Nahua impact on Lowland Mayan . . . in that era [Postclassic] . . . was considerable."

In addition to identifying the source language, loans can be dated by relating them to different periods of cultural interaction. Whorf (1948: 8) and later Campbell and Kaufman (1976: 82) note that a characteristic of loanwords is their concentration in specialized semantic domains, which reflect the types of contact between groups, including, for example, administration, religion, plants/animals foreign to the borrowing group, warfare, specialized knowledge, and material culture. Thompson (1948: 26) noted "extensive Maya borrowing of Nahuatl or Nahuatlized deities and religious concepts." For the Postclassic, Whittaker (1986), in his important article, identified three central Mexican Nahuatl names for deities associated with Venus and written in phonetic form in the Dresden Codex.

In light of the discussion of the importance of the Quetzalcoatl complex during the Postclassic by López Austin and López Luján (1999), it should be mentioned that there is also evidence of contact with reference to the gods named for the two aspects of Venus. On the one hand, Yucatec Mayan has *k'uk'ulkan*, a calque on Quetzalcoatl /*ke¢al-kowa:-tl*/ ("Precious.Feather-Snake-Abs") for the god corresponding to the morning star rising in the east. On the other, there is *Xolotl* /*šo:lo:tl*/ who is, of course, the nocturnal twin of Quetzalcoatl in central Mexican cosmology and thus very much a part of the Quetzalcoatl complex. Plausible semantic chains are necessary in those cases in which loans have shifted somewhat in meaning when passing from one language to another.

The Nahuatl word /*šo:lo:tl*/ clearly reconstructs to a Uto-Aztecan term *¢ɨ:-la'a-wɨ and is cognate with a number of northern Uto-Aztecan words, such as Southern Ute *sina'awe*, "trickster, coyote; copycat," and related terms refer to his older brother Wolf (cf. Dakin 2005). The mythical canine god Xolotl is always characterized as mischievous and is a sharp contrast to the serious Quetzalcoatl. For instance, in the Legend of the Suns (Sahagún 1953, bk. 7: 8), Xolotl runs away because he does not want to die and successively turns into twin cornstalks, twin magueys, and finally jumps into the water to become the *axolote*, a type of salamander. I would propose that there are borrowings of the word into Yucatec, Itzaj, and other lowland Mayan languages reflecting two meanings of the Nahuatl *[xolotl]* /šo:lo:tl/, "twin, double" and "trickster canine." In the entry for *xulab* in the Cordemex dictionary, Barrera Vásquez et al. (1995: 955) include the following comment: "*xulab*: la persona que se transformó en el planeta Venus según una leyenda de Belice" ("the person who transformed himself into the planet Venus according to a legend from Belize"). It seems certain that *xulab* /šulab'/ is a variant of /šulub'/. Yucatec has *lot* and Itzaj *šlot* for "twins," and Hofling and Tesucún's (1997) modern Itzaj dictionary includes *xulu'* /šulu'/ as "troublemaking." Word final /-'/ in Itzáj corresponds to /-b'/ in other Yucatecan languages, so that *xulu'* /šulu'/ corresponds to *xulub'* /šulub'/. The senses of the words borrowed from *xolotl* followed an interesting path related to the history of contacts within this area. Besides the Itzaj forms for "mischievous" and "twins," there is a form /šulub'/ as well, but with the meanings "devil, demon" and "horn." For the Hocabá Yucatec Mayan variant, Bricker et al. (1998: 265) give /šulub'/, "devil, demon; horns," but also include /č'ik-šulub'/ "Chicxulub, name of town—lit. devil's flea," a gloss that suggests that, rather than a devil, /šulub'/ was a canine. The final /b'/ is found on various loanwords into Mayan languages because it is a common final consonant for derived nouns, and has replaced the Nahua final absolutive suffix *-tl* (or perhaps *–t*, depending on the dialect), in some other words as well. Kaufman gives #*xulub'* /šulub'/ as the lowland and western Mayan word for "horn." The rest of the family has an entirely different form which Kaufman reconstructs to a proto-Mayan **'uk'aa'*. The only languages with the word *xulub'* and its variants are Yucatec, Mopan, Tzeltal, Mocho, and Tuzanteco. It would seem that *xolotl,* a god with the characteristics of a mischievous canine when introduced from central Mexico to northern Yucatán, became a Christian horned demon or devil under the Spanish missionaries. It was from this use that the word came to refer to the horns of cattle and deer.

There are also two day names, terms found in lowland Mayan languages that are important astronomically, for which a Nahuatl origin seems quite probable: *lamat*, "Venus," and *pek'*, "dog." The principal basis for arguing that they originate in Nahuatl is the classic one: They have Uto-Aztecan etymologies and therefore are not borrowed into Nahuatl but inherited from the parent language. Such evidence has much more weight than that of semantic domain or geographical precedence, since it is independent of nonlinguistic proofs and instead raises questions for other disciplines because migration theories need to explain all the linguistic evidence as well. If they are of Nahuatl origin, as argued here, they provide linguistic support for a Mexican highlands–northern Yucatán interaction that includes the cosmological system.

Lamat, "Venus," is the first astronomical term to be considered as a probable loan from early Nahuatl. Robertson (1984) calls attention to the fact that *q'ani:l* would be the proto-Mayan form for the eighth day name, and that the *Lamat* and *Lamb'at* terms are an innovation in western Mayan, mentioning Yucatec, Q'anjob'al, Chuj, and Tzeltal. Whittaker (n.d. [1980]: 55) proposed that "Lam(b)at, the glyph of the eighth day name, derives from the Zapotec glyph for the eighth day name, *Lapa* 'Drops' or 'Fragmented' *lam[b']at*, proto-Zapoteco #*lappa*." Apparently the *b'* is included as a possible part of the reconstruction because of the Q'anjob'al form *lamb'at*. Justeson et al. (1985: 48, 95) followed Whittaker's proposal in identifying *lam[b']at* as a loanword from pre-Zapotec but note that it is reconstructible for Western Mayan. However, a possibility that is phonetically much closer than the Zapotec one suggested by Whittaker would be that it comes from the Nahuatl agentive noun *ilamat*, "old woman," from *ilamati*, "to grow old (woman)." In some Sierra de Puebla Nahuatl dialects, for instance, *lamat* is "old woman" (cf. Hernández Vásquez n.d. [2008]), meaning that the loss of initial *i* is documented within Nahuatl, and it could thus have been borrowed into other languages. This source seems a much more reasonable one phonologically than for *Lamat* to have been borrowed from a pre-Zapotec *Lappa*.

An alternative explanation for the forms is that *Lamat* was borrowed from Nahuatl into Yucatec and from there into the other western Mayan languages; the *b'* could be an epenthetic consonant inserted by analogy with the word *b'at*, "hail," also connected with the heavens. Possibly *Lamat* was borrowed into Zapotec as "Venus" and reinterpreted as <*Lapa*>, "fragmented," because of the split identity of the planet, although it is also possible that the Zapotec gloss for the day name *Lapa* is simply mistaken. It should be noted that, although the Central Nahua tradition apparently does not include *ilamat* as a word for "Venus" in its terminology for the different phases of that planet (which do include *Quetzalcoatl*, *Xolotl*, *Tlahuizcalpantecuhtli*, and others), it is semantically feasible if one considers the parallelism in the metaphorical relationship between rabbits or hares and women, which is a productive source of word play on sexual themes in many Mexican indigenous and *mestizo* communities.

The semantic relationships are interesting because we need to take into account the fact that Nahuatl *sih-tli* refers both to "grandmother" and to "hare/jackrabbit," and the path, if the relationship implied by the etymology is correct, may be through the Mesoamerican image of the rabbit (or hare?) in the moon, and the astronomical relationships between the Venus cycle and human gestation. Aveni (2001: 84) points out that the Mesoamericans considered the cycle for the morning star aspect of Venus to be 250 days, and a nine-month pregnancy would be 270 days. Aveni (2001: 141), citing Spinden (1924: 103), also gives *Tochtli*, "rabbit," as the Aztec equivalent for the Mayan day name *Lamat*.

The change from *sih-tli*, "grandmother," to *[i]lamat*, "old woman," could be a replacement much like that used in many cultures for "wife" or "mother," when the term becomes "old lady." In addition, Whittaker (n.d. [1980]: 32–33) notes: "*The rabbit, or more precisely hare* [emphasis added], head that appears below the year-glyph on Period III stelae is to be taken as a variant way of representing the same yearbearer Tochtli" and concludes that *Lamat* and *Tochtli* could be equivalents. The linguistic evidence in the set of semantically related terms reflects what must be a relationship that *Lamat* has with both Venus and the moon. The cognate sets and correspondences for *Lamat* are given in the appendix to this chapter. In addition, Wichmann (personal communication, August 9, 2008) has pointed out that *ilama'*, "old woman," was also borrowed as such into Ch'orti', and Wisdom (1961: 311) notes that, in Ch'orti', a grandmother's sisters are sometimes called *tu' ilama*, "madre anciana" ("old mother"), that the borrowing of *ilama* is probably later than that of the day name, and that, in any case, it represents an independent semantic area.

<Pek> /*pek'*/, "dog," the second term argued here to be of Uto-Aztecan origin, is associated with the domesticated dog and is also a day name, thereby highlighting its importance in considering the depth of interaction between Nahuatl speakers and non-Nahuas in southern Mesoamerica. Whorf (1948: 8) identified both Yucatec Mayan *pek'*, "dog," and the Huastec calendar sign *piko* as borrowings from a term originating in proto-Uto-Aztecan **pu^{n}ku*, "domestic animal," a widely accepted reconstruction. (I would change the reconstruction slightly to *pu-l-ku.) Cognates include *buku* in Yaqui and *pooko* in Hopi, both meaning "dog." Kaufman (1971), on the other hand, reconstructed **peq^w'*, "dog," in Yucatec and Huastec but suggested it came from Zapotec. In Campbell and Kaufman (1976) and in Justeson et al. (1985: 21), the suggestion that it is Zapotec in origin is repeated and the proto-Zapotec form **pe'kku'* is proposed, which, it should be emphasized, is also very similar to the reconstructed Uto-Aztecan form *pu-l-ku.

Because cognates from **pu-l-ku-* are used to identify a *possessed* (and domesticated) animal in Uto-Aztecan languages, it would seem much more likely that Whorf was correct in his original suggestion that the word was diffused into southern Mesoamerican languages, including Zapotec, from early Nahuatl. There is one problem in the form, since initial *p's have been lost in Nahuatl nouns in a great number of cases, but the exact conditions for its occurrence are still not clearly understood; some initial *p's are retained, and that could be the case here. Campbell and Langacker (1978: 201, n. 43) argued that the initial *p was retained in forms usually preceded by prefixes. The *pu-l-ku cognate forms are almost always possessed when used in Uto-Aztecan languages, with examples like "my- *pu-l-ku animal," so that the *p would have been protected from loss by a possessive prefix. Another problem with the Uto-Aztecan proposal should be noted: neither *pek-* nor *pik* have been identified as words for "dog" in either colonial or modern dialects. Because the word is a day name, however, and thus imbued with ritual significance, it could have been replaced with terms related to /šo:lo:-tl/ or the Totonac borrowing /čiči/ for the animal name, much as the form *brethren* is replaced in normal English discourse by the regular plural *brothers* but is retained for a limited religious reference. This possibility is also noted by Justeson et al. (1985: 64) as a potential explanation for the loss of day names.

Conclusions

As noted earlier, López Austin and López Luján (1999: 141), in their consideration of the relationship between Nahuatl speakers and Mayan speakers from the northern lowlands and elsewhere, proposed the existence of a society with a multiethnic and multilingual population. Analysis of archaic traits in the colonial Nahuatl lingua franca provides evidence for such Pre-Hispanic multilingual contact between central Mexico and the Maya area. However, the evidence from linguistic diffusion of astronomical and other terms in southern Mesoamerica, such as the *xolotl* aspects of the Quetzalcoatl complex, also indicate the infusion of highland cultural beliefs into the area, perhaps creating the Zuyúa society proposed by López Austin and López Luján. However, the fact that there are terms for such early, culturally important entities as calendrical dates suggests that these Postclassic interactions follow and build on patterns of Nahuatl-Mayan interaction established at a much earlier date. It is interesting to go back to Whorf's (1948) early article, even though some of the correspondences he used to identify loans have now been corrected as a result of new research and access to many additional materials. His vision and intuitions about the social history behind the diffusion should be reconsidered in more detail. The development of glottochronology as a means of assigning time depth led away from proposals of an early Uto-Aztecan population in the southern part of Mexico because the Nahuatl variants, according to Swadesh's calculations, did not show great time depth. However, the layering of Nahuatl loanwords and what, in some cases, appear to be pre-Nahua forms diffused into lowland Mayan and other languages in the area lead us to the conclusion that the linguistic prehistory of the Maya lowlands must have included an important, if at times limited, Nahua presence. Evidence for this proposal, first suggested by Whorf, is supported by work on the reconstruction of a Uto-Aztecan lexicon that provides pedigrees for the diffused words, including a number discussed elsewhere (cf. Dakin 2001, 2003, 2005). This means that the more recent—and also more intense—Late Postclassic interaction between Yucatán and the central Mexican highlands implicit in the Madrid and Dresden codices and described in the papers in this volume, is probably the inheritance from a long tradition in that multicultural area.

Acknowledgments

I very much appreciated the invitation to participate in the Dumbarton Oaks symposium. I also especially wish to thank Gabrielle Vail and Christine Hernández, the organizers, and Martha Macri, Tony Andrews, Tony Aveni, Victoria Bricker, Richard Haly, Carmen León, Mercedes Montes de Oca, Michel Oudijk, Lloyd Anderson, and Søren Wichmann and the anonymous reviewers for their pertinent and thoughtful comments.

APPENDIX:
Proto-Uto-Aztecan Reflexes, Cognates, and Mayan Forms

A. **Lamat** from #[p]ila-ma or *pilV- "to twist (?) + *ma "to grow" (from author's personal database):
1. Uto-Aztecan forms
   a. Nahuatl *ilama-ti*, "to become old (woman)"; *ilamat, ilamah*, "old woman." The word is an agentive noun ("one who does action of verb") derived from the verb *ilama-ti*, "to become old (woman)," which is in turn a verb derived from what must be a noun or an adjective by adding the pUA *-tu*, Nahuatl *–ti* suffix "to become"; other Nahuatl verbs formed with *-ti*, such as *ilamati*, include *we:we:-ti*, "to become old (man)," from the adjective *we:we*, "old" from *we-* "big, long (time)."
   b. The Southern Paiute word *piŋwa-*, "wife, spouse," would suggest that *ilamat* derives from a pUA *pi-la-ma-* or *pi-la-wa* (pUA *p > Ø*, Nahuatl, *l* > southern Paiute *n > ŋ* before *w*. (In many Uto-Aztecan cognate sets *w ~* m; cf. Tarahumara *mehka*, Nahuatl *wehka* "distant"). Stubbs (2007: 217) notes that a pUA *ma'a*, "old (woman)," is reflected in Kawaiisu *ma'api-zi*, "old woman," and Chemehuevi *maapici* and Cupeño *wii-mamá-pɨ-ci*, "old lady."
2. Non-Uto-Aztecan forms
   a. Mayan (Robertson 1984): Yucatec *Lamat*; Q'anjob'al *Lamb'at*; Chuj *lamb'at*, Tzeltal *lambat*.
   b. Zapotec (Whittaker n.d.: 55): Zapotec glyph for the eighth day name, *Lapa*, "Drops" or "Fragmented," proto-Zapotec #*lappa*.
3. Uto-Aztecan words for "grandmother/Venus/moon"
   a. *su-'*, "grandmother; hare/jackrabbit" : *su* > Nahuatl *si-, sih-tli*, "(rabbit)/jackrabbit/grandmother."
      pUA root *su-* is reflected in Nahuatl *sih-tli* but is also part of *siwa:tl*, "woman"; *si:tlalin*, "star"; *se-n-tli/si-n-tli*, "corn ear"; *si-s-tli*, "conch"; and *si-lin*, "snail."

B. Yucatec *pek'* from pUA *pu-lV*, "keep, own," **pu-l-kV**, "possessed (especially animals)" (from author's personal database).

1. Northern languages
   a. Numic, Takic, Hopi, Tübatulabal: *p > p, *u > u; *l > n. Ø before .C.
   b. Southern Paiute *puŋku-*, "horse, domestic animal"; Hopi *pò:ko* (-*pko . pok-; pl. popkot*), "dog, domestic animal"; Mono *pukku*, "pet"; Northern Paiute *pukku*, "horse"; Shoshone *punku*, "horse; pet"; Kawaiisu *puku-*, "pet, dog"; and Tübatulabal *puŋgu-l*, "pet"; *pukubi-* "dog."

2. Southern languages
   a. Tarahumara, Guarijio, Yaqui, Tubar, Eudeve: *p > b, p, *u > u, *l > l, r and to h, Ø/__.C. Yaqui *buko*, "dog"; Guarijío *puhkú*, "possessed animal; cattle, cow, bull" (Medina Murillo n.d.); Tarahumara *bukú*, "possessed animal."
   b. Huichol, Nahuatl: pUA *p > h* or *p* in Huichol, and in Nahuatl initial *p > p* but also sometimes *h*. The *h* was then usually lost, except in some cases when it became preconsonantal as a result of a vowel loss, where it was retained as *h* and protected by an epenthetic initial *i; *u > ɨ* in Huichol, while in Nahuatl *u > i* or *e* or sometimes was lost, while the consonant *l > l* or *y* or was lost before a following *C*, as happened also in Yaqui above. Thus, *pula* becomes *piya*, the general Nahuatl transitive verb "to keep, possess," while *pulV-ku* must have become both *ihk-* found as the Nahuatl animate plural demonstratives *in-ihk-eh in* "these" or *in-ihk-eh on* "those," and as the noun *pik* "dog." The use of *pik* became limited to its function as a day name, and was replaced in general by the word *chichi* in most Nahuatl variants.

3. Borrowed into Mayan: Yucatec Mayan **pek'**, "dog"; Huastec **piko**, "calendar sign" (Whorf 1948); Kaufman (1971) reconstructs *peq$^{w'}$*, "dog," in Yucatec and Huastec.

Notes

1. The term *Nahuatl* is used to refer to all variants of the language, both eastern and western-central. Forms are cited with the phoneme *tl* unless otherwise noted. The term *pre-Nahua* refers to older (reconstructed) forms that had not yet undergone sound changes common to all dialects.

2. *Mayan* is used here and elsewhere in this chapter to refer to Mayan speakers or to the Mayan language.

3. Pochutec is classified with the western area because it is possible to reconstruct *tesi for "to grind" as the basis for Pochutec *tos* and not the eastern form *tisi. The dialect shares other features as well with the western area (see Dakin 1983).

4. For a more detailed description of the lingua franca, see Dakin (1996b, 2009).

5. Although the text is probably the source of their choice of the term *Zuyúa*, López Austin and López Luján's (1999) use of the word has a much broader reference than the cryptic mention discussed here.

6. For the discussions of etymologies and borrowings that follow, the principal source for Mayan cognates is Kaufman's (2003) Mayan etymological dictionary. The main source for Uto-Aztecan cognates is Hill (n.d. [1988]), with additions for Tubar and Eudeve from Lionnet (1978, 1986, respectively). Principal sources for Nahuatl besides my own notes are Lastra (1986), Molina (1970 [1571]), and Wimmer (2007).

7. I thank Victoria Bricker and Gabrielle Vail for bringing this to my attention.

8. I am particularly grateful to Beatriz Repetto whose 2003 course paper discussing Whorf's and Thompson's publications led me to reread them both with greater care.

References Cited

Amith, Jonathan D.
   1997   Tan ancha como tu abuela, adivinanzas en nahuatl del Guerrero central. *Tlalocan* 12: 141–222.

Aveni, Anthony F.
   2001   *Skywatchers*. Rev. ed. University of Texas Press, Austin.

Barrera Vásquez, Alfredo, director, with Juan Ramón Bastarrachea Manzano, William Brito Sansores, Refugio Vermont Salas, David Dzul Góngora, and Domingo Dzul Poot
   1995 [1980]   *Diccionario maya, maya–español, español–maya*. Editorial Porrúa, México, D.F.

Barrera Vásquez, Alfredo, and Silvia Rendón
   1982   *El libro de los libros de Chilam Balam*. Traducción de sus textos paralelos, basada en el estudio, cotejo y reconstrucción hechos por el primero, con introducción y notas. Fondo de Cultura Económica, México, D.F.

Bricker, Victoria, Eleuterio Po'ot Yah, and Ofelia Dzul de Po'ot
   1998   *A Dictionary of the Maya Language as Spoken in Hocabá, Yucatán*. University of Utah Press, Salt Lake City.

Campbell, Lyle
   1977   *Quichean Linguistic Prehistory*. Publications in Linguistics 8. University of California Press, Berkeley.

Campbell, Lyle, and Terrence Kaufman
   1976   A Linguistic Look at the Olmecs. *American Antiquity* 41: 80–89.

Campbell, Lyle, and Ronald W. Langacker
   1978   Proto-Aztecan Vowels: Part II. *International Journal of American Linguistics* 44 (3): 197–210.

Canger, Una

    1988   Nahuatl Dialectology: A Survey and Some Suggestions. *International Journal of American Linguistics* 54 (1): 28–72.

Canger, Una, and Karen Dakin

    1985   An Inconspicuous Basic Split in Nahuatl. *International Journal of American Linguistics* 54 (4): 258–261.

Dakin, Karen

    1982   *La evolución fonológica del protonáhuatl.* Instituto de Investigaciones Filológicas, Universidad Nacional Autónoma de México, México, D.F.

    1983   Proto-Aztecan Vowels and Pochutec: An Alternative Analysis. *International Journal of American Linguistics* 49 (2): 196–203.

    1991   Tepito y el origen de -kp- en náhuatl. In *Homenaje a Jorge Suárez* (Beatriz Garza Cuarón and Paulette Levy, eds.): 175–196. El Colegio de México, México, D.F.

    1996a   Long Vowels and Morpheme Boundaries in Nahuatl and Uto-Aztecan: Comments on Historical Developments. *Amerindia* 21: 55–76.

    1996b   El náhuatl de las memorias: Los rasgos de una lingua franca indígena. In *Nuestro pesar, nuestra aflicción: Memorias en náhuatl del valle de Guatemala dirigidas al Rey Felipe II alrededor de 1570* (Karen Dakin and Christopher Lutz, eds.): 167–189. Universidad Nacional Autónoma de México-CIRMA, México, D.F.

    2001   Animals and Vegetables, Uto-Aztecan Noun Derivation, Semantic Classification and Culture History. In *Selected Papers from the X International Congress of Historical Linguistics* (Laurel Brinton and Desiree Lundstrom, eds.): 105–118. John Benjamins, Philadelphia, Pa.

    2002   Isoglosas e innovaciones yutoaztecas. In *Avances y balances de lenguas yutoaztecas: Homenaje a Wick R. Miller* (José Luis Moctezuma Zamarrón and Jane H. Hill, eds): 313–344. *Noroeste de México* (número especial), Centro Instituto Nacional de Antropología e Historia Sonora, and CONACULTA-INAH, México, D.F.

    2003   Uto-Aztecan in the Linguistic Stratigraphy of Mesoamerican Prehistory. In *Language Contacts in Prehistory: Studies in Stratigraphy* (Henning Andersen, ed.): 259–288. John Benjamins, Amsterdam and Philadelphia, Pa.

    2005   Xolotl. In *La Metáfora en Mesoamérica* (Mercedes Montes de Oca, ed.): 193–223. Universidad Nacional Autónoma de México, Instituto de Investigaciones Filológicas, México, D.F.

    2009   Algunos documentos del sur de Mesoamerica. In *Visions del encuentro de dos mundos en América: Lengua, cultura, tradicción, y transculturación* (Karen Dakin, Mercedes Montes de Oca, and Claudia Parodi, eds.): 239–261. Instituto de Investigaciones Filologicas, Universidad Nacional Autónoma de México, and Centro de Estudios Coloniales Iberoamericanos, University of California, Los Angeles.

Dakin, Karen, and Søren Wichmann

    2000   Cacao and Chocolate: A Uto-Aztecan Perspective. *Ancient Mesoamerica* 11: 55–75.

Elliot, Eric Bryant
n.d.   Dictionary of Rincón Luiseño. Ph.D. dissertation, University of California San Diego, 1999.

Fowler, Catherine S.
1983   Some Lexical Clues to Uto-Aztecan Prehistory. *International Journal of American Linguistics* 49: 224–257.

Hernández Vázquez, Juan Ignacio
n.d.   Marcos de referencia y categorías de espacialidad en el nawat de Gardenias, Hueyapan, Puebla. Master's thesis, Centro de Investigaciones y Estudios Superiores de Antropología Social, México D.F., 2008.

Hill, Jane H.
2001   Proto-Uto-Aztecan: A Community of Cultivators in Central Mexico? *American Anthropologist* 103: 913–934.

n.d.   Uto-Aztecan and the Mesoamerican Linguistic Area. Paper presented at the 100th annual meeting of the American Anthropological Association, Washington, D.C., December 2001.

Hill, Kenneth C.
n.d.   Miller's Uto-Aztecan Cognate Sets, revised and expanded by Kenneth C. Hill, based on Wick R. Miller's Computerized Data Base for Uto-Aztecan Cognate Sets. Digital file, May 1988. Tucson, Ariz.

Hofling, Charles Andrew, with Félix Fernando Tesucún
1997   *Itzaj Maya-Spanish-English Dictionary, Diccionario maya itzaj-español-inglés.* University of Utah Press, Salt Lake City.

Justeson, John S., William M. Norman, Lyle Campbell, and Terrence Kaufman
1985   *The Foreign Impact on Lowland Mayan Language and Script.* Middle American Research Institute Publication 53. Tulane University, New Orleans.

Kaufman, Terrence
1971   Materiales lingüísticos para el estudio de las relaciones internas y externas de la familia de idiomas mayanos. In *Desarrollo cultural de los mayas* (Evon Z. Vogt and Alberto Ruz Lhullier, eds.): 81–136. Universidad Nacional Autónoma de México, Centro de Estudios Mayas, México, D.F.

1994   Languages of Meso-America. In *Atlas of the World's Languages* (Christopher Moseley and R. E. Asher, eds.): map 13, 34–41. Routledge, London.

Kaufman, Terrence, with the assistance of John Justeson
2003   *A Preliminary Mayan Etymological Dictionary.* A website and database available at www.famsi.org/reports/01051/index.html, accessed April 21, 2006.

Lastra de Suárez, Yolanda
1986   *Las áreas dialectales del náhuatl moderno.* Instituto de Investigaciones Antropológicas, Universidad Nacional Autónoma de México, México, D.F.

Lionnet, Andrés
1978   *El idioma tubar y los tubares. Según documentos inéditos de C. S. Lumholtz y C. V. Hartman.* Universidad Iberoamericana, México, D.F.

1986   *El eudeve: Un idioma extinto de Sonora.* Universidad Nacional Autónoma de México, México, D.F.

Longacre, Robert
1967   Systemic Comparison and Reconstruction. In *The Handbook for Middle American Indians*, vol. 5: *Linguistics* (Norman A. McQuown, ed.): 117–175. University of Texas Press, Austin.

López Austin, Alfredo, and Leonardo López Luján
1999   *Mito y realidad de Zuyuá.* Fideicomiso Historia de las Américas, El Colegio de México, and the Fondo de Cultura Económica, México, D.F.

Macri, Martha J., and Matthew G. Looper
2003   Nahua in Ancient Mesoamerica: Evidence from Maya Inscriptions. *Ancient Mesoamerica* 14: 285–297.

Medina Murillo, Ana Aurora
n.d.   *Diccionario morfológico de guarijío.* Universidad Nacional Autónoma de México, Instituto de Investigaciones Filológicas, México, D.F. (in press).

Mercenario Ortega, Mariana
2009   *Los entramados del significado en las adivinanzas de los antiguos nahuas.* Universidad Nacional Autónoma de México, Facultad de Filosofía y Letras and the Instituto de Investigaciones Filológicas, México, D.F.

Molina, Alonso de
1970 [1571]   *Vocabulario en lengua castellana y mexicana.* Edición facsímile, 4th ed. Editorial Porrúa, México, D.F.

Montes de Oca Vega, Mercedes
2005   *Niokculida, tïmahe, k'eojetik, huehuetlahtolli, telapnaawe:* La tradición oral de los pueblos nativos de México y Norteamérica. *Acta Poetica* 26 (1–2): 547–576.

Restall, Matthew
1997   *The Maya World: Yucatec Culture and Society, 1550–1850.* Stanford University Press, Stanford, Calif.

Robertson, John S.
1984   Of Day Names, Kin Names and Counting: Cultural Affinities and Distinctions among the Mayan Languages. *Anthropos* 79: 369–75.

Ruíz de Alarcón, Hernando
1975 [1629]   *Treatise on the Heathen Superstitions That Today Live among the Indians Native to this New Spain* (J. Richard Andrews and Ross Hassig, trans. and eds.). University of Oklahoma Press, Norman.

Sahagún, Bernardino de
1953   Book 7: *The Sun, Moon, and Stars, and the Binding of the Years.* Monograph 14, pt. 8 of *The Florentine Codex: General History of the Things of New Spain* (Arthur J. O. Anderson and Charles E. Dibble, eds. and trans.). University of Utah and School of American Research, Santa Fe, N.Mex.

Santamaría, Francisco J.
1983   *Diccionario de mejicanismos.* Cuarta edición corregida y aumentada, Editorial Porrúa, México, D.F.

Scholes, France V., and Ralph L. Roys, in collaboration with Eleanor B. Adams and
Robert S. Chamberlain
    1996   *Los chontales de Acalan-Tixchel* (Castellana de Mario Humberto Ruz,
            ed.; Mario Humberto Ruz y Rosario Vega, trans.). Universidad Nacional
            Autónoma de México, Instituto de Investigaciones Filológicas, Centro de
            Estudios Mayas, México, D.F.

Smith-Stark, Thomas C.
    1994   Mesoamerican Calques. In *Investigación lingüística en Mesoamérica*
            (Carolyn J. MacKay and Verónica Vázquez, eds.): 15–50. Universidad
            Nacional Autónoma de México, Seminario de Lenguas Indígenas, Instituto
            de Investigaciones Filológicas, México, D.F.

Spinden, Herbert
    1924   *The Reduction of Mayan Dates.* Papers of the Peabody Museum of
            American Archaeology and Ethnology Papers 6 (4). Harvard University,
            Cambridge, Mass.

Stubbs, Brian D.
    2007   *A Uto-Aztecan Comparative Vocabulary.* 2nd preliminary edition. South
            Blanding, Utah.

Suárez, Jorge A.
    1985   Loan Etymologies in Historical Method. *International Journal of American
            Linguistics* 51 (4): 574–577.

Swadesh, Mauricio
    1954   Algunas fechas glotocronológicas importantes para la prehistoria nahua.
            Revista mexicana de estudios antropológicos 14: 173–192.

Swadesh, Morris
    1950   Salish Internal Relationships. *International Journal of American Linguistics*
            16 (4): 157–167.

Thompson, J. Eric
    1948   *Pitfalls and Stimuli in the Interpretation of History through Loan Words.*
            Philological and Documentary Studies Publication 11. Middle American
            Research Institute, Tulane University, New Orleans.

Torre, Fray Tomás de la
    1944–1945   *Desde Salamanca, España, hasta Ciudad Real, Chiapas: Diario del
            viaje 1544–1545* (prólogo y notas por Franz Blom). Editorial Central,
            México, D.F.

Tozzer, Alfred M.
    1941   *Landa's* Relación de las cosas de Yucatan: *A Translation.* Papers of the
            Peabody Museum of American Archaeology and Ethnology 18. Harvard
            University, Cambridge, Mass.

Whittaker, Gordon
    1986   The Mexican Names of Three Venus Gods in the Dresden Codex. *Mexicon*
            8 (3): 56–60.
    n.d.   The Hieroglyphics of Monte Alban. Ph.D. dissertation, Yale University,
            New Haven, 1980.

Whorf, Benjamin L.

1948   *Loan Words in Ancient Mexico.* Middle American Research Institute, Philological and Documentary Studies Publication 11. Tulane University, New Orleans.

Wichmann, Søren

1999   A Conservative Look at Diffusion Involving Mixe-Zoquean Languages. In *Archaeology and Language II: Archaeological Data and Linguistic Hypotheses* (Roger Blench and Matthew Spriggs, eds.): 297–323. Routledge, London.

Wimmer, Alexis

2007   *Dictionnaire de la langue nahuatl classique.* Available at nahuatl.ifrance. com/, accessed August 17, 2006.

Wisdom, Charles

1961   *Los chortis de Guatemala.* Editorial del Ministerio de Educación Pública "José de Pineda Ibarra," Guatemala.

Chapter Eight

Nahua Vocables in a Maya Song of the Fall of Chichén Itzá

Music and Social Memory in the Construction

of Yucatecan Ethnicities

Timothy W. Knowlton

En su gentilidad y aora bailan y cantan al vso de los Mexicanos, y tenian y tienen su cantor principal, que entona y enseña lo que se ha de cantar, y le veneran, y reuerencian, y le dan assiento en la Iglesia, y en sus juntas, y bodas, y le llaman Holpop; a cuyo cargo estan los atabales, e instrumentos de musica, como son flautas, trompetillas, conchas de tortugas, y el teponaguaztli, que es de madera hueco, cuyo sonido se oye de dos, y tres leguas, segun el viento que corre. Cantan fabulas, antiguallas, que oy se podrian reformar, y darles cosas a lo diuino que cantan (Sánchez de Aguilar 1987 [1639]: 98).*

In the time of their paganism and now [the Maya] dance and sing according to the custom of the Mexicans. And they had and have their principal singer who sings and teaches what they are supposed to sing. And they venerate and revere him and give place to him in church and in their gatherings and weddings. And they call him *Holpop* whose responsibilities are the kettledrums and musical instruments like the flutes, trumpets, turtle shells, and the *teponaguaztli* that is made of hollow wood, and whose sound is heard two or three leagues, depending on the wind that blows. They sing fables and antiquities that today one could reform and give them divine things that they should sing (author's translation).

W RITING ALMOST A CENTURY after the beginning of the Spanish invasion of the northern Maya lowlands, yet many decades before this invasion's conclusion with the fall of the Peten Itzá polity at the close of the seventeenth century, the account of Creole priest Doctor Pedro Sánchez de Aguilar is a very valuable historical source during a crucial period in Colonial history. At the time he wrote in 1613 (published 1639), Maya life before the Spanish arrived had just passed beyond the point of living memory, but Maya lifeways and social memory of the Late Postclassic and even earlier periods persisted. In fact, this persistence of Maya social memory apparently was one of Sánchez de Aguilar's motivations for composing his *Informe contra idolorum cultores del Obispado de Yucatán* to begin with. As he did in the case of creation myths (Knowlton n.d. [2004]: ch. 3), Sánchez de Aguilar strongly urged the active replacement of these Maya songs of "fables and antiquities" with content he deemed sufficiently orthodox.

Sánchez de Aguilar's own personal efforts against "idolatry" and "heresy" included the continued persecution of Maya diviners and the seizure of hieroglyphic books that had begun in the mid-sixteenth century (Chuchiak 2001, 2004). During this same period, the Maya of the Yucatán Peninsula had begun a tradition of dialogue with the religious, historical, and other sources of Pre-Hispanic Maya and European civilizations in the form of the Books of Chilam Balam (Bricker and Miram 2002). The Chilam Balam, or "Prophet of the surname Jaguar" after whom the books are called, was a semilegendary figure purported to have predicted the arrival of the Spaniards. The Books of Chilam Balam, written throughout the colonial period and even afterward, were clandestine copybooks written by Maya themselves in the Yucatec Maya language, using a modified Latin alphabet. They were compiled, edited, and read aloud at community gatherings by Maya schoolmasters and choirmasters, out of sight of those non-Maya clergy like Sánchez de Aguilar who would have confiscated them.

Of particular interest to previous generations of ethnohistorians and archaeologists, these Books of Chilam Balam contain much in the way of indigenous histories (*kahlay*) which, like their Pre-Hispanic antecedents, were marked in terms of 20-year *katun* periods (Barrera Vásquez and Rendón 1948). But scholars have been frustrated as often as rewarded in attempting to reconcile the numerous histories of Pre-Hispanic events and personages in the Books of Chilam Balam with historical evidence from other sources (Miram 1994). Over the last several decades, the decipherment of the ancient Maya logosyllabic script has provided contemporaneous epigraphic references to personages previously known only from Maya and Spanish colonial histories (Grube 1994; Kelley 1976), but these data likewise have been difficult to reconcile with colonial *u kahlay katun* "*katun* history."

In addressing the relevance of the colonial documents to the topic of this volume, Maya and highland Mexican interaction during the Late Postclassic period, I will not attempt an interpretation of the *katun* histories of the Books of Chilam Balam. Instead, I have chosen primarily to examine a different genre in colonial Yucatec literature: *kay*, or "song." Given Sánchez de Aguilar's observation that Maya song in Yucatán during the colonial and Pre-Hispanic periods was like that found in highland Mexico, this seems a potentially fruitful avenue for pursuing the question of interaction between these different regions of Mesoamerica in late Pre-Hispanic times. Furthermore, because Aguilar states that the songs the Maya sang concerned their "antiquities," we may expect to encounter elements of Maya history (or, more precisely, Maya social memory) in their content. In this chapter, I first attempt to verify Sánchez de Aguilar's claim of highland Mexican influence on Maya music by an examination of extant colonial Yucatec Maya songs and then discuss the implications of Nahua influence for the social memory of Mesoamerican ethnic interaction as it was framed in colonial Yucatán.

Sources of Pre-Hispanic Song

One of the major problems facing an investigator of Pre-Hispanic songs from either highland Mexico or the Maya area is that, strictly speaking, none survive. Of course, murals and figurines depicting ancient Maya singers and musicians, the remains of Pre-Hispanic instruments, and other material artifacts have been recovered. But neither Pre-Hispanic transcriptions of song texts nor any unambiguous form of musical notation is known to exist in extant highland Mexican pictorial codices or in the logosyllabic texts of the Maya (although it has been suggested that signs appearing on drums and iconographic representations of drums among the Classic Maya may represent a form of musical notation; see Houston et al. 2006: 163). All extant song texts from both regions come from colonial period manuscripts written in indigenous languages in the modified Latin alphabets. Although in some cases it is a very reasonable supposition, we must still recognize it is still only a supposition that any of this colonial period evidence reflects Pre-Hispanic forms. The fact that Pre-Hispanic songs are preserved only in colonial period sources necessarily requires that the motivation for putting these songs to paper is derived from the colonial situations in Mexico and Yucatán. While examining these sources of evidence, we should never lose sight of the fact that the colonial "why" can and does determine "what" is dictated, even when the text in question is almost certainly derived from Pre-Hispanic antecedents. Incidentally, this same principle should be applied when examining any indigenous colonial document, whether from Mexico, Yucatán, or elsewhere, such as the K'iche' *Popol Wuj* of highland Guatemala.

Another factor to consider is the imbalance in the extant evidence for

Pre-Hispanic song from different regions and languages because the number of extant highland Mexican songs, specifically those in Nahuatl, far outweighs extant examples in Yucatec Maya. Almost 100 examples of Nahuatl language songs (*cuicatl*) are present in the *Cantares mexicanos* alone (Bierhorst 1985a), not counting other examples from the Florentine Codex, the *Romances de los señores de la Nueva España*, and other sixteenth-century manuscripts. The collection of autochthonous Nahuatl songs during the sixteenth century was stimulated in highland Mexico by the work of missionary-ethnographers such as Bernardino de Sahagún to an extent never realized for the Maya songs of Yucatán. As for the known songs transcribed in colonial Yucatec Maya, there exist the 15 *Cantares de Dzitbalché* and a few other texts identifying themselves as *kayob*, "songs," scattered throughout the Books of Chilam Balam. In contrast to those Nahuatl song collections that can be reliably dated to the middle to late sixteenth century, the dates of extant copies of Yucatecan examples are not as clearcut (see Barrera Vásquez 1965: 14, 22–23 for problems surrounding the dating of the *Cantares de Dzitbalché*). This imbalance in the number of datable extant examples from highland Mexico and the Yucatán Peninsula is also reflected in the quantity of previous scholarship on the subject. Voluminous studies of *cuicatl* as a branch of Aztec poetry exist from the period of the first missionary-ethnographers to the twentieth-century works of Garibay and others (see Bierhorst 1985a: ch. 13 for a brief history of this area of research). In contrast, systematic research into Maya song texts has yielded only a handful of very brief pioneering works by twentieth-century Mexican scholars. These include a facsimile with transcription and Spanish translation of the *Cantares de Dzitbalché* (Barrera Vásquez 1965) and a lexical study from colonial sources of Yucatec Maya dance theater, which necessarily touches on music (Acuña 1978). Therefore, we are much more likely to begin this investigation with an understanding of what constitutes the elements of the Nahuatl genre of *cuicatl* than we are with the Maya genre of *kay*.

Given this imbalance of known primary material and the quantity of subsequent scholarship on these subjects, it seems to me best to begin with surveying previous research concerning the identifying diagnostic elements of Nahuatl *cuicatl* and moving forward from there to examine extant Yucatec Maya songs for the presence or absence of these elements.

Recognizing Nahua Elements in Maya Song

Following the works of Garibay (1953–1954, 1: 59–106) and Karttunen and Lockhart (1980), Miguel León-Portilla (1985: 12–20) notes what he considers the outstanding features of the *cuicatl* genre. The most fundamental is their division into *units of expression* or "verses." These units are sometimes indicated in the orthography of the extant manuscripts through dots, spaces, indentations, or capital letters; in some cases, they are demarcated primarily by nonlexical elements called vocables. These vocables are ubiquitous to *cuicatl* and may have served to indicate meter. (English speakers also use vocables in their songs, such as *fa la la la la* in the Christmas carol "Deck the Halls.") Internal stylistic features of *cuicatl* include varieties of parallelism, *difrasismo*, and recurring sets of stock symbols.

John Bierhorst (1985a: 42–47), in his study of the *Cantares mexicanos*, provides an alternative approach to that followed by León-Portilla. Bierhorst sees the ideal structure of these *cuicatl* in terms of "stanzas" made up of verses and refrains organized in pairs with nonlexical elements serving as litanies. The use of dramatic monologue characterized by shifting voice and rhetorical questions highlights very important stylistic elements, which Bierhorst recognizes as common characteristics in the verbal art of many American Indian groups throughout the continent.

Both León-Portilla and Bierhorst caution that there is great irregularity in terms of meter as discernible from *cuicatl* manuscripts, noting that the idealized structures of scholars rarely predict the structure of the song texts themselves. Garibay explained this irregularity as "an artifice introduced by the songmaker, or as a consequence of bad transcription by an unskilled scribe" (León-Portilla 1985: 16). For León-Portilla, this apparent irregularity simply signifies that "there remains much to be clarified about the metric structure of the phrases and units of expression of the *cuicatl*" (León-Portilla 1985: 17). In contrast, Bierhorst argues that the *cuicatl* of the *Cantares mexicanos* are heterometric and heteromorphic, meaning that "they have no regularly recurring rhythm, at least not in the form in which they have been preserved" and "partly adapted to the dance, they continue to be strongly shaped by irregular patterns of speech. To students of American Indian music this should come as no surprise" (Bierhorst 1985a: 43). Thus, for León-Portilla, the standard metric structure of *cuicatl* has yet to be sufficiently defined, whereas for Bierhorst, the search for a standard metric structure is misguided, as it attempts to perceive in American Indian music structures more in keeping with European musical traditions.

In the absence of agreement as to what constitutes the metrical structure of *cuicatl*, what can we say is diagnostic about this genre that we should look for as evidence of influence in colonial Yucatec Maya song texts? Among the other qualities listed by León-Portilla and Bierhorst, stylistic forms such as parallelisms are a pan-Mesoamerican literary feature and thus cannot be used as evidence of specifically highland Mexican influence. *Difrasismo*, or diphrastic kennings, were once thought to have been diagnostic of highland Mexican verbal art and believed to have been introduced by Nahua speakers during the Postclassic period into the literatures of various Mayan language groups (Edmonson 1985: 112; Edmonson and Bricker 1985: 60). However, I have demonstrated elsewhere that *difrasismo* is in fact a relatively common stylistic element of Classic Maya hieroglyphic texts, predating Postclassic Nahua influence by several centuries (Knowlton 2002).

What then is left? It seems that the most consistent characteristic of Nahua song is the presence of vocables. Even if their precise function continues to elude scholars, these ubiquitous nonlexical elements are the most clearly definitive element of *cuicatl*, so much so that Bierhorst (1985b: 729–736) even appends a separate appendix of vocables in his dictionary-concordance of the *Cantares mexicanos*. A limited repertoire of vocables is attested to in the song traditions of some modern Mayan language groups, such as the Tzotzil speakers of Chamula (Gossen 1974: 224–227) and Zinacantán (Victoria Bricker, personal communication, April 2006), but they are not nearly as common and variable as vocables found in colonial Nahuatl documents. Therefore the presence of vocables of Nahua derivation would constitute evidence of Maya knowledge of highland Mexican musical forms and perhaps even Nahua influence on Yucatec Maya song itself.

Upon examining the 15 Maya songs contained in the manuscript of the *Cantares de Dzitbalché*, one quickly realizes that unlike *cuicatl*, vocables are not a common component of Yucatec Maya *kay*. A single vocable (*ay*) appears repeatedly only in the eighth of the 15 songs, the *u yayah kay* "the very painful song" (Barrera Vásquez 1965: 53–55). A form of this vocable *ay* does appear in Nahua *cuicatl*, though an interjection with the same form is also listed in the Motul dictionary as "particle with which one complains; it is a new word" (Ciudad Real 2001: 59; author's translation). Does "new" imply a borrowing from Nahuatl, or perhaps Spanish? In the absence of a method for determining whether this isolated instance is of Maya, Nahuatl, or Spanish origin, it appears there is little demonstrable highland Mexican influence in any of the 15 songs of the *Cantares de Dzitbalché*, at least in terms of vocables.

Although the songs of *Dzitbalché* form the largest corpus of Yucatec Maya *kay*, these are not the only extant examples of the genre. There are creation myths or parts of creation myths compiled in the "mythography" spanning pages 42.6 through 63.6 of the Book of Chilam Balam of Chumayel (Knowlton n.d. [2004]), which are referred to as *kay*. For example, the prologue to the creation myth attributed to the Pre-Hispanic *ah kin* ("divinatory calendar priest") Na Puc Tun states *lay kay uchci u sihil uinal*, "this song is how the *uinal* had come to pass" (Chumayel 60.5). Stylistically elegant in a variety of ways, this creation song does not include any elements of apparent highland Mexican derivation, including vocables.

Within the Chumayel mythography, however, there is one song in which numerous Nahua vocables occur. The song appears on manuscript pages 58.24–59.27 (see the appendix to this chapter), embedded within a Maya-Christian myth of the origin of human beings and of suffering as part of the human condition found on manuscript pages 58.1–60.2. This song is of interest to our investigation not only because it is the only example I am aware of in which Nahua vocables are present in a colonial Yucatec Maya song, but for two other principal reasons: Its subject is a historical event, the fall of Chichén Itzá due to the actions of Hunac Ceel (for more information about this individual, see Masson and Peraza Lope, ch. 3, this volume), and the song is represented not in the voice of a Yucatec Maya but in the voice of an Itzá inhabitant of that city. Later, I address the examples of Nahua vocables in this text, which I refer to here as the "Song of the Fall of Chichén Itzá." Thereafter, I explore why Nahua elements may appear in a song attributed to the Itzá Maya within the historical context of ethnic relations in Yucatán.

Contents of the "Song of the Fall of Chichén Itzá"

Unlike the Nahuatl *cuicatl* of the *Cantares mexicanos*, spacing and punctuation are not often reliable in distinguishing verse, or even word or morpheme, boundaries in this particular portion of the Book of Chilam Balam of Chumayel. Despite these challenges, it is still possible to discern the general framework of the song, although translations of the content of some lines are of course subject to alternate interpretations.

The setting of the "Song of the Fall of Chichén Itzá" is the feast (*uilim*) of the *ahau* Hunac Ceel (Chumayel 58.23), known from the Codice Pérez (page 135.23–25) as a *halach uinic* of Mayapán, whose scheming led to the overthrow of his fellow *halach uinic* at Chichén Itzá. In the song itself, we find a voice within a voice, the voice of a "servant of Chichén" framed by that of the compiler who is *bin yn kacuntah t in kay be*, "going to remember in my song thus" (Chumayel 59.21). Before the beginning of the song, a drum of the *t'unkul* or *teponaztli* type "is sounded" (*pecnahi*), indicating that the song is set to music (Ciudad Real 2001: 485; Alfonso Lacadena, personal communication, October 2006). The song is divided into six stanzas by a recurring litany. In the first stanza, this Itzá singer appeals on the basis of common ancestry (Chumayel 58.24, 59.19–20) against those who have come "to conquer the earth" and "vanquish the warlord" (Chumayel 58.28). In the second stanza, we learn that 1 Imix is the fated day of "heaven's capture," as determined by the "king to the west." The third stanza invokes a transition from "the first dry season" to a second period, with frequent references to shouting and to *muclam*, the "burial ground." The fourth stanza invokes a shift from a second period to the third time period in which "we bewail the day." In the fifth stanza, during "the sun of the third heaven," the Itzá singer identifies himself with the Classic period metaphor for generative sacrifice ("I am genesis, I am darkness"; see Knowlton n.d. [2004]: ch. 2) in his appeal to a *miscit* (Nahuatl: Misquitl) king, who is perhaps the "king to the west" mentioned earlier. From Chumayel 59.21 in the sixth and final stanza, the voice switches between that of the Itzá singer and the reported speech of the compiler. We learn that the Itzá singer is dead upon the fall of Chichén Itzá, the song being a ghostly elegy paralleling "the perfection of God the King's news" (Chumayel 60.1–2).

The compiler of the song presents it within a larger narrative of the origins of the first people. The inclusion of songs within such a narrative is similar to the insertion of songs within the Nahuatl narrative *Historia Tolteca-Chichimeca* (Alfonso Lacadena, personal communication, October 2006). Indeed, I note here that suffering accompanying migrations of the first peoples is a widespread Mesoamerican theme, which this part of the Book of Chilam Balam of Chumayel (58.8–10) shares with the otherwise different narratives of the *Historia Tolteca-Chichimeca* (Kirchoff et al. 1989: 157–158) and the *Popol Wuj*. The compiler of the Chumayel text expands this theme in various ways from the suffering of the first peoples to suffering as a recurring part of the human condition. As a way of accomplishing this extension, the compiler appears to be copying the "Song of the Fall of Chichén Itzá" into the larger mythic narrative from another source no longer extant. This is discernible because the orthography of the song is distinct from the creation text in which it appears. For example, in contrast to the lines of the myth preceding it, the song omits the *h* or replaces it with *g* for the phase initial particle *he*. Also, the word *kay* appears in the margin where the song proper begins, as if inserted as an afterthought to delimit where the intrusive text begins. So we can assume that the colonial period compiler of the song is its redactor but is probably not its author.

What follows is a list of the vocables and interjections that appear in the "Song of the Fall of Chichén Itzá" (see the appendix to this chapter). All but one of these is of Nahua derivation. Some Nahua vocables correspond to lexemes, but because scholars of Aztec literature usually assume they are present more for metric than semantic content, these vocables are frequently not represented in English or Spanish translations from Nahuatl. Differences between the forms of vocables as they appear in Nahuatl and Maya sources are explained phonologically in terms of place and manner of articulation (readers not familiar with phonetic terminology should consult Akmajian et al. 2000: 66–73):

AYANO: Nahuatl *ayamo* (Bierhorst 1985b: 730), with replacement of the voiced bilabial nasal [m] with the voiced alveolar nasal [n]. Number of occurrences in the Maya text: 11.
    Variants: *AYA*. Number of occurrences in Maya text: 1
    Ayamo and its variants in nonvocable contexts can correspond to the lexemes meaning "no longer" (Bierhorst 1985b: 48).

EYA: Nahuatl *hueya* (Bierhorst 1985b: 732). Voiced labiovelar glide [w] is under-represented or omitted when occurring between vowels in the Maya text. Number of occurrences in Maya text: 2

Variants include:

OEYA: o[hu]eya; number of occurrences in Maya text: 2.

OEYAN: o[hu]eyan; number of occurrences in Maya text: 1.

> Because *hueya hueyao* substitutes for the ubiquitous stanza final *ohuaya ohuaya* (or its variants *huiya ohuiya*) in some parts of the *Cantares Mexicanos* (Bierhorst 1985b: 380–384), I suspect OEYA in the Maya text represents a variant of the Nahuatl *ohuaya*.

LEE: Maya *le*—"partícula *dolentis*, y es de mugeres" (Ciudad Real 2001: 358). Number of occurrences in Maya text: 1.

O: Nahuatl interjection with the meaning "alas!" (Bierhorst 1985b: 245). *O* almost never appears in stanza final position in the *Cantares Mexicanos*. Number of occurrences in Maya text: 10.

OUA: Nahuatl *ohua* (Bierhorst 1985b:733). Synonymous with *ahua*, "hail, hey, ah" (Bierhorst 1985b: 32). Number of occurrences in Maya text: 1.

> Variants: *OA*: o[hu]a; voiced labiovelar glide [w] is apparently under-represented or omitted when occurring between vowels in the Maya text; number of occurrences in Maya text: 1.

YAE: Nahuatl *yahue*, corresponding to the lexeme meaning "alas!" (Bierhorst 1985b: 403). Occurs in the Maya text in identical contexts as *YAO*. Number of occurrences in the Maya text: 1.

YAO: Nahuatl vocable (Bierhorst 1985b: 735) that occurs in same context as *YAE* in the Maya text. Number of occurrences in the Maya text: 5.

Although these vocables are documented in colonial Nahuatl works such as the *Cantares mexicanos*, they do not appear to occur with the same frequency or distribution there as in the song under discussion. For example, *ohuaya ohuaya* is the nearly ubiquitous part of verse final litanies in the *Cantares mexicanos* (Bierhorst 1985a), yet it occurs rarely, if at all, in the "Song of the Fall of Chichén Itzá." On the other hand, variants of *ayamo* are the most common vocables in the song, particularly the litanies, although this is not true in the *Cantares mexicanos*. Thus it would appear that there is not a *direct* relationship between these colonial Nahuatl compilations and the "Song of the Fall of Chichén Itzá." Therefore, we are left with the possibilities that, first, the Nahua vocables were introduced into Maya song from an earlier and/or alternate tradition; and, second, this distribution reflects that their use was adapted to song structures based on Mayan languages. However, in the absence of additional examples, I am unaware of a viable method of determining the specific history of the introduction of the Nahua vocables into Yucatec Maya.

Song, Social Memory, and Ethnicity

> *Y si miramos a las costumbres, que antes de ser Christianos tenian, hallaremos, que en su gentilidad fueron tan politicos, y justicieros como los Mexicanos, cuyos vassallos auian sido seiscientos años antes de la llegada de los Españoles. De lo qual tan solamente ay tradicion, y memoria entre ellos, por los famosos, grandes, y espantosos edificios de cal y canto, y silleria, y figuras, y estatuas de piedra labrada, que dexaron en Oxumal, y en Chichiniza . . . y en las paredes destos dexaron los Mexicanos muchas figuras pintadas de colores viuos, que oy se veen de sus sacrificios, y bailes: por donde se colige ser obra de Mexicanos, y no de Cartaginenses como los nuestros pensaron.* (Sánchez de Aguilar 1987 [1639]: 94–95).

> And if we look at the customs that [the Maya] had before they were Christians, we will discover that in the time of their paganism they were as politic and austere in matters of justice as the Mexicans, whose vassals they were six hundred years before the arrival of the Spaniards. Of this there is only tradition and memory among [the Maya], on account of the famous, large, and awe-inspiring buildings of lime and stone, and masonry, and figures, and statues of carved stone that they left in *Oxumal* and in *Chichiniza* . . . and on these walls the Mexicans left many figures painted in living colors, that today one may see their sacrifices and dances; whereabouts they can be inferred to be the work of Mexicans, and not Carthaginians as we thought (author's translation).

According to Sánchez de Aguilar, Yucatec Maya "memory" of Maya-highland Mexican interaction during the Terminal Classic ("six hundred years before the arrival of the Spaniards") was reinforced by the remains of cities such as Chichén Itzá that made up their landscape (for archaeological perspectives on Maya-highland Mexican interaction in the Pre-Hispanic period, see Robles, ch. 2, and Masson and Peraza Lope, ch. 3, in this volume). Having established from examples in the "Song of the Fall of Chichén Itzá" some level of Nahua influence on Maya song in the northern lowlands, the question remains: What might this knowledge contribute to our understanding of indigenous Mesoamerican ethnic interaction?

Elite individuals bearing the name Itzá appear repeatedly in the epigraphic record of Terminal Classic period Chichén Itzá (Voss 2001). The later inhabitants of the Peten Itzá polity, who successfully maintained their independence and Pre-Hispanic religion until they were conquered in 1697, identified themselves as kin to these earlier Itzá from the Terminal Classic city (Jones 1998). Although Itzá are speakers of a mutually intelligible dialect of the Yucatecan language family, they are often (although not always; see Restall 2004: 66, 70–71) marked in colonial sources as distinct *itza uinicob* "Itzá people" (Codice Pérez 135.5, 10) from the *Maya* inhabitants of the peninsula. In light of this, I find it curious that, of all the extant examples of colonial Yucatec Maya songs, it is only in a song attributed to an Itzá that we find sufficient evidence of Nahua influence. This practice of attributing a song to a different ethnic group can also be found in collections of Nahuatl *cuicatl*, which often attribute songs to other ethnic groups, such as the Otomís. In the latter case, these Otomí songs are said to have been "translated into the Mexican language capturing the substance and soul of the song" (*Cantares mexicanos*, folio 6.6; Bierhorst 1985a: 148). It important to note that these "Otomí" songs probably better represent the Aztec perception of these different ethnic groups than direct evidence regarding these ethnic groups themselves. The same may be argued regarding this Yucatec Maya song attributed to the Itzá.

It appears that the use of Nahua vocables in an "Itzá" song is an artifact of the Yucatec Maya social memory of Maya and highland Mexican interaction at that Terminal Classic Maya city, as the statement by Sánchez de Aguilar seems to suggest. This "tradition and memory" of the Yucatec Maya represents the Itzá as associated with Nahua-speaking culture, just as the ruins of Chichén Itzá bespeak evidence of highland Mexican interaction. But how do we understand the relationship, if any, between this colonial period "Song of the Fall of Chichén Itzá" and the events of the Terminal Classic and later periods? That the extant version of the song is being presented from a colonial Maya perspective is evident because the final line asserts that the completion of the song is *v dzac lukanil y anumal ahau dios lae*, "perfection of God the King's news." Does this mean the song simply reflects the state of colonial period legend, without any real connection to the Pre-Hispanic past?

To make better sense of this anachronism and the relation between its colonial context and the Pre-Hispanic theme of the song, I propose that the "Song of the Fall of Chichén Itzá" is an example of the telescoping of characters and events from different historical epochs deemed alike in some fundamental way, as Victoria Bricker (1981) has argued of Maya myth and ritual in general. Memory of the Itzá of Terminal Classic Chichén Itzá is merged with that of the Itzá of Postclassic times, which in turn is merged with colonial Itzá groups contemporary with the redactor of the song.

The Terminal Classic inscriptions of Chichén Itzá provide some evidence of historical personages mentioned in the colonial sources. For example, the Itzá captain Kakupacal, first identified by David Kelley, carries the title *ah nun*, "barbarian" (Grube 1994: 335), which is applied to the Itzá as a people in later ethnohistorical sources. Although numerous individuals are known from the inscriptions of Chichén Itzá, to my knowledge Hunac Ceel is not among them. If there is a historical personage behind the accounts of Hunac Ceel, does he then belong to a period postdating the Terminal Classic inscriptions? According to accounts given in the Book of Chilam Balam of Chumayel (manuscript pages 10–11), Hunac Ceel was *halach uinic* and a fellow *ahau* of a person called Ah Mex Cuc at Chichén Itzá. The Chumayel account of their dominance of Chichén Itzá begins with an interesting parallelism: *ca hoppi u tepalobi ca hoppi ti y ahaulilobi*, "then their sovereignty began there, then their kingship began there." This is the pairing, in a context of syntactic and semantic parallelism, of two terms referring to rulership: *tepal*, ultimately deriving from Nahua (Jus-teson et al 1985: 25), and its autochthonous Maya equivalent *ahaulil*. When the Spanish invaded Yucatán in the sixteenth century, they encountered an ethnic distinction between the Yucatec Maya and the people who, according to indigenous chronicles, once inhabited Chichén Itzá. An important piece of evidence appears in the Morley manuscript (Whalen n.d.), a Yucatec Maya copybook that includes some texts which appear to have been composed originally no later than the late sixteenth century. This copybook contains the antecedents of Yucatec Maya texts later copied into the Books of Chilam Balam (Knowlton n.d. [2004]: ch. 3), as well as others later edited and published in 1620 by the Franciscans (Whalen n.d.). The Morley manuscript contains the following passage (Whalen n.d.: 169.10–170.1, with modifications):

> ta xocahi tac helel cech christiano
> hijbic sihsabcij yax anom adan ti lume
> u yumit tulacal vinicob yanob yokol cab tu sinile
> lacech dzulob laac francesob
> laac morosob laac judiob laac ekboxob
> laac ah mex cuc uincob laac ah maya uincob
> huntulili adan yax anom chunpahcij uinicilob loe
> bacac ix ua uecaanob ti petenob lae

> You read already now, you who are Christian,
> Just how the first man Adam had been born from earth
> To father all the men who exist upon the world everywhere
> Though they may be the foreigners [Spaniards], though French
> Though Moors, though Jews, though Blacks
> Though Ah Mex Cuc people, though Maya people
> It is only Adam, the first man, from who those people began
> Even though they are scattered to these lands.

This text has significant implications for Restall's (2004: 64) recent hypothesis that the Maya during the colonial period "did not call themselves that or any other name that indicated they saw themselves as members of a common ethnic group. Nor did Spaniards or Africans in colonial Yucatán refer to the Mayas as 'Mayas'." Furthermore, if an early colonial date of the Morley manuscript's original composition is correct, it seems very unlikely to me that this ethnic distinction is entirely the result of Spanish influence. Examining the context in which *ah mex cuc uinicob* and *ah maya uinicob* are juxtaposed (note how *ah mex cuc* refers to a people, not to an individual), the purpose here is to minimize an existing ethnic difference to better facilitate evangelization. Therefore, it seems very likely that a division of the inhabitants of Yucatán along these lines was present by at least the Late Postclassic period. As the presence of numerous Nahua vocables in the "Song of the Fall of Chichén Itzá" attest, inhabitants of the city such as the group associated with Ah Mex Cuc were at least *perceived* by later Yucatec Maya to have been more greatly influenced by Nahua-speaking culture.

Finally, we should address why the "Song of the Fall of Chichén Itzá" concludes with the anachronistic phrase "the perfection of God the King's news." In the Books of Chilam Balam, the term *ah nunil Itza* becomes the object of Christian Maya apocalyptic prophecies (e.g., Chumayel 47.28–48.8). This coincides with a shift at the beginning of the seventeenth century in which the difference between "Maya" and "Itzá" begins to take the form of a religious as well as an ethnic distinction. In a paper presented at Tulane University, John Chuchiak (n.d. [2005]) documented this growing distinction in the mid-colonial period between the *hahil Maya uinicob*, "true Maya people," who resided in towns and adopted many aspects of Spanish Christian culture, and the "barbarian" and "apostate" peoples of the interior of the peninsula. Chuchiak also presents documentary evidence that the *hahil Maya uinicob* participated with Spaniards in numerous campaigns against these "barbarians," eventually culminating in the fall of the Peten Itzá polity in 1697. I believe the apocalyptic prophecies regarding the *ah nunil Itza* in the Books of Chilam Balam likely represent an expression of this emerging mid-colonial state of affairs, in which ethnic relations between indigenous Yucatecans were marked by sectarian strife. A song about the fall of a previous Itzá polity is not just an account of past events, but a hope for "the perfection of God the King's news" to be realized in the colonial Yucatec Maya's struggle against their "apostate" Itzá contemporaries.

Conclusion

Thus in the voice of the singer of the "Song of the Fall of Chichén Itzá," we encounter a conflated representation of not one but three different groups of Itzá: the Itzá of the Terminal Classic Maya city, the Itzá that corresponded to Postclassic ethnic distinctions between Maya and "Ah Mex Cuc people," and the colonial period "apostate" Itzá occupying the unconquered areas of the lowland interior. The appearance of Nahua vocables in an "Itzá" song not only indicates highland Mexican influence on Maya music at some point in the Pre-Hispanic period but also marks colonial Maya ethnic distinctions as being rooted in indigenous social memory of these Maya-highland Mexican encounters.

Acknowledgments

I wish to thank Gabrielle Vail and Christine Hernández for inviting me to contribute to the 2006 Dumbarton Oaks Symposium. I also wish to thank Joanne Pillsbury, the staff of Pre-Columbian Studies, and symposium participants and attendees for creating a wonderful environment in which to exchange ideas and research. I am grateful to Judith Maxwell for originally suggesting I take a closer look into the relationship between colonial Maya song and the *Cantares mexicanos*. Victoria Bricker and Meredith Paxton shared much appreciated insights in response to earlier drafts of this paper. I wish to extend a very special thank you to Alfonso Lacadena for suggesting alternative readings for parts of the Yucatec text; I have incorporated several of these, resulting in some substantial changes in the present paper over the previous drafts. Any mistakes and omissions still present despite such wonderful feedback are, of course, my own.

APPENDIX

The following translation is a modified selection of one prepared for my dissertation (Knowlton n.d. [2004]). The chapter for the present volume has benefited from both my own reassessment of a few morpheme breaks and concomitant readings as well as very insightful suggestions by symposium participants, resulting in minor discrepancies between the previous version and the one presented here.

"Song of the Fall of Chichén Itzá"

BOOK OF CHILAM BALAM OF CHUMAYEL[1]

(58.22) *Ca pecnahi*	Then [the kettledrum] sounded
V uil im hunac ceel ahau	The feast (?) of Hunac Ceel the King
Kay	Song:
Ge ma et kinon	Are we not alike?
Tix kan thixal ti tun/e	And of the ripe gleanings(?) of this *tun*?
Mac u cobol y utztacil uinic	Who is the corn mold of the good people?
Yn nok ynu ex y alah oua	"My clothes and my pants" he said OUA
Kue	Oh deity
Balac au oktic	You mourn for this thing
Yx cijx mamace	And nobody better?
V munalen u chii ch'een	I am a servant of the Mouth of the Well
Cen ti uli	For me, when it arrived
O Chuc lum	O To conquer the earth
Dzidz v tah katun aya	To vanquish the warlord AYA

---

1. Manuscript pages 58.22–60.2. Page numbers are given in parentheses.

(59) *T u chi ch'een ytza*	At the Mouth of the Itzá's Well
O Antan he yao	O Stomp now YAO
Y ulu / u ayano	The moon arrives (?) AYANO
O [H]e ti hun imix u kijnil chuc / caan	O This 1 Imix is the day of heaven's capture
Bin ahau t u chiken ch'eene	According to the king to the west of the Well
[H]e taba/ech yane	Where will you be?
Kue	Oh deity
[H]e tun hun ymix v kin	Then this day 1 Imix
Y alah t u chi ch'een ytza oa	It declared to the Mouth of the Itzá's Well OA
Anta here yao	Stomp now YAO
Y ulu u ayano	The moon arrives (?) AYANO
Muclam muclam	Burial ground, burial ground
Cijx y aua/t	And so he shouts
O Muclam muclam	O Burial ground, burial ground
Ci xan y ohelob thun	So they also know the slit drum
Ci y aue	So he shouts
Ci xan y awat	So also it shouts
O T u hun te yaxkine	O In the first dry season
Chichil kinij ca te	A strong sun for the second time
Ak yabil ti tali	There were many tongues when it came
O Ayano ayano ayano	O AYANO AYANO AYANO
Y ulu u ayano	The moon arrives (?) AYANO
Yan/xin macxin	Who is it really?
Ahan uale	A defender, perhaps?
Chichil ni ca te / ayano	A strong tip the second time AYANO
Ox ten c acan v kine	Three times we bewail the day
Kue	Oh deity
C ah/ualob c ahualob	Our enemies, our enemies
Vui yao	Listen! YAO
Ma xan / ulom t u chi ch'een ytza oa	Will not arrive also at the Mouth of the Itzá's Well OA
Anta here yae	Stomp now YAE
Y ulu u ayano	The moon arrives (?) AYANO
Ox te caan u kin	The sun of the third heaven
He macen ua	If I am this man
T u than tan y ol vinice	In the word before the heart of the people
Cen u mac	I am the man
Lee eya	LEE EYA

Macen ua	If I am the man
T u than tan / y ol putun	In the word before the heart of the Putun
Men a nate oeyan	Because you may understand it OEYAN
Ch'aben / akaben	I am genesis, I am night
Coon ua sihij oeya	Is it we who are born? OEYA
Alakon / miscit ahau	We are comrades, Miscit King
Ho atal	Five are paid
Tix vlu	And arrive
Max / ela	Who burned it?
Bin yn kacuntah t in kay be	I was going to remember in my song thus
Antan here yao	Stomp now YAO
Y ulu u ayano eya	The moon arrives (?) AYANO EYA
Ci/milen y alah	He said "I am dead
T u men u kin cah oeya	Because of the town's day" OEYA
Ca/tacen y alahe	He said "I am two
T u men u sat cah	Because the town is lost"
O U ti u / lah ti y ol	O It all belongs to him in his heart
U tuclah t u pucsikale	He thought it in his core
Men u / sat cah	Because the town is lost
O Vali kacuntan in kay	O It stood memorialized in my song
O Antan / here yao ayano	O Stomp now YAO AYANO
Y ulu v ayano	The moon arrives (?) AYANO
(60) Lay kay t u lacal lae	This is all of the song
V dzoc lukanil y anu/mal ahau dios lae	The perfection of God the King's news

References Cited

Acuña, René
    1978   *Farsas y representaciones escénicas de los mayas antiguos.* Universidad Nacional Autónoma de México, México, D.F.

Akmajian, Adrian, Richard A. Demers, Ann K. Farmer, and Robert M. Harnish
    2000   *Linguistics: An Introduction to Language and Communication.* 4th ed. Massachusetts Institute of Technology Press, Cambridge.

Barrera Vásquez, Alfredo (trans.)
    1965   *El libro de los cantares de Dzitbalché.* Instituto Nacional de Antropología e Historia, México, D.F.

Barrera Vásquez, Alfredo, and Silvia Rendón
    1948   *El libro de los libros de Chilam Balam.* Fondo de Cultural Económica, México, D.F.

Bierhorst, John (trans.)

1985a *Cantares Mexicanos: Songs of the Aztecs.* Stanford University Press, Stanford, Calif.

1985b *A Nahuatl-English Dictionary and Concordance to the Cantares Mexicanos.* Stanford University Press, Stanford, Calif.

Bricker, Victoria R.

1981 *The Indian Christ, the Indian King. The Historical Substrate of Maya Myth and Ritual.* University of Texas Press, Austin.

Bricker, Victoria R., and Helga-Maria Miram

2002 *An Encounter of Two Worlds: The Book of Chilam Balam of Kaua.* Middle American Research Institute Publication 68. Tulane University, New Orleans.

Chuchiak, John F., IV

2001 Pre-Conquest *Ah Kinob* in a Colonial World: The Extirpation of Idolatry and the Survival of the Maya Priesthood in Colonial Yucatán, 1563–1697. In *Maya Survivalism* (Ueli Hostettler and Matthew Restall, eds): 135–157. Verlag Anton Saurwein, Markt Schwaben, Germany.

2004 The Images Speak: The Survival and Production of Hieroglyphic Codices and Their Use in Post-Conquest Maya Religion (1580–1720). In *Continuity and Change: Maya Religious Practices in Temporal Perspective* (Daniel Graña Behrens, Nikolai Grube, Christian M. Prager, Frauke Sachse, Stefanie Teufel, and Elisabeth Wagner, eds.): 167–183. Verlag Anton Saurwein, Markt Schwaben, Germany.

n.d. *Ah Otochnalob yetel Ah Chun Kaxob*: Indios de campana, indios idolatras, and the Colonial Re-Construction of Maya Ethnic Identity, 1590–1700. Paper presented at the symposium "Peoples and Institutions of the Colonial Americas" at the Gulf Coast Consortium of Latin American Colonialists, New Orleans, February 2005.

Chumayel, Book of Chilam Balam

n.d. Original manuscript in the Princeton University Library, N.J. See also Gordon 1993 [1913].

Ciudad Real, Antonio de

2001 *Calepino maya de Motul* (René Acuña, ed.). Plaza y Valdes Editores, México, D.F.

Codice Pérez

n.d. Photographic copy of original manuscript in Tozzer Library at Peabody Museum, Harvard University, Cambridge, Mass.

Edmonson, Munro S.

1985 Quiche Literature. In *Literatures, Supplement to the Handbook of Middle American Indians*, vol. 3 (Munro S. Edmonson, ed.): 107–132. University of Texas Press, Austin.

Edmonson, Munro S., and Victoria R. Bricker

1985 Yucatecan Mayan Literature. In *Literatures, Supplement to the Handbook of Middle American Indians*, vol. 3 (Munro S. Edmonson, ed.): 44–63. University of Texas Press, Austin.

Garibay K., Angel Maria
  1953–1954 *Historia de la literatura náhuatl.* Editorial Porrúa, México, D.F.

Gordon, George B.
  1993 [1913] *The Book of Chilam Balam of Chumayel.* Aegean Park Press, Laguna
         Hills, Calif.

Gossen, Gary H.
  1974 *Chamulas in the World of the Sun: Time and Space in a Maya Oral
         Tradition.* Harvard University Press, Cambridge, Mass.

Grube, Nikolai
  1994 Hieroglyphic Sources of the History of Northwest Yucatan. In *Hidden
         among the Hills: Maya Archaeology of the Northwest Yucatan Peninsula*
         (Hanns J. Prem, ed.): 316–358. Verlag von Flemming, Möckmühl, Germany.

Houston, Stephen, David Stuart, and Karl Taube
  2006 *The Memory of Bones: Body, Being, and Experience among the Classic Maya.*
         University of Texas Press, Austin.

Jones, Grant D.
  1998 *The Conquest of the Last Maya Kingdom.* Stanford University Press,
         Stanford, Calif.

Justeson, John S., William M. Norman, Lyle Campbell, and Terrence Kaufman
  1985 *The Foreign Impact on Lowland Maya Language and Script.* Middle
         American Research Institute Publication 53. Tulane University,
         New Orleans.

Karttunen, Frances, and James Lockhart
  1980 La estructura de la poesía náhuatl vista por sus variantes. *Estudios de
         cultura náhuatl* 14: 15–64.

Kelley, David
  1976 *Deciphering the Maya Script.* University of Texas Press, Austin.

Kirchoff, Paul, Lina Odena Güemes, and Luís Reyes Garcia (eds.)
  1989 *Historia Tolteca-Chichimeca.* 2nd ed. Centro de Investigaciones Superiores,
         Instituto Nacional de Antropología e Historia, México, D.F.

Knowlton, Timothy
  2002 Diphrastic Kennings in Mayan Hieroglyphic Literature. *Mexicon* 24
         (1): 9–14.
  n.d. Dialogism in the Languages of Colonial Maya Creation Myths. Ph.D.
         dissertation, Department of Anthropology, Tulane University, New
         Orleans, 2004.

León-Portilla, Miguel
  1985 Nahuatl Literature. In *Literatures, Supplement to the Handbook of Middle
         American Indians*, vol. 3 (Munro S. Edmonson, ed.): 7–43. University of
         Texas Press, Austin.

Miram, Helga-Maria
  1994 A Method for Recalibrating Historical Dates in the Books of Chilam
         Balam. In *Hidden among the Hills: Maya Archaeology of the Northwest
         Yucatan Peninsula* (Hanns J. Prem, ed.): 375–388. Verlag von Flemming,
         Möckmühl, Germany.

Restall, Matthew
   2004   Maya Ethnogenesis. *Journal of Latin American Anthropology* 9 (1): 64–89.

Sánchez de Aguilar, Pedro
   1987 [1639]   Informe contra idolorum cultores del Obispado de Yucatan. In *El alma encantada: Anales del Museo Nacional de México* (Fernando Benítez, ed.): 12–122. Instituto Nacional Indigenista, Fondo de Cultura Económica, México, D.F.

Voss, Alexander
   2001   Los Itzaes en Chichén Itzá—Datos epigráficos. *Investigadores de la cultura maya* 9 (1): 152–173.

Whalen, Gretchen
   n.d   An Annotated Translation of a Colonial Yucatec Manuscript: On Religious and Cosmological Topics by a Native Author. Available at www.famsi.org/reports/01017/index.html; accessed January 1, 2004.

Part III

Archaeoastronomy, Codices, and Cosmologies

Introduction

Gabrielle Vail and Christine Hernández

Studies of the Maya codices in recent years provide important information concerning the cultural context in which they were produced, most especially in terms of exhibiting evidence of highland Mexican influence in their almanacs and texts. Chapters 9–11 are concerned with examining the question of interaction between the northern Maya lowlands and highland central Mexico from the perspective of data contained in the screenfold books and other (post-conquest) indigenous documents.

The following discussion offers an overview of Mesoamerican calendrical systems and the workings of codical almanacs and tables as an introduction to the chapters contained in this part. We begin with a brief discussion of the codices and their proposed provenience.

Mesoamerican Codices: A Note Regarding Provenience

Before the arrival of Europeans, codices were produced by elite scribes in the central and southern highlands of Mexico and across the Maya area. The information recorded in these manuscripts relates to the numerous social concerns common to complex societies: political histories, royal genealogies, creation myths, tribute rolls, and calendrical and astronomical tools to divine fortunes for ceremonies and rituals pertaining to marriage, naming children, agriculture, beekeeping, feasts, artisan production, military raids, and travel (see, e.g., Boone 2000; Sahagún 1950–1982, bks. 4, 6–8).

Throughout the conquest and early colonial periods in Mesoamerica, Spanish ecclesiastical authorities confiscated and destroyed native screenfolds (Durán 1971: 55; Landa 1978: 82). The success of these extirpation campaigns can be measured by the fact that only 20 native screenfolds are known to still exist; 15 are most likely Pre-Hispanic, and five were produced just after the conquest (Boone 2000: 70). Of the pre-Columbian screenfolds, three or four divinatory books (the Dresden, Madrid, Paris, and Grolier codices) are of Maya origin, and the remaining 11 manuscripts come from the central Mexican highlands.[1] Five of the Mexican codices (the Zouche-Nuttall, Vindobonensis, Selden, Columbino, and Bodley codices) are genealogical/historical books from the Mixteca Alta area of southern Mexico. The remaining six screenfolds (the Borgia, Vaticanus B (3773), Fejérváry-Mayer, Cospi, Laud, and Aubin 20 codices) are divinatory in nature.[2] Although they are believed to have originated from various locales in central and southern Mexico (Boone 2003; Sisson 1983), all six are referred to as members of the Borgia Group codices (Seler 1887) because they exhibit similar stylistic, structural, and thematic attributes (Boone 2000: 71).

In the absence of historical records, codical specialists must rely on clues internal to the manuscripts to formulate theories about where and when the Maya and Borgia Group codices were painted. The consensus of researchers is that the Dresden, Madrid, and Paris codices are all from the northern Maya lowlands, as suggested by studies of their iconography, glyphic texts, calendrics, and overall content (Chuchiak 2004; Love 1994: ch. 2; Paxton 1991, 2004, n.d. [1986]; Thompson 1972: 16; Vail and Aveni 2004; Vail et al. 2003; see also Vail 2006). Although they were presumably painted during the Late Postclassic period, they are composed of almanacs and tables that were drafted at various times by a number of different scribes. This is similar to patterning documented in colonial Yucatec texts, such as the Books of Chilam Balam, which include copies of texts written over a period of several centuries (Bricker and Miram 2002).

It is not known where in central Mexico the five core screenfolds of the Borgia Group (excluding the Aubin 20) originated. They lack identifiable historical, genealogical, and geographical information that would allow us to pinpoint their proveniences within the central highlands. Instead, studies of art style and iconography and comparisons with archaeological remains have been used to identify possible sites of origin for each screenfold. To date, the general consensus holds that the Borgia and Cospi codices likely came from the Puebla-Tlaxcala region. The Laud and Fejérváry-Mayer codices seem tied stylistically to the Tabasco area of the Gulf Coast, and the Vaticanus B screenfold may have come from the Mixteca Alta region (see, e.g., Boone 2007; Nicholson 1966, 1982; Robertson 1966; Sisson 1983).

Numerous studies dedicated to comparing images of material culture in the Borgia Codex with artifacts, house styles, ceramics, and mural art recovered archaeologically from sites in the Puebla-Tlaxcala region support the attribution of the manuscript to that area of the central highlands (Chadwick and McNeish 1967; Contreras Martínez 1992, 1993; Lind 1994; Nicholson 1966, 1994; Pohl 1998; Sisson and Lily 1994a, 1994b; Uruñela et al. 1997). This suggests that the scribe or scribes who drafted the codex would have been fluent in

Nahuatl, if not native speakers of the language. The work of many scholars (see e.g., Kirchoff et al. 1989; Pohl 2003a, 2003b; Pohl and Byland 1994) has contributed to our growing understanding of the historical, ethnic, sociopolitical, and material contexts in which the Borgia Codex was likely to have been conceived and used.

In a recent discussion of Pre-Hispanic Mesoamerican codices, Elizabeth Boone (2003) considers relationships between the Maya and Borgia Group codices, citing evidence of Mexican elements found in the Dresden, Madrid, and Grolier manuscripts, but apparently lacking from the Paris Codex. She suggests that the manuscripts each reflect a different situation, implying a differential degree of adoption of Mexican ideology. The Dresden scribes, by including Nahua gods in the Venus table, indicate a familiarity with foreign deities and their realms and associations, but Boone sees this as an isolated occurrence in what is very much a Maya manuscript. The Madrid Codex, on the other hand, includes almanacs directly comparable to those found in the Borgia Group codices, suggesting a firsthand familiarity with Mexican divinatory codices (see Hernández and Bricker 2004; Just 2004 for an extended discussion). The best-known examples of Maya and Mexican almanacs with similar structures are those with an *in extenso* format (discussed later) focused on representing all 260 days of the ritual calendar explicitly (Boone 2003; Just 2000, 2004). In another recent publication, Christine Hernández and Victoria Bricker (2004) document other examples of connections between almanacs in the Madrid and Borgia Group codices, focusing on those that depict agricultural activities associated with planting and its attendant ceremonies and prophecies.

The Grolier Codex, if it is indeed Pre-Hispanic in date, is also relevant to this discussion. Both in terms of its style and the use of aberrant calendrical conventions, the Grolier appears to have derived from what Boone (2003: 220) describes as "a cultural frontier zone, far from the hearts of the two traditions [Maya and Mexican], but where their edges mixed." She notes that Coe (in Boone 2003: 220) may be correct in attributing it to the trading port of Xicalango on the southern Gulf Coast, in light of the fact that its population included Nahuatl traders as well as indigenous Chontal Maya speakers.

Pre-Hispanic Calendars and Codical Almanacs

Ancient Mesoamericans employed several interlocking calendrical cycles to track the passage of time (see, e.g., Aveni 2001: 125–166; Caso 1971; Edmonson 1988). A set of 20 day signs paired with the numerical coefficients 1–13 was combined to form a ritual calendar referred to as the *tzolk'in* by Mayanists and known as the *tonalpohualli* in Nahuatl (see Vail and Aveni 2004: 132, fig. 5.1 and Boone 2007: 37, fig. 12). The count begins with the first of the 20 days paired with the coefficient 1. The first day, 1 Imix or 1 Crocodile, is followed by 2 Ik' or 2 House, 3 Ak'b'al or 3 House, and so forth until the 260th day, 13 Ahaw or 13 Flower. The cycles and subdivisions of the ritual calendar convey important associations, fortunes, and omens that formed the basis for prognosticating, preparing for, and attempting to influence the outcome of future events and activities.

A second cycle of time is a "festival" round of 18 named periods of 20 days called *winals* in the lowland Mayan languages and *meztlipohualli* in Nahuatl (somewhat like the 12 months in the Western calendar) that produced a cycle of 360 days. Five additional days, referred to as Wayeb' or *nemontemi*, followed the last day of the festival round to complete a period of 365 days referred to as the *haab'* in Maya texts and *xihuitl* in Nahuatl. The Maya *haab'* was named for its initial day, whereas the Mexican *xihuitl* was named according to its terminal or 360th day.

The interlocking of the 260-day and 365-day cycles resulted in a perpetual sequence of solar years that all began or ended with one of only four days out of the 20 in the ritual calendar. These sets of four days are called "year-bearers." During the Late Postclassic period, the yearbearer days in the central highlands were Reed, Flint, House, and Rabbit (Caso 1971: 347; Edmonson 1988: 9–10); in the Maya area at the time of the conquest, they were K'an, Muluk, Ix, and Kawak (Tozzer 1941: 135). An earlier set from the Maya area, associated with the days Ak'b'al, Lamat, B'en, and Etz'nab', corresponds to the Late Postclassic highland yearbearers.

It requires 52 years to cycle through the years named by each yearbearer paired with the coefficients 1–13 (i.e., 1 Reed, 2 Flint, 3 House . . . 13 Rabbit). The enumeration of all 52 named years created yet another important cycle of time for ancient Mesoamericans, which Mayanists refer to as the Calendar Round (Thompson 1971: 123). In the Calendar Round, individual days within the *tzolk'in* couple with those in the *haab'* based on the initial pairing of 4 Ahaw (*tzolk'in*) with 8 Kumk'u (*haab'*) at the beginning of the present era.[3] The Nahuatl count of years is called *xiuhpohualli*, and people residing in the central highlands commemorated the completion of a 52-year cycle with a series of rituals and ceremonies referred to as *xiuhmolpilli*, "the binding of years," which is described in detail in the Florentine Codex (Sahagún 1953: 25–32).

The Mexican and Maya scribes who created codices organized their information within a variety of interrelated instruments used for divination, astronomical observation, and calendrical reckoning. Almanacs, which include a combination of pictures, calendrical information, and, in the case of the Maya screenfolds, hieroglyphic captions to place events of a secular or sacred nature into the 260-day ritual calendar, represent the majority of the content of the extant Pre-Hispanic codices. The Maya Dresden Codex also includes several astronomical tables that contain dates in the Long Count calendar used by the Maya, which allows events to be placed in absolute time. Almanacs differ from tables in that they do not contain explicit Long Count dates or mechanisms for calculating them, but recent research (described later) suggests that both types of instruments could be used for tracking events over a long period of time and that almanacs, like tables, frequently include references to datable events (i.e., rather than those that recur within a short cycle such as the 260-day calendar).

Cognate almanacs from the Borgia and Fejérváry-Mayer codices (figs. 1 and 2) and the Madrid Codex (fig. 3) reveal some of the key differences in almanac construction and calendrical reckoning between the two scribal traditions. The Mexican almanacs in figures 1 and 2 show a reliance on imagery alone to portray gods, activities, and associated omens in each of their compartments. The explicit depiction of days in the count of the almanac appears either as a row of day signs (fig. 1) or a combination of day signs and spacers represented by large colored dots (fig. 2).[4] In all but a few cases, the numerical coefficients of dates are not given and must be inferred. The Maya counterpart (fig. 3) contains hieroglyphic captions that supplement the imagery to name gods, describe the action portrayed, and reveal omens. The calendrical information in the almanac begins with an initial column of explicit day glyphs and a *tzolk'in* coefficient. In the example shown, the coefficient is 1 and the day glyphs refer to the following *tzolk'in* dates: 1 Ahaw, 1 Eb', 1 K'an, 1 Kib', and 1 Lamat. Mathematical notation for calculating the remaining dates in the almanac appears at the top of each frame as black-painted distance numbers (DNs) and red-painted *tzolk'in* coefficients. The complete calendrical structure of the almanac is detailed in figure 3 (see Vail and Aveni 2004: ch. 5 for an extended discussion of the calendrical structure of Maya almanacs).

Almanacs exhibit a number of different calendrical structures, depending on how they are organized. Their initial column may have four or five day glyphs (or sometimes multiples of these numbers). Almanacs with four day glyphs will have distance numbers totaling 65 ($4 \times 65 = 260$), whereas those with five day glyphs will have distance numbers totaling 52 ($5 \times 52 = 260$); they are therefore known as 4×65-day and 5×52-day almanacs.

Calendrical Studies of the Maya and Borgia Group Codices

An area of primary interest in the study of Maya codices in recent years has been the use of evidence internal to the manuscripts in order to date them in historical time. A number of scholars working with the Madrid Codex (e.g., Hatch 1975; Milbrath 1999) have focused on an astronomical interpretation of iconography to relate certain almanacs to a specific time period. This tradition is best exemplified in the work of Harvey Bricker and Victoria Bricker (H. Bricker et al. 1997; V. Bricker 1997a, 1997b; V. Bricker and H. Bricker 1988), who apply a methodology they developed in the 1980s to cross-reference iconographic parallels between almanacs in the Madrid Codex and the Dresden's

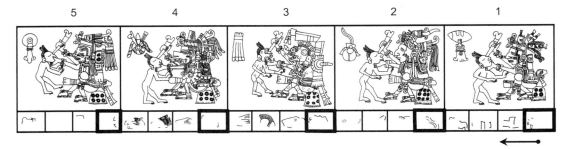

5   4   3   2   1

Reading order is from right to left

Compartment 3   **Compartment 2**   **Compartment 1**

Grass   Monkey   Dog   Water   Rabbit   Deer   Death   Serpent   Lizard   House   Wind   Crocodile

Compartment 5   **Compartment 4**

Flower   Rain   Flint   Movement   Vulture   Eagle   Ocelot   Reed

Fig. 1. The calendrical structure of Borgia 15c–16c. Artwork by Christine Hernández, after *Codex Borgia* (1976: 52).

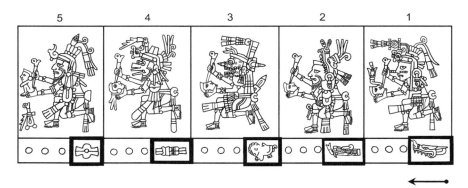

5   4   3   2   1

Reading order is from right to left

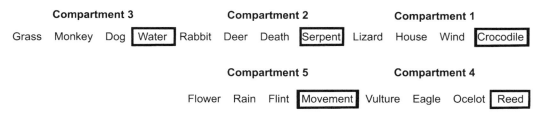

Compartment 3   **Compartment 2**   **Compartment 1**

Grass   Monkey   Dog   Water   Rabbit   Deer   Death   Serpent   Lizard   House   Wind   Crocodile

Compartment 5   **Compartment 4**

Flower   Rain   Flint   Movement   Vulture   Eagle   Ocelot   Reed

Fig. 2. The calendrical structure of Fejérváry-Mayer 23a–24a. Artwork by Christine Hernández, after *Codex Fejérváry-Mayer* (1994: 23–24).

astronomical and seasonal tables to propose unique dates for several sections of the Madrid Codex. Their studies suggest that the manuscript records astronomical and seasonal information pertaining to the tenth and fifteenth centuries. The fifteenth-century date is likely when the codex was actually created, whereas the earlier dates imply that almanacs originally composed in the tenth century were copied into the codex because they remained valuable to the fifteenth-century users.

These dating studies and recent research aimed at the identification of cognate almanacs shared by the Dresden and Madrid codices (Aveni 2004; Aveni et al. 1996; Drapkin n.d. [2002]; Vail and Hernández n.d.) have revealed interesting details about the Madrid's content and construction, as Hernández and Vail discuss in Chapter 11. In addition, several almanacs found at the beginning of the Madrid Codex contain what have often been referred to as "Mexicanized" elements. Julia Drapkin (n.d. [2002]: 155–156) suggests that these elements were incorporated by the Madrid scribes because they derived from an area that the elite of northern Yucatán viewed as a prestige center; their inclusion in the codex, therefore, served to express this important relationship and acted as a form of social currency. Marilyn Masson (2003) has proposed a similar model to account for International-style elements found in Maya murals from the coastal site of Santa Rita Corozal.

Although the calendrical study and historical dating of tables and almanacs in the Maya codices have been ongoing since the turn of the nineteenth century (see discussion in Vail 2006), only recently—long after Seler's (1904) initial commentaries—have these types of studies been reemployed to aid our understanding of astronomical references in the Borgia Group codices (see, e.g, Aveni 1999; Bricker 2001; Milbrath 1999, 2007). Studies by Aveni (1999) and Bricker (2001) reveal that at least five almanacs in the Borgia, Vaticanus B (3773), and Cospi codices concern the prediction of real-time movements of Venus during the fifteenth and sixteenth centuries. These five almanacs are sources of dated astronomical imagery that can be used to cross-date other almanacs in the Mexican and Maya codices using the Brickers' historical methodology (Hernández 2004, 2006), as Victoria Bricker discusses in Chapter 10.

Following the early work of Thomas (1884) and Seler (1904), there was a tendency to shy away from broad pan-Mesoamerican comparative research throughout much of the twentieth century. However, the early connections they demonstrated—between M. 75–76 and FM 1 and Venus instruments in the Borgia and Dresden codices[5]—form the foundation for much of the research done by later scholars (Hernández and Bricker 2004; Just 2000, 2004), including that reported in the present volume. Many of the comparisons involve almanacs with a format that differs from the standard structure described earlier. Typically, cognate almanacs are those that are structured in a circular format, as a "Formée cross," or as another type of *in extenso* almanac.

1 (+20 days)	8 (+10 days)	5 (+10 days)	2 (+12 days)
Ahaw	Ahaw	Ok	Ahaw
Eb'	Eb'	Ik'	Eb'
K'an	K'an	Ix	K'an
Kib'	Kib'	Kimi	Kib'
Lamat	Lamat	Etz'nab'	Lamat

Fig. 3. The calendrical structure of Madrid 99d. After *Codex Tro-Cortesianus* (1967); reproduced courtesy of the Museo de América, Madrid.

Almanac *in extenso*, a term coined by Anton Nowotny (2005: 248), describes a structural category of Mexican *tonalpohualli* almanacs in which all 260 day signs in the ritual calendar are explicitly represented in a horizontal layout. This is in contrast to the more condensed calendrical format generally found in almanacs in which only a subset of dates in the ritual calendar is highlighted (figs. 1–3).

Horizontal *in extenso* almanacs cover the introductory pages of three manuscripts in the Borgia Group—the Borgia, Vaticanus B, and Cospi codices. In the example illustrated here (fig. 4), pages 1 and 2 from a recent painted reconstruction of the Borgia Codex show the count of 260 days beginning in the lower right corner and reading continuously from right to left across eight pages in five rows of 52 day signs each. Reading from the bottom up, the rows are aligned to create vertical columns of five day signs with like coefficients (see right-hand column in fig. 4). A total of 13 columns fit across each pair of pages (four pairs in all) such that each set of 13 columns represents days with the coefficients 1–13, commonly referred to as *trecenas*.

In a recent study, Bryan Just (2004) contends that the scribes who painted the Madrid Codex adopted the format of the Mexican horizontal *in extenso* almanac to create four Maya versions of the expanded calendrical instrument.[6] One of these almanacs appears on pages 12b–18b of the Madrid manuscript (see ch. 11, fig. 5, this volume). The remaining three examples are on the obverse side of the codex, on pages 65–72 and 73b, 75–76, and 77–78.[7] Just (2004: 269–272) suggests that M. 12b–18b was centrally positioned in the manuscript so that the remaining three *in extenso* almanacs on the obverse side could be folded over and placed physically adjacent to pages 12–18, with the presumed intention of cross-referencing or aligning concordant data.

One of the Madrid *in extenso* almanacs, on pages 75–76 (plate 1), can be compared structurally to the almanac on FM 1 (plate 2). The two almanacs have essentially a quadripartite layout in relation to a center compartment, with an overall shape reminiscent of a Formée cross. Additional information is tucked into the corner spaces between the quadrants. The 260-day count of the ritual calendar outlines the quadrants, or "arms," and corners, or "lobes," of the almanac with each *trecena* (20 in all) indicated by a combination of explicit day glyphs and spacers. In addition, a second series of 20 day glyphs beginning with the day Imix, or Crocodile, is recorded in columns or around the perimeter of the central picture. These glyphs are grouped into four separate sets of five days, and each set is aligned with one of the four quadrants. They appear

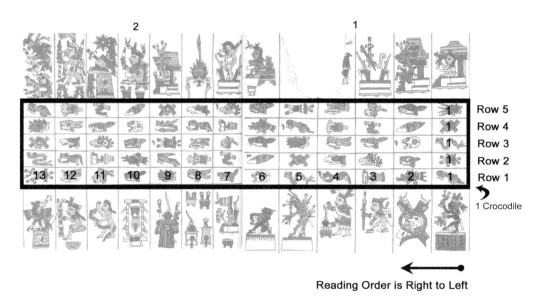

Fig. 4. Pages 1 and 2 of the almanac *in extenso* in the reconstructed version of the Borgia Codex. After Díaz and Rodgers (1993: pls. 1–2).

to represent a second embedded almanac (see Paxton, ch. 9, and Bricker, ch. 10, this volume).

A number of scholars interpret the almanacs on M. 75–76 and FM 1 as cosmograms that express the Mesoamerican vision of the universe in terms of a quadripartite structure with a central compartment that may be associated with creation (in the case of M. 75–76) (e.g., Aveni 2001; Boone 2003; Paxton 2001; Vail and Hernández 2006; see also Aveni, ch. 4, this volume). The four quadrants are related very specifically to certain deities, directions, and offerings and can be linked to the various calendars used by Mesoamerican cultures, including the 260-day and 52-year cycles. The four quadrants are associated with intervals of 65 days and of 13 years, as mapped by the structure of the almanacs (Vail 2004; see also Hernández and Vail, ch. 11, this volume). Aveni notes similar patterning in the architecture of Maya sites, as reported in Chapter 4.

Mesoamerican civilization has been defined on the basis of commonalities across cultures inhabiting a contiguous area beginning in northern Mexico and incorporating all of present-day Belize, Guatemala, and parts of Honduras and El Salvador. A common calendrical system, and significant similarities in underlying religious belief systems, cosmology, and creation stories are among the attributes shared. What make the studies that follow so compelling are correspondences that indicate more than a common cultural background, suggesting instead direct communication among priests and scribes from distant areas who were skilled practitioners in the indigenous astronomy of Mesoamerica.[8]

Notes

1. The authenticity of the Grolier Codex remains in dispute, as it has been since it was first publicly exhibited in 1973 in New York City. This question should be laid to rest by on-going studies being performed at UNAM in Mexico City (Milbrath 2002).

2. Scholars recognize a seventh colonial period manuscript, the Codex Porfirio Díaz, as containing a divinatory section of pages related to the Borgia Group codices (Boone 2000: 71).

3. In the Maya Long Count calendar, 4 Ahaw 8 Kumk'u represents the date 13.0.0.0.0, corresponding to August 11, 3114 BCE (Gregorian). The following day was 0.0.0.0.1 5 Imix 9 Kumk'u. The units of the calendar are the *k'in* (day), *winal* (20 days), *tun* (18 *winals*, or 360 days), *k'atun* (20 *tuns*, or 7,200 days), and *b'ak'tun* (20 *k'atuns*, or 144,000 days).

4. There is a precedent for the explicit depiction of day glyphs to represent a day count or span of time in Classic period texts from the Maya area. Several inscriptions, of which the best known is the Mural of the 96 Glyphs from Ek' Balam, include a sequential series of day glyphs to span the distance between two events, rather than a more standard distance number noting the number of days elapsed.

5. The following abbreviations are used here and in the chapters in this section to refer to a specific almanac within the Maya or Borgia Group codices: B = Borgia, D = Dresden, FM = Fejérváry-Mayer, M = Madrid; P = Paris.

6. Based on Lacadena's (2000: fig. 2.2) paleographic analysis, only two Madrid scribes can be credited with the construction of almanacs *in extenso*: Scribe 2, for M. 12b–18b, and Scribe 6, for M. 65–72 and 73b, 75–76, and 77–78. The classification of M. 12b–18b as an almanac *in extenso* is an issue discussed in Chapter 11, this volume.

7. The final example is not a true *in extenso* because it includes only the first 13 days, or one *trecena*, of the ritual calendar.

8. Although astronomical tables and calculations made by the Pre-Hispanic Maya were clearly intended to assist with divination and prophecy, we assert that the specialists who tracked the movements of the heavenly bodies were astronomers, rather than astrologers, as suggested by the very precise measurements and calculations they performed.

References Cited

Aveni, Anthony F.
1999   Astronomy in the Mexican Codex Borgia. *Archaeoastronomy* (Supplement to the *Journal for the History of Astronomy*) 24: S1–S20.
2001   *Skywatchers.* Rev. ed. University of Texas Press, Austin.
2004   Intervallic Structure and Cognate Almanacs in the Madrid and Dresden Codices. In *The Madrid Codex: New Approaches to Understanding an Ancient Maya Manuscript* (Gabrielle Vail and Anthony Aveni, eds.): 147–170. University Press of Colorado, Boulder.

Aveni, Anthony F., Steven J. Morandi, and Polly A. Peterson
1996   The Maya Number of Time: Intervalic Time Reckoning in the Maya Codices, Part II. *Archaeoastronomy* (Supplement to the *Journal for the History of Astronomy*) 21: S1–S32.

Boone, Elizabeth H.
2000   Guides for Living: The Divinatory Codices of Mexico. In *In Chalchihuitl in Quetzalli, Precious Greenstone, Precious Quetzal Feather: Mesoamerican Studies in Honor of Doris Heyden* (Eloise Quiñones Keber, ed.): 69–81. Labyrinthos, Lancaster, Calif.
2003   A Web of Understanding: Pictorial Codices and the Shared Intellectual Culture of Late Postclassic Mesoamerica. In *The Postclassic Mesoamerican World* (Michael E. Smith and Frances F. Berdan, eds.): 207–221. University of Utah Press, Salt Lake City.
2007   *Cycles of Time and Meaning in the Mexican Books of Fate.* University of Texas Press, Austin.

Bricker, Harvey M., Victoria R. Bricker, and Bettina Wulfing
1997   Determining the Historicity of Three Astronomical Almanacs in the Madrid Codex. *Archaeoastronomy* (Supplement to the *Journal for the History of Astronomy*) 22: S17–S36.

Bricker, Victoria R.

1997a The "Calendar-Round" Almanac in the Madrid Codex. In *Papers on the Madrid Codex* (Victoria R. Bricker and Gabrielle Vail, eds.): 169–180. Middle American Research Institute Publication 64. Tulane University, New Orleans.

1997b The Structure of Almanacs in the Madrid Codex. In *Papers on the Madrid Codex* (Victoria R. Bricker and Gabrielle Vail, eds.): 1–25. Middle American Research Institute Publication 64. Tulane University, New Orleans.

2001 A Method for Dating Venus Almanacs in the Borgia Codex. *Archaeoastronomy* (Supplement to the *Journal for the History of Astronomy*) 26: S21–S44.

Bricker, Victoria R., and Harvey M. Bricker

1988 The Seasonal Table in the Dresden Codex and Related Almanacs. *Archaeoastronomy* (Supplement to the *Journal for the History of Astronomy*) 12: S1–S62.

Bricker, Victoria R., and Helga-Maria Miram

2002 *An Encounter of Two Worlds: The Book of Chilam Balam of Kaua.* Middle American Research Institute Publication 68. Tulane University, New Orleans.

Caso, Alfonso

1971 Calendrical Systems of Central Mexico. In *Handbook of Middle American Indians*, vol. 10, pt. 1 (Gordon F. Ekholm and Ignacio Bernal, eds.): 333–348. University of Texas Press, Austin.

Chadwick, Robert, and Richard S. MacNeish

1967 Codex Borgia and the Venta Salada Phase. In *The Prehistory of the Tehuacan Valley: Environment and Subsistence*, vol. 1 (Douglas S. Byers, ed.): 114–131. University of Texas Press, Austin.

Chuchiak, John F., IV

2004 Papal Bulls, Extirpators and the Madrid Codex: The Content and Probable Provenience of the M. 56 Patch. In *The Madrid Codex: New Approaches to Understanding an Ancient Maya Manuscript* (Gabrielle Vail and Anthony Aveni, eds.): 57–88. University Press of Colorado, Boulder.

Codex Borgia

1976 *Codex Borgia.* Biblioteca Apostólica Vaticana (Messicano Riserva 28). Codices e Vaticanis Selecti, vol. 34. Akademische Druck- und Verlagsanstalt, Graz, Austria.

Codex Fejérváry-Mayer

1994 *Codex Fejérváry-Mayer.* Sociedad Estatal Quinto Centenario, Madrid; Akademische Druck- und Verlagsanstalt, Graz, Austria; and Fondo de Cultura Económica, México, D.F.

Codex Tro-Cortesianus

1967 *Codex Tro-Cortesianus (Codex Madrid): Museo de América Madrid* (mit Einleitung und Summary von Ferdinand Anders). Codices Selecti, vol 8. Akademische Druck- und Verlagsanstalt, Graz, Austria.

Contreras Martínez, José Eduardo

1992 Los hallazgos arqueológicos de Ocotelulco, Tlaxcala. *Arqueología* 7: 113–118.

1993   La pintura mural de la zona arqueológica de Ocotelulco, Tlaxcala. In *La escritura pictográfica en Tlaxcala* (Luis Reyes García, ed.): 54–61. Universidad Autónoma de Tlaxcala, Tlaxcala, Mexico.

Díaz, Gisele, and Alan Rodgers
1993   *The Codex Borgia: A Full-Color Restoration of the Ancient Mexican Manuscript*. Dover, New York.

Drapkin, Julia
n.d.   Interpreting the Dialect of Time: A Structural Analysis and Discussion of Almanacs in the Madrid Codex. Honors thesis, Department of Anthropology, Tulane University, 2002.

Durán, Fray Diego
1971   *The Book of the Gods and Rites and the Ancient Calendar*. University of Oklahoma Press, Norman.

Edmonson, Munro S.
1988   *The Book of the Year: Middle American Calendrical Systems*. University of Utah Press, Salt Lake City.

Hatch, Marion P.
1975   An Astronomical Calendar in a Portion of the Madrid Codex. In *Archaeoastronomy in Pre-Columbian America* (Anthony F. Aveni, ed.): 283–340. University of Texas Press, Austin.

Hernández, Christine
2004   "Yearbearer Pages" and Their Connection to Planting Almanacs in the Borgia Codex. In *The Madrid Codex: New Approaches to Understanding an Ancient Maya Manuscript* (Gabrielle Vail and Anthony Aveni, eds.): 321–364. University Press of Colorado, Boulder.
2006   Using Astronomical Imagery to Cross-Date an Almanac in the Borgia Codex. Special issue, *Human Mosaic* 36 (1): 125–143.

Hernández, Christine, and Victoria R. Bricker
2004   The Inauguration of Planting in the Borgia and Madrid Codices. In *The Madrid Codex: New Approaches to Understanding an Ancient Maya Manuscript* (Gabrielle Vail and Anthony Aveni, eds.): 277–320. University Press of Colorado, Boulder.

Just, Bryan R.
2000   Concordances of Time: *In Extenso* Almanacs in the Madrid and Borgia Group Codices. *Human Mosaic* 33 (1): 7–16.
2004   *In Extenso* Almanacs in the Madrid Codex. In *The Madrid Codex: New Approaches to Understanding an Ancient Maya Manuscript* (Gabrielle Vail and Anthony Aveni, eds.): 255–276. University Press of Colorado, Boulder.

Kirchoff, Paul, Lina Odena Güemes, and Luis Reyes García
1989   *Historia Tolteca-Chichimeca*. Fondo de Cultura Económica, México, D.F.

Lacadena, Alfonso
2000   Los escribas del códice de Madrid: Metodología paleográfica. *Revista española de antropología americana* 30: 27–85. Madrid, Spain.

Landa, Diego de
1978 [1937]   *Yucatan Before and After the Conquest* (William Gates, trans.). Dover, New York. Originally published by the Maya Society, Baltimore, Md.

Lind, Michael

    1994   Cholula and Mixteca Polychromes: Two Mixteca-Puebla Regional Sub-Styles. In *Mixteca-Puebla: Discoveries and Research in Mesoamerican Art and Archaeology* (H. B. Nicholson and Eloise Quiñones Keber, eds.): 79–99. Labyrinthos, Culver City, Calif.

Love, Bruce

    1994   *The Paris Codex: Handbook for a Maya Priest.* University of Texas Press, Austin.

Masson, Marilyn A.

    2003   The Late Postclassic Symbol Set in the Maya Area. In *The Postclassic Mesoamerican World* (Michael E. Smith and Frances F. Berdan, eds.): 194–200. University of Utah Press, Salt Lake City.

Milbrath, Susan

    1999   *Star Gods of the Maya: Astronomy in Art, Folklore, and Calendars.* University of Texas Press, Austin.

    2002   New Questions Concerning the Authenticity of the Grolier Codex. *Latin American Indian Literatures Journal* 18 (1): 50–83.

    2007   Astronomical Cycles in the Imagery of Codex Borgia 29–46. In *Skywatching in the Ancient World: New Perspectives in Cultural Astronomy* (Clive Ruggles and Gary Urton, eds.): 157–207. University Press of Colorado, Boulder.

Nicholson, Henry B.

    1966   The Problem of the Provenience of the Members of the "Codex Borgia Group": A Summary. In *Summa anthropologica en homenaje a Roberto J. Weitlaner* (A. Pompa y Pompa, ed.): 145–158. Instituto Nacional de Antropología e Historia, México, D.F.

    1982   The Mixteca-Puebla Concept Revisited. In *The Art and Iconography of Late Post-Classic Central Mexico* (Elizabeth H. Boone, ed.): 227–254. Dumbarton Oaks, Washington, D.C.

    1994   The Eagle Claw/Tied Double Maize Ear Motif: The Cholula Polychrome Ceramic Tradition and Some Members of the Codex Borgia Group. In *Mixteca-Puebla: Discoveries and Research in Mesoamerican Art and Archaeology* (Henry B. Nicholson and Eloise Quiñones Keber, eds.): 101–116. Labyrinthos, Culver City, Calif.

Nowotny, Karl Anton

    2005 [1961]   *Tlacuilolli: Style and Contents of the Mexican Pictorial Manuscripts with a Catalog of the Borgia Group* (George A. Everett Jr. and Edward B. Sisson, trans. and eds.). University of Oklahoma Press, Norman.

Paxton, Merideth

    1991   Codex Dresden: Late Postclassic Ceramic Depictions and the Problems of Provenience and Date of Painting. In *Sixth Palenque Round Table, 1986* (Merle Greene Robertson, general ed., and Virginia M. Fields, vol. ed.): 303–308. University of Oklahoma Press, Norman.

    2001   *The Cosmos of the Yucatec Maya: Cycles and Steps from the Madrid Codex.* University of New Mexico Press, Albuquerque.

2004   Tayasal Origin of the Madrid Codex: Further Consideration of the Theory. In *The Madrid Codex: New Approaches to Understanding an Ancient Maya Manuscript* (Gabrielle Vail and Anthony Aveni, eds.): 89–127. University Press of Colorado, Boulder.

n.d.   Codex Dresden: Stylistic and Iconographic Analysis of a Maya Manuscript. Ph.D. dissertation, Department of Art History, University of New Mexico, Albuquerque, 1986.

Pohl, John M. D.

1998   Themes of Drunkenness, Violence, and Factionalism in Tlaxcalan Altar Paintings. *RES: Pre-Columbian States of Being* 33: 184–207.

2003a   Creation Stories, Hero Cults, and Alliance Building: Confederacies of Central and Southern Mexico. In *The Postclassic Mesoamerican World* (Michael E. Smith and Frances F. Berdan, eds.): 61–66. University of Utah Press, Salt Lake City.

2003b   Royal Marriage and Confederacy Building among the Eastern Nahuas, Mixtecs, and Zapotecs. In *The Postclassic Mesoamerican World* (Michael E. Smith and Frances F. Berdan, eds.): 243–249. University of Utah Press, Salt Lake City.

Pohl, John M. D., and Bruce E. Byland

1994   The Mixteca-Puebla Style and Early Postclassic Socio-Political Interaction. In *Mixteca-Puebla: Discoveries and Research in Mesoamerican Art and Archaeology* (H. B. Nicholson and Eloise Quiñones Keber, eds.): 189–199. Labyrinthos, Culver City, Calif.

Robertson, Donald

1966   The Mixtec Religious Manuscripts. In *Ancient Oaxaca* (John Paddock, ed.): 298–312. Stanford University Press, Stanford, Calif.

Sahagún, Fray Bernardino de

1950–1982   *Florentine Codex: General History of the Things of New Spain*. 12 vols. (Arthur J. O. Anderson and Charles E. Dibble, trans. and eds.). University of Utah and School of American Research, Santa Fe, N.Mex.

1953   *Book 7—The Sun, Moon, and Stars, and the Binding of the Years*. Monograph 14, pt. VIII of *The Florentine Codex: General History of the Things of New Spain* (Arthur J. O. Anderson and Charles E. Dibble, eds. and trans.). University of Utah and School of American Research, Santa Fe, N.Mex.

Seler, Eduard

1887   Ueber die Namen der in der Dresdener Handschrift abgebildeten Maya-Götter. *Zeitschrift für Ethnologie* 19: 224–231.

1904   Venus Period in the Picture Writings of the Borgian Codex Group. *Bureau of American Ethnology Bulletin* 28: 355–391.

Sisson, Edward B.

1983   Recent Work on the Borgia Group Codices. *Current Anthropology* 24(5): 653–656.

Sisson, Edward B., and T. Gerald Lilly

1994a   A Codex-Style Mural from Tehuacan Viejo, Puebla, Mexico. *Ancient Mesoamerica* 5(1): 33–44.

1994b The Mural of the Chimales and the Codex Borgia. In *Mixteca-Puebla: Discoveries and Research in Mesoamerican Art and Archaeology* (Henry B. Nicholson and Eloise Quiñones Keber, eds.): 25–44. Labyrinthos, Culver City, Calif.

Thomas, Cyrus
1884 Notes on Certain Maya and Mexican Manuscripts. In *Third Annual Report of the Bureau of American Ethnology, 1881–82*: 3–65. Smithsonian Institution, Washington, D.C.

Thompson, J. Eric S.
1971 [1950] *Maya Hieroglyphic Writing: An Introduction.* University of Oklahoma Press, Norman. [Reproduced from the first edition published by the Carnegie Institution of Washington, Washington D.C.]
1972 *A Commentary on the Dresden Codex: A Maya Hieroglyphic Book.* Memoirs of the American Philosophical Society 93. Philadelphia, Pa.

Tozzer, Alfred M.
1941 *Landa's* Relación de las cosas de Yucatan: *A Translation.* Papers of the Peabody Museum of American Archaeology and Ethnology 18. Harvard University, Cambridge, Mass.

Uruñuela, Gabriel, Patricia Plunket, Gilda Hernández, and Juan Albaitero
1997 Biconical God Figurines from Cholula and the Codex Borgia. *Latin American Antiquity* 8 (1): 63–70.

Vail, Gabrielle
2004 A Reinterpretation of *Tzolk'in* Almanacs in the Madrid Codex. In *The Madrid Codex: New Approaches to Understanding an Ancient Maya Manuscript* (Gabrielle Vail and Anthony Aveni, eds.): 215–252. University Press of Colorado, Boulder.
2006 The Maya Codices. *Annual Review of Anthropology* 35: 497–519.

Vail, Gabrielle, and Anthony Aveni (eds.)
2004 *The Madrid Codex: New Approaches to Understanding an Ancient Maya Manuscript.* University Press of Colorado, Boulder.

Vail, Gabrielle, and Victoria R. Bricker (comps.), Anthony F. Aveni, Harvey M. Bricker, John F. Chuchiak, Christine L. Hernández, Bryan R. Just, Martha J. Macri, and Merideth Paxton
2003 New Perspectives on the Madrid Codex. *Current Anthropology* 44 (Suppl.): S105–S112.

Vail, Gabrielle, and Christine Hernández
2006 Fire Drilling, Bloodletting, and Sacrifice: Yearbearer Rituals in the Maya and Borgia Group Codices. In *Sacred Books, Sacred Languages: Two Thousand Years of Ritual and Religious Maya Literature; Proceedings of the 8th European Maya Conference, Madrid, November 25–30, 2003* (Rogelio Valencia and Geneviève Le Fort, eds.): 65–79. Verlag Anton Saurwein, Markt Schwaben, Germany.
n.d. Deities, Rituals, and Calendrical Cycles: A Comparative Analysis of Almanacs in the Maya and Borgia Group Codices. (In preparation.)

Chapter Nine

Solar-Based Cartographic Traditions of the Mexica and the Yucatec Maya

Merideth Paxton

S IMILARITIES IN THE ARCHAEOLOGICALLY KNOWN remains of Pre-Hispanic central Mexico and the lowland Maya of Yucatán have long engaged the interests of scholars, who have explained the resemblances in terms of cross-cultural interactions. For example, the low relief sculptures depicting warriors in nearly identical battledress that are found in the colonnades at Chichén Itzá and Tula, as well as other parallel features in the architecture of the two sites, inspired the theory that military conquerors from the latter area gained dominance in Yucatán (Tozzer 1957). The realization that manuscripts also contain detailed expressions of common themes was made during early studies by such pioneering researchers as Eduard Seler. His analysis of appearances of Venus portrayed in the Borgia Codex, Codex Vaticanus B, and Dresden Codex relied on descriptions of Mexica[1] beliefs that had been collected around the time of the conquest (Seler 1904; also see Förstemann 1906: 185 and Thomas 1884: 63). In recent investigations (e.g., Hernández 2004; Hernández and Bricker 2004; Just 2004), the importance of highland Mexican-Maya exchange in the construction of other sections of the codices has received special emphasis.

The present inquiry focuses on images that suggest the Mexica and Maya shared spatial concepts during the Late Postclassic and colonial periods. These include pages 75–76 of the Madrid Codex (Codex Tro-Cortesianus); two surveys of the lands of Yaxkukul, Yucatán; page 1 of the Codex Fejérváry-Mayer; folio 2r of the Codex Mendoza; and the map of San Mateo Ixtlahuacan, in central

Mexico. Evidently following the Pre-Hispanic conventions for mapping the apparent annual motion of the sun, all of these compositions are organized around rectangular forms with diagonals that link corners to carefully delineated center areas, and prominent lines of footprints are featured in two of the sources. The purposes of this study are to determine whether the formal resemblances indicate relationships in content and whether similarities in meaning signify communications between the geographic regions where the documents were produced.

Solar-Based Organization of Space in Yucatán

The diagram that fills pages 75–76 of the Madrid Codex (plate 1; for a photographic facsimile of the manuscript, see Anders 1967) has been widely studied as a statement of the solar-based definition of the directions that was followed in Late Postclassic Yucatán. Echoes of its most important concepts are apparently reflected in colonial records, such as the survey of the lands of Yaxkukul (see subsequent section) and the Book of Chilam Balam of Chumayel (Paxton 2001: 20–23). Even during the modern era, the same basic ideas can be traced through descriptions of rituals at such places as Xcacal (Villa Rojas 1988) and Yalcobá (Sosa n.d. [1985], 1989). The M. 75–76 diagram is the only direct map of the solar directions that has survived from pre-conquest Yucatán.

The Late Postclassic Yucatec Maya Directions and Pages 75–76 of the Madrid Codex
No known European documents describe the circumstances surrounding the acquisition of the Madrid Codex from the Maya who produced it. The theory that was most commonly followed during the twentieth century, developed from study of the content of the manuscript, is that it came from Yucatán. As is discussed in greater detail in the introduction to this volume, this working assumption has recently been challenged, but restudy of the question has supported the view that the codex is from Yucatán and is also Pre-Hispanic (Late Postclassic) in date. An illustration of the directions that seems to have held special significance, on account of its relatively large size, fills pages 75 and 76.

ORIENTATION AND BASIC STRUCTURE The manuscript now commonly known as the Madrid Codex is a screenfold that became separated, between pages 77 and 78, into pieces named the Codex Troano (or Tro) and Codex Cortesianus. The units had different owners and were once regarded as unrelated. The conclusion that the two fragments are part of the same document was reached by Léon de Rosny (1881; also see Glass and Robertson 1975: 154), who realized that a list of *trecena* dates (see Glossary) was continued across the break. From this it is also certain that the reading of page 78 precedes page 77. In addition, the listing of *trecena* days is prominently treated in the adjacent painting

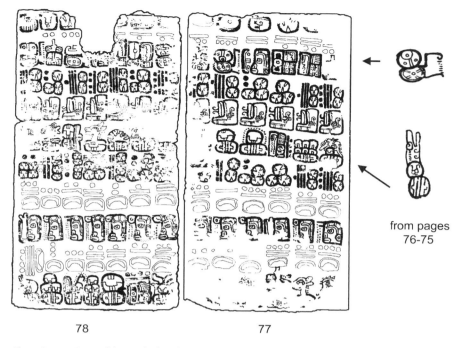

from pages
76-75

78   77

Fig. 1. Pages 78–77 of the Madrid Codex, with motif comparisons from pages 75–76. Redrawn after Anders (1967).

of the directions. As is shown in figure 1, pages 78 and 77 are further linked to this scene by the inclusion of hieroglyphs for the directions and by an offering motif that incorporates the affix T102. The columns of the table on pages 78–77 seem to supplement the diagram of the cosmos by describing the directions, deities, and offerings to be used in rituals for the days of the first *trecena*. Perhaps this established a pattern to be repeated during the rest of the cycle (Paxton 1997: 66–68; 2001: 32, 194–195, n. 4). It is important to note that interest in the *trecenas* is expressed directly in these four pages and that yearbearers are not listed in the M.78–77 table. Nor is iconography uniquely associated with yearbearer ceremonies included there or in the accompanying diagram.

From adjoining material (fig. 2), it can be seen that the four pages form a discrete unit that is upside down in comparison with the remainder of the side. The glyphs on pages 78 and 77 are uniformly aligned, and the table they make up is, with the possible exception of pages 75 and 76, obviously inverted with respect to the rest of the pages on that side of the screenfold. The page 76 portion of the spatial diagram is still attached to page 77, and page 75 remains attached to page 74. The subjects treated on page 74 are not obviously connected with pages 75–76.

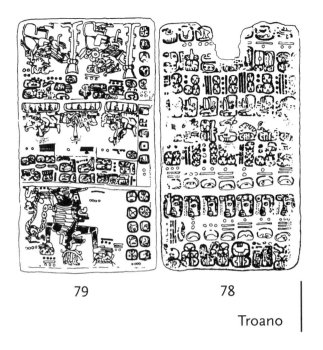

79 78

Troano

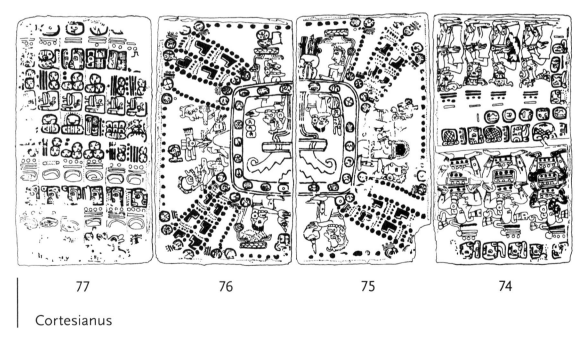

77 76 75 74

Cortesianus

Fig. 2. Pages 79–74 of the Madrid Codex. After Villacorta and Villacorta (1976).

The thematic relationship between the iconography of the diagram and the table on pages 78–77 argues that pages 76 and 75 should be consistent with the orientation of the table, not that of page 74, even though this inverts the central pair of figures. This inversion could have occurred because the artist inattentively turned the scene as he painted (Paxton 2001: 32–33). If such was the case, it should not have created major problems for the users of the codex, who could easily have rotated the illustration as they read. This is preferable to the other option, which places two of the three figure pairs in an upright position but inverts the adjacent *trecena* table. Thus the four pages that discuss directionally oriented offerings made during the *trecenas* constitute a separate section, and their correct sequence is 78, 77, 76, 75. From this it follows that east, the most important direction of the Maya system, belongs at the top of the map, as is also true of many other Mesoamerican spatial diagrams (for examples, see Aveni 2001: 149, fig. 60). Just (2004) has shown that, with this orientation, the diagram could have supplemented reading of the other side of the codex.

There are three associations of dates with the world directions on M. 76–75, the most prominent of which is made by the large dots and day glyphs arranged in a Maltese cross–like form (fig. 3). The glyphs for the directions, *lakin* (east, at top), *xaman* (north, at left), *chikin* (west, at bottom), and *nohol* (south, at right), are shown in the four large trapezoidal areas around the perimeter of the diagram. Earlier in the study of the manuscript, the dot and day glyph sequence was identified as a list of the 20 *trecenas* that make up the 260-day *tzolkin* cycle, which meshes with the days of the 365-day *haab* to form Calendar Round dates (see discussion in Introduction to Part III). The initial unit (1 Imix to 13 Ben) is located in the southeast corner (fig. 4). The second *trecena* (1 Ix to 13 Cimi) runs along the broad edge of the trapezoid in the east, to be followed by the third *trecena* (1 Manik to 13 Cauac). The pattern continues in a counterclockwise direction until the entire cross-like shape is completed and recycling begins at 1 Imix (Thompson 1950: 247–248).

INTERPRETATION   The overall shape of the Madrid illustration of space and time has been associated with the definition of the Yucatec world directions recorded by Bernardo de Lizana between 1606 and 1631 (discussed further in Paxton 2001: 17) and followed in modern Maya communities like Xcacal (fig. 5). The key concept of this system is that east and west are considered to be the locations of sunrise and sunset. Because of the apparent northward and southward migration of the sun along the horizons with respect to the central position of an observer, over the course of the solar (tropical) year the two directions make up the segments limited by sunrise and sunset on the dates of the summer and winter solstices. North and south are the faces of the horizons not included in east and west. Hence the directions consist of five sectors, the center location of the observer and four perimeter areas projected from it. The entire lengths

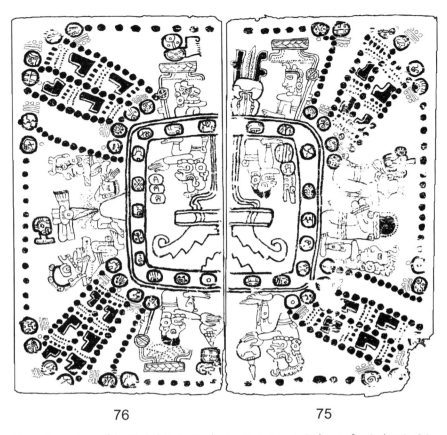

76   75

Fig. 3. Pages 76–75 of the Madrid Codex (Codex Tro-Cortesianus). Redrawn after Anders (1967).

of land defined according to the solstice corners of the universe are significant, but not to the exclusion of the cardinal points.

As noted by Aveni (1980: 154–157) and Villa Rojas (1988: 127–134), the depiction of the world directions in the Madrid Codex resembles the definitions stated in terms of the solar year. It features the center sector and the four perimeter areas created by sunrise and sunset at the solstice corners, with placement of the glyph labels in intermediate positions corresponding to the cardinal points. The angled paths linking the center sector to the corners emphasize the solstice connection. However, despite these general similarities, the manuscript scene seemingly does not represent the world directions precisely. These are created over the solar (tropical) year of 365.2422 days, but the 260-day *tzolkin* shown in the illustration falls well short of the required period.

The resolution of the apparent discrepancy is that the *haab,* the closest approximation to the tropical year that is possible in the Maya mathematical

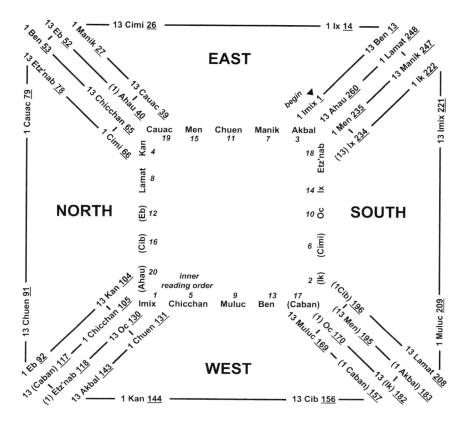

Fig. 4. Pages 76–75 of the Madrid Codex, transcription.

system, is also shown in the painting (fig. 6) (Paxton 1997, 2001: 39–42, 2004). The 18 footprints on the corner paths symbolize 18 intervals of 20 days in this period. They originate at the corners corresponding to sunrise and sunset on the solstices, the defining points of the directions over the tropical year, and thus are a likely symbol for the apparent annual motion of the sun. The group of six small dots in the southeast corner probably conveys the five-day *Uayeb* at the end of the *haab*. Although an extra dot is included, this is within the general expectation of accuracy for the pages, and the set is associated with the last *trecena* before recycling begins at 1 Imix. This is also the only unit painted outside the main line of large dots and *tzolkin* day glyphs. The question is still under discussion, but there is some evidence that every fourth *haab* cycle incorporated an extra day to correct for the difference with the tropical year (Tozzer 1941: 134; Tena 1987: 61–69). The small dots interspersed among the footprints on the paths can be explained as a second representation of the

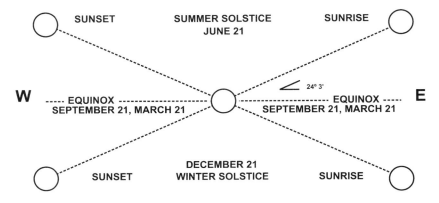

Fig. 5. World directions of the twentieth-century Maya of Xcacal, Yucatán. Redrawn after Villa Rojas (1988).

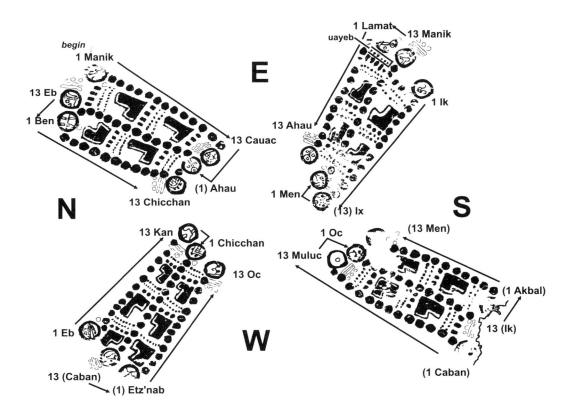

Fig. 6. *Uinals* at the solstice corners of the Madrid 76–75 painting. Redrawn after Anders (1967).

260-day cycle. Thus the Madrid diagram is an ideal map of space that also illustrates the two cycles that mesh to form Calendar Round dates, the *tzolkin* and the *haab*, at the solstice corners of the universe.

The Colonial Period: Surveying the Lands of Yaxkukul, Yucatán

Some time ago Michael Coe (1965) demonstrated the fundamental importance of the calendar in the political and spatial organization of the Pre-Hispanic Yucatec Maya, and the continuation of essential components from this system that are evidently related to the apparent annual motion of the sun can be traced into the colonial period. Their expression was through ritual land surveys known as *tzol peten,* which can be translated as "counting out, ordering, explaining (the) 'country, island, region'" (Hanks 1988: 351). The colonial *tzol peten* was effected through a series of walking visits by members of the Maya nobility to places where naming activities were performed. The ceremony has been related by Hanks (1989: 100, n. 8) and Edmonson (1986: 27–29) to the calendar, and to the reenactment of the creation of the world (Hanks 1988: 353–355).

DATING OF THE SURVEYS   The description of the Yaxkukul *tzol peten* is written in Maya, using the adaptation of the European alphabet that was created by the Spanish for such purposes. It is known from two accounts with different dates that are separated by only eight days, April 30, 1544 and May 8, 1544. According to this order, they are referred to as "Documents Numbers 1 and 2 of the Survey of the Lands of Yaxkukul." The date associated with the first version, which was composed by the governor, don Alonso Pech, is written once with numerals and spelled twice. Nevertheless, there are doubts about when it was actually compiled because it has a reference to don Tomás López, the royal *visitador* who did not reach Yucatán until 1552 (Farris 1984: 123). Moreover, because the founding of Mérida did not occur until 1542, it seems doubtful that a Maya scribe would have been trained in European writing as early as 1544. The Document 1 boundary survey, including reference to a now-lost map, answers the solicitation for such facts that López made, and 1554 has been proposed as a more likely date for the manuscript (Barrera Vásquez 1984: 9–12).

Document 2, dated in two places as May 8, 1544, was signed by Macan Pech, who is identified in the first account as the father of Alonso Pech and the first *batab* to rule under the Spanish (Barrera Vásquez 1984: 17, lines 28–30). Its actual date is uncertain as well, and the survey also lacks an accompanying map. Both documents mention that they were executed under the authority of don Francisco de Montejo, the *adelantado* of Yucatán (Barrera Vásquez 1984: 15, lines 6–11, 97). He died in 1553, having been removed from his position not long before April 1551 (Chamberlain 1948: 305–306, 310). Some of the chronological contradictions might indicate that the documents were recopied and that new information was inserted in the process.

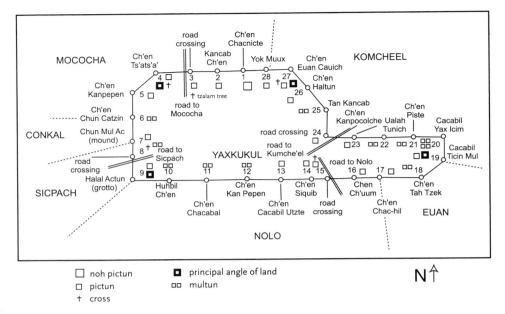

Fig. 7. Map from first survey description, Yaxkukul, Yucatán. Redrawn after Barrera Vásquez (1984: 102).

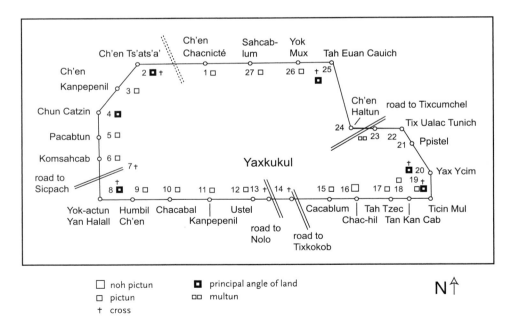

Fig. 8. Map from second survey description, Yaxkukul, Yucatán. Redrawn after Barrera Vásquez (1984: 104).

SURVEY DESCRIPTION By placing the settlement near the centers of the maps, the Barrera Vásquez reconstructions (figs. 7 and 8) portray the domain of Yaxkukul as the focus of the survey. In both versions, the first marker, in this instance an especially important stone (*noh pictun*), was observed at the north of the well of Chacnicté, a settlement located on the north side of the boundary line (Barrera Vásquez 1984: 22–23, lines 111–114, 92). Then the Yaxkukul representatives and those from the neighboring area of Mococha are described in both accounts as having moved west. The direction of the walking procession was consistently counterclockwise, with changes in membership as officials from a succession of adjacent territories rotated into the group when each new border was reached.

The total number of reference points differs slightly in the two presentations, but the overall shapes of the boundaries are similar. Seven of the significant features mentioned in Document 1 are missing from Document 2, and five from the latter are not included in the former. The characterizations of the roads clearly differ. One of those listed in Document 1 is omitted from the second version, which mentions a road in a place that is not indicated in the first account. The road shown only in Document 1, near the northwest corner of the survey, seems not only to have existed but to have held special importance. Its designation was observed through a *pictun* and a cross carved in the trunk of a *tzalam* tree, all of which are said to have been placed on the east side of the road.

COMPARISON WITH MADRID 76–75 The characterization of the Yaxkukul holdings in Document 1 includes several features that parallel Pre-Hispanic conventions also seen in the Madrid illustration of the cosmos. In addition to the counterclockwise direction of the circuit, roads angle toward the center of the map. The survey line is not exactly rectangular, but these routes can be approximately associated with solstice corners and with some of the corners where the directions of the survey path changed. Document 2 emphasizes the regular placement of markers for the survey line between the named sites along it. For example, it is stated that upon leaving the major corner of Dzadzá, the group went to the southwest, placing *pictuns* at regular intervals in anticipation of Kan Pepen (Barrera Vásquez 1984: 92–93). The action recalls the regular spacing of the large dots between the *tzolkin* days listed in the Madrid illustration of the cosmos.

The Solar Directions in Mexica Cartography

The Mexica used the same solar-based directions as the Yucatec Maya, with the creation of east and west by the apparent movement along the horizons of sunrise and sunset between the dates of the solstices. Observation of the changes over the year was made from a center sector (Matos Moctezuma 1987:

186–189; also see García-Zambrano 1994: 220, fig. 3; Nicholson 1971: 403–405; and Townsend 1979). Tenochtitlan was laid out to replicate this system (Matos Moctezuma 1987: 190), and at its center was the ceremonial precinct. The Templo Mayor, an essential symbol of Mexica power, was located there and was aligned to create a dramatic display as the sun rose between its twin structures on the date of the vernal equinox (Aveni 1992: 150–151).

The orientation of Tenochtitlan was guided by the dedication to solar ideology that was prominent in other aspects of the culture, and it is not surprising that the iconographic program of Late Postclassic and colonial Mexica art includes many works with solar themes (Matos Moctezuma and Solís 2004). Among the pieces in the Pre-Hispanic corpus is a group of sculptures, the most celebrated of which is probably the Aztec Calendar Stone (see Matos Moctezuma 2004: 60–75 for discussion and excellent photographs). In the center of the circular monument is a smaller circle that is filled by a face interpreted as the youthful solar deity Tonatiuh. Terrestrial attributes have been recognized in the image as well, and the possibility that it refers to other deities has been raised. Nevertheless, as a critical review of these theories by Michel Graulich (1998: 162–177) has established, the character of the motif is essentially solar. The design also features four squares, showing the previous world creations, which extend from the center in positions that suggest solstice symbolism.

Although there is not, so far as I am aware, a pre-conquest central Mexican representation of the solar-based directions that is as explicit as the Maya illustration on M. 76–75, a similar image is known from an outlying Mexica area. This is the painting of the cosmos on page 1 of the Codex Fejérváry-Mayer. From the depiction of the founding of Tenochtitlan on folio 2r of the Codex Mendoza and from the map of San Mateo Ixtlahuacan, it can further be seen that the organization of cartographic motifs according to the premise of the solar directions continued to be important in central Mexico during the colonial era.

A Late Postclassic Mexica Diagram of the Cosmos on Page 1 of the Codex Fejérváry-Mayer

PROVENIENCE AND DATE OF PAINTING   The Mesoamerican origin of the Codex Fejérváry-Mayer, like that of the Madrid Codex, is also undocumented. Study of the manuscript by Donald Robertson (1963) led him to conclude that it was probably painted in the Mixtec area, but other associations have subsequently emerged. Nicholson (2001: 99) comments that most researchers presently attribute the manuscript to the Gulf Coast area, and Boone (2001: 404) regards it as a primary source of information on Pre-Hispanic Aztec religion and calendrics. She notes that its style is less naturalistic than that of the Valley of Mexico and proposes Puebla, Tlaxcala, and Veracruz as possible places of origin (also see Pohl 2004; and Introduction to Part III, this volume).

The resemblance of the Madrid diagram of the directions and calendar to the image of space and time on page 1 of Fejérváry-Mayer (plate 2) is well known. Over a century ago, Cyrus Thomas (1884: 63) saw the closeness as "evidence of an intimate relation between the Maya and Nahua nations" (also see Seler 1901: 28–31 and Boone 2003: 219–220). As in the Madrid illustration, the sequence of the 20 *trecenas* that make up the 260-day *tonalpohualli* is arranged in a cross-like pattern that frames four individual scenes around a fifth, center sector. The Fejérváry-Mayer *trecena* series begins in the southeast corner, as does that of the Madrid diagram, but in this instance it is with the day 1 Crocodile. Nevertheless, the Fejérváry-Mayer painting differs from the Madrid scene in that it does not include the numbers associated with the *tonalpohualli* days. In both cases, the individual days of each *trecena* are marked as dots between the day glyphs, and Just (2004: 265–266) has interpreted this as evidence of direct influence on the Madrid diagram from the non-Maya notational system. The perimeter directions in the Fejérváry-Mayer painting are indicated, not by hieroglyphs, but by symbols. According to Anders et al. (1994: 150, 163), east (or up, symbolized by a sun disk) is shown at the top. The reading direction of the list of *trecenas* indicates that this direction is followed by north (on the left), west (down), and south (on the right). This creates the same counterclockwise progression as is shown in the Madrid scene.

The FM 1 representation of ritual space includes some concepts that are known to have been important in Pre-Hispanic Maya cosmology, although they are not shown on M. 76–75. For example, plant forms that are the counterparts of the Maya world tree markers,[2] used as symbols of the perimeter directions, are seen only in the Mexica manuscript (Anders et al. 1994: 160). In the Fejérváry-Mayer scene, the Nine Lords of the Night are depicted: Xiuhtecuhtli, the deity painted in the center, and the four pairs of deities that occupy the trapezoidal arms of the cross, rotating in a clockwise cycle (Anders et al. 1994: 164–165). The Nine Lords of the Night were recognized in Pre-Hispanic Maya civilization (Thompson 1950: 208–212), but they do not appear in the Madrid diagram. The primary deities there are, in three scenes along the east–west axis, the sun god and the moon goddess. This identification is based on the research of Thompson (1970: 205, 236–237), who saw the center figures as a creator pair. He recognized one of the deities as Itzamna, God D of the codices, whom he thought of as another aspect of God G, the sun god. Despite the inclusion of male attire, Thompson was certain that the second deity in the center section is female. As has been discussed in detail elsewhere, this assessment is correct (Paxton 2001: 145–149; also see 54–56). Thompson (1970: 233–235) reported wide acceptance of the sun and moon as a spousal pair among the modern Maya, and the Madrid goddess has been recognized as Goddess O, a deity with lunar associations (Ciaramella 1994; Milbrath 1999: 141–147; Vail n.d. [1996]: 148, 150).

The Fejérváry-Mayer image is more explicit in its presentation of some elements, yet it is not consistently so. A motif for the tropical year does not appear to be built directly into the Mexica representation, and the cycle is shown only by the overall configuration of the cross-like diagram of the *trecenas*, the yearbearers in circles carried on the backs of birds at the outer edges of the solstice corners and, as discussed later, calendrical intervals. As other scholars have observed (Aveni 2001: 148–149; Long 1923; Thomas 1884: 15; Vail 2004: 241–243), yearbearers can also be found in the Madrid painting. Nevertheless, the clarity of the meaning is much greater on Fejérváry-Mayer 1. The page shows only a single set of Mexica yearbearers, and its members (Reed-Flint-House-Rabbit) are highlighted by their circular frames. In contrast, all four possible groups of yearbearers from the Maya calendar system are shown on M. 76–75, without differential treatment of a particular set. In other words, the presence of the circular frames emphasizes the Fejérváry-Mayer yearbearers so that it is obvious at the level of formal analysis, without moving to the level of interpretation, that the days are special. Such is not the case on M. 76–75 (for a different view, see Hernández and Vail, ch. 11, this volume).

Using Fejérváry-Mayer 1 to Interpret the Third Tzolkin Motif in the Madrid Diagram

As noted earlier, the 260-day cycle is prominently represented in the Madrid illustration as a Maltese cross–like outline of dots, and the groups of small dots painted between the footprints at the solstice corners constitute a second representation. A third depiction of the *tzolkin*, which has received little attention over the years, is shown in a band around the center sector. From closer examination of Fejérváry-Mayer 1, it can be seen that the cross-like 260-day motif there is similarly accompanied by a second 260-day listing of the *trecenas*. This appears in columns at the sides of the loops in the solstice corners. As will be shown, this series can be used to explain the significance of the third *tzolkin* in the Madrid Codex diagram.

The second sequence in Fejérváry-Mayer begins in the interior of the northeast corner with the day [1] Crocodile (numbers in brackets refer to implied coefficients). Reading in a horizontal circle around the list, this is followed 13 days later, in the northwest corner, by [1] Jaguar; then, in the southwest corner, by [1] Deer. The next *trecena* begins in the southeast corner with [1] Flower, followed a *trecena* later by a return to the northeast corner and, moving outward, the day [1] Reed. The pattern continues until the entire list is read, and recycling begins at [1] Crocodile. Thus it can easily be seen that each *tonalpohualli* day in the solstice corner columns follows the preceding entry by four *trecenas*, and the positions of the 20 days that initiate the *trecenas* can be expressed

Table 1. The *trecenas* of the solstice corners, page 1, Codex Féjerváry-Mayer

Row	Northeast	Northwest	Southwest	Southeast
1	(1) 1 Crocodile *1**	(2) 1 Jaguar *14*	(3) 1 Deer *27*	(4) 1 Flower *40*
2	(5) 1 Reed *53*	(6) 1 Death *66*	(7) 1 Rain *79*	(8) 1 Grass *92*
3	(9) 1 Serpent *105*	(10) 1 Flint *118*	(11) 1 Monkey *131*	(12) 1 Lizard *144*
4	(13) 1 Movement *157*	(14) 1 Dog *170*	(15) 1 House *183*	(16) 1 Vulture *196*
5	(17) 1 Water *209*	(18) 1 Wind *222*	(19) 1 Eagle *235*	(20) 1 Rabbit *248*

*Tonalpohualli day numbers are italicized.

in tabular format (table 1). As is commonly recognized, the codex divides the *tonalpohualli* into five lines, each of which has four *trecenas* (52 days). Stated another way, this is a 5 × 52 construction of the *tonalpohualli*.

Returning to the *tzolkin* that frames the center of the Madrid diagram (fig. 4), it can be seen that this is equivalent to the solstice corner arrangement of the *tonalpohualli* on Fejérváry-Mayer 1 (see also discussion by Bricker, ch. 10, this volume). The first *trecena* day here, [1] Imix, is shown in the northwest corner. The first day of the second *trecena*, [1] (Ik)[3] is in the southwest corner, and the rotation continues with the beginning of the third *trecena*, [1] Akbal, in the southeast corner. The first rotation through the directions is completed with the *trecena* that begins on [1] Kan. As in the Fejérváry-Mayer painting, the user of the codex must supply the numerical coefficients that accompany the day names. The beginning of the fifth *trecena* is once again in the northwest corner, and the list continues in a counterclockwise direction through the distribution of the 20 *trecenas* over four rows, with five *trecenas* per row. The position of each successive *trecena* is four greater than that of the preceding entry, and the 5 × 52 structure of the Fejérváry-Mayer 1 columns is duplicated exactly.

The 52-day intervals have obvious utility for integrating dates from the 260-day and 365-day cycles, and this aspect of the Fejérváry-Mayer painting provides a convenient means for projecting *trecena* dates in terms of tropical years. Because 7 × 52 = 364, and a complete reading of the five-line table is 260 days in duration, a difference of two 52-day lines (104 days) remains. This period can easily be calculated by reading alternate lines of the solstice corner columns. For example, a user who desired to know the name of the *tonalpohualli* day that fell one 365-day year after the beginning of this diagram on the day [1] Crocodile would learn that the answer is the third entry in the day column, [1] Serpent. This date is 105 days after one complete 260-day cycle of the table, and it is also the beginning of the ninth *trecena*, which follows the completion of 104 days (8 *trecenas*) on 13 Lizard (not indicated on the codex page). This technique could have been applied to the third *tzolkin* representation in the Madrid diagram as well.

Accompanying Material

Examination of the FM 1 illustration of the cosmos in relation to the remainder of the obverse shows that there is considerable continuity. A prominent theme on page 1 is the Nine Lords of the Night, and the subject is elaborated further on pages 2–4 (Anders et al. 1994: 185–194). The remaining pages on the side show rituals associated with *tonalpohualli* days and bundles of offerings in carefully indicated quantities (Anders et al. 1994: 195–197; Boone 2001: 403; Nicholson 2001: 99–100). The concept parallels the apparent descriptions of offerings to be made on specific days of the 260-day cycle that is found on pages 78–77 of the Madrid Codex (Love 1994: 59–61).

It is interesting that the numbers that are used to quantify the Fejérváry-Mayer offering bundles hint at possible Late Postclassic influence from the Maya area. Although the Fejérváry-Mayer bars are typically vertical instead of horizontal, they do resemble Maya bar and dot notation, and numbers constructed with horizontal bars are scattered throughout the pages. Considered in the aggregate, the associations of FM 1 with the remainder of the manuscript suggest that it establishes the cosmological setting of other almanacs. The idea that page 1 has special importance beyond that of the typical Fejérváry-Mayer almanacs is further supported by its large format. The M. 76–75 large-scale painting of the universe may have served a similar function, at least in terms of its relationship to pages 78–77 and the almanacs on the reverse side of the codex.

Fig. 9. Codex Mendoza, folio 2r. Redrawn after Anawalt and Berdan (1992: 69).

Colonial Survival of Pre-Hispanic Mexica Cartography:
Folio 2r of the Codex Mendoza

The official characterization of the founding of Tenochtitlan in solar terms is consistent with the fundamental integration of the sun in the planning and construction of the city. This foundation is illustrated in the map on folio 2r of the Codex Mendoza (fig. 9) (for a facsimile reproduction, see Berdan and Anawalt 1992, 3: 11), a source created as an extensive compilation on Mexica social customs, conquests, and economic resources.

DATE OF PAINTING   The creation of the Codex Mendoza in or around Mexico City may well have occurred in response to a request made in 1541 by the viceroy of New Spain, Antonio de Mendoza. This is suggested by references in Spanish sources to a painted manuscript that could fit the description. However, there is no information in the codex that directly confirms the association, as Nicholson (1992: 1–5, 10) has commented in a review of the evidence on the painting date. The earliest possible date is 1529 because that is when Hernán Cortés received the title Marqués del Valle, which is used in the text. It also seems that the Codex Mendoza predates 1553, as it is reasonably certain that it was owned by the French clergyman André Thevet in that year. Although some lines of argument remain unsettled, Nicholson's general conclusion is that most information indicates a painting date toward the early 1540s. The derivation of the entire first part of the manuscript, including folio 2r, from Pre-Hispanic precedents is generally accepted (see Boone 1992: 35).

THE MOTIF OF THE DIRECTIONS   The painting on folio 2r combines the mapping of space with concepts of time, but in this instance the subject of the latter is human history instead of the cycles of the gods. A rectangular band of dates around the perimeter shows the 51-year reign of Tenoch, the leader of the migratory search for a permanent capital site (Anawalt 2001). Beginning in the upper left corner with 2 House (1325 CE), the founding date, the year series develops in a counterclockwise direction (Carrasco 1999: 22). Tenochtitlan is symbolized by the eagle perched on a cactus that had originally signaled the settlement location. The form is placed in the center of the island, indicated by a wavy blue rectangular frame. The canals that extend diagonally from the corners, crossing in the center sector, express the agreement of the city plan with divine instruction. According to Durán (Heyden 1994: 46), the solar deity Huitzilopochtli "spoke to his priest or steward and said, 'Tell the Aztec people that the principal men, each with his relatives and friends and allies, should divide the city into four main wards. The center of the city will be the house you have constructed for my resting place.'"

The creation of four quarters by diagonals suggests directions constructed according to solstice sunrise and sunset positions. From analysis of the subordinate leaders shown on the island, Van Zantwijk (1985: 58–72) has deduced that the Codex Mendoza map should be oriented with east at the top, and that the diagonals refer to the original mythic division of the site. Later, four cardinally oriented causeways that extended from the ceremonial precinct were superimposed, creating a spatial organization that he sees as an exact duplication of the FM 1 arrangement.

Colonial Solar Cartography and the Map of San Mateo Ixtlahuacan

The map of San Mateo Ixtlahuacan (fig. 10) is part of the collection of *Títulos de pueblos y tierras* now in the Archivo General de la Nación in Mexico City. This

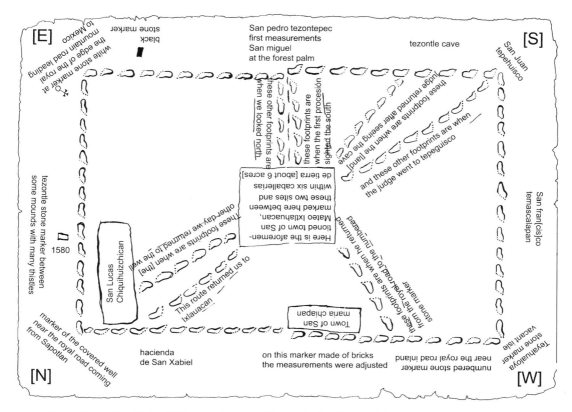

Fig. 10. Map of San Mateo Ixtlahuacan. Based on Montes de Oca Vega et al. (2003, 1: 204; 2: map 1480) and García-Zambrano (1994).

compilation filled the request from the Spanish colonial government for information that could be used to legitimize the rights of the Indians to remain on their traditional lands and to settle boundary disputes. The accounts record reenactments of the rituals of foundation that had been performed when the settlements were first established in places that fit cosmologically oriented criteria (García-Zambrano 1994). The *títulos* genre may well reflect pre-conquest custom because its distribution is widespread, ranging from central Mexico to Guatemala, and the member documents deviate from Spanish norms (Lockhart 1991: 56).

According to García-Zambrano's (1994) analysis, the members of the *Títulos de pueblos y tierras* present a common philosophical outlook in which these reenactments recall the creation of the universe and seek the intervention of the deities. With a conceptual derivation from the solar-based directional system, the maps are almost always built around two elements, the first of which is a circle that is usually open at one end to re-create both the mythical cave of origin and the actual cave required for the foundation of the settlement. The second key feature in the maps and in the urban planning is the quadrangle that marks the four corners of the earth. The form includes diagonals, measured from the solstitial points, that intersect in the center of the rectangle. The center functioned as a benchmark used to place structures at the settlements during the initial construction and later phases, creating the perception that the components rotate throughout the year in a counterclockwise direction (García-Zambrano 1994: 219, 221–222).

The processions that expressed the solar-based cosmological scheme underlying *Títulos de pueblos y tierras* paintings occurred in settings that ideally had, in addition to a centrally located mountain with a cave and a water hole, a mountain at each of the four solstice corners. The ritual of foundation began at the central mountain with the sighting of a diagonal that extended from the east corner mountain to that in the west. Then the members moved down the mountain and toward the north and began marking a circular route that progressed in a counterclockwise direction. As they completed this circuit, they defined the path with deposits of ropes and/or entwined boughs of grass and leaves as well as stone markers (García-Zambrano 1994: 218–220).

The San Mateo Ixtlahuacan map does not show mountains, but rather stone markers and roads at the east, north, and south corners. In this instance, the course of the procession was not a continuous counterclockwise circle. The first movement was from the town center to the north corner, then back to the center, and out to the midpoint between the east and the south corners, then to visit the cave near the south corner. From there a second diagonal was constructed with a segment to the center and a return to the south corner. The remainder of the circuit included the construction of a third diagonal that evokes another solstice line and travel around the remaining sides (García-Zambrano 1994: 224–226). Even though the map does not include diagonals to all four solstice corners, an underlying similarity to the solar organization of the Calendar Stone and the foundation map of Tenochtitlan on Codex Mendoza 2r remains clear.

PAINTING DATE   The date of painting that has been assigned to the map of San Mateo Ixtlahuacan is 1530 (García-Zambrano 1994: 223; Montes de Oca Vega et al. 2003, 2: map 1480, overleaf, and index, p. 6). However, the publication in 2003 of the large-scale color photograph of the map has made it possible to discern a detail (fig. 11) that was not legible in the earlier black and white photo. As the paleographer for the recent version notes (Montes de Oca Vega et al. 2003, 1: 204), the year 1580 is written on one of the stone markers used in the ritual survey. The summary of the accompanying *expediente* mentions that the earliest document is clearly dated 1530, and that its cover is marked 1744 (Mon-

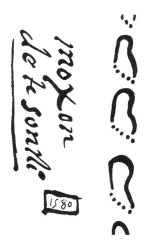

Fig. 11. Detail showing the date 1580, from the map of San Mateo Ixtlahuacan. Redrawn after Montes de Oca Vega et al. (2003, 2: map 1480).

tes de Oca Vega et al. 2003, 1: 24). There are, however, no surviving folios from the eighteenth century, and other pages state that the presiding judge for the survey, Juan de Mancilla de Castañeda, served on behalf of the viceroy Luis de Velasco. There were two viceroys with this name, a father and son, who were in office between 1550 and 1595 (Montes de Oca Vega et al. 2003, 1: 24).

It is known that the scribe (notary) who drew the map of San Mateo Ixtlahuacan was Luis de la Paz y Tapia (Montes de Oca Vega et al. 2003, 2: map 1480, overleaf), but the chronological range of his work is not, so far as I am aware, shown by the registers for the sixteenth century, nor does paleographic style establish a painting date.[4] If the paper on which the map is painted has a watermark that might indicate the earliest feasible date of the image, it is not visible in the color photograph. The motif of the dated survey marker does not appear to be a later addition, and the general need for the *títulos* was probably intensified by the Spanish congregation policies of the mid-sixteenth century (Wood 1998: 206). Therefore I would now say the map appears to have been compiled around 1580–1595.[5] Gibson (1964: 181) has found that by about 1590, Indian records no longer included pictorial components and native scribes were not generally used.

FOOTPRINT SYMBOLISM   The lines of footprints in the map of San Mateo Ixtlahuacan can be interpreted according to the general Pre-Hispanic Mesoamerican symbolism for roads and journeys and other early colonial Nahua maps where such sequences mark boundary perimeters. For instance, in a painting from the *Historia Tolteca-Chichimeca* (ca. 1545–1563, Ms. 46–50, folio 32v–33r, reproduced by Leibsohn 1994: 168–170, fig. 5), the boundary places and footprints are arranged in a rectangular pattern around the centrally located primary town. This probably continues Pre-Hispanic custom, as the map otherwise relies almost exclusively on pre-conquest stylistic and iconographic conventions.

COMPARISON WITH THE MADRID CODEX ILLUSTRATION Like the Madrid map, the San Mateo Ixtlahuacan map is rectangular, with a clearly delineated rectangular center sector and footprint lines toward solstice corners. Despite the questions of its date of painting and whether it is the original survey record or a later copy, the document has connections to the Pre-Hispanic past through its spatial organization and the use of footprints to define boundaries. Nevertheless, in comparison with M. 76–75, differences in the meanings of the footprints are evident. The total number shown—if this is what was originally intended and not merely the result of inattentive copying—is 117, with 73 footprints around the perimeter, 12 in the lower left, 5 in the lower right, 17 in the upper right, and 10 ascending toward the top. Certainly, the use of footprints to show roads or journeys is found in the pre-conquest Maya area; the Madrid illustration is one of several in which the passage of time is portrayed as travel along a road. Nevertheless, the Madrid footprints communicate a specific interval, and those in the Nahua map do not.

Summary and Conclusions: The Question of Cross-Cultural Exchange

The primary task of this research has been to determine whether a group of visually similar spatial diagrams can be interpreted as evidence of Mexica-Maya exchange during the Late Postclassic and colonial periods. The works under consideration have compositions that evoke the world directions as defined by observation from a center area of the apparent annual motion of the sun along the eastern and western horizons. East and west are the faces of the horizons marked by the solstice sunrises and sunsets, and north and south are the remaining segments. From the Maya area, the diagrams include pages 76–75 of the Madrid Codex and two surveys of the lands of Yaxkukul. The Mexica maps include page 1 of the Codex Fejérváry-Mayer, folio 2r of the Codex Mendoza, and the map of San Mateo Ixtlahuacan. These images feature generally rectangular formats with clearly marked center areas and crossed diagonals extending to corners; lines of footprints may also be incorporated.

The Late Postclassic Madrid and Fejérváry-Mayer diagrams share, beyond X-shaped compositions, large formats that indicate special importance within their respective manuscripts. Both paintings of sacred space are supplemented by other pages providing details on precisely itemized offerings, and the diagrams in turn provide cosmological contexts for additional passages. In my opinion, the two images should be oriented with east at their tops, and they further incorporate 5 × 52 divisions of the 260-day cycles that can correlate these dates with the 365-day *haab*. Nevertheless, the deities are not cognates, and the iconography of the Fejérváry-Mayer painting seems more complex in general. Although yearbearers are shown in both maps, one particular series is highlighted only in the Codex Fejérváry-Mayer. Moreover, the Madrid illustration includes a motif for the 365-day year that is not present in the Mexica version, possibly demonstrating a capacity for innovation in the Maya area. Thus it is clear that neither of the paintings was copied directly from the other.

Perhaps exchange existed at the general conceptual level rather than that of precise detail. However, this was evidently not in terms of the selection of the Maltese cross–like format, because the device has a long history in the Maya area. The hieroglyph meaning *kin*, or "day" (T544), also has this form. The representation of *trecena* days as individual dots in the main cross-like patterns could be a result of central Mexico-Maya communication or a technique for emphasis that was invented independently. The use of Maya-like bars on accompanying pages of the Late Postclassic Fejérváry-Mayer makes the explanation of exchange seem more probable. The most likely evidence of specific conceptual influence identified here lies in the association of the 5 × 52 division of the 260-day cycles with the solar year. Yet it would seem that this partition is so essential that it must have been devised well before the Late Postclassic. Broader comparisons in material culture indicate a long history of contact, and key aspects of this similar solar-based cartography may reflect early communications with widespread subsequent distribution.

In the colonial period, the Pre-Hispanic Mexica division of space according to solar directional definitions survives in the painting of the founding of Tenochtitlan on folio 2r (possibly copied from a lost pre-conquest source) of the Codex Mendoza. These ideas are less clearly incorporated in the later map of San Mateo Ixtlahuacan (SMI), which includes a center direction but has lines of footprints that angle toward only three of the four solstice corners. Footprints encircle the perimeter as well, recalling boundary markers painted on other colonial Mexica maps with Pre-Hispanic connections. In this respect, the SMI map is similar to the colonial land surveys of Yucatán known as the *tzol peten,* exemplified by the Yaxkukul survey, in which boundaries of surrounding towns were ritually visited in walking processions that have been related to the calendar. The spatial map on pages 76–75 of the Madrid Codex is an apparent prototype for the *tzol peten*, although its footprints are found only on paths to the solstice corners. Four roads on the first Yaxkukul survey recall these Pre-Hispanic solstice paths.

The scarcity of early documents and the post-conquest political situation make it difficult to evaluate colonial Mexica-Yucatec Maya interactions. It appears that in each region details of the Pre-Hispanic solar-based cartographic conventions disappeared, with retention of only broad forms. This preservation could have happened independently, but possible cross-cultural contact cannot be overlooked. Perhaps colonial Yucatec Maya solar concepts were reinforced by central Mexican ideas carried by Mexica in the service of Spaniards. Nevertheless, in my view, independent maintenance of ideas built through earlier exchanges is more likely.

Acknowledgments

I would like to thank the organizers of the symposium for which this chapter was written, Gabrielle Vail and Christine Hernández, for the opportunity to participate. I am also grateful to Karen Dakin for information on the recent publication of the map of San Mateo Ixtlahuacan in Mexico, and I have benefited from several enjoyable discussions of it with Ángel García-Zambrano. The comments of anonymous reviewers have been helpful as well.

Notes

1. In this chapter the term *Mexica* follows Pedro Carrasco's (2001: 297) definition: "The Mexica people were the last Nahua-speaking immigrants to enter the Basin of Mexico after the Toltec decline. Their place of origin was said to be Aztlán, an island in a lake, from which the name 'Aztec' is derived." Although the second name is still in common usage, it has acquired broader meanings (López Austin 2001: 68).

2. See pages 30c–31c of the Dresden Codex for some widely cited examples (Thompson 1972: 102). A motif that may represent a stylized tree symbol for the center sector is found in the M. 76–75 illustration, but not on FM 1.

3. The Madrid sequence includes errors, and the standard corrections (Thomas 1884: 15–16) are indicated here by parentheses.

4. Millares Carlo and Mantecón (1955: 89) comment that during the sixteenth and seventeenth centuries the most important Spanish styles were used concurrently in the New World.

5. Lockhart (1992: 410–411) would probably argue for a much later date; his view is that no known *título* predates 1650.

References Cited

Anawalt, Patricia Rieff
    2001   Mendoza, Codex. In *The Oxford Encyclopedia of Mesoamerican Cultures: The Civilizations of Mexico and Central America*, vol. 2 (Davíd Carrasco, ed.): 205–208. Oxford University Press, Oxford and New York.

Anawalt, Patricia Rieff, and Frances F. Berdan
    1992   The Codex Mendoza. *Scientific American* 266 (6): 60–79.

Anders, Ferdinand (ed.)

    1967   *Codex Tro-Cortesianus (Codex Madrid)*. Akademische Druck- und Verlagsanstalt, Graz, Austria.

Anders, Ferdinand, Maarten Jansen, and Gabina Aurora Pérez Jiménez

    1994   *El libro de Tezcatlipoca, señor del tiempo: Libro explicativo del llamado Códice Fejérvary-Mayer*. 2 vols. Akademische Druck- und Verlagsanstalt, Graz, Austria; and Fondo de Cultura Económica, México, D.F.

Aveni, Anthony F.

    1980   *Skywatchers of Ancient Mexico*. University of Texas Press, Austin.

    1992   Moctezuma's Sky: Aztec Astronomy and Ritual. In *Moctezuma's Mexico: Visions of the Aztec World* (Davíd Carrasco and Eduardo Matos Moctezuma, eds.): 149–158. University Press of Colorado, Niwot.

    2001   *Skywatchers*. Rev. ed. University of Texas Press, Austin.

Barrera Vásquez, Alfredo

    1984   *Documento n. 1 del deslinde de tierras en Yaxkukul, Yuc.* Colección Científica (Lingüística) 125. Instituto Nacional de Antropología e Historia (Centro Regional del Sureste), México, D.F.

Berdan, Frances F., and Patricia Rieff Anawalt (eds.)

    1992   *The Codex Mendoza*. University of California Press, Berkeley.

Boone, Elizabeth H.

    1992   The Aztec Pictorial History of the Codex Mendoza. In *The Codex Mendoza*, vol. 1 (Frances F. Berdan and Patricia Rieff Anawalt, eds.): 35–54. University of California Press, Berkeley.

    2001   Fejérváry-Mayer, Codex. In *The Oxford Encyclopedia of Mesoamerican Cultures: The Civilizations of Mexico and Central America*, vol. 1 (Davíd Carrasco, ed.): 402–404. Oxford University Press, New York.

    2003   A Web of Understanding: Pictorial Codices and the Shared Intellectual Culture of Late Postclassic Mesoamerica. In *The Postclassic Mesoamerican World* (Michael E. Smith and Frances F. Berdan, eds.): 207–221. University of Utah Press, Salt Lake City.

Carrasco, Davíd

    1999   *City of Sacrifice: The Aztec Empire and the Role of Violence in Civilization*. Beacon Press, Boston.

Carrasco, Pedro

    2001   Mexica. In *The Oxford Encyclopedia of Mesoamerican Cultures: The Civilizations of Mexico and Central America*, vol. 2 (Davíd Carrasco, ed.): 297–298. Oxford University Press, Oxford and New York.

Chamberlain, Robert S.

    1948   *The Conquest and Colonization of Yucatan, 1517–1550*. Carnegie Institution of Washington Publication 582. Washington, D.C.

Ciaramella, Mary A.

    1994   The Lady with the Snake Headdress. In *Seventh Palenque Round Table, 1989* (Merle Greene Robertson and Virginia M. Fields, eds.): 201–209. The Pre-Columbian Art Research Institute, San Francisco, Calif.

Codex Fejérváry-Mayer
  1971   *Codex Fejérvary-Mayer; 12014 M, City of Liverpool Museums*. Akademische
          Druck- und Verlagsanstalt, Graz, Austria.

Coe, Michael D.
  1965   A Model of Ancient Community Structure in the Maya Lowlands.
          Southwestern Journal of Anthropology 21 (2): 97–114.

Edmonson, Munro S.
  1986   *Heaven Born Merida and Its Destiny: The Book of Chilam Balam of
          Chumayel*. University of Texas Press, Austin.

Farriss, Nancy M.
  1984   *Maya Society under Colonial Rule: The Collective Enterprise of Survival*.
          Princeton University Press, Princeton, N.J.

Förstemann, Ernst
  1906   Commentary on the Maya Manuscripts in the Royal Public Library of
          Dresden. *Papers of the Peabody Museum of American Archaeology and
          Ethnology* 4 (2): 49–269. Harvard University, Cambridge, Mass.

García-Zambrano, Ángel J.
  1994   Early Colonial Evidence of Pre-Columbian Rituals of Foundation. In
          Seventh Palenque Round Table, 1989 (Merle Greene Robertson and Virginia
          M. Fields, eds.): 217–227. The Pre-Columbian Art Research Institute, San
          Francisco, Calif.

Gibson, Charles
  1964   *The Aztecs under Spanish Rule: A History of the Indians of the Valley of
          Mexico, 1519–1810*. Stanford University Press, Stanford, Calif.

Glass, John B., and Donald Robertson
  1975   A Census of Native Middle American Pictorial Manuscripts. In *Handbook
          of Middle American Indians*, vol. 14: *Guide to Ethnohistorical Sources*, pt.
          3 (H. F. Cline, C. Gibson, and H. B. Nicholson, eds.): 81–252. University of
          Texas Press, Austin.

Graulich, Michel
  1998   Reflexiones sobre dos obras maestras del arte azteca: La piedra del
          calendario y el teocalli de la guerra sagrada. In *De dioses y hombres* (Xavier
          Noguez and Alfredo López Austin, eds.): 155–207. El Colegio de Michoacán
          and El Colegio Mexiquense, A.C., México.

Hanks, William F.
  1988   Grammar, Style, and Meaning in a Maya Manuscript. Review of *Heaven
          Born Mérida and Its Destiny: The Book of Chilam Balam of Chumayel*
          (Munro S. Edmonson, trans. and annotator). *International Journal of
          American Linguistics* 54 (3): 331–365.
  1989   Elements of Maya Style. In *Word and Image in Maya Culture: Explorations
          in Language, Writing, and Representation* (William F. Hanks and Don
          S. Rice, eds.): 92–111. University of Utah Press, Salt Lake City.

Hernández, Christine
    2004   "Yearbearer Pages" and Their Connection to Planting Almanacs in the
            Borgia Codex. In *The Madrid Codex: New Approaches to Understanding an
            Ancient Maya Manuscript* (Gabrielle Vail and Anthony Aveni, eds.): 321–
            364. University Press of Colorado, Boulder.

Hernández, Christine, and Victoria R. Bricker
    2004   The Inauguration of Planting in the Borgia and Madrid Codices. In *The
            Madrid Codex: New Approaches to Understanding an Ancient Maya
            Manuscript* (Gabrielle Vail and Anthony Aveni, eds.): 277–320. University
            Press of Colorado, Boulder.

Heyden, Doris (trans.)
    1994   *The History of the Indies of New Spain, by Fray Diego de Durán.* University
            of Oklahoma Press, Norman and London.

Just, Bryan
    2004   *In Extenso* Almanacs in the Madrid Codex. In *The Madrid Codex: New
            Approaches to Understanding an Ancient Maya Manuscript* (Gabrielle Vail
            and Anthony Aveni, eds.): 255–276. University Press of Colorado, Boulder.

Leibsohn, Dana
    1994   Primers for Memory: Cartographic Histories and Nahua Identity. In
            *Writing without Words: Alternative Literacies in Mesoamerica and the
            Andes* (Elizabeth Hill Boone and Walter D. Mignolo, eds.): 161–187. Duke
            University Press, Durham, N.C.

Lockhart, James
    1991   *Nahuas and Spaniards: Postconquest Central Mexican History and
            Philology.* UCLA Latin American Studies 76. Stanford University Press,
            Stanford, Calif.
    1992   *The Nahuas after the Conquest.* Stanford University Press, Stanford, Calif.

Long, Richard C. E.
    1923   The Burner Period of the Mayas. *Man* 23 (108): 173–176.

López Austin, Alfredo
    2001   Aztec. In *The Oxford Encyclopedia of Mesoamerican Cultures: The
            Civilizations of Mexico and Central America*, vol. 1 (Davíd Carrasco, ed.):
            68–72. Oxford University Press, Oxford and New York.

Love, Bruce
    1994   *The Paris Codex: Handbook for a Maya Priest.* University of Texas
            Press, Austin.

Matos Moctezuma, Eduardo
    1987   Symbolism of the Templo Mayor. In *The Aztec Templo Mayor* (Elizabeth
            H. Boone, ed.): 185–209. Dumbarton Oaks Research Library and Collection,
            Washington, D.C.
    2004   El calendario azteca. In *El calendario azteca y otros monumentos solares*
            (Eduardo Matos Moctezuma and Felipe Solis, eds.): 13–75. CONACULTA-
            INAH and Grupo Azabache, México, D.F.

Matos Moctezuma, Eduardo, and Felipe Solís (eds.)

2004 *El calendario azteca y otros monumentos solares.* CONACULTA-INAH and Grupo Azabache, México, D.F.

Milbrath, Susan

1999 *Star Gods of the Maya: Astronomy in Art, Folklore, and Calendars.* University of Texas Press, Austin.

Millares Carlo, Agustín, and José Ignacio Mantecón

1955 *Album de paleografía hispanoamericana de los siglos XVI y XVII.* Instituto Panamericano de Geografía e Historia, México, D.F.

Montes de Oca Vega, Mercedes, Dominique Raby, Salvador Reyes Equigas, and Adam T. Sellen

2003 *Cartografía de tradición hispanoindígena.* 2 vols. Universidad Autónoma de México and Archivo General de la Nación, México, D.F.

Nicholson, Henry B.

1971 Religion in Pre-Hispanic Central Mexico. In *Handbook of Middle American Indians,* vol 10: *Archaeology of Northern Mesoamerica,* pt. 1 (Gordon F. Ekholm and Ignacio Bernal, eds.): 395–446. University of Texas Press, Austin.

1992 The History of the *Codex Mendoza.* In *The Codex Mendoza,* vol. 1 (Frances F. Berdan and Patricia Rieff Anawalt, eds.): 1–11. University of California Press, Berkeley.

2001 Borgia Group of Pictorial Manuscripts. In *The Oxford Encyclopedia of Mesoamerican Cultures: The Civilizations of Mexico and Central America,* vol. 1 (Davíd Carrasco, ed.): 98–101. Oxford University Press, Oxford and New York.

Paxton, Merideth

1997 Códice Madrid: Análisis de las páginas 75–76. In *Códices y documentos sobre México: Segundo simposio,* vol. 1 (S. Rueda Smithers, C. Vega Sosa, and R. Martínez Baracs, eds.): 63–80. Instituto Nacional de Antropología e Historia (Dirección de Estudios Históricos) and Consejo Nacional para la Cultura y las Artes (Dirección General de Publicaciones), México, D.F.

2001 *The Cosmos of the Yucatec Maya: Cycles and Steps from the Madrid Codex.* University of New Mexico Press, Albuquerque.

2004 The *Uinal* in the Books of Chilam Balam and Interpretation of Pages 76–75 of the Madrid Codex. *Latin American Indian Literatures Journal* 20 (2): 113–139.

Pohl, John M.D.

2004 Screenfold Manuscripts of Highland Mexico and Their Possible Influence on Codex Madrid: A Summary. In *The Madrid Codex: New Approaches to Understanding an Ancient Maya Manuscript* (Gabrielle Vail and Anthony Aveni, eds.): 367–413. University Press of Colorado, Boulder.

Robertson, Donald

1963 The Mixtec Religious Manuscripts. In *Ancient Oaxaca: Discoveries in Mexican Archaeology and History* (John Paddock, ed.): 298–312. Stanford University Press, Stanford, Calif.

Rosny, Léon de

1881   Les documents écrits de l'antiquité américaine: Compte-rendu d'une mission scientifique en Espagne et en Portugal (1880). In *Mémoires de la Société d'Ethnographie* n.s. 1 (3): 57–100.

Seler, Eduard

1901   *Codex Fejérváry-Mayer: An Old Mexican Manuscript in the Liverpool Free Public Museums.* T. and A. Constable, Edinburgh.

1904   Venus Period in the Picture Writings of the Borgian Codex Group. Bureau of American Ethnology Bulletin 28: 353–391. Government Printing Office, Washington, D.C.

Sosa, John

1989   Cosmological, Symbolic, and Cultural Complexity among the Contemporary Maya of Yucatan. In *World Archaeoastronomy: Selected Papers from the 2nd Oxford International Conference on Archaeoastronomy Held at Merida, Yucatan, Mexico (13–17 January, 1986)* (Anthony Aveni, ed.): 130–142. Cambridge University Press, Cambridge.

n.d.   *The Maya Sky, the Maya World: A Symbolic Analysis of Yucatec Maya Cosmology.* Ph.D. dissertation, State University of New York at Albany, 1985. University Microfilms, Ann Arbor, Mich.

Tena, Rafael

1987   *El calendario mexica y la cronografía.* Instituto Nacional de Antropología e Historia, México, D.F.

Thomas, Cyrus

1884   Notes on Certain Maya and Mexican Manuscripts. In *Third Annual Report of the Bureau of Ethnology, 1881–82*: 3–65. Smithsonian Institution, Washington, D.C.

Thompson, J. Eric S.

1950   *Maya Hieroglyphic Writing: An Introduction.* Carnegie Institution of Washington Publication 589, Washington, D.C.

1970   *Maya History and Religion.* University of Oklahoma Press, Norman.

1972   *A Commentary on the Dresden Codex: A Maya Hieroglyphic Book.* Memoirs of the American Philosophical Society 93. Philadelphia, Pa.

Townsend, Richard F.

1979   *State and Cosmos in the Art of Tenochtitlan.* Studies in Pre-Columbian Art and Archaeology 20. Dumbarton Oaks, Washington, D.C.

Tozzer, Alfred M.

1941   *Landa's* Relación de las cosas de Yucatan: *A Translation.* Papers of the Peabody Museum of American Archaeology and Ethnology 18. Harvard University, Cambridge, Mass.

1957   *Chichen Itza and Its Cenote of Sacrifice: A Comparative Study of Contemporaneous Maya and Toltec.* Memoirs of the Peabody Museum of American Archaeology and Ethnology 11–12. Harvard University, Cambridge, Mass.

Vail, Gabrielle

2004   A Reinterpretation of *Tzolk'in* Almanacs in the Madrid Codex. In *The Madrid Codex: New Approaches to Understanding an Ancient Maya Manuscript* (Gabrielle Vail and Anthony Aveni, eds.): 215–252. University Press of Colorado, Boulder.

n.d.   *The Gods in the Madrid Codex: An Iconographic and Glyphic Analysis.* Ph.D. dissertation, Tulane University, New Orleans, 1996.

Van Zantwijk, Rudolf

1985   *The Aztec Arrangement: The Social History of Pre-Spanish Mexico.* University of Oklahoma Press, Norman.

Villacorta, J. Antonio, and Carlos A. Villacorta

1976   *Códices mayas.* 2nd ed. Tipografía Nacional, Guatemala City.

Villa Rojas, Alfonso

1988   The Concepts of Space and Time among the Contemporary Maya. In *Time and Reality in the Thought of the Maya*, 2nd ed. (by Miguel León Portilla): 113–159. University of Oklahoma Press, Norman.

Wood, Stephanie

1998   The Social vs. Legal Context of Nahuatl Títulos. In *Native Traditions in the Postconquest World* (E. H. Boone and T. Cummins, eds.): 201–231. Dumbarton Oaks Research Library and Collection, Washington, D.C.

Chapter Ten

A Comparison of Venus Instruments in the Borgia and Madrid Codices

Victoria R. Bricker

IT HAS LONG BEEN KNOWN that the almanac on pages 53 and 54 of the Borgia Codex and the table on pages 24 and 46 to 50 of the Dresden Codex refer to 65 Venus revolutions, suggesting a shared interest in the movements of that planet among the peoples of central Mexico and the Maya area. The iconographic parallels between these two instruments—deities holding shields and/ or atlatls and spearing victims—were first noted by Eduard Seler in 1898. In the Maya codices, the Venus table in the Dresden Codex has attracted the most scholarly attention because of its undeniable beauty and elegance, but there are also almanacs in the Madrid Codex that are concerned with Venusian cycles, one of which shares both iconographic and calendrical parallels with almanacs in the Borgia Group of central Mexican codices. In this chapter, I will show that they are just as useful for understanding the flow of astronomical knowledge between the two regions as the better-known examples in the Borgia and Dresden codices.

The almanac on Borgia 53–54 is divided into five compartments, which are read in boustrophedon fashion from right to left in the lower register, changing to from left to right in the upper register (fig. 1). The compartments themselves contain two functionally distinct zones. In the center is a picture, and on two of the sides are boxes containing day signs and coefficients that refer to *tonalpohualli* dates associated with the picture. Two characteristics of the almanac imply a concern with the motion of Venus. The first is iconographic.

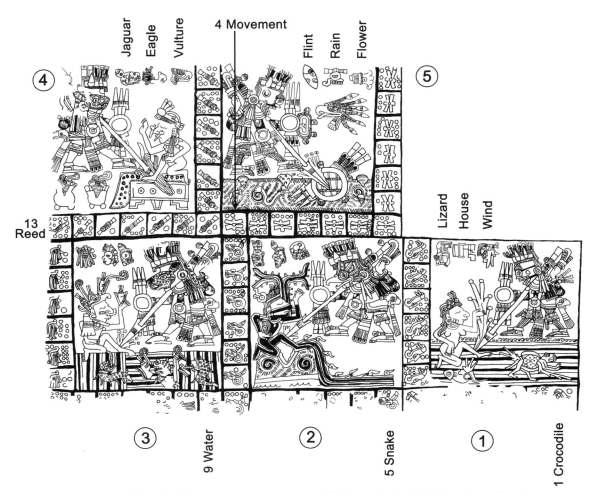

Fig. 1. The Venus almanac on pages 53–54 of the Borgia Codex. Circled numbers refer to the order of the compartments. Artwork by Christine Hernández, after *Codex Borgia* (1976: 53–54).

Tlahuizcalpantecuhtli, the Aztec god for Venus as morning star, is the principal figure in each of its five pictures. The second is calendrical. The *tonalpohualli* dates associated with adjacent pictures can be separated by intervals of 584 days, which correspond to the intervals between successive heliacal risings of Venus. It has been shown previously (Bricker 2001) that this almanac can be used efficaciously for predicting heliacal rises of Venus between 1473 and 1504 CE.

Even though the five representations are quite different (two death figures, one probable owl, one dog, and one rabbit) (fig. 1), they are all manifestations of Tlahuizcalpantecuhtli, who can be recognized in the pictures by his heron-

Fig. 2. Detail from page 53 of the Borgia Codex. After
Seler (1963: fig. 435). Reproduced with permission of
Fondo de Cultura Económica.

Fig. 3. Detail from folio 14v of the Codex
Telleriano-Remensis. After Seler (1963: fig.
432). Reproduced with permission of Fondo de
Cultura Económica.

feather crown studded with flint knives (fig. 2), the same crown he is wearing on
folio 14v of the Codex Telleriano-Remensis, where his name is associated with
Venus in one of the alphabetic glosses on the page (fig. 3). In the Borgia pictures,
he holds atlatl darts and a round shield in one hand and an atlatl in the other, and
he is spearing the legs of other deities—namely, Chalchiuhtlicue, the goddess of
running water, in the first picture (fig. 2); the black Tezcatlipoca in the second
picture; and Centeotl, the maize god, in the third (fig. 1). His victims are naked,
and their eyes are closed, indicating that they are dead. The victim in the fourth
picture has not been identified; there is no victim in the fifth picture, a shield and
darts serving as the target (Seler 1963: 12–14). This martial iconography is consistent with a passage in the *Anales de Quauhtitlan,* where Venus is described as
shooting people with darts when it emerges from the underworld after eight days
of invisibility at inferior conjunction (Bierhorst 1992: 36–37).

The pictures are framed on two sides by a series of 13 boxes containing
tonalpohualli dates, with both day glyphs and dots for the coefficients. Another
set of three day glyphs (without coefficients) appears above the victim in each

picture (fig. 1). They represent the days following the days on the sides of the compartments. For example, the first compartment (at the bottom right-hand corner of figure 1) has 1 Crocodile, now partially effaced, as its beginning date. The next three days in the sequence are [2] Wind, [3] House, and [4] Lizard, which are arranged in order from right to left above the victim of the spearer in the picture (the numbers in square brackets represent the missing coefficients). The next day is 5 Snake, which appears in the lower right corner of the second compartment. The next three days are [6] Death, [7] Deer, and [8] Rabbit, and the glyphs for these days are above the victim of the spearer in that compartment. The next day is 9 Water, which can be found in the lower right corner of the third compartment. The next three days are [10] Dog, [11] Monkey, and [12] Grass, which are mentioned above the victim of the spearer in that compartment. The next day, 13 Reed, is shown in the lower *left* corner of the fourth compartment, which, because it is in the *upper* register, is oriented in the opposite direction from the compartment below it.

The days following 13 Reed—[1] Jaguar, [2] Eagle, and [3] Vulture—appear above the victim of the spearer, this time on the right side of the compartment. The dates in the fifth compartment begin with 4 Movement (in the lower left corner) and continue with [5] Flint, [6] Rain, and [7] Flower. The next day, 8 Crocodile, is mentioned in the second box from the right at the bottom of the first compartment and begins the next run through the almanac. The 13 dates listed on the sides of each compartment suggest that this procedure should be followed 13 times in all. Each pass through the almanac covers a period of 20 days (= 5 × 4), and 13 passes equal one *tonalpohualli* of 260 days (= 13 × 20).

Although the almanac is nominally 260 days in length, the division of the 20-day period into five sets of four days (rather than, for example, into four sets of five days) calls to mind the structure of the much longer Venus table in the Dresden Codex, where dates of like Venus events, such as heliacal rise, are grouped into five columns and 13 rows (fig. 4). The mean length of Venus's synodic period is 583.92 days, which is rounded off to 584 days in the Dresden table. The sequence of days in the boxes on the sides of the five compartments on Borgia 53–54—Crocodile, Snake, Water, Reed, and Movement—can be separated by a number of intervals, among them 584 days. For example, the date reached by adding 584 days to 1 Crocodile is 13 *Snake* (the fourth date in the second compartment), which is followed 584 days later by 12 *Water* (the seventh date in the third compartment). The coefficients of the days continue to decrease by one whenever 584 is added to the previous date because the remainder is 12 after subtracting modules of 13 from 584 (table 1).

The pictures of Tlahuizcalpantecuhtli holding shields, darts, and atlatls and attacking other gods with spears in this Borgia almanac also have counterparts in the Venus table in the Dresden Codex, as Seler (1898) pointed out long ago. In fact, the caption over the picture of the spearer on Dresden page

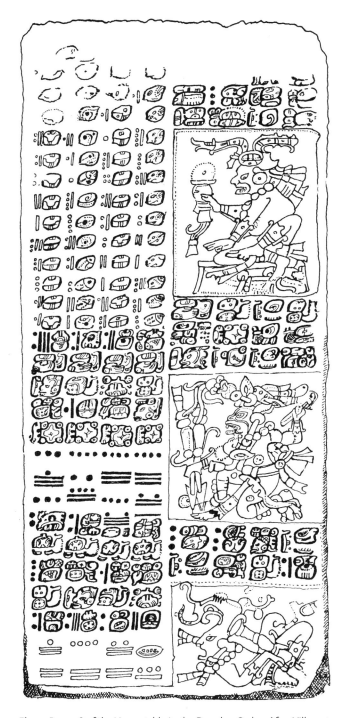

Fig. 4. Page 48 of the Venus table in the Dresden Codex. After Villacorta and Villacorta (1976: 106).

Table 1. Coefficients of the initial day of each Venus period represented
by the almanac on Borgia 53–54[1]

Crocodile	Serpent	Water	Reed	Movement
1	13	12	11	10
9	8	7	6	5
4	3	2	1	13
12	11	10	9	8
7	6	5	4	3
2	1	13	12	11
10	9	8	7	6
5	4	3	2	1
13	12	11	10	9
8	7	6	5	4
3	2	1	13	12
11	10	9	8	7
6	5	4	3	2

1. Reading from left to right in successive rows.

48 contains an abbreviated phonetic spelling of Tlahuizcalpantecuhtli's name
(at A2), spelled syllabically as **ta-wi-si-ca-la** (Whittaker 1986: 57) (figs. 5 and
6A), and the spearer on Dresden page 49 is wearing a heron-feather crown like
the one worn by the spearers in the Borgia Venus almanac (figs. 1 and 7). Thus
there are both iconographic and calendrical ties between the Borgia and the
Dresden Venus instruments.

The spearer on Dresden 49 represents the Aztec fire god, Xiuhtecuhtli, part
of whose name is spelled syllabically as **xi-wi-te-i** at A2 in the caption above
the picture (Taube and Bade 1991) (figs. 6B and 7). Boone (2007: 41, table 2)
has described the attributes of Xiuhtecuhtli as follows: "horizontal black band
through eye, fillet with two short and upright eagle feathers, turquoise pendant." The spearer on Dresden 49 has the first two attributes, but his pendant
is red with a white center, instead of turquoise. Except for the color of the pendant, he closely resembles the spearer shown on page 1 of the Codex Fejérváry-
Mayer, who also is holding atlatl darts in his right hand and an atlatl in his left
(fig. 8). Because the spearer representing Xiuhtecuhtli lacks the heron-feather
crown, he cannot be positively associated with the Venus gods in the Borgia
Codex, but his pose and weapons are similar to those of Tlahuizcalpantecuhtli
on Borgia 53–54 and his weapons to those of Xiuhtecuhtli on Dresden 49, where
he is clearly identified with Venus.

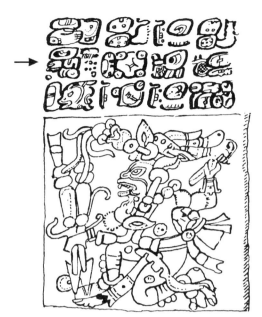

A

ta   ca
wi   la
si

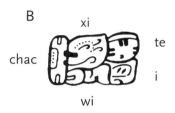

B

            xi
                       te
chac   i

        wi

Fig. 5. The middle picture on the right side of page 48 of the Dresden Codex. Arrow, reference to Tlahuizcalpantecuhtli. After Villacorta and Villacorta (1976: 106).

Fig. 6. Syllabic spellings of the names of Mexican gods pictured in the Venus table of the Dresden Codex. A. Tlahuizcalpantecuhtli (D. 48). B. Xiuhtecuhtli (D. 49). After Whittaker (1986: 57, figs. 2, 3).

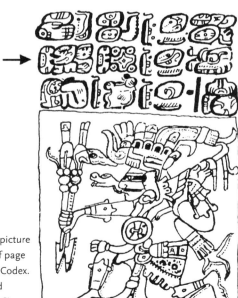

Fig. 7. The middle picture on the right side of page 49 of the Dresden Codex. After Villacorta and Villacorta (1976: 108).

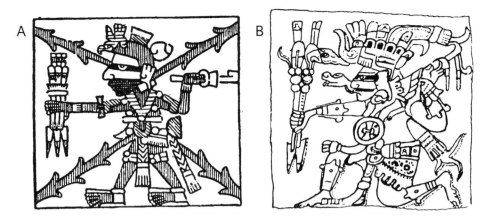

Fig. 8. A. Representation of Xiuhtecuhtli on page 1 of the Codex Fejérváry-Mayer. From Anders et al. (1994: 183). B. Xiuhtecuhtli on page 49 of the Dresden Codex. After Villacorta and Villacorta (1976: 108).

The almanac on the first page of the Codex Fejérváry-Mayer is of interest for our problem because of its structural similarity to the almanac on pages 75 and 76 of the Madrid Codex (cf. figs. 9 and 11; see also plates 1 and 2). Both almanacs have the shape of a Formée cross combined with a St. Andrew's cross (Boone 2007: 114), in which all the days of the 260-divinatory calendar known as the *tonalpohualli* in central Mexico and as the *tzolkin* in the Maya area are represented explicitly, either by day signs or by small circles or black dots, which are place markers for day signs not expressly pictured. What has not been recognized until now is that the Maya version of this cosmogram may also contain a Venus calendar.

I begin with the Fejérváry-Mayer version of this instrument because it, or something very much like it, seems to have served as the prototype for the Maya version (fig. 9). The ribbon of days forms four trapezoids arranged around a central square (the Formée cross). Three sides of each trapezoid are composed of a line of 12 small circles and one day sign, together representing the 13 days of a *trecena*. The side of the trapezoid facing the center is open. In the four corners between the trapezoids are two *trecenas* arranged as a horseshoe-shaped lobe, with the open side facing the center (the St. Andrew's cross). Together the days mentioned by the day signs or symbolized by the small circles represent the 20 *trecenas* that make up the 260 days of the *tonalpohualli* ([3 × 4] + [2 × 4] = 20).

The first day in the 260-day sequence is 1 Crocodile; it is represented by the crocodile glyph in the lower right corner of the upper trapezoid. The next *trecena* begins on 1 Jaguar, whose glyph appears in the upper right corner of the upper trapezoid. The third *trecena* begins on 1 Deer, and a deer sign can be seen in the upper left corner of the same trapezoid. The fourth *trecena* begins on 1

Fig. 9. Page 1 of the Codex Fejérváry-Mayer. For a color image of this page, see plate 2. After Anders et al. (1994: 183). Reproduced with permission of Fondo de Cultura Económica.

Flower, and a flower sign is shown at the base of the right side of the horseshoe in the upper left corner of the cosmogram. The sequence continues in this counterclockwise fashion, moving from right to left along that horseshoe and then continuing with the trapezoid on the left side of the cosmogram, followed by the next horseshoe, and so on through the almanac. Only day glyphs or small circles are shown. The coefficients are inferred from the structure of the almanac.

The area that is partially enclosed by each trapezoid contains a picture of two deities facing each other on either side of a tree (fig. 9). The gods in the picture at the top have been identified as Itztli, the personified knife, on the right and Tonatiuh, the sun god, on the left (Anders et al. 1994: 165). The tree that separates them grows out of a sun sign on a platform reached by steps. The presence of the sun suggests that the direction in question is east. The deities in the lower picture are Chalchiuhtlicue, the goddess of water, on the left and Tlazolteotl, the goddess of weaving and sexuality, on the right (Anders et al. 1994: 165). The platform on which they stand has a skull and skeletal arms on its side. The direction associated with this picture is thought to be west. The gods in the picture on the left side of the cosmogram are Tepeyollotl, the Heart of the Mountain, on the right and Tlaloc, the rain god, on the left (Anders et al. 1994: 165). The direction associated with this picture is considered to be north. The tree between them has thorns like a ceiba and emerges from a pot. The deities in the picture on the right side of the almanac are Centeotl, the maize god, on the right and Mictlantecuhtli, the lord of the Kingdom of the Dead, on the left (Anders et al. 1994: 165). The tree between them emerges from what appear to be the jaws of a crocodile. The remaining direction, south, has been assigned to this picture. The fifth picture, in a square defined by black lines in the center, not small circles and day signs, shows a single deity—Xiuhtecuhtli, the lord of fire, time, and the calendar—not two, and there is no tree. According to Anders et al. (1994: 164), "he can be recognized by the lower part of his face, painted black, and by the horizontal black band that passes across his eye. The blue hummingbird on his forehead is another diagnostic trait." He is shown holding a spear-thrower in his left hand and three darts in his right, and red rays emanate from his left eye, the back of his head, and his hips toward the corners of the picture. Boone (2007: 115–116) describes these rays as streams of blood that flow from the dismembered body parts of Tezcatlipoca, the god of war, rulership, and divination, on the left side of the trapezoids, "as if the body of the god of divination were nourishing the lord of time at the center" (fig. 10). On the other hand, because Tezcatlipoca is the second victim of the Venus god on Borgia 53–54 (fig. 1), it is possible that his dismembered body represents the victim of Xiuhtecuhtli on Fejérváry-Mayer 1 (fig. 10), whose pose and accoutrements resemble those of Tlahuizcalpantecuhtli in the Borgia Venus almanac and Xiuhtecuhtli in the Dresden Venus almanac, except that it lacks a heron-feather crown containing two flint blades (cf. figs. 2 and 8) (Vail and Hernández 2006: 74).

The nine gods in the pictures form a sequence representing the Nine Lords of the Night (Anders et al. 1994: 164), beginning with Xiuhtecuhtli in the center (1), followed by Itztli and Tonatiuh at the top (2 and 3), Centeotl and Mictlantecuhtli on the right side (4 and 5), then Chalchiuhtlicue and Tlazolteotl at the bottom (6 and 7), and Tepeyollotl and Tlaloc on the left side (8 and 9) (Anders et al. 1994: 167) (fig. 9). They introduce a clockwise element in that after Xiuhtecuhtli in the center, the series moves to 3 and 2 in the east, then 5 and 4 in

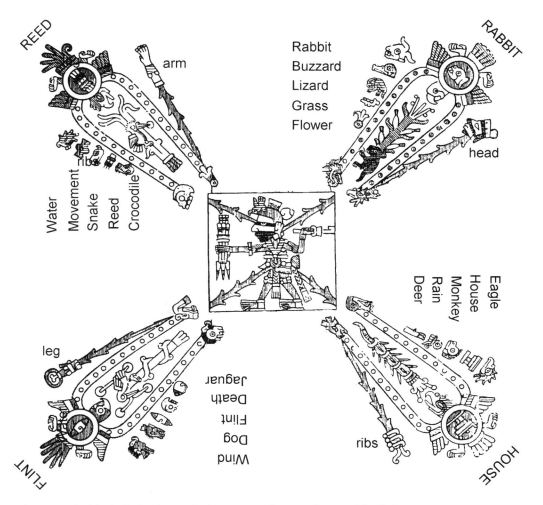

REED

RABBIT

arm

Rabbit
Buzzard
Lizard
Grass
Flower

head

rib

Water
Movement
Snake
Reed
Crocodile

Eagle
House
Monkey
Rain
Deer

leg

Jaguar
Death
Flint
Dog
Wind

ribs

FLINT

HOUSE

Fig. 10. Detail of the St. Andrew's cross in the corners and center of page 1 of the Codex Fejérváry-Mayer. Tezcatlipoca's head, ribs, leg terminating in an obsidian mirror, and arm appear on the right side of the corner lobes. After Anders et al. (1994: 183).

the south, 7 and 6 in the west, and 9 and 8 in the north. The order of pairs is clockwise, but the order of gods within pairs is counterclockwise, echoing the counterclockwise reading order of the day signs and small circles that mark the boundaries of the trapezoids and horseshoe-shaped lobes (see Boone 2007: 99, table 7, for the standard order of those deities).

The spaces demarcated by the horseshoes in the corners of the cross contain only plants, not trees or gods (fig. 10). Birds with long bills are shown perched on the plants in the upper and lower left corners; the plants on the right have either a small rodent (upper) or snake (lower) at their base. Above the plants, at

Table 2. The structure of the embedded almanac on page 1 of the
Codex Fejérváry-Mayer

[1] (+13) =	[1] (+13) =	[1] (+13) =	[1] (+13) =
Water	Wind	Eagle	Rabbit
Movement	Dog	House	Buzzard
Snake	Flint	Monkey	Lizard
Reed	Death	Rain	Grass
Crocodile	Jaguar	Deer	Flower

the top of the horseshoes, are birds, and embedded in their bodies are round, cartouche-like elements containing signs for the days Reed (upper left corner), Flint (lower left corner), House (lower right corner), and Rabbit (upper right corner). The days 1 Reed, 1 Flint, 1 House, and 1 Rabbit, which begin the *trecenas* at the top of the horseshoes, also begin the years that initiate the four quarters of the Calendar Round. Their large size and prominent placement in cartouches imply that they represent yearbearers in the central Mexican calendar.

A second almanac, also beginning on the day [1] Crocodile, is embedded in the corners of the cosmogram, between the horseshoes and the trapezoids (fig. 10); when read in a counterclockwise direction, it produces a table composed of 20 sequential *trecenas.* Assuming that the first *trecena* begins on [1] Crocodile (and reading from bottom to top), the table has the structure shown in Table 2. The day [1] Crocodile appears at the bottom of the left column. The next day mentioned in the table is [1] Jaguar (at the bottom of the second column from the left), 13 days after 1 Crocodile, indicating that the days within rows are separated by *trecenas.* The next *trecena* begins on [1] Deer (at the bottom of the third column from the left), 13 days after 1 Jaguar, which is succeeded by the *trecena* beginning on [1] Flower (at the bottom of the rightmost column). After four *trecenas,* the table returns to the first column, this time to the day [1] Reed, directly above [1] Crocodile. The table is read from left to right across the rows and from bottom to top in the columns. It has the structure of a 5 × 52-day Maya almanac, except that it is read from bottom to top (instead of from top to bottom). It echoes, in a compressed form (Boone 2007: 116), the sequence of 20 *trecenas,* all of whose dates are explicitly represented by day signs and circles in the ribbons marking the boundaries of trapezoids and horseshoes in the cosmogram.

Turning now to the Maya version of this cosmogram, we see that it has a similar layout, with four open trapezoids facing a central square (fig. 11). Here too the boundaries of the trapezoids are formed by lines of day signs and black

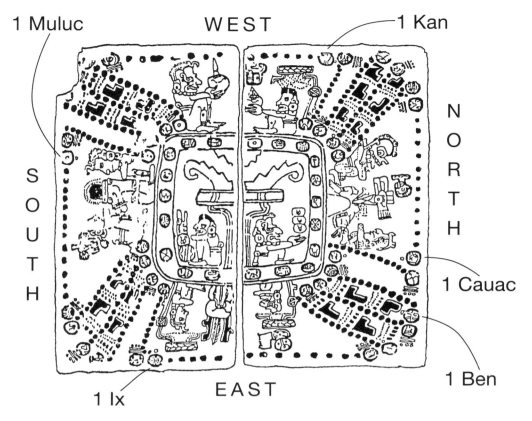

1 Muluc WEST 1 Kan

NORTH

1 Cauac

SOUTH

1 Ben

1 Ix EAST

Fig. 11. Pages 75–76 of the Madrid Codex. After Villacorta and Villacorta (1976: 374, 376).

dots (instead of small circles) representing *trecenas,* and the reading order is counterclockwise. Unlike the central Mexican version of this cosmogram, however, both the beginning and the ending days of *trecenas* are marked by day signs, and the days have coefficients (a single red dot for 1 and two red bars and three red dots for 13). Another difference is that, whereas the directional associations are inferred in the Fejérváry-Mayer version, here they are given explicitly as hieroglyphic collocations above the pairs of deities in the pictures within the trapezoids. There are fewer pictures in the Maya version and only one example of a stylized tree, in the center (there is no tree in the center of the Fejérváry-Mayer version) (cf. figs. 9 and 11). There are also no columns of day signs in the corners; instead, the picture in the center is framed by day signs.

One other difference that has attracted scholarly attention is that the almanac is oriented with west at the top, whereas the Fejérváry-Mayer version implicitly has east at the top. It is assumed that the Madrid version is in error, and one scholar (Paxton 2001: 36, fig. 3.2a; see also Paxton, ch. 9, this volume) has gone so far as to publish it upside down, arguing that it should have been oriented with east at the top. I suspect that the orientation of this page has nothing to do with the cardinal directions but is a result of the fact that the *trecena* marking the upper boundary of the upper trapezoid begins on 1 Kan, which was the senior yearbearer for the 52 years of the Calendar Round in the Mayapán calendar, according to a table on folio 20r of the Book of Chilam Balam of Tizimín (Edmonson 1982: 183). (The senior yearbearer of the central Mexican calendar was 1 Reed, which is shown at the top of the left horseshoe in the upper part of the almanac in the Fejérváry-Mayer [fig. 10], and 1 Ben, the Maya counterpart of 1 Reed, is located at the apex of the horseshoe-shaped lobe in the lower right corner of Madrid 75–76 [fig. 11]). This quadrant was associated with east in the Mayapán calendar (Edmonson 1982: 183), so the directional collocation is wrong, but turning the almanac upside down as Merideth Paxton (2001: 36, fig. 3.2a) has done creates a new problem: it places the *trecena* beginning on 1 Ix at the top of the page, whereas 1 Ix is the first year of the third quadrant of the Calendar Round, not the first (Edmonson 1982: 183). I suspect that, in trying to modify the Fejérváry-Mayer prototype to fit the Maya yearbearer scheme, the scribe who produced this cosmogram rotated it 180 degrees and then neglected to reverse the glyphs for east and west in the upper and lower trapezoids so that east would be associated with 1 Kan, as it is in the Book of Chilam Balam of Tizimín (Edmonson 1982: 183). That is the nature of the error, not a misunderstanding of which *trecena* should appear at the top of the page (see also Hernández and Vail, ch. 11, this volume, for another interpretation of the calendrical structure).

In the upper trapezoid (erroneously) associated with west, the god on the left is Itzamna, holding a maize seed or tortilla in his hand, and the one on the right, who is sitting in a house, has the parted hair often associated with goddesses, but the figure is wearing shin guards and a loincloth instead of a skirt, and the hair, although parted, is not obviously long. The theme of the trapezoid on the right, which is associated with north, is a human sacrifice. The chest of the victim has been pierced by a flint knife, and blood spurts from the wound. The death god sits to his left and the underworld god (*cisin*) to his right. In the lower picture, which is (erroneously) associated with east, both deities sit in houses facing an offering consisting of a tortilla or maize seed in a bowl, a stingray spine, and two obsidian eccentrics. The deity on the left is Itzamna; the identity of the one on the right is unknown. The picture on the left, which is associated with south, shows a headless captive with bound arms and legs flanked by two gods: the one on the right may be the flower god (*nic*); the identity of the one on the left is not known. The picture in the center contains the only tree in the cosmogram, which is providing shade for the two deities seated back to back beneath it. The one on the left sports a loincloth or a thong, which is typical attire for gods, but the parted hair implies a goddess, although one with atypically short hair. The single tooth in the lower jaw of the deities indicates that they are old.

It should be noted that in modifying the Fejérváry-Mayer template to accommodate the Mayapán yearbearers, the Madrid scribe preserved the clockwise reading order of the pictures and the placement of the death god in the right-hand trapezoid, which could not be accomplished by simply rotating the Madrid version 180 degrees. The orientation of the picture in the center and the day signs that surround it provide additional reasons for not turning the pages upside down.

The day signs in the cartouche around the central picture represent a second, embedded almanac, whose structure resembles that of the Venus almanac on Borgia 53–54. The glyphs above the picture are, from right to left, Imix, Chicchan, Muluc, Ben, and Eb (fig. 12). Intervals of four days separate the first four day signs from each other. The fifth day sign, Eb, is the day before Ben. To complete the pattern, it should be Caban, which is the third date on the right side of the picture, and, as I show later, Eb belongs in the slot occupied by Caban.

These five dates—Imix, Chicchan, Muluc, Ben, and Eb (corrected to Caban)—are the Maya counterparts of the five *tonalpohualli* dates (Crocodile, Snake, Water, Reed, and Movement) in the small boxes associated with the five Venus pictures on Borgia 53–54. The fact that they are found together, arranged in the same order (with one exception) as their counterparts in the Borgia almanac, suggests that they too have an astronomical function—namely, to predict dates of heliacal rise of Venus. The glyphs on the other three sides of the cartouche refer to other dates in the interval for predicting this celestial event. The ones on the left side of the cartouche refer to the days that immediately follow Imix, Chicchan, Muluc, Ben, and Caban—namely, Ik, Cimi, Oc, Ix, and Edznab, respectively. The order of Cimi and Ik is reversed, but both belong in the set of dates that should follow the ones at the top of the cartouche. The dates at the bottom of the cartouche must be read from left to right, beginning with Akbal (the day after Ik) and continuing with Manik (the day after Cimi), Chuen (the day after Oc), Men (the day after Ix), and Cauac (the day after Edznab). The dates on the right side of the cartouche are read from bottom to top: Kan (the day after Akbal), Lamat (the day after Manik), Caban (which should be Eb, the day after Chuen), Cib (the day after Men), and Ahau (the day after Cauac). The order of Cib and Ahau is reversed, but the two days belong in the same column. Thus the top row of day signs refers to canonical dates for Venus's first appearance as morning star after inferior conjunction, and those along the sides and the bottom refer to alternative dates in the four-day interval, arranged in the same order. The reading order for the dates in the cartouche is counterclockwise, except for the three transpositions I have described earlier (see also Paxton 2001: 37, fig. 3.2b; Thomas 1884: 15–17; Thompson 1950: 248), like the reading order of the embedded almanac in the Fejérváry-Mayer

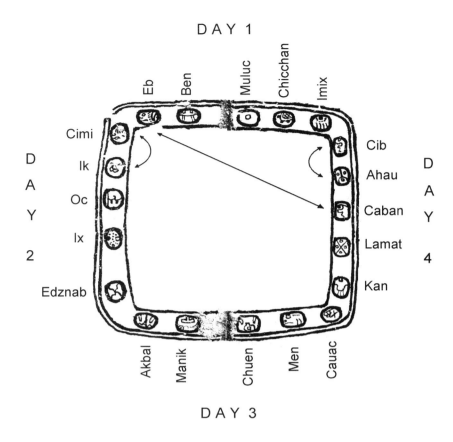

Fig. 12. The Venus almanac in the center of pages 75–76 of the Madrid Codex. After Anders (1967).

cosmogram but contrasting with the reading order of the dates in the Venus almanac on Borgia 53–54, which is clockwise.

The structure of this embedded almanac on Madrid 75–76 is, therefore, analogous to the structure of the almanac on Borgia 53–54. Both almanacs divide the 20 day signs into five sets, representing four-day intervals when heliacal risings of Venus are likely. The principal difference between them lies in where they place days 2–4 in the intervals. In the Borgia almanac, those days appear in sequence above their corresponding pictures, whereas in the Madrid almanac, they are grouped by their position in the sequence along the sides of the cartouche. The movement from day to day in sequence produces a counterclockwise spiral, beginning and ending in the upper right-hand corner.

This pattern can also be found in the almanac on page 25 of the Borgia Codex (fig. 13), which also probably refers to Venus's first appearance as morning star after inferior conjunction (Bricker 2001: S31–S35). It is also divided into five compartments, but in this case, there are only four pictures, each of which shows a deity carrying a small round shield, darts, and an atlatl, the same weapons carried by Tlahuizcalpantecuhtli on Borgia 53–54. The central compartment is smaller than the other four and contains only a day sign and its coefficient: 10 Movement (fig. 14). The prominence of this calendrical collocation, both its large size compared to the other dates in the almanac and its central placement, and the fact that it is the only day sign with an explicit coefficient, suggest that it was intended for use as the first day of the almanac. From it, one moves to [11] Flint (the day sign to the left of the central compartment), then to [12] Rain (the day sign directly below the central compartment), then to [13] Flower (the day sign to the right of the central compartment). (Note that the numbers in parentheses in figure 14 refer to the order of the days mentioned directly above them, not to their coefficients.) These four days correspond to the four days associated with the fifth compartment on pages 53 and 54.

The next day in the sequence is [1] Crocodile, which is the first of four dates above the central compartment. Then one moves to [2] Wind, [3] House, and [4] Lizard (above the picture in the lower left compartment). The glyph for Wind is connected by a short red line to the picture below it, indicating that it begins the sequence of days associated with that compartment and differentiating them from the glyph for Flint, which is related to the central compartment. Similarly, the glyph for the next day, [5] Snake, is connected by a short red line to the picture in the lower right compartment and represents the first in the sequence, [5] Snake, [6] Death, and [7] Deer, in the vertical band at the bottom of the page. They are followed by [8] Rabbit, [9] Water (connected by a short red line to the picture in the upper right compartment), and [10] Dog. The sequence continues with [11] Monkey (connected by a short red line to the picture in the upper left compartment), [12] Grass, and [13] Reed. The last three days in the sequence, [1] Jaguar, [2] Eagle, and [3] Vulture, appear in the upper left corner of the page. They seem to be leftovers, because they do not participate in the main structure of the almanac (Elizabeth Boone, personal communication, August 9, 1999).

The reading order of the first six days on Borgia 25 forms a counterclockwise spiral like that of the embedded almanac on Madrid 75–76 (fig. 14). After that, the sequence of days in the small boxes that frame the pictures is linear, as it is on Borgia 53–54. Thus the almanac on Borgia 25 is a hybrid instrument, combining the linear and spiral structures of the Venus almanacs on Borgia 53–54 and Madrid 75–76.

The outermost of the two almanacs on Madrid 75–76 is nominally 260 days in length. Gabrielle Vail (2004: 241–243) has argued that the division of the cosmogram into four quadrants with directional associations is just as relevant for the Calendar Round of 52 years, and she follows Merideth Paxton (1997, 2001: ch. 3) in interpreting the almanac as a commensuration of *tzolkin* and *haab*

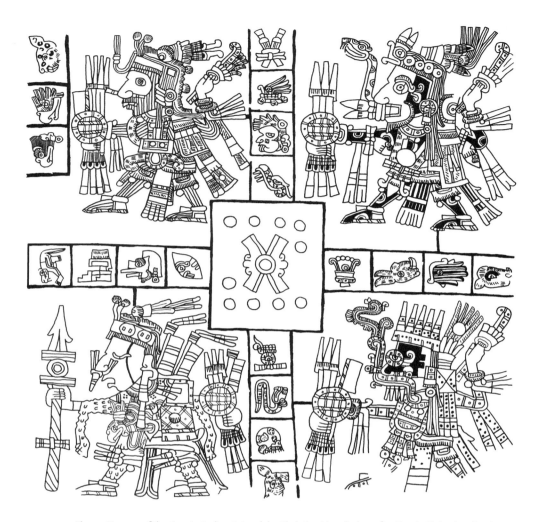

Fig. 13. Page 25 of the Borgia Codex. Artwork by Christine Hernández, after *Borgia Codex* (1976: 25).

cycles. She points out that the 13-year quarters into which the Calendar Round is divided begin on 1 Kan, 1 Muluc, 1 Ix, and 1 Cauac in the Mayapán calendar and that the *trecenas* beginning on these days are prominently placed along the sides of the cosmogram. However, neither Paxton nor Vail has proposed a function for the dates in the embedded almanac.

If I am correct in identifying the almanac embedded in the center of this cosmogram as a Venus instrument, then Madrid 75–76 could cover a much longer period of time, as much as two Calendar Rounds or 104 years, as is the case with the Venus almanac on Borgia 53–54 and the Venus table on Dresden

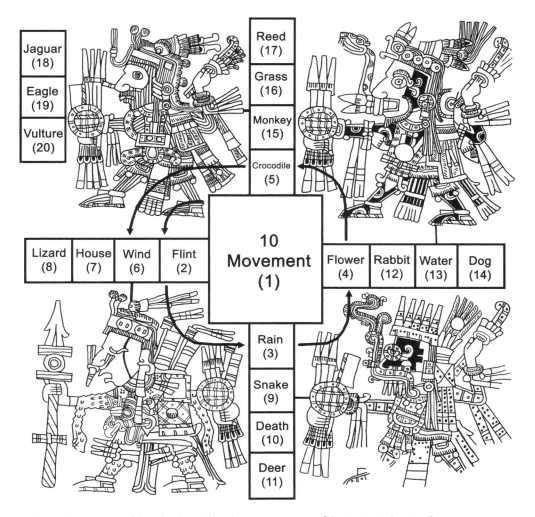

Fig. 14. Transcription of the calendrics in the almanac on page 25 of the Borgia Codex. Numbers in parentheses and arrows indicate the order of dates. Artwork by Christine Hernández; after Seler (1963: 3, plate 25).

24, 46–50. The cosmogram on Madrid 75–76 contains five pictures: four in the trapezoids along the sides and one in the center. The *tzolkin* and *haab* models can account for the four pictures in the trapezoids more easily than the one in the center. However, there are sets of five days in the embedded almanac, as well as in the Venus almanac on Borgia 53–54 and the Venus table in the Dresden Codex. After five Venus periods whose canonical heliacal rise dates are 1 Imix (or 1 Crocodile), 13 Chicchan (or 13 Snake), 12 Muluc (or 12 Water), 11 Ben

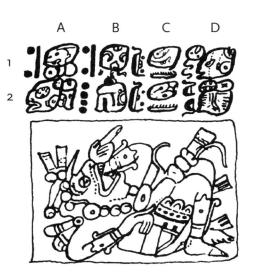

         A   B   C   D

1

2

Fig. 15. The lower picture on
the right side of page 49 of the
Dresden Codex. After Villacorta
and Villacorta (1976: 108).

Fig. 16. The upper picture on the right side
of page 47 of the Dresden Codex. After
Villacorta and Villacorta (1976: 104).

Fig. 17. The middle picture
on the right side of page 50
of the Dresden Codex. After
Villacorta and Villacorta
(1976: 110).

(or 11 Reed), and 10 Caban (or 10 Movement), the almanac returns to Imix (or Crocodile), this time with a coefficient of 9 (table 1). It is therefore possible that the pictures refer to the five Venus events implied by the embedded almanac, rather than to the divisions of the *tzolkin* or the Calendar Round. The picture on the left side of Madrid 75–76 includes a headless, bound captive (fig. 11), and the victim on Dresden 49 is named by a headless captive collocation (fig. 15, at B2). The death god and the god of the underworld (*cisin*) flank a victim whose chest has been cut open in the picture on the right side of the page (fig. 11); the death god is pictured sitting on a skyband in the upper register of Dresden 47 (fig. 16), and *cisin* seems to be the Maya counterpart of the central Mexican god Tezcatlipoca-Itzlacoliuhqui-Ixquimilli (Taube 1992: 110), who represents the spearer in the middle register of Dresden 50 (fig. 17). There is, then, some Venus iconography in at least two of the pictures in the trapezoids bracketing the Venus almanac in the center of the page, although the dates in it are not correlated with specific pictures.

Thus, in addition to the more obvious iconographic and calendrical ties between Madrid 75–76 and Fejérváry-Mayer 1, there are also hitherto unrecognized calendrical and astronomical links between the almanac embedded in Madrid 75–76 and the Venus calendar on Borgia 53–54. The structure of the embedded almanac echoes the structure of its central Mexican counterpart more closely than does the Venus table in the Dresden Codex, whose central Mexican ties are largely iconographic and linguistic (the pictures and names of central Mexican deities). In this respect, the embedded almanac on Madrid 75–76 is more deeply influenced by central Mexican conceptions of how Venus cycles interacted with the 260-day calendar than is the Venus table in the Dresden Codex.

Unlike the more prominent overlapping Formée and St. Andrew's crosses on Madrid 75–76, the Venus almanac on those pages is not a direct copy of any known central Mexican almanac. This implies that the person who produced the almanac in the center of the instrument understood the principles underlying the Venus almanacs in the Borgia Codex. His ethnic affiliation—Maya or central Mexican—is not known, nor can it be determined from information given on those pages. In either case, he must have been familiar with both manuscript traditions. Nor does it matter that we cannot pinpoint the cultural origin of the scribe responsible for the layout of the cosmogram on Madrid 75–76, because it is right in the middle of a Pre-Columbian Maya manuscript that we now know came from northern Yucatán (H. Bricker 2004; Chuchiak 2004). The presence of this and other hybrid instruments (e.g., Just 2004) in the Madrid Codex shows that some Maya intellectuals were interested in incorporating central Mexican models for representing solar and Venus cycles in their own books.

Acknowledgments

I am grateful to Anthony Aveni, Elizabeth Boone, Harvey Bricker, Christine Hernández, Susan Milbrath, Karl Taube, and Gabrielle Vail for their constructive comments on earlier versions of this paper.

References Cited

Anders, Ferdinand
    1967   *Codex Tro-Cortesianus (Codex Madrid)*. Akademische Druck- und Verlagsanstalt, Graz, Austria.

Anders, Ferdinand, Maarten Jansen, and Gabina Aurora Pérez Jiménez
    1994   *El libro de Tezcatlipoca, señor del tiempo: Libro explicativo del llamado Códice Fejérváry-Mayer*. Fondo de Cultura Económica, México, D.F.

Bierhorst, John (ed. and trans.)
    1992   *History and Mythology of the Aztecs: The Codex Chimalpopoca*. University of Arizona Press, Tucson.

Boone, Elizabeth Hill
    2007   *Cycles of Time and Meaning in the Mexican Books of Fate*. University of Texas Press, Austin.

Bricker, Harvey M.
    2004   The Paper Patch on Page 56 of the Madrid Codex. In *The Madrid Codex: New Approaches to Understanding an Ancient Maya Manuscript* (Gabrielle Vail and Anthony Aveni, eds.): 33–56. University Press of Colorado, Boulder.

Bricker, Victoria R.
    2001   A Method for Dating Venus Almanacs in the Borgia Codex. *Archaeoastronomy* (Supplement to *Journal for the History of Astronomy*) 26: S21–S44.

Chuchiak, John F.
    2004   Papal Bulls, Extirpators, and the Madrid Codex: The Content and Probable Provenience of the M.56 Patch. In *The Madrid Codex: New Approaches to Understanding an Ancient Maya Manuscript* (Gabrielle Vail and Anthony Aveni, eds.): 57–88. University Press of Colorado, Boulder.

Codex Borgia
    1976   *Codex Borgia*. Biblioteca Apostolica Vaticana (Messicano Riserva 28). Codices e Vaticanis Selecti quam Simillime Expressi, vol. 34. Academische Druck- und Verlagsanstalt, Graz, Austria.

Edmonson, Munro S. (trans.)
    1982   *The Ancient Future of the Itza: The Book of Chilam Balam of Tizimin*. University of Texas Press, Austin.

Just, Bryan R.

2004   *In Extenso* Almanacs in the Madrid Codex. In *The Madrid Codex: New Approaches to Understanding an Ancient Maya Manuscript* (Gabrielle Vail and Anthony Aveni, eds.): 255–276. University Press of Colorado, Boulder.

Paxton, Merideth

1997   Códice Madrid: Análisis de las páginas 75–76. In *Códices y documentos sobre México: Segundo simposio*, vol. 1 (Salvador Rueda Smithers, Constanza Vega Sosa, and Rodrigo Martínez Baracs, eds.): 63–80. Instituto Nacional de Antropología e Historia (Dirección de Estudios Históricos) and Consejo Nacional para la Cultura y las Artes (Dirección General de Publicaciones), Serie Historia, México, D.F.

2001   *The Cosmos of the Yucatec Maya: Cycles and Steps from the Madrid Codex.* University of New Mexico Press, Albuquerque.

Seler, Eduard

1898   Die Venusperiode in den Bilderschriften der Codex Borgia-Gruppe. *Zeitschrift für Ethnologie* 30: 346–383.

1963   *Comentarios al Códice Borgia*, 3 vols. (Mariana Frenk, trans.). Fondo de Cultura Económica, México, D.F.

1990 [1898]   The Codex Borgia. In *Collected Works in Mesoamerican Linguistics and Archaeology* (Frank E. Comparato, ed.), vol. 1: 54–73. Labyrinthos, Culver City, Calif. [Originally published in *Globus* 74: 299–302, 315–319.]

Taube, Karl A.

1992   *The Major Gods of Ancient Yucatan.* Studies in Pre-Columbian Art and Archaeology 32. Dumbarton Oaks Research Library and Collection, Washington, D.C.

Taube, Karl A., and Bonnie L. Bade

1991   *An Appearance of Xiuhtecuhtli in the Dresden Venus Pages.* Research Reports on Ancient Maya Writing 35. Center for Maya Research, Washington, D.C.

Thomas, Cyrus

1884   Notes on Certain Maya and Mexican Manuscripts. In *Third Annual Report of the Bureau of Ethnology*: 5–65. Smithsonian Institution, Washington, D.C.

Thompson, J. Eric S.

1950   *Maya Hieroglyphic Writing: An Introduction.* Carnegie Institution of Washington Publication 589. Washington, D.C.

Vail, Gabrielle

2004   A Reinterpretation of *Tzolk'in* Almanacs in the Madrid Codex. In *The Madrid Codex: New Approaches to Understanding an Ancient Maya Manuscript* (Gabrielle Vail and Anthony Aveni, eds.): 215–252. University Press of Colorado, Boulder.

Vail, Gabrielle, and Christine Hernández

2006 Fire Drilling, Bloodletting, and Sacrifice: Yearbearer Rituals in the Maya and Borgia Group Codices. In *Sacred Books, Sacred Languages: Two Thousand Years of Ritual and Religious Maya Literature*; *Proceedings of the 8th European Maya Conference, Madrid, November 25–30, 2003* (Rogelio Valencia and Geneviève Le Fort, eds.): 65–79. Verlag Anton Saurwein, Markt Schwaben, Germany.

Villacorta C., J. Antonio, and Carlos A. Villacorta

1976 *Códices mayas.* 2nd ed. Tipografía Nacional, Guatemala City.

Whittaker, Gordon

1986 The Mexican Names of Three Venus Gods in the Dresden Codex. *Mexicon* 8 (3): 56–60.

Chapter Eleven

A Case for Scribal Interaction

Evidence from the Madrid and Borgia Group Codices

Christine Hernández and Gabrielle Vail

EARLY SCHOLARLY RESEARCH on the Maya and Borgia Group codices
was responsible for identifying significant evidence of similarities between certain almanacs in the two distinct codical traditions, representing
products of the Late Postclassic northern Maya lowlands and various regions
of Late Postclassic highland Mexico (Seler 1904; Thomas 1884; see also ch. 1,
this volume). Later scholars of the twentieth century (Nowotny 2005: 241–250;
Taube 1992; Thompson 1934, 1972) also commented on similarities between
the Maya and the Mexican codices, although within a more general context
than earlier studies. Some points of comparison noted in these discussions include the identification of Mexican deities in the Dresden Venus table (Taube
and Bade 1991; Whittaker 1986), the identification of the central Mexican A-O
sign in the iconography of the Madrid Codex (H. Bricker et al. 1997; Vail 1997),
and the use of Mexican spacer counting in Maya almanacs (e.g., Carlson 1983a;
Drapkin n.d. [2002]: 82–83; Just 2000, 2004). Explanations put forth to account
for these similarities include a shared ancestral calendar system (Thompson
1934), a shared art style (Boone and Smith 2003), and occasions of cultural borrowing (Carlson 1983b).

Breakthroughs in the study of Maya and Mexican painted manuscripts within the past two decades have greatly improved our ability to understand the

333

significance of these similarities. These advances include (1) the decipherment of Maya hieroglyphic texts in the codices (see Vail 2006 and Vail and Hernández 2005 for a more comprehensive discussion and bibliography), (2) an improved understanding of the astronomical content of both the Mexican and the Maya codices (see, e.g., Aveni 1999, 2001; H. Bricker and V. Bricker 1983, 1992; V. Bricker and H. Bricker 1986; V. Bricker 2001; Milbrath 1999), and (3) the introduction of a methodology for situating Maya astronomical tables and divinatory almanacs in historical time, pioneered by Victoria Bricker and Harvey Bricker (1992).

Recent investigations aimed at cross-dating almanacs in the Maya and Borgia codices and placing them in real time have generated new information not only about the content of Mesoamerican codices but also about the scribes themselves and the process of codex production (Vail and Aveni 2004: 18–22). The results of these studies suggest that scribes from the Maya region and highland central Mexico may have been in close contact with each other over an extended period of time, exchanging information about calendars and codex construction, and may even have had access to each other's manuscripts.

In this chapter, we review some of the evidence from these studies in light of our own ongoing comparative and dating research. We believe similarities to Mexican almanacs or the inclusion of "Mexicanized" elements in the Maya Madrid Codex reveal a much more complicated and dynamic situation than that of remnants retained from a shared calendar system, borrowings, or the adoption of a cosmopolitan prestige art style. Rather, almanacs in the Madrid Codex recently dated by us and by our colleagues contain evidence of an active interchange and transformation of calendrical, astronomical, and iconographic information among codical scribes in northern Yucatán, the central Mexican highlands, and perhaps the Gulf Coast. In the discussion that follows, our emphasis is on connections among the Madrid and Borgia Group codices, specifically those focused on *in extenso* almanacs (see Glossary and Introduction to Part III, this volume).

A Case for Scribal Interaction

Our investigation focuses on evidence for pan-Mesoamerican communication that led to a series of almanacs in the Maya Madrid Codex having very similar structures and functions to almanacs in the Borgia and Fejérváry-Mayer codices from the highland Mexican tradition (see Introduction to Part III, this volume, for a summary of recent discussions of the proposed provenience of these manuscripts). Here, we briefly discuss current research on the construction and dating of these almanacs.[1] Such information is relevant for understanding how communication between scribes and/or the possible exchange of manuscripts may have taken place in the centuries just before European contact.

Madrid Codex

Using a methodology they developed in the 1980s to cross-reference icon-ographic parallels between almanacs and tables in the Maya codices, the Brickers (H. Bricker et al. 1997; V. Bricker and H. Bricker 1992) propose that the Madrid Codex contains almanacs that record astronomical and seasonal events dating to both the tenth and fifteenth centuries. The later almanacs are likely contemporaneous with the creation and usage of the manuscript, where-as the early dates for other almanacs suggest that scribes copied certain alma-nacs created for use in the tenth century into a much later codex.

These findings suggest that the Madrid Codex is composed of almanacs and texts that were drafted at various times by a number of different scribes. Alfon-so Lacadena (2000), who made a detailed paleographic study of the codex, con-tends that at least nine separate scribes painted the Madrid Codex. Linguistic evidence (Lacadena 1997; Vail 2000, n.d.c [2001]; Wald 2004) likewise points to a number of different authors and the possibility that texts were copied from earlier manuscripts. On the basis of recent research addressing this question from a number of different perspectives (reported in Vail and Aveni 2004), we believe that the Madrid Codex was composed by scribes from the northern Maya lowlands in a region where Yucatec was the principal language spoken, but where one or more Ch'olan languages were probably also understood, at least by merchants and members of the elite class.

Other significant advances in our understanding of the content and con-struction of the Madrid Codex have derived from comparative studies of cog-nate almanacs shared by the Dresden and Madrid codices (Aveni 2004; Aveni et al. 1996; Drapkin n.d. [2002]; Vail and Hernández n.d.). In an analysis of the first ten pages of the Madrid Codex, Julia Drapkin (n.d. [2002]) discusses two almanacs, Madrid 2a and Madrid 3a–6a, that have cognates in the Dresden Co-dex (Aveni et al. 1996; Seler 1990 [1906]). Madrid 2a is a counterpart to the Mars table on Dresden 43–45 (Aveni et al. 1996), which V. Bricker and H. Bricker (1986) discuss in detail. The iconographic and calendrical attributes of Madrid 3a–6a and its Dresden cognate suggest that both refer to rituals celebrating the start of the Maya *haab'* (Vail n.d.b [2005]).

Drapkin's (n.d. [2002]) analysis of Madrid 3a–6a (fig. 1) and Dresden 31b–35b (fig. 2) is especially relevant to our study of the scribal process. Compared to its cognate in the Dresden Codex, the almanac on Madrid 3a–6a is a more con-densed instrument. The number of frames in the Madrid version is reduced from eight to four, and the hieroglyphic captions are much abridged. The starting date is also different, suggesting that the Madrid scribe revised an earlier template (one such version represented by Dresden 31b–35b) for use in the Madrid Codex.[2]

Another important difference involves the black-painted 18s enclosed by serpents in each of the four frames of Madrid 3a–6a. These four 18s are the

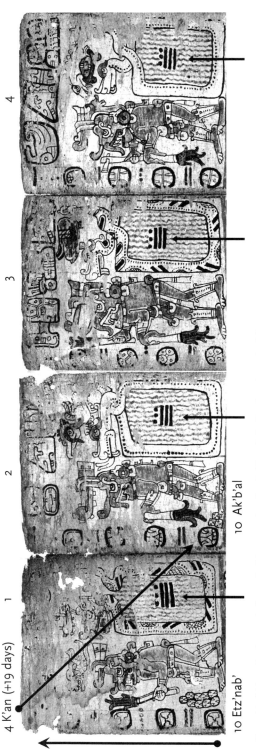

4 K'an (+19 days)

10 Etz'nab'

10 Ak'b'al

Fig. 1. Madrid 3a–6a. Arrows indicate the Maya notation for 18. After *Codex Tro-Cortesianus* (1967).

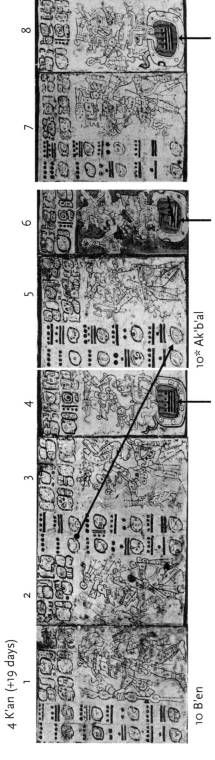

4 K'an (+19 days)

10 B'en

10* Ak'b'al

Fig. 2. Dresden 31b–35b. Arrows indicate the Maya notation for 19. *The numerical coefficient associated with the Ak'b'al date in the fifth compartment is interpreted as 10, although the scribe erroneously painted an 11. After Förstemann (1880).

distance numbers intended to advance the count of the almanac from one frame to the next. The Dresden version records 19s, the correct arithmetic quantity required to move across its pairs of frames. Drapkin (n.d. [2002]: 82–83) contends that the use of 18s by the Madrid scribe was not a mathematical error, as others have suggested (e.g., Seler 1990: 339 [1906]), but rather an intentional use of Maya notation to represent Mexican spacer counting. In other words, although 19 days must be added to move from 4 K'an in frame 2 to 10 Ak'b'al in frame 3 (see fig. 2), if one were simply to count the number of days between 4 K'an and 10 Ak'b'al, the result would be 18. A scribe operating in the central Mexican tradition would represent the same operation by placing 18 colored spacers between the day signs for K'an and Ak'b'al.

Madrid 3a–6a is one of several almanacs found at the beginning of the Madrid Codex that contains Mexicanized elements in its iconography and calendrical structure. Drapkin (n.d. [2002]: 155–156) suggests that the region encompassing highland central Mexico was a Postclassic period prestige center for the Maya elite of northern Yucatán and that the Madrid scribes may therefore have incorporated elements of Mexican almanacs into their codices to increase their value, power, and importance within their own local social milieu. Similar interpretations have been offered for the presence of International-style murals at the Maya site of Santa Rita Corozal (Masson 2003; see also Introduction to Part II, this volume, for a discussion of the International style).

Borgia Group Codices

The calendrical and astronomical study of tables and almanacs in the Maya codices, which attempts to place them in a historical context, has been ongoing since the turn of the nineteenth century (see Vail 2006). Only recently—long after Seler's (1904) initial commentaries—have these types of studies been re-employed to enrich our understanding of astronomical references in the Borgia Group codices and in the formulation of dating models to test when they might have been relevant (see, e.g., Milbrath 1999). Aveni (1999) and V. Bricker (2001), for example, reveal that at least five almanacs (on pages 25–28 and 53–54) in the Borgia Codex, along with their cognates and updated versions in the Vaticanus B. and Cospi codices, concern the prediction of real-time movements of Venus during the fifteenth and sixteenth centuries. The dated astronomical imagery in these almanacs can be used to cross-date other almanacs in the Mexican and Maya codices (Hernández 2004, 2006a, 2006b).

Two of those Venus-related almanacs are found on pages 27 and 28 of the Borgia Codex. Borgia 27 and 28 (figs. 3 and 4) contain circular almanacs consisting of five directionally linked compartments. The key iconographic elements on these pages—the Mexican rain god Tlaloc, streams of water, and maize plants—suggest a concern with agriculture and rain.

Four pairs of dates appear on Borgia 27: 1 Reed 1 Crocodile; 1 Flint 1 Death;

1 House 1 Monkey; and 1 Rabbit 1 Vulture (fig. 3 and table 1). The first date in each pair (underlined) names a year in the Mexican 52-year calendar. These four years are separated by 13-year intervals, thereby recording the first year of each quarter of a 52-year cycle (table 2). Using Caso's (1971) correlation of the year 1 Reed with 1519 CE, Aveni proposed a dating model for this almanac that correlates the starting date in the lower right compartment, 1 Reed 1 Croco-dile, with April 4, 1467 in the Gregorian calendar (Aveni 1999: S9–S10, table 2).[3] This date is significant because it coincides with a day on which Venus makes its last appearance as an evening star in the western sky (Aveni 1999: S10; V. Bricker 2001: S39). The first compartment in the lower right corner of Borgia 28 likewise records dates in a year 1 Reed (fig. 4). However, whereas the calendri-cal structure of Borgia 27 refers to an entire 52-year cycle (table 1) (Hernández and Bricker 2004: table 10.2), the five compartments on Borgia 28 (fig. 4) in-stead name dates in the early summer season of five sequential years in the first quarter of that 52-year cycle (table 3; see also Hernández [2006a] for a detailed reconstruction of Borgia 28 and its calendrical relationship to Borgia 27).

Borgia 27 and 28 are interpreted as paired instruments that concern the reckoning of the maize planting season with the start of the rains and concur-rent astronomical events of significance (Hernández 2006a). While the reckon-ing of Venus's visibility was instrumental in the dating of these almanacs, and some of the iconography on these pages may arguably refer to astronomical events, the overall theme for both pages is agricultural and meteorological. In fact, the scenes portrayed on Borgia 27 and 28 are strongly reminiscent of a sec-tion of almanacs in the Madrid Codex known as the "planting" pages.

The planting section on Madrid 24–33 is so named because much of the ico-nography on these pages concerns the planting of seeds, maize and other plants sprouting, pests attacking the crop, and rain falling. Hernández and Bricker (2004) were able to demonstrate specific calendrical and iconographic ties be-tween Borgia 27 and 28 and almanacs on the planting pages of the Madrid Co-dex. Cross-dating both sets of almanacs puts the beginning of the ritual cycle associated with the onset of the rainy season and the preparations for planting in late March and early April in both central Mexico and northern Yucatán. Hernández and Bricker (2004: 279–284) propose that there are so many nearly identical almanacs in the planting section of the Madrid Codex because each was intended to refer to individual years clustered around quarter intervals of a 52-year Calendar Round, a pattern that replicates that seen in the Mexican al-manacs on Borgia 27–28.

Hernández and Bricker (2004: 314) find the correspondences between the Borgia and the Madrid planting almanacs to be methodical and pervasive; as such, they are more suggestive of translation than of replication. They suggest that the scribe responsible for the Madrid's planting section may have had

Table 1. Gregorian and Julian equivalents of the dates on Borgia 27

Compartment	Mexican date	Gregorian
Lower right corner	1 Reed 1 Crocodile	April 4, 1467
Upper right corner	1 Flint 1 Death	March 31, 1480
Upper left corner	1 House 1 Monkey	March 28, 1493
Lower left corner	1 Rabbit 1 Vulture	March 26, 1506

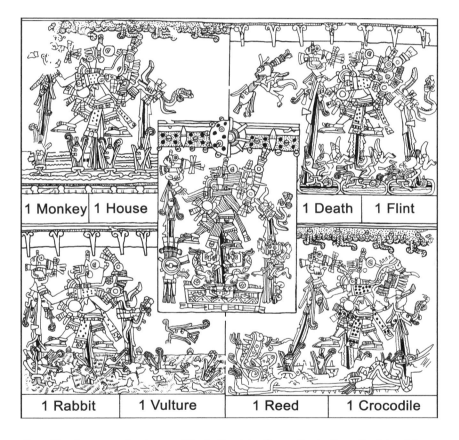

Fig. 3. The almanac on Borgia 27 and its starting date of year 1 Reed 1 Crocodile. Artwork by Christine Hernández, after *Codex Borgia* (1976: 27).

Table 2. The canonical 52-year calendar in the Postclassic Mexican calendar

1 Reed	1 Flint	1 House	1 Rabbit
2 Flint	2 House	2 Rabbit	2 Reed
3 House	3 Rabbit	3 Reed	3 Flint
4 Rabbit	4 Reed	4 Flint	4 House
5 Reed	5 Flint	5 House	5 Rabbit
6 Flint	6 House	6 Rabbit	6 Reed
7 House	7 Rabbit	7 Reed	7 Flint
8 Rabbit	8 Reed	8 Flint	8 House
9 Reed	9 Flint	9 House	9 Rabbit
10 Flint	10 House	10 Rabbit	10 Reed
11 House	11 Rabbit	11 Reed	11 Flint
12 Rabbit	12 Reed	12 Flint	12 House
13 Reed	13 Flint	13 House	13 Rabbit

access to a Mexican manuscript like the Borgia Codex, that he or she could read and understand its content, and that the scribe later used that knowledge of the Mexican agricultural almanacs to construct Maya equivalents.

Additional Evidence: *In Extenso* Almanacs

Another set of connections also suggesting scribal contact is highlighted by almanacs *in extenso* in the Madrid and the Borgia Group codices. Anton Nowotny (2005: 248) coined the term *almanac in extenso* to describe a subcategory of Mexican almanacs in which all 260 day signs in the ritual calendar are explicitly represented in a horizontal layout. This is in contrast to the more condensed calendrical format generally found in almanacs in which only a subset of dates in the ritual calendar is highlighted.

Horizontal *in extenso* almanacs cover the introductory pages of the Borgia, Vaticanus B, and Cospi codices. The count of 260 days begins in the lower right or lower left corner of the first page (depending on whether the screenfold was to be read from left to right or right to left) and runs continuously through five rows of 52 day signs each across eight pages (see Introduction to Part III, fig. 4, this volume). The five rows are aligned to create vertical columns of five day signs with a picture above and below each column. A total of 13 columns fits across each pair of pages (four pairs in all), such that each set of 13 columns represents days with the coefficients 1–13, commonly referred to as a *trecena*.

In a recent study, Bryan Just (2004) argues that the scribes who painted the

Table 3. Gregorian equivalents of the dates on Borgia 28

Compartment	Mexican year	First tonalpohualli date following the yearbearer sign	Gregorian
Lower right corner	1 Reed	5 Movement[1]	May 30, 1467
Upper right corner	2 Flint	5 Crocodile	May 28, 1468
Upper left corner	3 House	9 Water	May 31, 1469
Lower left corner	4 Rabbit	5 Water[1]	May 26, 1470
Center	5 Reed	1 Water	May 21, 1471

1. Reconstructed coefficient.

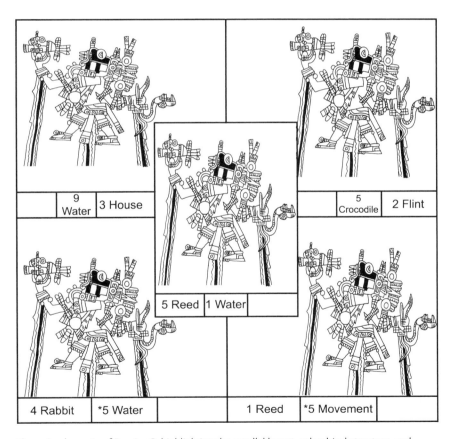

Fig. 4. A schematic of Borgia 28, highlighting the parallel layout, calendrical structure, and iconographic emphasis on the rain god (Tlaloc) also seen on Borgia 27. Artwork by Christine Hernández, after *Codex Borgia* (1976: 28).

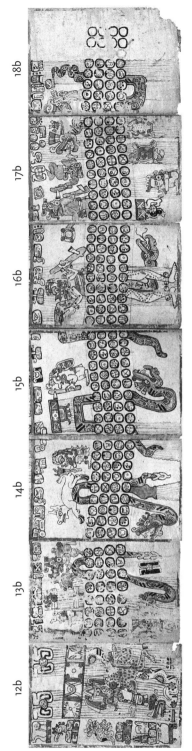

Fig. 5. The almanac on Madrid 12b–18b. After *Codex Tro-Cortesianus* (1967).

342

Madrid Codex adopted the format of the Mexican horizontal *in extenso* almanac to create four Maya versions of the expanded calendrical instrument.[4] One of these almanacs appears on pages 12b–18b (fig. 5) of the Madrid manuscript. Just (2004: 269–272) suggests that Madrid 12b–18b was centrally positioned in the manuscript so that the remaining three *in extenso* almanacs (Madrid 65–72, 73b, 75–76, and 77–78), found on the obverse side of the codex, could be folded over and placed physically adjacent to pages 12–18, presumably with the intention of cross-referencing or aligning concordant data.[5]

Madrid 12b–18b consists of an introductory section followed by the almanac *in extenso* (fig. 5). The introduction on page 12b includes a column of pictures depicting offerings along the left side of the page. To the right is a pair of eclipse glyphs above a skyband with rain falling below. The rain god, Chaak, wearing an A-O headdress, floats above a white-colored serpent that descends from the skyband. The second section of the almanac consists of an expanded calendrical register of day glyphs extending across the lower halves of the next six pages (13b–18b), with associated imagery, including zoomorphic figures, astronomical signs, gods, and depictions of rainfall appearing above and below the calendrical register. Five blue-colored serpents weave through the day glyphs on each page.

According to Just (2004: 259–260), Madrid 12b–18b and the Mexican *in extenso* almanacs share the following attributes (cf. fig. 5, this chapter, with fig. 4 in the Introduction to Part III, this volume): (1) both types list the 260 days of the ritual calendar (although Madrid 12b–18b actually records only 208 days explicitly); (2) both appear to begin with the first day of the ritual calendar, 1 Crocodile or 1 Imix; (3) the day signs are organized into parallel horizontal rows across multiple pages; and (4) imagery appears above and below the rows of day signs *in extenso*. However, the Madrid almanac differs from a Mexican *in extenso* in several important ways: (1) the imagery and text above and below the calendrical register are not aligned to specific columns of day signs; (2) the page breaks in the Madrid almanac do not align with groupings of 13 columns representative of *trecenas*; and (3) the calendrical register of Madrid 12b–18b has a 4 × 65-day structure and not a 5 × 52-day structure, as is the case for the Mexican *in extenso* almanacs, even though 52 day glyphs appear in each row (Just 2004: 261). Furthermore, 52 days (13 days at the end of each of the four rows) appear to be missing.

A total of 12 unfinished glyph blocks appear at the end of the rows on Madrid 18b (the first set of these has been partially erased). Various explanations have been offered to account for this: (1) the apparent miscounting of day glyphs and not leaving enough space to include all of the required day glyphs reveals carelessness on the part of the scribe constructing or copying the almanac (Förstemann 1902: 37; Milbrath 1999: 60; Thompson 1971: 26); (2) the scribe stopped in mid-construction and never finished the almanac (Lacadena

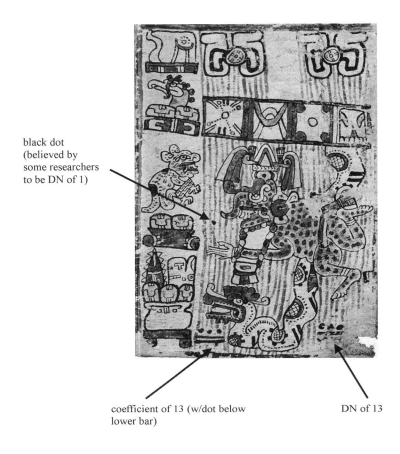

black dot
(believed by
some researchers
to be DN of 1)

coefficient of 13 (w/dot below
lower bar)

DN of 13

Fig. 6. Madrid 12b. After *Codex Tro-Cortesianus* (1967).

2000: 83–84); or (3) as Just (2004: 261–262) proposes, the scribe chose to complete the almanac's count using Maya arithmetic notation at the beginning of the almanac (on page 12b), perhaps to highlight the important distances of 1 and 13 upon which Mexican almanacs *in extenso* are based. He suggests that the "mistakes" in the almanac are symptomatic of a scribe trying to translate a Mexican *in extenso* template into a Maya one (Just 2004: 261).

Madrid 12b (fig. 6) contains two numerical notations: a red-painted 13, and a black-painted 13. If this black 13 was intended as a standard Maya distance number, then it would represent the 13 days added to the last day of each row on Madrid 18b (13 Eb', 13 Kab'an, 13 Ik', 13 Manik'). Adding these 13 days would advance the count of the almanac to the dates 13 Chikchan, 13 Ok, 13 Men, and 13 Ahaw that, in a standard format, should be represented by the red 13 on 12b. However, to enter the *in extenso* section on page 13b arithmetically, the addition of one day is required. Just (2004: 262), following H. Bricker et al. (1997), contends that an errant black spot near Chaak's nose on Madrid 12b represents a distance number of 1. What remains of the red *tzolk'in* coefficient 1 that should be paired with this distance number appears to the left of the first column of days in the *in extenso* section on Madrid 13b.

H. Bricker et al. (1997: S29–S30) interpret the almanac as beginning on Madrid 12b with the day 13 Manik' that appears explicitly at the end of the fourth row on Madrid 18b. Their interpretation of the calendrical structure is otherwise the same as Just's (who followed their model), except that they propose that the small red spot overlapping the red 13 at the bottom of 12b may represent a *tzolk'in* coefficient of 1, which is recorded a second time on 13b next to the day Imix in the first row (H. Bricker et al. 1997: S30).[6]

Despite similarities in the layout and structure of Madrid 12b–18b to the Mexican horizontal *in extenso* almanac, we believe that the 4 × 52-day structure of the explicit day glyphs on Madrid 13b–18b and the aberrant calendrical and iconographic characteristics of Madrid 12b may be better understood if we compare this almanac's structure with that of a second type of tabular 260-day almanac often referred to as a Formée cross almanac because of its four trapezoidal compartments. Maya and Mexican examples of such almanacs are found on Madrid 75–76 (plate 1) and on page 1 of the Codex Fejérváry-Mayer (FM) (plate 2), respectively. The close similarities between the two were described by early scholars, including Cyrus Thomas (1884) and Eduard Seler (1904), as evidence of cultural interchange (see also Introduction to Part III, this volume). In the final section of the chapter, we assert that the discrepancies between Madrid 12b–18b and the Mexican *in extensos* are *not* mistakes, but rather that the calendrical structure and layout of Madrid 12b–18b is complete and was designed this way intentionally by the almanac's scribe, who used structural and day-counting principles also found in the Formée cross almanacs. We also show additional connections between the Maya and the Mexican Formée cross almanacs that strongly suggest a pan-Mesoamerican exchange of information of an iconographic nature, relating to the format and layout of calendrical instruments.

Comparison of Madrid 12b–18b with the Formée Cross–Style Almanacs

Similarities between Madrid 75–76 and FM 1 have been the subject of extensive commentary since the earliest studies of the Maya and Borgia Group codices. The two almanacs have similar layouts, as described by Merideth Paxton in Chapter 9 and Victoria Bricker in Chapter 10 of this volume. As Plates 1 and 2 show, they are characterized by four large trapezoidal quadrants (arms) in the shape of a Formée cross, with a second set of four smaller quadrants (lobes) in the corner spaces between the larger quadrants. The 260 days of the ritual calendar are recorded along the arms and lobes, with each *trecena* (20 in all) forming a well-defined unit. A combination of day glyphs and spacers is used to mark the *trecenas*. A second count of days, represented by the 20 day glyphs without coefficients, forms an embedded almanac (see discussion, Introduction to Part III, this volume). These glyphs are grouped into four sets of five days, and each set is aligned with one of the four quadrants.

In FM 1 (Plate 2), the 39 days, or three *trecenas*, around a single arm are distinguished by color, thereby associating each arm with a world direction in the same manner as the costume colors of the rain gods on Borgia 27 (fig. 3). Two *trecenas* fill each corner lobe, where the day signs at the top—1 Reed, 1 Flint, 1 House, and 1 Rabbit—are encircled and highlighted to signify their yearbearer status. They are the same yearbearers as those recorded on Borgia 27.[7]

Each quadrant and associated lobe to its left therefore records a 65-day period beginning with the dates 1 Crocodile, 1 Death, 1 Monkey, and 1 Vulture. These same four *tonalpohualli* dates appear explicitly on Borgia 27 as well. The Maya equivalents of these four days, 1 Imix, 1 Kimi, 1 Chuwen, and 1 Kib', appear at the bottom right corner of each of the four "arms" of Madrid 75–76 (plate 2), and they are also the same days that begin the four rows of the *in extenso* portion of Madrid 12b–18b (fig. 7).

Each row on Madrid 13b–18b contains 52 explicit day glyphs (fig. 7). On Madrid 75–76 and FM 1 (figs. 8 and 9), these 52 days outline each "arm" of the almanac to the top of its adjacent corner lobe. The sets of 13 days not present at the end of each of the four rows on Madrid 18b correspond to the left sides of each of the four corner lobes (highlighted in figs. 8 and 9). On FM 1 (fig. 9), these remaining sets of days each begin with the highlighted day signs for 1 Reed, 1 Flint, 1 House, and 1 Rabbit. On Madrid 75–76 (fig. 8), two days are explicitly given at the top of each corner lobe: 13 Eb' and 1 B'en, 13 Kab'an and 1 Etz'nab', 13 Ik' and 1 Ak'b'al, and 13 Manik' and 1 Lamat. The first days in each set—13 Eb', 13 Kab'an, 13 Ik', and 13 Manik'—are the same days as those appearing in the final column on Madrid 18b (fig. 7). We contend that the missing *trecenas*—that is, the 13 days per row expected on Madrid 18b—are represented by the black-painted 13 on Madrid 12b.

Based on these comparisons with the tabular *tonalpohualli* almanacs, we assert that the scribe who painted Madrid 12b–18b *intended* the expanded calendrical register to contain only 52 days per row and that the remaining 13 days per row are represented by the bar-and-dot numbers on Madrid 12b (fig. 6). We agree with H. Bricker et al. (1997) that the red 13 on page 12b refers to the last column of explicit day glyphs on 18b and that the almanac begins with a day 13 Manik'. Our interpretation of the black 13 differs from that of previous researchers, however. We believe that it was not intended to function as an arithmetic distance number, but rather to signify the 13 days between

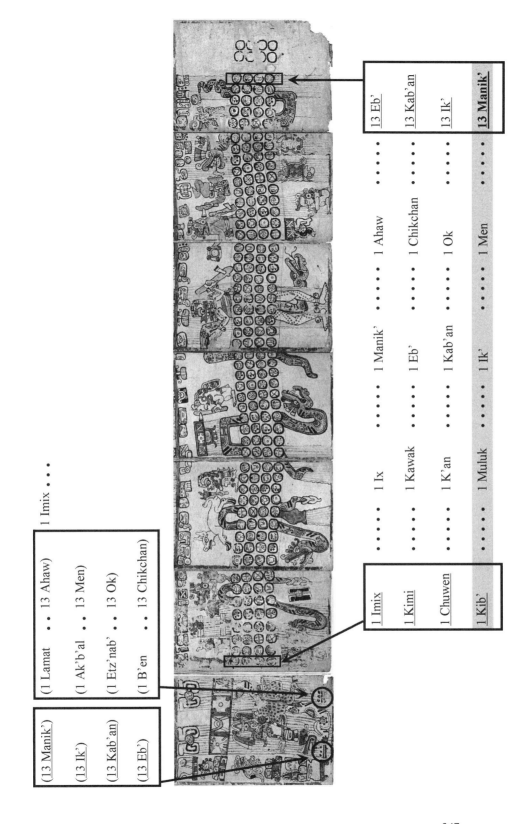

Fig. 7. Madrid 12b–18b, with expanded date structure. After *Codex Tro-Cortesianus* (1967).

347

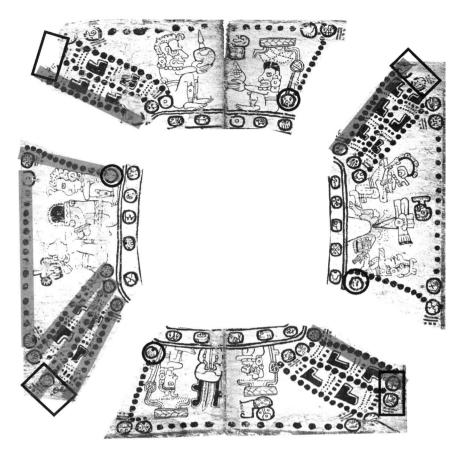

1 Imix		1 Ix		1 Manik'		1 Ahaw		13 Eb', 1 B'en		13 Chikchan
1 Kimi	..	1 Kawak	..	1 Eb'	..	1 Chikchan	..	13 Kab'an, 1 Etz'nab'	..	13 Ok
1 Chuwen	..	1 K'an	..	1 Kab'an	..	1 Ok	..	13 Ik', 1 Ak'b'al	..	13 Men
1 Kib'	..	1 Muluk	..	1 Ik'	..	1 Men	..	13 Manik', 1 Lamat	..	13 Ahaw

Fig. 8. Madrid 75–76, dissected. After *Codex Tro-Cortesianus* (1967).

the last day glyphs on Madrid 18b and the first day glyphs on Madrid 13b (fig. 7). It represents the same use of bar-and-dot numbers to count the days between frames that Drapkin (n.d. [2002]) suggested for the 18s in the almanac on Madrid 3a–6a. Moreover, it employs the same method of counting individual days as is used in the *in extenso* portion of the almanac, although the scribe

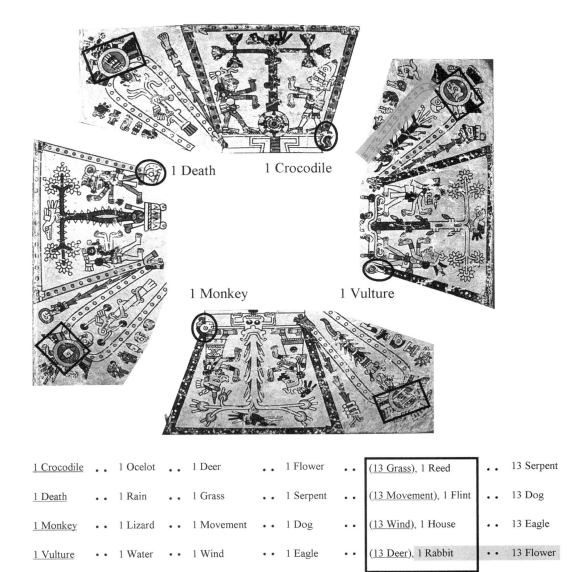

1 Crocodile	1 Ocelot	1 Deer	1 Flower	(13 Grass), 1 Reed	13 Serpent
1 Death	1 Rain	1 Grass	1 Serpent	(13 Movement), 1 Flint	13 Dog
1 Monkey	1 Lizard	1 Movement	1 Dog	(13 Wind), 1 House	13 Eagle
1 Vulture	1 Water	1 Wind	1 Eagle	(13 Deer), 1 Rabbit	13 Flower

Fig. 9. Fejérváry-Mayer 1, dissected. After *Codex Fejérváry-Mayer* (1994).

who painted page 12b chose to indicate this count of intervening days by using bar-and-dot numbers in the Maya style rather than with spacers as was typical of Mexican almanacs. This seems to us an ingenious conflation of Maya notation and Mexican counting to knit together the initial panel on Madrid 12b and the expanded calendrical format on 13b–18b.

Fig. 10. Chaak striding on a footprinted path in the seasonal table on Dresden 65b. After Förstemann (1880).

Another way in which to compare Madrid 12b–18b with the almanacs on FM 1 and Madrid 75–76 is through the iconography and calendrics on Madrid 12b (fig. 6). The pictures of vessels containing food and bound animals for sacrifice can be linked to other scenes in almanacs shown to refer to Wayeb' and New Year ceremonies (Vail 1997). Another definitive element is the A-O headdress worn by the blue-colored Chaak, which appears in several of the Madrid almanacs, where it has been linked to specific yearbearer dates (H. Bricker et al. 1997; Drapkin n.d. [2002]; Vail 1997). Certain pictures, as well as the calendrical structure represented on Madrid 12b, may refer to yearbearer ceremonies associated with the four 13-coefficient days implied by the red-painted 13, which also appear atop the corner lobes of Madrid 75–76. The days 1 B'en, 1 Etz'nab, 1 Ak'b'al, and 1 Lamat next to them are the Maya equivalents of the Late Postclassic yearbearer days (1 Reed, 1 Flint, 1 House, and 1 Rabbit) recorded atop the corner lobes of FM 1 (fig. 9).[8]

The corner lobes of Madrid 75–76 contain a set of inward-facing footprints topped by these pairs of *tzolk'in* dates. The appearance of these two dates with footprint iconography suggests that the dates may refer to the New Year station of the *haab'*. In their study of the Dresden seasonal table, V. Bricker and H. Bricker (1988: S21, S23) associate footprints painted in a right-to-left direction (fig. 10) or within a folded mat motif (fig. 11) with the midpoint of the *haab'*, or what they term the "Half Year."

Footprint iconography also appears in the almanac on Dresden 25–28 (fig. 12), where it concerns the New Year's station of the *haab'*. The left side of Dresden 25–28 includes a list of 13 paired day signs (Eb' and B'en, Kab'an and Etz'nab', Ik' and Ak'b'al, and Manik' and Lamat) that we believe correspond to the dates 0 Pop and 1 Pop in the *haab'*, thereby representing the last day of Wayeb' and the first day of the new year for all 52 years of the Calendar Round in the Classic period calendar. In the bottom register of each page, associated with the first day of the new year, is a motif symbolizing a directional tree. On page 25, the

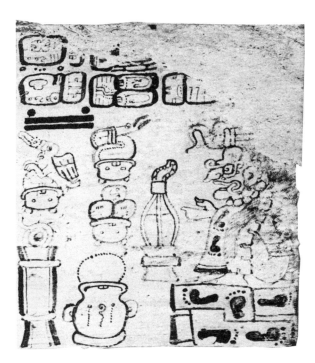

Fig. 11. Chaak wearing a footprinted scarf and sitting on a woven mat with footprints on Dresden 35a. After Förstemann (1880).

tree is represented by Chaak wearing a cape with a footprint oriented down-ward, in a fashion similar to the footprints in the corner lobes of Madrid 75–76 (fig. 8). The remaining three "trees" on pages 26–28 appear to be conflations of stone columns and living trees (see Vail n.d.a [2006]); they each wear a cape and a loincloth with downward-facing footprints, and a serpent coils at the top of the column. A Chaak wearing a similar cape is seated on a woven mat with footprints representing the Half Year station on Dresden 35a (fig. 11).

We suggest that the footprints in the corner lobes of Madrid 75–76 are equiv-alent to the footprint-patterned loincloths on the "trees" on Dresden 25–28,[9] thereby marking the explicit dates at the top of the lobes as the paired Wayeb' and New Year's dates in the Classic period calendar in the same way that the bird and vegetation iconography in the corner lobes of FM 1 and the Chaak with an A-O headdress on Madrid 12b also refer to yearbearer dates. If this is the case, then the count of 13 days along the left sides of each corner lobe on Madrid 75–76 (fig. 8) could also symbolize the 13 *haab*'s within the 52-year calendar separating the yearbearer dates (1 B'en, 1 Etz'nab', 1 Ak'b'al, and 1 Lamat) named at the top of the lobes (compare with the Mexican equivalent in table 2).

These Classic period yearbearers are not the only yearbearer dates recorded in this almanac, however. Elsewhere, we argue that Madrid 75–76 records the

Fig. 12. The Wayeb' pages on Dresden 25–28. After Förstemann (1880).

four yearbearers in the Mayapán calendar (1 K'an, 1 Muluk, 1 Ix, and 1 Kawak) that, like Borgia 27, mark the quarters of a canonical Calendar Round (table 4) (Vail and Hernández 2006).[10] These dates appear explicitly in the upper right corner of each arm, where they set off the four pictures around the perimeter of the almanac (fig. 13). If the Mayapán yearbearers are the focus of the almanac, as we believe, then the fact that the almanac is oriented 180 degrees vis-à-vis the obverse side of the document (see Paxton, ch. 9, in this volume) is, we argue, intentional.

Some scholars (see, e.g., Just 2004; Paxton 2001) suggest that Madrid 75–76 is positioned upside down within the screenfold, like its neighbor on Madrid 77–78, thereby presenting another example of incongruity between Maya and Mexican cognates. They believe this to be the case because the arm marked with the glyph for the direction east is at the bottom of the page, as is the starting date of the *tzolk'in* count, 1 Imix (plate 1 and fig. 8). To correct this, they believe that the almanac should be turned 180 degrees so that the east-related arm is at the top of the page, as is the case for the almanac on FM 1 (plate 2 and fig. 9). However, if it is the Mayapán system of yearbearers that is the focus of the almanac, and the canonical Mayapán Calendar Round begins with the year 1 K'an (table 4), then the placement of 1 K'an and its quadrant at the top of Madrid 75–76 is consonant with both the structure and reading order represented by its cognate on FM 1.

The canonical Mexican 52-year calendar begins with year 1 Reed. In the almanac on FM 1 (fig. 14), the arm associated with the 1 Reed yearbearer begins with 1 Crocodile (the starting date of the Mexican 260-day calendar), contains iconography (a flowering tree, quetzal bird, and temple with a solar disk) that associates it with the east direction, and is located at the top of the page. It is aligned with the set of five days (1 Crocodile, 1 Reed, 1 Serpent, 1 Movement, and 1 Water) in the upper left corner that begins a second embedded almanac. The reading order of the almanac proceeds counterclockwise with the years 1 Flint, 1 House, and 1 Rabbit associated with the directions north, west, and south, respectively. Madrid 75–76 does likewise with the Mayapán yearbearers, beginning with 1 K'an at the top and reading counterclockwise to 1 Muluk, 1 Ix, and 1 Kawak (fig. 14). The order of the day glyphs in the center of the almanac (fig. 15), representing an embedded almanac including all 20 of the day glyphs, follows that on FM 1—east (top), north (left), west (bottom), and south (right). As a result, the upper quadrant of the almanac is paired with the same set of five day glyphs (seen below the seated figures on fig. 14, left) as those associated with the top of FM 1. These include Imix, Chikchan, Muluk, B'en, and Kab'an, cognate with Crocodile, Reed, Serpent, Movement, and Water on FM 1.[11]

Despite these associations, it appears that the scribe maintained the pairing of the directional glyphs in each of the quadrants with the initial *tzolk'in* date recorded just to the right of the picture (i.e., east with 1 Imix [bottom], north

Table 4. A 52-year Calendar Round in the Mayapán calendar

1 K'an	**1 Muluk**	**1 Ix**	**1 Kawak**
2 Muluk	2 Ix	2 Kawak	2 K'an
3 Ix	3 Kawak	3 K'an	3 Muluk
4 Kawak	4 K'an	4 Muluk	4 Ix
5 K'an	5 Muluk	5 Ix	5 Kawak
6 Muluk	6 Ix	6 Kawak	6 K'an
7 Ix	7 Kawak	7 K'an	7 Muluk
8 Kawak	8 K'an	8 Muluk	8 Ix
9 K'an	9 Muluk	9 Ix	9 Kawak
10 Muluk	10 Ix	10 Kawak	10 K'an
11 Ix	11 Kawak	11 K'an	11 Muluk
12 Kawak	12 K'an	12 Muluk	12 Ix
13 K'an	13 Muluk	13 Ix	13 Kawak

The dates in each column are separated by one *haab'*, whereas the dates in each row are at 13 *haab'* intervals.

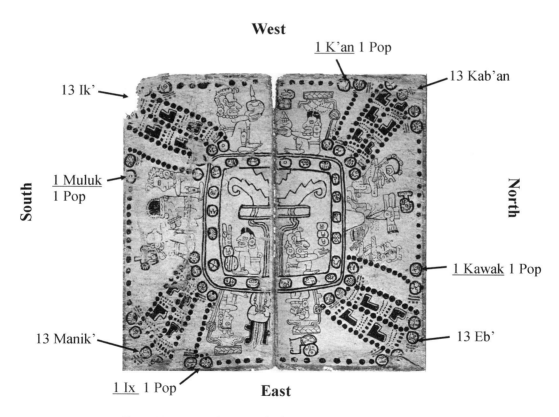

Fig. 13. Mayapán yearbearers in the four quadrants of Madrid 75–76. After *Codex Tro-Cortesianus* (1967).

354

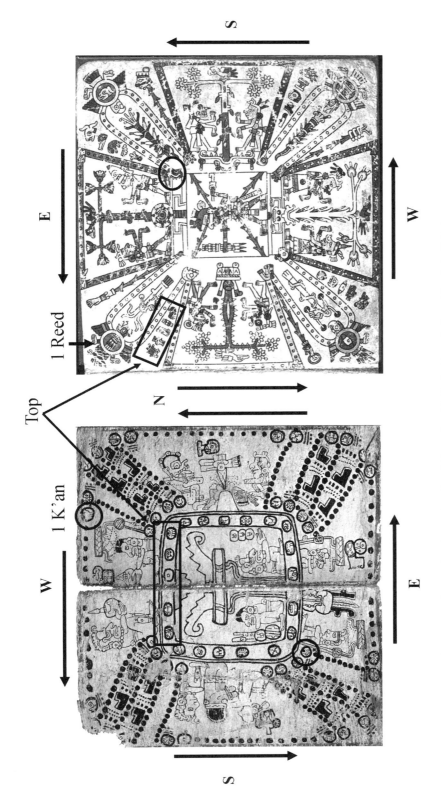

Fig. 14. A comparison of the top quadrant and reading order of Madrid 75–76 and Fejérváry-Mayer Codex 1. After *Codex Fejérváry-Mayer* (1994) and *Codex Tro-Cortesianus* (1967).

355

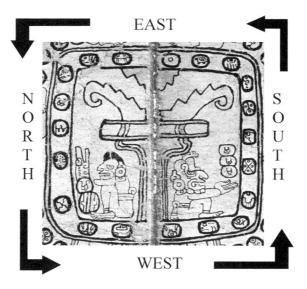

EAST

NORTH

SOUTH

WEST

Fig. 15. The reading order and directional association of the embedded almanac on Madrid 75–76. After *Codex Tro-Cortesianus* (1967).

with 1 Kimi [right], etc.), meaning that they coincide with the same directional pattern represented in the almanac on FM 1 (east with 1 Crocodile [top], north with 1 Death [left], etc.) (fig. 14). In other words, although east is associated with different quadrants in the two almanacs (the bottom on M. 75–76 and the top on FM 1), it is nevertheless matched with the appropriate day and quarter interval (of 65 days each) in the 260-day calendar in both cases. The iconography in each of the four quadrants of Madrid 75–76 likewise corresponds in abbreviated fashion to the Mexican system depicted in FM 1 and its cognates in the other codices of the Borgia Group (table 5). Note, for example, that the quadrants associated with the south direction on Madrid 75–76 and Borgia 49b–52b, which is cognate to both Madrid 75–76 and FM 1, include a red-painted decapitated victim (compare left quadrant in fig. 13 with fig. 16). The tabular layout of Madrid 75–76 shows that the scribe was clearly more interested in drawing parallels to the Mexican template for associating the quarters of the 260-day and 52-year calendars with the four world directions than using the iconographic formula found elsewhere in the Maya codices (see fig. 12 for an example from the Dresden Codex). Because the Late Postclassic yearbearer system used in the central highlands coincides with the Classic period Maya yearbearers, the tabular layout performs the dual function of contextualizing the Mayapán yearbearers within the 52-year Calendar Round and demonstrating the calendrical relationship between the Classic period yearbearers (lobes) and the Mayapán yearbearers (arms). It is therefore the case, we propose, that Madrid 75–76

Table 5. A comparison of directional iconography from Madrid 75–76 and Borgia Group cognates[1]

Borgia Group almanacs[2]

Direction	Mexican yearbearers[3]	Directional iconography[4]
East	1 Reed 4 House	Tonatiuh/solar god [B. 49b, FM 33b, Cospi 12a, PD 33, lower right)] Temple with solar disks and flowers [B. 49b, FM 1, FM 33b, Cospi 12a] Flowering tree w/ quetzal [B. 49b, FM 1, Vaticanus B 17] "Preciousness," turquoise jewels, flowers, and heart sacrifice [B. 49b, FM 1, FM 33b, Cospi 12a, Vaticanus B 17]
North	1 Flint 4 Rabbit	Ixtlacoliuhqui/god of frost, cold, and stone [B. 50b, Cospi 12b, FM 33b] Temple with lunar elements [B. 50b, Cospi 12b, FM 33b] Spiny cactus/tree with eagle [B. 50b, FM 1, Vaticanus B 17] Flint knives, symbols of punishment, heart sacrifice, autosacrifice [B. 50b, FM 1, FM 33b, Cospi 12b, Vaticanus B 18]
West	1 House 4 Reed	Centeotl/maize god [B. 51b, Cospi 13b, FM 34b] Temple with flower and sustenance symbols [B. 51b, Cospi 13b, FM 1, FM 34b] Maize plant/grassy tree with cotinga bird [B. 51b, FM 1, Vaticanus B 18] Heart sacrifice, *pulque*, earth goddess, female *tzitzimime*, fertility [B. 51b, Cospi 13b, FM 1, 34b, PD 33, upper left, Vaticanus B 19]
South	1 Rabbit 4 Flint	Mictlantecuhtli/underworld god [B. 52b, Cospi 13a, FM 34b, PD 33, lower left] Temple w/ death and underworld elements [B. 52b, Cospi 13a, FM 34b, PD 33, lower left] Thorny tree w/ macaw [B. 52b, FM 1] Red-painted sacrificial victim decapitated, crocodilian or earth maw [B. 52b, Cospi 13a, FM 1]

Madrid 75–76

Direction	Madrid 75–76 yearbearers[5]	Corresponding iconography in Madrid 75–76
East	1 Ix 1 B'en	Nik (flower god) and Itzamna (creator god) Maize and blood-letting instruments [lower quadrant]
North	1 Kawak 1 Etz'nab'	Underworld gods Kimil and Kisin Heart sacrifice, flint knife [right quadrant]
West	1 K'an 1 Ak'b'al	Itzamna and Chak Chel (creator couple) Maize and flint knives [upper quadrant]
South	1 Muluk 1 Lamat	Nik (flower god) and unidentified figure Bound and decapitated figure painted red [left quadrant]

1. Based on Seler's (1963, 2: 85–103) analysis. *B*, Borgia; *PD*, Porfirio Díaz; *FM*, Fejérváry-Mayer.
2. Summarized from FM 1 and cognate almanacs of the Borgia Group codices.
3. The upper set of yearbearers are recorded in the lobes of FM 1 and on Borgia 27; the lower set of yearbearers appear explicitly in the first four compartments of Borgia 49b–52b, 53c.
4. Cognates of FM 1 are FM 33–34, B 49b–52b, 53c, Cospi 12–13, PD 33, and Vaticanus B. 17–18, 24–27.
5. The upper set of yearbearers are the Mayapán dates in the quadrants; the lower set are the Classic period dates atop the lobes.

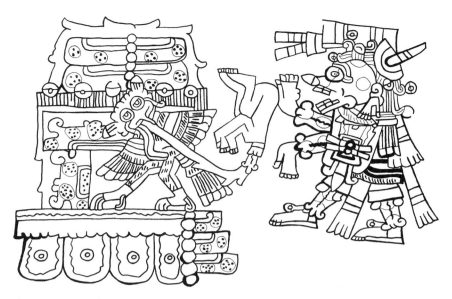

Fig. 16. Decapitated victim thrown to a temple associated with the south direction on Borgia 52b. Artwork by Christine Hernández, after *Codex Borgia* (1976: 52).

incorporates at least four embedded structures—the *tzolk'in* count (in which the directional associations match the start of each quadrant as well as the day preceding the Mayapán yearbearers); the Classic period yearbearers (and Postclassic Mexican yearbearers) recorded at the top of each set of footprints facing inward toward the center; the Mayapán yearbearers, with their associated iconography; and the central set of day glyphs, which are discussed by Paxton (ch. 9, this volume) and V. Bricker (ch. 10, this volume).

Discussion and Final Remarks

Mesoamerican scholars have been aware of iconographic and structural similarities between the Maya and the Mexican codices since the late nineteenth century. At that time, these similarities were explained by imprecise and Mexican-centric diffusionist theories, probably because the Borgia Group codices were at the time considered the more elevated and better understood body of work. The scribes themselves, particularly those responsible for the Maya codices, were portrayed as passive participants in the production, use, and revision of the codical arts and the knowledge contained therein.

Recent strides in our ability to decode and date Maya and Mexican codices have revealed that these manuscripts contain highly complex calendrical, astronomical, and divinatory instruments. Our enhanced understanding of how these instruments were created, copied, and revised has also begun to narrow the focus of study to the scribes themselves as individual artists, innovators, and agents of change. A fruitful component in these investigations of late has been the comparative study of almanacs in the Madrid and Borgia Group codices pertaining to astronomical and seasonal phenomena, which have uncovered systematic calendrical and structural connections, in addition to further iconographic ties between the two traditions not previously noted.

In this chapter, we further this inquiry by expanding on recent studies of almanacs *in extenso* in the Madrid Codex (H. Bricker et al. 1997; Hatch 1975; Just 2000, 2004; Lacadena 2000; Milbrath 1999; Paxton 2001). We chose to focus specifically on the almanac on Madrid 12b–18b because its expanded calendrical register and layout have recently been compared to the introductory almanacs *in extenso* found in three codices of the Borgia Group (Just 2000, 2004). Bryan Just (2004: 263–264) concludes that the attributes shared by Madrid 12b–18b and the Borgia Group *in extensos* are evidence of a Maya scribe adopting the Mexican *in extenso* format to construct a similar instrument to facilitate concordances of data across almanacs within the Madrid screenfold. He explains the numerous errors in the almanac as incongruities caused by the scribe's need to reconcile differences between the Maya and the Mexican systems of counting and almanac construction.

We contend that the scribe who drafted Madrid 12b–18b deliberately structured the almanac and its calendrics in its present form and that what are perceived as discrepancies and errors by other scholars stem from a mistaken comparison to the calendrical structure of *in extenso* almanacs. Rather, we have demonstrated that a comparison to the structure of the tabular 260-day almanacs on Madrid 75–76 and Fejérváry-Mayer 1 can better explain the peculiarities of the calendrics and layout of Madrid 12b–18b. Our comparison of all three almanacs not only maintains the original proposal made by Just (2000, 2004) that the almanac on Madrid 12b–18b represents an instance of intellectual interchange between Maya and Mexican scribes, but suggests that if such communication took place, it did so among scribes of similar standing, training, and talent.

The growing body of evidence for scribal interaction from the comparative study of Maya and Mexican almanacs continues to raise more questions than answers as to how and when such interchange took place, but it is helping scholars ask more penetrating questions of the codices and better define the parameters of where to look for answers. Based on the results presented in this chapter, we agree with other scholars (Hernández and Bricker 2004; Just 2004) who elsewhere have proposed that Maya scribes had access to actual Mexican screenfolds that they could read and understand. If this were so, then from whom did they obtain such documents and where?

The level of sophistication evident in the connections between the Borgia

Group and the Madrid codices suggests the importance of looking more closely at the lives scribes led and the places and occasions where they may have been in contact with others in their trade. Diego de Landa (1978: 12–13) recounts that the "high priest" of Yucatán, the *Ahkin May*, was held in great reverence by the chiefs and given many gifts as well as offerings and contributions in return for his counsel and ritual services. The *Ahkin May* and his disciples trained sons of the elite and other talented youths in the arts, sciences, and ritual life required to become priests. When they were ready, the *Ahkin May* gave them books to use when ministering in provincial towns. Perhaps a Mexican codex fell into the hands of the *Ahkin May* as a gift from a chief who had obtained it through trade or elite exchange. The maritime trade along the coasts of Yucatán described by Andrews (ch. 12, this volume) and Robles (ch. 2, this volume) may have provided opportunities for Maya chiefs and their scribes to have contact with Mexican scribes who were either residents in foreign enclaves or attendants to foreign traders (Hernández and Bricker 2004: 315). Landa (1978: 13) notes that priests in the provinces painted codices, so it is likely that a priest-scribe living in a coastal province would have had more opportunities to come into direct contact with traders and foreign objects, like a Mexican codex. Provincial scribes also painted codices and may have been more likely than those residing in the larger centers to be innovative when producing their own manuscripts. Whatever the situation may have been, the growing body of evidence for cultural interchange that scholars are gleaning from the Madrid and Borgia Group codices presents a picture of a more sophisticated and innovative society than had previously been imagined for the Late Postclassic Maya of northern Yucatán.

Acknowledgments

The ideas presented in this chapter stem from research funded by grant RZ-50311-04 from the National Endowment for the Humanities, held from July 2004 to April 2007. Any views, findings, conclusions, or recommendations expressed in this chapter do not necessarily represent those of the National Endowment for the Humanities. We would like to thank Anthony F. Aveni, Victoria R. Bricker, and Merideth Paxton for their helpful comments made on an earlier version of this work presented as part of a working group session at the 2006 Annual Meeting of the Society for American Archaeology held in San Juan, Puerto Rico. The revised version presented here benefited from additional comments made by Elizabeth H. Boone, Bryan Just, and Alfonso Lacadena.

Notes

1. For a more extensive treatment, see Vail and Aveni (2004) and Boone (2003).

2. Lacadena's (2000: fig. 2.2) paleographic study of the Madrid Codex suggests that at least three scribes were responsible for the almanacs on pages 2–18. Scribe 1 painted pages 2–9; Scribe 2 painted pages 10–13 and the middle and lower registers of pages 14–18; and Scribe 3 painted the upper register of pages 14–18 and pages 19–26. See also note 4, this chapter.

3. Aveni (personal communication, 2006) has amended the dates in his Table 2 from the 1999 article. We derived the Mexican dates and their Gregorian correlates for Borgia 27 from Aveni's original starting date of 1 Reed 1 Crocodile corresponding to March 26, 1467 in the Julian calendar.

4. Based on Lacadena's (2000: fig. 2.2) analysis, only two Madrid scribes can be credited with the construction of almanacs *in extenso*: Scribe 2, for Madrid 12b–18b, and Scribe 6, for Madrid 65–72 and 73b, 75–76, and 77–78.

5. The final example on Madrid 77–78 is not a true *in extenso*, as it includes only the first 13 days (*trecena*) of the ritual calendar.

6. This page might be better interpreted as having characteristics of a circular almanac, a type that appears fairly commonly in the Madrid Codex. In circular almanacs, distance numbers and coefficients are scattered around the central image, which generally encompasses the whole of the physical space allotted to the almanac. In a more standard almanac, the black 13 should appear *before* the red 13.

7. See Vail and Hernández (2006) for a more comprehensive discussion of how the color scheme and iconography in the corner lobes of FM 1 align it with Borgia 27.

8. See the discussion of the 4 × 13-year structure of Madrid 75–76 and Vail's (2002, 2004) suggestion that distance numbers in standard Maya almanacs may refer to a count of *haab's* rather than—or in addition to—days.

9. For a different interpretation of this iconography, see Paxton (2001: 41) and ch. 9, this volume.

10. It is important to note that we believe almanacs could contain a number of embedded calendrical cycles that were used for different purposes (i.e., not necessarily concurrently).

11. The scribe drew an Eb' glyph in place of Kab'an, apparently having transposed Eb' (associated with the right or south) with Kab'an (associated with the east and top). There are various other deviations from the order expected when reading these days as representing a 20 × 13-day almanac, as discussed in ch. 10.

References Cited

Aveni, Anthony F.
   1999   Astronomy in the Mexican Codex Borgia. *Archaeoastronomy* (Supplement to *Journal for the History of Astronomy*) 24: S1–S20.
   2001   *Skywatchers*. Rev. ed. University of Texas Press, Austin.
   2004   Intervallic Structure and Cognate Almanacs in the Madrid and Dresden Codices. In *The Madrid Codex: New Approaches to Understanding an Ancient Maya Manuscript* (Gabrielle Vail and Anthony Aveni, eds.): 147–170. University Press of Colorado, Boulder.

Aveni, Anthony F., Steven J. Morandi, and Polly A. Peterson

    1996   The Maya Number of Time: Intervalic Time Reckoning in the Maya Codices, Part II. *Archaeoastronomy* (Supplement to *Journal for the History of Astronomy*) 21: S1–S32.

Boone, Elizabeth H.

    2003   A Web of Understanding: Pictorial Codices and the Shared Intellectual Culture of Late Postclassic Mesoamerica. In *The Postclassic Mesoamerican World* (Michael E. Smith and Frances F. Berdan, eds.): 207–221. University of Utah Press, Salt Lake City.

Boone, Elizabeth H., and Michael E. Smith

    2003   Postclassic International Styles and Symbol Sets. In *The Postclassic Mesoamerican World* (Michael E. Smith and Frances F. Berdan, eds.): 186–193. University of Utah Press, Salt Lake City.

Bricker, Harvey M., and Victoria R. Bricker

    1983   Classic Maya Prediction of Solar Eclipses. *Current Anthropology* 24:1–23.

    1992   Zodiacal References in the Maya Codices. In *The Sky in Mayan Literature* (Anthony F. Aveni, ed.): 148–183. Oxford University Press, New York.

Bricker, Harvey M., Victoria R. Bricker, and Bettina Wulfing

    1997   Determining the Historicity of Three Astronomical Almanacs in the Madrid Codex. *Archaeoastronomy* (Supplement to the *Journal for the History of Astronomy*) 22: S17–S36.

Bricker, Victoria R.

    2001   A Method for Dating Venus Almanacs in the Borgia Codex. *Archaeoastronomy* (Supplement to the *Journal for the History of Astronomy*) 26: S21–S44.

Bricker, Victoria R., and Harvey M. Bricker

    1986   The Mars Table in the Dresden Codex. In *Research and Reflections in Archaeology and History: Essays in Honor of Doris Stone* (E. Wyllys Andrews V, ed.): 51–80. Middle American Research Institute Publication 57. Tulane University, New Orleans.

    1988   The Seasonal Table in the Dresden Codex and Related Almanacs. *Archaeoastronomy* (Supplement to the *Journal for the History of Astronomy*) 12: S1–S62.

    1992   A Method for Cross-Dating Almanacs with Tables in the Dresden Codex. In *The Sky in Mayan Literature* (Anthony F. Aveni, ed.): 43–86. Oxford University Press, New York.

Carlson, John B.

    1983a   The Grolier Codex: A Preliminary Report on the Content and Authenticity of a Thirteenth-Century Maya Venus Almanac. In *Calendars in Mesoamerica and Peru: Native American Computations of Time* (Anthony F. Aveni and Gordon Brotherston, eds.): 27–57. BAR International Series 174. Oxford, England.

    1983b   Venus-Regulated Warfare and Ritual Sacrifice in Mesoamerica. In *Astronomies and Cultures* (Clive L. Ruggles and Nicholas J. Saunders, eds.): 202–252. University of Colorado Press, Niwot.

Caso, Alfonso

    1971   Calendrical Systems of Central Mexico. In *Handbook of Middle American Indians*, Vol. 10, pt. 1 (Gordon F. Ekholm and Ignacio Bernal, eds.): 333–348. University of Texas Press, Austin.

Codex Borgia

    1976   *Codex Borgia*. Biblioteca Apostólica Vaticana (Messicano Riserva 28). Codices e Vaticanis Selecti, vol. 34. Akademische Druck- und Verlagsanstalt, Graz, Austria.

Codex Fejérváry-Mayer

    1994   *Codex Fejérváry-Mayer*. Sociedad Estatal Quinto Centenario, Madrid; Akademische Druck- und Verlagsanstalt, Graz, Austria; and Fondo de Cultura Económica, México, D.F.

Codex Tro-Cortesianus

    1967   *Codex Tro-Cortesianus (Codex Madrid): Museo de América Madrid* (mit Einleitung und Summary von Ferdinand Anders). Codices Selecti, vol. 8. Akademische Druck- und Verlagsanstalt, Graz, Austria.

Codex Vaticanus B

    1993   *Codex Vaticanus B. (3773)*. Sociedad Estatal Quinto Centenario, Madrid; Akademische Druck- und Verlagsanstalt, Graz, Austria; and Fondo de Cultura Económica, México, D.F.

Drapkin, Julia

    n.d.   Interpreting the Dialect of Time: A Structural Analysis and Discussion of Almanacs in the Madrid Codex. Honors thesis, Department of Anthropology, Tulane University, 2002.

Förstemann, Ernst

    1880   *Die Maya Handschrift der Königlichen öffentlichen Bibliothek zu Dresden*. Mit 74 Tafeln in Chromo-Lightdruck. Verlag der A. Naumannschen Lichtdruckeret, Leipzig, Germany.

    1902   *Commentar zur Madrider Mayahandscrift: Codex Tro-Cortesianus*. Verlag von L. Sauniers Buchandlung, Danzig.

Hatch, Marion P.

    1975   An Astronomical Calendar in a Portion of the Madrid Codex. In *Archaeoastronomy in Pre-Columbian America* (Anthony F. Aveni, ed.): 283–340. University of Texas Press, Austin.

Hernández, Christine

    2004   "Yearbearer Pages" and Their Connection to Planting Almanacs in the Borgia Codex. In *The Madrid Codex: New Approaches to Understanding an Ancient Maya Manuscript* (Gabrielle Vail and Anthony Aveni, eds.): 321–364. University Press of Colorado, Boulder.

    2006a The Fortunes for Planting Maize in the *Codex Borgia*. *Ancient America* 8:1–35.

    2006b Using Astronomical Imagery to Cross-Date an Almanac in the Borgia Codex. Special issue, *Human Mosaic* 36 (1): 125–143.

Hernández, Christine, and Victoria R. Bricker

2004   The Inauguration of Planting in the Borgia and Madrid Codices. In *The Madrid Codex: New Approaches to Understanding an Ancient Maya Manuscript* (Gabrielle Vail and Anthony Aveni, eds.): 277–320. University Press of Colorado, Boulder.

Just, Bryan R.

2000   Concordances of Time: *In Extenso* Almanacs in the Madrid and Borgia Group Codices. *Human Mosaic* 33 (1): 7–16.

2004   *In Extenso* Almanacs in the Madrid Codex. In *The Madrid Codex: New Approaches to Understanding an Ancient Maya Manuscript* (Gabrielle Vail and Anthony Aveni, eds.): 255–276. University Press of Colorado, Boulder.

Lacadena, Alfonso

1997   Bilingüismo en el códice de Madrid. In *Los investigadores de la cultura maya* 5: 184–204.

2000   Los escribas del códice de Madrid: Metodología paleográfica. *Revista española de antropología americana* 30: 27–85. Madrid.

Landa, Diego de

1978 [1937]   *Yucatan Before and After the Conquest* (William Gates, trans.). Dover, New York. [Originally published by the Maya Society, Baltimore.]

Masson, Marilyn A.

2003   The Late Postclassic Symbol Set in the Maya Area. In *The Postclassic Mesoamerican World* (Michael E. Smith and Frances F. Berdan, eds.): 194–200. University of Utah Press, Salt Lake City.

Milbrath, Susan

1999   *Star Gods of the Maya: Astronomy in Art, Folklore, and Calendars.* University of Texas Press, Austin.

Nowotny, Karl Anton

2005 [1961]   *Tlacuilolli: Style and Contents of the Mexican Pictorial Manuscripts with a Catalog of the Borgia Group* (George A. Everett, Jr. and Edward B. Sisson, trans. and eds.). University of Oklahoma Press, Norman.

Paxton, Merideth

2001   *The Cosmos of the Yucatec Maya: Cycles and Steps from the Madrid Codex.* University of New Mexico Press, Albuquerque.

Seler, Eduard

1904   Venus Period in the Picture Writings of the Borgian Codex Group. In *Bureau of American Ethnology Bulletin* 28: 355–391. Washington, D.C.

1963   *Comentarios al Códice Borgia.* 3 vols. (Mariana Frenk, trans.). Fondo de Cultura Económica, México, D.F.

1990   Parallels in the Maya Manuscripts. In *Collected Works in Mesoamerican Linguistics and Archaeology: English Translations of German Papers from Gesammelte Abhandlungen zur amerikanischen Sprach- und Alterhumskunde,* vol. 4 (Frank E. Comparato, ed.): 338–345. Labyrinthos, Culver City, Calif. [Originally published in *Globus,* 1906.]

Taube, Karl A.

1992   *The Major Gods of Ancient Yucatan.* Studies in Pre-Columbian Art and
Archaeology 32. Dumbarton Oaks Research Library and Collection,
Washington, D.C.

Taube, Karl A., and Bonnie L. Bade

1991   *An Appearance of Xiuhtecuhtli in the Dresden Venus Pages.* Research
Reports on Ancient Maya Writing 35. Center for Maya Research,
Washington, D.C.

Thomas, Cyrus

1884   Notes on Certain Maya and Mexican Manuscripts. In *Third Annual
Report of the Bureau of American Ethnology, 1881–82:* 7–65. Smithsonian
Institution, Washington, D.C.

Thompson, J. Eric S.

1934   *Sky Bearers, Colors and Directions in Maya and Mexican Religion.*
Contributions to American Archaeology 2 (10). Carnegie Institution of
Washington Publication 436. Washington, D.C.

1971 [1950]   *Maya Hieroglyphic Writing: An Introduction.* University of Oklahoma
Press, Norman. [Reproduced from the first edition published by the
Carnegie Institution of Washington.]

1972   *A Commentary on the Dresden Codex: A Maya Hieroglyphic Book.* Memoirs
of the American Philosophical Society 93. Philadelphia.

Vail, Gabrielle

1997   The Yearbearer Gods in the *Madrid Codex.* In *Códices y documentos sobre
México: Segundo simposio,* vol. 1 (Salvador Rueda Smithers, Constanza
Vega Sosa, and Rodrigo Martínez Baracs, eds.): 81–106. Instituto Nacional
de Antropología e Historia and Dirección General de Publicaciones del
Consejo Nacional para la Cultura y las Artes, México, D.F.

2000   Issues of Language and Ethnicity in the Postclassic Maya Codices. In
Language and Dialect Variation in the Maya Hieroglyphic Script (Gabrielle
Vail and Martha J. Macri, eds.). Special Issue of *Written Language and
Literacy* 3 (1): 37–75.

2002   Haab' *Rituals in the Maya Codices and the Structure of Maya Almanacs.*
Research Reports on Ancient Maya Writing 53. Center for Maya Research,
Washington, D.C.

2004   A Reinterpretation of *Tzolk'in* Almanacs in the Madrid Codex. In *The
Madrid Codex: New Approaches to Understanding an Ancient Maya
Manuscript* (Gabrielle Vail and Anthony Aveni, eds.): 215–252. University
Press of Colorado, Boulder.

2006   The Maya Codices. *Annual Review of Anthropology* 35: 497–519.

n.d.a   4 Ahaw Dates and Maya Creation Cosmology. Paper presented at the
Department of Anthropology, University of South Florida, Tampa,
February 2006.

n.d.b   Los sistemas calendáricos mayas del posclásico tardío del año nuevo.
Paper presented at the Segundo Congreso Internacional de Cultura Maya,
Mérida, March 2005.

n.d.c   Scribal Hands and Language Use in the Madrid Codex. Paper presented
at the working group "Current Research on the Madrid Codex: Issues of
Provenience and Dating" at Tulane University, June 2001.

Vail, Gabrielle, and Anthony Aveni (eds.)

    2004   *The Madrid Codex: New Approaches to Understanding an Ancient Maya Manuscript*. University Press of Colorado, Boulder.

Vail, Gabrielle, and Christine Hernández

    2005   The Maya Hieroglyphic Codices, Version 2.0. Website and database available at www.mayacodices.org.

    2006   Fire Drilling, Bloodletting, and Sacrifice: Yearbearer Rituals in the Maya and Borgia Group Codices. In *Sacred Books, Sacred Languages: Two Thousand Years of Ritual and Religious Maya Literature*; *Proceedings of the 8th European Maya Conference, November 25–30, 2003* (Rogelio Valencia and Geneviève Le Fort, eds.): 65–79. Verlag Anton Saurwein, Markt Schwaben, Germany.

    n.d.   *Deities, Rituals, and Calendrical Cycles: A Comparative Analysis of Almanacs in the Maya and Borgia Group Codices*. Ms. in preparation.

Wald, Robert F.

    2004   The Languages of the Dresden Codex: Legacy of the Classic Maya. In *The Linguistics of Maya Writing* (Søren Wichmann, ed.): 27–58. University of Utah Press, Salt Lake City.

Whittaker, Gordon

    1986   The Mexican Names of Three Venus Gods in the Dresden Codex. *Mexicon* 8: 56–60.

Part IV

Commentaries

Chapter Twelve

Travelers in the Night

A Discussion of the Archaeological Visibility of
Trade Enclaves, Ethnicity, and Ideology

Anthony P. Andrews

Caminante, no hay camino, sino estelas en la mar.

Traveler, there is no trail, only wakes in the sea.

—Antonio Machado, *Campos de Castilla* (1907–1917)

As MY COLLEAGUES in iconography and epigraphy gave their erudite presentations on the scribal evidence for interaction between central Mexico and the northern Maya lowlands at the fall 2006 symposium, I couldn't repress an occasional pang of jealousy at their images of maps and almanacs full of little footprints wandering all over the documents, inevitably leading them from one insight to the next. Why don't we find little footprints like that in the archaeological record? The fact is, we do have such footprints, but they are small, and few and far between. The physical footprint left by travelers and traders in ancient Mesoamerica is indeed small, and tracking the wanderings and activities of these individuals is a daunting challenge. Still, the chapters in this volume have made significant progress in exploring this subject, and following are some comments on the state of the current research in the archaeology relevant to the topic.

A major issue in the subject of interaction is how one goes about identifying it in the archaeological record, and how we interpret it. In this case, we are dealing primarily with the archaeological record in the Maya lowlands because there are few known traces, if any, of a Maya physical or cultural presence in Postclassic central Mexico (or Oaxaca).[1] In examining the material culture evidence from Yucatán, it is often not clear if we are dealing with the traces of commercial activities; shared ideological themes; or more ambivalent stylistic influence or mimicry, diffusion, or an outright foreign presence, as exemplified by unequivocal artifactual, architectural, and/or osteological evidence. In most instances, much of the archaeological evidence in Mesoamerica is equivocal. Some of the most compelling indications of an actual foreign presence are found, ironically, in sites of earlier periods, such as Teotihuacan (the Oaxacan and Merchants' barrios and their contents), Tikal (Teotihuacan architecture and stylistic influences in the sculpture and ceramics, central Mexican obsidian, all reinforced by epigraphic evidence), and Chichén Itzá (heavy architectural, sculptural, and artifactual evidence, reinforced by semihistorical texts). In the Postclassic period we also have linguistic data, native manuscripts and chronicles, and Spanish historical records, which may reinforce—or in some cases confuse—the archaeological picture.

An important central concern in defining the nature of interaction is the issue of the meaning of the word *style*, an ambiguous catch-all term that can mean anything from vague artistic mimicry to the actual presence of foreign artisans. As Marilyn Masson and Carlos Peraza have pointed out in chapter 3, style may spread and/or be filtered through varying routes and mechanisms and may have very different meanings in foreign contexts. Identifying the manner and significance of its diffusion will always be a risky endeavor in studies of cultural interaction.

Historical Background and Chronology

Fernando Robles (ch. 2) sets forth an updated historical foundation for the volume in time and space. Using native chronicles and archaeological data, Robles documents the early phase of the Postclassic in central Mexico and Yucatán and the establishment of an extensive mosaic of small polities following the collapse of Tula, and in the case of Yucatán, the decline of Chichén Itzá and the emergence of Mayapán. In central Mexico, he emphasizes the economic importance of Coaixtlahuacan, a strategic trading node and market city located at a major crossroads on the northern edge of the Mixteca Alta, at a key juncture of the Valley of Puebla, the Valley of Oaxaca, and Tuxtepec, gateway to southern Veracruz and the Gulf Coast. The trade networks and outposts spreading from Coaixtlahuacan extended into Oaxaca and beyond. On the lower Gulf Coast, they connected to other networks, which reached into every corner of the Maya world, as far as Cozumel and the coastal settlements of the Caribbean, and Nito on the Gulf of Honduras. Unfortunately, as he notes, early Postclassic Coaixtlahuacan was razed by the Aztecs, so we know little of the pre-Mexica emporium, over which the Aztecs built their own garrison and market town.

In Yucatán, the early development of Mayapán was no doubt linked to these trade networks, as attested to by both historic and archaeological evidence, which both Robles (in ch. 2, this volume) and Masson and Peraza (in ch. 3, this volume) discuss at length. Of particular note are the fine paste ceramics from the Gulf Coast—accompanied by historic references to ties between elites in Yucatán and Tabasco and iconographic elements in the murals and on the ceramics that reflect central Mexican influences in the Maya capital. Much of this follows on the tracks of earlier, post-Teotihuacan waves of central Mexican influence that began in the Terminal Classic period and are evident in the art and architecture of Chichén Itzá and the east coast.

Recent research on chronological issues in the historical and archaeological records of Mexico and Yucatán have brought these areas into closer alignment with one another. As Robles notes, the fall of Tula in 1064 CE is contemporaneous with the political decline and severe depopulation of Chichén Itzá, now believed by many to have taken place sometime in the eleventh century. This new chronological alignment would appear to indicate that Tula and Chichén Itzá reached their apogees and suffered their respective political declines during the Terminal Classic or Epiclassic period, which ended toward the middle of the eleventh century. If this is the case, then there is little basis for the "Early Postclassic" period, which has traditionally been dated from 900 to 1200 CE, because this period is anchored to the chronology of the sites mentioned earlier. Thus, as Robles argues, what used to be called the "Late Postclassic"—and what we now prefer to call the "Postclassic" period—in Mesoamerica begins after the fall of these two cities.[2]

This new "Postclassic" was by no means a monolithic horizon, and developments during the period varied from place to place. In central Mexico, the fallen Toltec capital was quickly replaced by a mosaic of competing city-states, both old and new. These polities were in turn absorbed by the expanding Mexica state, which originated in the fourteenth century and eventually established imperial rule over most of western Mesoamerica. In Yucatán, the collapse of the Itzá state in the eleventh century was followed by a political vacuum in the north and west, which was gradually replaced by the emerging power of the Cocom rulers of Mayapán sometime after 1100 CE, until its decline in the fifteenth century. To the east there was a renaissance of sorts along the Caribbean and adjoining inland regions, from northern Quintana Roo to Belize, where a number of small polities survived until the arrival of the Spanish.

The surge of development that we see along the east coast of Quintana Roo during the early part of the Postclassic period was also likely linked to the central Mexican trade florescence, as reflected in the presence of fine paste ceramics and the spread of central Mexican architectural and artistic motifs. Despite the wealth of archaeological remains in this region, we still know next to nothing about its history or its political structure before the conquest. Much remains to be worked out in this area. For example, we have yet to ascertain the exact location of the ancient Postclassic capital of Chetumal. Grant Jones and Anthony Andrews have long argued that Pre-Hispanic Chetumal was most likely located in the metropolitan cluster of sites around Ichpaatún, Tamalcab, and Oxtancah (Andrews and Jones 2001: 27–28; Jones 1989: 280–281, 337), but this has yet to be confirmed by archaeological research.

Another confusing issue is the history and configuration of the Postclassic "province" of Ecab. This territory, which purportedly encompassed much of northern Quintana Roo, was originally thought to be made up of a loose confederation of allied towns, from Conil in the north to Tulúm in the south (Roys 1957). Tsubasa Okoshi (1994) has argued that Ecab's status as a Postclassic province is a fiction created by colonial historians, as there is no mention of a political entity of that name in the native chronicles. However, Nikolai Grube and colleagues (2003) have more recently proposed that the emblem glyph of Cobá can be read as "Ek'-Hab-Ho," suggesting that this may be the name for the kingdom or domain of the Classic period city (see also Lacadena 2003). Whether this territorial designation survived into the Postclassic period is not clear. Did the last rulers of Cobá migrate to northern Quintana Roo and retain the name of their ancient kingdom for a diminished Postclassic province? Or did the Postclassic rulers of this region lay claim to the name of the ancient kingdom of Cobá to legitimize their own authority? Needless to say, this is a complex issue that can be resolved only through further historical and archaeological research. Still, at the time of the conquest, the port of Ecab was a major node in the maritime trading route that linked central Mexico to the network of towns and cities along the Caribbean coast.[3]

In sum, as Robles makes clear, much of the infrastructure for trade, travel, and the diffusion of ideas and social contacts, and possibly the intricacies of more subtle diplomatic networking, was solidly in place from the early stages of the Postclassic. In fact, the arguments advanced by Robles, Robertson (1970), Ringle et al. (1998), and others suggest that a Mesoamerican "cosmopolitan network" was in place from the Terminal Classic onward.

However that may be, it is clear that once the Mexican expansion began and the Aztecs consolidated their control over central Mexico and the Coaixtlahuacan trade networks, their access to the infrastructure beyond was a given. They did not need to do much to gain access to lowland Maya goods or to Maya political circles. All indications are that they had access to both. However, they did not have the time or the means to establish any kind of substantial physical presence before the Spanish arrived—or at least any kind of presence that has been identified in the archaeological or historical record. The process of Mexica expansion into the Maya area had begun: they had control of the Soconusco coast, trading outposts and possible garrisons on the Tabasco/southern Campeche coast, spies in the market at Zinacantán, and who knows what they were doing in the highlands of Guatemala (see Robles 2007 for details). As Robles notes, several scholars have wondered whether Tulúm was an Aztec outpost (e.g., Miller 1982: 75). One might also have similar thoughts about Ichpaatún and Nito, even though there is no concrete evidence to support any of these speculations. The final years before the conquest are a blur, and the events are lost to us; we see only fragments, like the whirling bits in a kaleidoscope.

Mayapán

Masson and Peraza make an important and historical chronological clarification at the beginning of Chapter 3, noting that any contacts between Mayapán and central Mexico would have preceded the imperial military expansion of the Mexica into southeastern Mesoamerica. As Robles has repeatedly pointed out over the years, and reiterates in this volume, the idea of an "Aztec"—that is, imperial Mexica—presence in Yucatán is out of the question, given that Mexica expansion began after 1450 CE, at about the same time as the abandonment of Mayapán, which is generally dated to between 1440 and 1460 CE. Moreover, direct Aztec influence in the Maya lowlands was probably not felt until around 1500 CE or thereafter, when Ahuitzotl and/or Moctezuma Xocoyotzin established trading centers, and possibly garrisons, at Cimatán and Xicalango. While this may be obvious to most Mesoamerican scholars, one still occasionally sees references to Aztec warriors at Mayapán or imminent Mexica invasions of the peninsula linked to Mayapán, based on a single confusing statement in Landa, who talks about Mexicans, but not Aztecs, at Mayapán (see Introduction to Part I, this volume).

To the best of my knowledge, we have yet to recover any evidence of an actual Postclassic Mexican physical presence on the peninsula proper—that is, in the area north of a line drawn between the Laguna de Términos and southern Belize—much less evidence of any kind of foreign enclave.

The recovery of traces of foreign ethnicity in the archaeological record is a daunting challenge. While the discovery of the Oaxacan Barrio at Teotihuacan is often held up as the gold standard for the identification of foreign ethnic groups at Mesoamerican sites, it bears keeping in mind that the Oaxacan Barrio is unique in the Pre-Hispanic archaeological world, and there may not be many places like it.[4]

Masson and Peraza's use of multiple lines of evidence, per the model developed by Santley et al. (1987), to identify potential foreign ethnic enclaves at archaeological sites is most appropriate for Mayapán, and they have covered all the bases. Most of their colleagues would agree with their interpretation of the data at hand—namely, that there is clear evidence of sustained cultural contact with central Mexico, but the physical evidence of actual groups of foreigners at the site is tenuous at best.

So far, we do not have a barrio *chilango*,[5] with folks wearing serapes and eating mole and salsa verde. Masson and Peraza's discussion of foodways is quite intriguing, but still, no cigar. However, a future line of research involves DNA studies, which might enable us to identify foreign populations at the city. In fact, short of actually finding a Oaxaca-type barrio in future excavations, DNA, strontium isotope studies, and other bio-osteological research may be the most promising future venues of documenting the presence of foreigners at Mayapán or other Postclassic Maya cities.[6]

In conclusion, one could argue that we have excavated only a small percentage of Mayapán and that with time a Mexican barrio might yet appear. Witness all the years of excavations and surface collecting at Edzná—by Alberto Ruz, Raul Pavón, Cesar Sáenz, Hector Gálvez, Román Piña Chan and his students, and Ray Matheny—before Luis Millet finally encountered a Postclassic neighborhood near the center of the site. Before that discovery, Edzná was thought to have been abandoned at the end of the Classic period.

On the other hand, maybe there is no Mexican barrio at Mayapán. Which does not mean that there were no Mexican merchants or dignitaries dispersed about the city. As Masson and Peraza note, there are subtle hints in the ideological dimension of the material culture. For example, the large volume of figurines in the city, even while not including any imported items, does not appear to be a Maya trait, whereas figurines are very common at Mexican sites. Eric Thompson's (1957: 621) suggestion that the Mexican effigy censers may reflect connections between central Mexican and local elite families is a very insightful observation. And such connections did not exist in a vacuum—obviously, individuals traveled back and forth between central Mexico and Yucatán to forge those ties. There may be a parallel with the kind of situation that Karl Taube (2003: 311–312) has suggested for the Merchants' Barrio at Teotihuacan: he has proposed that the elite Maya ceramics found there suggest not that it is a Maya barrio but that Maya elites were present in the Mexican capital. In similar fashion, it is quite likely that Mexican merchants, artisans, and dignitaries passed through Mayapán, and perhaps other Postclassic Maya cities, and even spent time in those communities without having special enclaves or barrios. Without the enclaves, they would not leave a large footprint in the archaeological record.

Archaeoastronomy

Aveni (ch. 4) summarizes the pertinent data from the codices and makes a strong case that there is indisputable evidence of (1) continuity of astronomical observation and recording in the Postclassic period and (2) transmission of certain kinds of astronomical information between central Mexico and the Maya area. He is then able to corroborate some of these patterns in the architecture, particularly at Mayapán. A strong dimension of this argument is the documentation of similar architectural alignments at Postclassic sites in the Mexican highlands and northern Yucatán.

Although it is not directly related to the Postclassic focus of this volume, it is intriguing that some of the cosmological components listed by Wendy Ashmore (1989, 1991) and cited by Aveni are found not only in some of the northern Postclassic Maya sites but in many of the large- and medium-size Middle Preclassic sites we have recently located in a survey of northwest Yucatán—especially the north-south axial alignment and the ballcourts. This would suggest that these cosmological components have deep roots in the layout of Maya settlements and have survived for more than 1,500 years.

Another very intriguing aspect of Aveni's chapter is the observation that Postclassic Yucatec architectural planning appears to reflect a primary concern with a 260-day calendar, summer solstices, and a possible solar alignment system. The solar alignments of the Mayapán observatory and the solar disks represented on the murals of Structure Q161 reinforce this notion and, as Aveni suggests, are substantive evidence of a solar cult at Mayapán. Does this shift to solar alignments and themes reflect a change in the view of the cosmos, or in how the Yucatec priests perceived the workings of the environment, or in their understanding of climatic change? After all, they must have understood that the great Classic culture of their ancestors came to an end, in large part owing to changes in the environment (Gill et al. 2007; Hodell et al. 2007; Yaeger and Hoddell 2009). The sun was likely seen as a major force behind the Late and Terminal Classic period droughts and thus needed to be acknowledged and placated to prevent future disasters. As the evidence indicates, the Postclassic Maya worldview of the cosmos had shifted, and this was no doubt owing to an awareness of changes that had taken place in the world around them.

Aveni's observations are based largely on the codices and the architecture of Mayapán. His suggestions could be reinforced by data from other sites. We still do not have a detailed plan of the observatory at Paamul, and there are other curious structures at Xcaret and Cozumel that need to be carefully measured. And we have yet to find a Postclassic ballcourt in the northern lowlands. With one possible exception,[7] they are absent from Postclassic sites throughout the lowlands but not uncommon in the highlands of central Mexico and Guatemala. Perhaps a closer examination of the astronomical alignments of Tulúm and Topoxte might also be of interest. However, the Postclassic architectural corpus is small, owing to the fact that most of it was absorbed into colonial construction, and we have forever lost a significant portion of it. As the work of Carlos Peraza at Mayapán has demonstrated, it is crucial that we preserve as much of the Postclassic architectural heritage as we can. A very fruitful region in this respect is the east coast of Yucatán, where many Late Postclassic sites are still relatively well preserved but threatened by ongoing development.

Aveni's chapter offers insightful new ideas on Postclassic astronomy and provides solid ground for the argument that the Maya and central Mexicans were truly fellow travelers in the night.

General Comments

Our understanding of the overall nature of interaction between central Mexico and the northern Maya lowlands in the Postclassic period is still at an early stage. Most scholars would not find this surprising, given the nature of the evidence. A limited number of native manuscripts; a slightly larger, but contradictory and confusing, corpus of contact period documents; and an extremely small archaeological sample, mostly from one site (and less than about 3 percent of that site) make up the bulk of the evidence presented in this volume. Most would agree that our strongest, and at the same time, most suspect evidence is historical. But the archaeological situation is not much better. There are scores of Postclassic archaeological sites in the lowlands that have yet to be explored and mapped, and the vast majority must still be tested. Even sites that have seen a fair amount of work, including architectural consolidation, have not yet seen systematic large-scale stratigraphic excavations. Tulúm is a good example. Simple statistics will inform anyone that this is not a satisfactory situation.

One would think that, given the historic evidence of commercial relations between the two areas, there would be more trade goods in the archaeological record, when in fact there are almost none. As Masson and Peraza explain, this is in large part owing to the fact that many of the items exchanged were perishable goods, such as cotton, textiles, dyes, cacao, salt, spices, pelts, and feathers. Moreover, most of the signature long-distance trade goods—ceramics and obsidian—found at Mayapán and other Postclassic Maya sites come from the Gulf Coast (Fine Orange ceramics) or from Guatemala (obsidian). Beyond a minimal amount of Mexican obsidian at Mayapán—less than 1 percent—and similar amounts from other Postclassic sites in the Maya lowlands, there is almost no physical evidence of trade with central Mexico at lowland Maya communities during this period.

In the same vein, we might ask why Maya architectural traits, iconographic motifs, or artifacts have not been reported in Postclassic Mexico. In earlier periods, we have evidence of a Maya presence or influence in Teotihuacan, Xochicalco, and Cacaxtla, but not later. Other than certain localities in and near Mexico City, such as the Templo Mayor, Tenayuca, and Malinalco, few Postclassic sites in central Mexico have been excavated in an intensive or extensive manner. Much is probably buried under Mexico City and is unlikely to be recovered. However, it is not difficult to imagine Postclassic Maya dignitaries, merchants, diplomats, and travelers visiting Mexican cities, as their ancestors did in earlier periods. In the 1960s, several Yucatecan friends and I traveled a few times to Mexico City and stayed at the homes of their relatives. These were invariably in or near the Colonia del Valle, where a large number of Yucatecans lived. There were even Yucatecan restaurants, serving up *cochinita*, *panuchos*, *salbutes*, and other regional dishes. In later years I often thought of the similarity of this neighborhood to the much older Merchants' Barrio at Teotihuacan. I find it difficult to believe that there was not such a barrio in Tenochtitlan.

One can only wonder what sort of evidence the modern Yucatecan residents of the Colonia del Valle would leave in the archaeological record of the future. Many of the items that come to mind—clothing, documents, photographs, books, state flags, and coats of arms—are all perishable. Nonperishable items, such as crafted souvenir items, audiovisual records (LPs, CDs, and DVDs), and bottles of Yucatecan beer and liqueurs (such as *Xtabentún*) could be construed as trade items. Needless to say, Yucatecan food would likely not survive, although traces of *recado rojo* (annatto) might survive in the ceramics.

The past and present work at Postclassic Mesoamerican sites has much to offer on the subject of Maya-Mexican interaction, but there is much more to be had. We still need to work on further integrating the political history of the lowlands with that of the highlands, and it is evident that many sites out there still await archaeological investigation. It is interesting, after all these years, that we do not have definite agreement on the exact location of three of the major Postclassic trading nodes—Xicalango, Chetumal, and Nito. Finally, a neat set of ideas to come out of this symposium was the contribution that astronomy was able to make to the subject of Maya-Mexican Postclassic interaction, both through architectural alignments and the codices and the mutual grounds found in both data sets.

In the past, what we knew about Mexican-Yucatec interaction was based primarily on historical documents written around the time of the conquest and on limited archaeological and iconographic evidence (architectural details, iconographic details in mural paintings). The present volume offers a new multidisciplinary approach to the subject. It combines a variety of different approaches, data, and materials: archaeological (architecture, ceramics, artifacts), epigraphic (glyphs in codices), historic (documents, codices), art historic (iconography of codices, mural paintings), linguistic (historical linguistics), and astronomical. This combination has yielded more insight into the subtle relationships among trade, material culture, and ideas, which have in turn provided us with more robust historical, economic, artistic, and ideological linkages between the two regions. Taken together, the chapters in this volume are a fine example of multidisciplinary research and of the results it can produce.

Notes

1. Unless otherwise specified, references to central Mexico will include not only the central basin but the highland areas of Oaxaca as well.

2. New data in both central Mexico and Yucatán support this scenario. Much of the new data in central Mexico are reported in the papers in volume 7 of *Ancient Mesoamerica*, compiled and edited by William Fowler (1996), and are reinforced by recently obtained unpublished radiocarbon dates from Tula (Patricia Fournier, personal communication to Fernando Robles, 2006; see also Introduction to Part I, n. 1, this volume). For recent revisions and discussions of the Yucatecan chronology, see the papers compiled and edited by Traci Ardren and William Fowler (1998) in volume 9 of *Ancient Mesoamerica* as well as Anthony Andrews et al. (2003), Rafael Cobos (1997, 1998), William Ringle et al. (1998), and Peter Schmidt (1998). Of special relevance is a series of new radiocarbon dates from Mayapán that indicate an earlier date for the emergence of the Cocom capital (Peraza et al. 2006; see Masson and Peraza, ch. 3, and Robles, ch. 2, this volume).

3. For descriptions of the colonial remains of Ecab and its history, see Benavides and Andrews (1979) and Andrews et al. (2006).

4. One such enclave may be the sector of Tikal known as the "Mundo Perdido" group, which may have been the residence of emissaries and/or merchants from Teotihuacan and/or elsewhere in the Early Classic period, although this has yet to be verified (cf. Laporte 2003; Martin 2003; Stuart 2000).

5. *Chilango* is a Mexican slang term denoting a person from or living in Mexico City or its environs.

6. In fact, such studies are under way at Mayapán (Marilyn Masson, personal communication, April 2006). For a discussion of a recent application of strontium isotope data to the identification of foreign versus local populations and a negative example from Tikal, see Lori Wright (2005).

7. One possible ballcourt occurs at the site of Laguna de On in northern Belize (Masson 2000: 99–100). To the best of my knowledge, this structure is the only known ballcourt in the Postclassic Maya lowlands.

References Cited

Andrews, Anthony P., E. Wyllys Andrews V, and Fernando Robles Castellanos
    2003   The Northern Maya Collapse and Its Aftermath. *Ancient Mesoamerica* 14: 151–156.

Andrews, Anthony P., Antonio Benavides Castillo, and Grant D. Jones
    2006   Ecab: A Remote Encomienda of Early Colonial Yucatan. In *Reconstructing the Past: Studies in Mesoamerican and Central American Prehistory* (David M. Pendergast and Anthony P. Andrews, eds.): 5–32. British Archaeological Reports International Series S1529. Oxford, England.

Andrews, Anthony P., and Grant D. Jones
    2001   Asentamientos coloniales en la costa de Quintana Roo. *Temas antropológicos* 23 (1): 20–35.

Ardren, Traci, and William Fowler (eds.)
  1998   Recent Chronological Research in Northern Yucatan. *Ancient Mesoamerica*
          9 (1): 99–182.

Ashmore, Wendy
  1989   Construction and Cosmology: Politics and Ideology in Lowland Maya
          Settlement Patterns. In *Word and Image in Maya Culture: Explorations
          in Language, Writing and Representation* (William Hanks and Don Rice,
          eds.): 272–286. University of Utah Press, Salt Lake City.
  1991   Site Planning Principles and Concepts of Directionality among the Ancient
          Maya. *Latin American Antiquity* 2: 199–226.

Benavides Castillo, Antonio, and Anthony P. Andrews
  1979   *Ecab: Poblado y provincia del siglo XVI en Yucatán.* Centro Regional del
          Sureste, Instituto Nacional de Antropología e Historia, México, D.F.

Cobos, Rafael
  1997   Katún y Ahau: Fechando el fin de Chichén Itzá. In *Identidades sociales en
          Yucatán* (María Cecilia Lara Cebada, comp.): 17–40. Facultad de Ciencias
          Antropológicas, Universidad Autónoma de Yucatán, Mérida.
  1998   Chichén Itzá y el clásico terminal en las tierras bajas mayas. In *XI simposio
          de investigaciones arqueológicas en Guatemala* (Juan Pedro Laporte and
          Hector Escobedo, eds.): 791–799. Museo Nacional de Guatemala, Guatemala.

Fowler, William (ed.)
  1996   Recent Chronological Research in Central Mexico [Special section].
          Ancient Mesoamerica 7: 215–331.

Gill, Richardson B., Paul A. Mayewski, Johan Nyburg, Gerald H. Haug, and Larry
C. Peterson
  2007   Drought and the Maya Collapse. *Ancient Mesoamerica* 18 (2): 283–302.

Grube, Nikolai, Alfonso Lacadena, and Simon Martin
  2003   Chichén Itzá and Ek Balám: Terminal Classic Inscriptions from Yucatán.
          In *Notebook for the XXVIIth Maya Hieroglyph Forum at Texas*, pt. 2 (March
          2003): 1–84. University of Texas, Austin.

Hodell, David A., Mark Brenner, and Jason H. Curtis
  2007   Climate and Cultural History of the Northeastern Yucatan Peninsula,
          Quintana Roo, Mexico. *Climatic Change* 83 (1–2): 215–240.

Jones, Grant D.
  1989   *Maya Resistance to Spanish Rule. Time and History on a Colonial Frontier.*
          University of New Mexico Press, Albuquerque.

Lacadena, Alfonso
  2003   El corpus glífico de Ek' Balam, Yucatán, México. (The Glyphic Corpus
          of Ek' Balam, Yucatan, Mexico). Foundation for the Advancement of
          Mesoamerican Studies, Inc. Available at http://www.famsi.org.

Laporte, Juan Pedro
  2003   Thirty Years Later: Some Results of Recent Investigations at Tikal. In *Tikal:
          Dynasties, Foreigners and Affairs of State: Advancing Maya Archaeology*
          (Jeremy A. Sabloff, ed.): 281–318. School of American Research, Santa Fe,
          N.Mex.

Martin, Simon
    2003   In Line of the Founder: A View of Dynastic Politics at Tikal. In *Tikal: Dynasties, Foreigners and Affairs of State: Advancing Maya Archaeology* (Jeremy A. Sabloff, ed.): 3–45. School of American Research, Santa Fe, N.Mex.

Masson, Marilyn A.
    2000   *In the Realm of Nachan Kan: Postclassic Maya Archaeology at Laguna de On, Belize.* University Press of Colorado, Boulder.

Miller, Arthur G.
    1982   *On the Edge of the Sea: Mural Painting at Tancah-Tulum, Quintana Roo, Mexico.* Dumbarton Oaks, Washington, D.C.

Okoshi Harada, Tsubasa
    1994   Ecab: Una revisión de la geografía política de una provincia maya yucateca. In *Memorias del Primer Congreso Internacional de Mayistas, San Cristóbal de las Casas, 1989*, vol. 3: 280–287. Universidad Nacional Autónoma de México, México, D.F.

Peraza Lope, Carlos, Marilyn A. Masson, Timothy S. Hare, and Pedro Candelario Delgado Kú
    2006   The Chronology of Mayapan: New Radiocarbon Evidence. *Ancient Mesoamerica* 17 (2): 153–175.

Ringle, William M., Tomás Gallareta Negrón, and George J. Bey III
    1998   The Return of Quetzalcoatl: Evidence for the Spread of a World Religion during the Epiclassic Period. *Ancient Mesoamerica* 9: 183–232.

Robertson, Donald
    1970   The Tulum Murals: The International Style of the Late Post-Classic. In *Verhandlungen des XXXVIII Internationalen Amerikanistenkongresses, Stuttgart-München, 1968*, vol. 2: 77–88. Kommissionsverlag Klaus Renner, Munich.

Robles Castellanos, Fernando
    2007   *Culhua México: Una revisión arqueo-etnohistórica del imperio de los mexica tenochca.* Instituto Nacional de Antropología e Historia, México, D.F.

Roys, Ralph L.
    1957   *The Political Geography of the Yucatan Maya.* Carnegie Institution of Washington 613. Washington, D.C.

Santley, Robert, Clare Yarborough, and Barbara Hall
    1987   Enclaves, Ethnicity, and the Archaeological Record at Matacapán. In *Ethnicity and Culture: Proceedings of the Eighteenth Annual Conference of the Archaeological Association of the University of Calgary* (Réginald Auger, Margaret F. Glass, and Scott MacEachern, eds.): 85–100. University of Calgary Archaeological Association, Calgary, Canada.

Schmidt, Peter J.
    1998   Contacts with Central Mexico and the Transition to the Postclassic: Chichén Itzá and Central Mexico. In *Maya* (Peter J. Schmidt, Mercedes de la Garza, and Enrique Nalda, eds.): 427–449. Rizzoli, New York.

Stuart, David

    2000   "The Arrival of Strangers": Teotihuacan and Tollan in Classic Maya
             History. In *Mesoamerica's Classic Heritage: From Teotihuacan to the
             Aztecs* (Davíd Carrasco, Lindsay Jones, and Scott Sessions, eds.): 465–513.
             University Press of Colorado, Boulder.

Taube, Karl A.

    2003   Tetitla and the Maya Presence at Teotihuacan. In *The Maya and
             Teotihuacan* (Geoffrey E. Braswell, ed.): 273–314. University of Texas
             Press, Austin.

Thompson, J. Eric S.

    1957   Deities Portrayed on Censers at Mayapan. *Current Reports* 40: 599–632.
             Carnegie Institution of Washington, Washington, D.C.

Wright, Lori E.

    2005   In Search of Yax Nuun Ayiin I: Revisiting the Tikal Project's Burial 10.
             Ancient Mesoamerica 16 (1): 89–100.

Yaeger, Jason, and David A. Hoddel

    2009   The Collapse of Maya Civilization: Assessing the Interaction of Culture,
             Climate, and Environment. In *El Niño, Catastrophism, and Culture Change
             in Ancient America* (Daniel H. Sandweiss and Jeffrey Quilter, eds.): 187–242.
             Dumbarton Oaks Research Library and Collection, Washington, D.C.

Chapter Thirteen

Highland Mexican and Maya Intellectual Exchange in the Late Postclassic

Some Thoughts on the Origin of Shared Elements
and Methods of Interaction

Alfonso Lacadena

Since thomas (1884) and Seler (1898, 1904) first noticed the existence of shared traits between Postclassic highland Mexican and Maya manuscripts, questions regarding exchange and interaction between both regions, its scope, and the historical contexts in which it occurred have become one of the most interesting subjects in Maya studies. However, while such a relationship is well accepted by scholars, many questions remain unanswered concerning crucial aspects—for example, what set of elements can be considered as resulting from this particular instance of cultural contact; what the specific origin of the presumed highland Mexican traits found in Maya contexts may be; and when, how, and why interaction occurred at this time.

Traditionally, the study of interaction between highland Mexico and the Maya in the Postclassic era has been restricted to the analysis of artistic style, focusing mainly on iconographic and stylistic traits found on late Maya mural paintings and their relation to the so-called Postclassic International style (Boone and Smith 2003; Masson 2003; Milbrath 1999; Miller 1982), with little attention given to non-iconographic shared elements or other media. Thus Maya codices, when included in analyses of art styles, have been used primarily as sources of iconographic representations, such as depictions of gods, but have generally been placed apart and considered as not belonging to the Post-classic International-style phenomenon (Boone and Smith 2003: 186).

Important research recently undertaken by scholars such as Anthony Aveni, Harvey Bricker, Victoria Bricker, Julia Drapkin, Christine Hernández, Bryan Just, Merideth Paxton, and Gabrielle Vail focusing on shared intellectual elements between highland Mexico and the Maya area, such as almanac content and structure, calendrical instruments, arithmetic tools, and scribal conventions represents a welcome addition that has greatly enriched the subject (see Aveni 2004; H. Bricker et al. 1997; V. Bricker 1997, 2001; V. Bricker and H. Bricker 1988, 1992; Drapkin n.d. [2002]; Hernández 2004, 2006; Hernández and Bricker 2004; Just 2000, 2004; Paxton 2001; Vail 2002, 2004, 2006; Vail and Aveni 2004; Vail and Hernández 2006; see also chs. 9–11, this volume). This fresh research incorporates the discussion of intellectual traits, which can be placed alongside the stylistic ones, radically changing the way we should approach the study of the interaction between highland Mexico and the Maya area in late Postclassic times. The codices, the actors involved, and the manner of interaction are key elements of this research.

The Identification of Highland Mexican Sources

Since the similarities between highland Mexico and the northern Maya lowlands in the Postclassic period were first noticed, there has been a disjunction between interpreting such connections as the independent product of an original shared tradition transmitted vertically, or as the product of borrowings or influences transmitted horizontally. How can we be sure that the presence of shared content and elements between highland Mexican and Maya cultural traditions are the result of a late intellectual exchange, instead of the result of a common tradition that began with the crystallization of Mesoamerica as a cultural region in Preclassic times? Why should we attribute certain content of the codices to the Borgia Group or more generally to highland Mexican traditions instead of attributing them to local development? Are those instruments and their contents really foreign?

Victoria Bricker, Christine Hernández, and Gabrielle Vail (this volume) assert that the similarities between the Maya codices and the Borgia Group codices are too regular and systematic to be attributed to a parallel development resulting from a common origin. According to these scholars, a horizontal transfer involving donors and borrowers must have existed, in which highland Mexico would have acted as the main donor, and the Maya lowlands as the main borrower.

One of the most clearly Mexican traits that has been identified is the Venus cult complex, which focuses on the heliacal rising of Venus, the looming up of Venus/Tlahuizcalpantecuhtli armed with a spearthrower and darts shooting

Fig. 1. Sequence Snake-Death-Deer on Jimbal Stela 1. Artwork by Alfonso Lacadena.

Fig. 2. Sequence Snake-Death-Deer on Jimbal Stela 2. Artwork by Alfonso Lacadena.

certain beings and causing bad fates, and the elaboration of arithmetical and calendrical instruments for its calculation. As some scholars have proposed, iconography and archaeology suggest that the transition from the Classic to Postclassic marks the introduction and spread of the Venus/Quetzalcoatl cult, which became a pan-Mesoamerican religious phenomenon (López Austin and López Luján 1999; Ringle et al. 1998).

I believe that there is epigraphic evidence that shows us precisely when Venus calendrical instruments were introduced to the Maya lowlands. Many years ago, scholars noticed that several tenth-cycle monuments from El Peten, Guatemala, bore non-Maya glyphs. These glyphs are easily recognizable by their squared shape and their graphic designs, which do not belong to the Maya tradition. Context and attached coefficients suggest that these glyphs are usually of a calendrical nature (Graham 1971: 146; Justeson et al. 1985: 53–54). Examples are found at the following Maya sites: Ucanal, Jimbal, Seibal, and Calzada Mopan. In three of the examples, the glyphs are in calendrical sequence. At Jimbal, on Stelae 1 and 2, the signs can be read as 12 Snake, 13 Death, and 1 Deer (Justeson et al. 1985: 53) (figs. 1 and 2). This same sequence (although truncated because the monument is broken) appears on a stone yoke recently found at Calzada Mopan, Peten by Juan Pedro Laporte, with the sequence (without coefficients) Snake and Death (fig. 3). The sequence of days Snake-Death-Deer (followed by Rabbit) is relevant

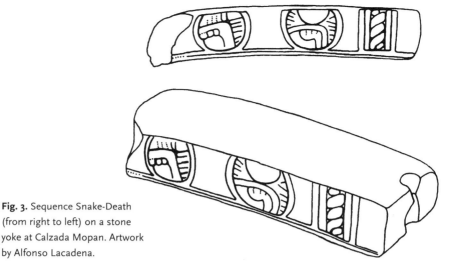

Fig. 3. Sequence Snake-Death (from right to left) on a stone yoke at Calzada Mopan. Artwork by Alfonso Lacadena.

to the Venus almanacs of the Borgia Group. Due to the mechanics of the calendar, Venus heliacal rise corresponds to the days Crocodile, Snake, Water, Reed, and Movement (see Bricker, ch. 10, this volume). Auguries associated with Tlahuizcalpantecuhtli correspond to those days of heliacal rising and to the following three days. Thus, the fate corresponding to the first heliacal rise of Venus on a day Crocodile would affect this day and the following days Wind, House, and Lizard; the second heliacal rise of Venus, on a day Snake, would affect this day and the following days Death, Deer, and Rabbit, and so on. The second series that starts on Snake and is followed by Death and Deer is the one present at Jimbal and Calzada Mopan, suggesting that the dates written in that foreign writing system might actually refer to a Venus almanac. It is interesting that non-Maya dates appearing on other contemporary tenth-cycle Maya monuments also belong to this calendrical pattern, such as 7 Crocodile and 5 Crocodile on Seibal Stela 3, and 7 Water on Seibal Stela 13. Crocodile and Water are key days involved in the Venus cycle.

Iconography can help confirm the possibility that these monuments were associated with Venus events. On the monuments discussed previously with non-Maya glyphs, as well as several other contemporary monuments, various figures float over the images of the rulers, placed in a celestial level (see, for example, Jimbal Stela 1, Ixlu Stela 2, Seibal Stela 18, and Ucanal Stela 3). Some of these figures are Maya and may be recognized as the so-called paddler gods, identifiable by the jaguar features displayed by the first of them and the stingray spine piercing the nose of the second; they have traditionally been related to day and night. The other figures who are represented with them are armed with spearthrowers and darts and have been interpreted as ancestral Tlaloc warriors (Schele and Freidel 1990: 386–391). However, I suggest that these armed figures can be related to Venus/Tlahuizcalpantecuhtli, who usually carries these weapons. The association of Venus with the paddler gods may be explained as follows: The Mexican epigrapher Erik Velásquez (n.d. [2005]) has recently demonstrated that the paddler gods do not actually represent day and night, but are the Maya counterparts of the Mexican deities Yohualtecuhtli and Yacahuitztli (*yacahuitztli* means "he of the spine in the nose"), who are the gods of dawn and dusk. Dawn and dusk are the moments of Venus's visibility as morning and evening star, thus providing another line of supporting evidence for interpreting these monuments as relating to Venus events.

If my interpretation is correct and the epigraphic and iconographic examples referred to constitute explicit evidence of the presence of a new Venus cult complex focused on the heliacal rising of the planet, we can suggest that, first, the introduction of Venus calendrical instruments among the Maya occurred around 850 CE; and, second, that, as V. Bricker, Hernández, and Vail claim, it had a foreign origin, as the absence of precedents in the Classic Maya period and the usage of non-Maya glyphs clearly shows. As V. Bricker (personal communication, October 2006) has pointed out, the base for calculation of the Dresden Venus table is 934 CE, close in time to the dedication of the tenth-cycle Peten monuments; in addition, the Brickers (H. Bricker et al. 1997; V. Bricker and H. Bricker 1992) have identified some almanacs in the Madrid Codex as dating to the tenth century, again pointing to the Terminal Classic as a special period when the adoption of certain calendrical instruments by the Maya took place.

The importance given to the *tzolk'in* and yearbearer dating system as the means for calculating Venus dates might explain the increasing interest of the Terminal Classic Maya in such calendrical instruments. On Seibal Stela 19, below an image of a personage with the attributes of the wind god (Graham 1990: 57; Green et al. 1972: 244; Just n.d. [2006]: 306; Ringle et al. 1998: 219), there is an eroded inscription that begins with a series of four *tzolk'in* dates with 1 as their coefficient (fig. 4). Only the first of the four *tzolk'in* dates is well preserved, and it represents the day B'en. The complete series might be reconstructed as 1 B'en, 1 [Etz'nab'], 1 [Ak'b'al], and [1 Lamat], representing a complete cycle of 52 years (4 × 13 years) in the yearbearer system (see ch. 11 and the Introduction to Part III, this volume). Although the traditional Maya New Year series in the Classic period was Eb'-Kab'an-Ik'-Manik' (see Stuart 2005), a B'en-Etz'nab'-Ak'b'al-Lamat series would make sense if we consider that the highland Mexican Venus calendar is related to the yearbearer series Reed-Flint-House-Rabbit. Because the Maya day B'en corresponds to the highland Mexican day Reed, the Seibal example might reflect a conscious attempt to correlate Maya and highland Mexican calendars by introducing a new set of yearbearers, based on advancing one position from the traditional Eb'-Kab'an-Ik'-Manik' series. The strategies followed by Maya scribes in adapting their calendar to include

Fig. 4. Calendrical sequence on Seibal Stela 19, A1–B2. Artwork by Alfonso Lacadena.

the new yearbearer series within the mechanics of the traditional Maya Long Count system and the opportunity this presents to correlate Maya and highland Mexican calendars at this time period deserves future in-depth study.

Shortly after these examples, the Venus cult is widely attested at Chichén Itzá, in the northern part of the Yucatán Peninsula, along with several other traits, including new iconographic programs, sculptural formats, and architecture (Ringle et al. 1998; Taube 1994) similar to those seen at "Toltec" Tula. As in the other regions discussed, there are a significant number of examples at the site of glyphs belonging to a different writing system. The full integration of Chichén Itzá in Terminal Classic economic, political, and religious networks probably peaked at the time of the greatest exchange between highland Mexico and the northern Maya lowlands in this period. Understanding the historical processes occurring at this time is extremely important because Late Postclassic highland Mexican-Maya interaction has its most immediate and closely related precedent in the Terminal Classic, as discussed by Fernando Robles (ch. 2, this volume). Unfortunately, the exact historical processes involved in the interaction are still far from completely understood, due to the archaeological and chronological problems that continue to plague comparisons between highland Mexico and the Maya area in this period (see Kowalski and Kristan-Graham 2007), as well as the difficulty of distinguishing the manner of interaction—whether it was based in commercial exchange, direct or indirect political control, and whether it involved the physical displacement of people, or a social process of elites adopting foreign ideology, styles, and symbols that were prestigious.

Historical linguistics can help in identifying the actors involved. In spite of suggestions of the presence of certain Otomanguean loans in Mayan languages (Justeson et al. 1985: 21–23; see also Macri, ch. 6, this volume), I think the evidence strongly suggests that the impact of Otomanguean languages such as Mixtec or

Zapotec on Mayan languages was irrelevant.[1] Although Mixtecs and Zapotecs played an important role in the general historical and cultural developments of the Postclassic period, they were not directly involved in the interaction that we are studying. That is not the case with Mixe-Zoque speakers, who provided some late loans into lowland Mayan languages (Justeson et al. 1985: 24), probably at a time of upheaval in the Isthmus region in the Terminal Classic, very likely in relation to events occuring at that time in the Maya lowlands.

The foreign component that is attested in the Postclassic in the northern Maya lowlands is accompanied by an important foreign linguistic input of clear Nahua affiliation (Justeson et al. 1985: 24–26; Whorf 1948; see also Dakin, ch. 7, this volume). As historical linguistics suggests, the Nahua input can be related to Eastern Nahuatl, the group to which the Gulf Coast variant and Pipil belong, and to Central Nahuatl, the last Nahua group to stabilize in central Mexico. These two different inputs from Nahua may well correspond to different moments or processes of interaction, the Central Nahuatl dialect being supposedly the later one. The mention of Nahua deity names spelled as **ta-wi-si-ka-la** (Tlahuizcalpantecuhtli), **xi-wi-te** (Xiuhtecuhtli), and **ka-ka-tu-na-la** (Cactonalli?) in the Venus table of the Dresden Codex (Taube and Bade 1991; Whittaker 1986; see also Macri, ch. 6, this volume) provides nice confirmation and strengthens suggestions of cultural exchange based on historical linguistics.

Seibal Stela 13 might provide some new data relevant to this question. Stela 13 belongs to the late sculptural program of Seibal rulers, starting around 10.3.0.0.0, or 889 CE (for a detailed discussion of Seibal sculpture programs, see Just n.d. [2006]). As noted, this sculpture program includes possible epigraphic references to Venus dates (7 and 5 Crocodile on Stela 3, 7 Water on Stela 13) and to the new B'en = Reed yearbearer series (Stela 19), as well as iconographic depictions of figures with the attributes of the Mexican Tlaloc rain god (Stela 3), the wind god (Stelae 3 and 19), and perhaps Venus/Tlahuizcalpantecuhtli (Stela 18). The hieroglyphic text on Seibal Stela 13 is certainly interesting (fig. 5). It starts with the 7 Water Venus date in the non-Mayan calendrical system mentioned earlier; except for the final statement, Ochk'in Kalo'mte' (west Kalo'mte', a Maya title), the rest of the text remains opaque and may indicate that the scribe was only semiliterate (see a discussion in Just n.d. [2006]: 328–330). However, at C1 there is a spelling that can be read as **e-je-ke**.[2] Considering the special sculptural program to which Stela 13 belongs, I wonder whether **e-je-ke** might be related to Nahua *ehecatl* (/e'ekatl/), the name of the wind god. The presence of **e-je-** instead of the expected *e-he-* or *e-e-* spellings can be explained by its late date, belonging to an epoch when the former distinction between glottal /h/ and velar /j/ spirants was no longer represented in Maya hieroglyphic writing by a distinct set of **h**V and **j**V signs, due to the collapse of /h/ and /j/ in the Ch'olan languages (see Grube 2004). The presence of a spirant instead of a glottal is not problematic, as both are actually

Fig. 5. The hieroglyphic text of Seibal Stela 13. Artwork by Alfonso Lacadena.

equally reconstructible for proto-Nahua (Dakin 1982; Terrence Kaufman, personal communication, March 2007). In any case, the **e-je-ke** spelling might reflect the way that Nahua *eheca(tl)* sounded to a Maya scribe and was thought to be written. If this suggestion is correct, Nahua speakers can be identified on the other side of the interaction at the very moment when the Maya adopted the new religious complex and calendrical instruments related to it.

The new Venus complex had come to stay. Beginning in the Terminal Classic period, and in the following centuries, the Maya began the process of assimilating and reelaborating the content borrowed from highland Mexico, and these elements were thereafter integrated into their own system. V. Bricker, Hernández, and Vail (this volume) have shown examples of almanacs that were translated, converted, and adapted to reflect Maya conceptions. If Nahuas from the Gulf Coast or highland Mexico were ever physically present at Chichén Itzá or other sites in the peninsula, they became completely assimilated within the Mayan-speaking population, leaving traces in patronyms and in a specialized vocabulary related to war and administration. This process is characteristic of warrior-elites, who usually become assimilated within the indigenous population within a few generations. This occurred during the period when Venus/Quetzalcoatl was transforming into Venus/Kukulcan. Yucatán suffered political upheavals at the time with the shift of the political center of the peninsula from Chichén Itzá to Mayapán. Relations with Nahua speakers of the Gulf Coast and highland Mexico continued, although probably through less intrusive mechanisms, such as commercial exchange.

The last main period of interaction with highland Mexico occurred during the final epoch of Mayapán and the time after its fall, before the Spanish conquest. There was again a strong Nahua component, but this time it seems to have involved speakers of Central Nahuatl. This scenario, which is suggested by historical linguistics, is confirmed by other lines of evidence. As Taube (1992; see also ch. 5, this volume) has pointed out, the presence of certain elements, such as the headdress of Quetzalcoatl in the Dresden Codex; figurines

of Mexican gods like Xipe Totec, Tlazolteotl, and Huehueteotl at Mayapán; and the representation of legged mollusks at Santa Rita, clearly points to the cultural tradition of late central Mexico, seemingly excluding Mixtec or Borgia Group sources.

Other iconographic traits support Taube's observations and also suggest a more complex scenario of interaction. In the Maya tradition, flint is represented by the graphic motif of the sign **TOK'**, "flint," consisting of an inner S-shaped line surrounded by dots, or by the graphic motif of the sign **ETZ'NAB'**, the day corresponding to "flint" in the Maya calendar, which consists of two wavy crossed diagonal lines. In the Postclassic highland Mexican tradition, flint is conventionally represented with its surface divided into two sectors, painted in red and white. This convention is present in the Mixtec, Borgia Group, and central Mexican traditions. However, there is a difference among them: in the Mixtec and Borgia Group pictorial tradition, the line dividing the two sectors is transversal; a variant of this transversal form, found in some Mixtec and Borgia Group codices, adds one or more parallel red lines to the main transversal red-white division. As a distinctive convention, the line is placed diagonally in the central Mexican tradition, which is probably an innovation.[3] In the Dresden and Madrid codices, which of course generally follow the Maya tradition of representing flint, it is of interest that in some cases the scribe-priests adopted the highland Mexican convention, painting the flint blade in red and white, as can be seen in color reproductions of Dresden pages 48, 49–50 (fig. 6) and Madrid pages 50 and 52–54 (fig. 7). It is also of interest that the Dresden Codex exhibits the transversal Mixtec and Borgia Group codices convention, specifically the variant that attaches red parallel lines to the main transversal division, while the Madrid Codex exhibits the central Mexico convention, with the dividing line painted diagonally. The scribe-priest of the Madrid Codex who painted

Fig. 7. Highland Mexican red-white flint (diagonal line) on page 52 of the Madrid Codex. After Villacorta and Villacorta (1976: 328).

these examples was perfectly aware of the central Mexican innovation and adopted it. If the differences between the Dresden Codex and the Madrid Codex cannot be explained in terms of temporal variation, this would suggest that different highland Mexican sources were merging in Yucatán at the same time.

Historical comparisons and correlations between Yucatán and highland Mexico are not easy to establish for this period because in both areas the political landscape was constantly changing—as witnessed, for example, by the rise and decline of Mayapán and a profound political restructuring of the Yucatán Peninsula after its fall, the rise and decline of several city-states and hegemonies in highland Mexico, and the later rise and rapid expansion of the Mexica hegemony. As some scholars have correctly reminded us (Masson 2003: 200; see also Masson and Peraza, ch. 3, and Robles, ch. 2, this volume), we must be careful when relating Late Postclassic Yucatán non-Maya traits to the Mexica expansion because, for the majority of the Maya Late Postclassic, the Mexica had not yet consolidated their power and could not have played the historical role that is attributed to them.[4] In fact, a Mexica impact on the northern Maya lowlands could have taken place only two or three decades before the beginning of the Spanish conquest of Yucatán.

The Manner of Interaction

Models to explain how interaction between highland Mexico and the Maya area could have occurred and how highland Mexican influences reached the Maya area are two of the main issues to be resolved. Macri (ch. 6, this volume) highlights the portable character of many objects with writing or painted images: codices, decorated ceramics, carved bones and shells, and textiles. All of these are items that can be transported easily within the packs of merchants and can be exchanged or purchased, thereby reaching the Maya area and serving as a model to Maya scribes and painters. Like Macri, Taube (ch. 5, this volume) highlights the importance of portable textiles as vehicles of transmission. He supports his proposal with persuasive evidence, including the stylistic relationship between painted textiles and mural paintings and textile motifs that are incorporated into the design of mural paintings, as well as ethnohistorical references to chambers and shrines adorned by painted textiles used as tapestries.

More than the other suggested media, Hernández and V. Bricker (2004) and Hernández and Vail (ch. 11, this volume) highlight the importance of written and painted codices as indispensable instruments of transmission, suggesting several possible scenarios in which codices coming from highland Mexico or the Gulf Coast could end up in the hands of a Maya scribe. Among them, they have highlighted the existence of international trade ports close to or within the Maya area (for a summary and listing of Postclassic international trade ports, see Gasco and Berdan 2003). The possibility that merchants traveled in the company of priests for the performance of ritual is highly probable, as is the suggestion made by Hernández and V. Bricker (2004: 315) about the necessity of establishing calendrical correlations among people belonging to different traditions to synchronize the times of meetings and transactions. Hernández and Vail (this volume), citing Landa, add the interesting scenario in which codices may have changed hands as gifts among priests, so that a codex acquired on the coast could end up in one of the cultural and political centers located inland.

Of all the suggested media, painted tapestries and codices seem to be the most plausible sources that could have served as models. Decorated ceramics and carved bones and shells bearing foreign iconographic representations or written inscriptions do not appear in the Maya archaeological record in a large enough quantity to be considered relevant as sources of inspiration. Because of the small surface area available, ceramics, shells, and bones also do not seem to be suitable for the inclusion of long and complex elements such as almanacs or full calendrical tables; even in highland Mexico, ceramics, shells, and bones were not regularly used for these types of content. Tapestries and textiles, although also lacking in the archaeological record (as may be explained by their perishable nature), might have been the perfect sources of inspiration, at least for Maya mural paintings. But codices must actually have been the main source of inspiration and provided the natural physical medium for the kinds of information discussed here, including almanacs and astronomical tables, and I believe they played a more important role than the one usually attributed to them.

In fact, Postclassic International-style traits, which have long been recognized on late Maya murals, are also widely present in the Maya codices,

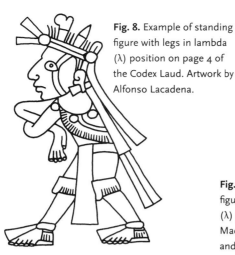

Fig. 8. Example of standing figure with legs in lambda (λ) position on page 4 of the Codex Laud. Artwork by Alfonso Lacadena.

Fig. 9. Example of standing figure with legs in lambda (λ) position on page 6 of the Madrid Codex. After Villacorta and Villacorta (1976: 236).

although not usually recognized.[5] I should note that I am not referring here to the almanacs previously mentioned or to depictions of highland Mexican deities. I am referring to the systematic use of iconographic traits that define a style. For example, the position of the legs of standing figures resembling the Greek letter lambda (λ), with both feet placed on the floor, one leg projected forward and the other bent backward, is not uncommon in the Postclassic International style (fig. 8). Along with other more general or idiosyncratic ways of representing legs in standing figures, it can be found in the Mixtec codices and in some manuscripts from central Mexico. This lambda position also appears in the Borgia Group codices where it is the most common way of representing legs in standing figures. The lambda position of legs in figures who are standing is also widely used in the Dresden, Paris, and Madrid codices (figs. 9 and 10), and, as far as I know, it has no antecedents in the Classic Maya period. This iconographic trait helps to confirm the special relationship between Maya codices and the Borgia Group.

Other iconographic traits can be also related to the Postclassic International style. In addition to the representation of flint blades in red and white mentioned previously, other traits include the A-O headdress of the Maya rain god on Madrid page 12 (H. Bricker et al. 1997; Vail 1997) (fig. 11) and the Mexican *ilhuitl*, "day," icon in skybands in the Dresden Codex (fig. 12). To this list we could also add the representation of darts with feather beds and concluding transversal lines, which have no antecedents in the Classic Maya period but closely resemble the way they are represented in highland Mexican manuscripts (fig. 13), and some other highland Mexican iconic conventions, such as the representation of water as a canal section in the Dresden Codex (fig. 14).

Other diagnostic traits should also be considered. Hernández and V. Bricker

Fig. 10. Example of standing figure with legs in lambda (λ) position on page 36 of the Dresden Codex. After Villacorta and Villacorta (1976: 82).

Fig. 11. Highland Mexican A-O headdress on page 12 of the Madrid Codex. After Villacorta and Villacorta (1976: 248).

Fig. 12. Highland Mexican *ilhuitl*, "day," icon in a skyband on page 53 of the Dresden Codex. After Villacorta and Villacorta (1976: 116).

Fig. 13. Highland Mexican-style darts with feather beds and transversal lines on page 32 of the Madrid Codex. After Villacorta and Villacorta (1976: 288).

Fig. 14. Representation of water as a canal section in highland Mexican style on page 34 of the Dresden Codex. After Villacorta and Villacorta (1976: 78).

(2004: 311–314) have recently suggested that the aberrant examples of Maya writing in the Madrid Codex with inverted reading orders from bottom to top and right to left could be explained in terms of the influence of Nahuatl writing, because that is the preferred reading order in that writing system. I completely agree with their interpretation. Moreover, I suggest another trait as an example of the influence of foreign systems. In highland Mexican pictorial compositions, objects, beings, and glyphic compounds fill the space, floating weightless around the figures. We can see this same convention in the Maya codices, where objects, beings, and glyphs float in the same way. On the same pages where these representational conventions occur, inverted reading orders pointed out by V. Bricker (in Hernández and Bricker 2004) also occur (fig. 15). These same conventions (floating objects, figures, and glyphs, some of them with reversed reading order) are also present on the Santa Rita murals, which have never been questioned as reflecting the Postclassic International style.

The scribe-priests who composed Maya codices not only knew the epigraphic contents of highland Mexican codices but also knew their pictorial conventions and were influenced by them. Without diminishing the importance of other methods of transmission, I must agree with V. Bricker and Hernández and Vail (this volume) regarding the crucial role played by codices in this interaction. In light of the epigraphic and iconographic evidence now available, the question of the placement of the Maya codices in relation to the Postclassic International style must be revised.

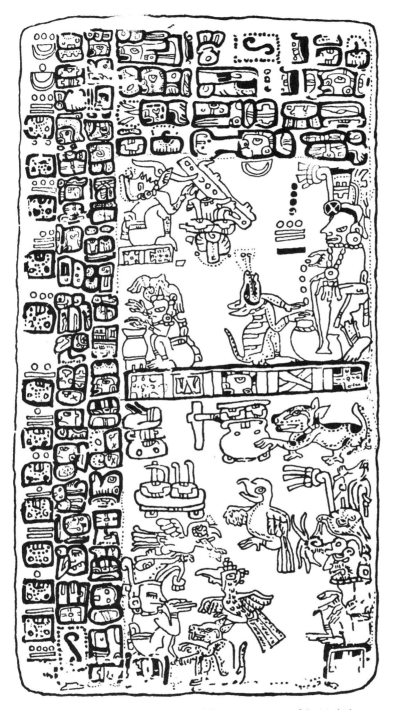

Fig. 15. Objects and beings floating around figures on page 37 of the Madrid Codex. After Villacorta and Villacorta (1976: 298).

Proposals regarding transmission focus on the movement of objects, not on the people involved. In the proposed scenarios, foreigners used to be imagined as far away—at trading ports on the edge of the Maya lowlands or bordering the Maya coast. However, I would like to highlight the fact that an inert object that travels and changes hands is not enough to bring about the processes and results that we have been discussing. It must be accompanied by the human element, which provides meaning to it. As far as I know, almost all of the shared traits that were presumably borrowed from one area to another not only keep their original formal referent but also their original meaning and function. This is an important point, because there does not seem to be disjunction in a Panofskian way. The Maya not only copied external forms of representation, but also their contents and meanings. This indicates that they understood perfectly what they were copying.

The Itzá song considered by Knowlton (ch. 8, this volume) illustrates the means by which forms are borrowed and adopted. The Maya who composed the Itzá song knew what a Nahuatl song was and how it sounded. In a world of limited technological development, where the only way to register sound is through writing (and we know that highland Mexican writing systems were never used to record songs), the only access to Nahuatl songs would have involved someone singing a *cuicatl* and being heard by a Maya. The process actually involves a bit more than just hearing a song. It is clear that the Maya who heard those Mexican *cuicatl* understood them linguistically, because the Maya composition does not include words or fragments of Nahuatl words embedded randomly, but rather perfectly placed vocables that conform to the structure and rhythm of Nahuatl poetry.

The manner in which Maya priests and artists used highland Mexican Postclassic traits was purposeful. It involved more than a casual meeting at a trading port or the acquisition of a foreign codex or a curious carved object. It was the result of a continuous intercommunication between literate people during long periods of time. V. Bricker, Hernández, and Vail have interpreted it in this way. Epigraphic and iconographic influences imply that Maya scribe-priests had access to and were able to read highland Mexican documents and that these were accessible and numerous enough to have influenced the recipients to make use of some of their conventions and contents. Postclassic International-style traits are so generalized in the Maya codices that it is hard to accept that they could be the result of sudden punctuated influences. Highland Mexican influence has to have been intense and constant over time, lasting for several centuries. The Dresden and Madrid codices, which were probably written by several scribe-priests (Lacadena 2000; Zimmermann 1956), confirm that the influence was of long duration, affecting successive generations of scribes.

The dynamics suggested by Masson and Peraza (ch. 3, this volume) for Mayapán involving foreign commercial agents and allies living in the city—

intermixed and married with the local population, and participating actively in the economic, political, religious, and social life—represent an accurate description of the kind of dynamic that we need by way of explanation, in that it extends far beyond casual access to painted or carved portable objects. In other words, they describe a situation of long duration involving meeting and exchange, in which qualified interpreters on both sides of the interaction process are able not only to explain the content of a given object but also to understand it. Mayapán could have been one of those places of intellectual exchange, as could other places in the Maya lowlands, such as Champotón, Campeche, Cozumel, or Chetumal.

However, among all these possible places, Mayapán was perhaps special because of its importance as a political center in the north of the peninsula in Late Postclassic times. Mayapán played a crucial role not only as a possible meeting place of highland Mexican and Maya cultural traditions but also because of the active role it played as an agent involved in the diffusion of styles and ideas in the northern Maya lowlands. According to ethnohistorical sources, Mayapán was a center where hieroglyphic codices were produced and distributed, a stable intellectual reference point for Postclassic Maya priests:

> They provided priests for the towns when they were needed, examining them in the sciences and ceremonies, and committed to them the duties of their office, and the good example to people and provided them with books (Tozzer 1941: 27).

The general iconographic and palaeographic uniformity that Postclassic Maya codices exhibit could well be the result, at least in part, of this kind of centralization during part of the Late Postclassic and the active role played by Maya religious elites themselves in the transmission. I think we can enrich our understanding of the process if we consider that much of the highland Mexican content, icons, and stylistic traits that we find in late Postclassic Maya murals and codices are probably not the result of direct influence and contact between Maya and foreigners occuring at the precise moment when a mural was being painted or an almanac for a codex was being composed but, rather, are the expression of an idiosyncratic late Maya style which had already incorporated those traits. The Postclassic International style spread, in the majority of cases, from Maya to other Maya following the regular process of cultural transmission. The perspective may change radically: My feeling when I see the famous almanac on pages 75–76 of the Madrid Codex (plate 1), with its calendrical instruments including the embedded Venus almanac (V. Bricker, ch. 10, this volume) and the Maya yearbearer series (Hernández and Vail, ch. 11, this volume), is that, paradoxically, the foreign Venus almanac is actually the older, more traditional instrument, while the Maya one, the K'an-Muluk-Ix-Kawak yearbearer series, is the fresh new element introduced by the scribe to the picture. Merideth Paxton, in chapter 9 (this volume), considers several other innovative features of the M. 75-76 almanac, indicating that the Maya scribe was not simply copying a canonical form but was interested in annotating it to include information relevant to those using the almanac.

Carefully avoiding any model of interaction that might suggest migration or movement of people or any kind of resulting political control, whether direct or indirect, the model of neutral commercial networks and long-distance trade as the process that frames the spread of cultural traits in Mesoamerica is currently the one most often accepted by scholars. However, although trade activities used to be presented as pacific and politically neutral, almost democratically established among peer participants who received equivalent benefits from the transactions, the fact is that we should not forget that commerce is always accompanied by politics. Merchants, goods, markets, and trading routes need to be protected. Merchants enrich themselves and the polities to which they belong; they act within factions and may influence or try to influence local politics (at home or abroad), according to their interests. And, depending on circumstances, they are favored by local political powers and factions with whom they are in contact and that can be used by them politically in internal competition. The same can be said of culture, which is borrowed because it is accompanied by some kind of preexistent social, religious, or political prestige; commerce and politics walk side by side and may be manifested in many different ways, including diplomacy, alliance, threat, or open war. Commercial blockades (like that of salt to Tlaxcala by the Mexica) provide a good example of how trade and politics relate to each other. Ill-treatment of merchants was one of the *casus belli* alleged by the Mexica for starting a war, and Mexica long-distance trading *pochteca* usually acted as spies on behalf of state interests. The attack suffered by the Acalan Chontals after establishing Tixchel by military forces from Champotón, Potonchán, and Xicalango—wasn't Xicalango an open international trade port?—resulted from what was probably considered by the attackers to be an intolerable intrusion of Acalan Chontals in coastal trade (Scholes and Roys 1996: 73–74, 315). I think we must accept that all of these things are not necessarily late innovations in the history of Mesoamerica. I wonder if scholars in the future will find us guilty of projecting too candidly the laissez-faire, laissez-passer principles of the Western ideal model of modern liberal free commerce and globalization on ancient Mesoamerica.

The process was a two-way road, and the Maya were clearly not passive actors in the interaction. Taube (ch. 5, this volume) gives eloquent examples of Maya elements that are found in highland Mexico and entered the Postclassic International style, including representations of the surface of the earth as a net, the use of flower motifs based on modified *k'in* designs, and even the representation of the Mexican deity Tonatiuh as a Maya solar king. Hernández and Vail point to the pairing of Nahua *ilhuitl*, "day," and Maya *k'in*, "day," icons in skybands found in the Dresden Codex and Codex Telleriano-

Remensis from central Mexico (see Macri, ch. 6, this volume). By no means should we see Late Postclassic Maya culture as generally being the debtor, but rather as an active, original, and extremely rich and complex intellectual culture that, through successive political collapses over centuries in an ever-transforming historical landscape, was able to preserve one of the oldest Mesoamerican intellectual traditions, enriching it with whatever new elements captured its interest.

As an example of the complexity and richness I am referring to and to visualize what the intellectual world of Postclassic Maya scribe-priests in Yucatán was like, let us look again at the priest who adopted the latest central Mexico fashion in drawing flint blades with diagonal red and white sections.[6] That scribe-priest is the same one who followed highland Mexican conventions concerning the representation of objects floating around figures in a weightless space; he is also the one who sometimes changed the reading order of glyphs, also following highland Mexican conventions. He understood the orthographic principles used by other contemporary writing systems and was probably trained in one of them. On the pages composed by him, he included almanacs similar to the Borgia Group tradition that contain many pictorial traditions that he also shared, probably because he learned them at a priestly school; these almanacs alternated with others referring to more than 1,000-year-old Maya myths about the flood that inaugurated the present era. And he can be identified as the same Yucatec-speaking (and Yucatec-writing) scribe-priest who included the old Ch'olan language of the Classic Maya period in some of the almanacs he copied, on the very eve of Spanish conquest.

Acknowledgments

I thank Gabrielle Vail and Christine Hernández for their kind invitation to be the discussant of the session on epigraphy, iconography, and linguistics at the 2006 Dumbarton Oaks Pre-Columbian Studies symposium. Being in the company of so many excellent scholars was a great honor for me. I also thank Dumbarton Oaks and the Library of Congress in Washington, D.C., for the excellent atmosphere they provided for exchange and work. Special gratitude goes to Gabrielle Vail, Christine Hernández, and Victoria Bricker for their comments on my paper, which has been greatly improved as a result.

Notes

1. Suggested loans, such as Otomanguean "snake" for the origin of a Maya variant of the syllabic sign **b'i**, or suggested Zapotec sources for the Maya *tzolk'in* day names Manik and Lamat, are unlikely. Lamat, at least, makes sense in Mayan, based on the root *lam* (**LAM, la-ma-**), "sink, diminish," plus an agentive/instrumental -V_1t suffix (Ignacio Cases, personal communication, September 2006).

2. In July 2007 I had chance to check the original monument at the site, confirming the presence of a **je** syllable between **e** and **ke**.

3. This may be seen in the main late Aztec scribal schools, including those centered in Tenochtitlan-Tlatelolco, Cuauhtinchan, Tlaxcala, and Huexotzinco. It is interesting that the Texcocan scribal school seems to favor a different convention, consisting of an empty uncolored flint blade.

4. Although usually labeled as "Aztec," the spread of the Postclassic International style predates Aztec expansion in Mesoamerica (Boone and Smith 2003; Umberger 1996; Umberger and Klein 1993).

5. For example, Boone and Smith (2003: 187) exclude the Maya codices from examples of the Postclassic International style.

6. According to my identification of scribal hands in the Madrid Codex, the scribe-priest I am referring to is Scribe 4, who composed pages 26 (lower section) to 55 (Lacadena 2000: 64–67).

References Cited

Aveni, Anthony F.
    2004   Intervallic Structure and Cognate Almanacs in the Madrid and Dresden Codices. In *The Madrid Codex: New Approaches to Understanding an Ancient Maya Manuscript* (Gabrielle Vail and Anthony Aveni, eds.): 147–170. University Press of Colorado, Boulder.

Boone, Elizabeth H., and Michael E. Smith
    2003   Postclassic International Styles and Symbol Sets. In *The Postclassic Mesoamerican World* (Michael E. Smith and Frances F. Berdan, eds.): 186–193. University of Utah Press, Salt Lake City.

Bricker, Harvey M., Victoria R. Bricker, and Bettina Wulfing
    1997   Determining the Historicity of Three Astronomical Almanacs in the Madrid Codex. *Archaeoastronomy* (Supplement to *Journal for the History of Astronomy*) 22: S17–S36.

Bricker, Victoria R.
    1997   The "Calendar-Round" Almanac in the Madrid Codex. In *Papers on the Madrid Codex* (Victoria R. Bricker and Gabrielle Vail, eds.): 169–180. Middle American Research Institute Publication 64. Tulane University, New Orleans.
    2001   A Method for Dating Venus Almanacs in the Borgia Codex. *Archaeoastronomy* (Supplement to *Journal for the History of Astronomy*) 26: S21–S44.

Bricker, Victoria R., and Harvey M. Bricker
    1988   The Seasonal Table in the Dresden Codex and Related Almanacs. *Archaeoastronomy* (Supplement to *Journal for the History of Astronomy*) 12: S1–S62.
    1992   A Method for Cross-Dating Almanacs with Tables in the Dresden Codex. In *The Sky in Mayan Literature* (Anthony F. Aveni, ed.): 43–86. Oxford University Press, New York.

Dakin, Karen

1982   *La evolución fonológica del protonáhuatl.* Instituto de Investigaciones Filológicas, Universidad Nacional Autónoma de México, México, D.F.

Drapkin, Julia

n.d.   Interpreting the Dialect of Time: A Structural Analysis and Discussion of Almanacs in the Madrid Codex. Honors thesis, Department of Anthropology, Tulane University, New Orleans, 2002.

Gasco, Janine, and Frances F. Berdan

2003   International Trade Centers. In *The Postclassic Mesoamerican World* (Michael E. Smith and Frances F. Berdan, eds.): 109–116. University of Utah Press, Salt Lake City.

Graham, John A.

1971   Non-Classic Inscriptions and Sculptures at Seibal. In *Papers on Olmec and Maya Archaeology.* Contributions of the University of California Archaeological Research Facility 13: 143–153.

1990   *Excavations at Seibal, Department of Peten, Guatemala: Monumental Sculpture and Hieroglyphic Inscriptions.* Memoirs of the Peabody Museum 17 (1). Harvard University, Cambridge, Mass.

Greene, Merle, Robert L. Rands, and John A. Graham

1972   *Maya Sculpture from the Southern Lowlands, the Highlands, and Pacific Piedmont, Guatemala, Mexico, Honduras.* Lederer, Street, and Zeus, Berkeley, Calif.

Grube, Nikolai

2004   The Orthographic Distinction between Velar and Glottal Spirants in Maya Hieroglyphic Writing. In *The Linguistics of Maya Writing* (Søren Wichmann, ed.): 61–81. University of Utah Press, Salt Lake City.

Hernández, Christine

2004   "Yearbearer Pages" and Their Connection to Planting Almanacs in the Borgia Codex. In *The Madrid Codex: New Approaches to Understanding an Ancient Maya Manuscript* (Gabrielle Vail and Anthony Aveni, eds.): 321–364. University Press of Colorado, Boulder.

2006   Using Astronomical Imagery to Cross-Date an Almanac in the Borgia Codex. Special issue, *Human Mosaic* 36 (1): 125–143.

Hernández, Christine, and Victoria R. Bricker

2004   The Inauguration of Planting in the Borgia and Madrid Codices. In *The Madrid Codex: New Approaches to Understanding an Ancient Maya Manuscript* (Gabrielle Vail and Anthony Aveni, eds.): 277–320. University Press of Colorado, Boulder.

Just, Bryan R.

2000   Concordances of Time: *In Extenso* Almanacs in the Madrid and Borgia Group Codices. *Human Mosaic* 33 (1): 7–16.

2004   *In Extenso* Almanacs in the Madrid Codex. In *The Madrid Codex: New Approaches to Understanding an Ancient Maya Manuscript* (Gabrielle Vail and Anthony Aveni, eds.): 255–276. University Press of Colorado, Boulder.

n.d.   The Visual Discourse of Ninth-Century Stelae at Machaquila and Seibal. Ph.D. dissertation, Departments of Art History and Linguistics, Tulane University, New Orleans, 2006.

Justeson, John S., William M. Norman, Lyle Campbell, and Terrence Kaufman
    1985   *The Foreign Impact on Lowland Mayan Language and Script.* Middle American Research Institute Publication 53. Tulane University, New Orleans.

Kowalski, Jeff, and Cynthia Kristan-Graham (eds.)
    2007   *Twin Tollans: Chichén Itzá, Tula, and the Epiclassic to Postclassic Mesoamerican World.* Dumbarton Oaks Research Library and Collection, Washington, D.C.

Lacadena, Alfonso
    2000   Los escribas del códice de Madrid: Metodología paleográfica. *Revista española de antropología americana* 30: 27–85.

López Austin, Alfredo, and Leonardo López Luján
    1999   *Mito y realidad de Zuyuá.* Fideicomiso Historia de las Américas, El Colegio de México, and the Fondo de Cultura Económica, México, D.F.

Masson, Marilyn A.
    2003   The Late Postclassic Symbol Set in the Maya Area. In *The Postclassic Mesoamerican World* (Michael E. Smith and Francis F. Berdan, eds.): 194–200. University of Utah Press, Salt Lake City.

Milbrath, Susan
    1999   *Star Gods of the Maya: Astronomy in Art, Folklore, and Calendars.* University of Texas Press, Austin.

Miller, Arthur G.
    1982   *On the Edge of the Sea: Mural Painting at Tancah-Tulum, Quintana Roo, Mexico.* Dumbarton Oaks, Washington, D.C.

Paxton, Merideth
    2001   *The Cosmos of the Yucatec Maya: Cycles and Steps from the Madrid Codex.* University of New Mexico Press, Albuquerque.

Ringle, William M., Tomás Gallareta, and George J. Bey
    1998   The Return of Quetzalcoatl: Evidence for the Spread of a World Religion During the Epiclassic Period. *Ancient Mesoamerica* 9: 183–232.

Schele, Linda, and David Freidel
    1990   *A Forest of Kings: The Untold Story of the Ancient Maya.* William Morrow, New York.

Scholes, France V., and Ralph Roys
    1996   *Los chontales de Acalán-Tixchel* (Spanish edition by Mario Humbeto Ruz). Centro de Estudios Mayas, Instituto de Investigaciones Filológicas, Universidad Nacional Autónoma de México, Centro de Investigaciones y Estudios Superiores en Antropología Social, México, D.F.

Seler, Eduard
    1888   Die Venusperiode in der Bilderschriften der Codex Borgia-Gruppe. *Zeitschrift für Ethnologie* 30: 346–383.
    1904   Venus Period in the Picture Writings of the Borgian Codex Group. *Bureau of American Ethnology Bulletin* 28: 355–391.

Stuart, David
    2005   New Year Records in Classic Maya Inscriptions. *The PARI Journal* 5 (2): 1–6. Available at www.mesoweb.com/pari/publications/journal/0502/NewYear.pdf.

Taube, Karl
    1992   *The Major Gods of Ancient Yucatan*. Studies in Pre-Columbian Art and Archaeology 32. Dumbarton Oaks Research Library and Collection, Washington, D.C.
    1994   The Iconography of Toltec Period Chichen Itza. In *Hidden among the Hills: Maya Archaeology of the Northwest Yucatan Peninsula* (Hans Prem, ed.): 212–246. Acta Mesoamericana 7. Verlag von Flemming, Möckmühl, Germany.

Taube, Karl, and Bonnie Bade
    1991   *An Appearance of Xiuhtecuhtli in Dresden Venus Pages*. Research Reports on Ancient Maya Writing 35. Center for Maya Research, Washington, D.C.

Thomas, Cyrus
    1884   Notes on Certain Maya and Mexican Manuscripts. In *Third Annual Report of the Bureau of American Ethnology, 1881–82*: 7–65. Smithsonian Institution, Washington, D.C.

Tozzer, Alfred M.
    1941   *Landa's* Relación de las cosas de Yucatán: *A Translation*. Papers of the Peabody Museum of American Archaeology and Ethnology 18. Harvard University, Cambridge, Mass.

Umberger, Emily
    1996   Aztec Presence and Material Remains in the Outer Provinces. In *Aztec Imperial Strategies* (Frances F. Berdan, Richard E. Blanton, Elizabeth H. Boone, Mary G. Hodge, Michael E. Smith, and Emily Umberger, eds.): 151–180. Dumbarton Oaks Research Library and Collection, Washington, D.C.

Umberger, Emily, and Cecilia Klein
    1993   Aztec Art and Imperial Expansion. In *Latin American Horizons* (Don S. Rice, ed.): 295–336. Dumbarton Oaks Research Library and Collection, Washington, D.C.

Vail, Gabrielle
    1997   The Yearbearer Gods in the *Madrid Codex*. In *Códices y documentos sobre México: Segundo simposio*, vol. 1 (Salvador Rueda Smithers, Constanza Vega Sosa, and Rodrigo Martínez Baracs, eds.): 81–106. Instituto Nacional de Antropología e Historia and Dirección General de Publicaciones del Consejo Nacional para la Cultura y las Artes, México, D.F.
    2002   Haab' *Rituals in the Maya Codices and the Structure of Maya Almanacs*. Research Reports on Ancient Maya Writing 53. Center for Maya Research, Washington, D.C.
    2004   A Reinterpretation of *Tzolk'in* Almanacs in the Madrid Codex. In *The Madrid Codex: New Approaches to Understanding an Ancient Maya Manuscript* (Gabrielle Vail and Anthony Aveni, eds.): 215–252. University Press of Colorado, Boulder.
    2006   The Maya Codices. *Annual Review of Anthropology* 35: 497–519.

Vail, Gabrielle, and Anthony Aveni (eds.)

2004   *The Madrid Codex: New Approaches to Understanding an Ancient Maya Manuscript*. University Press of Colorado, Boulder.

Vail, Gabrielle, and Christine Hernández

2006   Fire Drilling, Bloodletting, and Sacrifice: Yearbearer Rituals in the Maya and Borgia Group Codices. In *Sacred Books, Sacred Languages: Two Thousand Years of Ritual and Religious Maya Literature; Proceedings of the 8th European Maya Conference, Madrid, November 25–30, 2003* (Rogelio Valencia Rivera and Geneviève Le Fort, eds.): 35–49. Acta Mesoamericana 18. Verlag Anton Saurwein, Markt Schwaben, Germany.

Velásquez, Erik

n.d.   Los dioses remeros mayas y sus posibles contrapartes nahuas. Paper presented at the 10th European Maya Conference, The Maya and Their Neighbours: Internal and External Contacts through Time, Leiden, 2005.

Villacorta C., J. Antonio, and Carlos A. Villacorta

1976   *Códices mayas*. 2nd ed. Tipografía Nacional, Guatemala City.

Whittaker, Gordon

1986   The Mexican Names of Three Venus Gods in the Dresden Codex. *Mexicon* 8 (3): 56–60.

Whorf, Benjamin L.

1948   *Loan Words in Ancient Mexico*. Middle American Research Institute, Philological and Documentary Studies Publication 11. Tulane University, New Orleans.

Zimmermann, Günter

1956   *Die Hieroglyphen der Maya-Handschriften*. Abhandlungen aus dem Gebiet der Auslandskunde 62. Cram, de Gruyter, Hamburg.

Glossary

almanac: Almanacs in the Maya codices include dates in the 260-day ritual calendar (the *tzolk'in*), as well as pictures and hieroglyphic texts (those in the Borgia Group lack hieroglyphic texts).

biface: A lithic tool, such as a spear head, projectile point, or knife, that has been flaked on both sides.

boustrophedon: The writing of alternate lines in opposite directions (i.e., from left to right in one line and from right to left in the next).

cuicatl: Song; a Nahua genre of verbal art.

diphrastic kenning: Also referred to by its Spanish name *difrasismo*, meaning "diphrase," it is a common stylistic device in Mesoamerican verbal art in which two terms are paired to express metaphorically a third, often more abstract, concept.

E-type groups: Assemblages consisting of a radial pyramid on the west side of an open plaza and a low range building on the east surmounted by three small temples, usually associated with astronomical orientations.

Formée cross almanac: A category of almanac that explicitly depicts a full count of the 260-day ritual calendar in a form that combines four large trapezoidal quadrants (arms) in the shape of a Formée cross, with a second set of four smaller quadrants (lobes) in its open corner spaces between the larger quadrants.

glottochronology: A linguistic methodology that uses the rate of vocabulary replacement to estimate the date of divergence for distinct but genetically related languages.

Haab' (or haab): A 365-day calendar used by the Maya to approximate the length of the seasonal year. It consists of 18 months of 20 days, followed by a final five-day period at the end of the year called Wayeb' (Uayeb).

heliacal rise: The reappearance of a star or planet, usually at dawn, following a period of invisibility due to its apparent close proximity to the sun.

incensario: A vessel used for burning incense, usually made of pottery.

in extenso: *In extenso* almanacs contain all 260 days of the *tzolk'in* in order, sometimes represented by explicit day glyphs and sometimes by spacers.

isogloss: A boundary between regions that differ in a particular linguistic feature.

kahlay: Yucatec Maya term for "history, memory, or chronicle."

kay: Song; a Yucatec Maya genre of verbal art.

logosyllabic: A writing system that consists both of signs representing entire words (logograms) and signs representing syllables. Maya hieroglyphic writing is a logosyllabic writing system.

Long Count: A linear calendar used by the Pre-Hispanic Maya to place dates in absolute time. The Long Count is based on units of 20 and is organized as follows:

k'in (kin): The smallest unit of the Long Count, equivalent to a day.

winal (uinal): The second unit of the Long Count, equal to 20 *k'ins*, or 20 days.

tun: A *tun* is equivalent to 18 *winals*, or 360 days. This deviation from the vigesimal (20-based) system allowed for an approximation of the solar year. (Note that there was a separate calendar, the *haab'*, that was 365 days in length; see *haab'*.)

k'atun (katun): A period of 20 *tuns*, or 7,200 days.

b'ak'tun (baktun): A period of 20 *k'atuns*, or 144,000 days.

Mexica: One of several Nahuatl-speaking ethnic groups (referred to collectively as Aztecs) who migrated into and settled within the Basin of Mexico during the thirteenth century from a place they called Aztlan. The Mexica were one of the last groups to arrive, and because the area within the highland basin was already densely populated, they were forced to move from place to place and to serve the rulers of larger, more powerful polities. Thereafter, they fled into the marshes of Lake Texcoco, where they are said to have witnessed an eagle perched on a nopal cactus with a snake in its beak. Taking this as a sign from their patron god, the Mexica settled on this site and founded their capital of Tenochtitlan.

mythography: A written collection of myths, sometimes derived from disparate oral and written sources. One such collection of Yucatec Maya myths is found from page 42, line 6, though page 63, line 6, of the Book of Chilam Balam of Chumayel.

patronymic: A name derived from that of the father or a paternal ancestor, usually through the addition of an affix.

pochteca: A specialized merchant class that was widely used by the Mexica to provide information about neighboring regions in advance of conquest.

spacer: A colored circle used in central Mexican almanacs to represent a single day in a count of days. These are not to be confused with colored circles depicted in association with a single day sign that would be representative of a numerical coefficient.

spirant: A consonant such as /f/, /s/, or /sh/ that is produced by air flowing through a constriction in the oral cavity.

tonalpoualli: The name given to the Mexican 260-day ritual calendar (see *tzolk'in*).

toponym: A place name.

trecena: The 260-day calendar (see *tzolk'in*) contains 20 *trecenas*, periods of 13 days that begin with a day with a coefficient of 1 and count forward consecutively until reaching a day beginning with a coefficient of 13. An example is 1 Imix, 2 Ik', 3 Ak'b'al, 4 K'an, 5 Chikchan, 6 Kimi, 7 Manik', 8 Lamat, 9 Muluk, 10 Ok, 11 Chuwen, 12 Eb', 13 B'en. The following *trecena* would then begin on 1 Ix.

tzolk'in (tzolkin): A 260-day calendar used by the Maya and other Meso-american cultures for divination and prophecy. *Tzolk'in* dates consist of a number (or coefficient) ranging from 1 to 13 and a glyph referring to one of the 20 days of the *tzolk'in*. The starting point involves pairing the first number (1) with the first day name (Imix). One then moves forward by one day name and one coefficient for each of the 260 days in the cycle. The cycle ends on 13 Ahaw (day 260) and begins again on 1 Imix on the following day. For additional information, see mayacodices.org/calendar.asp.

vocable: Nonlexical elements characteristic of Nahuatl songs. Vocables in English songs include *fa la la* in the Christmas carol "Deck the Halls."

Yucatecan: A group of closely related Mayan languages, including Yucatec, Itzaj, Lacandón, and Mopan. This term is also used to refer to speakers of these languages.

Contributors

Anthony P. Andrews is a Professor of Anthropology at New College of Florida. His research interests embrace the archaeology, history, and historical archaeology of the Maya area, with a particular focus on the ecology, settlement patterns, economics, history, and historical cartography of the coastal regions.

Anthony Aveni is Russell Colgate Distinguished University Professor of Astronomy, Anthropology, and Native American Studies at Colgate University, where he has taught since 1963. Aveni helped develop the field of archaeoastronomy and is especially well known for his research into the astronomical history of the Aztec and Maya cultures of ancient Mexico. Aveni's recent books include *People and the Sky: Our Ancestors and the Cosmos*, *Uncommon Sense*, *Skywatchers*, a revised version of *Skywatchers of Ancient Mexico*, and *The Madrid Codex: New Approaches to Understanding an Ancient Maya Manuscript* (co-edited with Gabrielle Vail).

Victoria R. Bricker is an Emeritus Professor of Anthropology at Tulane University, where she taught for 36 years. Her research interests include Mesoamerican ethnology, ethnohistory, linguistics, epigraphy, and archaeoastronomy. She is a member of the American Philosophical Society and the National Academy of Sciences.

Karen Dakin is Investigador Titular ("Full Researcher") in the Seminario de Lenguas Indígenas in the Instituto de Investigaciones Filológicas of the Universidad Nacional Autónoma de México. Her research interests include the reconstruction, etymologies, and prehistory of Uto-Aztecan languages; Nahuatl dialectology and historical development; Nahuatl colonial period documents; and the use of Nahuatl as a lingua franca. Recent publications include "Xolotl" in *La metáfora en Mesoamérica* (Seminario de Lenguas Indígenas, Instituto de Investigaciones Filológicas, UNAM, 2005); "Final Features and Proto-Uto-Aztecan: A Contribution Using Morphological Reconstruction," in *Historical Linguistics 2005, Selected Papers from the XVII International Congress on Historical*

Linguistics (John Benjamins, 2007); "Nahuatl -ka Words: Evidence for a Proto-Uto-Aztecan Derivational Pattern," in *Sprachtypologie und Universalienforschung/ Language Typology and Universals* 50, no. 1 (2004); and "Animals and Vegetables: Uto-Aztecan Noun Derivation, Semantic Classification, and Cultural History," in *Selected Papers from the XIV International Congress of Historical Linguistics* (John Benjamins, 2001).

Christine Hernández holds a research position with the Middle American Research Institute at Tulane University in New Orleans, and is an Anthropology lecturer at Southeastern Louisiana University in Hammond, Louisiana. Her research interests are divided between an on-going archaeological study of the prehistory of the eastern Lake Cuitzeo Basin in Michoacán, Mexico, and comparative calendrical studies of the Maya and Borgia Group codices. She has published articles on both enterprises in several edited volumes and journals, including *Ancient Mesoamerica*, *Ancient America*, and *Arqueología*. She is currently working with Gabrielle Vail on completing an online database focusing on Mesoamerican codices and a new commentary of the Madrid Codex.

Timothy W. Knowlton earned his Ph.D. in Anthropology from Tulane University in December 2004. Knowlton was a Dumbarton Oaks Fellow and Visiting Professor at the Universidad del Valle in Guatemala in fall 2005 and spring 2006 and is currently Assistant Professor of Anthropology at Berry College in Georgia. Knowlton is the author of several articles in journals such as *Mexicon, Journal for the History of Astronomy*, and *Anthropological Linguistics*, and is currently completing a book manuscript on Classical Yucatecan creation myths.

Alfonso Lacadena received his Ph.D. in History from the Universidad Complutense de Madrid in 1995. His research interests include Mesoamerican writing systems, languages, and literatures, with a focus on Maya and Nahuatl. He has taught courses on Mesoamerican writing systems and Mesoamerican archaeology at the Universidad Autónoma de Yucatán, Mexico (1998–2003) and the Universidad Complutense de Madrid, where he has been a Professor in the Department of History of America II (American anthropology) since 2004.

Carlos Peraza Lope is an archaeologist with the Instituto Nacional de Antropología e Historia in the state of Yucatán, Mexico. He is the director of the INAH-Mayapán Project, which has annually investigated and restored sections of this city's monumental zone, open for tourism since 1996. He has also conducted investigations of hundreds of sites throughout the northern Maya lowlands, including Kuluba and Cozumel. His recent publications include articles on Mayapán in the journals *Arqueología mexicana, Mexicon*, and *Ancient Mesoamerica*, as well as a seminal monograph on Postclassic Maya pottery, *Estudio y secuencia del material ceramico de San Gervasio, Cozumel* (published by the Universidad Autónoma de Yucatán, 1993).

Martha J. Macri holds the Rumsey Endowed Chair in California Indian Studies at the University of California, Davis. Her research interests include the linguistic prehistory of the Americas, Native American revitalization, and the languages and scripts of ancient Mesoamerica. She is an enrolled member of the Cherokee Nation.

Marilyn A. Masson is Associate Professor in Mesoamerican Archaeology at the University at Albany–SUNY. She has co-directed the Proyecto Económico de Mayapán (PEMY) with Carlos Peraza (Centro INAH-Yucatán) and Timothy Hare (Moorehead State University) from 2001 to the present, as well as the Belize Postclassic Project. Her research focuses on economies, urban organization, religion, and political structure of ancient Mesoamerican states. Masson has worked in Mesoamerica since 1983. She is the author of three books, *In the Realm of Nachan Kan: Postclassic Maya Archaeology at Laguna de On, Belize* (University Press of Colorado, 2000), *Ancient Civilizations of Mesoamerica, A Reader* (with Michael E. Smith, Blackwell, 2002), and *Ancient Maya Political Economies* (with David Freidel, Altamira Press, 2002). Currently, she and Carlos Peraza are completing a book on Mayapán, titled *Kukulkan's Realm: The Postclassic Mesoamerican City of Mayapán* (University of Colorado Press, forthcoming).

Merideth Paxton is the author of *The Cosmos of the Yucatec Maya: Cycles and Steps from the Madrid Codex* and numerous articles and chapters contributed to edited volumes. Her research focuses on the Pre-Hispanic Maya codices and other painted scenes, as well as the influence of European intellectual traditions on the interpretation of this information. As part of her dissertation study concerning the provenience and date of painting of the Dresden Codex (*Codex Dresden: Stylistic and Iconographic Analysis of a Maya Manuscript*, University of New Mexico, 1986), she compiled a photographic survey of painted walls and capstones that have been found at the pre-conquest Maya settlements of Yucatán. She has subsequently continued to analyze these photographs, and she has returned to the peninsula to study recent discoveries. Paxton is also the Mesoamerican Manuscripts Editor for the *Latin American Indian Literatures Journal*.

Fernando Robles Castellanos is an archaeologist with the Instituto Nacional de Antropología e Historia in the state of Yucatán, Mexico. He is director of the Preclassic Xamán Susulá Archaeological Project near the city of Mérida. He has directed various archaeological projects, including El Meco, Xelhá, and Cozumel in northern Quintana Roo, and Costa Maya, Poxilá, and Caucel in Yucatán. He has also actively participated in other projects at Las Pilas in Morelos, Cobá in northern Quintana Roo, and Isla Cerritos on the north-central coast of Yucatán. His recent publications include articles in *Ancient Mesoamerica*, *Mexicon*, and *Colección científica del INAH*, as well as a seminal monograph on the Culhua Mexica (published by the Instituto Nacional de Antropología e Historia, 2007).

Karl Taube is a Professor in the Department of Anthropology at the University of California at Riverside. He received his Ph.D. in Anthropology from Yale University in 1988. His research interests include ancient Mesoamerican writing and religion. Although much of his research concerns the ancient Maya, he has also published studies concerning the Olmec, Teotihuacan, and the Aztec, as well as Pre-Columbian contact between Mesoamerica and the American Southwest. He has participated in archaeological projects in Yucatán and Chiapas, Mexico, Guatemala, and Honduras as well as coastal Ecuador and highland Peru and is currently serving as the Project Iconographer for the San Bartolo Project, co-directed by Dr. William Saturno and Monica Urquizu. Among his published books and monographs are *The Albers Collection*, *Aztec and Maya Myths*, *The Major Gods of Ancient Yucatan*, *The Writing System of Ancient Teotihuacan*, *Olmec Art at Dumbarton Oaks*, and *The Gods and Symbols of Ancient Mexico and the Maya*, the last co-authored with Dr. Mary Ellen Miller.

Gabrielle Vail holds research positions at New College of Florida and Tulane University. Her research interests focus on Late Postclassic Maya codices and murals and what these data sets can tell us about Maya religion, society, and daily life in the fourteenth and fifteenth centuries. She has co-edited two books on the Madrid Codex and published numerous articles and book chapters on the Maya codices, including an overview article in the *Annual Review of Anthropology* (2006). She and Martha Macri have recently completed volume 2 (on the codices) of *The New Catalog of Maya Hieroglyphs* (University of Oklahoma Press, forthcoming), and she and Christine Hernández are preparing a commentary on the Madrid Codex and its relationship to other Maya and Borgia Group codices.

Index

Numbers in **bold** type indicate illustrations or photos. Plates follow page 144.

astronomical tables, 266, 273n. 8, 334, 393

astronomy, 3, 127, 272, 376; and Maya-Mexican interaction, 377

Atónal, 41, 45, **47**; founded new royal dynasty, 46–47

Axayácatl, 64; and suppression of local dynasties, 49

Ayahualulco, **2**, 51, 139

Aztec Calendar Stone, 290, 298

Aztec expansion, 17, 20, 37, 65, 210, 220, 392; and access to infrastructure, 372–73; beginning of imperial expansion, 39; and cultural development, 56; intensification of, 49; Mayapán abandoned prior to, 6; and pilgrimages, 42; spread of International style predates, 402n. 4

Aztlán, 302n. 1

ballcourts, 22, 81, 118, 375; and Laguna de On, 378n. 7

barrios, 102, 374, 377. *See also* enclave, foreign; Merchants' Barrio; Mexican Barrio; Oaxacan Barrio

basal pyramids, 54, 59. *See also* temple-pyramids

Basin of Mexico, **2**, 3, 6, 8, 18, 19, 43, **43**, 44, 45, 48, 49, 62, 64, 67n. 5, 88, **139**, **218**, 302n. 1; Aztecs consolidate rule over, 64; and Aztec I ceramics, 44; expanding imperial networks from, 20; and figurine technology, 88; and founding of Toltec kingdom, 42; linguistic complexity within, **218**; and marriage alliances, 43; Nahuatl speakers from, 6; subdivisions of Postclassic period in, 18; Toltec lords revived their society in, 45

Belize, 24, 36, 145, 151, 229, 272, 371, 373; and knives, 96–97; possible ballcourt site, 378n. 7; and use of figurines, 85

Bernal, Ignacio, 48–49

Beyer, Hermann, 165, **167**

Bierhorst, John, 245–46

bilingualism, 210, 218, 222

birds, 161, 166–70, 172, 177, 292, 318, 320, 351; decapitated, 206; exotic, 165; precious, 146, 171, 178, 182; quetzal, 147, 148, 167, 353. *See also* cotinga; hummingbirds

bloodletting, 165, **166**

Book of Chilam Balam of Mani, 25

Book of Chilam Balam of Tizimin, 322

Books of Chilam Balam of Chumayel, 117, 138, 162, 222, 243, 247, 252, 280; apocalyptic prophecies in, 253; as clandestine copybooks, 242; and Hunac Ceel, 251; mythography in, 246; songs scattered throughout, 244; and suffering accompanying migration, 248; texts written over several centuries, 264

Borgia Codex, 264, 265, 269, 270, 279, 309–29, **311**; connections with Madrid Codex, 335; and *in extenso* almanacs, 340; Tlahuizcalpantecuhtli in, 318; transcription of calendrics in almanac from, 327; Venus almanac of, 314, 337

Borgia Codex, page 25 of, 325, **326**, **327**

Borgia Codex, page 27 of, 337, 338, **339**, 340, 341, 346, 351, 355n. 3, 355n. 4, 361n. 3, 361n. 7; agricultural and meteorological themes in, 338; calendrical structure of, 338; dating model by Aveni, 338

Borgia Codex, page 28 of, 337, 338, 339, 340, 341, 350

Borgia Codex, pages 49b–52b of: south direction on, 356

Borgia Codex, pages 53–54 of, 202, 309, **310**, 312, 315, 319, 323, 327, 328, 337; clockwise reading order of dates, 324; counterclockwise spiral reading order, 325; victims in, 311

Borgia Group codices, 1, 147, 149, 150, 167, 178, 182, 202, 264, 351, 356; astronomical references in, 337; parallels in structure and content with Maya codices, 5

borrowings, 4, 209, 210, 224–29, 231–32, 333, 384; and cosmopolitan art style, 334 bowls: hummingbird poised on rim of, **166**; inverted, and celestial symbolism, **168**; as open flowers, 168; polychrome, 171

breath, 156–58, 182; exhaled, 146

breath blossoms, 156

burials, 17, 81; cremation, 48, **92**, **93**, **97**, 97–98

butterflies, 150, 182; as brow piece, **152**; as design on bowl, **168**; as design on textile, **155**

Cacaxtla, **2**, 18, 149, 159; evidence of Maya influence in, 376

Calendar. *See* Maya calendar; Mexican calendar

Calendar Round, 283, 287, 320, 329, 353; 52-year, 266, 322, 325, 338, 350, **354**, 356; thirteen-year quarters of, 326

Calendar Stone, Aztec. *See* Aztec Calendar Stone

calendar systems: shared ancestral, 333

calendrical ritual program, 126

calendrical structures, 267, 384; Borgia Codex, **268**; Fejérváry-Mayer Codex, **268**; interpretation of, 322, 345; Madrid Codex, **270**

Calzada Mopan, 385, **386**

Campeche, 21, 25, 26, 45, 49, 51, 52, 56, 59, 65, 66n. 2, 66n. 4, 78, 217, 219, 373, 399

canal: and water representation, 394, **396**

Cantares de Dzitbalché, 246

Cantona, 18

Canul, 28; foreign group residing at, 25; as mercenaries, 24

Caracol. *See* Round Temples

cardinal directions, 116, 322. *See also* solar directions; world directions

Carnegie Institution, 22, 23, 81, 83, 88, 97

cartography: solar, 8, 279, 295, 296

cartouches, 163, 205, 320, 323

Castillo, 85, 122, 123, **123**, 124, **124**, 126, 182; at Chichén Itzá, **58**, **59**; comparison of Chichén Itzá and Mayapán, 123; at Tulúm, 27

Catherwood, Frederick, 21

celestial floral paradise, 168

celestial imagery, 199

Cenote X-Coton, 81, 97

censers, 80, 88, 91, 98, 102, 104n. 1, **174**, 374; effigy, 88, 90, 91, **91**, 100, 102, 374. *See also* Chen Mul modeled censers

Centeotl, 311, 318, **357**

Central Mexico, 1, 17–24, 27, 30n. 8, 37, 46, 51, 52, 56, 61, 64–66, 79, **100**, 116, 120, **121**, 126–28, 139, 140, 147, 159, 182, 202, 221, 229, 232, 263, 264, 279, 290, 297, 301, 309, 316, 338, 369–76, 378n. 1, 378n. 2, 389, 391, 394, 401; art from, 4; and chambered tombs, 97; Chollolan as principle Quetzalcoatl cult religious center of, 41; chronicles of, 21; and Codex Kingsborough, 150; commercial routes to Anahuac, 49; and contact between scribes, 334; and development of Classical Nahuatl, 137; and economic importance of Coaixtlahuacan, 370; and exchange with southwest Maya lowlands, 59; and homes of nobles, 82; and language, 64; migration of Nahuatl-speaking people from, to Basin of Mexico, 8; obsidian from, 103; period of heightened contact with, 28; as prestige center for Maya elite, 269, 337; scribes from, 8; similarity of knives and projectile points to those of Mayapán, 96; and a solar zenith-based calendar, 126; tennis courts of, 22; and trade goods, 21; trade with Mayapán, 59; traits linked to, 5; and use of figurines, 85; Venus represented by five-pointed star, 198

ceramics. *See* pottery/ceramics

Cerro Quemado, 183

Chaak, 91, 343, 345, **350**, 351, **351**; headdress worn by, 350

Chaak masks, 59, 178

Chac. *See* Chaak

chacmool statue, 22

Chacnicté, 289

Chak Chel, 153, 155, **359**. *See also* Ix Chel

chalchihuitl, 161

Codex Mendoza, 207, 279, 290, **295**, 295, 298, 300, 301; creation around Mexico City, 296; dating of, 296; and Mexican sign for "day," **208**; oriented with east at top, 296

Codex Telleriano-Remensis, 207, 208, **311**, 311, 400–1

Codex Vaticanus B, **153**, **155**, 167, **168**, 169, **169**, 171, 202, 264, 269, 270, 279, 337, **357**; and *in extenso* almanacs, 340

codices, 1, 5, 6, 28, 269, 377; astronomical content, 334; as gifts, 393; production of, 334; provenience of, 263–65, 290–92, 334; as screenfold, 156; and social concerns, 263

codices, by name: Codex Aubin, 20, 264; Codex Bodley, 264; Codex Borbonicus, 198; Codex Cortesianus, 280, **282**; Codex Kingsborough, 150; Codex Laud, **181**, 264, **394**; Codex Nuttall, 161, 202; Codex Pérez, 247; Codex Porfirio Díaz, 272n. 2; Codex Troano, 280; Codex Tro-Cortesianus, 279, **284**; Columbino Codex, 264; Cospi Codex, 182, 202, 264, 269, 270; Florentine Codex, 150, 154, 171, 222, 244, 266; Grolier Codex, 264, 265; Maya codices, 309; Mexican codices, 309; Paris Codex, 264; Selden Codex, 264; Tehuacán Codex, 150; Tudela Codex, 153; Vaticanus B Codex, 150, 167, 169, 202, 264, 270, 279, 337; Vindobonsis Codex, 264; Zouche-Nuttall Codex, 198, 264. *See also* Borgia Codex; Borgia Group codices; Codex Cospi; Codex Fejérváry-Mayer; Codex Vaticanus B; Dresden Codex; Madrid Codex

Colonia del Valle, 377

colors: use of, in description, 222

Comalcalco, 30n. 8

commerce, 26, 400. *See also* trade

commercial exchange, 388, 390. *See also* trade

commercial interaction: at variance with material record, 9

commodities: use and exchange of, 17

Conil, 372

conquered polity, **203**

conquest: verbs associated with war and, 201. *See also* Spanish conquest

correlations, calendrical, 119, 338, 393

Cortés, Hernán, 25, 26, 39, 53, 67n. 5, 161, 171, 172, 221, 296

cosmograms, 272, 316, 317, 320, 322, 327, 329

cosmology, 297; and alignment of important structures, 7; Maya and Mexican shared, 7; and Maya city plans, 118; Pre-Hispanic Maya, 291; and quadripartite designs, 118; role in city planning, 127

Cospi Codex, 150, 337; and *in extenso* almanacs, 340

cotinga, 357

couplets: paired, 222

Cozumel, **2**, 26, 52, 54, 56, 79, 83, 371, 375, 399; as pilgrimage center, 182

creation mythology, 98, 242, 246, 263

creation myths, 246

cremations. *See* burials, cremation

crosses, 289; Formée cross, 316, 329; St. Andrew's cross, 316, **319**, 329

cuicatl, 244, 245, 398; metrical structure of, 245

cuicatl genre: features of, 244–47

Culhua, 62; becomes dominant language of commercial trade, 64

Culhua Mexica, **63**, 65, 67n. 6; and expansion, 6

Culhua Toltec, 62

Culhuacan, 2, 41, 42–45; and commercial interaction, 44; end of ascendancy of Basin of Mexico, 45; rule over fertile region of Basin of Mexico, 43; territorial changes, 43–44

cultural interaction, 228, 345

cultural transmission, 399

culúa. *See* Culhuas

Cunduacán, 51, 66n. 4. *See also* pottery/ceramics, Fine Orange "U"

Cuzamil, **53**, 54; and diffusion of Mixteca-Puebla style, ideology, and iconography, 56; political innovations at, 56; as principal political-cultural entity, 53; structure at, **55**. *See also* Cozumel; San Gervasio

cycles of time, 265–66

darts, 150, 171, 176, 177, 318, 384, 386, 394, **396**; and atlatls, 311, 312, 314, 325

Davalos, Felipe, 146

day glyphs, 267, 271, 272n. 4, 283, 311, 317, 325, 337, 343, 346, 348, 350, 353, 358; blue-collared serpents weave through, 343; for Lamat, 196, 197; order of, 353

day names, 231

day signs. *See* day glyphs

decapitated victims, 358

deities. *See* gods

diphrastic kennings, 245

distribution of selected language families, **218**

DNA studies, 374; and foreign populations, 374

dog, 231

Dresden Codex, 120, 150, 159, 163, 165, 178, 194, 196, 200, 202, 209, 225, 228, 264, 265, 266, 269, 279, 302n. 2, 309, 312, 314, **328**, 392; flint in, 390; Mars table of, 335; Quetzalcoatl in, 390; skybands in, **394**, 400; and spacer counting, 337; Tlahuizcalpantecuhtli in, **315**; Venus table of, 3, 312–14, **313**, **315**, 318, 327, 333, 387, 389; water as a canal in, **396**; Wayeb' pages, 352; Xiuhtecuhtli in, 318

Dresden Codex, page 24 of, 326–27

Dresden Codex, pages 31b–35b of, **336**

Dresden Codex, page 36 of, 395

drought, 375

Dzadzá, 289

earspools, 158–61; serpents emerging from, **160**, 161

earth net, 149

east and west, geographic symbolism of, 147

Ecab, **2**, 372, 378n. 3

eclipses, 120

Edzná, **2**, 374

Ehecatl, 24, 46, **47**, 88, 98, 150, 389

Ek Balam, 20

Ek Chuah, 91

El Bellote, 29n. 8

El Chayal: mines at, 60

elites, 40, 44, 82, 140, 250, 337; adoption of foreign ideas by, 5; and intermarriage, 101

El Meco, **2**

El Tajín, 18

emblem glyphs, 201, 202

emergence, 179

enclave, foreign, 27, 56, 82, 101, 360, 373, 374. *See also* barrios

environmental changes, 7

equinoxes, 117, 120, **123**, 124, **124**, 126, **286**, 290

ethnic groups, ruling, **41**

evidence: archaeological, 9, 17, 20, 27, 66n. 1, 371; and colonial period, 8; ethnohistoric, 4; of interaction between lowland Maya and highland Mexico, 7; linguistic, 4; nature of, 370

exchange: Mexica-Maya, 279, 300, 301, 302, 383; exchange of manuscripts, 334; between highland Mexica and northern Maya lowlands, 388; of trade items, 194, 360. *See also* commercial exchange; information exchange

figurines, 85–95, **86–87**, 374; female, **88**; holding children, 85; and Mexican deities, 88

figurine technologies, 88

five-pointed stars, 198. *See also* half stars

flint: representation of, in Maya codices, 390

Imperial Aztec Triple Alliance, 80

imperial conquest, 4

Indians, 245, 297, 299

in extenso almanacs, 265, 269, 270, 271, **271**, 273n. 6, 273n. 7, 334, 340, 343–46, 348, 361n. 4, 361n. 5; in Madrid Codex, 359

information exchange: 5, 17; and Maya and Mexican scribes, 7, 334; and networks, 139

Inguiteria (architectural group), 48

intellectual exchange: models of, 207–8

intellectuals: interchange among Mexican and Maya, 18, 27

intellectual traditions: interrelatedness of, 203

interaction: central Mexico and northern Maya lowlands, 376, 383. *See also* exchange; intellectual exchange

International style, 24, 37–38, 53, 54, 65, 138, 148–49, 384, 393, 399; art themes, 182; first appearance of, 45; and floating objects, 396; in syncretic form, 38

interpreters, 27

investiture ceremonies, 4

Isthmian script, 194

Isthmus of Tehuantepec, **2**

Itzá, 8, 24, 53, 54, 57, 58, 65, 217, 247; conflation of three groups of, 253; song, 398. *See also* Itzaj

Itzaj: **218**, 224, 229; in contact with Nahuatl as a lingua franca, 217

Itzamkanac, 52, 53, 56

Itzamna, 91, **95**, **159**, 291, 322, 357

Itzcóatl, 62

Itzmal Ch'en, **84**, 85, **99**, **100**, **127**; as nexus of interaction and exchange, 83

Itztli, 318

Ix Chel, 26, 54, 56, 183. *See also* Chak Chel

Iximche, **2**

Ixlu, 386

Ixtlilxóchitl the Second, 67n. 5

Ixtepeque: mines at, 60

Izamal, 20

jade, 147–49, 152, 156, 158, **158**, 161, 163, **164**, 165, **166**, **167**, 171, 173, 182, 195, **197**

jaguar, 149, 162, **163**, 242, 292, **293**, 312, 316, 320, **320**, 325, 386; House of, 55; statue of, 29

Jimbal, **385**

Jiménez, Wigberto, 148; and reconstruction of Toltec history, 29n. 7

Kabah, 20

Kakupacal, 251

Katun 8 Ahaw, 62

katun ending, 117

katun period, 117

kay, 243, 246, 247, 248, **254**, **256**; as Maya genre, 244

Kiche' language, **136**

Kisin, **357**

knives, **96**, **100**, 318, 322; flint, 311, **357**; pointed, 96–97

Kukulcan, 101; and Hunac Ceel, 78; as Quetzalcoatl, 4, 21, 22, 24, 29n. 2, 39, 58, 66n. 3, 98, 99, **100**; temple to, **59**; and Venus, 390. *See* Quetzalcoatl

Lacandón Maya, 168

Laguna de Términos, 26

Lamat, 229–30. *See also* Venus

lambda position: figure with legs in, **394**

La Mojarra Stela 1, 195, **196**

Landa, Diego de (bishop), 21, 24, 28, 226, 360

language groups: evidence for dating the presence of, 223

languages: borrowings across Mesoamerica, 4; combined with visual art, 210; distribution of selected, families, 218; identification of source, 225; Postclassic Mesoamerican, 135–38; ritual, 222 *See also listings under individual language names*

Las Higueras, **2**

Lenca language, **136**

León-Portilla, Miguel, 245

Maya murals: and idiosyncratic late Maya style, 399. *See also* murals

Maya music, 243

Mayan languages: large consonant inventory in, 225

Mayan language speakers, 218; and contact with Nahuatl speakers, 219

Mayapán, 2, 21, 23, 25, 27, **53**, 322, 373–74; abandonment of, 6, 373; art and architectural programs of, 79; ascendancy of, 39; chronology of, compared to Tenochtitlan, 80; and commercial activity, 60, 61; contact with central Mexico, 79; contained most important temples dedicated to Quetzalcoatl, 66n. 3; date of abandonment, 29n. 3; diversity of artistic styles, 27; domestic architecture at, 82; emergence of, 370; and exotica, 104; fall of, 20, 80; feathered-serpent imagery, 24; governed by Cocom, 52; Gulf Coast Mexican agents settled at, 102; history of city of, 21; how chronology relates to Basin of Mexico, 6; imports, 103; international elements in monumental art, 98; and murals, 3; nature of foreign involvement in, 80; plan of, showing sunset alignments, **124**; as a political center, 390, 399; possibility of Mexican barrio in, 374; as principal political-cultural entity, 53; production and distribution of hieroglyphic codices, 399; provinces of, 59; pyramid at, compared to one at Chichén Itzá, 59; Round Temple at, 59, 122; ruled Yucatán after fall of Chichén Itzá, 57; settlement of, 24, 77; shared attributes with central Mexico, 100; solar cult at, 126; strong international ties and open exchange of ideas, 98; Temple of the Fisherman, **61**; Temple of the Niches, 60; and trade, 61; use of figurines at, 85

Maya scribes: physical access to Borgia Group codices, 6; and reading of Mexican documents, 398

Maya social memory, 242, 243

Maya song, 241–56; Nahua elements in, 244–47

Maya texts: Nahua words in, 208. *See also* hieroglyphic texts

Mendieta, Geronimo, 147

Mendoza, Antonio de, 296

merchandise: exchange of exotic, 47

merchants: 25, 26, 27, 47–49, 52, 65, two categories of, 102–3; and homes in Mayapán, 78

Merchants' Barrio, 102, 370, 374, 377

Mesoamerica: balkanization of, 39; calendrical systems of, 263; and cosmopolitan network, 372; figures from, **151**, **152**; spatial diagrams, 283

Mesoamerican symbols: combined with Christian symbols, 199–201

Mesoamerican themes: and suffering accompanying migration, 248

Mexica: 6, 7, 10, 64–66, 220, 290, 291, 292, 400; appointment of first king, 80; beginning of consolidation, 49; beginning of imperial expansion, 39, 373, 392; and maps, 301; razed Coaixtlahuacan, 48; rebel faction leaves, 62; and solar direction, 289; and yearbearers, 292. *See also* Culhua Mexica

Mexica art: solar themes in, 290

Mexican Barrio, 374

Mexican calendar, 320, 322, **340**, 387, 388

Mexican codices: contains highly complex calendrical, astronomical, and divinatory instruments, 358; parallels with Maya codices, 5; reconciling differences with Maya codices, 359; traits shared with Maya codices, 383. *See also listings for individual codices*

Mexican *in extenso* almanacs: attributes of, 343; and distances, 344. *See also in extenso* almanacs

Mexican influence, 8, 24, 65, 128, 245, 246, 398; and elements in murals and ceramics, 371; on Maya almanacs and texts, 263; on Maya area, 392; and Maya music, 243, 253; and murals, 139; probably not the result of migration, 7

Mexicans: pre-Aztec, 29n. 3

Mexican sculptures: some probably are Aztec, 29n. 5

Mexican-style artifacts, **94**; distribution of, 92, **93**

Mexico, central. *See* Central Mexico

Mictlantecuhtli, 318

migrations, 4, 7, 21, 22, 26, 29n. 7, 104, 136, 137, 210, 248, 283, 400

migration theories, 229

Millet, Luis, 374

Mixe language, **136**

Mixe-Zoque: loanwords from, 389; speakers of, 226

Mixteca Alta, 370

Mixteca-Puebla region, 3

Mixteca-Puebla style. *See* International style

Mixtec codices, 149

Mixtec language, **136**

Mococha, 289

Moctezuma, 25, 49, 64, 78, 117, **151**, 159, 173, 373

mollusks, 51, 150, **151**, 391

monkey panel, carved, **96**

Monte Albán, 176

Montejo, Francisco de, 287

Montezuma. *See* Moctezuma

monuments, 57, **93–94**, 98, 195, 207, 290, 385–87; similarities between Chichén Itzá and Tula, 38

Morley manuscript, 252

motifs, 138, 139, 168; death and gore, emblems of, 153; directional, 296; directional tree, 350; facial hair as sign of age, 177; flower, 400; netted earth, 149, 182; old man mountain, **179**; skull and crossed bones, 155; swirling grass motif, **153**, 154; vegetation, 148, 149, 163, 168, 171, 182, 350, 400

mountain cave maw, **180**

multepal (joint government), 58, 59

murals, 3, 24, 28, 54, 60, **61**, 139, 140, 153, 393; Bonampak, 194; at Cacaxtla, 173, 198; in International style, **55**, 65, 383; at San Bartolo, 175, 195; at Santa Rita, 161, 179; textile patterns in, 154; at Tulúm, 179. *See also listings by individual site*

Muyil, **2**

myths: creation, 79, 98, **100**, 101, 242, 246, 263, 272, 287, 290, 297; flood, 401

Naco, **2**, **139**

Nahua influence, 208, 243, 246, 250

Nahua loanwords, 208, 209, 210n. 2, 224–29, 232

Nahua-speaking peoples, 1, 26, 137, 217, 218; and contact with Mayan speakers, 219

Nahuatl, 136, 137, 140, 147, 265; as lingua franca, 217, 219; patronyms from, 228; in southern areas, 220

Nahuatl *cuicatl*, 244, 251

Nahuatl dialects: historical classification of, **221**

Nahuatl language, **136**, 217–34, 244

Nahuatl loans: listing of, 227–28

Nahuatl names, 25, 78, 200, 209, 228

Nahuatl speakers, 1, 4, 6, 17, 18, 26, 30n. 15, 135

Na Puc Tun, 246

New Year, 150, 161, 350, 351, 387

Nine Lords of the Night, 291, 294, 318

Nito, **2**; exact location unknown, 377; situated in Bay of Amatique, 61; trading posts established at, 56

Nonohualco, 49, 51, 64

North Yucatán, 18, **19**; alignment evidence from, 119; distribution of alignments in, 121; orientation of Late Postclassic sites, 128. *See also* Yucatán

Itzamna effigy ceramic face, **95**; Matillas Fine Orange, 51–52, **92**, **93**; Matillas Fine Orange Gulf Coast, 83; Mixteca-Puebla, 44; Palmul Incised, 82, 83, **84**, **90**, **91**, 101; Tulúm Red vessels, 54; Xipe effigy ceramic faces, **94**, **95**. *See also* censers; figurines; polychrome pottery

Preclassic period, 7, 193, 195

Pre-Hispanic song: sources of, 243–44. *See also* Maya song; Nahuatl *cuicatl*

prehistory: reconstruction of, 222–23

priesthood: specializations within, 3

priests, 9, 27, 41, 117, 120, 126, 202, 217, 219, 242, 246, 272, 296, 398; as belonging to elite class, 1; duties of, 1–2; educational background of, 3; high, 360; merchants traveling in the company of, 393; and painting of codices, 360; Spanish grammarian, 221; Yucatec, 375. *See also* priest-scribes; scribe-priests

projectile point, 96. *See also* knives

priest-scribes, 360. *See also* priests

Proto–Uto-Aztecan language, 233–34

Puebla-Tlaxcala region, 17, 264

Purepecha language, **136**

quadripartite arrangements, 169

quadripartite floral design, 200

quadripartite sign, 194

quadripartite star, 193

Quetzalcoatl, 21, 58, 65–66, 99, 171–77, 198, **199**, 202–3; dawn emergence of, 177; headdress of, 390; identified with Venus, 198; as Morning Star, 177; reborn at Tlahuizcalpantecuhtli, 176; temple-pyramid of, 59

Quetzalcoatl myth, 29n. 2

quetzalpanecáyotl, 171

quetzal. *See* birds

quetzal plumes, 158, **159**, 171, 172, **173**, 182

quincunx, 204–7

Quintana Roo, 20, 23, 52; east coast of, 24

radiocarbon dating, 57

rain, 228, **293**, 312, **320**, 337, 338; bringing of, 126, 148, 172, 176

Rancho Ina: murals of, 145; and Tulúm serpents, 175

record: archaeological, 9, 17, 18, 20, 27, 39, 77, 117, 369–77, 394

regions: named after occupying faction's ruling lineage, 40

Relación de las cosas de Yucatán (Landa), 1, 21, 226

Relación de la villa de Santa Maria de la Victoria, 25, 52, 64

religion, 228, 250, 290

religious specialists: travel by, 4

riddles, 222

Río Candelaria, 26

ritual calendar, 9, 273n. 7, 361n. 5; 260 days of, 265, 266, 270, 271, 340, 343, 346

roads, 205–6

Robertson, Donald, 24, 290

Rosny, Léon de, 281

Round Temples, 27, 30n. 14, 59, 98, **100**, 124, 126

sacred space, 300

sacrifice, 3, 154, 165, 250; animal, 350; captive, 97; generative, 247; heart, **357**; human, 322; mass, **100**; as motif, 153; and sun god, 161; and Venus, 202

sages, 3

de Sahagún, Bernardino, 244

salt beds, 28

San Angel, **2**; murals of, 145

Sánchez de Aguilar, Pedro, 242, 243, 250, 251; quoted, 241, 250

San Bartolo, 156, **158**, 175, 179, 195, **196**. *See also* murals

San Gervasio, **2**. *See also* Cuzamil

San Martin Jilotepeque: mines at, 60

San Mateo Ixtlahuacan, **2**; date of painting, 298; and Luis de la Paz y Tapia, 299; map compared to Madrid Codex, 300; map of, 279, 290, 296, **297**, 298, 300

Santa Rita Corozal, **2**, 24, 337; legged mollusks at, 391; and mountain imagery, 177; and plumed serpent headdress, 176; and Tulúm serpents, 175

Santa Rita murals, 3, 145–50, 178; deities in, 150; floating objects in, 396; strongly Maya, 146

screenfolds, 156, 266, 281, 340, 353, 359; compared to murals, 145; destruction of, 263; divinatory, 264; and hieroglyphic captions, 266; identification of possible sites of origin of, 264; and inverted material, 281; separation of Madrid Codex into two pieces, 280. *See also* codices

scribe-priests, 391, 393, 396, 399, 401; and exchange of information, 27. *See also* priests

scribes: as belonging to elite class, 1; codical, 334; familiar with more than one language, 207; as individual artists, innovators, and agents of change, 359; intellectual interchange between Maya and Mexican, 359; and painting of codices, 360. *See also* scribe-priests

sculptural features: and Mexican affinities, 23

sculpture, 22, 23, 27, 29n. 5, 38, **90**, 91, **91**, **99**, **100**, 104, 135, 279, 290, 370; Mayapán, 4; and sculptural program of Seibal rulers, 389

Seibal, 385

Seibal Stela 13, 389, **390**

Seibal Stela 19: calendrical sequence on, **388**

Seler, Eduard, 22, 279, 309, 345, 383; quoted, 45–46

semantic couplets, 202

semantic domains, 228

serpents, feathered, 24, 59, 79, 173, **173**, 174, **174**, 176, 182

serpents, intertwined, **173**, 174, **174**, 175, **175**, **176**, 176, 178

shells. *See* mollusks; turtles

sign, A-O, 333

site plans: late changes to, 7

skulls, 98, **99**, **100**, 153, **155**, 318

skybands, 171, 175, 182, 207, **209**

snakes, 203–4. *See also* serpents, feathered; serpents, intertwined

social memory, Maya, 250

Soconusco coast, 373

solar alignments, 375

solar cult, 375

solar directions, 280, 290, 301. *See also* cardinal directions; world directions

solar-related images: and polychrome bowls, 165

solar signs, 146, 162, 163, **164**, **166**

"Song of the Fall of Chichén Itzá," 241–56; contents of, 247–49; as example of telescoping of characters and events, 251; selected translation from, 254–56; setting of, 247; vocables and interjections found in, 248–49, 253

songs: Maya, 243–53; Mexican, 243–44; Pre-Hispanic, 243–44. *See also* cuicatl; kay

Sononusco, **2**

soothsayers, 3

sorcerers, 3

spacers, 267, 271, 333, 337, 346, 349

Spanish conquest, 5, 25, 26, 56, 67n. 5, 78, 210n. 2, 390, 392, 401

spatial concepts: comparison of Madrid and Fejérváry-Mayer codices, 291; Mexica and Maya shared, 279

spearthrowers, 202, 207, 384, 386; plumed serpent, **177**

Spinden, Herbert, 24

St. Andrew's cross, 316, 319, 329

star logograph, 195. *See also* Venus

Starry Deer Alligator, 197

Stephens, John L., 21

stingray spine, 322, 386

strontium isotope studies, 374, 378n. 6

style: ambiguous meaning of, 370; East Coast, 23; and position of legs in standing figures, 394. *See also* International style

sun, 375

sun deity, 162, **162**; turquoise mask of, 162; as war god, 162

surveys. *See tzol peten*

Swadesh, Morris, 223

symbols, 3, 5, 9, 138 serpents, feathered 40, 172, 202, 245, 291, 388; and butterflies, 147; Christian, 199; elite, 98; floral, 146; foreign, 88, 102; Mexican, 207; and Mexica power, 290; for motion of sun, 285; from non-Maya traditions, 193; quadripartite, 200; tree, 302n. 2; Venus, 196, 201, 207

Tabasco, 28; and cacao production, 25; commercial centers of, 26

Tabasco/Campeche coast: trading ports of, 21

Tancah: murals of, 145

Tayasal, **2**

Temosique, 26

Temple of Quetzalcoatl, **42**, 182

Temple of the Fisherman mural, Plate 4

temple pyramids, 58, 59

Templo Mayor, 99, 290, 376

Tenango del Valle, 18

Tenayuca, 376

Tenoch, 62, 296

Tenochtitlan, **2**, 296, 301; founding of, 295; orientation, 290

Teotihuacan, **2**, 183; discovery of Oaxacan Barrio at, 373; evidence of Maya influence in, 376; five-pointed stars from, 198; Merchants' Barrio at, 377

Tepeyollotl, 318

Terminal Classic Puuc: and city orientation axis, 119

Texcoco, 67, 96, **221**

textiles: and motifs, 153, 154, **155**, 393; painted, 393

texts, importance in linguistic reconstruction, 137. *See also* hieroglyphic texts

Tezcatlipoca, 66n. 3, 153, 155, 311, 318, **319**, 329

Thevet, André, 296

Thomas, Cyrus, 291, 345, 383

Thompson, Edward, 22

tianquiztli, 47, 49, 51. *See also* markets

Tikal, **2**, 172; and "Mundo Perdido" group, 378n. 4

Tikal's Twin Pyramid complexes, 118

time, reconfiguration of, 121

títulos, 297, 299

Tixchel, **2**, 400

Tlahuisical, 209. *See also* Tlahuizcalpantecuhtli

Tlahuizcalpantecuhtli, 176, 177, 310, 312, 314, 318, 325, 386

Tlaloc, 169, 318, 337, **341**, 386–87, 389

Tlapallan, 49

Tlazolteotl, 318, 391

Tochtepec, **2**

Tollan, 21, **38**; and development of International style, 37

Tollan Chollolan, **42**

Tolteca: rulers perpetuated the idea of descending from, 40

Tolteca-Chichimeca settlements, **46**

Toltec-Maya civilization, 22

Toltec migration myth, 22

Toltecs, 45; art of, 38; in the highlands, 65; limits of territory, **43**

tonalpohualli, 292, 293, 294, 309, 310, 311, 312, 316, 323, 346

Tonatiuh, 149, 176, 177, 182, 183, 290, 318; as Maya solar king, 400

Topoxte, **2**; astronomical alignments, 375

Toscano, Lourdes, 54

Totonac language, **136**

trade, 9, 24, 25, 51, 52, 56, 82, 371, 400; coastal, 400; control of, 49; and coveting of foreign objects, 91; and families living around Itzmal Ch'en, 85; and Mayapán nobles, 102; mediation of, 7; between Mexico and Yucatán, 21; ports of, 393; and Tulúm, 183 trade goods, 28, 376

trade networks, 4, 23, 27, 64, 140, 370, 371, 372

trade routes: control of, 26; and need for protection, 400

trecenas, 270, 271, 273n. 7, 280–81, 285, 292, 293, **293**, 294, 320–22, 326, 343; represented as dots, 301; as thirteen-day period, 316, 340, 346

tree, 116, 147, 167, 168, 169, **169**, 291, 318, 319, 322, 350, 351; cork, 217; directional, 350; flowering, 353, **357**; stylized, 302n. 2, 321; *tzalam*, 289

"Triple Alliance," 66n. 5, 80

Tula, **2**, 21, 22, 23, 29n. 6, 29n. 8, 42, 51, 66n. 3, **139**, 219, 279, 385; and architecture, 38; chronology, 29n. 1; declined at same time as Chichén Itzá, 38; excavation of, 22; fall of, 29n. 1, 39, **41**, 51, 65, 370, 371; and internal dissent, 39; major regional capital, 18; radiocarbon dates, 378n. 2; similarities with Chichén Itzá; 22, 38; and Toltec art, 38

Tulapan, 25

Tulúm, **2**, 20, 24, 56, 161; astronomical alignments, 375; as Aztec outpost, 373; deities in, 150; El Castillo at, **57**; established and abandoned suddenly, 56; and floral breath elements, 172; and floral symbolism, 156; flowers at, **157**; and mountain imagery, 177; and murals, 3, 145–50, 178; serpent images, 175; and trade, 183

tun, 254, 255, 272

turtles: and netted motif, 149; and shells, 149, 241; and stars of Orion's belt, 194

Tutul Xius, 25

Tuxtepec. *See* Tochtepec

tzitzimime, 357

tzolkin, 284, 285, 287, 289, 293, 294, 316, 325, 327, 329, 345, 350, 353, 358, 387

tzolk'in. See tzolkin

tzol peten, 287, 301

Uaxactun, **2**

Uayeb'. *See* Wayeb'

Ucanal, 385, 386; as Maya site, 385

uinal. See winal

Ulua, 26, 27, 62

Usumacinta Valley, 26

Utatlan, **2**

Uto-Aztecan languages, 136, 137, 147, 208, 210, **218**, 231, 233; and dispersal point for, 223; and Luiseño, 222; point of origin in Mesoamerica for, 223; as polysynthetic languages, 225

Uxmal, **2**, 20; ballcourts of, similar to Mexican "tennis courts," 22; House of the Governor, 122

Vaillant, George, 39

Valle, Marquis del, 296

Vargas, Leticia, 54

Velasco, Luis de, 299

Velásquez, Erik, 387

Venus, 194, 195, 309, 311, 386; associated with dawn, 199–200; associated with war and sacrifice, 202; and coefficients, **314**; and cult complex, 384, 388; cycle, 201; as great star, 195; iconography related to, 329; introduction of calendrical instruments to Maya lowlands, 385; as morning star, 310, 323, 324–25; movements of, 269, 337. *See also* Dresden Codex

Venus almanac, **310**, 323, **323**, 325, 329, 386; in Madrid Codex, 399

Venus calendar, 316

Venus glyph, 193, **194**, **196**, 198, 200

Venus/Quetzalcoatl cult, 385

Venus symbol. *See* Venus glyph

Veracruz-Tabasco coastal plain, **50**

vessels: floral rims on, **168**; inverted, 171. *See also* censers; pottery/ceramics

Virgin of Guadalupe, 199. *See also* Our Lady of Guadalupe

vocables, 8, 138, 241–56, 398

volutes, 156, 182

warfare, 62, 96, 97, 228

warrior, 25, 29n. 6, 155, 176, 279, 387, 390; Aztec, **100**, 147, 373

"water-hill" for town, 202

Wayeb', 266, 285, **286**, 350, 351, **352**

weaponry, 96–97

winal, 117, 246, 266, 272n. 3, **286**

wind, **47**, 148, 161, 182, **293, 312, 320, 325,** 386, 387; god of, 24, 156, **159**, 175, 198, 389; rain-bringing, 172; and breath, 147, 156, **157**, 158, **158**, 159, **159, 160,** 172, 173, 182

Wirikuta, 183

witz: and Witz Monster mountain, 178; and zoomorphic heads, 178, 182; and old man mountain motif, **179**; snout of, **180**

world directions, **286**. *See also* cardinal directions; solar directions

world systems theory, 5, 104

Xaltocan, **2**

Xcacal, 280, 283

Xcaret, **2**

Xelhá, **2**, 161; murals of, 145

Xicalanco. *See* Xicalango

Xicalango, **2**, 21, 25–28, 64, 373, 400; exact location unknown, 377; province of, 52, 61

Xipe Totec, 391; figurines of, **89, 100**

Xiu: destroyed city of Mayapán, 62; as part of confederacy government, 25; revolt by, 24; settlement at Mani, 25

Xiuhtecuhtli, **315**, 318; attributes of, 314

Xochicalco, 18, 83; evidence of Maya influence in, 376

xochicalli, 182

Xolotl, 176

Yacahuitztli, 387

Yalcobá, 280

Yaxkukul, **2**, 280, 287, 289, 301; map from first survey, **288**; map from second survey, **288**

yearbearers, 281, 292, 301, 322, 323, 351, 358, 387, 388, 389, 399; and cartouches, 320; Mayapán, **354**; tabular layout, 356

Yohualtecuhtli, 387

Yucatán, 26, 27; east coast of, 60; as economic unit, 25; historical comparisons with highland Mexico, 392; intellectual interchange with highland central Mexican cultures, 6; interaction with Mexico, 17; Itzá state replaced by Cocom rulers of Mayapán, 371; military conquerors and, 279; Postclassic period in, 20; trade goods from, listed, 21. *See also* North Yucatán

Yucatán Peninsula, **2, 53**, 53–54, 392. *See also* North Yucatán

Yucatec Maya, 7, 57, 58, **136**, 196; interchange with highland Mexicans, 9; Matillas Fine Orange ceramic used exclusively by elites of, 52; overlays of "Mexican" culture on, 137; political and cultural restructuring of, 53; and solar-based cartographic traditions, 279–302; and social memory, 251; and songs, 244–51

Yucatec Maya language, **136**; in contact with Nahuatl as a lingua franca, 217; introduction of Nahua vocables into, 249

Zapotec language, **136**, 204

zoomorphic figures, 52, 150, **154**, 156, 173, 178, **180**, 182, 343

Zoque language, 26, **136**

Zuyúa, 219; and secret language, 222